The Buddhist Art of Nāgārjunakoṇḍa

BUDDHIST TRADITION SERIES

Edited by
ALEX WAYMAN

VOLUME 25

The Buddhist Art of Nāgārjunakoṇḍa

ELIZABETH ROSEN STONE

MOTILAL BANARSIDASS PUBLISHERS
PRIVATE LIMITED • DELHI

First Edition: Delhi, 1994

ISBN : 81-208-0828-2

Also available at:

MOTILAL BANARSIDASS
41, U.A., Bungalow Road, Jawahar Nagar, Delhi 110007
120 Royapettah High Road, Mylapore, Madras 600 004
16 St. Mark's Road, Bangalore 560 001
Ashok Rajpath, Patna 800 004
Chowk, Varanasi 221 001

PRINTED IN INDIA
BY JAINENDRA PRAKASH JAIN AT SHRI JAINENDRA PRESS, A-45 NARAINA,
PHASE I, NEW DELHI 110028 AND PUBLISHED BY
NARENDRA PRAKASH JAIN FOR MOTILAL BANARSIDASS PUBLISHERS
PVT. LTD., BUNGALOW ROAD, DELHI 110 007

For
Stella Kramrisch

FOREWORD

It is a great pleasure to place before the interested Indian Art specialists, scholars of Buddhism, and Indian archaeologists this culmination of Elizabeth Stone's long preoccupation with the Buddhist Art of Nāgārjunakoṇḍa.

The basic work started when she was a student of Professor Alexander Soper and Professor Stella Kramrisch at the Institute of Fine Arts, New York University. For the wealth of photographs of Nāgārjunakoṇḍa, she enjoyed the permission of the Archaeological Survey of India and the encouragement of the late Dr. H. Sarkar, Joint Director General of the Archaeological Survey.

The editor's own researches by the book *The Lion's Roar of Queen Śrīmālā* (A. and H. Wayman) unexpectedly supported Dr. Stone's theories. This is because it provided a text which could be associated with the site. Since this work (*The Lion's Roar*) is also available in this Buddhist Tradition Series, it is easy for the reader to compare this scripture and its new Foreword with the evidence brought forth by Dr. Stone in her book.

New York, July 1992 *Alex Wayman*

ACKNOWLEDGEMENTS

My interest in Nāgārjunakoṇḍa began when the evolution of its sculpture was assigned to me as a Master's thesis topic by Professor Alexander C. Soper. The sculpture immediately appealed to me, not primarily for its aesthetic beauty (for some of the works are not beautiful), but for what appeared to be a relatively consistent style related to, but unmistakably different from that of Amarāvatī. When I came to learn of the richness of the epigraphic literature and the newly excavated archaeological material, my interest expanded beyond the purely stylistic problems.

I wish to express a very special thanks to Professor Herbert Härtel, former Director of the Museum für Indische Kunst in Berlin for allowing me to join his own students excavating at Sonkh, in Mathurā District, an experience which was invaluable in helping me to understand and interpret archaeological reports.

During the course of my work on Nāgārjunakoṇḍa, the appearance of the text of *The Lion's Roar of Queen Śrīmālā,* translated by Alex and Hideko Wayman, added a new dimension to my studies. What was serendipitous was that I was studying with Alex Wayman at the time of its publication, and I confess that I was initially perplexed by Professor Wayman's attribution of the text to Nāgārjunakoṇḍa. For its relevance was not immediately apparent to me until I re-examined the Nāgārjunakoṇḍa inscriptions and considered them in light of text. While I cannot thank the Waymans for translating and studying the text (for their interest in Nāgārjunakoṇḍa was totally independent of my own), I can thank Dr. Gary Tartakov and Dr. David Dell who, unwittingly coerced me into acknowledging my own conclusions regarding the relevance of the *Śrīmālā* text to Nāgārjunakoṇḍa.

Eventually, the bulk of the material presented here was to become the subject of my doctoral dissertation at New York University under the guidance of Professor Stella Kramrisch, a subject which I shall return to momentarily.

There is no question that this book could not have been written without the gracious permission of the Archaeological Survey of India. The Survey has been extremely generous allowing me to study this material. In this regard I wish to thank M. N. Deshpande and Dr. B. K. Thapar for allowing me to study at Nāgārjunakoṇḍa as a young student, and subsequently Dr. (Mrs.) Debala Mitra, Dr. M. S. Nagaraja Rao and Dr. M. C. Joshi for their encouragement with this project.

This study would never have been completed without the personal encouragement of the late Dr. H. Sarkar. My debt to his writings on Nāgārjunakoṇḍa may be seen throughout the pages of this book. While I was too young to have ever set foot on Nāgārjunakoṇḍa before the site was flooded, his memories of the excavation allowed me to pursue the project in spite of that handicap. I was able to share with him his excitement about the many aspects of the Nāgārjunakoṇḍa excavations, a site which to many of its excavators brought back only memories of isolation and blazing heat.

I wish to thank the curators of the Nāgārjunakoṇḍa Museum most particularly Mr. John Dawson. The gracious hospitality that has been extended to me by the families who lived and worked at Nāgārjunakoṇḍa has always been a source of great pleasure. In this regard, I wish to thank Mr. M.C.V. Prasad Rao, Mr. Muhammad Jallaludin, and Mr. Padma Rao and their families.

While the bulk of the material studied by me is at the Nāgārjunakoṇḍa Museum, many other museums and individuals have been helpful in allowing me access to study works in their institutions. In India, I wish to thank Dr. Laxmi P. Sihare and Dr. (Miss) Shashi Asthana (The National Museum, New Delhi) and Dr. V. V. Krishna Sastry (Director, State Archaeological Department, Andhra Pradesh). In London, Wladimir Zwalf (The British Museum) has always been helpful and informative, no matter what my inquiry was. In Paris, Françine Tissot (The Musée Guimet) and Dominique Darbois have been exceedingly helpful in helping me to acquire photographs. In the United States, Martin Lerner and Steven Kossack (The Metropolitan Museum of Art, New York) have always provided me with gracious and enthusiastic access to the storerooms to study the Andhra materials. Sincere thanks are also due to Dr. Stanislaw Czuma (The Cleveland Museum of Art), Dr. Pratapaditya Pal (Los Angeles County Museum of Art), and Amy G. Poster (The Brooklyn Museum) for sharing their respective institution's Andhra material.

It is very difficult to express my thanks to Professor Stella Kramrisch, even in the context of this book. My many years of association with her have had a profound impact upon me. I recollect the exciting years of instruction, recalling the ever so many important insights that came to her frequently and spontaneously, which she tested and re-tested in the most rigorous fashion.

From every practical point of view, Alex Wayman has been the main supporter of this book. He has seen it grow from its inception, as teacher, to its conclusion, as editor of *The Buddhist Tradition Series.* As colleague and teacher, not in my primary discipline, he has added new dimensions to my work, helping me to view Buddhism as an ongoing discourse, and to view Nāgārjunakoṇḍa not only through its art, but as the place where an important discourse was occurring.

In the course of my studies, generous funding has been provided to me for this project by The Breezewood Foundation, the Mary Livingston Griggs and Mary Griggs Burke Foundation, and The JDR 3rd Fund.

To Mr. N. P. Jain of Motilal Banarsidass Publishers Private Limited, and to the entire Jain family, I wish to express my thanks for their gracious hospitality, and their patience throughout the preparation of this book.

Most of all I wish to thank my husband Richard for his encouragement and for his invaluable help.

CONTENTS

LIST OF ILLUSTRATIONS

Unless otherwise indicated, all sculptural works are from Nāgārjunakoṇḍa, and are in the Archaeological Museum, Nāgārjunakoṇḍa. Likewise, unless otherwise indicated, all photographs are by the author.

CHAPTER I

THE IKṢVĀKUS AND THE BUDDHIST TRADITION OF NĀGĀRJUNAKOṆḌA

DISCOVERY AND DOCUMENTATION

On the 21st of February, 1920, an Andhra school teacher with the help of local villagers found his way into the remote jungle-ridden valley of Nāgārjunakoṇḍa.[1] (See map fig. 1) Upon finding an inscribed pillar there, the news was reported to the local press and to government officials. To our knowledge it was not until March 1926 that the site drew the attention of the more specialized scholarly community. At that time Shri Rangaswami Saraswati discovered that the site had several brick mounds. He was able to copy a sufficient number of inscriptions there to report that they were in the Prākrit language and probably belonged to the second and third centuries A.D. The news must have been widely spread, for shortly thereafter, in July 1926, Professor G. Jouveau Dubreuil of Pondicherry conducted a brief excavation at Nāgārjunakoṇḍa,[2] and seems to have removed some sculptures, bringing them to the attention of the Western world within only a year or two. A few months after Jouveau Dubreuil's visit, Mr. Hamid Kuraishi surveyed the site as deputy of A.H. Longhurst, then a Superintendant of the Archaeological Survey of India, to see if it would be worth conducting full-scale excavations. As Kuraishi had discovered that the site was extremely rich in Buddhist monuments,[3] Longhurst decided to undertake full-scale excavations. He worked there from 1927 to 1931, expanding upon the number of Buddhist monastic sites and sculptures. A summary of these finds was published by him in *Memoirs of the Archaeological Survey of India*, Volume 54.[4] The site was then re-excavated in 1938 by T.N. Ramachandran who made some additions to the Buddhist finds. His work was published in *Memoirs of the Archaeological Survey of India*, Volume 71.[5] These two monographs remain, in large part, the basis of all further studies on Nāgārjunakoṇḍa.

During the 1950s severe drought conditions in Andhra Pradesh ravished the countryside and coast many lives. It became clear that a massive irrigation scheme was required for the survival of the population. Consequently the magnificent Nāgārjunasāgar Dam was built, submerging the archaeological site of Nāgārjunakoṇḍa.

At that time the Government of India was keenly aware of the historic importance of Nāgārjunakoṇḍa, and had to balance the human need against the historic loss. The Archaeological Survey of India created a special project to salvage some of the monuments before their submersion.

As a result, between 1954 and 1960 the entire valley of Nāgārjunakoṇḍa was excavated under the supervision of Dr. R. Subrahmanyam, revealing remains from the Early Stone Age to late Medieval times. The final excavation report on the prehistoric finds has been published in *Memoirs of the Archaeological Survey of India*, Volume 75,[6] while the results of the excavations of the historic period as yet have been given only brief notice in *Indian Archaeology: A Review* from the years 1954-55 to 1960-61. While Dr. Subrahmanyam's excavations have expanded our knowledge of the Buddhist monuments of Nāgārjunakoṇḍa, and have given us an extremely important dated sculpture, equally important they have revealed the existence of what we had already expected from the Nāgārjunakoṇḍa inscriptions: the simultaneous construction of Hindu temples along with the Buddhist monastic complexes throughout the excavations.

With the knowledge of the coming submersion of the valley, small-scale models of each of the architectural remains were prepared. Several of the structures were actually removed from the valley and transplanted on the nearby hillsides. The sculptures, in accordance with the wishes of Jawaharlal Nehru to preserve them in their original area, were placed in a museum atop the fortified medieval hill of Nāgārjunakoṇḍa, the hill which lent its name to the ancient town of Vijayapurī, the original name of the Nāgārjunakoṇḍa valley. There, too, have been transplanted several major monuments including a great *stūpa* which originally housed "a corporeal remain" of the Lord Buddha.

Of a non-archaeological nature, two important studies on Nāgārjunakoṇḍa have been published. The first is a book by K. Krishna Murthy[7] fashioned after Sivaramamurti's well-known monograph on Amarāvatī. In it Krishna Murthy catalogues and analyzes all the artifacts represented at Nāgārjunakoṇḍa such as modes of dress, jewelry, furniture, architecture, etc. Where possible, he cites the Sanskrit name, relevant textual descriptions and comparative material. The completeness of his study makes it unnecessary to pursue this mode of research further. The other study, which is by H. Sarkar, first appeared as an article[8] and subsequently as a chapter to his book on *Studies in Early Buddhist Architecture of India*.[9] The chapter outlines the basic data regarding the Buddhist monuments of Nāgārjunakoṇḍa and proposes a chronology of these monuments based upon epigraphical and Buddhist doctrinal evidence. To the theories discussed in this specialized article, we shall return shortly. However, this article is not only important because of the opinions expressed, but also because of the excellent organizational structure underlying the article. Firstly, this is the only place where the groundplans of the major Buddhist structures have been published. The reader should refer to these plans frequently throughout the reading of this book (see our pl. 2). Secondly, Sarkar publishes a numbering system for the site which is considerably more logical than the ones previously adopted by Kuraishi, Longhurst, and Ramachandran, each of whom used his own method. The system for numbering the site is as follows. H. Sarkar uses the numbers ascribed to the *stūpas* by Longhurst as the site number, and then includes all the auxiliary monuments at that site under that number, regardless of any other numbers subsequently ascribed to the respective monument. Thus, Site 1 consists of Longhurst's *Stūpa* 1, Longhurst's Monastery 1, and Longhurst's Temple 1,[10] while Longhurst's Apsidal Temple 2 becomes part of Site 43, the number of the *stūpa* with which it was subsequently associated. T.N. Ramachandran, in his 1938 excavation, used an altogether different numbering system,[11] which Sarkar chose simply to ignore. Sarkar's system is used here, and it is hoped, will be used in all future works about Nāgārjunakoṇḍa.

This system has been excellent in helping us to view the monastic sites as units rather than as individual monuments.[12] The reader will shortly be chagrined to discover that as at many sites in India, there is no correlation between site numbers and chronology, they simply relate to the order in which Longhurst excavated them. Although the fact that, for example, Site 2 postdated Site 9 might be burdensome for many a reader, I have decided *not* to further complicate the matter by introducing a new system of my own and therefore creating an even more laborious task for future scholarship on the site. Sarkar's chapter, along with the deceptively modest looking guidebook to Nāgārjunakoṇḍa co-authored by H. Sarkar and B.N. Misra,[13] have provided an organizational framework upon which I have based my own study. Without them my task would have been almost hopeless, never having seen the layout of the valley with my own eyes before its submersion. The guidebook map showing the organization of the sites and layout of the valley is adapted herein (fig. 3). Again, I hope the reader will refer to it frequently to understand the layout of the valley.

Historical Introduction

Having reviewed the extant literature on Nāgārjunakoṇḍa, we will now turn to the site itself. Nāgārjunakoṇḍa, before its submersion, was a secluded valley about 23 square kilometers in area in the Palnāḍ Taluk of the Guṇṭūr District, Andhra Pradesh. It was surrounded on three sides by a group of hills which were offshoots of the Nallamalai range. In the northwest it was bounded by the Krishna river, thus providing it with both natural fortification and easy access to other areas along the Krishna river. At the time of its discovery, the area was occupied by only a small tribal hamlet known as Pullareddigudem, but it revealed several periods of habitation: the first belonging to the stone age, the Neolithic period beginning in the third millennium B.C.; a megalithic period of the second half of the first millennium B.C.; and historical periods principally of the third-fourth centuries A.D. under the Ikṣvāku Dynasty. Scanty remains of the Chalukyan Dynasty (7th-12th centuries) have also been reported, and the area seems to have again been important during the fifteenth and sixteenth centuries.[14] In this work, we confine ourselves largely to the third and fourth centuries A.D., the period of the reign of the Ikṣvāku Dynasty at Nāgārjunakoṇḍa.

Although it was the Ikṣvākus who were the major patrons at Nāgārjunakoṇḍa, one Buddhist donative inscription containing the name of the Sātavāhana King Vijaya Sātakarṇi (201-07 A.D.) has led to speculation that it was Vijaya who founded the ancient city of Vijayapurī before the coming of the Ikṣvākus.[15] While this inscription is important, as it is the only known epigraphic record of this king, as yet known only through the Purāṇas, it is not possible to ascertain what role he played in the Nāgārjunakoṇḍa area. For if in fact he did found the city of Vijayapurī, it must at that time have been a very minor settlement, for we have been unable to attribute any monuments to this king, with certainty and we have no evidence of his successors Chandaśrī and Puloma at the site. Nevertheless, this inscription is important to our sculptural study, for it helps us to explain the continuity of the Sātavāhana style at Nāgārjunakoṇḍa, and to shed light upon certain pieces which appear to be pre-Ikṣvāku.

History of the Ikṣvākus

The history of the Ikṣvāku Dynasty is known almost exclusively from inscriptions found at Nāgārjunakoṇḍa. The inscriptions, numbering over 100, are in the Prākrit and Sanskrit languages, both in a florid Brāhmī script exclusive to the Ikṣvāku Dynasty. They provide a complete Ikṣvāku genealogy of the Ikṣvāku king, as well as fascinating information pertaining to Ikṣvāku social history and religious affiliations. The early studies of these inscriptions by J. Ph. Vogel in *Epigraphia Indica*, Volumes XX and XXI, remain invaluable source material.[16] Further important discoveries and studies have been published in *Epigraphia Indica*, Volumes XX to XXVI, including important contributions by D.C. Sircar.[17] A useful, although incomplete handlist of these inscriptions is included in a book by M. Rama Rao for the reader's further reference.[18] My own sources for a chronology are largely the inscriptions themselves, and my understanding of Ikṣvāku history which has been aided by the relevant chapters in D.C. Sircar's *Successors of the Sātavāhanas in the Lower Deccan*,[19] Gopalachari's *Early History of the Andhra Country*,[20] and an unpublished Ph.D. Thesis on Andhra history by Ranjana Mukherjee.[21] Here I will discuss only questions of chronology and bring in other historical data only where relevant.

It is abundantly clear from numismatic, epigraphic, and perhaps Purāṇic evidence that the Ikṣvākus of Nāgārjunakoṇḍa were feudatories under the Sātavāhanas. At the time of the downfall of the Sātavāhana Dynasty, the Ikṣvākus (under the rule of Cāṁtamūla I) seem to have gained an independent ruling status and established their capital at Nāgārjunakoṇḍa. Thus Cāṁtamūla's ascendency is presumed to coincide with the fall of King Puloma, the last Sātavāhana king. As yet, none of the extant evidence has given us convincingly precise dates for this event, although dates between A.D. 223 and A.D. 231 have been suggested. A 1974 article by Karl Khandalavala suggests a date as early as A.D. 207, although he himself admits that his study is not a final solution to the "tangled" problem of Sātavāhana chronology.[22] For the sake of simplicity, we are here accepting the date of c. A.D. 225 for the date of Puloma's fall, with the hope that scholars who are partial to any of the alternative Sātavāhana dates will adjust the Ikṣvāku relative chronology to suit their own preference.

Regarding Ikṣvāku chronology, two basic approaches have been taken. The most simple approach starts with the assumption that the Ikṣvākus rose to power in Andhra Pradesh around the time of the fall of the Sātavāhanas in A.D. 225. According to an inscription bearing a genealogy,[23] we know of four kings ruling at Nāgārjunakoṇḍa. Inscriptional evidence provides us with regnal dates for these kings. If we total the final known regnal date for each king, we come to a total rule of 75 years. My own view presents a modification of this simple theory. A more complex approach will be discussed below.

The first known king of the Ikṣvāku Dynasty was Cāṁtamūla I. There are no inscriptions dating to his reign found at Nāgārjunakoṇḍa, but this merely indicates that no inscriptions were found, not that he did not rule there. Abundant numismatic evidence indicates that his coin types, as well as those of his successors, were fashioned after the Sātavāhanas.[24] That he was the first of his line is indicated by several factors. In the inscriptions pertaining to his reign found at the nearby sites of Reṇṭāla,[25] and Kesanapalli,[26] his father is never mentioned, indicating perhaps that his father was of lower rank. Conversely, he is consistently mentioned in the inscriptions of his successors at Nāgārjunakoṇḍa, in which his virtues are extolled at length.[27] Amongst them, he is described as performer of *aśvamedha*, a ritual usually reserved for a powerful king. His power though was most likely only of local significance, and dramatized by his successors, for as yet his name has not been identified in any but local sources. To date, his coins have been found only at Ongole[28] and Nāgārjunakoṇḍa.[29] The fact that his memorial pillar was found at Nāgārjunakoṇḍa would enhance the argument that this was his place of residence. His latest known inscription, found at Kesanapalli is dated in his thirteenth year. Upon such scanty evidence, we can in no way assume that this was his last regnal year. According to the inscriptions of his successors, Cāṁtamūla was a devotee of

Mahāsena although he clearly tolerated Buddhism as many of his relatives gave pious donations to that faith.

It was from the time of the second king onward, King Vīrapuruṣadatta, that we have many of the extant Nāgārjunakoṇḍa inscriptions. Vīrapuruṣadatta's reign may have covered broader territory than Cāṁtamūla's, for inscriptions attesting to his reign have been found at Jaggayapeta,[30] Uppugundur[31] and Rāmireḍḍipaḷḷi.[32] At Nāgārjunakoṇḍa one of these appears on a dated sculpture. A memorial pillar to his father bears the controversial date "*vijaya*" (fig. 51). Vīrapuruṣadatta was known to have five wives. It was under his reign that many of the Buddhist monuments of Nāgārjunakoṇḍa were built, patronized to a large extent by royal ladies and lay members of the community. The site must have at this time been an extremely important Buddhist center, for inscriptional evidence tells us monks were attracted to the area from as far away as Śrī Lanka. The latest known date of Vīrapuruṣadatta is his 24th regnal year.[33]

Vīrapuruṣadatta was succeeded by his son Ehuvala Cāṁtamūla. The reign of Ehuvala was clearly a period of great building activity. He may have consolidated the Ikṣvāku empire, for only one inscription was found outside of Nāgārjunakoṇḍa, that was found in nearby Kottampalugu.[34] As with the other kings, little of significance is known of Ehuvala Cāṁtamūla, except that he was considered equal to such epic heroes as Sagara, Dilīpa, Ambarīśha, Yudhiṣṭhira and Rāma,[35] and that he formed a matrimonial alliance with a Śakå queen who was the daughter of a Mahākṣatrapa of the Bṛhatphalāyana *gotra*.[36] The power of King Ehualav Cāṁtamūla is attested to by archaeological, epigraphic and art historical evidence, for the remains show us that there was a vast amount of building activity under Ehuvala. This included several Buddhist monastic establishments, unique experiments in Hindu temple architecture dedicated to Śaiva deities, and some unique examples of secular architecture which vie with the wonders of the ancient world. The latest known inscription of Ehuvala Cāṁtamūla is on a sculptured slab dated to his 24th regnal year.[37]

The last known king of the Ikṣvāku dynasty is King Rudrapuruṣadatta. He is known from an inscription at Gurzāla[38] dated to his fourth regnal year, and one on a sculptured memorial pillar from Nāgārjunakoṇḍa. This is dated to his eleventh regnal year.[39] His latest known inscription belongs to his fourteenth regnal year.[40]

If we take the most parsimonious approach based on known regnal years, we arrive with the following short chronology starting with the year 225:

Cāṁtamūla I	225-238
Vīrapuruṣadatta	238-262
Ehuvala Cāṁtamūla	262-286
Rudrapuruṣadatta	286-300

Thus the entire Ikṣvāku reign would be a minimum of 75 years. This approach has been recently accepted by several scholars.[41] My own approach is archaeologically less provable, for I have attempted to extend the dynasty very slightly farther. My reasons for this are ultimately based on stylistic evidence, for as we shall see in Chapter II, the sculptures of the Ehuvala Cāṁtamūla period closely foreshadow the paintings of Ajantā done in the fifth century. Although a hiatus will always exist between the two sites, I choose to select the longest reasonable chronology. My literary evidence here is unfortunately Purāṇic, evidence which, as we know from the endless disputes on Sātavāhana chronology, must be taken with extreme caution.

A group of people known as the Andhra Śrīpārvatīyas or the Andhra Bhṛtyās (servants of the Andhras) are mentioned in the Purāṇas. The Śrīpārvatīyas would refer to the Andhras who lived in the Śrīparvata region. The Nāgārjunakoṇḍa inscriptions seem to indicate that Śrīparvata is the ancient name for the Nallamalai hills, the hills which surround Nāgārjunakoṇḍa. Thus we assume that the Andhra Bhṛtyās or Andhra Śrīpārvatīyas are none other than the Ikṣvākus. According to the *Matsya Purāṇa*, the Ikṣvākus ruled for 100 years, while according to the *Vāyu Purāṇa* they ruled for 52 years. Epigraphic evidence has shown us that the *Vāyu Purāṇa* account is too short while the *Matsya Purāṇa* account of 100 years lies within reason.[42] But to accept the Purāṇic evidence we must, in the tradition of Sātavāhana scholarship, complicate our reasoning, for the *Matsya Purāṇa* tells us that there were seven Ikṣvāku kings while epigraphic and numismatic evidence give us only four. If we are to use the Purāṇic evidence we can only suggest that the four known members of the dynasty rules for the appropriate 100 years while three other kings belonged to collateral branches of the Ikṣvāku dynasty and ruled simultaneously. Granted, our main rationale for even considering such a hypothesis is that the time span involved seems appropriate to the development of the sculptural style at Nāgārjunakoṇḍa. Thus without being dogmatic about our acceptance of the Purāṇic reference, and using the epigraphic evidence as a guide to time spans rather than actual dates, we propose the following chronology:

Cāṁtamūla I	c. A.D. 225-c. A.D. 240-250
Vīrapuruṣadatta	c. A.D. 240-250-c. A.D. 265-275
Ehuvala Cāṁtamūla	c. A.D. 265-275-c. A.D. 290-300
Rudrapuruṣadatta	c. A.D. 290-300-c. A.D. 315-325

One argument from silence, suggested to me by H. Sarkar, may posit 320 as a cut-off date for the Ikṣvāku dynasty. The well-known, posthumous Allahabad pillar listing the conquests of Samudragupta makes no reference to the Ikṣvākus in the list of conquests in Andhra Pradesh.[43] At that time they may have either been of little significance or non-existent. It is hoped that our readers will accept these dates as a useful hypothesis for our art historical chronology rather than concrete fact, in hopes that newly discovered sites in Andhra Pradesh will one day give us more corroborative evidence.

For scholars of Ikṣvāku history, we have conspicuously omitted two problems: the inscriptions belonging to the so-called Jovian cycle and an inscription which has been interpreted as referring to an Ābhīra interregnum within Ikṣvāku rule. The question of the Jovian cycle inscriptions we refer to briefly here, but as our final conclusions are ultimately based on stylistic considerations, this discussion will be elaborated upon in Chapter II. Briefly, two inscriptions are dated in the year *vijaya* (Sanskrit for "victory"). The first of these is on a memorial pillar to Cāṁtamūla I (fig. 51) dated in the year *vijaya* in the reign of his son Vīrapuruṣadatta.[44] The second is dated to the reign of Ehuvala Cāṁtamūla, Vīrapuruṣadatta's son and successor.[45] It was found on a limestone pillar near Site 126. As has been pointed out by D.C. Sircar, the word *vijaya* not only means "victory", but is the name of the 27th year of the sixty-year cycle of Jupiter. However, it would seem illogical that this is the implication of this word in this context, for no other names of Jovian years appear in the Nāgārjunakoṇḍa inscriptions. If we accepted these inscriptions as belonging to Jovian years, the plausible dates within Ikṣvāku rule would be A.D. 273-74 in the reign of Vīrapuruṣadatta for the first inscription, and A.D. 333-34 in the reign of Ehuvala Cāṁtamūla for the second inscription. As the reader will see in Chapter II, if we accept the dates of 273-74 for the memorial pillar to Cāṁtamūla I, we would have to place the development of Ikṣvāku sculpture within too short a time span. Regarding the date of A.D. 333-34 for the inscription belonging to the time of Ehuvala Cāṁtamūla, it seems to stretch beyond historical plausibility the reign of Ehuvala Cāṁtamūla. We thus simply discard the use of Jovian reckonings in these inscriptions and will return to the problem in Chapter II.

The so-called "Ābhīra Interregnum" inscription records the dedication of a temple to Aṣṭabhujsvāmin (Site 29) a form of Viṣṇu.[46] It was dedicated in the 30th regnal year of the Ābhīra King Vasuṣeṇa who had ruled from the region around Nāsik. Instead of considering the year 30 as a regnal year, D.C. Sircar suggested that the year 30 was that of an era, and chose the Kalachuri-Chedi era of A.D. 248. Thus the dedication of this temple at Nāgārjunakoṇḍa would have occurred around A.D. 278. In order to reconcile this with Ikṣvāku chronology, Sircar suggested that the Ābhīras subdued the Ikṣvākus for a brief time, perhaps between the reigns of Vīrapuruṣadatta and Ehuvala,[47] and then lost their power again. This seems to be another one of D.C. Sircar's flights of fancy which has required scholarly retort. The most comprehensive discussion of this inscription lies in the Ph.D. dissertation of Dr. Ranjana Mukherjee.[48] Her approach is considerably more straightforward. Based on her own palaeographic study of the inscription, she placed the inscription to near the close of the Ikṣvāku dynasty or even later, and thus considered the year 30 as a regnal year. Unable to find dates for King Vasuṣeṇa she sought the dates of one of his contemporaries mentioned in the same inscription, that of Śaka Rudradāman of Avanti. According to her, the only known Rudradāman of Śaka extraction was Rudradāman II, known through the coin legends of his son Mahākṣatrapa

Rudrasena III. The date of his florescence seems to be somewhere between 332 and 348. Consequently, it would seem that the inscription, as well as the Aṣṭabhujsvāmin temple, was of a post-Ikṣvāku date, and there was never an Ābhīra interregnum at Nāgārjunakoṇḍa. We know from the Nāgārjunakoṇḍa inscriptions that the Ikṣvākus were supporters of the Śaivite and the Buddhist faiths. It seems unlikely that Vaiṣṇavism would have found favor at that time. But one further fact argues against the Ābhīra interregnum at Nāgārjunakoṇḍa. A pair of elaborately carved pillars was excavated at the Aṣṭabhujsvāmin temple (fig. 267). As we will see in an addendum to Chapter II, they are post-Ikṣvāku in style.

The Architecture of Nāgārjunakoṇḍa: Secular Remains

The Ikṣvāku dynasty ruled from a citadel overlooking the Krishna river (see fig. 4) The citadel was walled on all sides except that facing the river with ramparts of mud construction later strengthened with brick. The citadel was a fortified residence although the palace buildings themselves have never been found. There were, however, surviving barracks, stables, and especially cisterns. Two structures found in the citadel (Site 93) have been interpreted as having royal significance. The first (fig. 5) is a plastered stepped brick tank 27 feet square and 8 feet 6 inches deep at its greatest depth. A drainage system was provided for water when it reached the 7 foot level. The tank was made of brick and coated with a thick coat of plaster. It originally had a wooden superstructure, and the structure appears to have been destroyed in a fire. About thirty feet from this was found another tank of similar construction (fig. 6), measuring 18 x 12 feet with a depth of four feet six inches. The shape of this tank is generally described as that of a tortoise. Both the uniqueness of these structures, and the fact that they seem to have formed some sort of ritual function, have led scholars to suggest that these structures were used as part of the *aśvamedha* ceremony of Cāṁtamūla I.[49] At present, such a hypothesis can neither be confirmed nor denied.

Outside the citadel, numerous residential structures have been found, largely made of rubble. These are of little significance in our present study with the exception of two structures that are of particular importance in understanding Ikṣvāku art. The first is a magnificent bathing *ghāṭ* excavated at Site 34,[50] (fig. 7 is a detail), and currently transplanted onto the island of Nāgārjunakoṇḍa (fig. 8). As one can see from its location on the map (fig. 3), it originally flanked the Krishna river. In the spring, when the river was low, the bottom portion of the *ghāṭ* was in use whereas after the rainy season entrance to the Krishna was through the upper area. The *ghāṭ* was constructed of brick and then faced with limestone. Based on a study of mason's marks[51] at Nāgārjunakoṇḍa, H. Sarkar has placed the *ghāṭ* to the reign of Ehuvala Cāṁtamūla. The splendor of this *ghāṭ*, with its elaborate system of staircases, shows the Ikṣvākus to have been extremely sophisticated in constructional method and to have had a very strong taste for luxury, which can be experienced even today in its transplanted state.

Another find of great significance is a striking stadium (figs. 9-10), a structure which ranks amongst the most important finds of ancient India. It was originally found at Site 17, and is currently transplanted on the eastern bank of Nāgārjunakoṇḍa along the modern road to Macherla. The rectangular enclosure has an area of 16.46 x 13.72 meters. Around the four sides are tiered galleries providing seating for about 1000 people.[52] It is of the same mode of construction as the bathing *ghāṭ*, and based on a study of mason's marks, is probably contemporary with it.[53] As it has excellent acoustic properties, it has been assumed to have been used for theatrical purposes. This may well have been the case, but if it is so, it was also apparently used as a boxing arena, and was moreover a structure whose function was not unique. In a recent study of the city of Mathurā, Dr. Usha Nilsson cited a Purāṇic passage describing what seems to have been a very similar structure at Mathurā.[54] The structure in question was a boxing arena. As there were numerous sculptures of boxers at Nāgārjunakoṇḍa (for example fig. 140), it was not unlikely that this structure had the same function. In terms of the form of this monument, all scholars have commented that it is Roman in inspiration. This is not quite the case, but what is more likely of Roman inspiration is the technique, i.e., the use of stone facing over a less expensive core.[55] In India the use of this architectural technique is unique to Nāgārjunakoṇḍa, although it was used much earlier in Andhra *stūpa* architecture. The form of the arena has no relation to the true Roman amphitheater, which is oval in shape. In fact, it is closer in shape to a Greek *bouleterion*, a structure which would seem to have no functional parallel in India. The closest comparison we have found is the *bouleterion* at Priene, in Western Turkey (fig. 11). It dates from about the second century B.C., but later examples must have existed. If indeed the notion of the amphitheater is foreign, it seems to have borrowed ideas from two different cultures and reorganized them into a new Indian structure. For we will see, as a current running through this thesis, that India in the third century A.D. seems to have had access to a considerable amount of information from the West, information which was built up through many years of active trade.

When we speak of trade with the West, we refer here not only to trade with Rome, but to the entire Roman Empire and to all the intermediate seaports along the coastal trade route.[56] Thus goods seem to have been brought from the entire Mediterranean area to Alexandria (see map, fig. 12). From there they were transported overland by caravans until they reached the Red Sea. These routes seem to have ended at the ancient port of Myos Hormos before the goods were shipped by sea. From there the traders went down the Red Sea and skirted the coast of the Arabian peninsula, trading with merchants along the way. The trader continued his journey up the Persian Gulf toward Iraq, down toward Iran, and eventually reached the mouth of the Indus. From there he skirted the entire coast of India leaving behind him Roman currency as well as objects of glass, bronze, gold, silver and Roman wines. In return, he was to receive such items as cloth, gem stones, and the still favored spices of the East, especially pepper. Although these trade routes seem rather theoretical to us, for they are known largely through Roman literary evidence and through a small number of Roman hoards found throughout the Indian sub-continent, we cannot underestimate their importance as having had both an economic and artistic influence upon India. The entire extent of this trade is only partially documented archaeologically, but the extent of it must have been quite vast. For Strabo, writing at the time of Augustus, wrote that 120 ships left the port of Myos Hormos alone each year in order to trade with the East.[57] That this trade continued for a considerable amount of time is known from both literary and archaeological evidence, and is underscored by the fact that in 408 A.D. Alaric the Goth demanded 3,000 pounds of pepper in his treaty with Rome.[58]

It has been suggested by M.N. Deshpande that due to this trade there existed an actual Roman settlement at the nearby town of Ter.[59] If in fact there was a Roman settlement at Ter, this would be an obvious solution to our architectural problems. For trade goods that came into India from the West could easily have provided the source for sculptural styles and motifs. But to build a large structure in a well-known foreign technique, implies that there must have been actual foreigners nearby to provide an example. In this context, we must recall that the *Periplus of the Erythrean Sea* mentions the existence of a temple of Augustus at the town of Muziris (modern Cranganore) on the Malabar coast.[60] One would assume that such a temple was built with Roman techniques, and that these techniques went on several generations before the traders became Indianized. Unfortunately, the Augustus temple has never been found, but the general accuracy of the *Periplus* seems to indicate that it must have existed at one time.

The Architecture of Nāgārjunakoṇḍa: Hindu Remains

The religious architecture of Nāgārjunakoṇḍa falls into two groups employing different but sometimes related forms. Although Nāgārjunakoṇḍa is known largely for its numerous Buddhist remains, a number of Hindu temples were discovered around the citadel and along the banks of the citadel. Unfortunately all but one of these has been submerged, and the rest are known only through old photographs or reconstructions. Most of these temples are called Hindu because they are physically separated from the Buddhist community and/or because they do not conform to the traditionally Buddhist apsidal form. Others bearing inscriptions mostly belong to the Śaivite faith, except for the post-Ikṣvāku Vaiṣṇavite Aṣṭabhujsvāmin temple (Site 29) mentioned above.[61] For a broad study of these temples, we await the publications of the Archaeological Survey, but two will be cited for they convey to us the ecumenical nature of the Ikṣvāku Dynasty, for as we can tell from the Nāgārjunakoṇḍa inscriptions, the Ikṣvāku kings were Śaiva while their wives and consorts patronized the Buddhist faith. The very same stone masons must have worked for both, producing a great deal of experimentation in the Hindu architectural form.

Of the available temples about which we have definite information, two are of particular significance for their unique form. Both were built during the reign of Ehuvala Cāṁtamūla, c. A.D. 265-75-A.D. 290-300. The first was once a temple (fig. 13) found at Site 99 along the banks of the Krishna river. According to an inscription which existed in six or seven versions, the monument was built in the eleventh regnal year of Ehuvala Cāṁtamūla.[62] It was built by a local army general and was an abode of Sarvadeva (i.e., Śiva), built by the grace of Kārttikeya. In contrast to the predominantly Prākrit inscriptions used by the Buddhists at Nāgārjunakoṇḍa, the Hindu inscriptions are in pure Sanskrit. Seen here is a small central shrine containing two massive pedestals. The walls of the shrine are constructed of rectangular stone pillars with brick infills. Flights of steps lead upward to a huge L-shaped pillared *maṇḍapam*, the floor of which was once covered with stone slabs upon a coarse brick core, the same technique used in the contemporary bathing *ghāṭ* and "arena". The use of stone veneers on the Hindu temples at Nāgārjunakoṇḍa seems to mark a transition point between the use of brick in pre-Gupta times and the abundant use of stone during the Gupta period. According to its excavators, the Sarvadeva temple was originally multi-storied.[63]

The other shrine is the Mahādeva Puṣpabhadrasvāmin temple (Site 34 figs. 14-15) dedicated only five years after the Sarvadeva temple, i.e., in the sixteenth regnal year of Ehuvala Cāṁtamūla.[64] The temple was dedicated by the king's and possibly also by the young man's mother, the reigning queen. The form of the temple is perhaps surprising. The main shrine is apsidal, a form usually associated with the Buddhists.[65] Around the edges are pillars which either indicate that it was an open pillared structure similar to one shown on a Buddhist relief at Nāgārjunakoṇḍa (fig. 192), or that the outer wall was created by filling the spaces between the pillars with brick-work, encasing the brick with a stone veneer.[66] This latter technique would be consistent with experimental techniques of architecture used by the Hindus at Nāgārjunakoṇḍa as observed in the Sarvadeva temple. At present both suggestions should be kept in mind as the physical remains of the temple do not permit a clear answer.

The Architecture of Nāgārjunakoṇḍa: Buddhist Remains

The Buddhist architectural remains of Nāgārjunakoṇḍa[67] present an entirely different problem than the Hindu remains. Many of them are well documented both by abundant remains and inscriptions. The monuments are well distributed throughout the valley with a large concentration in the central portion. In contrast to the Hindu architecture found in Nāgārjunakoṇḍa, the basic design elements of the Buddhist monuments are not unusual in form. They consist of simple apsidal *caitya* halls and *vihāras* in the standard quadrangle arrangement. In general, the *stūpas* follow the well-known Andhra Pradesh conventions and consist of a dome resting on a round drum. Projecting from these drums are four platforms on each of the four axes. On each of these platforms is a row of five pillars referred to as *āyaka* pillars (*āyaka khambha*) in the inscriptions. The platforms have subsequently been called *āyaka* platforms. The structure is best illustrated in a reconstruction of the Amarāvatī *stūpa* (fig. 16). A proposed meaning for both the platforms and the pillars will be discussed in Chapter II, for the meaning of them is closely allied to the meaning of the sculpture which has been found upon them.

But beyond the meaning of the individual architectural forms at Nāgārjunakoṇḍa, there is a great importance in the juxtaposition of these forms. They show a definite chronological evolution which has largely been worked out by H. Sarkar,[68] and this evolution is completely consistent with my own stylistic evolution of the Buddhist sculptures at the site. Further, they show an evolutionary phase within Andhra Buddhism which can be supported by the Nāgārjunakoṇḍa inscriptions, an evolution which marks a transition from Hīnayāna to Mahāyāna; this, too, has been worked out by H. Sarkar, and has also been considered by Sukumar Dutt.[69] Both concluded that the architecture of Nāgārjunakoṇḍa, while clearly Hīnayāna Buddhist in origin, was built by Hīnayānists who were taking the path to the Mahāyāna, with monks gradually acceding to both *stūpa* and image worship. From a purely historical point of view, these religious changes have been explained by Akira Hirakawa in "The Rise of Mahāyāna and its Relation to *Stūpas*."[70] Worship of Beginning with the premise that the rise of the Mahāyāna faith in Indian Buddhism was based upon doctrines of both the Sarvāstivādin and Mahāsaṁghika schools, Hirakawa demonstrates how the development of the cult of *stūpa* worship, through the activities of the lay community, for which we have only diffuse and scant documentation, was an important factor in the development of the Mahāyāna faith. His study contains the assumption that the worship of the *stūpa* could not have been an intrinsic part of the Hīnayāna faith because there exist necessary distinctions within the *triratna*, the Buddha, the *dharma*, and the *saṁgha*. As the *stūpa* is a symbol of the Buddha, it could not be included within the properties of the *saṁgha*.

Subsequent to the work of Sarkar, Dutt, and Hirakawa has come the translation of the anonymous text of *The Lion's Roar of Queen Śrīmālā* by Professor Alex Wayman and Hideko Wayman. The text is one of the chief scriptural sources for the theory that all sentient beings have the potentiality of Buddhahood within them. The heroine of the text is a Buddhist queen, and presumably a contemporary of the Buddha.

The Waymans were able to demonstrate, through documentary and circumstantial evidence, that *The Lion's Roar*, though clearly Mahāyāna, was probably written during the third century for one of the later Mahāsāṁghika sub-sects at Nāgārjunakoṇḍa.[71] The addition of the text to our present knowledge of the architecture and inscriptions helps us to expand upon Sarkar's carefully thought out speculations upon the coming of the Mahāyāna faith to that site. It also helps to envision the Nāgārjunakoṇḍa monuments in a broader cultural framework. Thus I would like to restate, with several variations and explanations, Sarkar's evolution of the Buddhist architecture which shows a transition from Hīnayāna to Mahāyāna. The inclusion of epigraphical evidence, as well as a parallel discussion of the crucial text, *The Lion's Roar of Queen Śrīmālā*, greatly enhances our understanding of Nāgārjunakoṇḍa's architectural history and the evolution of Buddhism at Nāgārjunakoṇḍa.

The Great *Stūpa* or *Mahācetiya* at Nāgārjunakoṇḍa (fig. 17) is, as yet, the earliest monument at the site with a dated inscription. It was a large *stūpa* covered with plaster. No remains of stone decoration were reported to be found near the *stūpa*. It rested on a drum which was 5 feet high and 106 feet in diameter. The original height of the *stūpa* was approximately 70 to 80 feet.[72] Its importance is attested to by its size and also by the fact that it housed corporeal remains of the Buddha.[73] Even today, Buddhists from all over India, and especially many Tibetans, come to worship at what is essentially a reconstruction of the original monument on the present island of Nāgārjunakoṇḍa in the middle of Nāgārjunasāgar. The *stūpa* contained the usual Andhra rectangular projection on each of the four axes, each surmounted by five stone pillars bearing donative inscriptions. Such pillars may be seen represented on sculptural relief panels from both Amarāvatī and Nāgārjunakoṇḍa (figs. 150-51). In this case, all the pillars bear an identical date, that is, the sixth regnal year of King Vīrapuruṣadatta,[74] i.e., c. 246-56. This would probably be the date of the completion of the *stūpa*.

The inscriptions tell us that the monument was dedicated to the Aparamahāvinaseliya sect.[75] The Aparamahāvinaseliyas were a branch of the later Mahāsāṁghikas. Amongst their doctrines, according to Vasumitra, we find it stated that the worship of a *stūpa* or the worship of a *caitya* does not produce much fruit.[76] Nevertheless, the fact that one of the largest *stūpas* in India was built for the benefit of this sect indicates that they were willing to alter their practices to fit more modern times. A lady named Cāṁtisiri is identified as the major donatrix; also identified are her relatives. The most interesting of these is King Cāṁtamūla I, deceased father of Vīrapuruṣadatta, brother of the donatrix and first known king of the dynasty. Cāṁtamūla is described as a worshipper of Kārttikeya of Mahāsena. His Śaivite affiliation mentioned on a Buddhist monument is at first surprising, but all the men of the royal family were Hindus, usually Śaivites, as I have said, while most of the royal women were Buddhists and patronized Buddhist monuments for the benefit of their Hindu spouses and kin.

A major role was played by the chief donatrix, Cāṁtisiri. She is praised, or rather praises herself, in the inscriptions for her munificence and compassion, especially for those who are destitute and poor. She carefully lists her material donations, and asks in return for the attainment of nirvāṇa for herself and for the welfare and happiness of all the world. Thus her self-image was not one of passivity but of spiritual participation. The historical Cāṁtisiri seems to have her counterpart in Queen Śrīmālā, the interlocutor of *The Lion's Roar.* The Waymans suggest that the Śrīmālā text was written at Nāgārjunakoṇḍa to honor the royal patronesses. For Queen Śrīmālā, on her own path to nirvāṇa, is also an active participant. She takes a vow to teach the doctrine and to give to the poor; the wording of her vow is similar to that of the Nāgārjunakoṇḍa inscriptions. In her eighth vow, Śrīmālā addresses the Buddha:

> Lord, from now on, and until I attain enlightenment, I hold to this eighth vow, that when in the future I observe sentient beings who are friendless, trapped and bound, diseased, troubled, poor and miserable, I shall not forsake them for a single moment until they are restored. Lord, seeing them afflicted by suffering, I shall liberate them from each of those sufferings; having conferred goods upon them, I shall leave them.[77]

As if echoing Śrīmālā's words, the historical Cāṁtisiri is described as follows in the Aparamahāvinaseliya inscriptions:

> . . .she who, out of compassion for Śramanas, Brahmins, and those that are miserable, poor and destitute, is wont to bestow on them a matchless and ceaseless flow of Velāmic gifts, she the great mistress of munificence, devoted to all the virtuous, having due regard for the past, future and present (members) of both the houses to which she belongs, for the attainment of welfare and happiness in both the worlds and in order to attain herself the bliss of Nirvāṇa and for the attainment of welfare and happiness by all the world, has erected this pillar.[78]

The request for nirvāṇa by the laity in return for charitable acts is indeed a Mahāyāna practice. Such a request also appears in early inscriptions from Taxila, as has already been pointed out by Sarkar.[79] But the wording of the Taxila texts[80] is so entirely different that these cannot be closely associated with the Nāgārjunakoṇḍa inscription or with *The Lion's Roar of Queen Śrīmālā.* At Nāgārjunakoṇḍa, the phraseology of *The Lion's Roar* is confined to the Aparamahāvinaseliya sect, and most particularly with donations by Queen Cāṁtisiri.

If Cāṁtisiri was a potential candidate for nirvāṇa, what then was her place in Ikṣvāku society? If we continue to compare her to Queen Śrīmālā, Śrīmālā is referred to in the text as the "good daughter of the family" and in that capacity she is also a bodhisattva. According to the Waymans, she would be a member of the *bodhisattvagaṇa*, a separate lay organization whose ultimate origins probably went back to about a century after the Buddha, at the time of the original split between the orthodox Buddhists and the Mahāsāṁghikas.[81] Textual validation of this group in the early *Mahāyāna saṁgha* is provided by Akira Hirakawa, who demonstrates that the function of the *bodhisattvagaṇa* was to teach the Mahāyāna faith.[82] It seems to have remained separate from the *bhikṣusaṁgha* and was not a renunciant group. The role of Cāṁtisiri was as the lay equivalent to the monks, who were dependent upon her for their sustenance.

Even though in the opinion of Vasumitra the Aparamahāvinaseliya monks were not in themselves dedicated to *stūpa* worship, it was through donations to the *stūpa* that the lay bodhisattva could express support for the monastic community and devotion to the Buddha. Hirakawa has demonstrated that the development of a powerful lay group, with a justifiable place within Buddhism, was one of the major factors which helped to bring about the Mahāyāna faith. One of the most important roles of the laity was to give donations to the *stūpa*.[83] The role of the lay bodhisattva is further stated in the Śrīmālā text when Śrīmālā says to the Buddha:

> Lord, at the time of the decline of the Doctrine, when monks, nuns, and male and female laymen quarrel with each other to break up into many sects, whatever good son of the family or good daughter of the family delighting in the Doctrine which is without deceit and falsehood, for the sake of maintaining the Illustrious Doctrine, creates a bodhisattva group of those who have the Doctrine, would certainly be the good son of the family or good daughter of the family to obtain a prophecy from all the Buddhas because of that activity.[84]

Such sectarianism was precisely the case at Nāgārjunakoṇḍa. There were several sects, all Hīnayāna. Most seem to have acceded to image worship, *stūpa* worship, and other activities associated with lay practice. But, as we shall see, many of their steps were tentative.

As I have said, the worship of the *stūpa* by the brotherhood was not only frowned upon by the Aparamahāvinaseliyas, but was generally averse to Hīnayāna monastic tradition. In the *Mahā-parinibbāna-sutta* the Buddha specifically says to Ānanda that it is the job of the laity rather than the job of the monks to worship the corporeal remains of the Buddha. In the text, Ānanda says to the Buddha:

> What are we to do, Lord, with the remains of the Tathāgata?

The Buddha replies:

> Hinder not yourselves, Ānanda, by honoring the remains of the Tathāgata. Be zealous, I beseech you, Ānanda in your own behalf! Devote yourselves to your own good! Be earnest, be zealous, be intent on your own good! There are wise men Ānanda, among the nobles, among the Brāhmans, among the heads of houses, who are firm believers in the Tathāgata; and they will do honor to the remains of the Tathāgata.[85]

Yet, as documented by inscriptions, nine years after the completion of the Great *Stūpa* at Nāgārjunakoṇḍa (Vīrapuruṣadatta's 15th regnal year), a monastery was built right next to it,[86] and three years after that (Vīrapuruṣadatta's regnal 18th year), a simple *caitya* hall containing a small *stūpa* was added right outside the monastic precinct (fig. 18).[87] Indeed, the complex was financed by the laity, or rather a member of the *bodhisattvagaṇa*, but it was built for the monks who had immediate access to the *stūpa*.

The next monastic unit I would like to cite also belongs to the Aparamahāvinaseliya sect. This unit, Site 9 (fig. 19), had four structural phases. The complex was begun at the time of Vīrapuruṣadatta or even earlier, and appears to have been completed during the eighth regnal year of his son Ehuvala Cāṁtamūla (c. A.D. 273-83).[88] (This is nearly contemporary with the two Hindu structures discussed above.) There is at least a twenty year time difference between the completion of this group and the completion of the Great *Stūpa* at Site 1. The monastic unit as a whole is similar to Site 1 except that two small votive *stūpas* were set up in front of the *caitya gṛha* which contains a *stūpa*. Facing this is yet another *caitya gṛha* which originally contained a standing Buddha image. The second *caitya* seems to have been added in one of the later phases of construction, which seems to indicate that the worship of the free standing Buddha image (a practice associated with Mahāyāna Buddhism) did not come into vogue at Nāgārjunakoṇḍa until the time of Ehuvala Cāṁtamūla, that is, during the latter part of the third century. (As we will see in Chapter II, the Buddha image in narrative relief was used during the reign of Vīrapuruṣadatta, but only gained prominence during Ehuvala's reign.) But the Buddha image did not really dominate the monastic complex. The worshipper monk faced a choice; if he went into one *caitya gṛha* he worshipped a *stūpa*, in the other, a complete standing image of the Buddha. Sarkar has suggested that the introduction of the Buddha at Nāgārjunakoṇḍa may indicate that the Aparamahāvinaseliyas were divided into two subsects.[89] Indeed, this may be the case, but the addition of the Buddha image, as an icon of equal importance to the *stūpa* contained in the chapel opposite it, may also indicate an evolutionary phase within the Mahāsāṁghika subsect whose tenets were obviously predisposed to such worship. We must also recall that the presence of the Buddha image in Andhra Pradesh had already appeared in a narrative context at Amarāvatī over a century before its appearance as a free standing image at Nāgārjunakoṇḍa, and many of the late Amarāvatī narrative scenes containing figures of the Buddha seem to belong to an Ikṣvāku phase. Again, as we will see in Chapter II, the Amarāvatī school most strongly influenced Nāgārjunakoṇḍa from Ehuvala's reign onward. Before that, other groups had an impact on Nāgārjunakoṇḍa.

The inscriptions belonging to Site 9 are also of great interest. They tell us that the monument was dedicated by an *upāsaka* named Chadasiri, who has bestowed many religious gifts at prominent cities, prominent townships, and prominent hills in connection with festivals celebrated in honor of the Buddha, the *dharma*, and the *saṁgha*. In return for his donations, he was to attain nirvāṇa.[90] The term *upāsaka*, not used in the above Cāṁtisiri means "those who serve" in contrast to the *bhikṣus*, "those who beg". This is different from the Mahāyāna member of the *bodhisattvagaṇa*, whose purpose is his own nirvāṇa and the conversion of others to the Great Vehicle. The inclusion of the Hīnayāna term, however, does not indicate Hīnayāna practice. Following the Mahāyāna tradition, as seen in Cāṁtisiri's inscription, and defined in the Śrīmālā text, the *upāsaka* asks for his own nirvāṇa.

The ground-plan of Site 4 (figs. 20 and 21) shows us an ideal Nāgārjunakoṇḍa ground-plan toward which the architects of Site 9 seem to have been striving. Unfortunately, this site has little documentation. In this case, the *caityas* were actually included within the monastic complex, indicating beyond a doubt that the monks actually participated in both the worship of the *stūpa* and the Buddha image. In actual practice, the monk entered the courtyard. If he walked to the right, he entered a *caitya* containing a *stūpa* around which *pradakṣinā* could have been performed. If he walked to the left, he entered a shrine containing an over-life-size Buddha placed firmly against the back wall of the shrine. Outside the complex was a large *stūpa* to which either the monk or the laity could have had access. This particular Buddha image (fig. 22) is presently housed in the Nāgārjunakoṇḍa Museum for safety, while a replica of it is placed in a full-scale model of the site and is used for worship by present-day visitors to the island of Nāgārjunakoṇḍa.[91]

The Aparamahāvinaseliyas show us yet another variation in structure, a rectangular shrine housing the image of a seated female deity (figs. 23 and 24).[92] The shrine was within a precinct which included places for assembling and washing. It was found nearly contiguous to the amphitheater of Site 17. The shrine itself was reached by a flight of steps leading up a hill and was flanked by two large rooms. The inscription concerning it is quite fragmentary and undated, but it clearly belongs to the Aparamahāvinaseliya sect.[93] It has been conjectured that the structure post-dates the Ikṣvākus. If this is the case, we have clear evidence of the continuation of Buddhism after the decline of this dynasty in the mid-fourth century A.D. However, it is clear in any case, that the Aparamahāvinaseliyas had no objection to image worship at the time, and that they did not confine their structures to the traditionally Hīnayāna independent *stūpa*, *caitya* and *vihāra* forms.

The other identifiable sects residing at Nāgārjunakoṇḍa were the Mahīśāsakas, the Bahuśrutīyas, and the Theravādins from Ceylon. While it was the Aparamahāvinaseliyas who seem to have been the first to introduce imagery at Nāgārjunakoṇḍa, it was the Mahīśāsakas who were the most conservative. From their extant literature, which survives only in the Chinese version translated by Buddhajīva in A.D. 424, their work seems to be quite similar to the Pāli *Vinayapiṭaka* of the Theravādins.[94] According to Bareau,[95] they believed that it was more meritorious to give to the monastic community than to the Buddha (*Buddha=stūpa*). Because the Buddha is part of the *saṁgha*, he may be considered a monk (*Śramaṇa*). Having long since entered into nirvāṇa, he cannot enjoy the fruits of this gift. However, the *saṁgha*, which is composed of living persons, could well profit from such a gift, and the gift could produce much fruit. Nevertheless, if there is a gift to the Buddha, the material properties must be kept separate from that of the *saṁgha*. This is clearly consistent with the ground-plan of the Mahīśāsaka monastic area, Sites 7-8 (fig. 25), which shows two small *stūpas* placed outside the monastic precinct, with neither a *stūpa* nor a Buddha image within the confines of the simple compound. The inscription belonging to the site tells us that the monastery was built during the eleventh regnal year of King Ehuvala Cāṁtamūla, that is three years after the completion of the Aparamahāvinaseliya Sites 9. Site 7-8 was built by the sister of the king, who was also the wife of the Mahārājā of Vanavāsi, "for the benefit of the Masters of the Mahīśāsaka sect, on behalf of the community of the Four Quarters, and for the sake of the welfare and happiness of all sentient beings."[96] In this inscription, there is neither a request for nirvāṇa, nor any other reflection of either the Śrīmālā text nor of specific Mahāyāna practice.

The Bahuśrutīyas at Nāgārjunakoṇḍa were offshoots of the Mahāsāṁghikas, whose literature showed a strong affiliation to that of the Sarvāstivādins. The Bahuśrutīya text, the *Satyasiddhiśāstra*, which exists in the Chinese translation of Kumārajīva, originated in central India around the third century A.D., and expresses a doctrine which is half way between Hīnayāna and Mahāyāna including the supramundane teachings of the Buddha. The Bahuśrutīyas did not believe that the Buddhas existed within the *saṁgha*, and believed that gifts to the *saṁgha* and gifts to the Buddha were both meritorious.[97] Again, this was reflected in their monastic unit, Site 5 (fig. 26), which was being built during the second regnal year of Ehuvala Cāṁtamūla.[98] Outside the *vihāra* were two *caityas* facing each other, both meant for enshrining a *stūpa*. At a later date, a *caitya*, rectangular in shape, was built within the residential part of the monastery. In front of it was a pillar portraying the seated figure of a Buddha (fig. 27).[99] Thus the Bahuśrutīyas first included *stūpa* worship, and subsequently image worship into their practices.

The last group for which we have clear evidence at Nāgārjunakoṇḍa is the Theravādins from Ceylon who were referred to as the Theravādins of the Mahāvihāra and also as Vibhajyavādins.[100] This is the group which we expect to be most conservative, but such was not the case. An inscription dated in the fourteenth regnal year of Vīrapuruṣadatta, the second king of the dynasty, records the donation of a *caitya* at Site 43 (fig. 29) by a female lay worshipper (*upāsikā*) named Bodhisiri. Bodhisiri does not seem to have been connected with the Ikṣvāku royal family. She refers to the Theravādins from Ceylon as having converted the monks from twelve different regions of India (perhaps a bit of formulaic exaggeration) including Gandhāra and Kashmir. The donation was made for the sake of at least thirty-one of her relatives, all listed by name. The *caitya* was dedicated "for the endless welfare and happiness of the assembly of saints and for that of the whole world."[101]

The site consisted of a monastic unit, a *caitya*, and a *stūpa* very similar in arrangement to the Aparamahāvinaseliya Site 1. But at a later date, an oblong shrine with a pedestal for a Buddha image was placed inside the residential enclosure.[102] Another residential unit also belonging to this sect,[103] Site 38 (fig. 28), was completed by adding a *caitya*, perhaps means for enshrining a Buddha image, and the *stūpa* right inside the residential enclosure. Thus, not surprisingly, we find among the doctrines of the Theravādins of the Mahāvihāra, that a gift to the Buddha produces much fruit (*mahāphala*).[104]

We all realize that for centuries before the building of Nāgārjunakoṇḍa, many of the trends which we are showing, that is, the gradual incorporation of the *stūpa* and the Buddhist image into monastic worship, had already begun; and were more evidence available, we might be able to show similar happenings at other sites. But the best available evidence is at Nāgārjunakoṇḍa, a Śaivite and Buddhist region where a large lay community poured its vast funds into *stūpa* construction and repair. The monks, of all cults except the Mahīśāsakas, gradually incorporated both *stūpa* worship and image worship into their precincts, thus breaking down the traditional Hīnayāna distinctions between the Buddha, the *dharma*, and the *saṁgha*. Thus, the *Mahāsāṁghika-vinaya* stated that the land of the *saṁgha* and the land of the *stūpa* must not encroach upon each other. However, the *Sarvāstivāda-vinaya-vibhāṣa* qualifies this by saying that a *stūpa* must not be erected upon the land of the *caturdiśa saṁgha* with the exception that it be permitted with the approval of the whole membership of the *saṁgha*.[105] Such a vote must indeed have been taken at Nāgārjunakoṇḍa.

The laity, too, needed to find their position within the Buddhist community. Following the tradition of the pious patroness Cāṁtisiri, who was influenced by, or had influence upon *The Lion's Roar of Queen Śrīmālā*, the patronesses became the "good daughters of the family", who gained merit, and sometimes even nirvāṇa, through their support of the Buddha, the *dharma*, and the *saṁgha*, as we have seen in the architecture of Nāgārjunakoṇḍa, the Aparamahāvinaseliya inscriptions, and in *The Lion's Roar of Queen Śrīmālā*.

As we will see in Chapter II, these architectural and doctrinal developments are strongly reflected in the sculpture at Nāgārjunakoṇḍa. For the Buddhist sites at Nāgārjunakoṇḍa with simple monastic complexes reveal an early style. Changes began at Site 9, which is the first documented monument to use the double chapel system. It also ushers in a new style which is strongly reflected at two undated monasteries of the more complex arrangement, those of Sites 2 and 3 in the northeast part of the valley (see plates 2 and 3).

CHAPTER II

THE EVOLUTION OF THE NĀGĀRJUNAKOṆḌA STYLE

The sculpture of Nāgārjunakoṇḍa is generally considered a stylistic bridge between the fully developed Amarāvatī style of the second century A.D. and the florescence of the Gupta style of North India in the fifth century. Nāgārjunakoṇḍa is frequently represented as the late phase of the art of Amarāvatī, that is, its period of aesthetic decline. Indeed, many of the themes represented at Nāgārjunakoṇḍa are the same as those found at Amarāvatī, executed in a flat decorative style, sometimes carved by sculptors less technically skilled than those who made the richly modeled and carefully finished reliefs of the neighboring site. Nevertheless, the Nāgārjunakoṇḍa school is one of variety and experimentation. Such experimentations, along with those at the neighboring sites of Goli and Gummididurru, help us to understand works such as the Begram ivories; they also provide transitions to works of the Gupta, Vākāṭaka, Cālukya, and Pallava styles.

Consistent with the frustrations of art history, most dated inscriptions from Nāgārjunakoṇḍa are not associated with sculptures. In fact, there are relatively few dated inscriptions. Although we have at least one inscribed work for each of three successive kings of the Ikṣvāku dynasty, these works are only in part representative of the bulk of material discovered. Nevertheless, these must be used as a chronological basis, while the remainder of the works can be dated in association with them.

While the sculpture of Amarāvatī shows a relatively consistent pattern of development from an early phase, through a mature phase, and subsequently through a phase of decline, the sculpture of Nāgārjunakoṇḍa shows no such consistent development. The close proximity to Amarāvatī permitted the sculptors from Nāgārjunakoṇḍa easy access to that site, allowing sculptors from Nāgārjunakoṇḍa to borrow freely from all its sculptural phases, frequently repeating themes almost *verbatim*, while at the same time transforming the style into an idiom entirely of their own.

As we shall demonstrate in this chapter, the stylistic changes in the art of Nāgārjunakoṇḍa are allied to the development of the architectural ground-plans of the site. For there is a definite sculptural style associated with the works of art found at sites using the Site 1 type ground-plan. As Site 9 showed a ground-plan which was transitional toward the "ideal" Nāgārjunakoṇḍa ground-plan, so too was its sculptural style transitional. Consequently, the sculptures belonging to the monastic complexes with the "ideal" ground-plan formed a consistent group, and they, in turn, imply a date for the florescence of the "ideal" ground-plan.

Before discussing the sculptures of Nāgārjunakoṇḍa, we wish to discuss some of the basic characteristics of the mature Amarāvatī school, which reached its heights during the latter part of the second century A.D. and seems to have continued production well into the third century. For, not only is Amarāvatī the more well-known of the two art centers, but it appears to be one of the most sculpturally sophisticated and most creative centers of the Buddhist narrative tradition in India. Thus, we must first look at the Amarāvatī tradition to understand the extent to which the Nāgārjunakoṇḍa school was dependent upon it, and to see what the innovations of the parent school were.

The sculpture of Amarāvatī has by no means homogeneous tradition, for it contains within it many subtrends, as has been discussed by Stella Kramrisch in 1933.[106] The Amarāvatī styles are in themselves a subject suitable to a monographic study, but here we confine ourselves to some general characteristics relevant to the Nāgārjunakoṇḍa problem.

The decorative scheme of the Amarāvatī *stūpa* provided all the basic compositional formats used at Nāgārjunakoṇḍa. Thus, as centuries earlier at Bharhut in the Madhya Pradesh, the sculptors of the railing were required to decorate the interiors (figs. 31, 84 and 161) and exteriors[107] of the coping stone dealing with problems of continuous horizontal compositions. On the uprights of railings, roundels contained either lotuses, or were filled with elaborate compositions (i.e., figs. 32 and 156). Although there were few railing fragments at Nāgārjunakoṇḍa, the artists employed this roundel form to decorate the bases of *āyaka* platforms (i.e., fig. 155). The Amarāvatī *stūpa* had no gateways, but vertical compositions associated with railing uprights at Sāñcī are found between the lotus roundels of railing *staṁbhas* (fig. 30). Such vertical compositions are not employed at Nāgārjunakoṇḍa except in the case of memorial pillars (figs. 51, 57, 60, 61 and 63) which seem to have both a format and origin which is independent of *stūpa* decoration. The body of the *stūpa*, which was decorated in Gandhāra but not in other areas of the Indian subcontinent, showed the way for a new set of decorative elements at Amarāvatī. The drum was decorated with rectangular panels each representing an entire *stūpa* (figs. 153 and 154). These were separated by narrow vertical panels containing symbolic forms or episodes from the life of the Buddha,[108] and were surmounted by the narrow drum friezes (fig. 50). Such drum friezes were absent at Nāgārjunakoṇḍa, but provided a compositional source for long narrow panels decorating *āyaka* platforms (fig. 64). The lower portion of the dome was decorated with vertical panels. These were surmounted by a frieze of running animals which in turn was surmounted by a row of *triśūlas.*[109] The Nāgārjunakoṇḍa dome slabs were simply variants of the Amarāvatī type (fig. 218). Thus by the time of the building of the *stūpas* at Nāgārjunakoṇḍa, a whole series of satisfactory solutions had already been worked out at Amarāvatī for the basic compositional types. However, in one major area, the decoration of *āyaka* platforms, Nāgārjunakoṇḍa was to produce her most innovative art.

The sculptors of Amarāvatī used a technique of spatial representation totally unique to that school. Figures are carved in low relief, but are so deeply undercut that they stand away from their background creating shadow pools from which emerge figural groupings (figs. 30, 31 and 32). They stand away from their background plane which rarely retains a unified level, thus heightening the shadows at the deepest points. Yet on the upper surfaces, figures become united by harmonious linear rhythms or parabolic curves (figs. 29 and 30), leading the viewer's eye through the main events of the narrative sequence. This technique appears never to have been successfully achieved in any other school of Andhra Pradesh or elsewhere in India, and seems to be the technical point on which Amarāvatī so successfully distinguishes itself from all other schools. While the linear unity is retained in Nāgārjunakoṇḍa, the deep under-cutting is conspicuously absent, so that the viewer's eye moves fluidly plane (i.e., fig. 158). It is clear that the Amarāvatī mode of carving required far more skill and time on the part of the sculptors, while the Nāgārjunakoṇḍa sculptors could have produced works in more rapid succession with an even ground plane rarely more than 1/4 inch in depth, the carving frequently being reduced to a series of flat incised lines on a single plane.

The two modes of carving are paralleled in the approach toward linear perspective of the two schools. While throughout the schools of Amarāvatī and Nāgārjunakoṇḍa architectural settings usually serve as scene dividers, at Amarāvatī they are also a field for the artists' perspectival achievements. For example, in representing the Buddha's Return to Kapilavastu (fig. 31), each section of the palace ramparts on the left is seen from two angles, while on the far right we see a unique head-on view into a *caitya,* while the moonstone before it is seen as if from above, and the *stūpa* raised above its ground level to emphasize its significance. The large *stūpa* virtually dominating the composition is of the type which existed throughout Andhra Pradesh. All the details must have been of extreme significance to the local worshippers, for each is shown from its optimum viewpoint. The front portion of the *stūpa* is shown straight on, exaggerating the depth of the railing entrance, while showing the moonstone step as if seen from above. The side entrances are in "correct" perspective, but the *āyaka* pillars, the important symbolic innovation of the Andhra Buddhists, are shown in reverse perspective, so that their numbers, and therefore their symbolic significance, cannot be mistaken by the viewer. In terms of architectural representation, this particular *stūpa* representation exemplifies the achievements of the Amarāvatī artist in his most flamboyant manner. At Nāgārjunakoṇḍa, perspective representations of architecture appear not to have been significant to the artist's aims. The structures selected are usually very simple in form (figs. 180, 226 and 231), while scene dividers are frequently pillars as seen from the front (fig. 203).

Both schools use the overlapping figures to suggest recession in depth, but this perspectival technique is frequently negated for reasons of inconographic significance. For instance, in the Return to Kapilavastu from Amarāvatī, the Buddha figure in the middle ground "rises above" obscuration, as he performs a miracle before the onlookers. His physical proportions vie with that of the *stūpa* and the tree, his aniconic counterparts.

Cāṁtamūla I (c. A.D. 225-40 to 250)

THE PROBLEM OF THE MAHĀCETIYA AND SITE 6

The earliest phase of the art of Nāgārjunakoṇḍa is clouded in obscurity. It stands aside from both the fully mature Amarāvatī style, and does not even seem to foreshadow the fully mature Nāgārjunakoṇḍa style in any obvious way. There are no clearly documented surviving monuments at Nāgārjunakoṇḍa from the reign of the first known king, Cāṁtamūla I. His inscriptions were however found at the nearby sites of Reṇṭāla[110] and Kesanapalli;[111] but unfortunately these are not connected with surviving sculpture. As we have mentioned in Chapter I, the most important monument from the reign of Vīrapuruṣadatta, or for that matter all of Nāgārjunakoṇḍa, was the *Mahācetiya* of Site 1. It bore numerous inscriptions indicating that it was completed in Vīrapuruṣadatta's sixth regnal year, at which time the *āyaka* pillars were installed. This *stūpa*, according to all archaeological accounts was undecorated. In almost all of the inscriptions of the *Mahācetiya*, not only is Vīrapuruṣadatta mentioned, but also his father Cāṁtamūla I, who, according to inscriptional evidence, was a follower of Mahāsena. Yet the Reṇṭāla and Kesanapalli inscriptions clearly indicate that donations on behalf of the Buddhist community were made during his reign.[112] Although these inscriptions were found on architectural remains, it seems reasonable to believe that a whole sculptural tradition did originally accompany these works. Although we cannot document any sculptural works at Nāgārjunakoṇḍa from Cāṁtamūla I's reign on epigraphical grounds, stylistic and circumstantial evidence indicates that such a school did exist.

The *Mahācetiya* of Site 1 at Nāgārjunakoṇḍa was one of the largest *stūpas* of the ancient Indian world and purportedly housed a corporeal relic of the Buddha. The relic was placed deep within the dome of the *stūpa* toward the outer rim.[113] After the relic was safely enclosed, the dome was completed and encased with plaster. Most likely, the *āyaka* platforms and the pillars bearing the dated inscriptions were added toward the end of the construction. This would be consistent with the building scheme of the Jaggayyapeta *stūpa*, for we know that the *āyaka* pillars dating to Vīrapuruṣadatta's twentieth regnal year[114] were added to a *stūpa* of an earlier date. Although there is no reason to give such a long span to the building of the *Mahācetiya*, an extra generation or two to the usually presumed date would not be unreasonable.

As we will see in subsequent pages, we have excellent evidence for a distinct sculptural style produced under Vīrapuruṣadatta and his successors. Thus, if one could find a group of sculpture which could be reasonably associated with the *Mahācetiya*, or cannot fit in with any other group, one could both test the hypothesis for a long duration of the building of the *Mahācetiya* and for a yet undefined sculpture style belonging to Cāṁtamūla I.

In 1930, J. Ph. Vogel published an inscription which has since gone unnoticed. The sculpture on which the inscription appeared (fig. 33) was never published, nor was its find spot, even though Vogel was careful to indicate such information whenever known. Further, Vogel questioned his own reading of the inscription even though this is one of the clearest inscriptions of the Nāgārjunakoṇḍa group. For by 1930, Vogel must have already known that the inscription contradicted the reported archaeological evidence from the site, which was that the *Mahācetiya* was an undecorated *stūpa*. The inscription and his translation reads as follows:[115]

> (Line 1) Sidhaṁ namo bhagavato aga-pogalasa Budhasa chhadakapavitch[e]na Paduma[vā]-niya gharhaniya sagaya saputakānaṁ Hagas [i]r[i]sa sagasa Nagatarasa cha sabhaja[sa] (Line 2) saputakāna[ṁ] cha deyadham[o] paṭo unisa cha mahāchetiye patiṭh[a]vito
>
> Success. Adoration of the Lord Buddha, the best of beings.
>
> A meritorious gift (consisting of) a slab and a coping stone, has been dedicated at the Great Chaitya by Chhadakapavaticha, Padumavānī his house-wife, together with their sons Hagasiri and Nagatara with his wife and together with their daughters.

The significant term in this inscription is clearly the reference to the *Mahācetiya* or Great *Caitya*. This term in the Nāgārjunakoṇḍa inscriptions has been applied only to the Great *Caitya* of Site 1. The other term of significance is *Patiṭhavito* (skt. *pratiṣthāpito*).[116] The term is usually translated as "installed" or "consecrated". Thus the inscription tells us that a slab (this one?) and a coping stone were installed at the Great *Caitya*. Yet this epigraphic information contradicts our own archaeological understanding of Site 1, for, according to Longhurst, no sculpture whatsoever was found within the proximity of Site 1,[117] and the *stūpa* was considered to be totally unadorned. If this piece actually did come from Site 1, how is it that only one piece remains of a *stūpa* of 106 feet in diameter? If the *stūpa* did bear sculpture and a stone railing, they would have left some traces, even if most of the sculpture had been removed and burnt for lime. The answer remains enigmatic, but let us examine the possibility of this piece coming from *Stūpa* 1.

The *stūpas* of Andhra Pradesh are generally considered to follow an evolution from unadorned to that of being richly decorated with reliefs. Consequently, the Nāgārjunakoṇḍa *stūpa* should be an elaboration of the Great *Stūpa* at Amarāvatī. However, the archaeological evidence defies this notion. On the other hand, we believe that the drum slabs depicting *stūpas* from Nāgārjunakoṇḍa represent, with a certain degree of accuracy, *stūpas* which actually did exist. No plain *stūpa*, with *āyaka* pillars and platforms has been represented on these slabs. In fact, demonstrably early examples, those of the Site 9 type, show us a *stūpa* with a decorated drum frieze (figs. 93, 94, 100 and 105), and, in one case (fig. 104) only a decorated *āyaka* platform. In fact, a relief similar to the inscribed one appears in figure 93.

It would be logical then that these early *stūpa* slabs were representing the *Mahācetiya* which must have been only partially decorated. Still this contradicts the archaeological evidence which insists that no traces of stone, except for the *āyaka* pillars, were found at Site 1. There are a few small clues to the problem. Upon first excavating Site 1 in 1926, Kuraishi reported that ". . .the *stūpa* was excavated by some treasure seekers or amateur archaeologists long before its existence became known to the officers of the Archaeological Department."[118] This could easily account for the loss of some pieces, but not all. We have searched in vain through both public and private collections in both India and in the West and have been unable to find any sculpture which we could attribute to the *Mahācetiya*. Yet the wording of the inscription is undeniably clear.[119] Further, when an inscription on a panel from nearby Site 6 (figs. 36, 41-42) was published by Vogel, he stated that the piece was from Polugubōḍu (the contemporary name of the mound of Site 6). Regarding the so-called *Mahācetiya* inscription, he gave no find spot, indicating that there was a confusion in the archaeological data.

Sarkar, seemingly aware of an inconsistency, suggested that one of the early drum slabs (fig. 101) belonged to Site 1.[120] This slab, however, would be consistent with the early Site 9 type to be discussed below, as is the slab dedicated at the *Mahācetiya* consistent with the style of the *āyaka* panel of Site 6. As we shall shortly see, it is possible that the inscribed slab, as well as other stones, was intended to be installed at Site 1 but never was. Regarding the *unisa* or coping stone mentioned in the inscription, we have no evidence of its existence. The *Mahācetiya*, as the largest and most important *stūpa* at Nāgārjunakoṇḍa, must have been represented numerous times on various drum slabs sculpted at the site. As mentioned above, on these slabs we have no evidence of a totally unadorned *stūpa*. Enigmatic as the evidence is, we believe that the *Mahācetiya* must have been decorated, at least on the *āyaka* platforms. Even if the inscribed slab did not decorate the *Mahācetiya*, it was intended to do so. Thus one could assume that the slab was carved before the installation of the *āyaka* pillars of the *Mahācetiya* in the sixth regnal year of Vīrapuruṣadatta. Further, the inscribed slab, as we shall demonstrate, is stylistically related to another slab from Site 6. Thus, from the point of view of style, we will consider the inscribed slab in relation to a group of works from Site 6.

The sculpture bearing the donative inscription appears to be part of an *āyaka* platform. Its subject is easily recognizable as an aniconic representation of the Buddha's First Sermon at Banaras. The central scene is flanked by two *mithuna* couples which are set off from it by a rail pattern containing three protruding lotus roundels on each group of cross-bars. The figural style is squat and heavy. The figures are set upon a shallow stage, and protrude beyond the borders of the composition. This is quite surprising, for it does not conform to the flat low relief which we have already defined as typifying the Nāgārjunakoṇḍa style which we consider to be a direct outgrowth of the Amarāvatī tradition. The female figures in the *mithuna* couples are seen arranging their hair. This theme is well-known in classical antiquity, and was popular at Mathurā, an observation whose significance we shall elaborate on shortly.

Other sculptures from Nāgārjunakoṇḍa clearly demonstrate that the so-called *Mahācetiya* sculpture was not an isolated example but related to a larger group of works. Though we have no reason to suggest that these were part of the *Mahācetiya*, the entire group is stylistically related. A scene of the Worship of the Bodhi Tree (fig. 34) shows similar features; squat heavy figures protruding beyond the borders. The facial types in these two panels are noteworthy. These are broad with relatively small chins, while noses are flat. In an upright panel found at Site 6, these features are even more squat (fig. 44). These same features will be reflected at a later time in the sculptures from Site 9.

Regarding yet another *āyaka* panel of this group (fig. 35), its compositions are more complex and less hieratic than the other examples. On the right half of the panel, we see a remaining fragment of the Champeyya Jātaka. From the point of view of style, this panel clearly derives from a more elegant example of the same theme from Amarāvatī (fig. 40). This theme will be reused in the more traditional Nāgārjunakoṇḍa style (see fig. 89) during the reign of Vīrapuruṣadatta.

We said we intend to consider the so-called *Mahācetiya* panel in context with the sculpture from Site 6. Site 6 was amongst the earliest to be excavated by Hamid Kuraishi in 1926.[121] (It was originally called Site 4 but has since been renumbered by Longhurst and others.) Its early discovery was a mixed blessing, for it provided the source for several Nāgārjunakoṇḍa sculptures which were removed from the site before it was selected by Madras Presidency for government preservation. Further, in the context of the work of Longhurst and subsequent archaeologists, it was of minor significance, so that these important works took a subsidiary role in the literature.

Site 6 is about three-eighths of a mile to the west of the *Mahācetiya*. It has no dated or datable inscriptions, but it appears to us that it was erected during the building of the *Mahācetiya* by monks coming into the area, perhaps from Gummididurru. If we look at the ground-plan in our fig. 2, we notice that the site consists of a simple *stūpa* with a few monastic cells nearby. This is consistent with the simple ground-plan used by the monks at Site 1 and should be nearly contemporary with it.

The most informative piece from Site 6 is an *āyaka* slab representing the Dream of Queen Māyā, the Casting of the Horoscope, and the Nativity the Seven Steps.[122] The piece bears a donative inscription with neither a date nor the name of a donor.[123] It was considered so pedestrian in appearance that it was never published. But it is the mundane nature of this work which gives it its significance. We shall discuss the piece in sections, for each adds to our knowledge in a different way.

The first section (fig. 37) is one which is stylistically so close to the *Mahācetiya* example and the panel showing the Worship of the Bodhi Tree that we once believed it to be part of the "unknown findspot" group. But, as the *in situ* photograph shows (fig. 36), it is, in fact from Site 6. It represents a couple with a child resting on its mother's hip, and uses the same type of heavy figures resting on a shallow stage, protruding beyond its borders as in the aforementioned group. The child in the scene is the only example of a naturalistic baby appearing at Nāgārjunakoṇḍa; for the Birth and the Seven Steps are always represented aniconically there. The active movement of the child, in contrast to the more subdued babes of Mathurā,[124] reminds us at once of the well-known Hāritī compositions from Gandhāra,[125] and of the much later sixth-century Mother and Child sculptures from Śāmalāji in Rajasthan.[126] But the comparison here does not suggest a lineage from Gandhāra to Nāgārjunakoṇḍa, and then to Śāmalāji, for each has its own stylistic idiom. Instead, each seems to have been independently looking at a now unknown Classical source.[127] The fact that this type was also found on the Begram ivories (fig. 38) with mother and child in an almost identical posture (the posture of the mother is Indian) indicates that this type was being produced by artisans who were in close contact with Western material.[128] To demonstrate that at least one part of the mother and child composition was definitely known on Indian soil, we illustrate here (fig. 39) a Roman bronze handle found at Akota. The bronze, illustrating a small figure of Cupid with outstretched arms, compares closely with the child in our fig. 37. According to Karl Khandalavala, the bronze is of Alexandrian manufacture of about the second century.[129]

The remainder of the *āyaka* panel is also of importance. With regard to the inscription, it is significant in that it bears paleographic similarities to the inscription on the *Mahācetiya* panel. The major feature which they share is that neither inscription contains the elongated vowels which are characteristic of the Nāgārjunakoṇḍa inscriptions in their mature phase.

The panel originally ended in a *bhadraghaṭa* (vase of plenty), a motif which reoccurs at Site 9. Regarding the narrative compositions of the Site 6 panels, two different styles appear. If we look at the Dream of Queen Māyā (fig. 41), we appear to be seeing, at once the compositional prototype for the same theme on *āyaka* panel 2 (fig. 83) and the reclining King Ugrasena on *āyaka* panel 3 of Site 9 (fig. 86), both reflecting an Amarāvatī figure style. But if we look at the composition of the Nativity and the Seven Steps (fig. 42), we find a format totally atypical of Andhra Pradesh. Four male figures (the Great Brahmas) hold up a cloth bearing the footsteps of the Buddha to represent the Seven Steps. The figures, which are quite stumpy, stand in a space box with their heads protruding slightly beyond the border. The knees of all the figures are bent, and are aligned so as to form a horizontal rhythm parallel to the cloth. There is practically no variety in pose, and what is left of Queen Māyā forms a plain vertical. Such compositions, as well as the format of the whole, as we shall see, influenced the general rigidity of *āyaka* panel 1 of Site 9. See, for example, figures 64 and 81. Thus, as we can see, the style of the *āyaka* panel from Site 6 conforms well to the *Mahācetiya* group. It is quite possible that the so-called *Mahācetiya* panel was originally intended for the *Mahācetiya*, but was actually placed at Site 6, while the rest of the group hailed from Site 6 itself.

What caused this unexpectedly simple style of the Site 6-*Mahācetiya* group which in turn was transmitted to *āyaka* panel 1 of *Stūpa* 9 ? A similar panel of the Nativity and Seven Steps (fig. 42) was excavated at Ghāntaśāla,[130] and may have had some influence upon it. In use of space, the closest comparison we have is from a *toraṇa* excavated at apsidal temple 2 at Sonkh in Mathurā District, perhaps representing the *Nāginī* Jaratkārū and the *Nāga* Vāsukī (fig. 43).[131] The figures, set puppet-like across a shallow stage, are united horizontally through their hand gestures and slight bends in their bodies. It would thus seem that the artists of Andhra were very well aware of the Mathurā style, and in fact in this early group, chose it over the indigenous Andhra tradition.

We have shown instances of the borrowing of motifs from the classical West and shall continue to do so throughout this study. We would very much like to have discovered a large group of classical objects in the Nāgārjunakoṇḍa region to demonstrate the mode of transmission. But the lack of such finds does not indicate that these objects did not exist in ancient times. Regarding the problem of Classical influence, Site 6 again helps clarify our understanding. At that site were found two clear gold imitations of Roman gold coins (fig. 45), pierced at the top to be hung on a string. These were found in a reliquary of the *stūpa* along with gold flowers, jade, coral, pearl beads, and a piece of bone[132] indicating that the coins were of extreme importance. Aside from these imitations, actual Roman coins were found at Nāgārjunakoṇḍa: one of Hadrian (A.D. 117-38), one of Faustina, wife of Antoninus (A.D. 138-68), and one which remains unidentified.[133] According to P.L. Gupta, the unidentified coin is probably an imitation,[134] and according to Manfred Raschke,[135] the Faustina coin also fits that category. In 1977, a group of eight Roman gold coins presumably found in South India were offered to the American Numismatic Society for sale.[136] Of the eight coins, two of them bearing crude legends were determined to be imitations which were actually manufactured in India by a process which could reproduce the broad images, but left the legends illegible. In a study of these coins, William Metcalf states that although Roman coinage had a monetary function in India in the first century A.D., in the second and third centuries A.D. they more likely functioned as jewelry, as many of them such as the one from Site 6 had holes meant for suspension on a string.[137] That fact that both Roman gold and imitations of it were found at Nāgārjunakoṇḍa shows an Ikṣvāku interest in the imagery of the West, and imagery which can be discerned in the sculptures of Site 9. That such copies were more widely in use at Nāgārjunakoṇḍa than we had hitherto expected is indicated by the find of a small group of terracotta pendants (*bullae*) excavated at Nāgārjunakoṇḍa (fig. 46). These pendants are again copies of Roman coins[138] intended to be hung on a string and worn around the neck.[139] The fact that these imitations existed in clay as well as in gold indicates a widespread interest in the Western type.

We have begun our section on the period of Cāṁtamūla I with a discussion of a piece of sculpture which was intended to be placed on the *Mahācetiya*. This was apparently associated with other works from nearby Site 6, perhaps the earliest completely decorated *stūpa* at Nāgārjunakoṇḍa. These sculptures clearly reflect a Mathurā idiom and were probably also influenced by sculptures from neighboring Andhra sites. Combined with this, we find elements of Western classicism, which were probably directly copied from imported trade goods. In the subsequent period of Vīrapuruṣadatta, we shall see that the indigenous Andhra element begins to assert itself, and combines with the Mathurā style to produce an unusual experimental style.

Was the indigenous Andhra tradition totally absent at the inception of the Nāgārjunakoṇḍa sculptural tradition? For we actually see its beginnings in the panel representing the Dream of Queen Māyā (fig. 41) from Site 6. Nāgārjunakoṇḍa's proximity to the great site of Amarāvatī would make the total absence of the Amarāvatī style highly unlikely. For as a sub-style it seems to have been present from the beginning on a sculptured slab excavated at Site 23 at Nāgārjunakoṇḍa (fig. 47). The roundels are similar to those found on the small drum friezes of late Amarāvatī (figs. 49 and 50), and share with them the same animal frieze beneath the sculptural composition. The theme of the Viśvaṁtara Jātaka (fig. 47) shares the sketchy elongated figures as the same theme from a late Amarāvatī coping stone (fig. 48), a phase of the Amarāvatī style where limbs are stretched beyond plausibility. The panel bears a fragmentary inscription which refers to the setting up of the sculptured stone at the *Mahārāja Vardhamāna* at Vichayapura (Vijayapurī). This is of little significance except that the paleography of the letters is distinct from the other inscriptions at the site. D.C. Sircar attributes the squat letters to lack of space.[140] However, it is more likely that the letters indicate an early date as confirmed by H. Sarkar.[141] This may belong to the time of Cāṁtamūla, or even before, for as we have said above, there is evidence of Sātavāhana presence at Nāgārjunakoṇḍa.[142] However, it is clear from this piece that the Amarāvatī style entered Nāgārjunakoṇḍa at an early date along with imported styles of the Site 6 group.

While there is no epigraphical proof that there was a sculptural style that predated the reign of Vīrapuruṣadatta, the sculptures from the *Mahācetiya,* Site 6, and Site 23 certainly stand apart from the remainder of the group. It seems most likely that the panel from Site 6 belongs to the period of Cāṁtamūla I. It is further possible that the *Mahācetiya* work, as well as that from Site 23 date back even farther, perhaps even to the reign of Vijaya Sātakarṇi (A.D. 201-07). If this were the case, then each work would have represented the paradigm for the two stylistic elements found in the *āyaka* panel of Site 6: the *Mahācetiya* work representing the Mathurā idiom, and the work from Site 6 representing that of Amarāvatī.

Vīrapuruṣadatta (c. A.D. 240-50-c. A.D. 265-75)

The sculpture which we shall attribute to the reign of Vīrapuruṣadatta elaborates upon the stylistic trends already introduced at Site 6 during the reign of Cāṁtamūla I. Elements of the Mathurā style were expanded upon and Classical elements continued to appear. The indigenous Andhra elements began to assert themselves more forcefully, to become even more dominant during the reign of Vīrapuruṣadatta's successor, Ehuvala Cāṁtamūla.

Memorial Pillars

Before discussing the Buddhist sculptures of the reign of Vīrapuruṣadatta, we wish to discuss a group of memorial pillars assignable to Vīrapuruṣadatta's reign. For it is these pillars which help to assign a date to Vīrapuruṣadatta's style. The earliest of these is an inscribed dated memorial pillar found at Site 9 (fig. 51), which we have already referred to in Chapter I. It was erected in memory of King Cāṁtamūla I. Unfortunately, the date of this inscription of Vīrapuruṣadatta has become a source of continuous debate.

The inscription, known as pillar inscription I, was originally published by J. Ph. Vogel.[143] Vogel read the date as *saṁvachhara viṁsayam,* which he took to be the Prakrit equivalent of *saṁvatsara viṁśaka,* meaning the twentieth regnal year of King Vīrapuruṣadatta. The well-known inscription from Jaggayapeta of this date is of no direct assistance to us as the number twenty is indicated in ciphers rather than by a word.[144] An examination of the impression of the inscription read by Vogel,[145] reveals that the word which Vogel read as *Viṁsayam* is nearly obliterated, and thus the interpretation was merely a guess on his part. Under the supervision of D.C. Sircar, new impressions were prepared in 1960, and indeed the new rubbings were much clearer and Sircar's reading more convincing.[146] Sircar reads the date in question as *saṁvachhara(ṁ) vijaya(ṁ),* which introduces a totally new term for the notation of regnal years. The Sanskrit term *vijaya* generally means "victory" or "conquest". It is also the name of the twenty-seventh year of Jupiter's sixty year cycle as known in both North and South India at a later date. Sircar, as we have mentioned in Chapter I, takes the term *vijaya* as referring to a date in this cycle as counted in South India and accordingly assigns the inscription to A.D. 273-74.[147] This interpretation is highly unlikely, since the first appearance of the use of the sixty year cycle of Jupiter in Indian inscriptions is in the Mahākūṭa pillar inscription of the Early Cālukya king Maṅgaleśa of A.D. 602-03.[148]

In this context, it should be mentioned that there exists a second inscription mentioning the year *vijaya*.[149] This inscription belongs to the reign of Vīrapuruṣadatta's son, Ehuvala Cāṁtamūla. If we consider this too to be part of the Jovian cycle, there are only two possibilities for its date. The first possibility is that it is the same year as pillar inscription I, and the second possibility is that it is sixty years later, corresponding to the year *vijaya* in the next cycle, i.e., A.D. 333-34. Both possibilities seem to pass beyond historical plausibility. In the first case, it is hardly likely that father and son ruled simultaneously. In the second case, the reign of either king could hardly have been so long as to make these two inscriptions fall sixty years apart. Further, there are no other inscriptions from Nāgārjunakoṇḍa using the Jovian system of reckoning.

We therefore must point to the more logical suggestions given by V.V. Mirashi[150] and B. Vidyadhara Rao[151] that the term *saṁvachhraṁ vijayaṁ* simply means "victorious year". Mirashi's argument is quite simple. He cites an inscription found at Reṇṭāla referring to the fifth regnal year of king Cāṁtamūla I, the first king of the dynasty. In this inscription, the term *vijaya-(saṁ)vachhara(ṁ)* is given along with the regnal year. In this context, the term *vijaya* clearly means "victorious". Vidyadhara Rao convincingly argues that the "victorious year", when no other regnal year was given indicated the victorious year of a king's accession to the throne. This would be consistent with the terminology used in later Telugu inscriptions.

Vidyadhara Rao's theory is more than plausible in that it is consistent with the other known facts of Ikṣvāku chronology. Cāṁtamūla I seems to have overthrown the Sātavāhana overlords in c. A.D. 225. The latest known inscription belonging to his reign is dated to his thirteenth regnal year. It is not really known just how long Cāṁtamūla ruled, but dates between A.D. 240 and 250 have been suggested for the accession of his son Vīrapuruṣadatta to the throne.[152] This would be the most logical time for a memorial to be built to the late king by his "Sisters, mothers, and consorts."[153]

This pillar, as well as most of the other sculptures from Nāgārjunakoṇḍa, is made of a greenish white limestone, although the tones of pink and grey were also used. There is absolutely no distinction between this stone and the stones used at the other nearby Andhra sites. When freshly excavated the colors are quite vibrant and lustrous, but as the stones weather they take on a white powdery look and begin to decompose,[154] with progressive loss of surface decoration. A major problem is the great variety in the quality of the stone. The stones of lesser quality, as the one containing pillar inscription L, frequently spall, sometimes causing losses of one-quarter to one-half an inch in depth, leaving only the silhouette of the sculpture.

The sculptural relief above pillar inscription L is in an extremely poor state of preservation, and has unfortunately undergone extensive deterioration since its excavation. Yet in spite of its condition, the compositions are still quite intelligible. The pillar consists of four scenes crowned by a domed structure which echoes the curve of the top of the pillar (fig. 51). In the center of the structure is a small object which has been described by Sastri as a *stūpa* containing a *dhātu* of the Buddha,[155] but from an examination of the old photograph seen in figure 51 it would seem that the object in the shrine is a small *liṅga*. (This has been completely obliterated by time and cannot be seen in more recent photographs.) Placing a *liṅga* on a memorial to Cāṁtamūla I would not be inconsistent with the king's beliefs as he is described in the inscriptions of Nāgārjunakoṇḍa as a worshipper of Mahāsena.[156]

Reading from top to bottom, in the first panel (fig. 52) we see a corpulent man seated in a relaxed pose. On either side of him are female figures with extremely slender bodies and elongated limbs. Behind the group are two smaller standing figures, one on each side, who appear to be holding fly whisks. The composition of the heads of the figures forms an arc, again echoing the top of the pillar. When viewed separately, it seems almost as if this circular composition was meant to be tipped forward at the bottom and placed within a *tondo* form. This compositional device, in a more elaborate form, is well-known in the railing *tondi* from Amarāvatī from its middle phase onwards (figs. 32 and 137).[157] The circular movement of the composition continues downward as the legs of the women slant toward each other as if to complete the circle and tilt the bottom of it slightly toward the viewer. With the addition of the king's legs to the other two, the legs form a triangle leading down to the visual center of the composition below. Virtually the same composition may be observed on a *stūpa* slab from Amarāvatī (fig. 55).

The second panel (fig. 53 top) shows the same corpulent figure seated on a throne. A small figure stands behind him. To the king's right, visually separated from him by a vertical void, are two female figures in a moment of play. These attenuated figures strikingly resemble those found in the latest phase of the art of Amarāvatī.[158] Below are three barely visible figures filling the entire lower part of the composition, forced into a block-like form by the perimeters of the available space. Again the legs of two of the figures join, pointing downward, leading the viewer's eye to an umbrella which breaks into the border of this panel from the composition beneath it.

Circular motion is implied in the third panel (fig. 53 bottom). A king is riding an elephant with an attendant seated behind him. The composition is extended into the square form by two figures behind the elephant. At the base of the trunk is a small child-like figure, and above it is a figure bearing what appears to be a small table or stool on his head. Again, the formula for this type of composition may be observed on a small relief on a *stūpa* panel from Amarāvatī (fig. 56) of which this seems to be a simplification. Such miniature reliefs on the Amarāvatī *stūpa* panels provide an excellent source for no longer extant full-sized compositions.

The bottom panel is the most important as it gives us a possible clue to the iconography of the panels (fig. 54 bottom). Eight figures are gathered around a large mound. The main figure, a corpulent gentleman, bears a staff in his left hand, while an umbrella is held above his head. His right hand is placed upon a pot which is held by the figure to his right. It is clear from the presence of the water pot that an act of donation is being performed. The strange looking mound seems to be identified in the pillar inscription. In it, Cāṁtamūla is described as "the giver of myriads of gold, hundred thousands of kine, and hundred thousands of ploughs (of land).[159] The scene in question, as has been suggested by M. Rama Rao, seems to represent the *hiraṇyakoṭidāna,* or "giver of myriads of gold" referred to in the inscription.[160] The corpulent figure dominating the composition is a representation of Cāṁtamūla I preparing to donate the mound of gold before him. Interpretations have been offered for the other panels as representing various other members of the Ikṣvāku royal family, but inscriptional evidence does not permit us to confirm these speculations.[161] As all the panels are dominated by the same corpulent figure, they are most likely Cāṁtamūla himself, surrounded by his entourage, showing different aspects of his life.

Although the pillar of Cāṁtamūla I has been hitherto considered the only dated monument in the reign of King Vīrapuruṣadatta, Cāṁtamūla's successor, it would appear that there were at least two more memorial pillars to the founder of the dynasty, both almost identical in format with the well-known example. This would not be illogical due to the importance of Cāṁtamūla I. The first known pillar bore the names of thirty-two donors consisting of "sisters", "mothers", "wives", and "concubines".[162] Indeed it would not have been unlikely for other members of the community to have honored the great hero. Although the other pillars survive only in fragmentary condition, the surface of one of them is in better condition than the first pillar, thus giving better definition to the style of the period.

The evidence for the existence of more than one memorial pillar (fig. 57) to Cāṁtamūla I is both epigraphic and iconographic. The existence of only four faintly visible Brāhmī letters, clearly once part of a longer inscription, is highly suggestive. The letters 𑀅𑀲𑀫𑀥 (Prakrit *asam[e]dha*) is a clear reference to one of Cāṁtamūla's major epithets, i.e., *asamedhayāji,* or performer of the *aśvamedha* sacrifice. Not only do we find the use of the word of great interest in this context, but the placement of it is almost the same as on the previous pillar.[163] Unfortunately, this is all of the inscription that is legible, the rest having been long since destroyed. Further evidence for the identification is in the bottom panel of the pillar (fig. 58). The composition is nearly identical to the known Cāṁtamūla pillar, but what is clearly a mound of gold, consisting of tiny little coins in figure 54 is here reduced to a low, *stūpa*-like form. However, close examination of the remaining surface area, especially in the lower left hand corner, reveals the same gold coins as in the previous example. In fact, the weightiness of the figures, and the exaggerated roundness of the heads, as well as the near identical duplication of the composition leads us to believe that the two pillars are by the same hand. The upper panel of what we shall now call the second memorial pillar to Cāṁtamūla I (fig. 59) is again nearly identical to the first, and again it is in a better state of preservation, emphasizing the rotundity of forms and the impossibly small size of the elephant who bears the weight of the portly king.

Aside from these two contiguous panels, it appears that the upper portion of the second Cāṁtamūla I pillar still survives. A detached fragment (fig. 60) may be compared to figures 52 and 53 top, where we see the identical composition with only minor variations in posture, leaving us a much clearer representation of the hefty king, his *cauri* bearers, and his feminine cortége. This panel compares well, not only to the top portion of the first Cāṁtamūla I memorial pillar, but also to what is now called the bottom part of the second memorial pillar. The sculptor in question took a special delight in the rotundity of Cāṁtamūla's form and the contrasting elongated slenderness of his companions. The pendulous abdomen of the king is conspicuously separated from the breast area by a bow-like line which gives special fullness to the chest area, which is perhaps a direct observation from nature. The original composition, which appears at Amarāvatī (fig. 55), is still retained.

The notion of two identical memorial pillars by the same hand seems at first surprising to the modern onlooker, but the notion of uniqueness was in no way pertinent to the artisans of Andhra Pradesh. As we shall see in the Buddhist art of Nāgārjunakoṇḍa, the repetition of themes, frequently almost *verbatim,* was most often the artist's task, and it was through this praxis that the tales of the Buddha were represented. Likewise, once a standard visual formula for representing Cāṁtamūla I was laid down, there was no reason to alter the formula. The artistic device has its parallels in the epigraphs. Within all the epigraphs from

Nāgārjunakoṇḍa containing the name of Cāṁtamūla I, only a limited set of epithets were applied to his name, listing the chief deeds by which his successors wished to remember him. Thus, both the visual and verbal expressions are conventional dynastic formulas which gain currency through repetition.

In this vein, we would like to suggest that there was perhaps a third memorial pillar to Cāṁtamūla I, in this case surviving only as shadow of its former self. Again (fig. 61) we see the top panel representing the king and his two consorts. Largely due to the decomposition of the stone, these appear as stick-like figures, more animated than in the two previous pillars. On the top, we see the faint traces of an architectural pavilion, a feature which may have had symbolic significance in the memorial pillars of Nāgārjunakoṇḍa.

Until recently the memorial pillars of Nāgārjunakoṇḍa seemed to play a unique role in Indian art history, and stood as the earliest known predecessors of the later, more common, hero stones of Medieval India. But as new Sātavāhana and Ikṣvāku sites have been discovered throughout Andhra Pradesh, Tamil Nadu, and Karnāṭaka States, we find that many of the features that we have hitherto seen as unique to Nāgārjunakoṇḍa were actually part of a broader cultural and artistic complex, extending throughout vast areas of South India and the Deccan, with its limits still in the process of definition. The site of Sannati, as well as the nearby site of Jewargi, in Karnāṭaka State, yielded a group of memorial pillars similar in format to the Nāgārjunakoṇḍa examples.[164] Although the compositions vary from pillar to pillar, the Karnāṭaka examples were frequently erected in memory of a deceased couple rather than an individual. A recurrent feature found throughout all examples is the existence of the architectural pavilion on top. In Sannati and in two other Nāgārjunakoṇḍa examples (figs. 62 and 63) the heads of the main figures, presumably the deceased, are seen peering out of the architectural pavilion. Dr. M.S. Nagaraja Rao has suggested that the pavilion represented the heavenly abode of the deceased.[165] Although we have been able to find no textual precedent for this notion, it would appear to have loose parallels in the façades of the rock-cut caves of the Western Ghāṭs where the figures contained within the architectural framework in the upper portions of the façade are known to represent the heavenly abode of the gods.

Further evidence for the extensive use of memorial pillars may be found in the *Maṇimekhalai*, an ancient Tamil text set in the city of Puhār, or modern Kaveripattinam. Recent archaeological evidence[166] indicates the existence of Ikṣvāku type structures in that region, confirming the usefulness of this text, as well as the companion text, the *Śilappadikāram*, for evidence of Ikṣvāku art. The *Maṇimekhalai* refers to "monuments of various sizes bearing inscriptions of those whose dead remains they cover. These inscriptions give the details of the name, caste, mode of life and station in society, and the manner of death of those whose monuments they happen to be, each one of them."[167] This evidence is completely consistent with the inscribed evidence found on the memorial pillars of Nāgārjunakoṇḍa.[168]

The memorial pillars are the only sculptures from Nāgārjunakoṇḍa which we can, on inscriptional evidence, assign to the reign of Vīrapuruṣadatta. Yet we know that his reign was one of great building activity. Indeed, the Buddhist sculptural decoration already underway during his father's time must have been continued. The only evidence we have for this is based on the style of *Stūpa* 9, for inscriptional evidence implies that the *stūpa* is of a later date.

The Problems of Site 9

Stūpa 9 belongs to the Aparamahāvinaseliya site which was dedicated during the eighth regnal year of Ehuvala Cāṁtamūla, the third king of the dynasty.[169] If we accept the date of Vīrapuruṣadatta's accession to the throne as c. A.D. 240-50, and we know that Vīrapuruṣadatta reigned for at least 24 years,[170] we may place this site around the third quarter or beginning of the fourth quarter of the third century A.D. Although the dated inscription was found in the *maṇḍapam* of Site 9, and not on the *stūpa* itself, it is generally accepted that the two are contemporary.[171] The validity of this date as applicable to the sculptural work, will be contested here.

At this point, we must note an unfortunate situation regarding the accuracy of find spots. Many of the find spots from the early Nāgārjunakoṇḍa excavations were left unrecorded and frequently a piece was described in a publication but not illustrated. Thus, our ascription of many of the pieces to a given site is based frequently upon stylistic considerations or brief, and not always unambiguous, published descriptions of the sculptures.

Amongst the sculpture found at *Stūpa* 9 were four beams, originally used as friezes on the upper portion of *āyaka* platforms. In general, the *āyaka* friezes at Nāgārjunakoṇḍa are the best preserved of the sculptures at the site, and it is these friezes which illustrate the unique character of the art of Nāgārjunakoṇḍa. As we are certain that these beams were used to decorate the front portion of the *āyaka* or projecting platforms, as was the panel from Site 6 (fig. 40), we shall use these here for two purposes: first to discuss the general problem of the meaning of the *āyaka* panels, and second to discuss the style of the reliefs and their relevance to Ikṣvāku chronology, two issues which cannot be separated. Similarly, we shall examine other parts of Site 9 to the same ends. Parenthetically, the numbers here given to the *āyaka* panels do not reflect the order in which they appear on the *stūpa*, as this information seems to have been left unrecorded. They indicate simply the order in which they were listed in Longhurst's excavation report.

In general, the length of *āyaka* panels varies according to the size of a *stūpa*, and most frequently, they are about one foot high. They are illustrated with a series of rectangular reliefs consisting of stories of the Life of the Buddha or of *Jātaka* tales. The scenes are most frequently separated by playful *mithuna* couples (i.e., fig. 65). At the ends of the panels are *vṛkṣa devatās* standing either alone or with a male companion. Beneath them are elaborate composite animals (i.e., figs. 171 and 200). These bracket-like devices are conspicuous by their absence on the panels of Site 9. At the bottom of each panel is a row of bird and leonine motifs.

Of the friezes belonging to Site 9, only two were illustrated by Longhurst, and the other two merely described.[172] We illustrate here the first three panels which were clearly identified by Longhurst (figs. 64, 65 and 66). These beams vary in format, some reflecting the smaller panels that we have seen in the *Mahācetiya*—Site 6 group, and some foreshadowing a later trend.

The best preserved panel from Site 9, *āyaka* panel 1 (fig. 64) has both a unique format and a unique style within the group from Site 9. The panel consists of five major scenes which are to be read from right to left as: Prince Siddhārtha in his Pleasure Garden, the *Māndhātu Jātaka*, an illustration to the theme of the "Man in the Well", a Chakravartin with his Seven Jewels, and the Buddha Protected by the Nāga Mucilinda. The ends of the beams are decorated with richly carved *pūrṇa ghaṭa* motifs. The scenes are separated by vertical decorative bands with incised carving. Between these bands are three lotus flowers carved in high relief. An examination of the Amarāvatī predecessors of the Nāgārjunakoṇḍa carvings has shown that these seemingly decorative patterns represent the cross-bars of a *stūpa* railing decorated with lotuses, while the vertical low-relief carving represents the railing uprights, thus creating the reinterpretation of a structural element (the cross-bar) into a vertical decorative motif.[173] A similar format is found throughout late Amarāvatī drum friezes (figs. 49-50) as well as at Site 6 group, of which these seem to be an immediate successor. The abstracted rail pattern is also found on late Amarāvatī representations of a *stūpa* to separate individual scenes along the drum frieze (figs. 55 and 67).

At the bottom of the Nāgārjunakoṇḍa panel is the typical frieze of alternating bird and leonine motifs. On the Amarāvatī representations of a *stūpa*, these have their correspondence in quadrilateral forms, or beam ends, beneath the drum frieze (figs. 55 and 67), and in animal forms beneath the *āyaka* portion (fig. 68). On the actual drum friezes of the Amarāvatī *stūpa*, the motif occurs with animal heads (fig. 69), and even a human head (fig. 70). The function of these animal motifs is not at first obvious, but just as we can interpret the lotiform bosses as signifying the rail pattern whose original form was in wood, we may also wish to see this motif as having an ultimate wood prototype. Interestingly, the combined railing motif and frontal animal frieze occurs only as part of the decoration of the drum of the *stūpa*, never on the dome, whether it be small drum friezes of the Amarāvatī *stūpa* or the larger *āyaka* friezes protruding from the drum on the *stūpas* at Nāgārjunakoṇḍa. Thus, they occur only a few inches below the drum platform. Comparative representations of the rail motif combined with the animal heads occur in Gandhāra,[174] while the simple quadrilateral beneath the rail form occurs throughout the early Indian art of Bharhut and Sāñcī.[175] It is interesting to note that here are projecting beams beneath the railing frequently used to support a balcony, and sometimes peg-like supports to secure the rail. In both Andhra Pradesh and in Gandhāra, these beams have been turned into decorative animal forms. In turn, the tradition of representing such beams in animal form is carried into Gupta temple architecture, where we can see them represented above door frames. These appear, for example, both on the Vāmaṇa temple at Maṛhiā and the Viṣṇu temple at Deogarh,[176] where they are an even more remote reference to an original wood prototype. They also have their parallels on Roman sarcophagi, where similarly they are a sculptural representation of a previous architectural form.[177]

What then would be the reason for placing the railing motif with beam ends on the *āyaka* platform of the *stūpa?* The face is that the existence of a railing always had symbolic importance to the *stūpa*. We may recall that many early Indian *stūpas* were composed of a dome resting on a drum. The drum was surrounded by a railing which formed an upper *pradakṣinā* path, which can be seen both by the remains of *stūpa* 1 at Sāñcī, and by sculptural representations of early *stūpas*,[178] where it is ambiguous as to whether these were decorative or actual. The whole complex was surrounded by an outer railing, leaving a space for *pradakṣinā* between the railing and the *stūpa*. A large gateway or *toraṇa* was frequently added at the entrance or entrances of the outer gateway.

Based on the finds at Nāgārjunakoṇḍa, the Andhra *stūpa* presents a new variant. The *toraṇa* disappears, and usually also the outer railing. At the same time, *āyaka* platforms are added to the drum of the *stūpa*. On each of these platforms are five pillars known as *āyaka* pillars.[179] Although their function will be elaborated upon subsequently, they seem to represent at one level the idea of "entrance", and are somehow a symbolic substitute for the *toraṇa*.[180] At the same time, the upper railing disappears from the *stūpa*, leaving a vestigial railing motif at the top of the drum.

At present we know very little about early activity at Amarāvatī, but we do know that its history goes back to Mauryan times.[181] From the few remaining fragments, we cannot reconstruct the form of earlier *stūpa*. However, one fragment from the main *stūpa* at Amarāvatī clearly shows that a *stūpa* with an upper rail, either actual or conceptual, was known there (fig. 71). This particular example is complete with the rectangular support beams for the upper railing. In the great *stūpa* at Amarāvatī, and its Nāgārjunakoṇḍa successors, the upper railing disappeared, leaving only the drum friezes and *āyaka* panels as a memory of its existence. To strengthen the equation between *āyaka* frieze and rail, we may cite a small votive *stūpa* belonging to the latest phase of Amarāvatī, where the rail motif and *āyaka* frieze are represented interchangeably on *stūpa* slabs (fig. 72). Thus the *āyaka* panels as a whole exist as a memory of a railing which no longer exists. Whether it was a memory of the upper railing, or outer railing, was probably a point of confusion, for it seems to partake of aspects of both.

The *āyaka* panels of Site 9 have yet another feature which gives an unusual character to the art of Nāgārjunakoṇḍa, and again this feature has its origins in the drum friezes from Amarāvatī and predecessors at Site 6. On the Amarāvatī examples, we note that the narrative scenes are divided not only by the rail motif, but further by couples placed between the *stambhas.* Such couples are adapted by the Nāgārjunakoṇḍa artist. In the case of Site 9, panel 1, the couples have attendants (fig. 64), but more commonly (fig. 65) they are alone. They are represented so frequently at Nāgārjunakoṇḍa that they, along with the distinctive style of the sculpture, appear to be the signature of the school.

The proliferation of playful couples separating Buddhist narrative reliefs has caused a great deal of curiosity amongst the viewers of the art of Nāgārjunakoṇḍa. The couples have become so popular that they are frequently illustrated out of context, independent of the Buddhist narratives which they accompany. Indeed, at first glance the couples seem inappropriate to the decoration of the sacred monuments of the Buddhists, and thus Longhurst has considered them to be "merely" decorative.[182] However, if we consider them in the light of the *āyaka* panel as a rail motif, they are completely consistent with the known Buddhist tradition. Auspicious couples form a part of the earliest known decorated *stūpas* in India and continue their appearance throughout the history of Hindu temple architecture. Such figures are found on the railing of Sāñcī 2,[183] Bharhut,[184] and Bodhgayā,[185] frequently in association with other auspicious symbols. Similarly, they are found on the façade of Buddhist *caitya* halls where the figures are almost always in association with a railing motif (fig. 73).[186] In erotic postures, they appear around the door frame of Cave III at Nāsik (a Buddhist monastic *vihāra)* showing, as has been pointed out by Devangana Desai, that they were indeed a well established convention. Here the couples were still associated with a railing, as the entire entrance is surrounded by the representation of a *toraṇa*, with the auspicious couples placed on the uprights.[187] Thus the figures are invariably placed at the point of entry into a sacred or meditative place. At the point of entry, there is almost always a rail, whether it exists in actuality, as around the early Buddhist *stūpas*, or symbolically, as on the façade of the early Buddhist caves (fig. 73).

In the early Buddhist monuments, auspicious couples, as well as other auspicious symbols, are never placed on the dome of the *stūpa*. They belong to the exterior of the monument as part of the auspicious symbols of the secular world and mark the transition to the sacred. In both the early *stūpas* and those in the early *caitya* halls, the *stūpa* is left undecorated, thereby juxtaposing the two worlds.[188] But in Andhra Pradesh, the whole pattern of *stūpa* representation has changed, and the *stūpa* itself seems to be in a state of transition. At Amarāvatī, the *stūpa*, along with its railing, became the repository for representations of both *jātaka* tales and scenes from the life of the Buddha. As an independent motif, both auspicious couples and *vṛkṣa devatās* are practically absent on the railing at Amarāvatī. The couples begin to make their appearance only in the latest phases of the art of Amarāvatī, which is probably contemporary with the earlier phases at Nāgārjunakoṇḍa. The place where they begin to appear is on the drum friezes, which is the representation of a railing. At Nāgārjunakoṇḍa, where the auspicious couples become a major feature at the site, there are no major stone railings. The *Mahācetiya*, which was the largest *stūpa* at the site, is believed to have been unadorned. If it did have an outer railing, it was in wood and is no longer preserved.[189] The remaining *stūpas* at Nāgārjunakoṇḍa were all considerably smaller, ranging in size from approximately 20 to 60 feet in diameter.[190] Most of them were part of monastic complexes, and many of them were on square platforms. Lack of space may indeed have been one of the factors in eliminating the railing. Iconographically this was indeed a loss. However, some of its motives were preserved. They were thus placed on the *stūpa* itself, but, at Nāgārjunakoṇḍa, placed in such a manner that they were still part of the symbolic entrance, i.e., *āyaka* platforms which project from the *stūpa* and are thus probably a symbolic combination of both railing and *toraṇa*. Consistently, the woman and tree motif, which is part of the railing or gateway of all early Indian *stūpas*, is also incorporated into the *āyaka* platform. Thus we conclude that the auspicious couples are symbolically not to be considered part of the *stūpa* proper, as they are found only on those parts of the *stūpa* which indicate the idea of the leave-taking from the secular world.

When auspicious couples are introduced into the drum friezes of Amarāvatī, some of them appear in a style which clearly shows a recrudescence of a type directly influenced by the Classical West, an influence which, from this period onward, is more and more in evidence in the art of Andhra Pradesh. This was already hinted at in the context of Site 6. In figures 74 and 75, the female figures are definitely in classical drapery, while the female represented in figure 74 has her counterpart in an incised ivory plaque from Begram (fig. 76). The stylistic sources for these figures may have been small classical metal figures of a type which could have been easily imported into India, such as the statuette of a goddess (figs. 77 and 78) of the second to third centuries A.D. reported to be from Lebanon or Syria.[191] This statuette is currently in the Toledo Museum of Art. Also of specific Western origin is the mirror held by the male in figure 50. Similar mirrors have been found in the excavations at Brahmapuri[192] and are depicted on the Begram ivories.[193] These Western type mirrors are represented frequently on the sculpture of Nāgārjunakoṇḍa. Opposite the mirror-bearing male, a graceful female figure stands in a posture reminiscent of the popular Classical theme of Venus drying her hair, a theme also known at

Mathurā.[194] As we have seen, this theme appeared in Site 6 group (fig. 33) and Begram. Thus, it was in this context, with an awareness of Western modes and Western objects, that the *āyaka* panels of *Stūpa* 9 of Nāgārjunakoṇḍa were created. But using the formulae and knowledge of the Amarāvatī pieces, the sculptors of Nāgārjunakoṇḍa greatly simplified the compositions, using a new figural style of their own.

The use of dividing couples, as seen on the Amarāvatī panels, is on Site 9 panel 1 (fig. 64) awkwardly adopted, in this case flanking only the central panel (figs. 64, 79 and 80). Each pair is here accompanied by a third member. The figures have a stark, heavy, block-like shape. The females lack the ample hips and narrow waist associated with the school of Andhra Pradesh. In figure 79, the male and female coiffures are barely distinguishable from each other. Further, the turban and the elaborate female coiffures so common to the sculptors of Andhra Pradesh are abandoned, leaving a hair style reminiscent of the coiffure of an aphrodite.

In composition, the reliefs have a foreign appearance while representing Buddhist narrative scenes. While being sufficiently removed from the classical style, we see in them a definite use of Classical motifs. For example, in the composition known as the "Man in the Well" (figs. 64 and 81), we see a figure lunging forth with a spear in his hand, being restrained by his female companion. The lunging figure is reminiscent of numerous Classical compositions of Meleager killing the boar while being restrained by one of the Dioscuri.[195] An example of this type is seen in a late second century A.D. Roman sarcophagus, now in the Palazzo, Doria Rome. In it (fig. 82) Meleager lunges forth with a spear held horizontally. At Nāgārjunakoṇḍa, the composition is in reverse and the lunge of the protagomist is weak and ineffectual. It would seen that the original Meleager type was known to the Nāgārjunkaṇḍa artists, but underwent numerous transformations in the hands of artists employing a fairly uncongenial motif. In this way, *āyaka* panel 1 of *Stūpa* 9 remains a compositional hybrid set apart from the mainstream of Nāgārjunakoṇḍa sculpture. As at Site 6, it shows some of the Mathurā weightiness of form and the use of classical sources. But on this panel, they are poorly integrated. The broad features and small chin of the spear-bearing figure have at times been considered portraiture. These same features are clearly seen in other panels from Site 9 (figs. 111 and 202). Yet if we consider them in light of Site 6 (i.e., fig. 42), their source is readily apparent, for this facial type is clearly inherited from one already in common use at Nāgārjunakoṇḍa.

Stūpa 9 shows us yet another stylistic facet. *Āyaka* panel 2, as described by Longhurst, illustrates Queen Māyā's Dream, Casting the Horoscope, the Nativity, and the First Sermon.[196] Of these, only Queen Māyā's Dream is illustrated by Longhurst and this, along with the contiguous scenes of the Casting of the Horoscope and the Nativity are here illustrated by figures 65 and 83. Unfortunately, this last scene is broken off and I have been unable to trace it. The themes which represent the major events in the life of the Buddha had become quite standardized at Amarāvatī and Nāgārjunakoṇḍa, making many of the scenes immediately identifiable. They usually vary only in the number of accompanying figures, or small details of accessories and furniture, as well as, of course, the degree of the mastery of the anonymous sculptors. For example, the scene of Queen Māyā's Dream has been stylized into a luxurious court scene of a reclining lady surrounded by her entourage (fig. 83). The Buddhist message is clarified only by a tiny elephant, as in the Amarāvatī example (fig. 84), relegated to the border of the panel, while in the Nāgārjunakoṇḍa example, the miniscule beast appears to be taking a nose dive toward the reclining female, through the crowded space. (Notice here how much more slender these figures are in comparison to the same theme from Site 6, fig. 41). By this time, we have come more than three centuries from the well-known representation of the same theme at Bharhut wherein the basic elements of the message are stressed, giving the queen and the elephant equal size, and further labelling the composition *bhagavato ukraṁti*, "the Descent of the Blessed One". The Bharhut example suggests a comparison with early Buddhist literary didacticism while the Andhra works may better be compared to early *kāvya* literature, poetic rather than doctrinal.[197] In fact, as we will see later, a clear source for some of the Andhra works may be found in the writings of Aśvaghoṣa. Nevertheless, by the time of the florescence of Buddhist art at Amarāvatī and Nāgārjunakoṇḍa, the major Buddhist themes were so well-known that there was no need to define all the iconographic details. Instead, many of the religious events became part of the luxurious court scenes which no doubt appealed to the wealthy patrons. In this context, we should repeat that *Stūpa* 9, as discussed in the previous chapter, was dedicated to the Aparamahāvinaseliya sect, a sect which seems to have had an extremely active lay patronage who were seeking their own enlightenment.

The style of *āyaka* panel 2 (fig. 65) varies distinctly from *āyaka* panel 1 (fig. 64). Using the same format, that is, scenes divided by the lotuses of a railing cross-bar, with *mithuna* couples between each pair, we find a teeming mass of figures in a crowded composition. The number of lotuses in each row has increased from three to four. The separating *mithuna* couples are slender and lively, spilling over the confines of the borders allotted to them. Figures are carved on a shallow stage of about an inch deep at the bottom, and shallower at the top. Linear rhythms are obscured. Each figure is given minimum space and is encroached upon by its neighbor. The stark, orderly compositions of *āyaka* panel 1 and its Amarāvatī and Site 6 predecessors are not seen here. Likewise, the intrusive foreign elements are relatively undiscernible. Compare, for example, the Indianized staff bearers of *āyaka* panel 2 (fig. 83) with the Romanized version from Amarāvatī (fig. 75). Whatever elements are introduced from the Classical West are here melted into a truly Indian composition leaving us only faint Classical reminiscences such as the use of contraposto which are already well-known to us from the art of Amarāvatī.[198] Even though the style of *āyaka* panel 2 does not derive from the small drum friezes which the artist of *āyaka* panel 1 seems to have been aware of, the panel does have its parallels in another style of the Amarāvatī school. A drum frieze showing the Śibi Jātaka, the "Subjugation of the Mad Elephant" and the Sasa Jātaka (fig. 85)[199] illustrates the same linear attenuation and straining of the composition over the limits of its borders, even while retaining reminiscences of the rhythmic parabolic curves of the school of Amarāvatī.

Panel 3, four scenes from the Champaka Jātaka (fig. 66), seems a compromise between the unresolved appearance of *āyaka* panel 1 and the vibrant but disorderly extreme of *āyaka* panel 2. As in panels 1 and 2, scenes are divided by the lotus railing; there are four *sūcīs* as in panel 2. As panel 2 survives only in a fragmentary state, we are unable to discuss the format in its entirety, so that *āyaka* panel 3 as a whole may be compared only to *āyaka* panel 1. Interestingly, we note that the beams, although co-ordinated to a certain extent in their formal elements and their size (c. 11 feet wide x 1 foot high), were not necessarily "matched" decorative motifs. While the center of *āyaka* panel 1 bears a Buddhist tale (fig. 81), the near center of *āyaka* panel 2 bears a *mithuna* couple. Peculiarly, in this case, the dividing device is the figure of a standing Buddha in *abhaya mudrā* (figs. 66 and 86). At Nāgārjunakoṇḍa, the use of the Buddha figure as a central motif in a non-narrative context is unique to this panel. The figure of the Buddha, while centrally placed, is nevertheless visually insignificant; moreover, it is the only place on this entire panel where the anthropomorphic figure of the Buddha appears. As if placed in descending order of hierarchy, the other two dividing devices are in pairs, the Buddha figure being the only figure appearing only once. As we go outward, we find rather charming *cauri* bearers, and further outward, two pairs of *mithuna* couples. But these figures are of little visual impact, for the narrow spaces in which they are placed, flanking crowded compositions, provide no resting place for the eye along the entire panel.

The placement of the Buddha image as a dividing figure was not exclusive to Nāgārjunakoṇḍa, but again can be found on the small drum friezes of late Amarāvatī. In a standing position, in an almost identical representation to the Nāgārjunakoṇḍa type, the figures appear in two fragments of a drum frieze from Amarāvatī which appear no longer to be extant. These fragments were published in line drawings by James Fergusson in 1863. At the time, the unexpected placement of the image on the drum frieze caused Fergusson to suggest a fourth or fifth century date for these pieces.[200] However, throughout the art of Gandhāra, the standing Buddha image is placed on pilasters separating narrative scenes,[201] while in the Swat Valley we find that the standing Buddha image is juxtaposed with the *mithuna* couple.[202] If we think in terms of monumental architecture, we note that the earliest known

Buddha images in Western *Ghāṭs* [203] are placed modestly on a large pillar in the forecourt of Cave 3 at Kaṇheri (fig. 81). According to Marilyn Leese, "they seem to serve inconspicuously as sentinels, surveying all who might enter the site's main sanctuary."[204] The notion of the Buddha image appearing almost surreptitiously at Site 9 should not surprise us, for we believe that the large Buddha image as a major object of worship did not appear at Site 9 until toward the end of its construction. For the Buddha image entered slowly, giving time for the new ways to gain acceptance. Further, Buddhism seems to have been known in Amarāvatī since Mauryan times, and we have documentation for the continuation of Buddhist narrative from the second century B.C. onwards,[205] a point that has become obscured since the publication of Douglas Barrett's short choronology of the Amarāvatī *stūpa.*[206] Thus, the Buddhists of Nāgārjunakoṇḍa could rely strongly on their own traditions, and would not necessarily feel a great need to adopt all the latest iconographic trends of the northwest and Mathurā. Even when the tradition of making Buddha images came into vogue, iconic representation never wholly replaced the aniconic, and the image of the Buddha rarely dominated the compositions.

Āyaka panel 3 ends with the usual *pūrṇa ghaṭa* motif, but projecting is a small *bhadraghaṭa* (fig. 88). This also appeared at Site 6. More than likely, all the *āyaka* panels of Site 9 originally bore this motif, which was to be supplanted in later *stūpas* by a woman and tree motif, or a *mithuna* couple.

Although this panel is the best preserved of the group at Site 9, it is indeed much cruder than the previous two examples, and thus has never been published in its entirety. The scenes have neither the dynamism of *āyaka* panel 2 nor the simplicity of *āyaka* panel 1. The figures are extremely flat and squat, crudely carved, and cramped by the rectangular frames which house them. The scene of the snake charmer catching the Nāga King Champaka (fig. 89)[207] is one which was handled with great charm at Amarāvatī (fig. 40),[208] showing the companions of the snake charmer harmoniously urging on the capture of the Nāga King. In the Nāgārjunakoṇḍa example, the flat figures give only the essential narrative details of the message. (Cf. fig. 35 for the Site 6 example.) If we compare the second scene, King Ugrasena visited by the wife of the Nāga King (fig. 86),[209] to a similar scene of repose in Queen Māyā's Dream of *āyaka* panel 2 (fig. 83), the difference is clearly defined. Surprisingly, both panels are the same height and proportions, but the artist the *āyaka* panel 3 felt no need to embellish the story to its limits, even though the text speaks of the chief queen visiting King Ugrasena with a company of "sixteen thousand female Nāgas". It was almost as if the artist tried to return to a simpler, more lyrical style of an earlier phase of the school of Amarāvatī (fig. 84), but was not up to the effort. When the Nāgārjunakoṇḍa style is defined as the decline phase of the Amarāvatī school, it is particularly this panel which suits such a definition. It shows neither a fruitful innovation, nor a competent continuation of the Amarāvatī tradition.

The fourth panel excavated at *Stūpa* 9, described by Longhurst,[210] represents the Śibi Jātaka and the "Subjugation of the Mad Elephant". I have looked in vain for such a panel, expecting to find a panel quite similar to the late Amarāvatī drum frieze of the subjects (fig. 85), but I have been unable to find it. It would seem that what Longhurst was referring to as *āyaka* beams were two pieces (not originally fragments of a larger piece) which were perhaps placed at the sides of the *āyaka* projection at a ninety degree angle to the main *āyaka* beam (figs. 90 and 91). These panels are clearly in the same stylistic tradition as *āyaka* panel 3, with the elements of the composition reduced only to the bare minimum. The absence of the bird and leonine motif beneath the composition may indicate that these were side panels, as one might surmise from the representation on figure 67. As for the fourth panel, there are several extremely mutilated fragments which, by their format, may be candidates for this position. However, they are so fragmentary that they do not add to our knowledge of the style of *Stūpa* 9.

Regarding the theme of the Subjugation of the Mad Elephant, we note that the Buddha is represented as a flaming pillar. But the pillar is humanized by the appearance of feet placed at a diagonal upon a lotus pedestal. This innovative looking feature had appeared previously in a relief from Amarāvatī in a scene representing the Conversion of the Kāśyapas,[211] and is most charmingly represented in a small fragment from Nāgārjunakoṇḍa (fig. 92).

A small group of drum slabs belonging to *Stūpa* 9 have been excavated at Nāgārjunakoṇḍa. Of these, only two have been documented in the literature,[212] while others may be added to the group by similarities of style and format. The two known examples which definitely belong to *Stūpa* 9 (figs. 93 and 94) are at first rather startling to those only superficially familiar with the evolution of Andhra sculpture. Through the works of Douglas Barrett[213] and Stern and Bénisti[214] we have come to expect a "development" of the representation of the *stūpa*, basically from a simple unadorned version to a more elaborate structure, complete with railing, *āyaka* platform and pillars, a fully decorated drum and dome, and a Buddha image. This latter type is presumed to be most fully realized at Nāgārjunakoṇḍa and characteristic of the school (for example, figs. 144-46 *et al*). But while such a concept is plausible in the broadest sense, it ceases to function in many specific examples, as admitted by both Barrett and the French. Thus not surprisingly, the *stūpas* of Site 9 have not been included in the literature. In this regard, we must restate that both monographic and individual studies on Amarāvatī place Nāgārjunakoṇḍa motifs at the end of the Andhra sequence, but we must allow for many unexpected variants, especially at Site 9, which recall apparently simpler forms. With regard to the specific examples from Site 9, we are perhaps seeing the representation of an "unadorned" or "partially adorned" rather than an "earlier" type *stūpa*, as has been suggested by Longhurst,[215] for the co-existence of adorned and unadorned *stūpas* at Nāgārjunakoṇḍa has been well documented. Further, these *stūpas* are represented without railings. Again, this was a feature common to the smaller *stūpas* of Andhra Pradesh.

The notion of the appearance of a simple type *stūpa* at the end of the Amarāvatī sequence has been suggested by the authors concerned. The representation of the simple type *stūpa* at Rāmagrāma (fig. 95) is hesitantly considered by Stern and Bénisti to belong to the late phase of Amarāvatī's evolution, based on the style of the standing Nāga on the right side of the composition. But as Stern and Bénisti suggest, these figures appear to have been recut at a later date, perhaps much later,[216] and may combine a late style figure with an early type *stūpa*. This indeed seems to be a logical solution to the problem, based not only of figural style, but also on the lack of the appearance of *āyaka* platforms and pillars common to the late phase of the style as seen on the drum slabs from Amarāvatī. A small slab in the British Museum (fig. 96) whose original position on the *stūpa* is not known, clearly shows the simultaneity of early and late features. A simple type *stūpa* with a crossed "collar" on the dome is combined with a seated Buddha image in the center of the drum of the *stūpa* which has been divided into three sections. Barrett has placed this image in the late phase of Amarāvatī.[217] The fact that the *āyaka* platforms and pillars are absent here is of less significance than in the previous example, for the piece appears not to have been a drum slab, but belonged to another part of the *stūpa* where an older form *stūpa* was represented on late phase sculpture.[218] The very fact that the illustration of Rāmagrāma *stūpa* was recut rather than replaced by another work is a further indication that the early type *stūpa* continued to be favored along with later forms.

Archaeological evidence from Amarāvatī further confirms the co-existence of simple and elaborate types. The small votive *stūpa* excavated by Rea[219] (fig. 72) shows the co-existence of both. The elaborate variants are typical examples of a late Andhra *stūpa* abundantly represented by Ikṣvāku art in Nāgārjunakoṇḍa. The more simple type co-exists with it, and although we might be tempted to pre-date the earlier appearing slab (fig. 97), it seems highly doubtful that a *stūpa* of such small proportions would require a rebuilding phase. The figure style, as we can see, is actually typical Ikṣvāku (cf. *mithuna* couple in fig. 65), although at first glance belonging to the more archaic tradition of the early phase of Amarāvatī and Jaggayyapetȧ.[220] Most likely, the juxtaposition of an archaizing type with the more "modern" form finds its justification not in questions of chronology, but more in contemporary attitudes toward religious worship, just as the *stūpa* and Buddha image are placed in facing chapels of Site 9, therefore forming an equivalency between old and new forms.

Further evidence for the use of simple *stūpa* forms at a later date comes from the nearby *stūpa* at Goli village, excavated by Jouveau-Dubreuil in 1926.[221] A *caitya* slab from the Goli *stūpa* bears an inscription which has been assigned to the late phase of Amarāvatī.[222] The *stūpa* represented has an unadorned drum and a cantilevered *harmikā* to the *Stūpa* 9 examples. *Āyaka* pillars are present, and the dome of the *stūpa* bears three representations: one at the center of the supposed *āyaka* platform and one on either side. This is essentially the same format as in the Nāgārjunakoṇḍa examples. Another example, currently in the Los Angeles County Museum (fig. 98), which we have ascribed to Goli (see Chapter III), belongs to this group but has a representation of the Buddha in the center, further confirming the co-existence of the simple and elaborate *stūpas* at a later date.

The very notion of the continuity of early simple architectural forms may indeed have historic as well as iconographic justification. The Great *Stūpa* at Jaggayyapeta appears to have been constructed mostly during the first century B.C. From that site, there is no surviving evidence of the mature style, and only one fragment reflects the late Amarāvatī tradition.[223] But it is clear from several fragmentary inscriptions that during the twentieth year of the reign of the Ikṣvāku King Vīrapuruṣadatta, significant additions were made to the *stūpa*.[224] We know that the region was a center of activity for the *Aparamahāvinaseliya* sect, the Buddhist sect for which both Site 1 and Site 9 were dedicated, perhaps enhancing the intercourse between the two sites.[225] The Jaggayyapeta *stūpa*, from which only a few pieces of sculpture survive today, stands atop a small mountain, and when complete must have been visible from a great distance. During Ikṣvāku times, it must have been one of the most splendid sights of the ancient Buddhist community. Thus the Ikṣvākus chose to contribute to that site and be influenced by the early forms, consequently causing occasional confusion between an archaic tradition and a later variant of that tradition. Thus the *stūpa* representations (figs. 93 and 94) take on the same tripartite arrangement of the central altar of the Buddha and flanking panels as was found in the Jaggayyapeta representation of the altar placed within the temple (fig. 99). The format was transferred onto the representation of the *stūpa*, as the requirement of the Ikṣvākus was to decorate the drum with numerous representations of *stūpas*, as if radiating from the latter monument.[226]

The Jaggayyapeta representation demonstrates another feature relevant to our Nāgārjunakoṇḍa study. The altar appears to be placed within a multi-storied structure, of which the first storey was an open pillared pavilion. This type must have remained in use for objects of worship in Andhra Pradesh for it is represented on the two documented *caitya* slabs from Site 98, two other slabs which clearly belong to the same tradition (figs. 100 and 101),[227] and in a miniature representation on a *caitya* slab from Amarāvatī placed along the representation of the drum frieze (fig. 102). In this case it contains what appears to be an Aśokan type pillar protected by a domed pavilion. Unfortunately, we have no direct archaeological evidence for these structures, but the art of Nāgārjunakoṇḍa, as well as that of all the major early Buddhist sites, contains several representations of no longer extant architectural forms.

The *stūpas* represented at Site 9 are placed on a double lotus pedestal. This, in fact, does represent a feature which survives in actual structures. It is a stone molding (fig.103) which had been placed around the base of votive *stūpas* which were contained within *caitya gṛhas* at Nāgārjunakoṇḍa. The appearance of this feature is highly supportive of recent hypotheses of John Irwin on the origin of the *stūpa*. Irwin suggests that the *stūpa* originally represented the creation of the universe and, as such, was originally conceived of as the Primordial Mound resting on the Cosmic Ocean. Vestigial representations of this notion appear in the representations of aquatic motifs placed beneath the *stūpa* at Bharhut, Sāñcī, and Amarāvatī.[228] The placement of the lotus beneath the *stūpa* at Nāgārjunakoṇḍa provides further evidence for Irwin's conjectures. G. Roth, in a discussion of *stūpa* symbolism, provides confirmative textual parallels for the existence of the lotus at the base of the *stūpa*. In a descriptive passage on the *stūpa* contained within the *Kriyāsaṁgraha,* a text of about the eighth century, the lotus is actually stated to be in full blossom, containing sixteen petals. A ritual commentary following the passage states:

> after he has realized the bright wheel of eight spokes with the sound of *bhrūm*, upon that the lotus of all-pervading petals which originates from the sound *āḥ*. . .[229]

This passage gives further support to Irwin's notion of aquatic symbolism. However, concerning specifically the *stūpas* of Nāgārjunakoṇḍa, this passage is of still further interest. We recall that the majority of the *stūpas* at Nāgārjunakoṇḍa had a wheel-like inner structure. It has long been debated whether this structure has a symbolic or purely a structural justification.[230] The mention of "the bright wheel of eight spokes" seems to favor the symbolic interpretation, or perhaps the late text is a justification of what was formerly a structural necessity.

From the point of view of figural style in the *stūpa* panels we find the same weightiness of forms (figs. 93 and 94) that we find on *āyaka* panel 1 of Stūpa 9 (cf. figs. 79 and 80). The *vidyādharas* placing garlands on the *stūpa* look as if they are going to slip under their own weight, lacking the light soaring quality that we will see in many of the late Nāgārjunakoṇḍa sculptures. Note that on figure 93 the appearance of the lotus cross-bars in sets of three while in figure 94 they appear in sets of four. These cross-bars are represented on the drum of the *stūpa*. Interestingly, this corresponds to the actual situation of *Stūpa* 9, for we have noticed the group of three on *āyaka* panel 1 (fig. 64) and the groups of four on *āyaka* panel 2 (fig. 65) and panel 3 (fig. 66), indicating the level of accuracy of these small *stūpa* representations. Two other *caitya* slabs are essentially the same pattern as the documented examples from Site 9. The first shows the worship of the throne at the center of the *āyaka* platform (fig. 104). Note here the unexpected, exaggerated use of perspective in the representation of the *āyaka* platform. The second (fig. 105) shows the same theme only here represented as a Buddha image. As we have stressed before, the appearance or lack of appearance of the Buddha image is not of chronological significance, for the notion of equivalence of iconoic and aniconic imagery at Nāgārjunakoṇḍa[231] has been seen in the Nāgārjunakoṇḍa monastic site with the "ideal" ground-plan.

The *caitya* slabs from Site 9 originally belonging to the drum of the *stūpa* are in general consistent in style with *āyaka* panel 1 of the same *stūpa*, consisting of relatively simple compositions and rather lifeless figures. But only one slab survives from the dome of the *stūpa* which is more characteristic of the Nāgārjunakoṇḍa *oeuvre* in general than are the others from Site 9. The fragment represents the Sasa Jātaka[232] (fig. 106), a theme in which the bodhisattva, in the form of a hare, leaps into a fire in order to provide food for Śakra disguised as an old hungry Brahman. The tale, mentioning numerous animals, provides an opportunity for the Nāgārjunakoṇḍa artist—whose *forte* was as a miniaturist—to give loving attention to the hare leaping into the fire on the left, or talking to the jackal on the right. It was in compositions such as this one that the artist could dwell on the lively animals seen in nature, rather than on the static reproduction of the well established conventions of the major scenes in the life of the Buddha. It was here that he excelled his predecessors who in the same scene at Amarāvatī showed the leaping hare reduced to a small figure at the bottom of the composition, totally dominated by the figure of Śakra (fig. 85, right panel). The Goli variant of the same scene (fig. 107) is closer to the Nāgārjunakoṇḍa example, but even though only a part of the Nāgārjunakoṇḍa composition survives, we can see the slender elegance of human and natural forms of which the Nāgārjunakoṇḍa artist was the master. Interestingly, this love for delicated natural details appears in none of the *āyaka* panels or *caitya* slabs from the same site.

A small but important fragment, not attached to the *stūpa* itself, was excavated at Site 9. It shows the left leg and right foot of what was originally a seated Buddha image (fig. 108). It bears an inscription on its base which is fragmentary and of little significance. It simply tells us that the image was installed by a lady who was the wife of Koḍabudhi.[233] Nothing else is known about this donatrix and no date or other significant information has been supplied. Seated Buddha images in the round from Gandhāra and Mathurā have long been well-known, but from Andhra Pradesh these figures are extremely scarce. An image formerly in the collection of Mr. Ernest Erickson (fig. 109), now in the Brooklyn Museum, has hitherto been the best known example. The fact that it appeared on the market with no clear provenance and no parallels within the Andhra *oeuvre* has caused this piece to be frequently overlooked within scholarly discourses upon Andhra art. But the appearance of the excavated fragment from Site 9 clearly substantiates the type even though we have no knowledge of its exact function or find spot. Based upon the sculptural style of Site 9, we would not suspect that the Erickson Buddha belonged to that stylistic group, but appears to be of a later date as will be discussed below. More likely, an unpublished seated Buddha figure excavated at Nāgārjunakoṇḍa (fig. 110) fulfils the requirements for the Site 9 type. At best, the figure may be described as coarse and clumsy. It is as if cut from a square block producing broad shoulders, enormous thighs, short chest, and a waistline so broad as to be nearly obliterated. The hair appears like an even cap of curls and the *uṣṇīṣa* is almost non-existent as in many Nāgārjunakoṇḍa examples. In its heavy corporeality, this figure would not immediately suggest Andhra Pradesh where it was indeed made, but rather the well-known Mathurā images from Sitala Ghati and Set Mahet.[234] Since it was Douglas Barrett who suggested that Mathurā was the source for the "idea" of the Andhra Buddha image, he readily acknowledges that the Mathurā predecessors provide none of the naturalism found at Amarāvatī.[235] But if there is a dependence on works from Mathurā, as we have already demonstrated, this particular Buddha image would provide one more of the connecting links, and not the more slender examples so abundant within the Andhra tradition.

To justify the seated Buddha image as not necessarily coming from Site 9, but belonging to the Site 9 type, we can compare it to the *āyaka* panel reliefs representing the seated Buddha figure. Note the similar corpulence of the seated figure, in this case possibly an ascetic (fig. 81) showing excessively broad shoulders and body as found on *āyaka* panel 1 and a more refined variant of it showing the Buddha seated under Nāga Mucilinda's hood (fig. 111). Even the standing variant of *āyaka* panel 3 (fig. 86) lacks the slender elegance to be seen in the bulk of Buddha images from Andhra Pradesh, while a free standing variant of this type has been found at the nearby site of Guntapalli (fig. 112) in Andhra Pradesh.

Site 9 and Later Works from Site 6

The corpulent Buddha type, popular with the artists of Site 9, is found in a well-known fragment currently in the Musée Guimet in Paris. Its main remaining theme is the story of the Man in the Well (fig. 113) and the Buddha-like figure is again that of an ascetic. That the corpulence is a stylistic rather than an iconographic feature is demonstrated by comparing it to another representation of the same scene from Amarāvatī (fig. 68) and to another example from Nāgārjunakoṇḍa to be discussed below (fig. 223). The pot bellied representation of the seated ascetic with a tree appearing like a mushroom behind his head is nearly identical to the *āyaka* panel 1 example from Site 9 (fig. 81), but other aspects of this panel make us reluctant to ascribe it to Site 9. In fact, many stylistic features of this panel would cause us to remove it entirely from the school of Nāgārjunakoṇḍa and ascribe it to the nearby school of Gummididurru. The stylistic features, particularly a certain perkiness of the female faces, which will be discussed in Chapter IV, are characteristic of Gummididurru. But in spite of this, accumulated evidence compels us to consider this piece as the style of Gummididurru as practised at Nāgārjunakoṇḍa.

The chief evidence concerns not only this panel but one currently in the Metropolitan Museum of Art which is clearly by the same hand (fig. 114). The sculpture, representing Māra's Temptation of the Buddha and the Great Departure is also in the style of Gummididurru, but information regarding this piece does not permit us to ascribe it to that site. It was acquired by the Metropolitan Museum in 1928. According to an article by the then curator Maurice Dimand, this work and another currently owned by the Metropolitan Museum (fig. 115) were unearthed at Nāgārjunakoṇḍa in 1926 along with two pieces acquired by the Musée Guimet.[236] This statement already contains a gross inaccuracy, although it cannot be completely ignored. In reference to the two Guimet "Nāgārjunakoṇḍa" pieces, Dimand cites figures 2 and 3 in an article by Renée Grousset.[237] One of the pieces, Grousset's figure 3, is indeed the Guimet Man in the Well composition, the clear companion to the Metropolitan Departure and Temptation. Unfortunately, the other work, Grousset's figure 2, is the well-known Temptation scene from Ghāṇṭaśāla previously published by Rea in 1894.[238] As for figure 115, although it may be from Nāgārjunakoṇḍa, we would not ascribe it to the same *stūpa* as figures 113 and 114, for it shares none of their stylistic features. But further information given by Dimand is significant. According to him, the pieces were obtained by Jouveau-Dubreuil and C.T. Loo before the site of Nāgārjunakoṇḍa was classified among the ancient monuments selected by the Madras Presidency for conservation.[239] This story is of the type which the present author generally regards with great caution, but further evidence helps us to confirm it. According to a note in the Metropolitan Museum (which may date back to the time of Dimand) the sculpture was unearthed at Nāgārjunakoṇḍa in July 1926. According to the first official Nāgārjunakoṇḍa excavation report which was published by Hamid Kuraishi, "Professor Jouveau-Dubreuil of the Pondicherry College had removed two beautiful reliefs in July 1926" from Site 4 at Nāgārjunakoṇḍa[240] (now called Site 6 by Longhurst and others) before Kuraishi's trial excavations had begun. This site, which as we have said above has never been well documented, is most likely the source for the Guimet representation of the Man in the Well and the Metropolitan Museum Departure and Temptation. As we have seen, this site bears close stylistic affinities to Site 9. As the site was amongst the first to be discovered, and was visited early by Jouveau-Dubreuil, it appears to have supplied some of the pieces currently in European and American museums. However, as we shall see later, many of the pieces in Western museums which are traditionally considered to belong to Nāgārjunakoṇḍa are in fact from other sites; consequently, one may state that no *masterpiece* has ever left the site of Nāgārjunakoṇḍa, except for those pieces given to the National Museum in New Delhi.

The crude, corpulent Buddha type also appears in another context at Site 6, this time uniquely placed on the *āyaka* pillars of the *stūpa*. Here again (figs. 116-17) we see an overweight, full-bellied, full-chested type whose hair is placed upon his head as if it were a tight fitting cap. This indeed is suggestive of the seated Buddha figure (fig. 110) discussed above and it is indeed possible that this figure is also from Site 6. A very crude but similar figure is currently in the possession of the Victoria and Albert Museum in London (fig. 118). It bears the same full breasts and pot belly as figure 116, while it has the same cap-like coiffure and crudely cut open staring eyes as the seated Buddha figure (fig. 110), again suggesting that the Victoria and Albert piece is from Site 6.

The meaning of the Buddhas represented on the *āyaka* pillars from Site 6, a stylistic companion to the images of Site 9, has long been a source of speculation along with the meaning of the *āyaka* pillars themselves. Longhurst first suggested that the pillars represent the major events in the life of the Buddha.[241] But this is unlikely, as these events are clearly represented elsewhere on the *stūpa*. The fact that the Buddha figures existed on the pillars indicated that the pillars themselves represented the Buddha, an idea well expressed by Mireille Bénisti.[242] But why would the pillars represent the Buddha, when the *stūpa* with its central axis represents the Buddha principle, while the narrative reliefs represent the present and former lives of Śākyamuni Buddha? By adding the *āyaka* pillars, we are adding a third type of Buddha, which, when considered in this light, immediately suggests the notion of the Buddhist *trikāya*, or the notion of the three body theory of the Buddha. This would be comprised of the *dharmakāya* or Law Body referring to the ultimate nature of the Buddha. It is also known as the *svabhāvakāya* or self-existent body. The *saṁbhogakāya* or Bliss Body refers to the celestial manifestation of the Buddha nature visible only to the gods. The *nirmāṇakāya* or assumed body of the Buddha is the only body through which the inhabitants of this earth may learn of the true Buddha nature.[243] If we apply this doctrine to the parts of the *stūpa*, we see the following scheme. The *stūpa*, with its central axis would be the *dharmakāya* or Law Body. The tall *āyaka* pillars pointing up to the sky would represent the *saṁbhogakāya* or Bliss Body meant for the gods, and the low reliefs against the drum and dome of the *stūpa* would represent the *nirmāṇakāya* or assumed body of the Buddha (i.e., scenes of Śākyamuni Buddha in his present and former lives). The notion of the *trikāya* system first appeared in the *Avataṁsaka Sūtra* (c. 200-400 A.D.) and in the *Laṅkāvatāra Sūtra* (4th century A.D.). In the *Lion's Roar of Queen Śrīmālā*, the *trikāya* is absent, but the two body theory is presented.[244] According to Mireille Bénisti, *āyaka* pillars were first constructed around the early part of the second century A.D.[245] The fact that this predates the literary evidence is of no significance, for whether or not we are talking about the *trikāya* as understood in the *Avataṁsaka* and *Laṅkāvatāra Sūtras* is impossible to say. But the visual evidence presented by the Andhra *stūpas* makes it clear that some sort of triple notion of representing the Buddha was intended.

But the question of the pillars appearing in four groups of five is a bit more difficult. Mireille Bénisti considers the five pillars as representing the five Buddhas of the *kalpa*, i.e., Krakucchanda, Kanakamuni, Kāśyapa, Śākyamuni (indicated without pre-eminence), and Maitreya (who symbolizes the coming). These four groups of five project from the top of the drum in the four cardinal directions. Thus according to her, the Buddhas of the spatio-temporal world, here represented by pillars, are projections or successive manifestations, which are temporary and local, of the noumenal principle symbolized by the central axis of the *stūpa*. Thus, according to Bénisti, the outer pillars would represent the Buddha and his teachings, while the central pillar would be the law.[246] But this does not agree with our notion of the pillars representing the *saṁbhogakāya*, for each of the Buddhas cited by Bénisti would indicate manifestation. But if her interpretation that the pillars are the five Buddhas is correct, perhaps we can attempt to co-ordinate the two ideas. Perhaps the pillars in groups of five, when placed above the Buddhas of the present (the reliefs of Śākyamuni) indicate the *saṁbhogakāya*, for one may say that the simultaneous appearance of the past, present, and future is perceivable only to the gods. Bénisti considers the *stūpas* of Andhra Pradesh to be spectacular representation of early Mahāyāna doctrine, at the same time indicating the early roots of *tantra* (the notion of the *dharmakāya*, the Jina, etc.).[247] While she points to the fact that the Mahāsāṁghikas gradually became aware of the Buddhist notion of the *trikāya*,[248] she makes no attempt to apply this vocabulary to the parts of the *stūpa*. But a major point which Bénisti stresses throughout the article is the very fact that these pillars existed in a particular region at a particular time indicates that there must have been a major doctrinal change in Andhra Pradesh, a change which was represented on the *stūpas* in a conspicuous fashion. The exact nature of this doctrinal change we do not know, but it clearly included some sort of *trikāya* system.[249] Thus, the small Buddha figures on the pillars of Site 6 help to provide for us a theory which is of far greater significance than their aesthetic insufficiencies would seem to indicate.

In discussing the style and symbolism of Site 9, we have found it necessary to include works from Site 6, for it becomes clear that Site 6 (and probably Site 9) had a long building history and many of the works from the two sites are contemporary and shed light upon each other. Thus, we shall include a few more examples from Site 6 in this section, for they indeed seem to have cross-fertilized each other.

Other remains from Site 6 present a miscellany of formats and styles. A long panel (fig. 119) unique in format was published by Longhurst.[250] The main scenes are separated from each other by a squat *yakṣa* flanked by rectangular buildings surmounted by *gavakṣas*. This arrangement does not correspond to any examples in the *āyaka* panels at Nāgārjunakoṇḍa. The piece has a sharp curve and appears to have been a base molding either for a *caitya gṛha* or for a *stūpa* (cf. fig. 103). The scenes have been identified by Vogel as representing the Śrīkinnarī Jātaka, a theme well-known through its representation on Barabuḍur.[251] The scenes are delicately carved and show a miniaturist's technique quite apart from the other examples from Site 6, anticipating a later style which we will see in the more fully developed Nāgārjunakoṇḍa style. For example, in scene 2 (fig.120), Prince Sudhāna is seen sitting in the center cross-legged. Before him is the cross-legged Kāśyapa seated between the trees. The visual focus is not at the center, but on the hermit on the left, a type of composition which becomes popular in many scenes from Nāgārjunakoṇḍa. In the third scene (fig. 121), the prince and his companions are mounted on the back of the monkey king. The soaring diagonal composition easily anticipates the noteworthy composition of the Buddha and Nanda flying over heaven in panel representing scene from the *Saundarānanda* (fig. 179).

Other sculptures from Site 6 are problematic due to the scanty nature of the excavation reports. According to Longhurst, the drum of the *stūpa* contained vertical slabs "with the usual representations of *stūpas* and figures of worshippers standing at the foot of the pillars supporting Buddhist symbols such as a wheel or a *stūpa.*"[252] We believe in this case that Longhurst's description was over-generalized. What he seems to be referring to is, in fact, best represented in the Cleveland Museum of Art (fig. 122) showing a representation of the Buddha as a flaming pillar which originally issued forth immediately behind a throne. This is similar to many such representations from Gummididurru (fig. 124). (For the assignment of this work to Gummididurru, see Chapter III.) These were originally placed between *caitya* slabs along the drum of the *stūpa*. The Cleveland slab first appeared in an exhibition catalogue published by C.T. Loo in 1935. The piece was then described as "art tardif d'Amarāvatī[253]." But a nearly identical fragment remains at Nāgārjunakoṇḍa, and it would appear that the Cleveland piece was associated with Jouveau-Dubreuil's early visit to Site 6. Interestingly, both works are broken at approximately the same places. They probably flanked the same *caitya* slab. Sometime during the original destruction of the *stūpa*, the same horizontal breaks must have covered the three slabs, thus leaving the Cleveland and Nāgārjunakoṇḍa slabs in such a similar condition. The facial types represented on this pillar are a variant of other examples belonging to the early Nāgārjunakoṇḍa style. The widely opened eyes, producing a hollow lifeless stare, may be seen on the seated Buddha image (fig. 110) and partakes of a similar quality as figures from Gummididurru (fig. 123). This facial type is also apparent on the Guimet Man in the Well (fig. 113). As we have mentioned before, representations of the Buddha as a flaming pillar were common to Gummididurru. At Nāgārjunakoṇḍa, this theme is mostly found in the early representations from *Stūpas* 6 and 9 (figs. 91, 93 and 100).

Regarding the *caitya* slabs of Site 6 (figs. 36 and 124), we feel it would be most logical to discuss them here, in the Vīrapuruṣadatta section, even though one could conceivably create a rationale for placing them anywhere from the period of

Cāṁtamūla I to that of Ehuvala Cāṁtamūla. One of these panels (fig. 124) bears a mason's mark 𑀥𑀫𑀲 (Prakrit dhamasa =Sanskrit *dharmasya*) "of dharma" and has been included in an article on the *Chronological Aspects of Mason's Marks at Nāgārjunakoṇḍa* by H. Sarkar.[254] This article contains several errors which led the author to erroneous conclusions. In one section of the article (p. 227) the slab is described as coming from Site 6 which is dated to the second regnal year of Ehuvala Cāṁtamūla. In fact, Site 6 bears no date, while the date of the second regnal year of Ehuvala Cāṁtamūla is the date associated with Site 5. The original *in situ* photograph of the piece (fig. 36) confirms that it is indeed from the undated Site 6. On the basis of epigraphical and paleographical evidence (on pp. 230-31 of the same article) Sarkar ascribes the *dharma* mason's mark to the reign of Vīrapuruṣadatta, the period to which we are ascribing Site 9 and some parts of Site 6. This would be the appropriate time period for the Site 6 *caitya* slabs, for they contain both Amarāvatī and non-Amarāvatī elements, a combination which is typical for the reign of Vīrapuruṣadatta. The non-Amarāvatī elements are the appearance of recumbent animals along the drum frieze of the *stūpa*, as well as the simplicity of the drum frieze representations (cf. figs. 93, 94, 100 and 105). To this is added a railing typical of the late Amarāvatī school and common in the later *caitya* slabs of Nāgārjunakoṇḍa.

In 1933, Stella Kramrisch referred to "an altogether heavy physique" peculiar to the site of Nāgārjunakoṇḍa.[255] It is particularly at the *Mahācetiya* and Sites 6 and 9 where this feature dominates. The *Mahācetiya* followed by Site 6 were the earliest to fit this description, showing strong influences from Mathurā, possibly through the intermediary of Gummididurru. This was followed by Site 9 which combined the style of the *Mahācetiya* and Site 6 with features from Amarāvatī, particularly influenced by the small late phase drum friezes. With regard to Site 9, we have also spoken of Classical influences. Many of these are fore-shadowed in the drum friezes from Amarāvatī. In the case of the squat portly Buddha images and the stumpy figures lined up against a flat ground show some influence from Mathurā, an influence which may have been partly filtered through Gummididurru, Ghantaśāla, or other regional sites.

We began our discussion of *Stūpa* 9 standing that a date of the eighth regnal year of Ehuvala Cāṁtamūla (c. 273-83 A.D.) was associated with the site. With it we have included a discussion of Site 6 and have shown several different stylistic trends on some of these monuments. It would seem that the trends were not necessarily simultaneous, and that the group showed a definite evolution. As we have stated before, the inscription at Site 9 was found in the *maṇḍapam* and is not necessarily the date of the *stūpa* itself. According to the excavation reports, *Stūpa* 9 underwent four phases of construction and the monument may go back to the time of Vīrapuruṣadatta or even earlier.[256] From the time of Vīrapuruṣadatta, we have discussed three memorial pillars (figs. 51, 57-60 and 61) dating to around the first year of Vīrapuruṣadatta's reign (c. 240-50 A.D.). These pillars were found at Site 9, and it is likely that at least an early stage of the *stūpa* existed when they were placed there. If we look at the bottom panel of the inscribed memorial pillars (figs. 54 and 58) we note the portliness of the two major figures in the scene wearing cap-like coiffures. This bears comparison with the Guimet Man in the Well and the Metropolitan Departure from Site 6 (figs. 113 and 114). Although King Cāṁtamūla was probably quite a robust figure, and his representation certainly bore a large element of portraiture, it would seem that this feature probably occurred simultaneously with the Buddha images of Sites 6 and 9, which as we have said showed influences from Mathurā. But we wonder if there was not a conceptual equation being made between the Buddha and the revered King Cāṁtamūla, and that this did not somehow influence the choice of the introduction of the Mathurā aesthetic. We remember that in the inscriptions, for three generations (Vīrapuruṣadatta, Ehuvala Cāṁtamūla, Rudrapuruṣadatta) the virtues of Cāṁtamūla I, as performer of Aśvamedha, etc., were extolled at far greater length than that of the Buddha himself. Thus, it would not be difficult to imagine that at least a sculptural comparison was perceived. The pillars also include Amarāvatī elements, as in the animated elongated couple (fig. 53 top) and the rear view figure at the left (fig. 54). This is also the case with the Guimet Man in the Well and the Metropolitan Departure panels. It would seem therefore that panel 1 (fig. 64) of *Stūpa* 9 belonged to the same period as the memorial pillars, followed shortly by panel 2 (fig. 65) and panel 3 (fig. 66), as well as the two smaller panels (figs. 90 and 91). The Guimet Man in the Well and the Metropolitan Great Departure from Site 6 would also be contemporary as would be the seated Buddha image of the Site 6/9 type (fig. 110). These would be followed shortly by the *āyaka* pillars (figs. 116-17) from Site 6 as well as the Victoria and Albert Museum seated Buddha image (fig. 118). This group was preceded by the *āyaka* panel of Site 6 (figs. 36, 37, 41 and 42) dating to the time of Cāṁtamūla I, and perhaps the Site 9 drum slabs (figs. 93-94). Both the Sasa Jātaka from Site 9 (fig. 106) and perhaps the Śrīkinnari Jātaka from Site 6 (fig. 119) belong to the early years of Ehuvala Cāṁtamūla, the time when the complex of Site 9 was probably completed. For as we shall see their stylistic characteristics belong to a later time.

Thus the earliest Ikṣvāku sculptural remains at Nāgārjunakoṇḍa at Site 6 (the *āyaka* panels) date to the time of Cāṁtamūla I (c. 225-240-50 A.D.) as do perhaps the drum slabs of Site 9. The *Mahācetiya* whose *āyaka* panels were inscribed during the sixth regnal year of Vīrapuruṣadatta (c. 246-56 A.D.) must have been in existence well before that time and attracted new establishments to that area. Site 9 must also have been in existence before the beginning of Vīrapuruṣadatta's reign, for in the first year of the reign Vīrapuruṣadatta placed his father's memorial pillar there, and in the probability shortly thereafter he had the *āyaka* panels added to *Stūpa* 9. Around the same time, the scene of the Man in the Well and the Great Departure were added to Site 6, as well as the *āyaka* panels. But we know of the inscription at Site 9, dating to the eighth regnal year of Ehuvala Cāṁtamūla (c. 273-83 A.D.). It was probably around this time that the Sasa Jataka of Site 9 and the Śrīkinnarī Jātaka of Site 6 were added.

Ehuvala Cāṁtamūla (c. 265-75-c. 290-300 A.D.)

It would seem that the style of Nāgārjunakoṇḍa, which more or less represents what we would call the continuation of the late phase of Amarāvatī (or the traditional Andhra style) flourished during the reign of Ehuvala Cāṁtamūla. To this reign, we have only two inscribed and securely dated pieces.

To the thirteenth regnal year of Ehuvala Cāṁtamūla (c. A.D. 278-88) belongs an inscribed and dated memorial pillar (fig. 125) found in a ruinous state of preservation at Site 61. According to its inscription it was raised in memory of Mahāsenāpati Kumāra Elī Ehuvaladāsamṅaka, who appears to have been a step-brother of King Ehuvala Cāṁtamūla.[257] It is hardly possible for us to speak of style, for the surface of this image has been nearly totally destroyed. The general idea of the seated figure of the deceased surrounded by female figures has been found in all the memorial pillars thus far discussed. But from what remains, we see none of the heaviness of the Cāṁtamūla and early Vīrapuruṣadatta groups. Instead, it seems to be reasserting a slenderness of form characteristic of the school of Amarāvatī.

The Kumarānandin Panel and Site 3

Amongst the pieces of sculpture at Nāgārjunakoṇḍa bearing a dated inscription, we find one which is outstanding in its conception. The piece known as the Kumarānandin panel was found in a *caitya* hall at Site 106 at Nāgārjunakoṇḍa (fig. 126). According to R. Subrahmanyam,[258] it was found "a little in front of a platform raised at the apsidal end" and appears to have been a casing slab that was set at the top edge of the platform. The panel (fig. 127) consists of four scenes from the life of the Buddha: from right to left, Siddhārtha in his palace, the Great Departure, the Temptation and the Devas congratulating the Buddha after his enlightenment. The scenes are flanked by five large *mithuna* couples, equal in their visual significance to the small figured scenes of the Buddha medallions. The entire format of this panel is unique. The scenes from the life of the Buddha are placed within lotus roundels reminiscent of the numerous roundel representations on the railing of the Great *Stūpa* at Amarāvatī. The *mithuna* couples (figs. 128-32) on the Kumarānandin panel are placed on small platforms as if in front of the railing (in the realm of desire). The variety of their emotional expressions and varied postures represent phases and moments of loving togetherness. The scenes from the life of the Buddha are likewise animated and show a full understanding of the sculptural opportunities of the iconographic themes. In the scene of Siddhārtha in his palace (fig. 133), the figures in both front and rear views are placed carefully within the roundel, in a manner fully understood at Amarāvatī. However, the roundel with the Prince on his throne has a truly peculiar feature. The throne is tilted. The mastery of the panel makes it clear that this was not clumsiness on the part of the sculptor. The slanted throne may indicate the inner commotion of Siddhārtha before his renunciation, in contrast to the calm of figures 135 and 136. The panel of the Departure (fig.134) shows the Prince proceeding on his horse, held horizontally to the business at hand, while his groom and personal bearer protrude beyond the borders of the roundel. In the scene of the Temptation (fig. 135) and in the post-Enlightenment scene (fig. 136), the Buddha sits serenely, taking no notice of the events around him.

On the slab is an inscription bearing the date of the twenty-fourth regnal year of Ehuvala Cāṁtamūla (c. A.D. 289-99). Dr. R. Subrahmanyam has contested that the date refers to the slab.[259] According to D.C. Sircar,[260] the inscription says that in the twenty-fourth regnal year of Ehuvala Cāṁtamūla, Kumarānandin installed a stone image *(śailamayī pratimā)* of the Buddha. Sircar interprets the stone image to be the frieze under discussion. Subrahmanyam, on the other hand, believes that the "stone image" was not this slab, but must have referred to an image placed on top of the platform beneath which the Kumarānandin was found. Based on the unexpected inclusion of the word for "stone" *(śailamayī)*, he believes that the "stone image" was a replacement for an earlier wood or stucco image on the platform. To him, the Kumarānandin panel was contemporary with the earlier wooden or stucco image. When the stone image was set up, the inscription was added to the empty space on the panel. Based on the appearance of the roundel form, and several features of middle Amarāvatī style, he placed the sculptures at the very beginning of the Ikṣvāku period. His arguments only make sense if one assumes that the artist imitated earlier artists in neat art historical order. The female in figure 131 indeed shows a knowledge of the female figures in the Amarāvatī scene of Sūjātā offering Rice to the Buddha[261] and the Kumarānandin scene of Siddhārtha in his Palace (fig. 133) also shows that the sculptor had recently seen an Amarāvatī representation of the Muga Pakkha Jātaka (fig. 137). This is not disturbing, as during the third century A.D., the Amarāvatī *stūpa* was still intact, and artists could draw from the early, middle, and late phases simultaneously.

There is, in fact, a decorated roundel from the Ikṣvāku period, as we have seen in figure 47. In this case it is on the lotus decoration of the *sūcīs*. Subrahmanyam is quite correct in pointing out that the decorated lotus roundel was more common to Amarāvatī. This is indeed because the Amarāvatī *stūpa* had a decorated lotus railing. But the decorated roundel is equally valid for later times, as we will see that it is most common at Nāgārjunakoṇḍa in the period of Ehuvala Cāṁtamūla. Thus we will have no hesitation in accepting the date of the twenty-fourth regnel year of Ehuvala Cāṁtamūla (c. A.D. 289-99) as the correct date for the Kumarānandin panel. For the stylistic elements in the panel which derive from Amarāvatī do not negate the Ikṣvāku elements of the piece: the low flat carving, unique composition, and a find spot which shows no indication of Sātavāhana habitation.

While we have stated before that the *stūpas* of Nāgārjunakoṇḍa had no railings, the *Mahācetiya* may have had a wooden one. Fragments of stone railings have been found out of context and Sarkar suggests they may have formed rectangular railings around apsidal temples. Numerous undecorated cross-bars have been found and a few decorated ones including a traditional lotus *sūcī* (fig. 138) and a roundel containing two elephants, one behind the next (fig. 139). Sarkar believes this piece to be from Site 3.[262] Another example of the decorated roundel form shows a plaque of boxers on the obverse (fig. 140) and a dancing *yakṣa* or *gaṇa* on the reverse (fig. 141). A fragment of a railing with a roundel on the cross-bar and a *mithuna* couple on the upright (fig. 142) is probably contemporary with the Kumarānandin panel. The female figure with her full rounded bosom, narrow waist and languid grace compares well with the females in figures 129 and 130. This couple can in no way be considered an early work.

Subrahmanyam's interest in the roundel form opens up for us a new area of investigation involving a consideration of the *caitya* slabs at Nāgārjunakoṇḍa. As we have mentioned above, the *caitya* slabs represent with a general accuracy the architecture of contemporary *stūpas*. In searching for roundel forms along the drum of the *stūpa*, we have found the following. In the Madras Government Museum one such representation exists. It is on a late phase *stūpa* slab (fig. 143) which is of clear Ikṣvāku workmanship of the fully developed Ikṣvāku style. If one looks at the left side of the drum frieze (behind the pillar) one sees what appears to be a lotus roundel. This is also seen on the Metropolitan *caitya* slab (fig. 115). A similar example (fig. 144) was excavated at Nāgārjunakoṇḍa (lotus roundels behind lions) where the corners of the square are filled in with lotus leaves as in the Kumarāṇandin panel. Each of the drum slab panels is separated by a decorated vertical band again similar to the Kumarānandin format. Other examples (figs. 145 and 146) show the vertical band containing further lotus roundels. In figure 147 (detail of fig. 146), the roundel is used to contain a decoration other than a lotus. Although to our knowledge the Kumarāṇandin panel is not a *stūpa* drum slab, we would suppose that contemporary *āyaka* panels once existed in that format, as represented on the *stūpa* slabs. Thus the *caitya* slabs bearing the roundels should be approximately contemporary with the Kumarānandin panel.

A *caitya* slab from Site 3 at Nāgārjunakoṇḍa (figs. 148 and 149) helps us to indicate that we are here approaching a late date in Ikṣvāku stylistic evolution. Superficially, this panel reminds us of a *caitya*, also showing the Buddha protected by Nāga

Mucilinda, from Amarāvatī (fig. 150). But after further examination, the comparison weakens. At the base of the Nāgārjunakoṇḍa panel is a lotus roundel border. Is this a reference to the Kumarānandin type of panel? Here we shall return to the method of motif analysis used by Stern and Bénisti. Although we have pointed out that in certain specific examples, their system falls short, it is still useful in broad terms. In their evolution of the *stūpa figurée*, Stern and Bénisti conclude their evolutionary sequence at Amarāvatī with a panel such as our figure 150, showing a Buddha figure at the opening of the railing, and a ground balustrade which is either decorated with the usual garland motif or with a row of rearing animals and humans.[263] According to them, this phase is abundantly represented at Nāgārjunakoṇḍa. Figure 145 partially corresponds to this type, but only if you ignore the roundels on the drum frieze. In fact, the drum friezes represented on the Amarāvatī *caitya* slabs correspond to the *āyaka* panels of the Cāṁtamūla and Vīrapuruṣadatta period, but not to the early drum slabs. They show no reflection of what we will see of the *āyaka* panels of the Ehuvala Cāṁtamūla period. A feature which the French team does not take into account is the appearance of free-standing pillars situated within the *pradakṣinā* path of the *stūpa*. This is apparent in figures 143 and 146 and absent in Nāgārjunakoṇḍa figures 144 and 145. But in a *caitya* slab from *Stūpa* 2 (fig. 151), we see that these pillars have been moved outside the railing, placed on a platform, and are honored by adoring worshippers. The sequence is brought to its culminating stage at Site 3 (fig. 148) where the pillars with elaborately decorated shafts are placed on plinths and are surmounted by corbeled capitals which bear the Wheels of the Law (fig. 148). From the hub of the wheel hang large garlands, but the most important aspect of the wheel is that it is rendered in perspective, a feature associated with the Gupta era and with the Sārnāth Preaching Buddha.[264] Standing around the pillar are worshipful female figures in bracket-like poses. These appear to be a link between the bracket figures of the early Buddhist *stūpas* and those of the early Cālukyas.[265] Other features which help to place this panel to a late date are the animals represented on the coping stone. The Amarāvatī type coping stone with rearing animals has taken a new form. Here, on one side of the coping stone, a man wrestles with a rearing lion, while on the other he rides the beast (fig. 149). The animal's tail merges with the leaf-like form behind, as do the *makara* tails of the Gupta era. In a small narrative relief on the *stūpa*, to the right of the *āyaka* pillars (fig. 148) we see two *nāgas* surrounded by a group of female figures as if forming an illusionistic halo, an idea which may reflect knowledge of painting. The *caitya* panel of Site 3 must be quite close in time to the Kumarānandin panel because of the roundels appearing on the drum frieze and the similarity in the Buddha figures (compare figs. 149 and 135). Thus, the date inscribed on the Kumarānandin panel, c. A.D. 289-99, would be the appropriate time realm for both the Kumarānandin panel and the *caitya* slab from Site 3.

Other panels from Site 3 are of great interest. Figure 152, a relatively narrow *caitya* slab, lack the free-standing pillars of figure 148, but shares with it the decorative border at the base. Thus we do not find here as much of a matched set as we found on the panels of Site 9. The central portion of the composition is nearly identical to the Metropolitan *caitya* slab (fig. 115), and the proportions of the Buddha are the same, indicating that the Metropolitan *caitya* slab is closer in time to Site 3 than to the Metropolitan Great Departure from Site 6 (fig. 114). Regarding the proportions of the Buddha, these are inherited from Amarāvatī indicating a recession of the Mathurā-Gummididurru idiom, and a resurgence of the Amarāvatī style, as can be seen in the well-known British Museum palimpsest from Amarāvatī (fig. 153). The drum frieze on the palimpsest shows the rare occurrence of *mithuna* couples on *caitya* slab drum friezes showing the same format as the *āyaka* slabs from the early Nāgārjunakoṇḍa periods.

Site 3 yielded unique drum slabs of a type not found elsewhere. They consisted of large roundels on a rail pattern originally placed on the drum of the *āyaka* projection. A similar type may have existed at Amarāvatī as they are placed, with two roundels, on several Amarāvatī *caitya* slabs (for example fig. 154). A panel showing the transportation of the Buddha's alms bowl to heaven (fig.155)[266] is placed upon a railing closely reminiscent of an early Amarāvatī rail pillar. The addition of rich leaves around the lotus creates a slight variation. The representation in the roundel is also restating an Amarāvatī theme (fig. 156). The Amarāvatī example shows a *horror vacuii* best known in its late sculptural phase, a phase whose Nāgārjunakoṇḍa counterpart we have seen in *āyaka* panel 2 of *Stūpa* 9 (fig. 83). The Ehuvala Cāṁtamūla period, as seen in the Site 3 example, tries to reorder the composition by adopting a flat decorative style and to change the composition slightly to thin out and linearize the Amarāvatī example. Other examples of this type show the Buddha and the Devas (fig. 157) and the Buddha in the Deer Park in Benares.[267]

The *āyaka* panels of Site 3 represent the fully mature Nāgārjunakoṇḍa style. Panel 1 (fig. 158) consists of a series of five scenes from the Life of the Buddha. The scenes are separated by both *nāga* and human *mithuna* couples in relatively active poses. At the bottom of the panel are the usual bird and leonine beam ends, while at the ends the *bhadraghaṭas* of the early *stūpas* are replaced by beautiful *vṛkṣa devatās* standing upon composite animals. The old railing motif of the earlier *āyaka* panels has disappeared, and is now replaced by slender decorative pilasters, a transition which also took place on the drum friezes of the Amarāvatī *stūpa* (figs. 159 and 160) Although columns as scene dividers were well-known in Gandhāra, this does not seem to be the source of the motif in Andhra. Most likely, the Andhra dividing columns were adaptations from buildings or they expressed the narrow walls which culminated in a saddle roof seen in profile view. These were successfully used as scene dividers at Amarāvatī (figs. 85 and 161). An *āyaka* panel from Site 2 (fig. 221) to which we shall return later, seems to be transitional in this regard. In the Nāgārjunakoṇḍa composition as a whole there is the slightest hint that the whole panel itself is an architectural pavilion.

The scenes on the panel (fig. 158), reading from right to left, represent the Nativity and the Seven Steps, the Departure, the Temptation, the First Sermon, and the *Parinirvāṇa*. In the scene of the Nativity and the Seven Steps (fig. 162), the straight lined simplicity of the Site 6 panel of the same theme (fig. 42) is gone. Instead, the composition of late Amarāvatī (fig. 161) is adopted. The theme, however, is reorganized and simplified as in the case of the Transportation of the Buddha's alms bowl (cf. figs. 155-56). By a comparison of the Amarāvatī and Nāgārjunakoṇḍa Nativity scenes, we can see the essential difference between the Amarāvatī and Nāgārjunakoṇḍa styles. One of the many *fortés* of the school of Amarāvatī is the large number of planes appearing in one composition. This we have spoken about in the beginning of this chapter. Such technical mastery appears nowhere else in the art of India. The Nāgārjunakoṇḍa artist of the Ehuvala Cāṁtamūla period abandons this technique completely. There is only one flat ground level, and the shallowly carved figures, even when they overlap, are in fact on the same picture plane, almost as a reversion to the techniques used at Bharhut. The cause of this change is difficult to document. We know that Amarāvatī was the truly creative center of the region. From the sculptural, architectural, and epigraphic finds at Nāgārjunakoṇḍa, it would seem that the Ikṣvākus were a wealthy and cosmopolitan dynasty, more than capable of engaging the best sculptors of the period. Ikṣvāku genius during the reign of Ehuvala Cāṁtamūla can be seen in the technical innovations of the Puṣpabhadraswāmin temple, the Sarvadeva temple, and the boxing arena. Vīrapuruṣadatta, Ehuvala Cāṁtamūla's predecessor, seems to have patronized works at Jaggayyapeta, Uppugundur, Rāmireḍḍipaḷḷi[268] and probably some of the late phase work at Amarāvatī. Ehuvala Cāṁtamūla, on the other hand, seems to have concentrated his patronage at Nāgārjunakoṇḍa. Only one inscription of his was found outside the site at nearby Kottampalugu.[269] Under his reign, the earliest surviving stone Hindu temple was produced. It would seem that before his reign, the *Mahācetiya* at Amarāvatī was just about complete. It was time for Ehuvala to consolidate his efforts at the site of Nāgārjunakoṇḍa, consolidating what may have been an over-expanded empire. With the ability to draw upon several hundred years of work at Amarāvatī, the sculptors and masons were asked to complete major building projects within one generation. In order to do so, the technical complexities of Amarāvatī had to be sacrificed, while its themes were copied. To compensate for the technical loss, the sculptor added numerous decorative elements, while reducing the number of figures, and flattening the relief. Although we have no evidence of this, it is possible that modelling was added through the use of pigments.[270] To the modern viewer, it appears that art under Ehuvala Cāṁtamūla is entering the realm of the decorative and would thus be entering a decline phase, especially in the treatment of Buddhist themes. But Ehuvala's devotion to Śaivism, his great expansion of the Buddhist monasteries at Nāgārjunakoṇḍa, indicates that under his rule Nāgārjunakoṇḍa was a truly great center of innovative religious thought.

In a comparison between the Nāgārjunakoṇḍa scene of the Great Departure (fig. 163) with an Amarāvatī version of the same theme (fig. 164) we can again state the differences. In the Nāgārjunakoṇḍa example, the depth of carving is about one-fourth that of the Amarāvatī example. The figures are greatly flattened. In the Amarāvatī example, the leaping figure in front of the horse shows his joy at the event, while the one behind the horse is so seized with passion that he nearly leaps out of the composition. In the Nāgārjunakoṇḍa version, the limits of human physiognomy are ignored; the figure's arm is stretched beyond its possibilities to square off the composition. The linear component of the composition is stressed, rather than the composition of lights and darkness produced by the figures held firmly away from their background in the Amarāvatī example. In the Amarāvatī example, clearly architectural structures are used as dividers. In the Nāgārjunakoṇḍa example, the dividing pillars are conspicuously decorated. But the dependence of the Nāgārjunakoṇḍa composition upon the Amarāvatī example is beyond doubt. Looking at the scene of the Temptation (fig. 165) we see no surprises. The Buddha's right hand is in *abhaya mudrā*. *Bhūmi sparśa mudrā* is never used at Nāgārjunakoṇḍa. The Buddha's robe is wrapped around his left shoulder twice, in exactly the same manner as in the Kumarānandin panel (fig. 135). The flat placement of the halo against the *bodhi* tree is also the same. But small details add charm and interest to an otherwise standard composition (fig. 166). The provocative stance of Māra, with his unusual bristling coiffure, is perhaps more amusing than terrifying, especially when placed near Māra's daughters, here rather timid temptresses.

We have spoken extensively in Chapter I about the gradual introduction of the free standing Buddha image within the monastic complex, and how this image was frequently placed opposite a *stūpa*, both within *caitya gṛhas*. Such is the configuration found at Site 3. In examining the *āyaka* panel of *Stūpa* 3 (fig. 158) we see a loose parallel. The Birth and Seven Steps are represented aniconically, the Departure and Temptation iconically, and the First Sermon and *Parinirvāṇa* aniconically. One generally considers the development of early Buddhist narrative sculpture as a development from the aniconic imagery of Bharhut and Sāñcī to the iconic imagery of the Gupta narratives of the Sārnāth school. But the Buddhist art of Andhra Pradesh defies this developmental sequence. When we speak of aniconic art on the *āyaka* panel from Site 3, which belongs to the end of the third century A.D., we can no longer speak of the use of aniconic form as purely an archaism. Clearly, from the form of the *stūpas* being worshipped, the people of Andhra Pradesh were not developing along the line of the Buddhists of the Northwest of India.

This is most clear in considering the scene of the *parinirvāṇa* (fig. 158 left). The *parinirvāṇa* is here represented by the *stūpa.* The standard Gandhāran representation of this scene consists of a Buddha reclining on a couch. This mode of representation is conspicuous by its absence in Andhra Pradesh. The *parinirvāṇa* does exist in aniconic form, in a relief from Amarāvatī of about 100 B.C. The theme is indicated simply by an empty bed (fig. 167) with an inscription nearby indicating that this was a *parinirvāṇa* scene.[271] If the Andhra artist wanted simply to retain an archaism, this would have been the chosen form. But obviously, the Andhra artist had a conscious reason for seeking another form, that of the *stūpa.* Jorinde Ebert, in a study of the relationship between the *stūpa* and the *parinirvāṇa* refers to a study of Bareau, in which he says that the *stūpa*, after the beginning of the Christian era must have been more than just a symbol of the Buddha, but was the part which remains in this world after the *parinirvāṇa.*[272] In her own words, she refers to this as the "*nirvāṇa* body" of the Buddha.[273] If we consider this in relation to our conception of the Andhra *stūpa* as a whole, this might be a restatement of the multiple body theory, and the so-called representation of the *parinirvāṇa* scene would in fact be the *dharmakāya*, especially in a context where it is juxtaposed against iconic themes. While we have no documentation to expand upon this notion, it is clear that the use of the *stūpa* at the end of the life cycle was a conscious decision rather than simple conventionalization.

Returning to the compositional problems of the panel from Site 3 (fig. 158) we can see that the unifying visual elements of the panel are the *mithuna* couples. These can serve as framing elements as in the couples flanking the scene of the Nativity or can give a directional sense as the figures point toward the Great Departure. The thrust of the movement is toward the central composition of the Temptation as can be seen by the couples flanking and leaning toward it. Thus, during this period, the *mithuna* couples have become a fully integral part of the composition of the *āyaka* panels. Regarding the couples themselves (i.e., figs. 168-71), they show none of the formal constraints which iconographic necessity demanded in the narrative scenes They show a wide variety of compositional interaction and coquettish charm while lacking some of the emotional sensitivity we have observed in the Kumarānandin panel.

While we have stated above that the Mathurā element of the Nāgārjunakoṇḍa school receded during the Ehuvala Cāṁtamūla period, there is one conspicuous exception. The *vṛkṣa devatās* at the end of the panel (fig. 171) retain some of the weighty sumptuousness of their Mathurā predecessors. Again, the best comparison is from apsidal temple 2 at Sonkh (fig. 172). But instead of the lovely broad hipped lady standing upon an individual dwarf or other figure, her *vāhana* at Nāgārjunakoṇḍa is novel creation of addorsed leonine and marine animals. The composite best has its three-dimensional counterpart in what appears to be the end of a *toraṇa* from

Andhra Pradesh (fig. 173) currently housed with the Andhra State Department of Archaeology in Hyderabad.[274]

Before leaving the discussion of *āyaka* panel 1 of Site 3, we would like to return to a discussion of a piece which we have touched upon briefly before, and which deserves consideration in a discussion of the Ehuvala Cāṁtamūla period: the Erickson Buddha currently in the Brooklyn Museum (fig. 109). Readers looking at the illustration of the Buddha as it appears today may question the authenticity of this piece due to its highly-polished surface and slick appearance. These are unknown in Andhra Pradesh. The piece was exhibited at Asia Society in 1962, and a photograph of it was published by Aschwin Lippe (fig. 174).[275] The published photograph does not exactly correspond to the piece as it appears today. It was provided by the dealer C.T. Loo and shows the piece before it was cleaned by an over-zealous restorer. In its pre-cleaned state, the piece was without doubt the work of a late Andhra craftsman. During cleaning, the surface was polished. The fingers and toes of the Buddha were slightly shortened and much of the surface detail was obliterated. The deeply incised folds of the drapery were reduced and many of the surface blemishes were planed down. In examining the piece, let us look at the pre-cleaning photograph and remember that the present state of the Buddha image is unfortunate mishap.

The Buddha is seated on a tripartite throne of a type represented on an *āyaka* pillar from Site 6 (fig. 117). The Buddha, whose missing right hand was most likely in *abhaya mudrā,* is represented as delivering the First Sermon as indicated by the addorsed deer on the throne. The motif of the crouching lion, with the head turned backwards, as well as the use of addorsed animals, was known at Nāgārjunakoṇḍa on the Site 9 type *āyaka* panels (fig. 175). The Buddha type clearly belongs to the time of Site 3. The Buddha's robe, which covers the left shoulder, is twisted around the armpit with the end resting on the Buddha's forearm as in Site 3 (figs. 157 and 165) as well as on the Kumarānandin panel (fig. 135). Indeed, it can be seen on the earlier Victoria and Albert seated Buddha (fig. 118) but the essential differences here are quite clear. On the Victoria and Albert Buddha, the drapery is wrapped carelessly around the arm as an Indian lady might wrap a *sārī* tightly about her while doing household chores. In the Erickson Buddha, as well as in the Site 3 examples, the drapery is studiously arranged in a decorative, monumental shape which could only be retained while remaining still. In the Kumarānandin example dating toward the end of the reign of Ehuvala Cāṁtamūla, it becomes a purely decorative element whose exact drapery prototype is impossible to recreate. The well marked waist and firmness of modelling of the Erickson Buddha again compare best to those of Site 3, quite different from the corpulent Buddhas of the Vīrapuruṣadatta period. The Erickson Buddha in its pre-cleaned state (fig. 174) was thus the only known surviving Buddha image from the Ehuvala Cāṁtamūla period. In its current condition, it is but a memory of that.

Stylistically consistent with Site 3 is the beautiful *āyaka* panel representing the Conversion of Nanda (fig. 176).[276] This panel, while consistent with the scenes from the life of the Buddha from Site 3, rises sharply above it in quality, reflecting the poetic expression of Aśvaghoṣa's *Saundarānanda*. The scenes in question have been identified by Vogel.[277] The first (fig. 177) represents the Buddha with Nanda and his wife Sundarī. Sundarī points to her face in reference to the promise extracted from her husband that he will return before the face paint dries. The second panel (fig. 178) represents Nanda's ordination, while the third scene (fig. 179) poetically represents the Buddha and Nanda flying to the celestial world so that the Buddha might ultimately point out to Nanda that his wife's beauty is like that of a one-eyed monkey. It is a condensation of several passages from Canto X as follows:

> *X. 3.* Then the Blessed One, seeing Nanda to be wandering in the darkness which is called 'wife', grasped his hand and flew up into the sky to rescue him, like a cormorant which has caught a fish in the water and, wishing to bring it up, comes to the surface.
>
> *X. 5.* Quickly they came to Mount Himavat, supremely fragrant with deodars, possessing many rivers, lakes and torrents, full of gold ore and of divine seers.
>
> *X. 14.* Monkeys wandered along the mountains, keeping the deodars in perpetual commotion, and finding they bore no fruit, departed from them, as from rich men whose favor is empty of gifts.
>
> *X. 15.* The sage saw in that herd a female monkey, with one-eye gone and its face red as if lac had been pressed on it, which was playing the laggard,. . .
>
> *X. 35.* And Nanda beheld the grove of Indra on all sides with eyes staring with surprise; and the Apsaras, full of joy and eyeing each other haughtily, came round him.
>
> *X. 36.* They were ever young, ever busied in love alone and enjoyed jointly by those who have earned merit; celestial beings, union with them was no sin. In them centered the reward of austerities of the divine world.[278]

The flight of Nanda and the Buddha is imbued with the picturesque imagery of the poetry. They soar over Mount Himavat, enjoying the view of the maidens, who, in their relaxed poses, show that they are full of joy. The identification of the fourth scene on the panel (fig. 180) was not clear to Vogel. It seems to represent Nanda's return to Kapilavastu in order to preach salvation (Canto XVIII.62).

That the *Saundarānanda* panel reflects poetry rather than having the didactic purpose of many of the other reliefs is enforced by C. Sivaramamurti in a discussion of *mithuna* motifs. He says that, "Ordinarily it may mean nothing more than an amorous couple, but treated in proper artistic form, and the imagination and fancy of the sculptors given its full scope, it has given us some of the loveliest commentaries on literary passages and an insight into the rich and glorious life of the best period of art in India."[279] Regarding one of the *mithuna* couples on the *Saundarānanda* panel (fig. 181), he finds that it reflects a passage in the *Amaruśataka*:

> The young lady of the house, terribly tormented by shame at the utterance of the pet parrot in the presence of the elders in the morning of all that it had heard spoken by the wedded couple during the night, stops its prattle by putting in its beak her ruby-set ear-ring as if it were a pomegranate fruit.[280]

Sivaramamurti has suggested literary parallels for several other *mithuna* couples at Nāgārjunakoṇḍa. Whether or not we can justify these parallels historically is somewhat irrelevant. The fact is that the artistic treatment of these figures compels us to make these poetic associations. This new, more poetic form of expressing Buddhist themes at Nāgārjunakoṇḍa attains its height during the period of Ehuvala Cāṁtamūla. Modern scholars often tend to view this elaboration of themes as decadent, as did most likely contemporary readers of Buddhist *kāvya* literature. For even Aśvaghoṣa, at the end of the *Saundarānanda* felt compelled to defend his style:

> *XVIII. 63.* This poem dealing with the subject of salvation has been written in Kavya style, not to give pleasure but to further the attainment of tranquillity and with the intention of capturing hearers devoted to other things. For, that I have handled other subjects in it besides salvation is in accordance with the laws of Kavya poetry to make it palatable, as sweet is put into a bitter medicine to make it drinkable.
>
> *XVIII. 64.* Since I saw mankind mainly given over to the pleasures of the objects of the senses and averse from Salvation, I have here told of the final truth under the guise of Kavya, considering Salvation to be supreme. Let the reader understand this and study attentively in it that which leads to tranquillity and not that which is merely pleasurable, as only the residue of gold is taken after it has been separated from the metal dust.

A comparison with other Andhra examples of the conversion of Nanda helps to show the innovativeness of this piece. At Amarāvatī, we cite three different panels which are clearly identifiable as representing the conversion of Nanda. The first (fig. 182) is on the well-known British Museum palimpsest (fig. 153) showing Nanda's wife Sundarī at her toilet. Another example on a small drum frieze condenses four scenes into one panel: Nanda leaving his wife, Nanda dreaming of his married life, Buddha and Nanda on the way to heaven, and Indra's celestial grove (fig. 183).[281] The scene is expanded into four surviving panels (the bottom one to be read as two) in an upright (fig. 184) showing Nanda and his wife Sundarī, Nanda following the Buddha, Nanda at his ordination, and Nanda and the Buddha (standing behind a wall as observers) in the Paradise of Indra. It is in the Nāgārjunakoṇḍa version that instead of a contraction of the story, as in many of the early Buddhist narratives, we begin to get an expansion and an inclusion of nature within the panel. The scenes are being expounded upon rather than being summarized.

A comparison of the panel of the conversion of Nanda with the same scene from Goli village (fig. 185) shows the narrative in further elaboration. (For the identification of this piece as being from Goli, see Chapter III.) The Goli panel, which probably postdates the Ehuvala Cāṁtamūla period and belongs to the early fourth century A.D., subdivides the scenes even further, as in the text. For example, in one scene we see Nanda and the Buddha flying over heaven gazing at the one-eyed female monkey who is sitting in front of a "deodar....which bore no fruit" (X. 14 and X. 15). The next scene shows Indra's heaven full of *apsarās* (X. 35 and X. 36). These as we have seen were condensed into one panel into earlier Nāgārjunakoṇḍa example (fig. 179). The expansion of poetic themes in the narratives of the conversion of Nanda is here clearly taking on a directional development and that is toward the expanded version on the wall of Cave XVI at Ajantā.[282] Thus the conversion of Nanda panel signals the coming of a new era, not looking back to the past, but foreshadowing a new style.

The *vṛkṣa devatā* at the end of the conversion of Nanda beam (fig. 186) is the most representative that has survived Nāgārjunakoṇḍa. She stands with her knee resting on a lion's head while her eyes look down pensively. She is on a composite animal of the type seen in figure 171. In simpler form, these addorsed beasts make their appearance at Amarāvatī,[283] but at Nāgārjunakoṇḍa they are two different beasts, leonine and aquatic. They have their counterparts in addorsed composite animals from Begram,[284] which in turn are probably related to Western *grilli.*

An extraordinary slab was found in a sculptor's workshop. It is an incised sketch on white limestone (fig. 187) seemingly intended as a sketch for an *āyaka* beam-end. The slender proportions of the *vṛkṣa devatā*, enhanced by the fact that the stone is not carved, point toward the elegant figures of Ajantā. A servant accompanying her is a unique introduction. We have no idea what her *vāhana* was intended to be, but above her is a composite animal placed as if it were the end of a lintel on a door frame. The animal consists of a rearing horse being spewed forth from the mouth of a *makara*, which is being held open by a small human figure. The rearing horse, otherwise unknown in early Indian art, seems to contain within it a confusion, for the rounded ears and heaviness of the front legs seem more leonine than equine (cf. the horse in the Great Departure, fig. 163).[285]

Site 3 yielded a number of magnificent dome slabs exceeding in both quality and interest those from Amarāvatī. Unfortunately, a study of them becomes hopelessly confused with sculptures from nearby Site 2. Most of the sculptures from these sites were excavated by Longhurst between 1927 and 1929. It appears to us that the majority of sculptures published in the Archaeological Survey for the years 1927-28 belonged to *Stūpa* 2.[286] Those published in the subsequent year seem to belong to Site 3.[287] Yet the often published National Museum *āyaka* panel was published by Longhurst in his final report,[288] and is listed as coming from Site 3, while in the

1927-28 report it seems to come from Site 2. The major purpose of Longhurst's excavation seems to have been the removal and preservation of the monuments, a mission successfully completed. The exact find spots of the pieces seem to have been a matter of only secondary consideration, as can be seen by the large number of sculptures for which no find spot has been recorded. Particularly in the case of Sites 2 and 3, which were contiguous, the pieces seem to have been hopelessly scrambled. Thus, in speaking of the sculptures from these sites, we will be taking great liberties in our ascription of a given piece to a given site based partly on our own selective consideration of Longhurst's reports, and partly on style. Thus, a piece indicated as Site 3 implies that it is stylistically consistent with that site, and one indicated as coming from Site 2 would have the same implication.

Largely due to its high aesthetic quality, and to its appearance in the 1928 excavation report,[289] we will ascribe a dome slab currently in the National Museum, New Delhi (fig. 188) to Site 3. The type reflects in format the dome slabs of Amarāvatī,[290] but elaborates on it, both in decorative intent and in compositional knowledge gained from Amarāvatī's late phase. The scenes are rendered in extremely low relief. The modelling of the figures is minimized so that the outer surfaces of the figures are united and flattened to produce an even frontal plane. No figure steps beyond this plane, either in actuality or through the use of visual perspective. This flatness is emphasized by the rendering of the architecture. For example, in the architectural renderings of the upper panel, walls are placed at very shallow angles. Though they should perhaps be read as coming toward us and separating the individual scenes into separate compartments, the walls are pushed to the side, emphasizing the planar effect of the composition. This composition may be seen as a striking contrast to a middle Amarāvatī example (fig. 189) illustrating some of the same themes. In the Amarāvatī version, architectural elements are placed at sharp angles to each other, producing separate rooms or space compartments. These compartments are read as being on four different planes. Linear perspective is used so that figures may be read as one behind the next. Each figure is deeply cut around its bodily form so that it appears to have abundant space in which to move. Such movement would be unthinkable in the Nāgārjunakoṇḍa composition, for the figures have no undercutting and are bound together by the frontal plane. The scene on the upper left of Siddhārtha's presentation in the temple is clearly an elaboration and a flattening of the middle Amarāvatī composition (fig. 189) with an obvious re-ordering of the scenes. The middle panel showing the Nativity and the Seven Steps, as well as the bottom panel showing the Casting of the Horoscope, flattens and reorganizes the same compositions from late Amarāvatī (figs. 159 and 190). This is the same relationship we have seen between several other Site 3 examples and their Amarāvatī predecessors. The elegant figure of Queen Māyā in the Birth scene shows the same relationship of forms and proportions as the *vṛkṣa devatā* and her servant in the Site 3 sketch (fig. 187).

The following drum slabs also seem to include the requirements for Site 3: The National Museum Transportation of the Buddha's Headdress (fig. 191), the Exhortation of the Gods to the Bodhisattva and the Descent of the Bodhisattva in the Form of a White Elephant (fig. 192), a panel including the Exhortation of the Gods and Māra's Assault (fig. 193),[291] and a panel representing both the conversion of the Kāśyapas and the Sāgata and the Nāga of Mango Ferry (fig. 194).[292] In the bottom panels, the Buddha is represented twice in one scene, a feature more common to the panels of Site 3.

Site 2

The *āyaka* panels from Site 2 show a different stylistic trend from those of Site 3. Both through the choice of subject-matter and the treatment of composition they reflect a nervous tension and elasticity of form which was seen already at Amarāvatī. The artistic intention was not a serene simplification, as in Site 3, but an emphasis on bodily movement frequently stretching human limbs beyond their limits. Faces are particularly crude, showing coarse features on a three quarter profile. Heavily arched brows are placed over the eyes, producing an anguished facial tension, a tension which is maintained regardless of the subject-matter. The best documented panel from Site 2 has been broken in four parts, thus making it feasible for part of it to have been exhibited in the United States in 1964.[293] The entire panel consists of six scenes (figs. 195-200), not all of which have been identified. Although this panel uses the same planar technique which we have seen at Site 3, the visual impact of this technique is quite different here. A far greater area of the frontal plane is used and areas of the background are so small as to produce deep shadows on the background. The transition between foreground and background is here produced by almost perpendicular cutting. The modelling of these figures is far less subtle than at Site 3 (cf. for example fig. 188) so that they are barely individualized, but seem to form group silhouettes, while the details of anatomy are simply incised upon the body rather than softly modelled. The limbs of the figures are greatly attenuated and gain importance in structuring the compositions. As a group, they form arc-like curves emphasizing violent movement (fig. 196) or a gentle sway (fig. 198). If we compare the battle scene (fig. 196) to a composition from Amarāvatī and one from Site 3 at Nāgārjunakoṇḍa, the differences are quite clear.

The battle scene (fig. 196) shows an exaggerated stretching of human limbs so as to create a curving diagonal motion. Unlike Amarāvatī where we see a richness of texture (fig. 201), here the composition is reduced to abstract curving elements losing all sense of the individual figures. Compare this also to the Site 3 Departure (fig. 163) where the individual figures retain their own integrity. Even in the more calm scene of Siddhārtha stringing the mighty bow (fig. 200), the arms of Siddhārtha's female companion are so stretched that their shoulders have disppeared. They are in fact stretched to the point that they reflect the curves only of the tautly held string. The radical change in style from the earlier style of Site 9 can be seen if we compare the Chakravartin and His Seven Jewels (fig. 198) and the Subjugation of the Mad Elephant (fig. 199) to their earlier counterparts at Site 9 (figs. 202 and 91). In the Site 2 Chakravartin and His Seven Jewels (fig. 198) the composition is crowded, including more figures than necessary to define the theme. We read the swaying group of figures in one mass which is incised to define the individual bodies. From these bodies protrude narrow limbs which accentuate the darkness of the shadowed ground.

In the Site 9 example of the same theme (fig. 202), the figures have retained their fullness and individual integrity, still showing careful modelling and the portliness of their Site 6 predecessors as well as their Mathurā influences. The comparison between the Site 2 Subjugation of the Mad Elephant (fig. 199) and that of Site 9 (fig. 91) illustrates a slightly different point, for the flatness of the elephant at Site 9, and the cutting which is nearly perpendicular to the plane, are indications that this fragment postdates the *āyaka* 1, approaching the style of the Ehuvala Cāṁtamūla period.

The ends of the beams of this *āyaka* panel (figs. 195 and 200) present us with a variant of the type found at Site 3. Here they are occupied by auspicious couples beneath the tree, anticipatory of similar sixth century brackets in Bādāmī Cave 3.[294] The couples stand on yet another variant of the mythical beast. This consists of two addorsed *makaras*, with the outer *makara* spewing forth a "rearing" lion. One might wish to see this as a further development from the Site 3 type (fig. 186), but this cannot really be maintained. In general the sculptures of Site 2 seem to represent a different trend rather than a development from Site 3. The artisans of the contiguous Sites 2 and 3 were most likely in close contact with each other. It is possible that these compositions came from some sort of contemporary three-dimensional prototype that was available to them. Thus, we cannot see the *Stūpa* 2 type as coming out of the Site 3 type, but the artisans were varying the original as they saw fit. Similarly, though the use of the individual *vṛkṣa devatā* reflects a past tradition, and the couples foreshadow a future one, we lack sufficient evidence of Ehuvala Cāṁtamūla.

The best preserved of the *āyaka* panels from Site 2 is currently in the National Museum in New Delhi (figs. 203, 204-08).[295] The panel has a compactness and compositional vigor of its own. The shallow relief, with details incised on the body is similar to that of the aforementioned panel in the Nāgārjunakoṇḍa Museum. Facial types are similar as is the rendering of the draped garments. Their folds are rendered by narrow incised lines which almost make them appear striped (cf. figs. 205 and

198). However, the figural groupings are here more unified. Though placed within a rectangular panel, a circular composition is implied. Figures at the rear recede slightly into depth so that one is reminded of the roundel forms of Amarāvatī which we have spoken of in connection with the memorial pillars of the Vīrapuruṣadatta period. If we compare the second (fig. 204), third (fig. 205), and sixth (fig. 206) panels from the right, these seem to reflect the same workshop as figure 195. The last panel (fig. 207)[296] has a similar lyrical charm to the last panel of the previous example as seen in figure 200 (cf. slant of the seat with fig. 133). Yet when it comes to representing a seated Buddha figure (fig. 208), the required compositional restraints are adhered to, with the massive and calming central figure of the Buddha quieting both this composition, and from a distance, the whole panel.

Two other major panels of the Sites 2 and 3 group remain at Nāgārjunakoṇḍa. The first of these (fig. 209) has remained unpublished most likely due to its heavily abraded surface. It consists of seven small panels and shows, more than any of the other examples, a cursory technique. The scenes represented are the Nativity and the Seven Steps, the Visit of Asita and Presentation in the Temple, Siddhārtha in His Palace the night before his departure, the Departure, the Temptation, the Enlightenment, and the Return to Kapilavastu. In terms of a "matching set" they are not completely consistent with the *āyaka* panels of either Sites 2 or 3. Instead they seem to reflect the numerous shallowly carved representations on the *caitya* slabs belonging to the late phases of Amarāvatī,[297] and to the Ehuvala Cāṁtamūla period at Nāgārjunakoṇḍa (for example, figs. 67, 68, 115, 143-46, 150, 151, 153 and 154), which in turn contain illustrations of drum and dome slabs. The artist of the *āyaka* panel has clearly spent his energy elsewhere and rapidly filled in the required seven scenes. The Birth and Seven Steps (fig. 210) retains the basic format of late Amarāvatī (fig. 161) but here miniaturized and reduced to a mere sketch. Regarding the bracket figures from the site (fig. 210) they appear to be a variant of the aforementioned type, couples as in the Site 2 examples, and addorsed *makara* and leonine forms as in Site 3.

The last of these panels (fig. 211), illustrating a veritable *potpourri* of Buddhist literature, contains some of the most charming passages of the group. While the bracket figures are of the Site 2 type (figs. 212 and 213), the modelling of the figures (figs. 212-17) is considerably softer than the Site 2 types. Facial expressions are less strained and the limbs of the figures adhere closer to the limits of human anatomy. The grace and charm of the *mithuna* couples are equal to those of the Kumarānandin panel (cf. fig. 214 and figs. 128-32), and even go beyond it in the shy, youthful coquettishness of the figures (fig. 215). This has its closest counterpart in a *mithuna* couple from Site 3 (fig. 170). Reading from right to left, in order of *pradakṣiṇā*, the themes illustrated are the Transport of Relics, the Śibi Jātaka, Māra's Assault, the Mandhātu Jātaka, and the Nāga King Apalāla subdued by the Buddha. While the first scene is relatively conventional, that of the Śibi Jātaka (fig. 216) continues a type which is specific to Andhra Pradesh. King Śibi is kneeling on one knee while he stretches his left leg to slice off his flesh. The striking position of Śibi, so different from its Gandhāran and Mathurā predecessors,[298] seems to imply a source outside of India, a source which we shall discuss below. But the most interesting of the events here is the story of the Subjugation of the Nāga King Apalāla, (fig. 217), for in contrast to most other representations at Nāgārjunakoṇḍa, this was not one of the themes known at Amarāvatī, but had a local significance for the artists of Gandhāra, and more specifically, Swat Valley.[299] The artists of Nāgārjunakoṇḍa developed the theme more dramatically than in the Northwest, for a Vajrapāṇi smites the mountain with his thunderbolt, in which the Nāga lived, we get a true dramatic sense of a cracking of the rock rather than the neat, orderly examples of gandhāra.[300] The scene twice more in Nāgārjunakoṇḍa (fig. 218 bottom, fig. 219, det. fig. 220). In the first of these scenes, the artist's 'split' in the mountain created by Vajrapāṇi extends right through to the composition of the Indraśaila cave above it, uniting the two cave events into one composition. It is here that the dwelling of Apalāla (rather than the Indraśaila cave as in Gandhāra) is heavily endowed with naturalistic forms and rock-like structures. In fact, the Indraśaila cave is so sketchily represented that one might be tempted to think that the missing rocks and animals on the cave were originally painted in. As Dr. Soper has pointed out, the significance of the cave imagery was so misunderstood that it is totally forgotten in the first panel of Indra's visit.[301] The elaboration of the Apalāla cave, in contrast to the Indraśaila example, is more clearly defined in figures 219-20. In this case, the Gandhāran Indraśaila cave, strewn with animals, seems to have been the prototype, thus totally transforming the imagery. The artist's lack of assuredness is further seen in the figure of Vajrapāṇi, for while attempting to carve a rear view, he created a frontal upper body. We must therefore conclude that the *āyaka* panel containing the Apalāla scene is a type unto itself. While using the *mithuna* couples of the Site 2 type, it retains much of the style of Site 3 and the Kumarānandin panel. We cannot be certain to which site it belonged originally. However, the panels bearing the Apalāla representation stand conspicuously apart. With these the artists were seeking beyond their own tradition, experimenting with different ways to carve in stone a natural grotto. The visual source of these experimentations was most likely Gandhāra,[302] the source of the Apalāla myth.

We shall return briefly to one more panel which we have stated is from Site 2 (fig. 221). This piece was excavated by T.N. Ramachandran,[303] who seems to have recorded his find spots more accurately than Longhurst. Ramachandran stated that this piece was from the *āyaka* platform of *Stūpa* 2. We have spoken of this piece in regard to the heavy columns as a type which probably preceded the types 2 and 3 *āyaka* panels. In regard to the style, there is very little we can say due to the very heavy surface erosion, but the appearance of two scenes within one long panel, separated by a tree, is unique in the *āyaka* panel format. Further, the frieze at the base consists of a row of pecking geese rather than the architecturally derived bird and leonine motif. These variations are not consistent with the matching groups we have referred to above, and one suspects that this panel belonged either to an earlier phase of Site 2, or to a different part of the *Stūpa* (perhaps the base) or both.

The dome panels of Site 2 show a distinctive style, although every dome panel assigned to that group might not be totally consistent with it. In general, they show the attenuated bodies and exaggerated forms as the panel illustrated in figures 195-200 and the National Museum *āyaka* panel (figs. 203-08), and some even show the attenuated and sketchy forms of the Site 2 scenes of the Life of the Buddha (figs. 209-10). One of these, using themes we have illustrated before, shows the style well: the first panel shows in the Śibi Jātaka and the second the Story of the Man and the Well (fig. 222). In them the movement of the figures is so sketchy that our eyes are left only with a sense of diagonal lines rather than human figures. In the Man in the Well composition the lunging posture of the figure holding the spear (fig. 223) was perhaps difficult for the artist to fully realize, for he found it expedient to hide the feet behind bushes, rather than to deal with their appropriate foreshortening. Yet this flat, spindly figure seems closer in spirit to the Roman Meleager type (fig. 82) than the earlier example from Site 9 (fig. 81). This panel, in exception to almost all others at Nāgārjunakoṇḍa, uses a tripartite vertical decorative border rather than the railing motif. Other dome slabs from Site 2 use the exaggerated human form to express a sense of human pathos, as in a panel representing one of the Four Sights, a rare example showing a corpse (fig. 224), or in a scene of Śākyamuni exchanging clothes with the hunter (fig. 225 bottom), and on the top panel, his father's grief at the news of his son's renunciation (fig. 225), or in an unidentified panel (fig. 226). Other panels (figs. 227 and 228) exaggerate the human form beyond visual reason. Thus, the effect that this group produces is one of very limited spatial depth with figures united through linear accents.

One more panel, reported by Longhurst to be from Site 2,[304] merits mention. In three registers it shows successive episodes in the Life of the Buddha (fig. 229) including two episodes in the first two panels, reading from bottom to top, and one in the top panel. The first scene represents the Buddha's Walk after his Enlightenment, then the Buddha protected by Nāga Mucilinda, two episodes in which two merchants feed the Buddha after his Enlightenment, and the first sermon at Benares. The panel, although interesting in itself for the appearance of two representations of the Buddha within each panel, foreshadows in format although not in the specific iconography the numerous Sārnāth Gupta steles of the Life of the Buddha, steles whose origins and functions have remained rather mysterious.[305]

The construction of new *stūpas* and additions to old ones certainly continued beyond the time of Ehuvala Cāṁtamūla, but for this we have no clear documentation. The fact that we have ascribed particular sculptures to particular reigns does not mean that the works cannot overlap into the preceding or subsequent reign. The large bulk of inscriptions found at Nāgārjunakoṇḍa give us a clue to periods of activity rather than dates of the sculpture. For as these inscriptions have provided us with excellent information about Ikṣvāku history and given us a relative architectural sequence, only one inscription helps us with a firm dating of the sculpture, that of the Kumarānandin panel in the twenty-fourth regnal year of Ehuvala Cāṁtamūla. Thus in broad terms we have divided the Ikṣvāku sculpture based on style as follows. To the period of Cāṁtamūla I (c. A.D. 225 to 240-50) we have placed the *āyaka* panels of Site 6. (the so-called *Mahācetiya* panel pre-dating the Ikṣvākus), and perhaps the Site 9 drum slabs. It is generally believed that because there are no extant inscriptions of the time Cāṁtamūla I at Nāgārjunakoṇḍa, that there was no sculptural activity there. We know that the *Mahācetiya* was completed in the early years of his successor, and must have been under construction during his time. The nearby Sites 6 and 9 were also already under construction. In fact, the placement of Cāṁtamūla's memorial pillar at Site 9 may even indicate a degree of affiliation. To the period of Vīrapuruṣadatta (c. A.D. 240-50 to 265-75) belong the memorial pillars to Ehuvala Cāṁtamūla, the *āyaka* panels of Site 9, and the remainder of sculpture from Site 6. During this time the style begins to reflect that of Amarāvatī and shows the format seen on the late phase drum friezes and on the *caitya* slabs. At this time there was probably still considerable activity at Amarāvatī. By the time of Ehuvala Cāṁtamūla (c. A.D. 265-75 to 290-300), the sculptural efforts at Amarāvatī seem to have moved to Nāgārjunakoṇḍa, first completing Site 9 and then moving to the Northeast part of the valley to work on Sites 2 and 3, and whatever associated monuments the many unrecorded slabs reflect. This style shows new developments in Amarāvatī's late phase, flattening the forms of the sculpture while expanding upon and varying visual devices, anticipating the expansion of the narrative into the paintings of Ajantā.

Rudrapuruṣadatta (c. 290-300 to c. 315)

To the period of Rudrapuruṣadatta, the *fourth king* (c. 290-300 to c. 315), an unusual memorial pillar (figs. 230-31) remains to reflect upon many of the problems we have hitherto discussed. The pillar, though in a poor state of preservation, sums up many of the problems we have faced in Nāgārjunakoṇḍa sculpture. It shows how the artisans both continued in the traditions of Amarāvatī and were keenly aware of objects imported from the classical world, as were their predecessors. Finds at Begram,[306] and Brahmapuri,[307] as well as evidence from Nāgārjunakoṇḍa, all attest to the easy availability of Western luxury goods.[308] These objects were actually represented on Buddhist narrative art from Amarāvatī and Nāgārjunakoṇḍa. With the importation of these objects came the development of new techniques, especially in the art of terracotta manufacture.[309] What I wish to demonstrate through this work of art is that objects imported from the West had a direct influence upon compositions in Buddhist narrative reliefs from Amarāvatī and Nāgārjunakoṇḍa, and that this influence was at its height from the latest phases of the art of Amarāvatī and continued through the early part of the fourth century A.D.

The pillar in question (figs. 230-31) was first reported in *Indian Archaeology, A Review 1955-56*,[310] as having come from Site XIII at Nāgārjunakoṇḍa (now called Site 24 by H. Sarkar).[311] It was found in a votive *Stūpa* opposite a *caitya gṛha*. The pillar records a complete genealogy of the Ikṣvāku kings, and was dedicated in the eleventh regnal year of the fourth and last known king, Rudrapuruṣadatta, i.e., c. 301-11. According to the inscription, it was raised as a memorial pillar to a deceased Queen Varmabhattā, step-mother of King Rudrapuruṣadatta. Varmabhattā is further stated to have been the daughter of a Mahākṣatrapa of the Bṛhatphalāyana *gotra*, thus showing a second instance of an Ikṣvāku marital alliance with *kṣatrapas* of Western India.

As the pillar was found in a Buddhist monastic complex, naturally a Buddhist interpretation was suggested first. The main figure (fig. 231) was called Prajāpati Gotamī, foster mother of the Buddha, holding the Buddha as a child in a scarf.[312] Subsequently, D.C. Sircar and K.G. Krishnan[313] reinterpreted the sculpture as representing none other than the deceased Queen Varmabhattā who was dressed as a foreigner as she indeed was. The deceased queen is represented at her toilet holding a mirror and accompanied by two other figures. Portrait sculpture on a memorial pillar is indeed the logical identification, and a precedent for it had already been well-established at Nāgārjunakoṇḍa.

In the earliest memorial pillar at Nāgārjunakoṇḍa, that bearing the well-known pillar inscription L (fig. 51), the deceased King Cāṁtamūla I is described as *hiraṇyakoṭidāna* or "giver of myriads of gold". As we have stated above, the memorial pillar represents just that aspect of the king's deeds. The dominant corpulent figure, with the umbrella over his head, would obviously be the king. His right hand is placed on a water pot, thus indicating a donation. In the center of the composition is the mound of gold which the king is giving away.

Although it seems relatively simple to represent a king in a heroic or generous act, we have no clear convention, at this time, for representing a deceased queen. We know that many of the queens at Nāgārjunakoṇḍa were active supporters of the Buddhist faith, and for their support they expected to gain merit or even *nirvāṇa*.[314] About Queen Varmabhattā we have no such concrete information; but the find spot of the pillar may indicate that the lady was at least sympathetic to Buddhism.

In the realm of Buddhist art, the closest comparison we have to the representation on the Rudrapuruṣadatta pillar is on the well-known palimpsest in the British

Museum (fig. 153) belonging to the late phase of the art of Amarāvatī. As the nearby Amarāvatī *stūpa* was still in worship throughout the sculptural activity at Nāgārjunakoṇḍa, this would be the most likely source for the composition of the memorial pillar. In a small panel (fig. 182) representing a scene from the Conversion of Nanda,[315] we see Nanda's lovely wife Sundarī, accompanied by an attendant holding a mirror in front of her. (Contrast this to Varmabhattā holding the mirror herself.) Sundarī is surrounded by numerous attendants, here reduced to one in the representation of Varmabhattā. However, in spite of some obvious visual similarities, the theme of the *Saundarānanda,* with the completely negative light in which it casts the vain wife Sundarī, would hardly be a suitable source for a memorial pillar, presumably intended to elevate the memory of the dead Queen Varmabhattā. For in the *Saundarānanda*, Sundarī is referred to as the "darkness which is called 'Wife." '

Rather than proposing that the scene from the *Saundarānanda* was the compositional source for the Rudrapuruṣadatta pillar, I wish to suggest that both works were independently arrived at from a common Classical prototype or prototypes, even though the two works may have been done over a hundred years apart. As I wish to stress again, there was active trade between India and the Classical West. Just when this trade ceased is not clear, but we do know that Roman *amphorae,*[316] as well as Roman coins, were found during the Ikṣvāku phase at Nāgārjunakoṇḍa.[317] Objects similar to those found at Begram in Afghanistan have been represented in the art of Amarāvatī,[318] while similar comparisons may be seen between Roman objects and Nāgārjunakoṇḍa reliefs. The existence of what appears to be an arena, or perhaps a Classical *bouleterion* (a rectangular stepped assembly hall) at Nāgārjunakoṇḍa (discussed in Chapter I), seems to indicate an Ikṣvāku receptiveness to certain Western notions. In terms of sculptural relief, unlike in the art of Gandhāra, this receptiveness was received upon a foundation of Buddhist narrative art which was already over four centuries old. Thus, when we see a *mithuna* couple in Roman style dress on a late Amarāvatī drum frieze (fig. 69), we are seeing the imposition of a Roman style figure (figs. 77-78) on an already pre-existing Indian concept. In another vein, we wonder if the well-known Scythian type guardian figure, represented on a pillar from Nāgārjunakoṇḍa (fig. 232), is a borrowing from Kushān art, or from reality, or from both. For the contemporary Tamil text, the *Śilappadikāram*, in speaking of the region of Madurai, refers to the "best Yavana swordsmen" who acted as guards.[319]

To return to the question of the Rudrapuruṣadatta pillar, we will be able to see that this Classical influence lasted the end of the Ikṣvāku tradition. Objects found at Brahmapuri give an excellent notion of the type of objects imported from the Classical world into India. For example, a small mirror case representing Perseus and Andromeda,[320] probably produced in the workshops of Alexandria, has been found at Brahmapuri. In a discussion of this piece, Karl Khandalavala cites comparative examples in the British Museum, stating that such mirrors were in demand in India and local copies were made of them.[321] This is quite indisputable, as they have been clearly represented on sculptures from both Amarāvatī and Nāgārjunakoṇḍa.[322] One of the comparative Classical mirrors which Khandalavala cites is the small mirror case representing the Toilet of Venus, now in the British Museum.[323] To the left proper of the central figure of Venus is the small figure of Cupid, and opposite her is a servant-like figure on a pedestal. The mirror cited by Khandalavala is indeed pertinent to this argument, as a composition such as this one must have served as the prototype for the Rudrapuruṣadatta pillar. Both show the central figure of a lady at her toilet. The small figure of Cupid becomes, in the Nāgārjunakoṇḍa example, a female, as would be suited to the private quarters of Queen Varmabhattā. The Rudrapuruṣadatta pillar is, in fact, closer to the Classical inspiration than it is to the Amarāvatī Conversion of Nanda, indicating that Classical objects of this nature must have been in constant use during the Ikṣvāku period at Nāgārjunakoṇḍa. The notion that the Rudrapuruṣadatta pillar is based on a Venus is quite plausible, as the small *putto* placed beneath the seated female figure is a standard representation of Venus known throughout the Classical world, as can be seen in this second century Roman sarcophagus composition of Venus and Adonis (fig. 233), as well as in numerous other examples.[324] Such sarcophagus compositions were not seen directly by Indian artists. They seem to have been copied onto the more portable luxury goods, and in that form transmitted to India. The mode of transmission into the art of Amarāvatī and Nāgārjunakoṇḍa, in my opinion, was not indirect, as for example via the art of Gandhāra. More likely, the objects entered through the well-known ports of Western India and/or of Maisolia in Andhra Pradesh, and reached Amarāvatī and Nāgārjunakoṇḍa in the same way they reached Brahmapuri and Ter.[325] Most likely, there was a good store of Classical objects at Nāgārjunakoṇḍa which is now lost to us.

Before continuing with the problem of Classical influence in general, I think we should try to answer the next obvious question, that is, "Why was Queen Varmabhattā represented as a figure of Venus?" I feel quite certain in stating that the source of the Venus composition at Nāgārjunakoṇḍa does not alter, in any way, Sircar and Krishnan's interpretation that this was simply the portrait of the dead queen. Only the composition influenced the artist, not the iconography. It is indeed possible that the queen herself owned such a mirror, and that the composition appealed to the artist. On the other hand, we cannot forget that the pillar itself was found within a Buddhist monastic complex, and that many of the royal women of Nāgārjunakoṇḍa were known to be supporters of Buddhism. Thus might we consider that the sculpture represented the figure of the Queen at her toilet looking into a mirror, at the same time taken from a Classical composition, was also imbued with a Buddhist meaning? As I have already eliminated the *Saundarānanda* as a source for the subject-matter,

I admit now to entering the realm of pure speculation. However, a series of articles by Alex Wayman on mirrors and their associated symbolism has been quite suggestive.[326] In them, Wayman states that "Buddhism takes prestigious and imposing symbols of secular life and transforms them into religious symbols."[327] In his interpretation of a passage from the *Saddharmapuṇḍarīka*, Wayman refers to the necessity of obliterating one's image in the mirror, because the image in the mirror is the projection of the phenomenal world.[328] In later texts, Wayman has found that the obliteration of the image is a symbolic death, or even an actual omen of death (i.e., the disappearance of the phenomenal world).[329] This latter interpretation would be most suitable to a memorial pillar, but must be considered independently from the compositional source.

Although a chronology for the art of late Amarāvatī is only known in a general way, it seems clear that Classical compositional sources found their way into the illustration of Buddhist *stūpas* in Andhra Pradesh, and in this case, a memorial pillar. The preponderance of these that I have thus far observed occurs from the beginning of the third century A.D. through the early part of the fourth century A.D. As I have already cited above, conspicuous examples from Amarāvatī are on the late phase drum friezes showing the typical *mithuna* couples of the Andhra *stūpas* here in Classical dress and pose, on the British Museum palimpsest showing Sundarī, wife of Nanda, at her toilet, taken from the Classical composition of Venus. Another noteworthy example is found at both Amarāvatī and Nāgārjunakoṇḍa and involves the well-known Śibi Jātaka. As we can see in the Nāgārjunakoṇḍa example (fig. 216), the posture of King Śibi is quite close to the figure of Adonis about to be wounded in the thigh (fig. 234). This motif is the central motif of numerous Roman sarcophagi showing Venus and Adonis. Again we have an example of an ancient Indian tale borrowing a brief motif from a Roman sarcophagus in order to best represent the theme, and again, the borrowing is purely compositional, and in no way symbolically or iconographically significant. Note that the borrowing is from the Venus and Adonis story, a myth which seems to provide a number of compositional borrowings.

Although Classical influences in the art of Nāgārjunakoṇḍa is a subject which is in itself of great interest, the implications of this influence go beyond the site itself. In Andhra Pradesh, motifs from the Classical world appear on traditional Indian narrative art inherited from the indigenous traditions of Bharhut, Sāñcī, and Amarāvatī itself. The Rudrapuruṣadatta pillar, because of its dated inscription, shows that such passages continue into the fourth century A.D. The whole notion of the mixture of Andhra style, combined with Classical motifs, has been seen elsewhere, that is, in the ivories from Begram in Afghanistan. Here again, on Coffret IX from Begram (fig. 235), we observe a Venus type seated at her toilet, in traditional Indian style surrounded by clearly Classical motifs. The late date of the Rudrapuruṣadatta pillar helps us to confirm that these hybrid compositions persisted in India at least through the early part of the fourth century A.D. and perhaps even later. Many of the passages of Classical influence which we might guess to be of the second century A.D. survive easily into the fourth century. Thus, the dated Rudrapuruṣadatta pillar of the dead Queen Varmabhattā-*cum*-Venus is another support for the late date of Coffret IX at Begram, a theme to be discussed in Chapter IV.[330]

ADDENDUM TO CHAPTER II: THE POST-IKṢVĀKU STYLE

While it has been our intention to concentrate this study on the Buddhist art of the Ikṣvāku period, we wish to cite an example of post-Ikṣvāku workmanship. For it is this work which helps to narrow the gap between the Buddhist narrative tradition of Nāgārjunakoṇḍa and the traditions of Ajantā.

Two beautifully carved *maṇḍapa* pillars from Site 29 (fig. 236) display a quality of carving which far surpasses that of the Ikṣvāku period, while the sculpture on these pillars is totally subordinated to their decorative quality. They measure about seven feet tall and ten inches wide. They were found in association with the Vaiṣṇavite Aṣṭabhujsvāmin temple.[331] As we have already discussed in Chapter I, an inscription associated with this temple shows that it was dedicated in the thirtieth year of the Abhira king Vasuṣeṇa. Two hypotheses regarding the date of the inscription have been cited. The first is that of D.C. Sircar who dated it to c. 278, while the latter, that of Ranjana Mukherjee, placed it between 332 and 348 A.D. The historical plausibility for the date of Vasuṣeṇa favors the latter date, as does the style of the carving and its distinctness from the Ikṣvāku school.

The pillars have a square base. Moving upwards, it turns into an octagon, and then into a round shaft. The point of transition between the bottom square and the octagon is marked by a human figure. This complex pillar shape is totally absent amongst Ikṣvāku pillar remains, for the standard Ikṣvāku pillar shape is either a plain square pillar (fig. 23) or combines a square pillar with an octagonal shaft, with the point of transition marked by a half lotus (fig. 240). The only exception to this type is a pillar found in the Bhauśrutīya monastery, Site 5 (fig. 27), which appears to have been a later addition. In fact, when we look at the Aṣṭabhujsvāmin pillars both in shape and decoration, we are reminded not of the early Buddhist tradition of India, but of a subsequent era, that of the Vākāṭakas who produced the richly decorated columns of Ajantā. Although there is no specific column at Ajantā which takes on this form, many of the elements of the columns are common to the Ajantā *oeuvre* spanning almost its entire history. While the shape has its counterpart in Ajantā Cave 4,[332] the elements of decoration are seen throughout. For example, the use of horizontal bands of decoration on the columns (figs. 237-38) can be seen at Ajantā in both painted and sculpted forms.[333] The use of square and round decorative motifs contained within a pearl border (figs. 237-38) is elaborated upon at Ajantā[334] as is the use of the human figure (fig. 237) placed at the point of transition between the square and octagonal portion of the pillar.[335] For those seeking the source of these complex pillar forms at Ajantā, indeed a study of the Nāgārjunakoṇḍa post-Ikṣvāku pillars must be included. Other elements of these pillars, indeed, point to a late date in relation to Ikṣvāku works. Even a small detail such as the deeply undercut flower held by the woman at the base of the column (fig. 239) has no counterpart in the flat, decorative Ikṣvāku style, but seems to be approaching the rich floral decoration of the ceiling paintings of Ajantā Cave II,[336] while the scroll inhabited by small dwarf figures on the octagonal portion of the shaft (fig. 237) forms a transition between the early Buddhist scroll forms and those of the Gupta-Vākāṭaka era.[337] Thus, while we have seen throughout this chapter works containing pre-Ajantā elements, the Aṣṭabhujsvāmin pillar contributes to narrowing the gap toward the later site.

CHAPTER III

RELATED SITES IN ANDHRA PRADESH: GUMMIDIDURRU AND GOLI

While the sites of Amarāvatī and Nāgārjunakoṇḍa have met with numerous misfortunes, they were considerably more fortunate than many of the smaller sites, whose works disappeared or were destroyed before the sites could be fully published or characterized. Many of the pieces from the smaller sites eventually reached Europe and America, where they entered into museums and private collections whose curators and owners were at a loss for proper identification. Since they were usually compared with only readily accessible information on famous sites, many of them became labelled "Amarāvatī", "Amarāvatī School", or more ambitiously, "Nāgārjunakoṇḍa", or "Late Andhra". Scholars sometimes even took a stab at giving it the name of a smaller site. Indeed, it is in no way fallacious to apply these terms to some of the smaller sites, as Amarāvatī during the second century A.D., and Nāgārjunakoṇḍa during the third century, were the major centers of Andhra art, and their patrons, as is well-known, contributed works to the smaller sites.[338] Thus it would indeed be a mistake to attempt to define all the small sites in the region as belonging to separate schools. For sculptors from the main centers indeed worked at other places, and an identification of many of these fragments would in no way contribute to our knowledge. Yet, two sites in particular, those of Gummididurru and Goli, merit individual discussion, for not only do they have individual styles of their own, but their styles can be seen to interact with that of Nāgārjunakoṇḍa.[339]

GUMMIDIDURRU

The site of Gummididurru lies in a small village of that name in the Krishna District of Andhra Pradesh (see fig. 1). It is situated only about six miles to the east of the Great *Stūpa* at Jaggayyapeta and therefore the monks of that area must have had contact with that region as well as with Nāgārjunakoṇḍa. To the modern scholar the site appears rather obscure, but in ancient times it must have been quite important, for there is evidence that Buddhist monks inhabited the region from the second century A.D. through medieval times.[340]

Gummididurru was first excavated in 1926 by Hamid Kuraishi, that is in the same year in which he first excavated Nāgārjunakoṇḍa.[341] The finds were described in the *Annual Report of the Archaeological Survey of India* for that year and has received almost no mention since, except for a description in Debala Mitra's survey volume *Buddhist Monuments*[342] and a brief mention in Stella Kramrisch's *Indian Sculpture*.[343] The remains consisted of a large main *Stūpa* about 55 feet in diameter and several subsidiary *Stūpas*. The main *Stūpa* appears to have been decorated in a manner similar to the *Stūpas* of Amarāvatī and Nāgārjunakoṇḍa. The sculptures from the site have been moved to the Amarāvatī Museum for safety while other examples appear in American collections. An important group of these is currently in the Los Angeles County Museum of Art, along with an example from Goli village. It is this small group in the Western collections that we shall dwell upon, for they help to show us an important stylistic trend in the early style of the art of Nāgārjunakoṇḍa.

In 1976, Pratapaditya Pal published five fragmentary pieces of sculpture from Andhra Pradesh, in the Los Angeles County Museum. In writing about them, Pal clearly recognizes that four of them (figs. 241, 242, 244 and 245) are from the same *Stūpa,* while a fifth is from elsewhere. Pal labels them Amarāvatī style, but goes on to state that "there is no way to determine the exact provenance of the reliefs, but very likely they are from the area around Goli village."[344] As we shall see, from the point of view of style Goli is the least plausible of the choices, for the major trend of the Goli *Stūpa* stands quite apart from the rest of the Andhra tradition. A more plausible guess for their attribution would have been Nāgārjunakoṇḍa, for we will demonstrate that these works have close ties with the Nāgārjunakoṇḍa school from the time of Cāṁtamūla I and Vīrapuruṣadatta. While an examination of the style might leave us hovering between Nāgārjunakoṇḍa and Gummididurru, and examination of the literature gives us the precise answer.

Dr. Pal has identified figure 241 as representing the rare scene of the Miracle Below the Jambu Tree. The episode took place when Siddhārtha as a young man sat beneath the tree in meditation. While the shadows of other trees could be seen moving, that of the Jambu tree remained still. When the miracle occurred, a messenger was sent to King Śuddhodhana, who came to worship his meditating son. Above this scene is Siddhārtha's Great Departure.[345] The episode at the Jambu tree is indeed rare, but such a scene has already been identified by Hamid Kuraishi in his excavation report of Gummididurru.[346] If one looks at the general view of Gummididurru reproduced by Kuraishi, one can in fact recognize the piece now in the Los Angeles Museum. It appears although miniscule in size slightly to the left of the center of the reproduction.[347] Although we have no datable inscriptions from Gummididurru, this fragment probably dates to the early Ikṣvāku period. Through comparison with works from Nāgārjunakoṇḍa, we can see that the fleshiness of the seated figures from Gummididurru is similar to examples from the *Mahācetiya* and Site 6 (figs. 33-37).

Another fragment from the Los Angeles group (fig. 242) compares well to a Gummididurru work currently in the Amarāvatī Museum (fig. 243). For on the railing of both fragmentary *Stūpa* slabs there are similar representations of the Taming of the Mad Elephant,[348] while the figure standing to the left of the *Stūpa* entranceway in the Amarāvatī Museum example has its counterpart to the right of the entranceway in the Los Angeles example.

As we look at the two Los Angeles fragments discussed above, we begin to note the distinguishing feature of the school of Gummididurru. The corners of the mouths of the figures are almost invariably turned upwards. This can be read as a gentle smile as in figure 244 or as the rather perky expression in figure 245. In fact, figure 245 is extremely important to our study of Nāgārjunakoṇḍa. Its attribution to Gummididurru is beyond doubt as it belongs to a group of reliefs found between the *Stūpa* slabs on the drum of the *Stūpa* at Gummididurru. These have been described by Kuraishi as "generally decorated with the figure of a pillar or a tree with a wheel or trident above and deer, svastika, or the feet of the Buddha below, accompanied by the usual devotees and donors."[349] Kuraishi does not state how many of these he found, but his description implies that there were several. Kuraishi only published one example of the group in a cropped photograph whose center was upon another piece.[350] The Los Angeles example is either a fragment of that piece or one identical to it. A more complete version of the same type has already been seen in figure 123. Its similarity to the Los Angeles piece is beyond dispute, and its attribution to Gummididurru has already been noted by Debala Mitra.[351]

We have cited the Cincinnati Gummididurru (fig. 123) sculpture in the context of its similarity to an example from Site 6 (fig. 122). But equally important are its stylistic features, particularly the rather perky faces with small chins. These show a similarity in facial type to the Mahācetiya *āyaka* panels (figs. 33 and 34). Even closer are the facial types of the Site 6 Musée Guimet panel of the Man in the Well (fig. 113) and the Metropolitan Museum Great Departure (fig. 114). In fact, so many of the elements of the style are similar that, had there not been abundant evidence that these pieces were from Nāgārjunakoṇḍa, we might have, on the basis of the facial types, assigned them to Gummididurru. For those faces which are still intact (see detail of the Metropolitan Great Departure, fig. 246) show this quality. The fleshiness of the figures, as well as the relatively high relief in comparison to later Nāgārjunakoṇḍa sculptures are also features shared by the Site 6 figures and Gummididurru. In fact, a fragment in the Asian Art Museum of San Francisco (fig. 247) clearly from Gummididurru both from its style and its similarity to the Los Angeles fragment seen in figure 244, shares a decorative border which is identical to that on the Guimet Man in the Well and the Metropolitan Great Departure. This particular border is not seen elsewhere on the sculptures of Nāgārjunakoṇḍa.

Unfortunately, we have seen no dome slabs from Gummididurru which could be compared with the Guimet and Metropolitan works. Nor in fact do we have relevant comparative dome slabs from Nāgārjunakoṇḍa. What seems most likely to have occurred is that sometime during the construction of Site 6, there was active contact between the two sites. More than likely, the Nāgārjunakoṇḍa artists seem to have copied the Gummididurru type. For as we have seen in Chapter I, the facial type seems to have been transmitted to *āyaka* panel 1 of *Stūpa* 9, where it becomes broadened and slightly flattened (fig. 248).

Goli

While the site of Gummididurru relates to early Nāgārjunakoṇḍa, the site of Goli[352] relates to its later tradition. Although Goli has a definite style of its own, it is frequently mistaken for Nāgārjunakoṇḍa. In fact, while it does relate to the Nāgārjunakoṇḍa style, it has a style unique to itself. We shall concentrate our discussion of Goli on an *āyaka* panel currently in the Metropolitan Museum of Art (fig. 185), for not only is it the finest work from Goli village, but it serves to clearly define the Goli style.

The small mound near Goli village was excavated in 1926 by Dr. G. Jouveau-Dubreuil, and the results of his work were published in 1929 by T.N. Ramachandran in the *Bulletin of the Madras Government Museum*.[353] The site was first referred to by James Sewell in his *List of Antiquarian Remains in Madras Presidency*, 1882, under the heading of Mallavaram (Mullawarum).[354] Present-day Mallavaram is only three miles west of the original mound and a half a mile northwest of Goli village. Goli is on a stream which joins the Krishna River about eighteen miles below to the site of Nāgārjunakoṇḍa.

After a brief description of the visible remains, which consisted of a small decorated *Stūpa*, Sewell suggested "that the place should be carefully watched and examined as soon as possible. The discovery may be one of great importance."[355] Sewell's intuition was absolutely correct. By the time that Ramachandran published a description of those pieces excavated by Jouveau-Dubreuil, several pieces had been sent to the Madras Government Museum, while other pieces had come into the hands of local villagers. The Goli *nāga*,[356] which had been described by Sewell, came into worship and could not be removed from the site. Among others described by Ramachandran, there is one which he mentions as:

> "a long frieze about the length of frieze No. 2 (figs. 251-55) of those now in the Museum, containing about seven panels, most of them illustrating scenes from the Buddha's life. We can locate this frieze as from the South of the stūpa as the other friezes which have reached us were found by Dr. G. Jouveau-Dubreuil in the other three directions. The villagers, who did not know what the scenes on the sculpture

meant, did not know what to do with it. So the stone was left uncared for until the construction of the room around the naga when they fixed it on one of the walls. The frieze, like two of those that have reached us [at the Madras Government Museum] is not complete."[357]

Ramachandran published his small excavation report in 1929, and from then on Goli ceased to play an important role in the literature of Andhra Pradesh. Goli is usually characterized by one piece preserved in the Madras Government Museum, frieze No. 2,[358] referred to above by Ramachandran and discussed subsequently. In 1930, the Metropolitan Museum of Art in New York acquired a piece of sculpture which was identified by Maurice Dimand, then Curator of the Oriental Collection, as coming from Nāgārjunakoṇḍa[359] (fig. 185, det. figs. 249, 250). The piece in question has seven scenes, and according to Dimand's calculations measures 7 feet $5^1/_2$ inches by $10^3/_4$ inches. Frieze No. 2 from Goli, according to Ramachandran's measurements, is 7 feet 6 inches by $11^1/_2$ inches.[360] If we take into account that both pieces are in a poor state of preservation, and that each scholar was probably measuring from a slightly different point, the measurements correspond sufficiently well for the Metropolitan piece to be the "missing piece from the South side of Goli *Stūpa*." Stylistically, not only is there a complete correspondence between the Metropolitan Conversion of Nanda and Goli frieze No. 2, representing the Vessantara Jātaka, but there is a definite disparity between the style of these two blocks and the friezes of Nāgārjunakoṇḍa. While we have attributed the Metropolitan Conversion panel to Goli on the basis of style and circumstance, Mrs. Debala Mitra came to the same conclusion independently. For she discovered an *in situ* photograph of the panel, proving beyond doubt that the work currently in the Metropolitan Museum is the missing piece from the south side of the Goli *Stūpa*.[361] We are most fortunate in having a beautifully preserved panel from Nāgārjunakoṇḍa representing the same scene for clear contrast (figs. 176-80).

The stylistic attribution of the Metropolitan's piece to Goli is confirmed if we recall that the Andhra narrative reliefs, while fulfilling a religious function, were unified as an ensemble by unified decorative borders. The most common border decorations on the Goli reliefs are a small row of circlets at the top of the *āyaka* panel and a rectangular module at the bottom of the relief, as can be seen in Goli frieze No. 2. These features are absent at Nāgārjunakoṇḍa where the immediate upper border of the *āyaka* panel is generally left plain, relieved only by small *kuḍus* which form the top of pillars separating the individual scenes of the narrative. The "module" at Nāgārjunakoṇḍa is generally replaced by an animal figure with the face of a lion or a bird. It was by this means that Mireille Bénisti attributed a very important piece in the Musée Guimet to Goli[362] a piece which undoubtedly is connected to both frieze No. 2 at Goli and to the Metropolitan Conversion of Nanda.

But there are other features, too, which are characteristic of Goli. The figures in the Goli reliefs have a box-like rigidity and lack the graceful languor of those on the Nāgārjunakoṇḍa pieces. The torsos are disproportionately large in comparison to the heads. The hands and arms have a tubular quality and, when represented crossing over the body, they seem to form a slight depression as if pressed against a balloon. The necks are very short, and in fact the heads look as if sprouting directly from the shoulders. There is a stylized naiveté to the faces, with very little variation in carving. These characteristics are all direct contradictions to the style of the Nāgārjunakoṇḍa cornice, wherein the languorous couples may be seen moving about in a graceful variety of poses and with rather more individualized physiognomies.

The most important distinction, however, is in the method of separating the individual scenes of the story. At Nāgārjunakoṇḍa, individual scenes are invariably separated by playful *mithuna* couples framed by a pair of pilasters. These couples, although they appear on narrative panels, have nothing whatsoever to do with the story. They seem rather to have been so integrated into the Nāgārjunakoṇḍa identity, that they never fail to appear. Whereas the Nāgārjunakoṇḍa artist used rigid architectural devices rather like those used in Gandhāra to separate their scenes,[363] the sculptors of Goli employed devices more consistent with the ancient and with the later pictorial representations at Ajantā.[364] For example, in the last scene of the Metropolitan version (fig. 249, see also fig. 255) the figures are completely framed by an architectural pavilion, a device in common use at Ajantā. Most of the scenes are divided by columns, which have been puffed up like balloons and have lost the vertical rigidity of those in the Nāgārjunakoṇḍa reliefs. This is again more consistent with the decoration of Ajantā, where the verticality of the architectural members is broken by the use of cushion capitals and the use of decorative horizontal bands.[365] Interestingly, the plump columns with crossing over linear decorations have their counterpart also in a relief from Swat Valley.[366] All these features are indeed shared with Goli frieze No. 2, where there is even a greater use of architectural devices to separate scenes.

The Goli version has another feature which is characteristic of Ajantā. The artists of Ajantā were fond of creating architectural settings and filling spaces by the abundant use of cubistically represented rocks.[367] This feature is so abundant in both the Metropolitan frieze and in frieze No. 2 from Goli, that we must think there was an individual artist who took special delight in the creation of these rocks. If we look at the Nāgārjunakoṇḍa version of the *Saundarānanda* (fig. 179), the flowers, garlands, and splendors of heaven are greatly emphasized. The monkey sits on a small pile of rocks, which takes on no more importance than a chair. The Goli version, on the other hand (fig. 250), represents the rocks emphatically as a major aspect of the pictorial setting, and in this case they seem to represent all of Mount

Himavat. The monkey sits off to one side, and next to him is probably the remains of the "deodar" which they found "bore no fruit". The Ajantā version of this scene is illustrated clearly in a line drawing published by Begley.[368] It is very much closer to the Goli prototype wherein the rocks on which the monkey sits represent the great Mount Himavat. The Buddha and Nanda, in these two versions, are rising up almost vertically in contrast to their soaring diagonal movement in the Nāgārjunakoṇḍa scene.

Another work which definitely belongs to the Goli group is an unfinished relief in the Cleveland Museum clearly representing the Javasakuṇa Jātaka (fig. 256).[369] There is little doubt that the rocky wilderness setting, which completely surrounds the scene, is the creation of the Goli rock artist.

Another fragment,[370] formerly in the collection of Mr. George P. Bickford, fulfills all the stylistic characteristics for a definite ascription to Goli. Indeed, it is stylistically identical to the Goli fragment in the Musée Guimet, and one wonders whether the two might not be from the same panel.

One more fragment, previously assigned to Nāgārjunakoṇḍa and now in the Los Angeles County Museum, must be assigned to Goli (fig. 98),[371] for not only does it show the Goli figural type, but it shows an unusual way of draping the Buddha's robe, a way which in Andhra Pradesh is unique to Goli village. The panel is a fragment of a *caitya* slab with the central portion occupied by the Buddha Protected by Nāga Mucilinda's Hood. Flanking him on one side is a worshipping Nāga, and presumably another was originally on the other side. The format of the tripartite *Stūpa* drum is the same as we have seen on another example from Goli which is a simple and perhaps earlier variant of the type (See note 222). The seated Buddha in the center wears his robe over the left shoulder except that the drapery is arranged so as to produce an extra flap which appears almost like an epaulet. While this flap is absent at Nāgārjunakoṇḍa, it is characteristic of Goli (cf. fig. 255). A similar motif is found elsewhere in the art of India, for it appears in several variants in Swat Valley.[372] It is well-known that certain works from Swat show characteristics of Andhra Pradesh, and an interesting subject for future consideration might be the particular relationship between Swat and Goli.

Other examples from Goli are in fact closer to Nāgārjunakoṇḍa examples. The Goli version of the Sasa Jātaka (fig. 107) reminds us of the Nāgārjunakoṇḍa version of the same subject (fig. 106). Two *āyaka* friezes, numbered 1 (figs. 257-63) and 3 (figs. 264-65) by Ramachandran, share features with Nāgārjunakoṇḍa and differ somewhat from Goli frieze No. 2 and the Metropolitan Conversion of Nanda. Both of these friezes make use of *mithuna* couples as separating devices. Frieze 3 also uses the device of the railing motif to separate scenes, as well as the animal heads on the lower borders. Both of these devices were used on *Stūpas* 6 and 9 at Nāgārjunakoṇḍa. However, this group is separated from Nāgārjunakoṇḍa by the exceptionally wide compartments in which the figural groupings are contained, a feature seen in only one example from Nāgārjunakoṇḍa (fig. 221). Further, the approach to figural grouping is different. In frieze 1 (fig. 260), figures are separated into two distinct ovoid compositional groups with only one figure tying the two compositions together, as if one were combining two separate Nāgārjunakoṇḍa panels. Frieze 3, on the other hand, harks back to the style of the Site 6-*Mahācetiya* group at Nāgārjunakoṇḍa, consisting of figures in a row lined up against a flat ground (cf. especially fig. 42). Although the artist of this work was cognizant of the Site 6-*Mahācetiya* group, the Goli works are neither contemporary with, nor mere copies of, the Nāgārjunakoṇḍa group. The Goli figures are considerably more elongated in their proportions, while their postures are much more varied, with each figure moving independently within its own space. In fact, while frieze 3 seems to be derived from a Nāgārjunakoṇḍa type, it looks forward to the Gupta era as seen in a lintel from Garhwā with its gracefully elongated figures all in a row, but each having its own space and its own movement. But more precisely, it prefigures the Garhwā pillars in compositional arrangement and figural type.[373]

Thus, the sculptures from the Goli *Stūpa* are clearly dependent upon the Nāgārjunakoṇḍa *oeuvre*, both in its earlier and later styles. Yet, these works seem to post-date the early style of Nāgārjunakoṇḍa by a considerable period of time and seem also to fall after the Ehuvala Cāṁtamūla period in which the Conversion of Nanda was completed. The lack of any dated inscriptions at Goli makes it impossible to assign a date to the sculptures with precision. The elongated figures of frieze 3 may be compared both to the memorial pillar dated to the eleventh regnal year of Rudrapuruṣadatta (fig. 231), as well as with the figures on the Aṣṭabhujsvāmin temple pillars of the post-Ikṣvāku period. The paucity of securely dated pieces from the Rudrapuruṣadatta period and the post-Ikṣvāku period makes it difficult to assign a precise date to the Goli works, but the Goli *Stūpa* was probably begun during the reign of Rudrapuruṣadatta and continued into the post-Ikṣvāku period. Thus we would assign the major works from the Goli *Stūpa* to the first half of the fourth century A.D., and consider them as further evidence of the transmission of the Andhra style into the Gupta-Vākāṭaka era.

CHAPTER IV

THE BEGRAM IVORIES

In studying the Buddhist sculpture of Nāgārjunakoṇḍa and its neighboring sites we have mapped out the general development of narrative reliefs in Andhra Pradesh from c. A.D. 225 to c. A.D. 350 However, an understanding of the late Andhra contribution to Indian art cannot be complete without a consideration of the Begram ivories, which very closely parallel the Andhra tradition and reflect an ivory production which must once have existed on the soil of Andhra Pradesh. Not only do the Begram ivories reflect an Andhra style, they fall into a context of similar art historical problems. The ivories were found along with a hoard of classical luxury goods. We believe that such a hoard must once have also existed at Nāgārjunakoṇḍa. Furthermore, in both areas these native sculptural productions were heavily influenced by Western artistic imports and in turn influenced the art of the Gupta-Vākāṭaka period. We shall not attempt to show that the Begram ivories were produced at Nāgārjunakoṇḍa, although in certain examples we do believe this to be a possibility. For the classical elements used in the Begram ivories retain more of their original classical flavor, rather than being inconspicuously integrated into the native style, as at Nāgārjunakoṇḍa. As I have already published an article on the Begram ivories several years ago, I shall not herein repeat my entire argument, which was to assert that the Begram ivories are part of the late Andhra tradition, and date to the third and fourth centuries A.D.[374] Instead, I shall cite only two of the major works from Begram so that the reader may understand my older study in a new context, and view the problem of the Begram ivories and the late Andhra tradition as companion problems, forming a bridge to the Gupta-Vākāṭaka era. I do not believe that I would have been able to begin to understand the problems of either Begram or Andhra had I not worked on both simultaneously.

The Begram ivories were discovered in 1936. In that year, Joseph and Ria Hackin opened a sealed chamber near the modern city of Begram (Afghanistan), or ancient Kapiśa, the place where, according to Hsüan-tsang, the Kushan King Kanishka was said to house hostages from China during the summer.[375] In this chamber, and in subsequent finds, there were found numerous treasures. Amongst them were objects which have been identified as Hellenistic bronzes, Greco-Roman plaster casts, Alexandrian glass, lacquer work from China, and an exquisite hoard of ivories which clearly point to an Indian origin. In an effort to bring them into public view quickly, J. Hackin published their finds in the *Memoires de la délégation archéologique française en Afghanistan* (hereafter referred to as *M.D.A.F.A.*), Volume IX, supplying a catalogue, photographs of the major finds, and a brief discussion of the works of major importance. In discussing the ivories, he compared some of them to the carvings on the gate of *Stūpa* 1 at Sāñcī, while one extremely important one, which he referred to as Coffret IX (fig. 235), he placed at the end of the third of the beginning of the fourth century A.D.[376]

The Hackins continued excavating at Begram until 1940, at which time they insisted upon returning to France to serve in the French army. They were both killed in February 1941. Fortunately, their notes had been left in safe hands and were subsequently published in *M.D.A.F.A.* XI, 1954, along with articles by Philippe Stern, Jeannine Auboyer, Otto Kurz, and others.[377]

Philippe Stern compared individual motifs on the ivories with motifs which appear throughout early Indian art. Judging from these comparisons he dated the ivories from the end of the first to the beginning of the second century A.D., concluding that they were consistent with works which appear in Mathurā. Yet, had Stern had the opportunity to write this book only ten years later, after he and Mireille Bénisti had completed their motif analysis of Amarāvatī (*Evolution du style indien d'Amarāvatī*), the question of the date and stylistic affiliation of these ivories would probably have been different. For, in fact, the method of motif analysis would have shown the late Andhra affiliations.

Kapiśa lies at the junction of the Panjshīr and Ghorbend Rivers near the village of Begram, twenty-five miles northeast of Kabul and just south of the Hindu Kush. In ancient times it was the most important city of Afghanistan. It has been identified as Nissa (or Nikea), a town mentioned in the chronicles of the conquests of Alexandar the Great, but this identification remains uncertain.[378] Based on the finds of numerous coins and structures, we know that it was the capital of Indo-Greek kings and of the first rulers of the Kushan Dynasty. On the foundation of this capital were raised new foundations with variants in structure known as the New Royal City, which was believed to be the capital of Kanishka and his successors.[379] It was in the New Royal City that the Begram ivories, along with other objects, were found in two contiguous chambers, believed to have been sealed against coming invaders. Based upon the mere historical situation, we can see that Kapiśa was an area which must have been extremely cosmopolitan in its tastes, an area whose art must have been in constant state of flux.

When the rooms were sealed is again a matter of conjecture. The major proposal has been put forth by R. Ghirshman who suggested that the rooms were sealed to protect the treasures against the invading armies of Shāpur I between 241 and 250 A.D.[380] Ghirshman based his assumption on the interpretation of an inscription discovered on the wall of Naksh-i-Rustam pertaining to the conquests of Shāpur I. If Ghirshman's theory is correct, the mid-third century would thus have to be the *terminus ante quem* for the ivories. Yet the tenuous nature of the archaeological evidence, and the fact that we see most of our comparative stylistic evidence in Andhra Pradesh from the period of Vīrapuruṣadatta onwards, compels us to abandon his hypothesis.

The finds at Begram also attest to a third level of occupation containing Hephthalite coins. This has led Hackin to conclude that the New Royal City was destroyed in the fifth century A.D. and was then occupied by Hephthalite invaders.[381] Ghirshman, maintaining the mid-third century date, suggests a temporary abandonment of the city before the coming of the Hephthalites.[382] The most explicit information that we have about Kapiśa is that it was still in existence at the time of the visit of Hsüan-tsang in the seventh century and that objects of merchandise could be found there "from all parts".[383]

The Begram ivory which is closest in style to works of Andhra Pradesh is the back of an exquisite ivory throne (figs. 267-69) of a type frequently represented in the art of Mathurā and Andhra Pradesh (fig. 266). The major decoration on the back of the throne is a group of thirteen ivory plaques arranged in two registers. The figures represented on the plaques are all women, as is suitable to objects belonging to private women's quarters, yet they are definitely based on typical *mithuna* couples found throughout early Indian art. These couples have at times been compared to couples appearing in the art of Mathurā, to those appearing at Kārlā or in Kondāñe (fig. 73), comparisons which become less significant when we compare them to the works of Andhra Pradesh. Any of the earliest sites show figures which are reserved and self-contained. Although the earlier figures display some degree of physical contact, nowhere in early Indian art do we find the degree of interplay, and of overlapping of playful poses, as in the Begram ivories and the sweet couples separating Buddhist narrative scenes on the *āyaka* panels of Nāgārjunakoṇḍa. These languorous couples, with elongated bodies, which first appear in the latest phases of the art of Amarāvatī are developed to their fullest extent in the third and fourth century art of Nāgārjunakoṇḍa. The closest comparison to the Begram couples belongs, in fact, to the period of Ehuvala Cāṁtamūla and possibly later. It is during this period that we see the widest variety of poses and most active interaction between the figures. If we compare these couples to those on the Buddhist narratives (i.e., figs. 128-32; 169-71; 181, 214-15), we notice a similar type of playful interaction between the figures. Such a comparison does not hold true for works of the Cāṁtamūla I or Vīrapuruṣadatta periods, but is again relevant in the post-Ikṣvāku period. A pillar from Nāgārjunakoṇḍa (fig. 270) which is probably contemporary with the Aṣṭabhujsvāmin pillars, shows a similar liveliness of form.

One particular plaque on the ivory throne (fig. 271) seems rather remote from the *mithuna* couples from Nāgārjunakoṇḍa. It probably represents a lady about to place a necklace about her neck with the aid of an attendant, but is closest to a representation of a Buddhist theme, that of Siddhārtha stringing the mighty bow to show his skill in archery (fig. 200). The compositional similarity of the two central figures, one holding a string and the other a necklace at the same height, clearly shows an exchange of artistic ideas between secular ivory workers and Buddhist stone workers. For just as we have sculptors of Andhra Pradesh adopt Roman compositional motifs into their own Buddhist art, there must have been a similar relationship with the ivory carvers of Begram. In this case, however, the relationship was most certainly reciprocal.

To further our comparison we would like to cite an extremely curious object excavated by T.M. Ramachandran at Nāgārjunakoṇḍa (fig. 272 obverse, fig. 273 reverse). The object in question comes from a *caitya* hall at Site 3 and has been identified by Ramachandran as a coping stone.[384] Amongst the numerous coping stones excavated in Andhra Pradesh, no other has shown this decorative pattern. If we consider it in relation to the Begram works, it becomes obvious that it is a translation into stone of the type of throne back under discussion. At the bottom is a decoration which represents the round spools of the ivory throne. This is followed, in successive registers, by a decorative animal frieze and by a row of plaques which in this case represent dwarflike figures, elephants, and figure groupings. The small vertical ivory spokes between the plaques on the ivory throne are translated into a decorative bead and reel motif surrounded by a twisted rope, a motif which is common on the ivories of Begram (fig. 274). How such a throne would have been used in the context of a Buddhist *caitya* hall is not known, but it is evident that the ivory examples were well-known to the artisans of Nāgārjunakoṇḍa and similar reliefs must have been known to the ivory carvers.

If one needs to be reminded at this point, that there could have been contact between Andhra Pradesh and Afghanistan, one need only to cite a Prākrit donative inscription from Nāgārjunakoṇḍa mentioning the gift of a *caitya gṛha* containing a *stūpa*, dated in the fourteenth regnal year of King Vīrapuruṣadatta, for the benefit of the Theravādin monks from Ceylon, who converted the peoples of "Kashmir, Gandhāra, China, Chilāta (=Skt. Kirāta), Tosali, Avaraṁta (=Skt. Aparānta), Vaṅga, Vanavāsi, Yavana(?), Damila(?), Palura(?), and the isle of Tambapaṁni (Sri Lanka)."[385] As we know that there was contact between Afghanistan and Gandhāra, and from our inscription, Gandhāra and the South, we need not be hampered in thinking that there was a transmission of works and/or artisans between Andhra Pradesh and Kapiśa.

Although it is well-known that there was classical influence in the art of the Northwest, and classical influence in the Begram ivories, we have demonstrated that there was also Western influence in the art of the Sātavāhanas and Ikṣvākus. We believe that the Begram ivory carvers and the artists of Begram both had accessible to them similar types of Western material, and each used it in his own way. To underscore this fact, we illustrate a Roman steelyard weight found at Begram (fig. 275), an object easily accessible to the ivory carvers. A very similar object, here either a steelyard weight or incense burner, is seen in the left hand of a female figure represented on a no longer extant relief from Amarāvatī.[386]

While attempting to draw parallels between Andhra Pradesh and Begram, showing that they were both influenced somehow by the West, we would like to turn our attention to the much debated Coffret IX, which everyone agrees is a "late" work and is the most exquisite of the Begram ivories (figs. 235 and 276 for both the coffret and its reconstruction). The coffret consists of two plaques set contiguously. They are united by a common border consisting of a meander, a so-called acanthus *rinceau* inhabited by floral motifs of animals with composite animals or *grilli* in each corner, and a bead and reel motif. The technique employed in the rendering of the main figures of the coffret, as well as the small plaques on the sides, is "sunk relief", a technique peculiar to Egyptian art. However, the border decorations are incised while a *rinceau* of elephants on the lower part of the coffret is carved in low relief with a pierced background. The units were originally held together by wooden supports which have since decomposed.

The style of the central portion of the coffret, and the details of the jewelry, costumes and coiffure suggest that this is the work of an Indian craftsman.[387] Such figures (see especially second figure from the left) would derive ultimately from types found in the middle phases of the art of Amarāvatī and would have their successors in the early fifth century door jambs from Garhwā (see note 373), the wall paintings of Ajantā (note particularly the eyelash of the farther eye on the background as a precursor to the slightly extended farther eye),[388] a ceiling painting in the niche of the 53 meter Buddha at Bāmiyān,[389] and a fresco in Sīgiriya in Sri Lanka[390] showing the same sort of elongated body, attention paid to the modelling of the abdomen, and elongated hands. Perhaps the most interesting comparison is another wall painting from Sīgiriya where the female figures seem almost to be derived from our Begram example.[391] Yet at the same time we have seen that the figural grouping on the right hand of the composition is similar to that of the memorial pillar from Nāgārjunakoṇḍa dated to early fourth century A.D. (fig. 231). Both works must thus have been derived from similar classical prototypes.

Concerning the specific coiffures represented in the ivories, we have not found any such coiffures in the art of Sāñcī or Mathurā. The chignon, appearing somewhat like a pony-tail, and the use of an ornament in front is well-known in the art of Nāgārjunkoṇḍa (fig. 277) and variants also appear in the art of Amarāvatī. The hip girdle, bracelets, and ankle bangles are consistent both with Nāgārjunakoṇḍa and its antecedents in Indian art.

Western influence, or rather western motifs in this ivory have been discussed at great length with the dominant emphasis being on the so-called acanthus *rinceau* around the border of the plaque. The *rinceau* has been compared to Roman examples of the first century A.D., a Sinhalese example, and examples from Amarāvatī.[392] As each of these comparisons were clearly weak, scholars have sought elaborate theories of an Indian decomposition of an original motif in order to justify their comparisons. The scroll is, in fact, a Roman type, and not an Indian variant of such. An almost identical vine scroll can be seen on the lid of a sarcophagus from Tripoli (fig. 278). The sarcophagus was either imported from the Eastern Mediterranean or was of local manufacture, and is dated to the thrid century A.D.[393] The Begram artist was clearly looking at a late Roman version of this scroll. Yet, comparisons with Amarāvatī should not be totally dismissed. For the Amarāvatī vine scroll seen in figure 279 shows a similar approach, and yet there is a fundamental difference. The Begram example appears Western; the Amarāvatī example does not. If the Amarāvatī artist had, in fact, been looking at a Roman vine scroll, he totally transformed it based on his local knowledge and skill. For when the Andhra artist borrowed from the West, he frequently concealed the borrowing in a traditional Indian motif. There is, however, one Begram vine scroll which stands between the two traditions. For the scroll on the ivory throne back shows not only birds inhabiting the scroll, but also the humped bull (figs. 268-69). As we have said above, this particular throne back is stylistically closest to the Andhra tradition.

Another instance in which we can contrast the approach of an Andhra and Begram artist is the approach to composite animals. On the corners of the main plaque of Coffret IX are *grilli* (fig. 235, upper right corner) or composite animals which have been identified as having an ultimate Iranian prototype and were used in the West until the third century A.D.[394] The *grilli* or amulets have their counterparts in India for one was found at Nevase in Ahmednagar District.[395] The Coffret IX type is clearly Western in inspiration,[396] while again the composite animal on the ivory throne back appears as an intermediate type (fig. 268). At the same time, the motif of the *makara* at Nāgārjunakoṇḍa becomes transformed into a fantastic composite animal (figs. 186-87). In this case, we do not see that the Begram or Andhra artists were copying from each other. Instead, they were both looking at similar source material and each adapted it to his own preference.

Thus, the problem of the Begram ivories exists as a parallel problem to the art of Nāgārjunakoṇḍa. They both reflect an Indian tradition and show an avid interest in works from the West. Most of the Begram ivories were probably produced somewhere in the Northwest, with a very strong influence from the Andhra tradition. For as in the art of Gandhāra, their Classical influence is conspicuous, whereas the Andhra artist carefully absorbed Classical elements into his own tradition. If there is an object which bridges the two traditions, it is the ivory throne back in figure

267. As we have pointed out in our article on Begram, the ivories stand as a bridge to the Gupta-Vākāṭaka tradition, and therefore stand in the function with the contemporary Buddhist narratives from Nāgārjunakoṇḍa.

If we accept the Begram ivories as contemporary with late Nāgārjunakoṇḍa, how do we explain the problem of Shāpur's supposed destruction of Begram in A.D. 241? It has been hoped for some time that the Archaeological Survey of India would excavate at Begram and perhaps arrive at a conclusion archaeologically. Recent events in Afghanistan have made this impossible. We have learned from our study of Nāgārjunakoṇḍa, that when the archaeological evidence contradicts both stylistic and epigraphic evidence, the artistic remains must be examined in their own right.

CHAPTER V

CONCLUSION

The basic aim of this book has been to establish a chronology for the Buddhist art of Nāgārjunakoṇḍa. In Chapter I, we dealt largely with the framework in which this chronology was to be set. Our opinion as to a chronology of the four kings of the Ikṣvāku dynasty, under which the large part of the Nāgārjunakoṇḍa sculptures was created, is as follows:

Cāṁtamūla I, c. A.D. 225-c. A.D. 240-50
Vīrapuruṣadatta, c. A.D. 240-50-c. A.D. 265-75
Ehuvala Cāṁtamūla, c. A.D. 265-75-c. A.D. 290-300
Rudrapuruṣadatta, c. A.D. 290-300-c. A.D. 315-25.

We have expanded upon and varied a theory, previously proposed by H. Sarkar, that the monastic sites of Nāgārjunakoṇḍa showed a definite evolution in their ground-plan, and that this evolution was largely conditioned by doctrinal changes in the Buddhism practised at Nāgārjunakoṇḍa. This has been aided by the recent translation of a text, *The Lion's Roar of Queen Śrīmālā*, probably written at Nāgārjunakoṇḍa during Ikṣvāku times. We have also shown that during this period, important Hindu and secular structures were created at Nāgārjunakoṇḍa with technical innovations perhaps introduced from the West.

Chapter II deals largely with the evolution of the sculptural style, which essentially follows the evolution of the monastic units in which these works were placed. In summary, we have assigned to the reign of Cāṁtamūla I the sculptures of Site 6, a group of sculptures which have rarely been seen and never discussed as part of the Nāgārjunakoṇḍa style. This group seems to have been heavily influenced by the art of Mathurā as was its pre-Ikṣvāku predecessor a work which was intended for the *Mahācetiya*, a Nāgārjunakoṇḍa *Stūpa* which was previously considered to be unadorned and to belong to the period of Vīrapuruṣadatta. During the same time the building of *Stūpa* 9 may have already begun.

Several important works were produced during the reign of Vīrapuruṣadatta. Of particular interest is a group of memorial pillars. These belong to the realm of secular art. Yet we have seen in one instance that a particular composition was repeated or copied, just as we have come to expect repetition in the realm of Buddhist narrative art. The most important Buddhist works of this time were the *āyaka* panels of Site 9, which continued the traditions of Site 6 and added examples which reflected the late style of Amarāvatī. This period probably coincided with the latest phases of the Amarāvatī *Stūpa*. At the same time, the dome slabs were added to Site 6.

During the reign of Ehuvala Cāṁtamūla, Sites 6 and 9 appear to have been completed, while new structures were built at Sites 2, 3 and 106. This period marks an evolutionary phase of the late style of Amarāvatī, both repeating its themes and adopting a less complex mode of carving.

In the reign of Rudrapuruṣadatta, we have discussed only one work, a memorial pillar to the King's deceased mother. The pillar is in too poor a state of preservation to discuss from a stylistic point of view, yet we have shown how the composition of this pillar, while possibly Buddhist in meaning, was borrowed from the classical West. Such compositional borrowings have been seen throughout the art of Nāgārjunakoṇḍa, and have been cited as they appeared chronologically. An addendum to Chapter II discusses a pair of pillars belonging to the post-Ikṣvāku period. These stand as a transition to works of the Gupta-Vākāṭaka era.

Chapter III deals with the nearby Andhra sites of Gummididurru and Goli. These sites help to give us some notion that there was a generalized Andhra style and that there was a great deal of communication between the sculptors of the individual schools. While the style of Gummididurru seemed to influence the early phase of Nāgārjunakoṇḍa, that of Goli seems to have inherited the Nāgārjunakoṇḍa tradition and carried it into the post-Ikṣvāku phase.

The site of Begram, discussed in Chapter IV, proposes an altogether different problem, for the ivories found there seem to have been produced at the same time as the Nāgārjunakoṇḍa sculptures. The ivories embody some of the same art historical problems, especially that of combining Western influence with a native Indian tradition.

Throughout this study, the reader may have observed that in ancient times Nāgārjunakoṇḍa was a truly cosmopolitan area. Yet this observation had already been made by a Nāgārjunakoṇḍa artist some time ago. For he created a pillar on one side of which he placed a guardian figure in Scythian dress (fig. 232). On the next side he placed a togate figure, quasi-Roman in appearance (fig. 280), while on a third side he placed a figure in classical dress or posture holding a rhyton (fig. 281). On the fourth side, he placed the *yakṣī* or *vṛkṣa devatā* (fig. 282), one of India's most ancient indigenous motifs.

NOTES

1. R. Subrahmanyam, "Nāgārjunakoṇḍa (1954-60)", Vol. I, *Memoirs of the Archaeological Survey of India,* 75, New Delhi, 1975, p. xvii.
2. Hirananda Sastri, "Report on Indian Epigraphy", in *Annual Report, Archaeological Survey of India, 1925-26,* p. 141; Hamid Kuraishi, "Trial Excavations at Alluru, Gummadidurru, and Nāgārjunikoṇḍa", *Annual Report, Archaeological Survey of India, 1926-27,* p. 160. The unpublished results of these excavations are discussed in Chapter II.
3. Kuraishi, pp. 56-161.
4. A.H. Longhurst, "The Buddhist Antiquities of Nāgārjunakoṇḍa, Madras Presidency," *Memoirs of the Archaeological Survey of India*, 54, Delhi, 1938.
5. T.N. Ramachandran, "Nāgārjunakoṇḍa, 1938", *Memoirs of the Archaeological Survey of India,* 71, Delhi, 1953.
6. See note 1.
7. K. Krishna Murthy, *Nāgārjunakoṇḍā : A Cultural Study,* Delhi, 1977.
8. H. Sarkar, "Some Aspects of Buddhist Monuments at Nāgārjunakoṇḍa", *Ancient India,* No. 16, 1962, pp. 65-85.
9. H. Sarkar, *Studies in Early Buddhist Architecture of India,* Delhi, 1968, Chapter 5.
10. Longhurst, *Buddhist Antiquities,* p. 10.
11. Ramachandran, *Nāgārjunakoṇḍa,* pp. 9ff.
12. Sarkar, *Studies in Early Buddhist Architecture,* pl. XIII.
13. H. Sarkar and B.N. Misra, *Nāgārjunakoṇḍa,* Delhi, 1972.
14. Sarkar and Misra, pp. 8-19.
15. H. Sarkar, "Nagarjunakoṇḍa Prakrit Inscription of Gautamiputra Vijaya Satakarni, Year 6", *Epigraphia Indica,* XXXVI, 1964-65, pp. 273-74; for a variation of this theory see H. Sarkar, "The Nāgārjunakoṇḍa Phase of Lower Kṛṣṇā Valley Art" in *Indian Epigraphy: Its Bearing on the History of Art,* Ed. Frederick M. Asher and G.S. Gai, New Delhi, 1985, p. 30.
16. J. Ph. Vogel, "Prakrit Inscriptions from a Buddhist Site at Nāgārjunakoṇḍa", *Epigraphia Indica*, XX, 1929-30, pp. 1-36; "Additional Prakrit Inscriptions from Nāgārjunakoṇḍa", *Epigraphia Indica,* XXI, pp. 61-71.
17. D.C. Sircar, "More Inscriptions from Nāgārjunakoṇḍa, *Epigraphia Indica,* XXXV, 1963-64, pp. 1-36; "Nāgārjunakoṇḍa Inscription of the Time of Abhira Vasushena, Year 30", *Epigraphia Indica,* XXXIV, 1961-62, pp. 197-204; "Some Brahmi Inscriptions", *Epigraphia Indica,* XXXIV, 1961-62, pp. 207-12; D.C. Sircar and K.G. Krishnan, "Two Inscriptions from Nāgārjunakoṇḍa", *Epigraphia Indica,* XXXIV, 1961-62, pp. 17-22; D.C. Sircar and L.N. Lahiri, "Footprint Slab Inscription from Nāgārjunakoṇḍa", *Epigraphia Indica,* XXXIII, 1960, pp. 247-50.

18. M. Rama Rao, *Inscriptions of the Andhradeśa,* 2 Vols., (Sri Venkatesvara University Historical Series, No. 5), Tirupati, 1967.
19. D.C. Sircar, *Successors of the Sātavāhanas in the Lower Deccan,* Calcutta, 1935, Chapter 1.
20. K. Gopalachari, *Early History of the Andhra Country,* Madras University Historical Series, No. 16, 2nd ed., Madras, 1976.
21. Ranjana Mukherjee, *The History of the Āndhra Region c. A.D. 75 to A.D. 350,* Ph. D. Thesis, University of London, 1965; this thesis is discussed in my own unpublished M.A. Thesis, Elizabeth Rosen, *The History and Buddhist Architecture of Nāgārjunakoṇḍa,* M.A. Thesis, New York University, 1970.
22. Karl Khandalavala, "An Inscription of the Year 11 of Caṣṭana and Its Implications", *Journal of Indian History,* Vol. 52, 1974, pp. 206-301.
23. Sircar and Krishnan, pp. 20-22.
24. R. Subrahmanyam, *A Catalogue of Iksavaku Coins in the Andhra Pradesh Government Museum* .(Andhra Pradesh Government Series, No. 5), Hyderabad, 1962; Brajadulal Chattopadhyaya, *Coins and Currency Systems in South India,* New Delhi, 1977, p. 105.
25. R. Sankaranarayanan, "Rentala Pillar Inscription of Siri-Chamtamula I, Year 5", *Epigraphia Indica,* XXXVII, 1965-66, pp. 29-32.
26. Md. Abdul Waheed Khan, *A Monograph on an Early Buddhist Stūpa at Kesanapalli,* (Andhra Pradesh Government Archaeological Series, No. 27), Hyderabad, 1969, p. 5.
27. For example, Pillar inscription L, Vogel, "Additional Prakrit Inscriptions", pp. 63-64.
28. Subrahmanyam, *Catalogue of Coins,* p. 1.
29. *Indian Archaeology, A Review 1955-56,* p. 26.
30. James Burgess, *The Buddhist Stūpas of Amarāvatī and Jaggayyapeta,* Archaeological Survey of Southern India, London, 1887, p. 10ff, pls. LXII and LXIII.
31. *Indian Archaeology, A Review 1959-60,* p. 67.
32. N.P. Chakravarti, "Summary of Epigraphical Work during 1933-34", *Annual Report, Archaeological Survey of India,* 1930-34, p. 238-39.
33. Sarkar and Misra, p. 15. The inscription bearing the date of the 24th regnal year of Vīrapuruṣadatta was discovered toward the end of the Archaeological Survey's work at Nāgārjunakoṇḍa. It was first reported in *Indian Archaeology, A Review, 1967-68,* p. 52, and was therefore unmentioned in the earlier literature on Nāgārjunakoṇḍa.
34. Sircar, *Successors of the Sātavāhanas,* p. 35.
35. Sircar and Krishnan, "Two Inscriptions", p. 18.
36. Sircar and Krishnan, pp. 20-21.
37. Sircar, "More Inscriptions", pp. 11-13.
38. K.A. Nilakanta Sastri, "Gurzala Brahmi Inscription", *Epigraphia Indica,* XXVI, 1941, pp. 123-25.
39. Sircar and Krishnan, pp. 20-22.
40. This inscription was reported to me by H. Sarkar and is incorporated in his version of a short chronology in "The Nāgārjunakoṇḍa Phase", p. 31.
41. Subrahmanyam, *Catalogue of Coins,* p. 7; Krishna Murthy, *Nāgārjunakoṇḍa,* pp. 7-8; and a variation in H. Sarkar, "The Nāgārjunakoṇḍa Phase", p. 31.

42. This problem has been discussed by Gopalachari, pp. 132-33, in which he accepts a shorter chronology of 52 years. His book, now in its second edition, first appeared in 1951 before the discovery of the "later" Ikṣvāku inscriptions, which would make the 52 year chronology obsolete. This section appears not to have been updated in the second edition.
43. J.F. Fleet, Inscriptions of the Early Gupta Kings, *Corpus Inscriptionum Indicarum,* Vol. III, 3rd rev. ed., Varanasi, 1970. Page 13 mentions Hastivarman of Veṅgī, but there is no mention of any members of an Ikṣvāku lineage in that area.
44. Sircar, "More Inscriptions", pp. 1-4.
45. Sircar, "More Inscriptions", pp. 4-7.
46. Sircar, "Nāgārjunakoṇḍa Inscriptions", pp. 197-204.
47. Sircar, "Nāgārjunakoṇḍa Inscriptions", p. 201.
48. See note 21. See also V.V. Mirashi, "Epigraphic Note", *Epigraphia Indica,* XXXVII, 1967, pp. 72-73, as well as M. Mehta, *The Abhiras: Their History and Culture* (M.S. University Archaeology and Ancient History Series, No. 6), Baroda, 1962, pp. 100-102.
49. *Indian Archaeology, A Review 1956-57,* p. 30; Sarkar and Misra, pp. 29-30.
50. *Indian Archaeology, A Review, 1955-56,* pp. 25-26. Another, but considerably less elaborate bathing *ghāṭ,* has been excavated at the contiguous site of Yelleśwaram. Unfortunately, the *ghāṭ* and the site were submerged along with Nāgārjunakoṇḍa. Waheed Khan ascribes the *ghāṭ* to the first to second centuries A.D. Md. Abdul Waheed Khan, *A Monograph on Yēllēśwaram Excavations,* Andhra Pradesh Archaeological Series, XIV, Hyderabad, 1963, pl. XI and p. 11.
51. H. Sarkar, "Chronological Aspects of Mason's Marks at Nāgārjunakoṇḍa", *Bhāratī* (Bulletin of the Department of Ancient History, Culture and Archaeology), 1968-71, Nos. 12-14, p. 232. According to Sarkar, the *ghāṭ,* which was found within the proximity of the Puṣpabhadrasvāmin temple, may have had a religious function.
52. Sarkar and Misra, p. 22.
53. Sarkar, "Mason's Marks", p. 232.
54. Harivamsa, *Viṣṇuparva,* 26:30, p. 298. The amphitheatre where this competition was to take place was inspected by Kamsa himself. He found that the architect had designed platforms upon platforms. They were all very securely placed. There were very beautiful balconies also. Some balconies had six pillars each; some were supported only by one. The pillars, balconies and platforms added decorative touches to the amphitheatre which was very large. It was set on a very good foundation. For climbing the platforms there were stairs that were high, wide, and with closely set steps. The *rang bhavan* looked grand. There were thrones placed for the various kings. It had many exits and entrances. It had the capacity to hold a large number of people comfortably. Kamsa added his order, "For tomorrow, decorate all the platforms, balconies and pathways with paintings, garlands and flags. Sprinkle perfumed water so that everything is fragrant. Decorate it so that it is pleasing to the eye. Spread white coverlets on the seats. Nice curtains should be hung. Strong poles should be fixed deep in the ground. Put stands at regular intervals and place gold pitchers on them, filled with water and juice. . . Invite the people who know the rules

of wrestling, also invite the merchants and artisans along with their chiefs. Tell the wrestlers and judges to arrive punctually. . ." This passage was quoted by Usha Nillson in a seminar on "The Cultural Heritage of Mathurā" held in New Delhi, January 1980.

55. The use of brick faced with stone was the common constructional method used throughout the Roman Empire from the second century onward. The Roman method consisted of a brick and concrete core faced with stone. Axel Boethius and J.B. Ward-Perkins, *Etruscan and Roman Architecture,* Harmondsworth, 1970, pp. 245-63.
56. Sir Mortimer Wheeler, *Rome Beyond the Imperial Frontiers,* London, 1954, Ch. 9, gives a good description of the coastal sea route to India.
57. Wheeler, p. 129.
58. Wheeler, p. 122.
59. M. Deshpande, "Classical Influences on Indian Terracotta Art", *Huitiéme congrés inernational d'archéologie classique,* Paris, 1963, 1965, pp. 606ff.
60. Wheeler, p. 121.
61. A recent sculptural find in Andhra Pradesh, at the site of Koṇḍamoṭu, gives us further evidence of early Andhra Vaiṣṇavism. The frieze, depicting Narasiṁha, is in the style of Nāgārjunakoṇḍa, but we have no evidence of an Ikṣvāku affiliation for this work. (Md. Abdul Waheed Khan, *An Early Sculpture of Narasiṁha,* Andhra Pradesh Government Archaeological Series, No. 16, Hyderabad, 1964; W.E. Begley, *Viṣṇu's Flaming Wheel: The Iconography of the Sudarśana-Cakra,* New York, 1973, pp. 2-3, fig. 2.)
62. As can be noted on the inscription belonging to this temple, the donor of the temple does not seem to have belonged to the Ikṣvāku royal house. The donor is male, while most of the Buddhist monuments at the site were patronized by women, most of whom were part of the Ikṣvāku royal family. For a complete discussion of the inscription, see B. Ch. Chhabra, "Nāgārjunakoṇḍa Inscription of Ehavalasri's Time, year 11", *Epigraphia Indica,* XXXIII 1966, 147-49. The inscription was originally cited incorrectly in *Indian Archaeology, A Review 1956-57,* p. 36, and corrected in *Indian Archaeology, A Review 1957-58,* p. 54, as well as in the above-mentioned article.
63. Sarkar and Misra, p. 27; *Indian Archaeology, A Review 1956-57,* p. 36. This temple, as other Śaivite temples at Nāgārjunakoṇḍa, was found along the banks of the Krishna river, while the valley was occupied by contemporary Buddhist structures. The proximity of one side of the temple to the river caused A.H. Longhurst to identify it as a wharf before the excavations were complete. (Longhurst, *Buddhist Antiquities,* pp. 7-8.)
64. The prince in question is commonly referred to as Vīrapuruṣadatta II. Although he seems to have been commander of Ehuvala Cāṁtamūla's armies, he does not seem to have succeeded to the throne, as we know that Ehuvala Cāṁtamūla's successor was Rudrapuruṣadatta. (D.C. Sircar and K.G. Krishnan, "Two Inscriptions", pp. 17-22.)
65. Another extant example of a Hindu apsidal temple found was at the site of Sonkh in Mathurā district. This temple, belonging to the Kushan period, was worshipped by followers of the Nāga cult. The temple had a pre-Kushan phase which could have

been Buddhist. H. Härtel, "Some Results of the Excavations at Sonkh: A Preliminary Report", *German Scholars in India, Contributions to Indian Studies* II, Bombay, 1976, pp. 93-99. For a proposed reconstruction of the Nāga temple, see Härtel, "Aspects of Early Nāga Cult in India", *Journal of the Royal Asiatic Society,* October 1976, fig. 20.

66. This latter suggestion was made by K.V. Soundara Rajan, *Architecture of the Early Hindu Temples of Andhra Pradesh,* Andhra Pradesh Government Archaeology Series, No. 21, Hyderabad, 1965, p. 15. Similar temples are also represented on early Indian coins; see J.N. Banerjea, *The Development of Hindu Iconography,* 2nd ed., Calcutta 1956, p. I, No. 16, and p. 118. Note that the temple cited was also a Śaiva temple.
67. The Buddhist architecture of Nāgārjunakoṇḍa was discussed by me in a symposium on *Stūpa* symbolism held in 1978 at the University of Heidelberg. See E. Rosen, "The Buddhist Architecture and Lay Patronage at Nāgārjunakoṇḍa", in *The Stūpa: Its Religious, Historical and Architectural Significance,* ed. A.L. Dallapicolla, *Beiträge zur Südasien Forschung,* Bd. 55, Wiesbaden 1980. See also Alex Wayman and Elizabeth Rosen, "The Rise of Mahāyāna Buddhism and Inscriptional Evidence at Nāgārjunakoṇḍa, *Indian Journal of Buddhist Studies,* Varanasi, Vol II, No 1, 1990.
68. Sarkar, *Buddhist Architecture,* Chapter 5.
69. Sukumar Dutt, *Buddhist Monks and Monasteries of India,* London, 1963, Chapter 4.
70. Akira Hirakawa, "The Rise of Mahāyāna and Its Relation to *Stūpa* Worship", *Memoirs of the Toyo Bunko Research Society,* Vol. 22, 1963, pp. 57-106.
71. Alex Wayman and Hideko Wayman, *The Lion's Roar of Queen Śrīmālā,* New York and London, 1974, pp. 1-3.
72. For proposed shape of dome, see Longhurst, *Buddhist Antiquities,* pl. XIIa.
73. The relic, which is mentioned in the inscriptions, was excavated on the outer rim of the Great *Stūpa.* Longhurst, *Buddhist Antiquities,* pl. XIIb, XIIId. It is presently housed in Sārnāth in a temple belonging to the Mahābodhi Society.
74. See J.Ph. Vogel, "Prakrit Inscriptions", p. 17 inscriptions C1 and C3, and p. 18 inscription B1. The name of Vīrapuruṣadatta was known several decades before the discovery of Nāgārjunakoṇḍa, as a pillar inscription bearing his name was first noticed at Jaggayyapeta by James Burgess in 1882. (James Burgess, *The Buddhist Stūpas of Amarāvatī and Jaggayyapeta,* Archaeological Survey of Southern India, Vol. 1, London, 1887, p. 110f., pls. LXII and LXIII.) These inscriptions are dated in the twentieth regnal year of Vīrapuruṣadatta.
75. The wording of the inscription is as follows (Vogel, "Prakrit Inscriptions" p. 17, C1): ". . . for the benefit of the masters of the Aparamahāvinaseliya sect, this pious foundation of the Mahācetiya has been completed by the Reverend Ānanda... a disciple of the Masters of the Ayira-Haṁgha (Skt. Ārya-Sangha) . . . . who are preachers and preceptors of the Dīgha, Majjhima-(nikāya) and of the five 'Mātukas'." André Bareau (*Les Sectes bouddhiques du petit véhicule,* Saigon, 1955, p. 104) observes that the divisions of the *sūtrapiṭaka* of this group were designated under the name of *nikāya* and not under the name of *āgama* as in the Northwest. As we shall see, Theravādins from Ceylon were living at Nāgārjunakoṇḍa side by side with the Aparamahāvinaseliyas.

This may indeed have had some effect on terminology as well as on doctrine and architecture. As for the confusing term *mātuka*, Bareau states that it refers to a group of the *abhidharma*, a work which all sects collected late and which remained in the form of separate *mātṛkās*. This is in contrast to the opinion expressed by Nalinaksha Dutt (*Buddhist Sects in India,* Calcutta, 1970, p. 63), who believes that the five *'mātukas'* refers to the *vinaya piṭaka* of the *Mahāsāṁghikas* (of which the Aparamahāvinaseliyas were a branch) whose texts had five divisions like other schools. See also Wayman and Wayman, *The Lion's Roar,* pp. 5-6, footnote 8.

76. Bareau, *Les Sectes bouddhiques,* p. 105.
77. Wayman and Wayman, *The Lion's Roar,* p. 65.
78. Vogel, *Prakrit Inscriptions,* p. 17, C3.
79. Sarkar, *Studies in Early Buddhist Architecture,* p. 57.
80. Indeed, the Taxila inscriptions pre-date the Nāgārjunakoṇḍa inscriptions, and Taxila may have provided part of the inspiration to the early Mahāyāna faith at Nāgārjunakoṇḍa. But some interesting points of contrast between the inscriptions should be noted. The Taxila Silver Scroll inscription reads as follows:

"Anno 136, on the 15 day of the first month Āshādha, on this day were established relics of the Lord by Urasaka, of the Iṁtavhria boys, the Bactrian, the resident of the town of Noacha. By him these relics of the Lord were established in his own bodhisattva chapel, in the Dharmarājikā compound of Takshaśilā, for the bestowal of health on the Great King, the King of Kings, the Son of Heaven, the Khushana, in honour of all Buddhas, in honour of the Pratyekabuddhas, in honour of the Arhats, in honour of all beings, in honour of mother and father, in honour of friends, ministers, kinsmen, and blood-relations, for the bestowal of health upon himself. May this thy right munificence lead to Nirvāṇa."

(Sten Konow, Kharoshthī Inscriptions: With the Exception of Those of Aśoka, *Corpus Inscriptionum Indicarum,* Vol. II, pt. 1, reprint ed., Varanasi, 1969, p. 77; see also the Hidda inscription of the Year 28, p. 158.) According to the Taxila inscription, the donor deposited a relic in his own bodhisattva chapel, while the Nāgārjunakoṇḍa donatrix expressed a more direct involvement with the monastic community. The benefits obtained from the donations were mainly for the king and for the donor's kinsmen, while the Nāgārjunakoṇḍa inscriptions implied an active involvement in both the secular and monastic community. Indeed, while Andhra Buddhism may have been connected with that of Taxila, it is much more consistent with the Mahāyāna faith as outlined in *The Lion's Roar of Queen Śrīmālā.* The most obvious contrast here is that the donor of the Taxila inscriptions was a male, while the donatrices of Nāgārjunakoṇḍa may be more closely associated with the heroine of *The Lion's Roar,* and with what seems to be a general trend of southern Buddhism.

81. Wayman and Wayman, *The Lion's Roar,* p. 8.
82. Hirakawa, "The Rise of Mahāyāna", pp. 79-84.
83. Hirakawa, "The Rise of Mahāyāna", pp. 102-106.
84. Wayman and Wayman, *The Lion's Roar,* p. 76.

85. Mahā-parinibbāna-sutta, V, 24, in *Buddhist Suttas,* tr. T.W. Rhys Davids, *Sacred Books of the East,* Vol. XI, Oxford, 1881; Dover reprint, New York, 1969, p. 91.
86. J. Ph. Vogel, "Additional Prakrit Inscriptions from Nāgārjunakoṇḍa", *Epigraphia Indica,* XXI, 1930-31, pp. 64-68.
87. Vogel, "Prakrit Inscriptions", pp. 21-22, Inscription E.
88. *Indian Archaeology, A Review, 1957-58,* pp. 8-9.
89. Sarkar, *Studies in Early Buddhist Architecture,* p. 77.
90. D.C. Sircar, "More Inscriptions from Nāgārjunakoṇḍa", *Epigraphia Indica,* XXXV, 1963-64, pp. 7-10.
91. This particular image has been greatly restored, giving it a somewhat "Classical" face. One should therefore avoid any attempt to take this image into account from a stylistic point of view.
92. *Indian Archaeology, A Review, 1954-55,* pp. 22-23. The identification of the seated image in this temple with Hāritī is highly speculative.
93. D.C. Sircar, "*Some Brahmi Inscriptions*", pp. 210-11, Inscription III.
94. Bareau, *Les Sectes bouddhiques,* p. 182; Hirakawa, "The Rise of Mahāyāna", p. 99.
95. Bareau, *Les Sectes bouddhiques,* p. 185; Hirakawa, "The Rise of Mahāyāna", p. 99.
96. Vogel, "Prakrit Inscriptions", pp. 24-25, Inscription H.
97. Bareau, *Les Sectes bouddhiques,* pp. 81-83.
98. Vogel, "Additional Prakrit Inscriptions", pp. 61-63, Inscriptions G2 and G3.
99. Sarkar, *Studies in Early Buddhist Architecture,* p. 79 and pl. IXB.
100. Vogel, "Prakrit Inscriptions", pp. 22-23; D.C. Sircar and A.N. Lahiri, "Footprint Slab Inscription from Nāgārjunakoṇḍa", *Epigraphia Indica,* XXXIII, 1970, p. 250.
101. Vogel, "Prakrit Inscriptions", pp. 22-23.
102. Sarkar, *Studies in Early Buddhist Architecture,* p. 77.
103. Sarkar considers that Sites 43 and 38 were made for two different Sinhalese sects, the Theravādins from Ceylon and the Mahāvihāravasins (Sarkar, *Studies in Early Buddhist Architecture,* p. 77). Sircar and Lahiri ("Footprint Slab Inscription", p. 248) have shown that many of the epithets belonging to the supposed two sects are the same, and thus concludes that they are one sect. Sarkar (p. 77, footnote 4) objects to this idea because Sircar and Lahiri interpret the term "Mahāvihāravasin" as "Dwellers of the Mahāvihāra" at Nāgārjunakoṇḍa, who were in fact Aparamahāvinaseliyas. But the term "Mahāvihāravasin", in this case, refers to the dwellers of the Mahāvihāra in Ceylon from which this group probably came. The group in question was also known as Vibhajyavādins. (See Bareau, *Les Sectes bouddhiques,* pp. 205-11, 167.) Interestingly, the inscriptions from Sites 43 and 38 both give a long list of names of regions which were converted by the Theravādins from Ceylon residing at Nāgārjunakoṇḍa. At least six out of the twelve names mentioned at Site 43 (Vogel, "Prakrit Inscriptions", p. 23) may be found in the *Mahāvaṁsa* under the list of countries converted by the Theravādins (*The Mahāvaṁsa,* tr. Wm. Geiger, London, 1912, reprint ed., 1969, p. 82). All of the names on the footprint slab inscription belonging to Site 3 are found on the same list.

Sircar and Lahiri (p. 248) also note that the orthography of the inscription belongs to the time of Vīrapuruṣadatta, the second king of the dynasty. The inscription was placed on a footprint slab found within the monastery recording the donation of the Lord's feet (Buddha-*pāda*). Although this date may be satisfactory for the Buddha-*pāda,* it is highly unlikely that the *caitya-gṛha* and the *Stūpa* would have been added before the time of Ehuvala Cāṁtamūla, the third king.

104. Bareau, *Les Sectes bouddhiques,* pp. 223-34, 171.
105. Hirakawa, "The Rise of Mahāyāna", pp. 98-99.
106. Stella Kramrisch, *Indian Sculpture,* Calcutta, 1933, pp. 46-53.
107. Douglas Barrett, *Sculptures from Amarāvatī in the British Museum,* London, 1954, pls. XXXVIII-XLI.
108. Barrett, pls. VIII and IXa.
109. Barret, pls. XIX.
110. See note 25.
111. See note 26.
112. The Reṇṭāla pillar inscription specifically refers to a dedication to the Buddhist *saṁgha* on a stone (Sankaranarayanan, pp. 30 and 32), while the Kesanapalli inscription appeared on an *āyaka* pillar of a *stūpa* recording the dedication of a *stūpa* to the Bahuśrutīya sect (Waheed Khan, *Kesanapalli,* p. 2), a sect also known at Nāgārjunakoṇḍa.
113. Longhurst, *Buddhist Antiquities,* p. 17.
114. See note 30.
115. Vogel, "Prakrit Inscriptions", p. 25, Inscription J.
116. I have had the great pleasure of discussing the inscription with H. Sarkar and C. Sivaramamurti, and subsequently with Professor Alex Wayman.
117. Longhurst, *Buddhist Antiquities,* p. 16.
118. Kuraishi, "Trial Excavations", pp. 156-57.
119. Vogel, "Prakrit Inscriptions", p. 15 Inscription K.
120. H. Sarkar, "Some Aspects of Buddhist Monuments at Nāgārjunakoṇḍa", *Ancient India,* 1962, p. 84 and pl. XLVI.
121. Kuraishi, pp. 160-61.
122. Mentioned by Kuraishi, "Trial Excavations", p. 60, under Site 4; Longhurst, "Excavations at Nāgārjunakoṇḍa", *Annual Report, Archaeological Survey of India, 1929-30,* p. 145, under Site 6.
123. J. Ph. Vogel, "Prakrit Inscriptions from a Buddhist Site at Nāgārjunakoṇḍa", *Epigraphia Indica,* XX, 1929-30, p. 15, inscription K.
124. H. Härtel and J. Auboyer, *Indien und Südostasien (Propyläen Kunstgeschichte)* 16, Berlin, 1971, pls. 30b and 41b; M. Bussagli and C. Sivaramamurti, *Five Thousand Years of the Art of India,* New York, n.d., fig. 13.
125. I. Lyons and H. Ingholt, *Gandharan Art in Pakistan*, Hamden, Conn., 1971, pls. 340, 342 and 344.
126. For example, R.C. Agrawala, "Mother and Child Sculptures from Śāmalāji and Rajasthan", *Bulletin of the Museum and Picture Gallery, Baroda,* Vol. XXIII, 197, pl.

LX, fig. 12, LXI, fig. 13; J. Harle, *Gupta Sculpture,* Oxford, 1974, fig. 92. The suggestion of P. Pal in "Indian Art from the Paul Walter Collection", *Bulletin of the Allen Memorial Art Museum, Oberlin College,* Vol. XXIII, No. 2, 1971 (cited by J. Harle) that these figures are Skanda Mātās is interesting in this context. We know that the cult of Kārttikeya was popular at Nāgārjunakoṇḍa and one would be tempted to suggest that the Śāmalāji figures were related to Nāgārjunakoṇḍa. However, these comparisons are only coincidental.

127. This type seems to have been ultimately derived from the Kephisodotus Eirene and Ploutos of the fourth century B.C. and known from a copy in the Glyptotek in Munich. Gisela Richter, *The Sculpture and Sculptors of the Greeks,* 4th ed., New Haven and London, 1970, fig. 197.
128. A plaster cast, which has been identified as representing Nysa with the infant Dionysus, perhaps of Alexandrian manufacture, has been excavated at Begram. Although this particular representation clearly did not serve as a prototype for the ivory, other examples of this theme may have originally existed at Begram which did. (J. Hackin, *Nouvelles recherches archéologiques à Begram,* Paris, 1954, Vol. I, p. 114, Vol. II, figs. 277 and 293.)
129. Karl Khandalavala, "Brahmpuri: A Consideration of the Metal Objects Found in the Kundangar Hoard", *Lalit Kala,* 7, 1960, fig. 6.
130. A Rea, *South Indian Buddhist Antiquities, Archaeological Survey of India, New Imperial Series,* XV, Madras 1894, pl. 82. It is difficult to speak of style in this line drawing, but we may easily assume that the style is quite similar to the Site 6 piece.
131. "Some Results of the Excavations at Sonkh, A Preliminary Report", *German Scholars in India,* Vol. II, 1976, p. 98.
132. Longhurst, "Excavations, 1929-30", p. 147.
133. Parmeshwari Lal Gupta, *Roman Coins from Andhra Pradesh,* Andhra Pradesh Government Museum Series, No. 10, Hyderabad, n.d., pp. 61 and 74-75.
134. Gupta, p. 75.
135. Unpublished paper cited in William E. Metcalf, "Roman Aurei from India". The American Numismatic Society, *Museum Notes,* Vol. 24, 1979, p. 125, footnote 2.
136. Metcalf, pp. 123-27.
137. Metcalf, p. 127.
138. Both Manfred Raschke and William Metcalf have kindly looked at the photographs of these *bullae.* Both believed them to be imitations of a coin rather that a direct copy.
139. The popularity of coin necklaces at Nāgārjunakoṇḍa is attested to by their representation on sculptural reliefs. In fact, in the Jaina *Kalpa Sūtra,* such coin necklaces are referred to as *urattha-dinara-mālayā,* "a string of *Dinaras* on the breast". (K. Krishna Murthy, *Nāgārjunakoṇḍa: A Cultural Study,* Delhi, 1977, p. 80., fig. 6, No. 19.) Even if the coins were not literally fashioned on Roman *denarii,* they once presumably were.
140. Sircar, "More Inscriptions", p. 19, No. II.
141. Compare this inscription, "More Inscriptions", pl. VI, BII, with any other from Nāgārjunakoṇḍa. All others show an exceptionally elongated decorative script

characteristic of the Ikṣvāku period. I thank H. Sarkar for generously sharing his opinions on this inscription with me.

142. Sarkar, "Nāgārjunakoṇḍa Prakrit Inscription", pp. 273-74.
143. J. Ph. Vogel, "Additional Prakrit Inscriptions from Nāgārjunakoṇḍa", *Epigraphia Indica,* XXI, 1930-31, pp. 63-64.
144. J. Burgess, The Buddhist Stūpas of Amarāvatī and Jaggayyapeta, *Archaeological Survey of Southern India,* Vol. I, London, 1887, reprint ed. Varanasi, 1970, p. 110 and pl. LXIII, No. 1.
145. Vogel "Additional Prakrit Inscriptions", facing p. 63.
146. D.C. Sircar, "More Inscriptions", pp. 1-4.
147. Sircar cites no reference to works on the Jovian cycle when he gives this date. A convenient source and computation table for the Sixty Year Cycle of Jupiter is provided by A. Cunningham, *Book of Indian Eras,* Calcutta, 1883, reprint ed. Varanasi, 1970, pp. 18-25 and table on p. 146.

   The *Bārhaspaty-Māna*, or Sixty Year Cycle of Jupiter, consists of five twelve year cycles of Jupiter around the sun. Each year is given a specific name, *vijaya* being the twenty-seventh year. In order to adhere to astronomical accuracy, it is necessary to drop one year from the cycle in every 86. There are three basic systems used in India for this cycle. The first is that expounded by Varāhmihira in the *Sūryasiddhānta,* dating to the sixth century A.D. Computations for the system begin with the beginning of the *Kali-Yuga*, and according to Varāhamihira, the first year of the *Kali-Yuga* corresponds to the twenty-seventh year of the first Jovian cycle. The second system, known as the Jyotishtava reckoning, is similar to that of the *Sūryasiddhānta,* but makes the first year of the *Kali-Yuga* correspond to the first year of the Jovian cycle. However, the actual difference between a given year in each cycle is computed to be only one year apart. In both these systems, the necessary omission of one year in eighty-six is taken into account.

   The third system is that known as the Telinga reckoning, and is peculiar to South India. It is this system that D.C. Sircar has chosen to reckon the year *vijaya* in pillar inscription L. By the Telinga reckoning the Jovian cycle began twelve years before the *Kali-Yuga.* This system has abandoned the astronomical accuracy of the previous two systems, and makes the 1/12 of the Jovian year (i.e., one-fifth of a cycle of the sixty year Jupiter) correspond exactly to the solar year. The system drops the necessary omission of everyone year in eighty-six. As a modification of the more logical and astronomically accurate northern system, the Telinga system must post-date the previous two, i.e., the system post-dates the sixth century A.D. According to all three systems, the only remotely plausible dates for pillar inscription L are the twenty-seventh year of the fifty-seventh Jovian cycle, that is 273-74 A.D. according to the Telinga system, or 279-80 A.D. according to the system of the *Sūryasiddhānta.* However, we have no evidence of any of these systems being used as early as the third century A.D.
148. J. Fleet, "Sanskrit and Old Kanarese Inscriptions", No. 185—Mahākūṭa Pillar Inscription of Mangaleśa, *Indian Antiquary,* 19, 1890, pp. 7-20; *Bombay Gazeteer,* Vol. I, pt. 11. pp. 348-49.

149. Sircar, "More Inscriptions", pp. 4-7.
150. V.V. Mirashi, "Is Vijaya Mentioned in Nāgārjunakoṇḍa Inscriptions the Name of a Cyclic Year ?", *Journal of the Oriental Institute,* M.S. University of Baroda, Vol. 18, pt. 4, June 1969, pp. 318-22; Mirashi, "Epigraphic Notes", *Epigraphia Indica,* XXXVII, 1965-66, pp. 70-73.
151. B. Vidyadhara Rao, "Occurrence of Sexagenary Cycles in Two Inscriptions from Nāgārjunakoṇḍa", *Journal of the Oriental Institute,* M.S. University of Baroda, Vol. 18, pt. 4, June 1969, pp. 323-25.
152. For the various chronologies of the Ikṣvāku kings, see S. Dutt, *Buddhist Monks and Monasteries of India,* London, 1962, p. 25; D.C. Sircar, *The Successors of the Sātavāhanas in the Lower Deccan,* Calcutta, 1939, p. 390. This book contains Sircar's assessment of Ikṣvāku history before his reinterpretation of pillar inscription L. R. Subrahmanyam, *A Catalogue of Ikshvakus Coins of the Andhra Pradesh Government Museum,* (Andhra Pradesh Government Museum Series, No. 5), Hyderabad, 1962, p. 7; M. Rama Rao, *Ikṣvākus of Vijayapurī,* Tirupati, 1967, p. 19. A chronology containing the date of 273 A.D. as a possibility is given in R. Mukherjee, *The History of the Andhra Region c.* A.D. *75-*A.D. *350,* unpublished Ph.D. diss., University of London, 1965. This chronology is summarized by E. Rosen, *The History and Buddhist Architecture of Nāgārjunakoṇḍa,* unpublished M.A. thesis, New York University, 1970, p. 27.
In an attempt to give an approximate Ikṣvāku chronology, Sheila Weiner cites the fall of the Sātavāhana dynasty as c. A.D. 200. She is therefore left with a seventy year interval in which only the reign of Cāṁtamūla I can be placed. This extremely unlikely chronology is the inevitable result of accepting pillar inscription L as part of the Jovian cycle. Further, Dr. Weiner has omitted the fourth king of the Ikṣvāku dynasty, king Rudrapuruṣadatta. It is known that he ruled for at least eleven years, but there is no remaining space for this king in Dr. Weiner's chronology. See Sheila L. Weiner, *Ajantā: Its Place in Buddhist Art,* Berkeley, Los Angeles, London, 1977, pp. 17 and 119.
153. The term "mothers" refers to the fact that the Ikṣvāku kings had several wives. Most likely, one of them was mother of king Cāṁtamūla.
154. Experiments with the Amarāvatī sculptures in the British Museum have attempted to solve this problem. In 1973, the sculptures were placed in a humidity chamber, and within only few days, the original of the stone began to return. The stone then showed some of the greenish color usually associated with the site of Nāgārjunakoṇḍa.
155. H. Sastri, "Sanskrit Epigraphy", *Annual Report, Archaeological Survey of India, 1929-30,* p. 165.
156. Vogel, "Additional Prakrit Inscriptions", p. 62, inscription G 2.
157. See also for example, P. Stern and M. Bénisti, *Évolution du style indien d'Amarāvatī* (Publications du Musée Guimet, recherches et documents d'art et d' archéologie, t. VII), Paris, 1961, Pls. XXVb, LXIII. Douglas Barrett, *Sculptures from Amarāvatī in the British Museum,* London 1954, Pls. XX and XXXV.
158. Barrett, Pl. XXVII, female figures in the roundel portion of the pillar. Barrett's identification of this scene (p. 70) as representing Nanda and his beautiful wife seems to have no basis. This scene bears no relation to the well-known scenes of the

Conversion of Nanda from Nāgārjunakoṇḍa and Goli which will be discussed below. James Fergusson's identification of this roundel as representing the Harem at Kapilavastu seems more satisfactory. (J. Fergusson, *Tree and Serpent Worship,* reprint ed. Delhi and Varanasi, 1971, p. 175 and pl. LX right.)

159. Vogel, "Additional Prakrit Inscriptions", pp. 63-64. The expression *"hirana-koti-gosata-sahasa-hala-satasahasa-padayisa"* is equivalent to Sanskrit "*hiranya-koti-gośatasahasra-hala-śatasahasra-pradāyin",* but was left untranslated by Vogel in this inscription. It appears, however, in inscription G2, p. 62.
160. M. Rama Rao, *Ikṣvākus of Vijayapurī,* Tirupati, 1967, pp. 29-30.
161. "Nāgārjunakoṇḍa Inscriptions" in Hirananda Sastri, "Sanskrit Epigraphy", *Annual Report, Archaeological Survey of India, 1929-30,* pp. 165-66.
162. Sircar, "More Inscriptions", p. 3.
163. Sircar, "More Inscriptions", fig. 1A. For a list of the recurrence of this phrase, see the epigraphical glossary, p. 22 of Sircar's article.
164. M.S. Nagaraja Rao, "Brāhmī Inscriptions and their Bearing on the Great *Stūpa* at Sannati", in *Indian Epigraphy, eds.* Asher and Gai, pp. 41-45. These pillars are not *āyaka* pillars as had been suggested by M. Seshadri ("Buddhist Monuments in Mysore", *Artibus Asiae,* 34, 1972, pp. 169-70).
165. M.S. Nagaraja Rao, "Brāhmī Inscriptions", p. 43. This idea was elaborated upon in oral presentation.
166. *Indian Archaeology, A Review, 1964-65,* p. 25, reports the finds of a Buddha-*pada* and *a vihāra* showing affiliations with Amarāvatī and Nāgārjunakoṇḍa.
167. S. Krishnaswami Aiyangar, *The Maṇimēkhalai in its Historical Setting,* London, 1928, p. 25.
168. Sircar, "More Inscriptions", pp. 1-2, 13-17.
169. Sircar, "More Inscriptions", pp. 7-10, inscriptions 2A and B.
170. *Indian Archaeology, A Review, 1967-68,* p. 52.
171. H. Sarkar and B.N. Misra, *Nāgārjunakoṇḍa,* 2nd ed., New Delhi, 1972, p. 46.
172. A.H. Longhurst, "Excavations at Nāgārjunakoṇḍa", *Annual Report, Archaeological Survey of India, 1929-30,* pp. 149-51, and pl. XXXIX.
173. The theme of the evolution of railing motif at Amarāvatī has been studied by Stern and Bénisti (*Évolution du style,* pp. 11-20). The Nāgārjunakoṇḍa *āyaka* panel is evolved from the type illustrated in Stern and Bénisti, p. 19, fig. 14.
174. John Marshall, *The Buddhist Art of Gandhāra,* Cambridge, 1960, pls. 86 and 87.
175. At both of these sites, the motif is omnipresent. For clear illustrations see for example Heinrich Zimmer, *The Art of Indian Asia,* ed. Joseph Campbell, 2nd ed. New York, 1964, Vol. 2, pl. 9 (Sāñcī) and pl. 36 (Bharhut).
176. James Harle, *Gupta Sculpture,* Oxford, 1974, fig. 109 (Marhia) and fig. 104 (Deogarh).
177. An example of this may be seen on a sarcophagus in the Capotoline Museum, Rome, representing the Discovery of Achilles Amongst the Women and dating to the first decade of the third century A.D. (C. Robert, *Die Antiken Sarkophag-Reliefs,* Vol. 2, "Mythologische Cyklen", Rome, 1968, p. 36 and pl. 25.

178. For Bharhut examples see Ananda Coomaraswamy, *La Sculpture de Bharhut,* Paris 1956, pls. XXIV, fig. 64; XXV, fig. 65. For Sāñcī, see Zimmer, *The Art of Indian Asia,* pl. 23 (south gate, rear view, top architrave, inscribed Śātakarṇi panel).

179. For a summary of the form of the Andhra *stūpas* see Barrett, pp. 27-39.

180. K. Gopalachari, *Early History of the Andhra Country,* Madras 1941, p. 140, footnote 67; Stella Kramrisch, "The Four Cornered Citadel of the Gods", *Journal of the American Oriental Society,* 75, 1955, p. 185, footnote 13.

181. H. Sarkar and S.P. Nainar, *Amarāvatī,* New Delhi, 1972, pp. 11-13.

182. Longhurst, *Buddhist Antiquities,* p. 30.

183. John Marshall and Alfred Foucher, *The Monuments of Sanchi,* Calcutta, 1940, Vol. III, pls. LXXIV, 1a, 1b; LXXXII, 49a; LXXXVI, 66c, 71a; XCI, 88b.

184. Coomaraswamy, *Bharhut;* pls. VIII, fig. 24; XV, fig. 37.

185. Ananda Coomaraswamy, *La sculpture de Bodhgayā,* Paris, 1935, pls. XVIII, XVI, XXXIII.

186. Zimmer, *The Art of Indian Asia,* Vol. 2, pl. 80.

187. Devangana Desai, *Erotic Sculpture of India: A Socio-Cultural Study,* New Delhi, 1975, p. 24; and James Fergusson and James Burgess, *The Cave Temples of India,* 1880, reprint ed. Delhi, 1969, pl. 20.

188. The *stūpa* railing, as well as the exterior of the *caitya* halls, would correspond to the *kāma-dhātu* or "Realm of desire", A. Wayman, "The Role of Art Among the Buddhist Religieux", *East-West Dialogues in Aesthetics,* ed. Kenneth K. Inada, Buffalo, N.Y., 1978, p. 5.

189. Longhurst, *Buddhist Antiquities,* p. 16.

190. H. Sarkar, *Studies in Early Buddhist Architecture of India,* Delhi, 1966, p. 80.

191. Andrew Oilver, *Silver for the Gods,* Toledo, 1977, p. 157. The Indian artist, of course, chose to vary his source, for when copying a bronze of this type, he added Indian anklets to the figure. An inscription beneath the Amarāvatī example reads as follows: Adoration to the sun, the truly enlightened one, the chief of men, the best (of all beings)! The gift of Nākhā, the wife of the lay worshipper, the Nārasala, the merchant (Nāgatishya) with her two sons, the goldsmith Budhi, Mūla . . . (Burgess, *Amarāvatī and Jaggayyapeta,* p. 82.)

The association of this piece of sculpture with a merchant is not surprising, since such objects as the Toledo statue were carried into India by merchant traders.

192. Karl Khandalavala, "Brahmapuri: A Consideration of Metal Objects Found in the Kundangar Hoard", *Lalit Kala* 7, 1960, figs. 14 and 15. These mirrors, according to Khandalavala, are probably of Alexandrian workmanship. Khandalavala's fig. 17 is a Sātavāhana copy of this type. Originally they probably had ivory handles, perhaps of the type recently unreathed at Ter (Prince of Wales Museum, Bombay, *Dawn of Civilization in Maharashtra,* Bombay, 1975, pl. 61).

193. Illustrated in J. Auboyer, "Ancient Indian Ivories from Begram", *Journal of the Indian Society of Oriental Art,* XVI, figs, 73, 74 and 75. For a Roman example found at Pompeii see J. Hackin, *Nouvelles rescherches archéologique á Begram,* (Memoires de la délégation archéologique française en Afghanistan T. XI), Paris, 1954, Vol. 2, fig. 392.

194. R.C. Sharma, *Mathura Museum Introduction,* Mathura, 1971, fig. XL. For Classical versions of this type, see S. Reinach, *Répetoire de la statuaire grecque et romaine,* T. H, V. 1, 3rd ed., Paris, 1904-30, p. 343.
195. For variants of this type, see Guntram Koch, *Die Mythologischen Sarcophage,* Teil 6, *Meleager,* 12, Bd., Berlin, 1975.
196. Longhurst, "Excavations", 1929-30, p. 151.
197. This comparison was very loosely suggested to me by Wayman's article, "The Role of Art", p. 1; for the Bharhut example see Coomaraswamy, *Bharhut,* fig. 61.
198. Many of the principles of the Andhra style have been carefully described by Stella Kramrisch in 1933. To date, her chapter on "Classical Sculpture" of India stilll contains the only discussion of the style of this region, the other works being restricted mainly to questions of motif analysis, epigraphy, or archaeology. See Stella Kramrisch, *Indian Sculpture,* Calcutta, 1933, particularly pp. 46-53.
199. Douglas Barrett, *Amaravati,* p. 73, No. 116, reports that this piece bears an unpublished inscription. Neither my own photographs nor notes could validate this fact. Mr. Wladimir Zwalf of the British Museum has kindly examined the piece for me. Zwalf writes, ". . . there is nothing that I can in all conscience call an inscription." The only possibility that Zwalf could suggest is that the inscription may have existed on the bottom, but there is no evidence to confirm this notion. (Wladimir Zwalf, personal correspondence, July 15, 1980.) The notion of an inscription on this piece has been tantalizing to me. The stylistic similarity between this piece and *āyaka* panel 2 is so close, that one would expect such an inscription to show Ikṣvāku characteristics.
200. James Fergusson, *Tree and Serpent Worship,* reprint ed., Delhi, 1971, p. 207 and pls. LXXXIV, 2 and 3.
201. For example, see Marshall, *Gandhāra,* pl. 47.
202. D. Facenna. *Sculptures from the Sacred Area of Bhutkara I (Swat, Pakistan),* Istituto Italiano per il Medio ed Estremo Oriente, Centro studi e Scavi Archeologici in Asia, Reports and Memoirs, Vol. II, pt. 2, pl. CCXXXIX; Vol II, pt. 3, pl. CCCLVIII.
203. I thank Mr. B.V. Shetti for pointing out these images to me on a trip to Kaṇheri Caves taken in 1971.
204. Marilyn Leese, "The Early Buddhist Icons in Kanheri's Cave 3", *Artibus Asiae* 41, No. 1, p. 83.
205. Recent excavations at Amarāvatī, conducted by Dr. R. Subrahmanyam have yielded the remains of another small *stūpa* about one mile from the great *stūpa* give us further evidence of the extent of the Buddhist settlement of about the second century B.C. R. Subrahmanyam, "On the Utilization of Epigraphs for Art History", *Indian Epigraphy,* eds. Asher and Gai, pp. 25-26. See also, H. Sarkar and S.P. Nainar, *Amaravati,* New Delhi, 1972, pp. 11-14.
206. Barrett, *Amaravati.*
207. *The Mahāvastu,* Vol. II, tr. J.J. Jones, *Sacred Books of the Buddhists,* Vol. XVIII, London, 1976, p. 172.
208. See also, Barrett, *Amaravati,* p. XXVII.
209. *Mahāvastu,* p. 173.

210. Longhurst, "Excavations", p. 151.
211. For a discussion of the Amarāvatī Conversion of Kasyapa, see M. Bénisti, "Les stūpa aux cinq piliers", *Bulletin de l'école français d'Extreme Orient,* Vol. 58, 1971, p. 143.
212. Longhurst, "Excavations", pl. XL c and d.
213. Barrett, *Amaravati,* pp. 49-50.
214. Stern and Bénisti, *Évolution du style,* pp. 9-16; P. Stern and M. Bénisti, "Évolution du *stupa* figurée dans les sculptures d'Amarāvatī", *Bulletin de la sociéte des études indochinois,* Vol. XXVII, no. 4, 1952, pp. 1-7.
215. Longhurst, *Buddhist Antiquities,* pp. 13-14.
216. Stern and Bénisti, *Évolution du style,* p. 76.
217. Barrett, *Amaravati,* p. 74, No. 121. This piece appears to have been only illustrated once in a very small photograph by Fergusson, *Tree and Serpent Worship,* pl. XCIII.
218. For example, Barett, *Amaravati.* pl. XLIV.
219. A. Rea, "Excavations at Amaravati", *Annual Report, Archaeological Survey of India, 1905-06,* p. 6.
220. The difference between the late Andhra figural style and the early traditions is sometimes confusing. However, the earlier style always shows a more abrupt articulation of limbs (Burgess, *Amaravati and Jaggayapeta,* pl. LV, 3), while the later style, as depicted at Nāgārjunakoṇḍa, almost always reveals a careful transition between the parts of the body, showing a knowledge of Western *contraposto* known in Andhra Pradesh since the middle phase of Amarāvatī.
221. T.N. Ramachandran, *Buddhist Sculptures from a Stūpa near Goli Village,* Bulletin of the Madras Government Museum, New Series, Vol. I, pt. 1, 1929, p. 1.
222. Ramachandran, *Goli,* p. 41, pl. X.
223. The fragment is a small frieze representing alternate seated Buddha figures and *stūpa.* Illustrated by D. Mitra, "Observations on Buddhist Remains at Jaggayapeta", *Indian Historical Quarterly* 35, No. 3, 1959, fig. 2. Similar panels from Amarāvatī are illustrated by Burgess, *Amaravati and Jaggayapeta,* pl. XLIII, no. 3-13.
224. Burgess, *Amaravati and Jaggayapeta,* pp. 110-11.
225. I thank H. Sarkar for pointing out this inscriptional evidence to me. *Annual Report of Indian Epigraphy,* 8 of 1957-58.
226. Most of these panels were approximately of equal size. Their numbers varied according to the size of the *stūpa.*
227. Other examples of this type have been illustrated in line drawing by Jeannine Auboyer and Jean-François Enault in *La vie publique et privée dans l'Inde ancienne,* Fascicule I, *L'architecture civile et religieuse,* Publications du Musée Guimet, recherches et documents d'art et d'archéologie, T. VI, Paris, 1969, pl. 29.
228. John Irwin, "The Stūpa and the Cosmic Axis: The Archaeological Evidence", *South Asian Archaeology 1977.* Papers from the Fourth International Conference of South Asian Archaeologists in Western Europe, Naples, 1979, pp. 825-33 and figs. 19-22.
229. G. Roth, "Symbolism of the Buddhist Stūpa", in A.L. Dallapiccola, ed., *The Stūpa: Its Religious, Historical and Architectural Significance,* (Beiträge zur Südasienforshung, Bd. 55.) Wiesbaden, 1980, pp. 201-02.

230. Sarkar, *Buddhist Architecture,* pp. 84-90. Sarkar here has no real clear idea of the meaning, but it is clear that the spokes are suggestive of both a symbolic and a structural meaning.
231. For an excellent discussion of the equivalency of the different aniconic symbols of the Buddha being equal to the image itself, see M. Bénisti, "Les Stūpa aux cinq piliers", *Bulletin de l'école francais d'Extreme Orient,* Vol. 58, 1971, pp. 140-45.
232. Longhurst, *Buddhist Antiquities,* p. 24; *The Jātaka,* ed. E.B. Cowell, London 1895, reprint 1973, Vol III, pp. 34-37 (No. 316).
233. Sircar, "More Inscriptions", p. 19, No.1.
234. For Sitala Ghati and Set Mahet images see respectively L. Bachhofer, *Early Indian Sculpture,* reprinted ed., New York, 1972, pls. 84 left and right respectively.
235. Barrett, *Amaravati,* pp. 57-59.
236. M. Dimand, "Two Reliefs from the Amarāvatī School", *Bulletin of the Metropolitan Museum of Art,* Vol. XXIII, No. 10, October 1928, p. 238.
237. R. Grousset, "The Great Periods of Indian Art", *Indian Art and Letters,* N.S., Vol.I, No. 2, 1927, pp. 104-09.
238. A. Rea, *South Indian Buddhist Antiquities,* Archaeological Survey of India, New Imperial Series, Vol. IV, Madras, 1894, pl. XXVIII.
239. Dimand, "Two Indian Reliefs", p. 238.
240. Kuraishi, "Trial Excavations", p. 160.
241. Longhurst, "Excavations", pp. 145-46.
242. Bénisti, "Les Stūpas", p. 143.
243. T.O. Ling, *A Dictionary of Buddhism,* New York, 1972, pp. 50-51.
244. Wayman and Wayman, *The Lion's Roar,* p. 1.
245. Bénisti, pp. 135-36.
246. Bénisti, pp. 151-53.
247. Bénisti, pp. 158 and 162.
248. Bénisti, p. 168 citing A. Bareau, *Les sectes bouddhiques du Petit Véhicule*, Saigon, 1955, p. 302.
249. In the Śaivite expression *par excellence,* the great Śiva cave at Elephanta, the triple level of experiencing deity is most clearly expressed: the *liṅga* (transcendental), sadāśiva (manifest in the cosmic directions), and the reliefs of the *līlā mūrti* (Śiva in his play). It would thus appear that the Śaivite triple view of anthropomorphic deity and the Buddhist *trikāya* notion may somehow be interconnected. Further investigation will show that this concept had a wide reaching function in the development of Indian art. But a further point may be relevant for our further study. The Ikṣvāku kings of Nāgārjunakoṇḍa were Śaivites, while their wives supported the Buddhist faith. It is particularly at this site where there must have been a great cross-fertilization of ideas. (For a thorough understanding of the Śaiva cave at Elephanta, see Stella Kramrisch, *The Presence of Śiva,* Princeton, 1981, appendix.)
250. Longhurst, *Buddhist Antiquities,* p. 29 and p. XXVII c.
251. J.Ph. Vogel, "The Man in the Well and Some Other Subjects Illustrated at Nāgārjunīkoṇḍa", *Revue des arts asiatiques,* Vol. XI, No. 3, Sept. 1937, pp. 119-21.

252. Longhurst, "Excavations", p. 145.
253. C.T. Loo & Co., *Exposition de sculpture et bronzes anciens de l'Inde* (14 Juin au 31 Juillet 1935), Paris, 1935, pl. IV, No. 7, p. 5.
254. H. Sarkar, Chronological Aspects of Mason's Marks from Nāgārjunakoṇḍa", *Bharati, Bulletin of the Department of Ancient History, Culture and Archaeology,* 1968-71, No. 12-14, pp. 226-35.
255. Kramrisch, *Indian Sculpture,* p. 211.
256. *Indian Archaeology, A Review 1958-59,* p. 6 reports an inscription found at Site 9 reading "Kumara Siri-Vira . . .". This is interpreted to refer to Vīrapuruṣadatta. But if this were the case, then Vīrapuruṣadatta would have been a prince *(kumarasa)* and not the reigning monarch, thus putting the inscription back to the time of Cāṁtamūla I. The inscription, as recorded by D.C. Sircar, "*More Inscriptions*", p. 20, reads "Si dha m . . .Kumarasa Vira-Ar ibha". Though it has a slight similarity to the name of Vīrapuruṣadatta, we would not venture to say that the inscription belongs to the monarch. But the problem of the inscription is somewhat irrelevant, because based on stylistic considerations, the *stūpa* more than likely went back to the time of Cāṁtamūla I.
257. Sircar, "*More Inscriptions*", pp. 10-11.
258. R. Subrahmanyam, "On the Utilization of Epigraphs for Art History: Some Andhra Examples", in *Indian Epigraphy,* eds. Asher and Gai, p. 27.
259. Subrahmanyam, "*Epigraphs*", p. 27.
260. Sircar, "More Inscriptions", pp. 11-13.
261. Barrett, *Amarāvatī,* pl. XXV.
262. Sarkar, *Buddhist Architecture,* p. 88.
263. Stern and Bénisti, *Evolution du style* p. 14, fig. 9.
264. Harle, *Gupta Sculpture,* pl. 70.
265. Philippe Stern, *Colonnes indiennes d'Ajantā et d'Ellora,* Publications du Musée Guimet, Recherches d' art et d' archéologie, T. XI, Paris, 1972, fig. 76 for Aurangabad III; Zimer, *The Art of Indian Asia,* pl. 131 (Bādāmī, Cave III) pl. 227 (Ellora, Rameśavara Cave).
266. Published in fragmentary condition by Longhurst, *Buddhist Antiquities,* pl. XIV b; for the Amarāvatī pillar see Barett pl. XXI.
267. Published in fragmentary condition by Longhurst, *Buddhist Antiquities,* pl. XIV c and XIVa respectively.
268. *Indian Archaeology, A Review, 1959-60,* p. 67; N.P. Chakravarti, "Summary of Epigraphical Work during 1933-34", *Annual Report, Archaeological Survey of India 1933-34,* pp. 238-39.
269. D.C. Sircar, *Successors of the Sātavāhanas in the Lower Deccan,* Calcutta, 1933, p. 35.
270. Traces of red pigment can be seen on a Buddha image currently preserved in the Amarāvatī Museum. This may indicate that the Buddha images, or even all the sculpture, were painted red. Stucco fragments were found extensively at Nāgārjunakoṇḍa. Pigment must have been used to provide a visual cohesiveness

between the stone and stucco parts. But the style of the sculpture seems to require considerably more "help" than monochromatic painting would have provided. With new sites continually being excavated in Andhra Pradesh, we expect to one day find evidence of the use of polychromy.

271. Jorinde Ebert, "*Parinirvāṇa and Stūpa: Was the Stūpa only a 'Symbolical' Depiction of the Parinirvāṇa ?*", in Dallapiccola, *The Stūpa*, p. 221 and fig. 2A. This fragment originally, belonged to the same piece of sculpture as Ebert fig. 1.
272. Ebert, p. 220; A. Bareau, "La construction et le culte du stūpa d'après les *Vinayapiṭaka", Bulletin de l'école français d'Extreme Orient,* Vol. 50, fasc. 2, p. 269.
273. Ebert, p. 220.
274. It has been suggested to me by Douglas Barrett that this piece is from Amarāvatī.
275. Aschwin Lippe, *The Art of India: Stone Sculpture,* New York, 1962, fig. 26.
276. This appears to be the panel found at Site 3 and illustrated in a miniscule photograph by Longhurst in *Buddhist Antiquities,* p. XVa.
277. Vogel, "Man in the Well", pp. 115-18.
278. E.H. Johnston, ed. and trans., *The Saundarānanda of Aśvaghoṣa,* Lahore, 1921 (reprint ed., Delhi, 1975).
279. C. Sivaramamurti, *Sanskrit Literature and Art-Mirrors of Indian Culture,* Memoirs of the Archaeological Survey of India, Vol. 73, New Delhi, 1970, p. 13.
280. Sivaramamurti, pp. 15-16.
281. See: C. Sivaramamurti, *Amaravati Sculptures in the Madras Government Museum,* Bullletin of the Madras Government Museum, N.S. IV, 1942, pp. 254-55 and pl. LXII.
282. See: W. Begley, "The Identification of the Ajantā Fragment in the Boston Museum", *Oriental Art,* XIV, no. 1, Spring 1968, pp. 25-32.
283. A.K. Coomaraswamy, *Yakṣas,* reprint ed., New Delhi, 72, part 2, 37, No. 5.
284. Hackin, *Nouvelles recherches,* fig. 57.
285. Regarding the artist's visual source, we are inclined to think that it was nothing other than horse. A rearing *śārdūla* (Hackin, *Nouvelles, recherches,* fig. 156) issues forth from a *makara* in an ivory bracket from Begram. This is the only visual comparison we have been able to find for one animal issuing forth from another. But a rearing lion, upon which this figure seems to be based, has many examples in the West and Near East. It seems to be best illustrated in a rearing lion found at Taxila, which originally formed the handle of a censer (R. Ghirshman, *Parthes et Sassanides,* 1962, pl. 41C). A similar object must have been in the hands of the Nāgārjunakoṇḍa sculptor at the time this unique representation was being made. (See also: Smithsonian Institution, *7,000 Years of Iranian Art,* Washington, 1964, pl. 427.) Earlier examples of this type (2nd century B.C.) may by observed on ivory *rhyta* from Nysa (Ghirshman, pl. 41). The artists from Nysa must have had some contact with Indian art for one of the *rhyta* is decorated with a clearly Indian elephant (G. Herrmann, *The Iranian Revival,* Oxford, 1977, p. 46).
286. A.H. Longhurst, "Excavations at Nāgārjunikoṇḍa", *Annual Report, Archaeological Survey of India, 1927-28,* p. 121, pls. LI, LI(a), and LII. Hereafter referred to as "Excavations 1927-28".

287. A.H. Longhurst, "Excavations at Nāgārjunikoṇḍa", *Annual Report, Archaeological Survey of India, 1928-29,* p. 104, pls. XLVII-XLIX. Hereafter referred to as "Excavations 1928-29".
288. Longhurst, *Buddhist Antiquities,* pl. XXVI(b). The other half of this panel is published by Longhurst, *Buddhist Antiquities,* pl. XXIIIc.
289. Longhurst, "Excavations 1928-29", pl. XLVIII, XLIX(a).
290. For example, Barrett, pl. XXa.
291. The artist of this work seems to have been cognizant of the Andhra Pradesh scene of the same subject in the Boston Museum, which we would attribute to Ghantaśāla, a site which would benefit from further study. See A.K. Coomaraswamy, "Andhra Sculptures", *Bulletin of the Museum of Fine Art,* Boston, Vol. 27, 1929, p. 22.
292. The top panel was identified by M. Bussagli, "Eine nicht gedeutete Figur aus Nāgārjunakoṇḍa", *Artibus Asiae,* Vol. VIII, 1940-45, pp. 258-64, before it was attached to the bottom two panels.
293. S. Lee, *Ancient Sculpture from India,* Cleveland, 1964, fig. 146.
294. Zimmer, *Indian Asia,* pl. 130.
295. This has been recorded as coming from Site 2 in Longhurst, "Excavations 1927-28", p. 21; and as Site 3 in Longhurst, *Buddhist Antiquities,* caption to pl. XXVI(b).
296. Sivaramamurti provides a lovely but late literary parallel for this panel:

 "Those (damsels) shone like rivers with their flowing stream of love filling the deep nave lake and flowing past the soft line of hairs above it, with the jingling of the anklets resounding like swans as they moved with graceful sway." (Śiśupāla, VII.23).

 As Sivaramamurti puts it, the damsels here are actually "swimming in the stream of love". (Sivaramamurti, *Sanskrit Literature,* p. 28.)
297. Compare fig. 187 to the same scene represented on a late Amarāvatī drum frieze, published by Jeanning Auboyer, *Introduction à l'étude de l'art de l'Inde,* Serie Orientale Roma XXXI, Rome, 1965, pl. XXIII.
298. For types from Gandhāra and Mathurā, see Dieter Schlingloff, "Der König mit dem Schwert: Die Identifizierung einer Ajantā Malerei", *Wiener Zeitschrift für die Kunde Südasiens,* XXI, 1977, figs. 3 and 5.
299. J. Ph. Vogel, *Indian Serpent Lore,* 1926 (reprint ed., Varanasi, 1972, pp. 121-23); Longhurst, *Buddhist Antiquities,* pp. 45-46.
300. For contrast, see N.P. Joshi, *Gandhāra Sculptures in the State Museum,* Lucknow, 1969, fig. 20.
301. A.C. Soper, "Aspects of Light Symbolism in Gandharan Sculptures, III", *Artibus Asiae,* 13, 1950, p. 72.
302. For a classical variant of this type of cave, see H. Buchthal, "The Western Aspects of Gandhara Sculpture", *Proceedings of the British Academy,* Vol. XXXI, fig. 39. The ideal place for the Nāgārjunakoṇḍa artist to have borrowed from would be Swat; the surviving example of the Submission of Apalāla in Swat is too fragmentary to consider. Facenna, *Bhutkara,*Vol. II, part 2, pl. CVII.
303. T.N. Ramachandran, "Nāgārjunakoṇḍa, 1938", *Memoirs of the Archaeological Survey of India,* 71, Delhi, 1953, p. 23 and pl. XXXIIIb.

304. Longhurst, *Buddhist Antiquities*, p. 61 and pl. L.

305. For the various types of Sārnāth Gupta Buddhist narrative stelae, see Joanna Williams, "Sārnāth Gupta Steles of the Buddha's Life", *Art Orientalis* X, 1975, pp. 171-92. See also Patricia Eichenbaum Karetzky, "The Art of Pilgrimage and Guptan Steles with Scenes from the Life of the Buddha", *Oriental Art,* XXIII, 1987, 268-74.

306. J. Hackin, *Recherches archéologiques á Begram,* (Memoires de la délégation archéologique française en Afghanistan, tome IX), Paris, 1939, Vol. II, pls. IV-XXVII; J. Hackin, *Nouvelles recherches,* figs. 250-358.

307. K. Khandalavala, "Brahmapuri: A Consideration of the Metal Objects Found in the Kundangar Hoard", *Lalit Kala,* Vol. VII, 1960, pp., 56-62.

308. K. Khandalavala, "Brahmapuri", pl, XV, fig. 12; pl. XXV, fig. 59 and p. 69.

309. M.N. Deshpande, "Classical Influence on Indian Terracotta Art", *Huitième congrés international d' archéologie classique , Paris, 1963,* Paris, 1965, pp. 603-10; E. Rosen, "The Begram Ivories", *Marsyas,* Vol. XVII, 1974-75, p. 42.

310. *Indian Archaeology, A Review, 1955-56,* p. 24. This pillar is discussed in an article by E. Rosen, "A Dated Memorial Pillar from Nāgārjunakoṇḍa", in *Indian Epigraphy,* eds. Asher and Gai, pp. 35-40.

311. H. Sarkar, *Buddhist Architecture,* p. 81 and p. XIII.

312. See note 310.

313. D.C. Sircar and K.G. Krishnan, "Two Inscriptions from Nāgārjunakoṇḍa", *Epigraphia Indica,* XXXIV, 1961-62, pp. 20-22.

314. See for example *āyaka* pillar inscription C3 in J.Ph. Vogel, "Prakrit Inscriptions from a Buddhist Site at Nāgārjunakoṇḍa,"*Epigraphia Indica,* XX, 1929-30, pp. 15-17. For the significance of these inscriptions see E. Rosen, "Buddhist Architecture and Lay Patronage at Nāgārjunakoṇḍa", *The Stūpa: Its Religious, Historical and Architectural Significance,* ed. A.L. Dallapiccola, (Beiträge zur Südasienforschung; Bd. 55), Wiesbaden, 1980, pp. 114-15.

315. D. Barrett, *Amaravati,* p. 72; Aśvaghoṣa, *Saundarānanda,* Canto X, 3, p. 54.

316. *Indian Archaeology, A Review, 1957-58,* p. 9.

317. P.L. Gupta, *Roman Coins from Andhra Pradesh,* pp. 6, 74-75.

318. E. Rosen "Begram", p. 42, pl XIII.

319. Iḷango-aḍigaḷ, *The Śilappadikāram (The Ankle Bracelet),* trans. with introduction and notes by V.R. Ramachandra Dikshitar, Oxford, 1939, p. 201. According to Dikshitar (p. 201, footnote 6), the term *yavana* may be a reference to Greeks. However, he feels that the term applies equally well to all foreigners. Such foreigners were employed by Tamil kings for military service.

In another passage of the *Śilappadikāram* (p. 128) the existence of seaborne trade is cited. In reference to the ancient city of Puhār, the author states:

> "In these stretches of white sand can be seen different kinds of goods brought in ships by foreign merchants, who have left their native homes and settled here."

Ancient Puhār is modern Kaveripattinam. The excavations of Buddhist material at that site show that there was an affiliation between the ancient port city and Amarāvatī and Nāgārjunakoṇḍa (*Indian Archaeology, A Review, 1964-65,* p. 25, pls. XVII-XVIII).

The date of the *Śilappadikāram* is a matter of dispute. Although traditionally belonging to the second or third century A.D., Kamil Zvelebil (*Mehfil,* Vol. IV, no. 3-4, 1968, pp. 1-12) places it between the end of the fifth and the beginning of the seventh centuries A.D. However, even if the text is late, it seems to represent a historical situation of an earlier time, and remains a good source for South Indian cultural history. See also E. Rosen, Review of Prince Iḷango Aḍigaḷ, *Śhilappadikāram (The Ankle Bracelet),* translated by Alain Daniélou, in *Artibus Asiae,* Vol. 37, No. 1-2, 1975, pp. 148-50.

320. Khandalavala, "Brahmapuri", fig. 7.
321. Khandalavala, "Brahmapuri", p. 60.
322. For example see Barrett, *Amarāvatī,* pl. XI; A.H. Longhurst, *Buddhist Antiquities,* pls. XXVIIIb, XXXVa.
323. In the early part of the century, the mirror was cited by H.B. Walters as being of Roman workmanship (H.B. Walters, *Catalogue of the Silver Plate* (Greek, Etruscan, and Roman) in the British Museum, London, 1921, p. 16, No. 71). Later scholarship places it into the Hellenistic period (D.E. Strong, *Greek and Roman Silver Plate,* London, 1966, p. 104, pl. 29B). Although the date of the mirror seems still open to question, its precise date is, in this instance, not crucial to our argument. For it is this type of representation which must have seen in India, not this specific example. (Illustrated in Rosen, "A Dated Memorial pillar", fig. 46.)
324. See C. Robert, *Die Antiken Sarkophag Reliefs,* Vol. 3, No. 1, *Einzelmythen,* Rome, 1969, pl. 2, figs. 3, 4, 5 and 10.
325. Khandalavala, "Brahmapuri", 49ff; D. Barrett, *Ter,* Bombay, 1960, pp. 3-5.
326. A. Wayman, "A Jotting on the Mirror: Those of Ladies", *Mehfil,* Vol. VII (1971), pp. 209-12; "Mirror-Like Knowledge in Mahāyāna Buddhist Literature", *Asiatische Studien,* Vol. 25 (1971), pp. 353-63; "The Mirror as a Pan-Buddhist Metaphor-Simile", *History of Religious,* Vol. 13, 1974, pp. 251-69; "Notes on Mirror Words and Entities in the Area of India", *Ural-Altaische Jahrbücher,* Bd. 47, 1955, pp. 204-06.
327. Wayman, "The Mirror as a Metaphor-Simile", p. 263.
328. Wayman, "The Mirror as a Metaphor-Simile", p. 263; and U. Wogihara and C. Tsuchida, eds., *Saddharmapuṇḍarīka-sūtram,* Tokyo, 1936, Chapter 18, verse 62.
329. Wayman, "The Mirror as a Metaphor-Simile", p. 264.
330. See also E. Rosen, "Begram", pp. 39-48.
331. *Indian Archaeology, A Review, 1955-56,* p. 24, Sarkar and Misra, pp. 25 and 60.
332. Philippe Stern, *Colonnes Indiennes d'Ajantā et d'Ellora,* Publications du Musée Guimet, Recherches et Documents d'Art et d'Archélogie, Tome XI, Paris, 1972, fig. 27.
333. Stern, *Colonnes,* figs. 13, 39-43.
334. Stern, *Colonnes,* figs, 37, 53, 64. Ghulam Yazdani, *Ajantā,* Oxford, 1931-46, Vol. IV, pl. 2.
335. Stern, *Colonnes,* fig. 41.
336. Yazdani, *Ajantā,* Vol. II, pl. Xb.
337. Ajanta Cave XVII, Odette Viennot, *Les divinités fluviales Gaṅgā et Yamunā,* Publication du Musée Guimet, recherches et documents d'art et d'archéologie, tome X, Paris, 1964,

pl. IVb; Bhumara, Pramod Chandra, *Stone Sculpture in the Allahabad Museum,* Poona, n.d., fig. 124.

338. For example, it is well-known through an inscription that a Buddhist lay worshipper named Bodhisiri (one of the important benefactresses at Nāgārjunakoṇḍa) contributed "a stone *mandava* at the eastern gate of the Great *Caitya* at Kaṇṭakasela (= Sanskrit, Kaṇṭakaśaila)". J.Ph. Vogel, "Prakrit Inscriptions from Nāgārjunakoṇḍa", *Epigraphia Indica,* XX, 1929-30, p. 23. D.C. Sircar has suggested that this is most likely the Great *Caitya* at Ghantaśāla. D.C. Sircar, *Successors of the Sātavāhanas in the Lower Deccan,* Calcutta, 1939, p. 33.
339. A study of these smaller sites grew partly out of a sense of frustration. For when museums and scholars generously supplied me with photographs of various Andhra works for inclusion in my Nāgārjunakoṇḍa study, I found it impossible to place them within the Nāgārjunakoṇḍa *oeuvre,* but could not in good conscience eliminate them, for they were clearly of importance and deserved to be assigned to their original sites.
340. Debala Mitra, *Buddhist Monuments,* Calcutta, 1971, p. 212.
341. Kuraishi, "Trial Excavations", p. 156.
342. Mitra, p. 315.
343. Mitra, p. 212.
344. Pratapaditya Pal, "South Indian Sculptures in the Museum", *Bulletin of the Los Angeles County Museum of Art,* Vol. XXII, 1976, p. 30.
345. Pal, pp. 30-34.
346. Kuraishi, p. 154, footnote 9.
347. Kuraishi, pl. XXXa.
348. Pal, pl. XXIII, no. 3.
349. Kuraishi, p. 154.
350. Kuraishi, pl. XXXVIa.
351. Mitra, *Buddhist Monuments,* p. 212.
352. My interest in the Metropolitan Goli fragment began some years ago when I was asked to provide an article for the Dr. Moti Chandra Memorial issue of the *Bulletin of the Prince of Wales Museum.* The article, "Observations on Some Buddhist Sculptures from Goli Village", is still in press. I wish to thank Mr. Martin Lerner of the Metropolitan Museum of Art for graciously allowing me continuous access to the Goli piece as well as the other Andhra works in the store-rooms.
353. T.N. Ramachandran, "Buddhist Sculptures from a Stūpa Near Goli Village", *Bulletin of the Madras Government Museum,* N.S., Vol. 1, pt. 1, Madras, 1929.
354. R. Sewell, *List of Antiquarian Remains in Madras Presidency,* Madras, 1882, p. 60.
355. *Ibid,* p. 60.
356. T.N. Ramachandran, *Goli,* pl. XII.
357. Ramachandran, p. 2.
358. Ramachandran, pl. IV bottem, pl. V and pl. VI.
359. M.S. Dimand, "A New Relief of the Amarāvatī School", *Bulletin of the Metropolitan Museum of Art,* Vol. 25, 1930, p. 131; and "An Indian Relief of the Amarāvatī School", *Bulletin of the Metropolitan Museum of Art,* Vol. 28, 1933, p. 125.

360. R.N. Ramachandran, *Goli,* p. 7.
361. Debala Mitra, "A Frieze from Goli in the Metropolitan Museum of Art, New York", *Damilica* (Journal of the Tamil Nadu State Department of Archaeology), Vol. II, pt. 3, 1973, pp. 19-20, pl. I.
362. Mireille Bénisti, "Un Relief inedit de l'Āndhradésa", *Arts asiatiques,* Vol. IV, 1957, pp. 299-307, figs. 1-2.
363. See, for example, the Sikri *Stūpa,* A. Foucher, *L'Art gréco-bouddhique du Gandhara,* Paris, 1905, fig. 73. See also figs. 157, 158, etc.
364. Both the Goli and Nāgārjunakoṇḍa pieces have already been pointed out by Wayne Begley as prototypes for the Conversion of Nanda in Cave XVI at Ajantā. Because his article was mainly concerned with an Ajantā problem, he was not aware of the great differences between the two Andhra versions and that it was Goli which was a better source for the Ajantā painting. (See Wayne Begley, "The Identification of the Ajantā Fragment in the Boston Museum", *Oriental Art,* Vol. XIV, No. 1, Spring 1968, pp. 25-32.)
365. Begley, p. 27, fig. 3.
366. Domenico Facenna, *Sculptures from the Sacred Area of Bhutkara (Swat, W. Pakistan), Istituto Italiano per il Medio ed Estremo Oriente, Reports and Memoirs,* Vol. 2, No. 2, Rome, 1962, pl. CXLII.
367. This convention may be seen as early as Cave IX (G. Yazdani, *Ajantā,* 4 Vols., Oxford, 1931-46; Vol 3, pl. XVa) and continue into Cave XVI (Vol. 3, pl. LI) and XVII (Vol. 3, pl. LXII; Vol. 4, pl. XXV), and as late as Cave 1 (Vol. 1, pl. XVa) and Cave II (Vol. 2, pls. VII, XXXa and b).
368. Begley, fig. 2.
369. *An Exhibition of the Sculpture of Greater India,* C.T. Loo & Co., New York, 1942, pp. 31-32; E.B. Cowell, *The Jātaka,* London, 1879, Vol. 34, pp. 17-18, No. 308.
370. Published as Amarāvatī School, probably from Nāgārjunakoṇḍa, in Stainslaw Czuma, *Indian Art from the George P. Bickford Collection,* Cleveland, 1975, No. 5.
371. This has been attributed by Pal to Nāgārjunakoṇḍa (?), "South Indian Sculptures", fig. 1.
372. Faccenna, pls. CCX, CCXI.
373. Harle, *Gupta Sculpture,* figs. 70 and 75 for the Garhwā lintel; Joanna Williams, *The Art of the Gupta Empire,* Princeton, 1982, pls. 241 and 242 for the pillars.
374. My interest in the Begram ivories first arose in 1973, when the late Dr. Moti Chandra urged me to go to Afghanistan to see them. My first impressions were in fact that the ivories and the sculptural production of Nāgārjunakoṇḍa were closely allied. From this visit eventually arose my article "The Begram Ivories", *Marsyas* XVII, 1974-75, pp. 39-48.
375. Samuel Beal, *Buddhist Records of the Western World,* London 1884, reprint edition, Delhi, 1969, pp. 6-7.
376. *M.D.A.F.A.* IX, p. 22.
377. J. Hackin, *Nouvelles recherches archélogique à Begram,* 1939-40, *M.D.A.F.A.* XI, Paris, 1954.

378. *M.D.A.F.A.* IX, pp. 3-4; John Rosenfield, *The Dynastic Arts of the Kushans*, Berkeley and Los Angeles, 1967, p. 47.
379. *M.D.A.F.A.* IX, pp. 5-7.
380. R. Ghirshman, *Begram, M.D.A.F.A.* XII, Paris, 1946, pp. 99-100.
381. *M.D.A.F.A.* XI, p. 15.
382. *M.D.A.F.A.* XII, p. 99.
383. Beal, p. 54.
384. *Nāgārjunakoṇḍa, 1938,* pls. XVIa and b.
385. Vogel, "Prakrit Inscriptions", p. 23.
386. Illustrated in Fergusson, *Tree and Serpent Worship,* pl. LXXXV right.
387. The notion of an Indian style combined with a foreign technique has architectural parallels in the "arena" at Nāgārjunakoṇḍa.
388. Dr. Susan Huntington pointed out to me the relationship of these figures to those in the Vidhurapaṇḍita Jātaka at Ajantā Cave 2. She considers this comparison a support for Walter Spink's fifth-century dating of the cave.
389. B. Rowland, *The Wall Paintings of India, Central Asia and Ceylon,* Boston, 1938, pl. 13.
390. B. Rowland, *The Wall Paintings,* pl. 24.
391. B. Rowland, *The Art and Architecture of India,* third edition, Baltimore, 1967, pl. 140.
392. See Rosen, "Begram", p. 44.
393. J.M.C. Toynbee and J.B. Ward-Perkins, "Peopled Scrolls: A Hellenistic Motif in Imperial Art", *Paper of the British School at Rome,* Vol. XVIII, N.S. V, 1950, 33, 40, and pl. XXI, 3.
394. A. Roes, "New Light on the Grilli", *Journal of Hellenic Studies,* LV, 1935, pp. 32-35.
395. Prince of Wales Museum of Western India, Bombay, *Dawn of Civilization in Maharashtra,* Bombay, 1975, fig. 56.
396. *M.D.A.F.A.* IX, p. 21.

BIBLIOGRAPHY

Agrawala, R.C., "Mother and Child Sculptures from Śāmalāji and Rajasthan", *Bulletin of the Museum and Picture Galllery,* Baroda, Vol. XXIII, 1971, pp. 101-11.

Annual Report of Indian Epigraphy, 1957-58.

Aśvaghoṣa, *The Saundarānanda,* E.H. Johnston, ed. and trans., Lahore, 1921 (Reprint ed. Delhi, 1975).

Auboyer, J., "Ancient Indian Ivories from Begram", *Journal of the Indian Society of Oriental Art,* Vol. XVI, pp. 34-46.

——, *Introduction a l'étude de l'Inde,* Serie Orientale *Roma,* Vol. XXXI, Rome, 1965.

——, and Jean-François Enault, *La vie publique et privée dans l'Inde ancienne,* Fas. I, *L'architecture civile et reliegieuse,* Publications du Musée Guimet, Recherches et documents d'art et d'archéologie, Paris, 1969.

Bachhofer, Ludwig, *Early Indian Sculpture,* reprint ed., New York, 1972.

Banerjea, J.N., *The Development of Hindu Iconography,* 2nd ed., Calcutta, 1956.

Bareau, A., "La construction et le culte des *stūpa* d'aprés les Vinayapiṭaka", *Bulletin de l'école français d'Extreme Orient,* Vol. 50, fasc. 2, pp. 229-74.

——, *Les sectes bouddhiques du petit vehicule,* Saigon, 1955.

Barrett, D., *Sculptures from Amaravati in the British Museum,* London, 1954.

Beal, S., *Buddhist Records of the Western World,* London, 1884 (Reprint ed. Delhi, 1969).

Begley, W., "The Identification of the Ajantā Fragment in the Boston Museum", *Oriental Art,* Vol. XIV, No. 1, Spring 1968, pp. 25-32.

——, *Viṣṇu's Flaming Wheel: The Iconography of the Sudarśana Cakra,* New York, 1973.

Bénisti, M., "Les stūpa aux cinq piliers", *Bulletin de l'école français d'Extreme Orient,* Vol. 58, 1971, pp. 131-62.

——, "Un relief inédit de l'Āndhradeśa", *Arts Asiatiques,* Vol. IV, No. 3, 1957, pp. 299-307.

Boethius, A. and J.B. Ward-Perkins, *Etruscan and Roman Architecture,* Harmondsworth, 1970.

Buchthal, H., *The Western Aspects of Gandhara Sculpture, Proceedings of the British Academy,* Vol. XXXI, London, 1945.

Burgess, J., *The Buddhist Stūpas of Amaravati and Jaggayapeta,* Archaeological Survey of Southern India, London, 1887 (Reprint ed. Varanasi, 1970).

Bussagli, M., "Ein Nicht Gedeutete Figur aus Nāgārjunakoṇḍa", *Artibus Asiae,* Vol. VIII, 1940-45, pp. 258-64.

——, and C, Sivaramamurti, *Five Thousand Years of the Art of India,* New York, n.d.

Chakaravarti, N.P., "Summary of Epigraphical Work during 1933-34", *Annual Report, Archaeological Survey of India,* 1933-34.

Chandra, P., *Stone Sculpture in the Allahabaḍ Museum,* Poona, n.d.

Chattopadhyaya, B., *Coins and Currency Systems in South India,* New Delhi, 1977.

Chhabra, B. Ch., "Nāgārjunakoṇḍa Inscription of Ehavalasri's Time, Year 11", *Epigraphia Indica,* XXXIII, 1966, pp. 147-49.

Coomaraswamy, A.K., "Andhra Sculptures", *Bulletin of the Museum of Fine Arts,* Boston, Vol. 27, 1929, pp. 20-23.

——, *La Sculpture de Bodhgayā, Ars Asiatica,* Vol. XVIII, Paris, 1935.

——, *La Sculpture de Bharhut,* Annales du Musée Guimet, Bibliotheque d' Art, N.S. Vol. VI, Paris, 1956.

——, *Yakṣas,* reprint ed. New Delhi, 1972.

Cunningham, A., *Book of Indian Eras,* Calcutta, 1883 (Reprint ed. Varanasi, 1970).

Czuma, S., *Indian Art from the George P. Bickford Collection,* Cleveland, 1975.

Davids, T.W.R., trans., *Buddhist Suttas, Sacred Books of the East,* Vol. XI, Oxford, 1881 (Reprint ed. New York, 1969).

Desai, D., *Erotic Sculpture of India: A Socio-Cultural Study,* New Delhi, 1975.

Deshpande, M.N., "Classical Influence on Indian Terracotta Art", *Huitième congrès international d' archéologi classique, Paris, 1963,* Paris, 1965, pp. 603-10.

Dimand, Maurice S., "An Indian Relief of the Amarāvatī School", *Bulletin of the Metropolitan Museum of Art,* Vol., XXVIII, No. 7, July 1933, pp. 124-25.

——, "A New Indian Relief of the Amarāvatī School", *Bulletin of the Metropolitan Museum of Art,* Vol. XXV, No. 5, May 1930, pp. 131-34.

——, "Two Indian Reliefs from the Amarāvatī School", *Bulletin of the Metropolitan Museum of Art,* Vol. XXIII, No. 10, October, 1928, pp. 238-44.

Dutt, N., *Buddhist Sects in India,* Delhi, 1970.

Dutt, S., *Buddhist Monks and Monasteries of India,* London, 1962 (Reprint Delhi, 1988).

Ebert, J., "*Parinirvāṇa and Stūpa:* Was the *Stūpa* only a 'Symbolical' Depiction of the Parinirvāṇa?" in A.L. Dallapiccola, ed., *The Stūpa: Its Religious, Historical and Architectural Significance, Beiträge zur Südasien Forschung,* Vol. 55, Wiesbaden, 1980.

Facenna, D., *Sculptures from the Sacred Area of Bhutkara I (Swat, Pakistan),* Istituto Italiano per il Medio ed Estremo Oriente, Centro Studi e Scavi Archaeologici in Asia, *Reports and Memoirs,* Vol. II, pt. 2, Rome, 1962.

Fergusson, J., *Tree and Serpent Worship,* London, 1863 (Reprint ed. Delhi and Varanasi , 1971).

——, and J. Burgess, *The Cave Temples of India,* 1980 (Reprint ed. Delhi, 1969).

Fleet, J.F., "Inscriptions of the Early Gupta Kings", *Corpus Inscriptionum Indicarum,* Vol. III, 3rd rev. ed., Reprint ed. Varanasi, 1970.

——, "Sanskrit and Old Karanese Inscriptions, No. 185, Mahākūṭa Pillar Inscription of Maṅgaleśa", *Indian Antiquary,* Vol. 19, 1890, pp. 7-20.

Foucher, A., *L'Art Gréco-Bouddique du Gandhāra,* 2 Vols., Paris, 1905-18.

Ghirshman, R., *Begram: Recherches archéologiques et historiques sur les Kouchans, Memoires de la délégation archéologique française en Afghanistan,* Vol. XIII, Paris, 1946.

——, *Parthes et Sassanides,* Paris, 1962.

Gopalachari, K., *Early History of The Andhra Country,* Madras University Historical Series, No. 16, Madras, 1941; 2nd ed., Madras, 1976.

Grousset, R., "The Great Periods of Indian art", *Indian Art and Letters,* N.S. Vol. I, No. 2, 1927, pp. 104-09.

Gupta, P.L., *Roman Coins from Andhra Pradesh,* Andhra Pradesh Government Museum Series, No. 10, Hyderabad, n.d.

Hackin, J., *Nouvelles recherches archéologique à Begram, Memoires de la délégation archéologique française en Afghanistan,* Vol. XI, Paris, 1954 (2 vols.).

——, *Recherches archéologique á Begram, Memoires de la délégation archéologique française en Afghanistan,* Vol. IX, Paris, 1939.

Härtel, H., "Aspects of Early Nāga Cult in India", *Journal of the Royal Asiatic Society,* Oct. 1976, pp. 663-83.

——, "Some Results of the Excavations at Sonkh: A Preliminary Report", *German Scholars in India, Contributions to Indian Studies,* Vol. II, Bombay, 1976, pp. 69-99.

——, and J. Aubyoer, *Indien und Südostasien, Propyläen Kustgeschichte,* Vol. 16, Berlin, 1971.

Härle, J., *Gupta Sculpture,* Oxford, 1974.

Herrmann, G,. *The Iranian Revival,* Oxford, 1977.

Hirakawa, A., "The Rise of Mahāyāna and Its Relation to *Stūpa* Worship", *Memoirs of the Toyo Bunko Research Society,* Vol. 22, 1963, pp. 57-106.

Ilango-aḍigal, The Śilappadikāram, trans. with intro. and notes by V.R. Ramachandra Dikshitar, Oxford, 1939.

Indian Archaeology: A Review, 1954-55.

Indian Archaeology: A Review, 1955-56.

Indian Archaeology: A Review, 1956-57.

Indian Archaeology: A Review, 1957-58.

Indian Archaeology: A Review, 1958-59.

Indian Archaeology: A Review, 1959-60.

Indian Archaeology: A Review, 1964-65.

Indian Archaeology: A Review, 1967-68.

Irwin, J., "The Stūpa and the Cosmic Axis: The Archaeological Evidence", *South Asian Archaeology, 1977,* Papers from the Fourth International Conference of South Asian Archaeologists in Western Europe, Naples, 1979, pp. 799-845.

The Jātaka, ed. E.B. Cowell, London, 1895 (Reprint 1973), Vol. III, pp. 34-37, No. 316.

Joshi, N.P., *Gandhāra Sculptures in the State Museum,* Lucknow, 1969.

Karetzky, Patricia Eichenbaum, "The Act of Pilgrimage and Guptan Steles with Scenes from the Life of the Buddha", *Oriental Art,* XXIII, 1987, pp. 268-74.

Khan, M.A.W., *An Early Sculpture of Narasimha,* Andhra Pradesh Government Archaeological Series, No. 16, Hyderabad, 1964.

——, *A Monograph on an Early Buddhist Stūpa at Kesanapalli,* Andhra Pradesh Government Archaeological Series, Vol. 14, Hyderabad, 1963.

——, *A Monograph on Yēllēśwarm Excavations,* Andhra Pradesh Government Archaeological Series, Vol. 27, Hyderabad, 1963.

Khandalavala, K., "An Inscription of the Year 11 of Caṣṭana and its Implications", *Journal of Indian History,* Vol. 52, 1974, pp. 269-301.

——, "Brahmapuri: A Consideration of Metal Objects Found in the Kundangar Hoard", *Lalit Kala,* Vol. 7, 1960, pp. 29-75.

Koch, G., *Die Mythologischen Sarcophage,* Part 6, *Meleager,* Vol. 12, Berlin, 1975.

Konow, S., ''Kharoshṭhī Inscriptions: with the Exception of Those of Aśoka'', *Corpus Inscriptionum Indicarrum,* Vol. II, pt. 1, reprint ed., Varanasi, 1969.

Kramirsch, S., ''The Four Cornered Citadel of the Gods", *Journal of the American Oriental Society,* Vol. 75, 1955, pp. 184-87.

——, *Indian Sculpture,* Calcutta, 1933, Reprint Delhi, 1979.

——, *The Presence of Śiva,* Delhi, 1988.

Krishna Murthy, K., *Ṇāgārjunakoṇḍa: A Cultural Study,* Delhi, 1977.

Krishnaswami Aiyanagar, S., *The Maṇimekhalai in its Historical Setting,* London, 1928.

Kuraishi, M.H., "Trial Excavations at Alluru, Gummadidurru and Nāgārjunikoṇḍa", *Annual Report, Archaeological Survey of India,* 1964.

Lee, S., *Ancient Sculptures from India,* Cleveland, 1964.

Leese, M., "The Early Buddhist Icons in Kaṇheri's Cave 3", *Artibus Asiae,* Vol. 41, No. 1, pp. 83-93.

Ling, T.O., *A Dictionary of Buddhism,* New York, 1962.

Longhurst, A.H., The Buddhist Antiquities of Nāgārjunakoṇḍa, Madras Presidency, *Memoirs of the Archaeological Survey of India,* No. 54, Delhi, 1938.

——, Excavations at Nāgārjunikoṇḍa", *Annual Report, Archaeological Survey of India, 1927-28,* pp. 113-21.

——, "Excavations at Nāgārjunikṇḍa", *Annual Report, Archaeological Survey of India, 1928-29,* pp. 100-04.

——, "Excavations at Nāgārjunikoṇḍa", *Annual Report, Archaeological Survey of India, 1928-29,* pp. 145-51.

Loo, C.T. & Co., *Expositions de sculpture et bronzes anciens de l'Inde (14 Juin au 31 Juillet 1935),* Paris, 1935.

Lyons, I. and H. Ingholt, *Gandhāran Art in Pakistan,* Hamden, Conn., 1971.

The Mahāvaṁsa, trans. W. Geiger, London, 1912 (Reprint ed. 1969).

The Mahāvastu, Vol. II, trans, J.J. Jones, *Sacred Books of the Buddhists,* Vol. XVIII, London, 1976.

Marshall, J., *The Buddhist Art of Gandhāra,* Cambridge, 1960.

——, and A. Foucher, *The Monuments of Sāñcī,* 3 vols., Calcutta, 1940. Mehta, M., *The Abhiras: Their History and Culture* (M.S. University Archaeology and Ancient History Series, No. 6), Baroda, 1962.

Metcalf, W.E., "Roman Aurei from India", *The American Numismatic Society, Museum Notes,* Vol. 24, 1979, pp. 123-27.

Mirashi, V.V., "Epigraphic Notes", *Epigraphica Indica,* Vol. XXXVII, 1967, pp. 70-73.

——, "Is Vijaya Mentioned in Nāgārjunakoṇḍa Inscriptions the Name of the Cyclic Year?", *Journal of the Oriental Institute,* M.S. University of Baroda, Vol. 18, pt. 4, June 1969, pp. 318-22.

Mitra, D., *Buddhist Monuments,* Calcutta, 1971.

——, "A Frieze from Goli in the Metropolitan Museum of Art, New York", *Damilica* (Journal of the Tamil Nadu State Department of Archaeology), Vol. II, pt. 3, 1973, pp. 19-20.

——, "Observations on Buddhist Remains at Jaggayapeta", *Indian Historical Quarterly,* Vol. 35, No. 3, 1959, pp. 274-75.

Mukherjee, R., *The History of the Āndhra Region c. A.D. 75-350,* Ph.D. Thesis, University of London, 1965.

Nagaraja Rao, M.S., "Brāhmī Inscriptions and their Bearing on the Great Stūpa at Sannati", in *Indian Epigraphy: Its Bearing on the History of Art,* eds. Frederick M. Asher and G.S. Gai, Delhi 1985, pp. 41-45.

Nilakanta Sastri, K.A., "Gurzala Brahmi Inscription", *Epigraphia Indica,* XXVI, 1941, pp. 123-25.

Oliver, A. *Silver for the Gods,* Toledo, 1977.

Prince of Wales Museum, Bombay, *Dawn of Civilization in Maharashtra,* Bombay, 1975.

Ramachandran, T.N., "Nāgārjunakoṇḍa, 1938", *Memoirs of the Archaeological Survey of India,* Vol. 71, Delhi, 1953.

——, "Buddhist Sculptures from a Stūpa Near Goli Village", *Bulletin of the Madras Government Museum,* N.S. Vol. 1., pt.1, Madras, 1929.

Rama Rao, M., *Inscriptions of the Andhradesa,* 2 Vols., Sri Venkatesvara University Historical Series, No. 5, Tirupati, 1967.

Ray, Amita, *Life and Art of Early Andhradesa,* Delhi, 1983.

——, *Ikṣvākus of Vijayapuri,* Tirupati, 1967.

Rea, A., "Excavations at Amarāvatī", *Annual Report, Archaeological Survey of India,* 1905-06, pp. 116-19.

——, *South Indian Buddhist Antiquities,* Archaeological Survey of India, New Imperial Series, Vol. XV, Madras, 1894.

Reinach, S., *Répetorie de la statuaire Grecque et Romaine,* Paris, 1904-30.

Richter, G., *The Sculpture and Sculptors of the Greeks,* 4th ed., New Haven and London, 1970.

Robert, C., Die Antiken Sarkophag Reliefs, Vol. 3, No. 1, *einzelmythen, 'rome, 1969.*

Roes, A., "New Light on the Grilli", *Journal of Hellenic Studies,* Vol. LV, 1935, pp. 232-35.

Rosen E., "The Begram Ivories", *Marsyas,* Vol. XVII, 1974-75, pp. 39-48.

——, "Buddhist Architecture and Lay Patronage at Nāgārjunakoṇḍa", *The Stūpa: Its Religious, Historical and Architectural Significance,* ed. A.L. Dallapiccola. *Beiträge zur Südasien Forschung,* Vol. 55, Wiesbaden, 1980, pp. 35-40.

——, "A Dated Memorial Pillar from Nāgārjunakoṇḍa", in *Indian Epigraphy: Its Bearing on the History of Art,* Eds. Frederick M. Asher and G.S. Gai, Delhi, 1985, pp. 35-40.

——, *The History and Buddhist Architecture of Nāgārjunakoṇḍa,* unpublished M.A. Thesis, New York University, 1970.

——, "Observations on Some Buddhist Sculptures from Goli Village", in press in *Bulletin of the Prince of Wales Museum of Western India.*

——, Review of Prince *Ilango Aḍigal, Śilappadikāram (The Ankle Bracelet),* trans. by Alain Dainélou, in *Artibus Asiae,* Vol. 37, Nos. 1-2, 1975, pp. 148-50.

——, and A. Wayman, "The Rise of Mahāyāna Buddhism and Inscriptional Evidence at Nāgārjunakoṇḍa", *Indian Journal of Buddhist Studies* (Varanasi), II, 1, 1990.

Rosenfield, J., *The Dynastic Art of the Kushans,* Berkeley and Los Angeles, 1967.

Roth, G., "Symbolism of the Buddhist Stūpa", *The Stūpa: Its Religious, Historical and Architectural Significance,* ed. A.L. Dallapiccola, *Beiträge zur Südasien Forschung,* Vol. 55, Wiesbaden, 1980, pp. 183-209.

Rowland, B., *The Art and Architecture of India,* 3rd ed., Baltimore, 1967.

——, *The Wall-Paintings of India, Central Asia and Ceylon,* Boston, 1938.

Sankaranarayan, S., "Rentala Pillar Inscription of Siri-Chamtamula I, Year 5", *Epigraphia Indica,* XXXVII, 1965-66, pp. 29-32.

Sarkar, H., "Chronological Aspects of Mason's Marks at Nāgārjunakoṇḍa", *Bharati* (Bulletin of the Department of Ancient History, Culture, and Archaeology), 1968-71, Nos. 12-14, pp. 226-35.

——, "The Nāgārjunakoṇḍa Phase of the Lower Kṛṣṇā Valley Art: A Study Based on Epigraphical Data", in *Indian Epigraphy : Its Bearing on the History of Art,* Eds. Frederick M. Asher and G.S. Gai, Delhi, 1985, pp. 29-34.

——, "Nāgārjunakoṇḍa Prakrit Inscription of Gautamiputra Vijaya Satakarni, Year 6", *Epigraphia Indica,* XXXVI, 1964-65, pp. 273-74.

——, "Some Aspects of the Buddhist Monuments at Nāgārjunakoṇḍa", *Ancient India,* No. 16, 1962, pp. 65-85.

——, *Studies in Early Buddhist Architecture of India,* Delhi, 1966.

——, and B.N. Misra, *Nāgārjunakoṇḍa,* 2nd ed., Delhi, 1972.

Sarkar, H. and S.P. Nainar, *Amaravati,* New Delhi, 1972.

Sastri, H., "Report on Indian Epigraphy", *Annual Report, Archaeological Survey of India* 1925-26, pp. 141-42.

——, "Sanskrit Epigraphy", *Annual Report, Archaeological Survey of India,* 1929-30, pp. 164-65.

Schlingloff, D., "Der König mit dem Schwert: Die Identifizierung einer Ajantā Malerei", *Wiener Zeitschrift für die Kunde Südasiens,* Vol. XXI, 1977, pp. 75-80.

Seshadri, M., "Buddhist Monuments in Mysore", *Artibus Asiae,* Vol. 34, 1972, pp. 169-70.

Sewell, R., *List of Antiquarian Remains in Madras Presidency,* Madras, 1882.

Sharma, R.C., *Mathura Museum Introduction,* Mathura, 1971.

Sircar, D.C., "More Inscriptions from Nāgārjunakoṇḍa", *Epigraphia Indica,* XXXV, 1963-64, pp. 1-36.

——, "Nāgārjunakoṇḍa Inscription of the Time of Abhira Vasushena, Year 30", *Epigraphia Indica,* Vol. XXXV, 1961-62, pp. 197-204.

——, "Some Brahmi Inscriptions", *Epigraphia Indica,* XXXIV, 1961-62, pp. 207-12.

——, *The Successors of the Sātavāhanas in the Lower Deccan,* Calcutta, 1939.

——, and K.G. Krishnan, "Two Inscriptions from Nāgārjunakoṇḍa", *Epigraphia Indica,* XXXIV, 1961-62, pp. 17-22.

——, and L.N. Lahiri, "Footprint Slab Inscription from Nāgārjunakoṇḍa", *Epigraphia Indica,* XXXIII, 1960, pp. 247-50.

Sivaramamurti, C., Amaravati Sculptures in the Madras Government Museum, *Bulletin of the Madras Government Museum,* N.S. Vol. IV, Madras, 1942.

——, "Sanskrit Literature and Art—Mirrors of Indian Culture", *Memoirs of the Archaeological Survey of India,* Vol. 73, New Delhi, 1970.

Smithsonian Institution, *7,000 Years of Iranian Art,* Washington, 1964.

Soper, A.C., "Aspects of Light Symbolism in Gandharan Sculpture, III", *Artibus Asiae,* Vol. 13, 1950, pp. 63-85.

Soundara Rajan, K.V., *Architecture of the Early Hindu Temples of Andhra Pradesh,* Andhra Pradesh Government Archaeology Series, No. 21, Hyderabad, 1965.

Stern, P., *Colonnes indiennes d'Ajantā et d'Ellora,* Publications du Musée Guimet, *Recherches d'art et d'archéologie,* Vol. XI, Paris, 1972.

——, and M. Bénisti, "Évolution du stūpa figurée dans les sculptures d'Amarāvatī", *Bulletin de la société des études indochinois,* Vol. XXVII, No. 4, 1952, pp. 1-7.

——, and ——, *Évolution du style Indien d'Amarāvatī,* Publications du Musée Guimet, Recherches et Documents d'Art et d'Archéologie, Vol. VII, Paris, 1961.

Strong, D.E., *Greek and Roman Silver Plate,* London, 1966.

Subrahmanyam, R., *A Catalogue of Ikshvaku Coins in the Andhra Pradesh Government Museum,* Andhra Pradesh Government Museum Series, No. 5, Hyderabad, 1962.

——, *Nagarjunakonda (1954-1960),* Vol. I, *Memoirs of the Archaeological Survey of India,* Vol. 75, New Delhi, 1975.

——, "On the Nature of Utilization of Epigraphs for Art History", in *Indian Epigraphy: Its Bearing on the History of Art,* eds. Frederick M. Asher and G.S. Gai, Delhi, 1985, pp. 25-27.

Toynbee, J.M.C. and J.B. Ward-Perkins, "Peopled Scrolls: A Hellenistic Motif in Imperial Art", *Papers of the British School at Rome,* Vol. XVIII, N.S. V, 1950, pp. 1-43.

Vidyadhara Rao, B., "Occurrence of Sexagenary Cycles in Two Inscriptions from Nagarjunakonda", *Journal of the Oriental Institute, M.S. University of Baroda,* Vol. 18,

No. 4, June 1969, pp. 323-25.

Viennot, O., *Les divinités fluviales Gaṅgā et Yamunā*, Publications du Musée Guimet, Recherches d'Art et d'Archéologie, Vol. X, Paris, 1964.

Vogel, J. Ph., "Additional Prakrit Inscriptions from Nagarjunikonda", *Epigraphia Indica*, Vol. 21, 1930-31, pp. 61-71.

——, *Indian Serpent Lore*, 1926 (Reprint ed. Varanasi, 1972).

——, "Prakrit Inscriptions from a Buddhist Site at Nagarjunikonda", *Epigraphia Indica*, Vol. XX, 1929-30, pp. 1-36.

——, "The Man in the Well and Some Other Subjects Illustrated at Nāgārjunikonda", *Revue des Arts Asiatiques*, Vol. XI, No. 3, Sept. 1937, pp. 109-21.

Walters, H.B., *Catalogue of the Silver Plate (Greek, Etruscan, and Roman) in the British Museum,* London, 1921.

Wayman, A., "A Jotting on the Mirror: Those of Ladies", *Mahfil*, Vol. VII, 1971, pp. 209-12.

——, and H. Wayman, *The Lion's Roar of Queen Śrīmālā*, New York and London, 1974.

——, "The Mirror as a Pan-Buddhist Metaphor-Simile", *History of Religions*, Vol. 13, 1974, pp. 251-69.

——, "Mirror-Like Knowledge in Mahāyāna Buddhist Literature", *Asiatische Studien*, Vol. 25, 1971, pp. 353-63.

——, "Notes on Mirror Words and Entities in the Area of India", *Ural-Altaische Jahrbücher*, Vol. 47, 1955, pp. 204-06.

——, "The Role of Art Among the Buddhist Religieux", *East-West Dialogues in Aesthetics*, ed. Kenneth K. Inada, Buffalo, N.Y., 1978, pp. 2-15.

Weiner, S.L., *Ajantā: Its Place in Buddhist Art,* Berkeley, Los Angeles and London, 1977.

Wheeler, M., *Rome Beyond the Imperial Frontiers*, London, 1954.

Williams, J., "Sārnāth Gupta Steles of the Buddha's Life", *Arts Orientalis*, Vol. X, 1975, pp. 171-92.

——, *The Art of Gupta India: Empire and Province*, Princeton, 1982.

Yazdani, G., *Ajantā*, 4 Vols., Oxford, 1931-46.

Zimmer, H., *The Art of Indian Asia*, ed. J. Campbell, 2 Vols., 2nd ed., New York, 1964.

Zvelebil, K., *Mahfil*, Vol. IV, Nos. 3-4, 1968, pp. 1-12.

INDEX

ERRATA

Page xxii	- line 7	-	*Read* "Detail of fig. 105" for "Detail of fig. 104".
Page 9	- line 8	-	*Read* "(fig. 237)" for "(fig. 267)".
Page 12	- line 23	-	*Read* "(Site 34, figs. 14-15)" for "(Site 34 figs. 14-15)".
Page 20	- last line	-	*Read* "figs. 2 and 3" for "plates 2 and 3".
Page 23	- line 21	-	*Add* "across the surface of the" after "fluidly".
Page 31	- line 34	-	*Read* "pillar inscription L" for "pillar inscription I".
Page 32	- line 20	-	*Read* "inscription L," for "inscription I".
Page 37	- line 29	-	*Read* "(fig. 36)" for "(fig. 40)".
Page 39	- line 32	-	*Read* "the earlier *stūpa*" for "earlier *stūpa*".
Page 45	- line 2	-	*Read* "fig. 87" for "fig. 81".
Page 48	- line 34	-	*Read* "Site 9" for "Site 98".
Page 55	- line 20	-	*Read* "fig. 123" for "fig. 124".
Page 56	- line 31	-	*Read* "stating" for "standing".
Page 57	- line 39	-	*Read* "all probability" for "the probability".
Page 60	- line 1	-	*Read* "regnal year" for "regnel year".
Page 61	- line 14	-	*Read* "on the" for "of the".
Page 62	- line 2	-	*Read* "lacks" for "lack".
Page 72	- line 33	-	*Add* "to greatly separate these two works in time. Both are best assigned to the reign" *after* "evidence".
Page 74	- line 12	-	*Read* "Gandhāra" for "gandhāra".
	- line 13	-	*Add* "is illustrated" *after* "The scene".
Page 76	- line 11	-	*Read* "Site 6," for "Site 6."
	- line 14	-	*Read* "of Cāṁtamūla I" for "Cāṁtamūla I".
	- line 19	-	*Read* "Cāṁtamūla I" for "Ehuvala Cāṁtamūla".
Page 77	- line 19	-	*Read* "Prajāpatī" for "Prajāpati".
Page 78	- line 28	-	*Read* "fig. 74" for "fig. 69".
Page 89	- line 27	-	*Read* "fig. 250" for "fig. 255".

Page 89	- line 35	- *Add* "published" *after* "(figs. 264-65)".
Page 96	- line 10	- *Read* "third" for "thrid".
Page 105	- line 16	- Read 'Nāgārjunakoṇḍa" ', for "Nāgārjuna konda,"
Page 107	- line 41	- *Read* "Site 38" for "Site 3".
Page 126	- line 17	- *Read* "archéologie" for "archéologi".
Page 127	- line 12	- *Read* "*à*" for "*á*".
	- line 18	- *Read* "*Kunstgeshichte*" for "*Kustgeschichte*".
Page 128	- line 5	- *Read* "Yēllēśwaram" for "Yēllēśwarm".
Page 129	- line 39	- Read "Einzelmythen, Rome" for "einzelmythen, rome".
Caption to fig. 175		- *Read* "fig. 105" for "fig. 104".

ILLUSTRATIONS

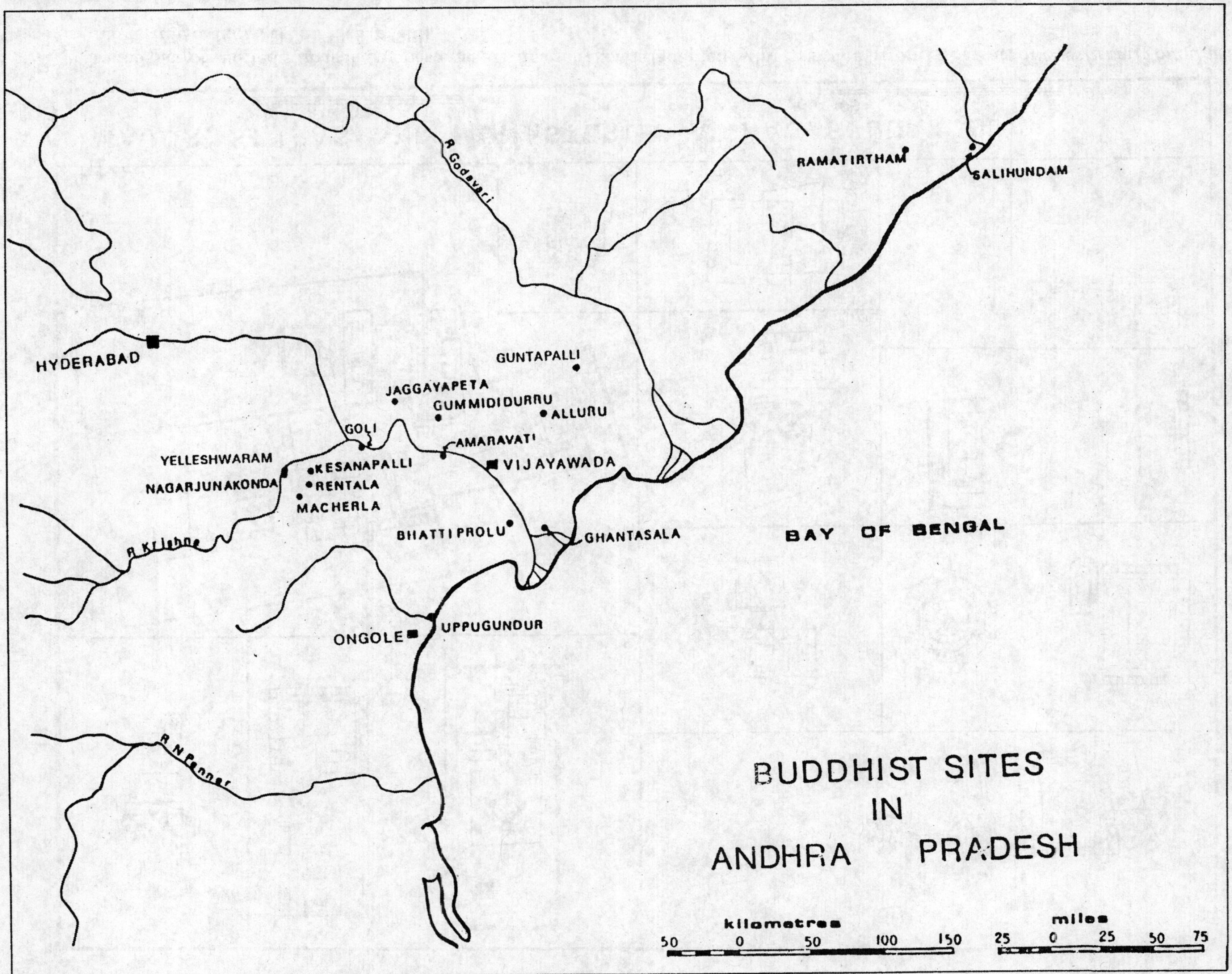

1. Map of significant Buddhist sites in Andhra Pradesh (adapted by Swagata Guha from K. Krishna Murthy, *Nāgārjunakoṇḍa: a Cultural Study*, Delhi, 1977, fig.1).

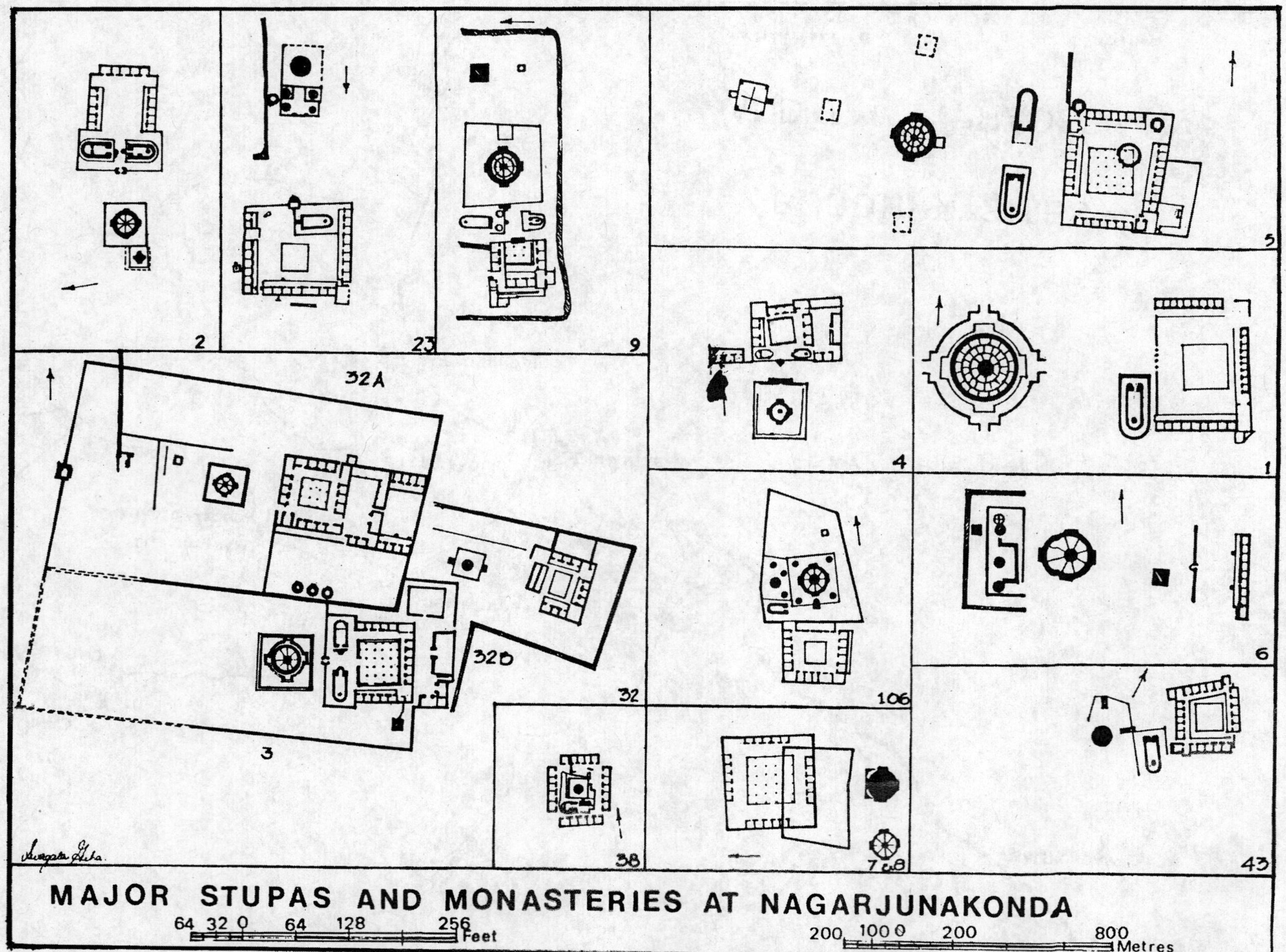

2. Ground plan of selected *stupas* and monasteries at Nāgārjunakoṇḍa (adapted by Swagata Guha from H. Sarkar, *Studies in Early Buddhist Architecture of India,* Delhi, 1966, p. xiii).

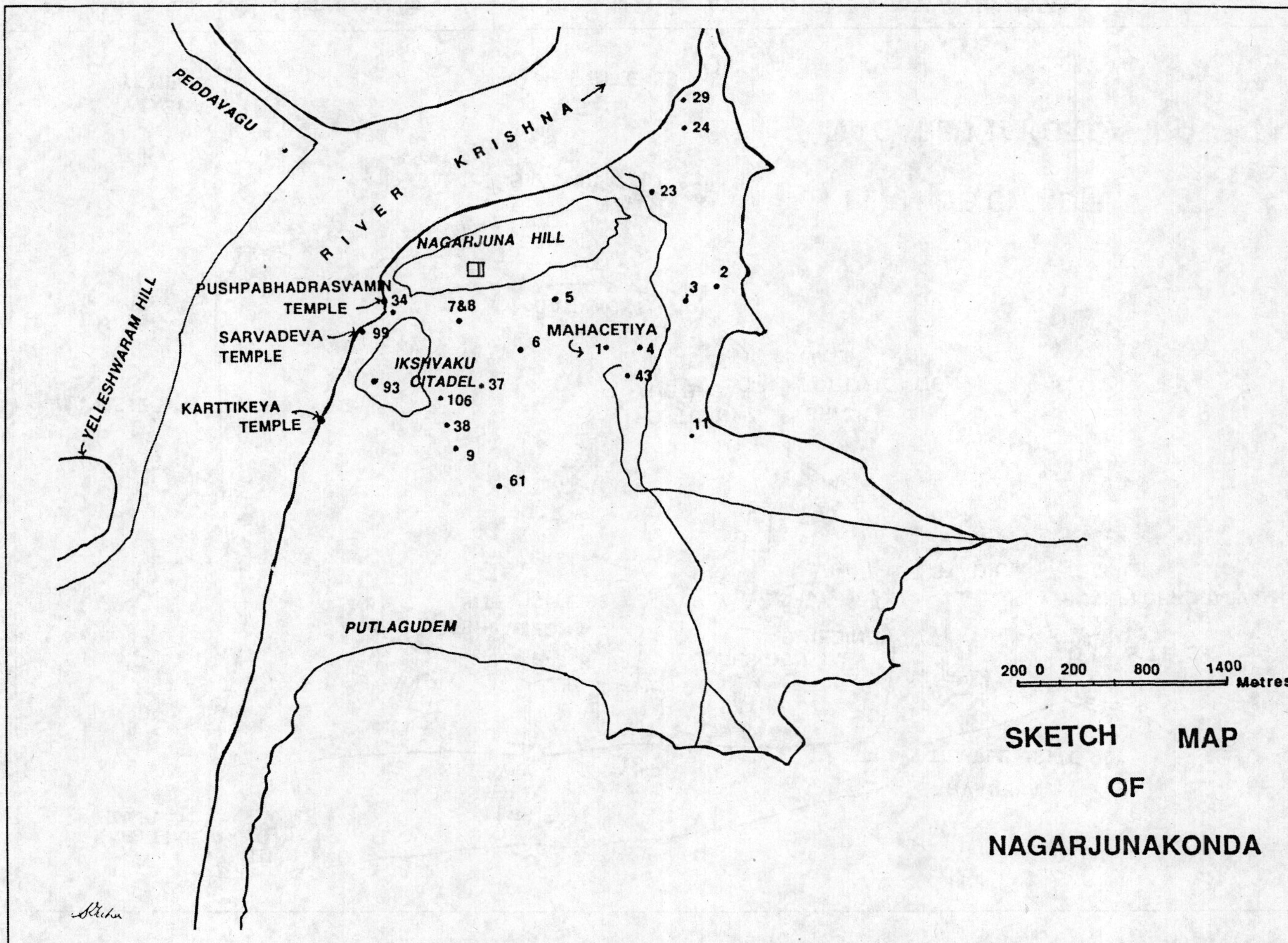

3. Site plan of Nāgārjunakoṇḍa (Swagata Guha, adapted from H. Sarkar and B.N. Misra, *Nagarjunakonda,* New Delhi, 1966, pl. XIII).

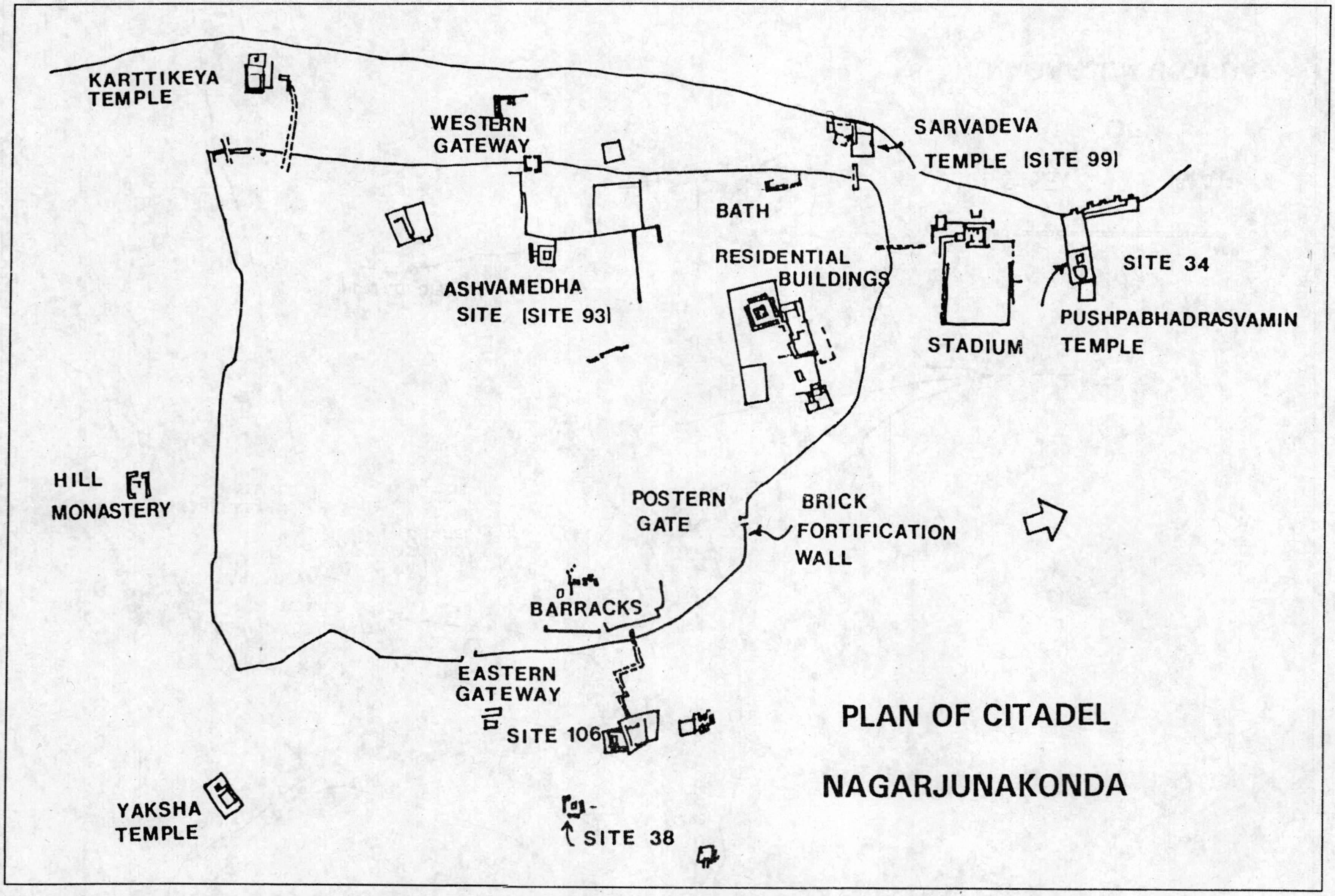

4. Plan of the Citadel of Nāgārjunakoṇḍa (Swagata Guha, based upon plan in *Indian Archaeology, A Review 1957-58*, p. 7).

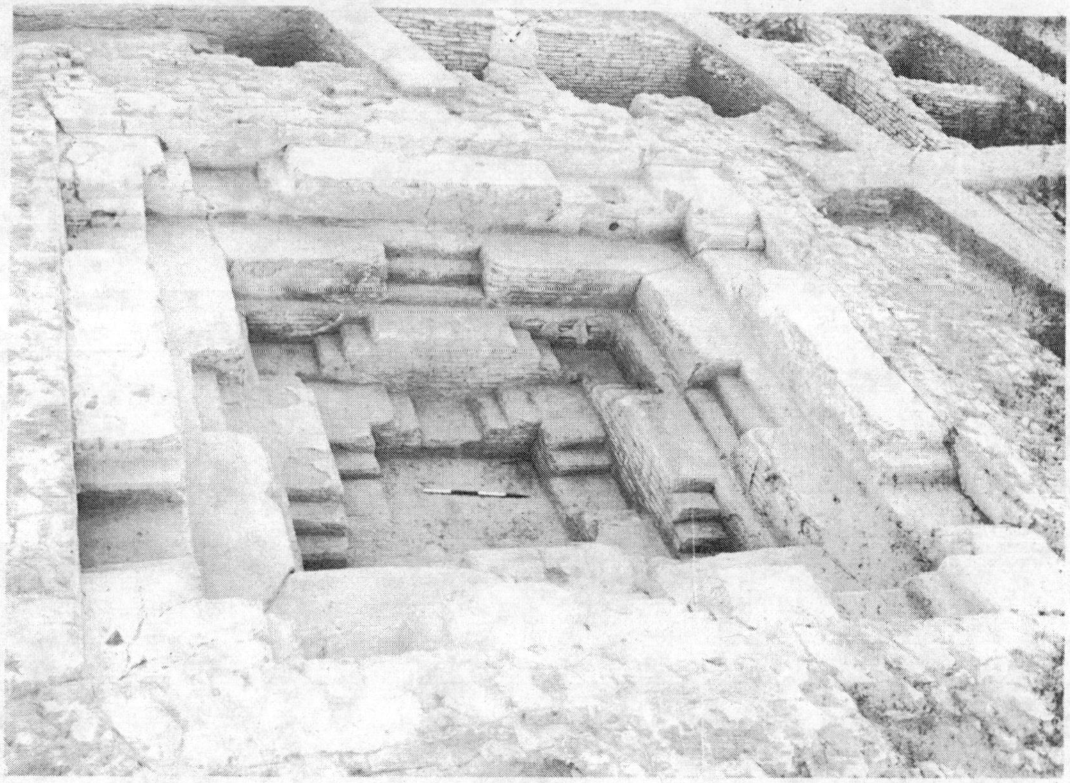

5. So-called *Aśvamedha* tank, Nāgārjunakoṇḍa (Photo: Archaeological Survey of India).

6. So-called *Kūrma* tank, Nāgārjunakoṇḍa (Photo: Archaeological Survey of India).

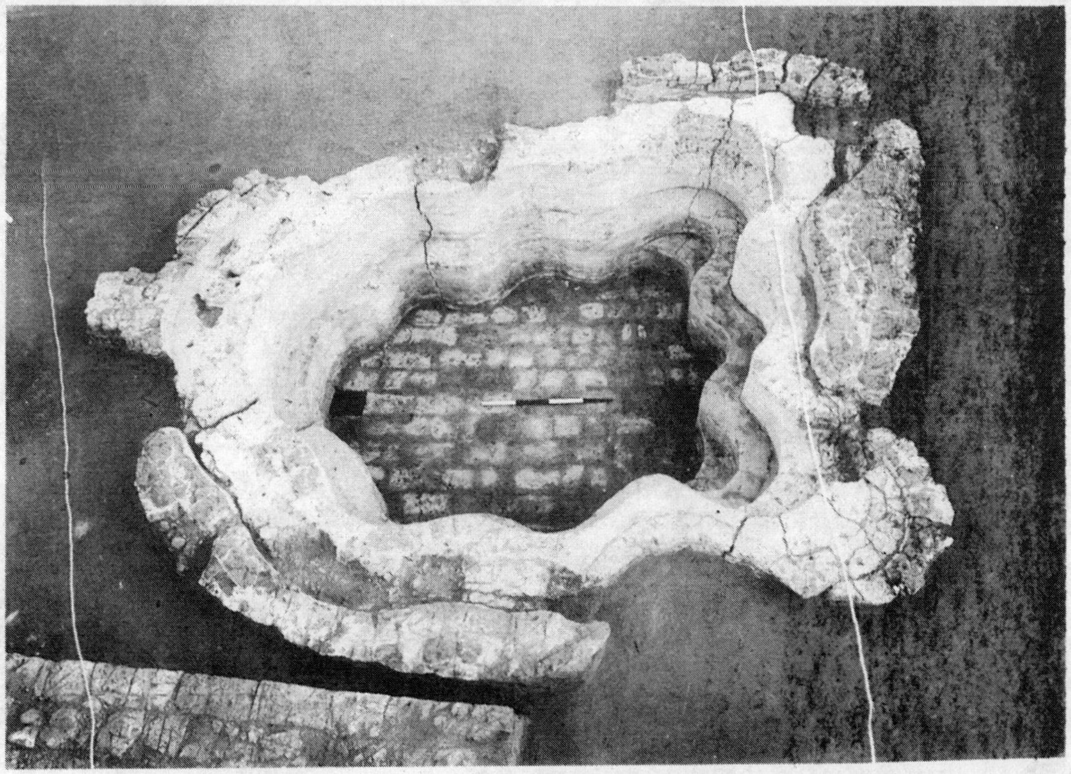

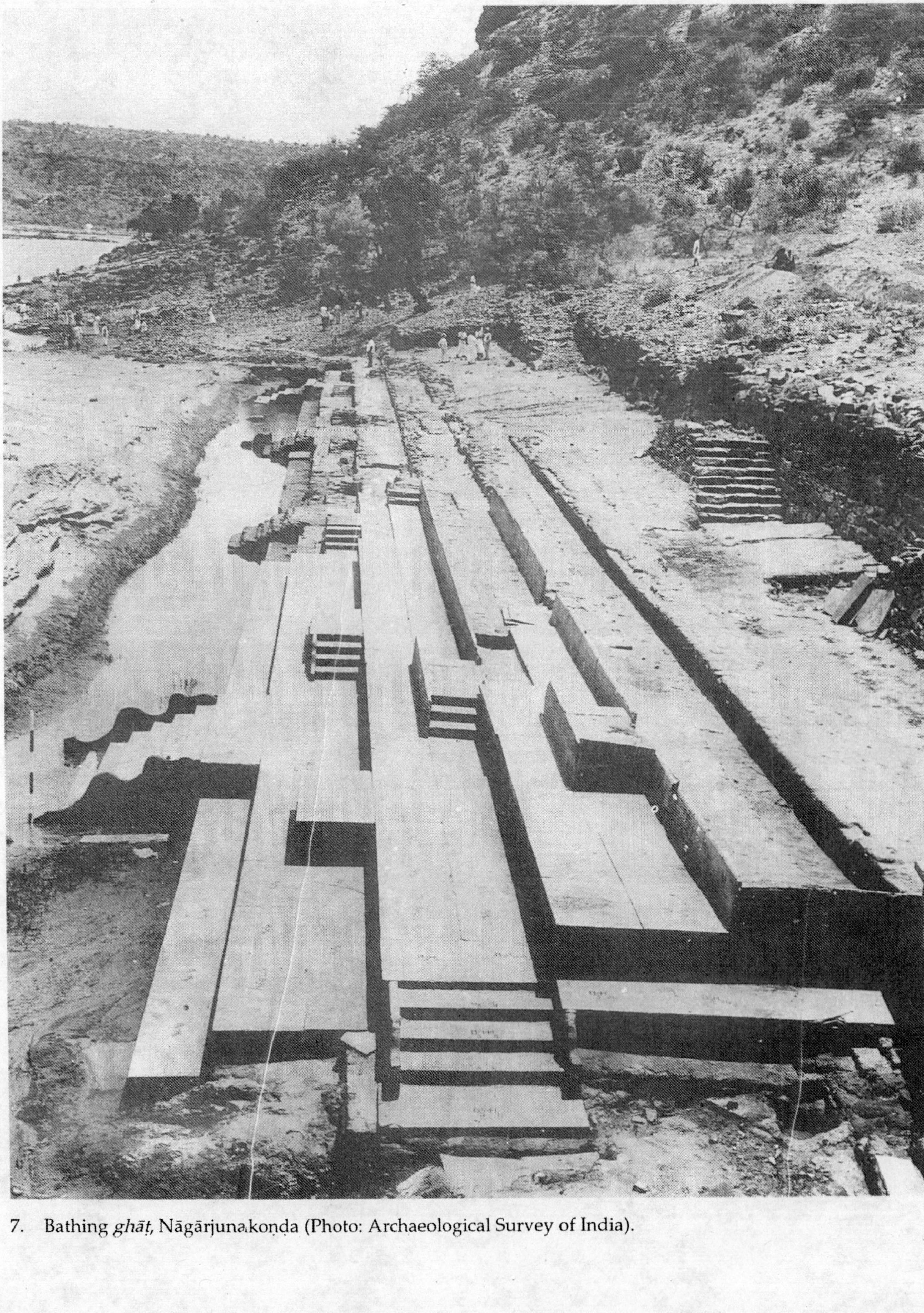

7. Bathing *ghāṭ*, Nāgārjunakoṇḍa (Photo: Archaeological Survey of India).

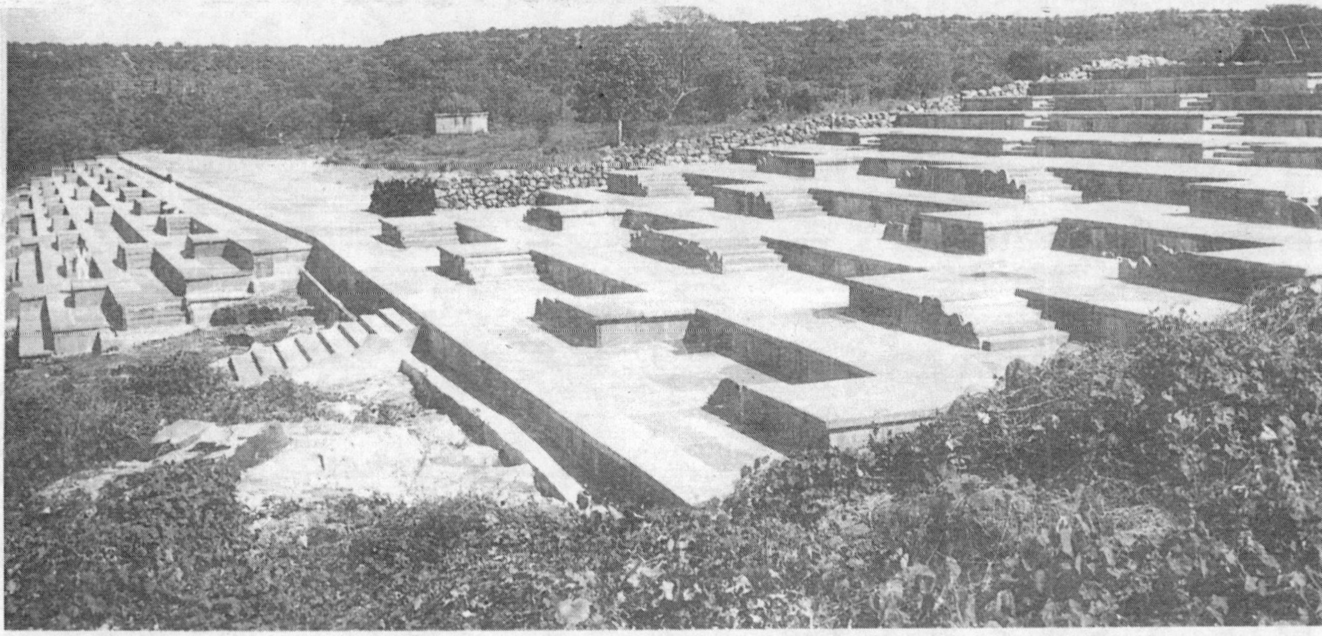

8. Reconstructed bathing *ghāṭ,* Nāgārjunakoṇḍa (Photo: Archaeological Survey of India).

9. Stadium, Nāgārjunakoṇḍa (Photo: Archaeological Survey of India).

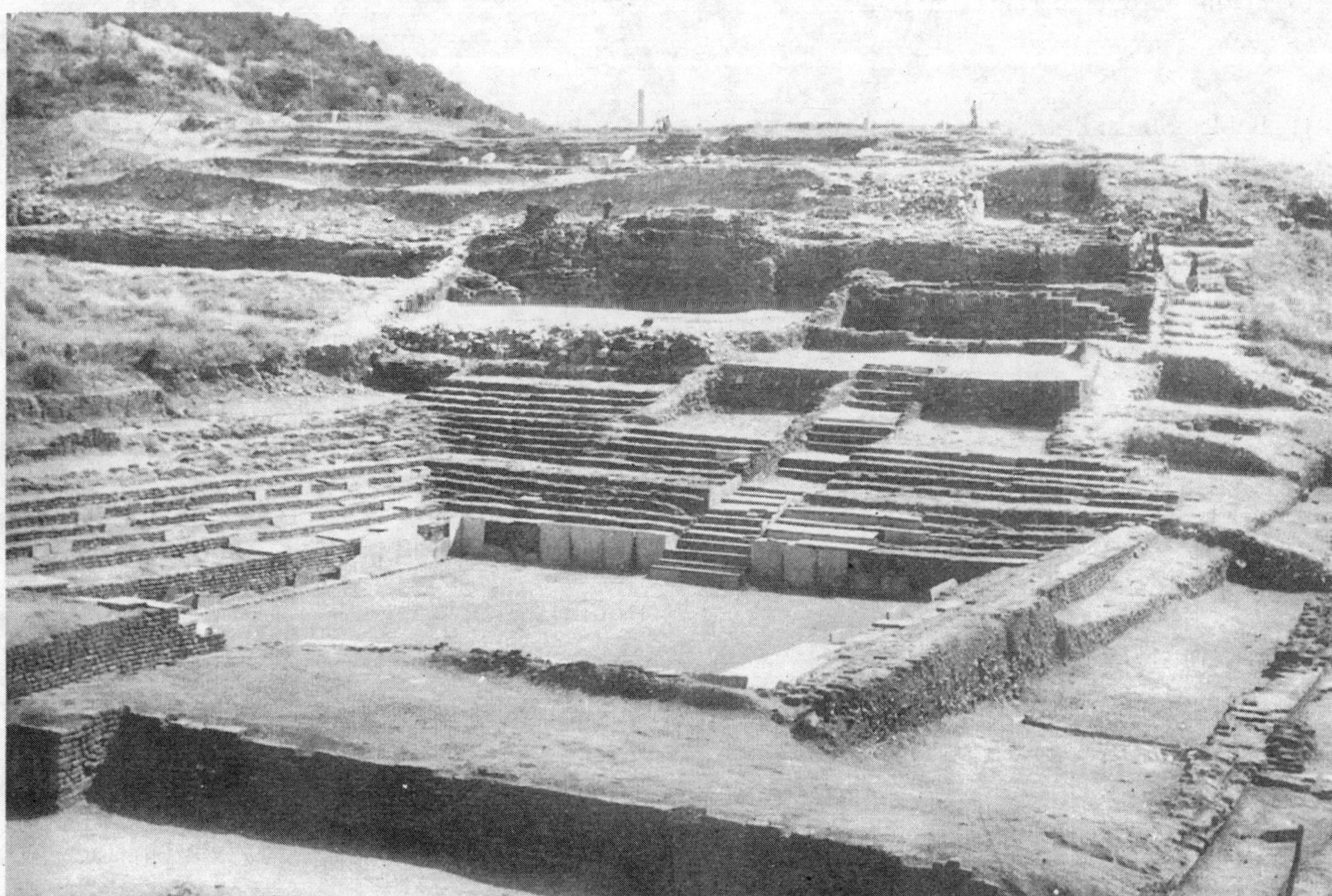

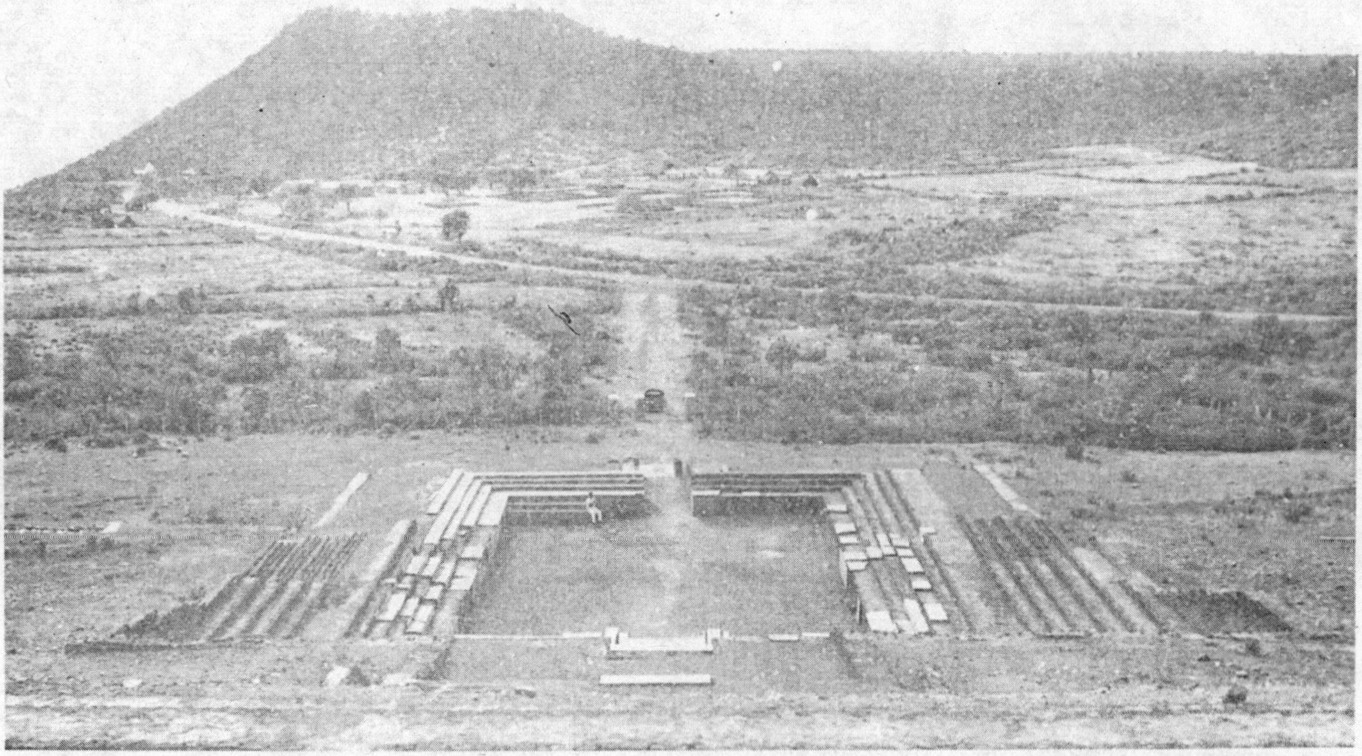

10. Stadium from top, Nāgārjunakoṇḍa.

11. Bouleterion at Priene, Western Turkey, 2nd century B.C. (Photo: Joan Aruz).

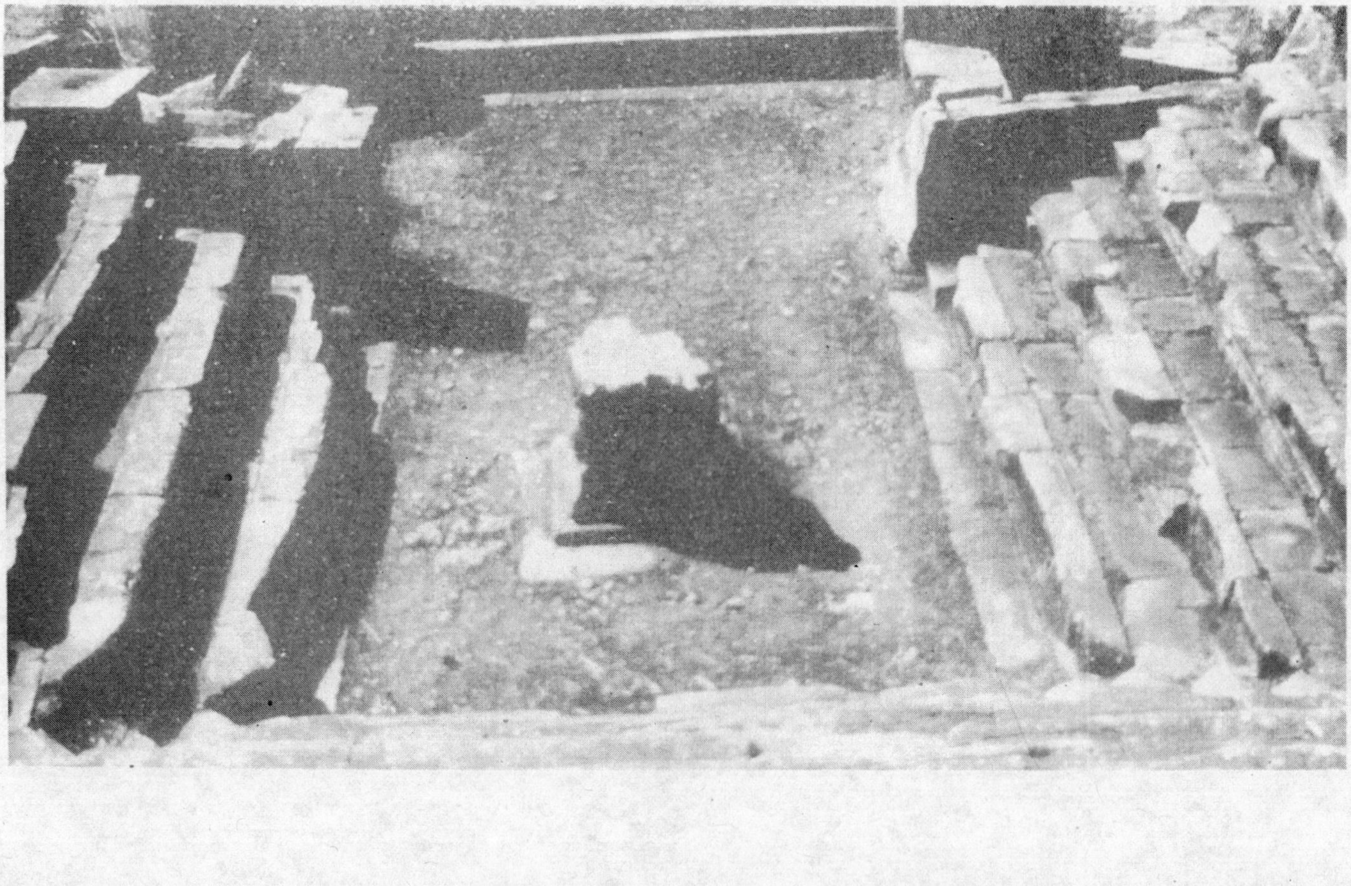

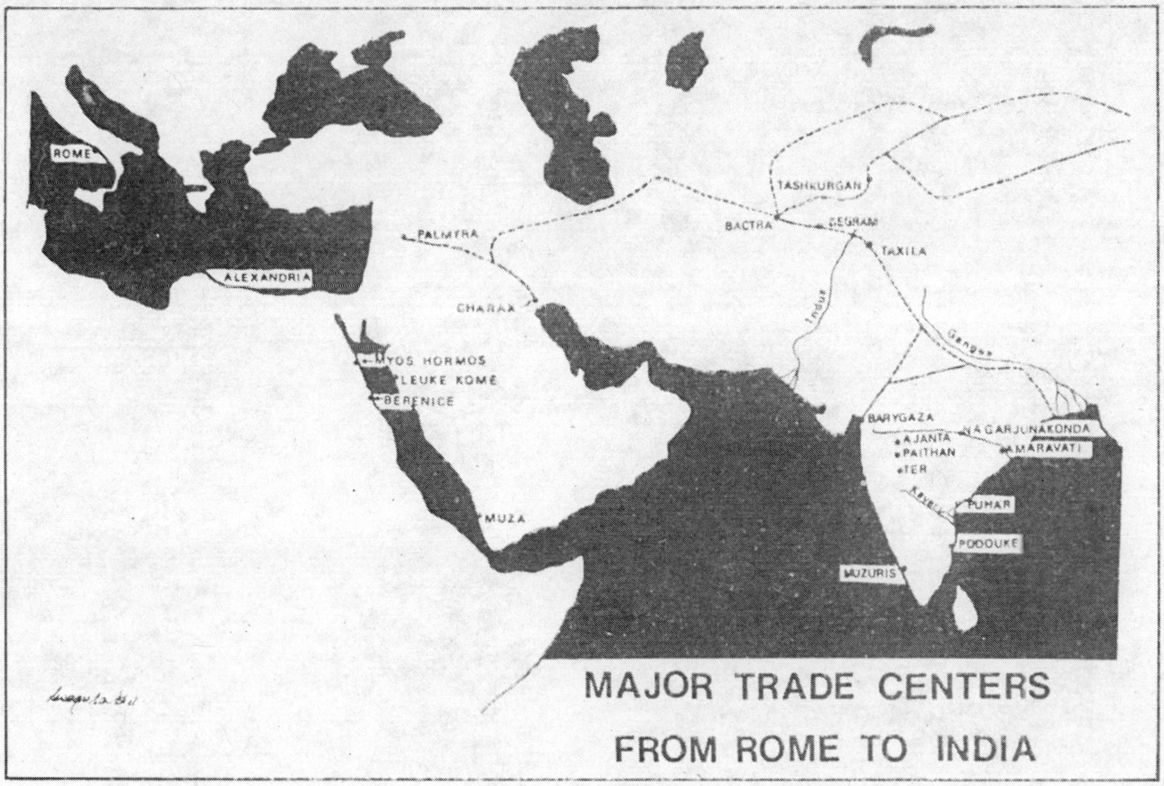

12. Map showing centers of trade (adapted by Swagata Guha from Sir Mortimer Wheeler, *Rome Beyond Imperial Frontiers*, London, 1954).

13. Sarvadeva temple, Nāgārjunakoṇḍa (Photo: Archaeological Survey of India).

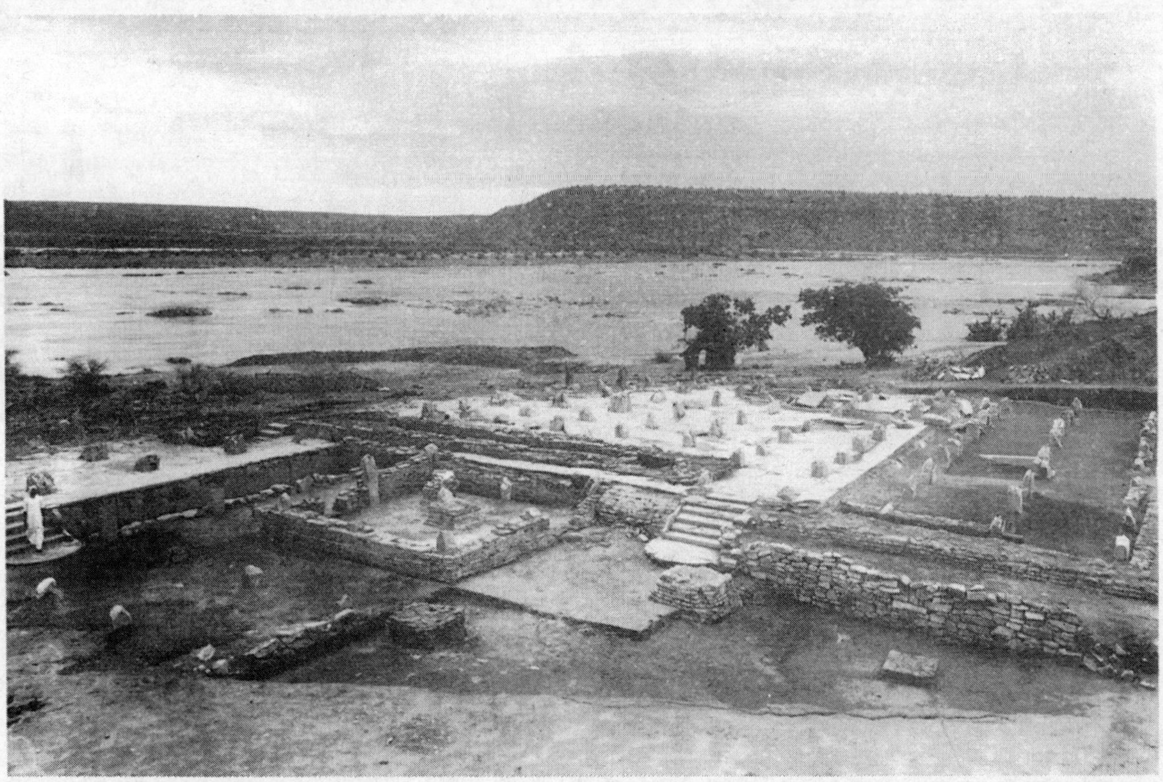

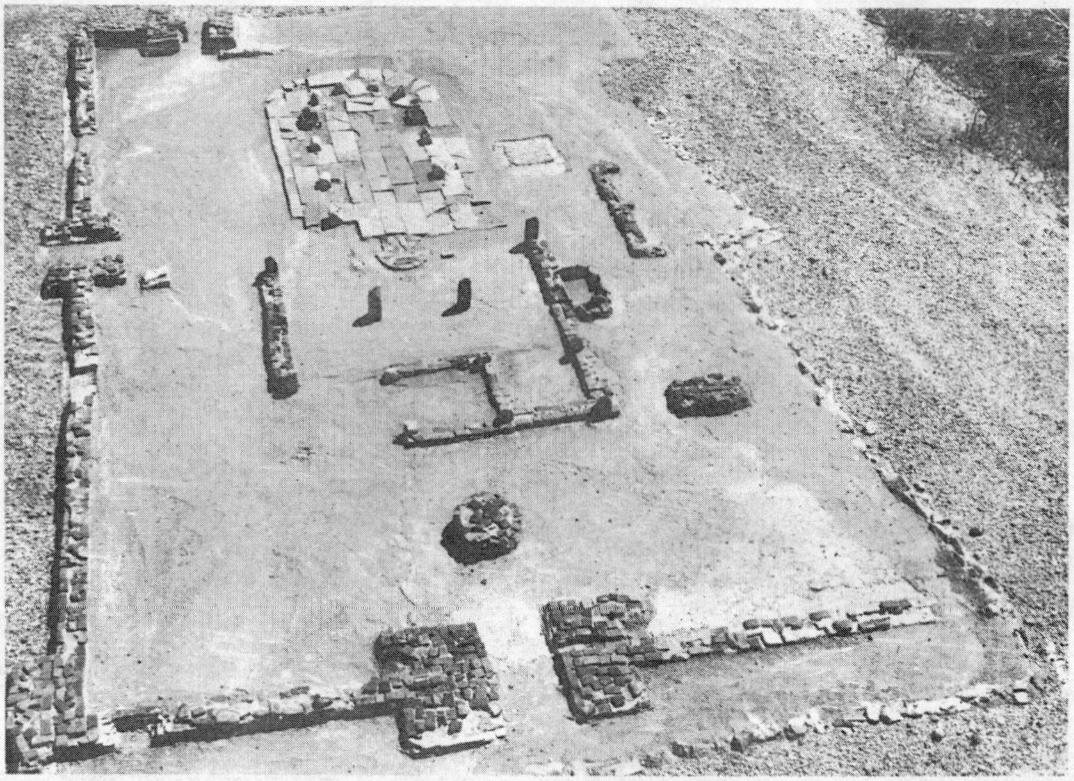

14. Puṣpabhadrasvāmin temple (model), Nāgārjunakoṇḍa (Photo: Archaeological Survey of India).

15. Plan of the Puṣpabhadrasvāmin temple (adapted by B. Forman after K.V. Soundara Rajan, *Architecture of the Early Hindu Temples of Andhra Pradesh*, Andhra Pradesh Government Archaeological Series, No. 21, Hyderabad, 1965, fig. 2).

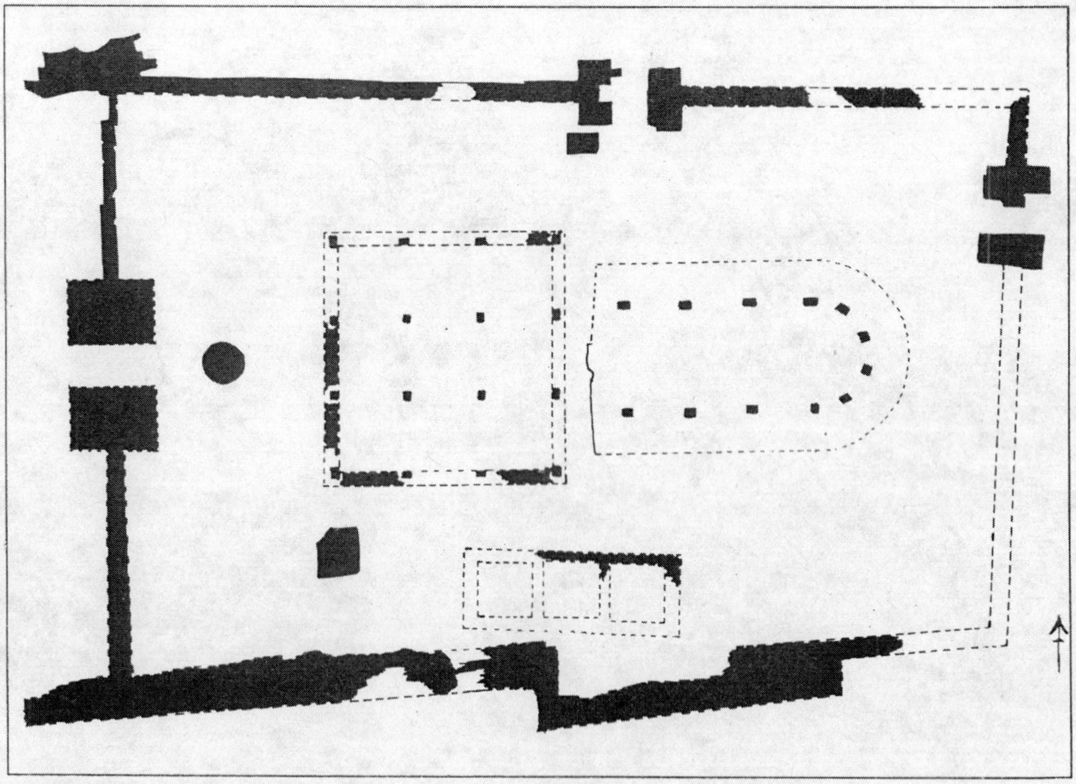

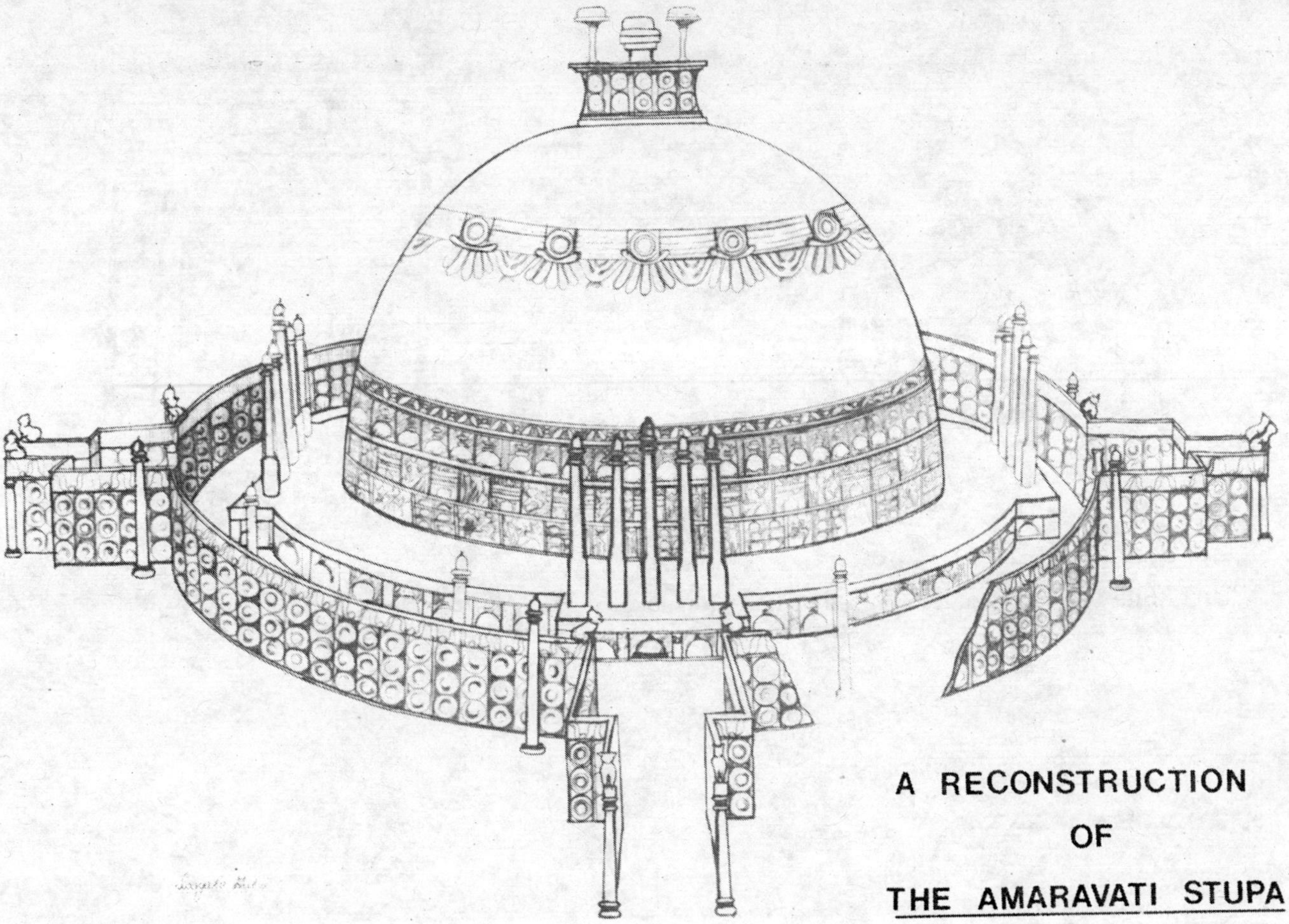

16. Reconstruction of the Amarāvatī *Stūpa* (Swagata Guha, based upon the model in the Archaeological Museum, Amarāvatī).

17. The *Mahācetiya*, Site 1, Nāgārjunakoṇḍa (Photo: Archaeological Survey of India).

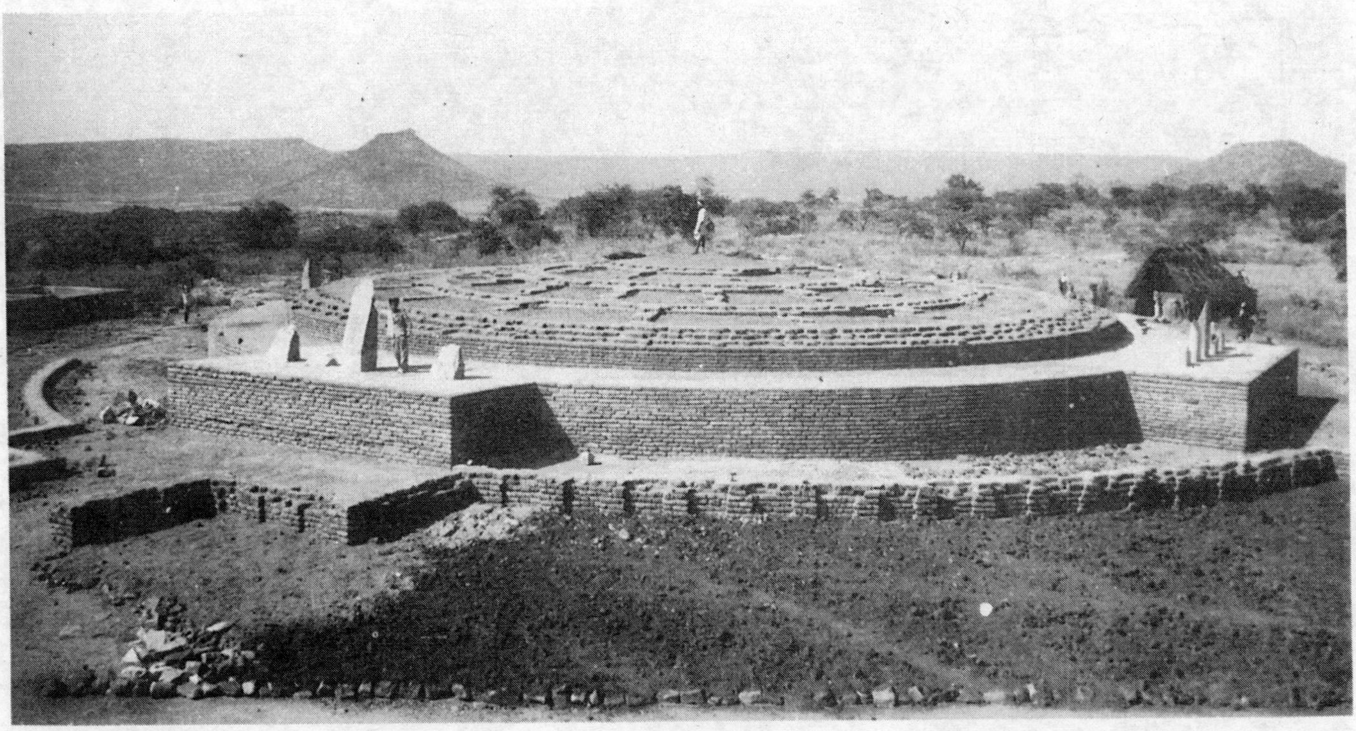

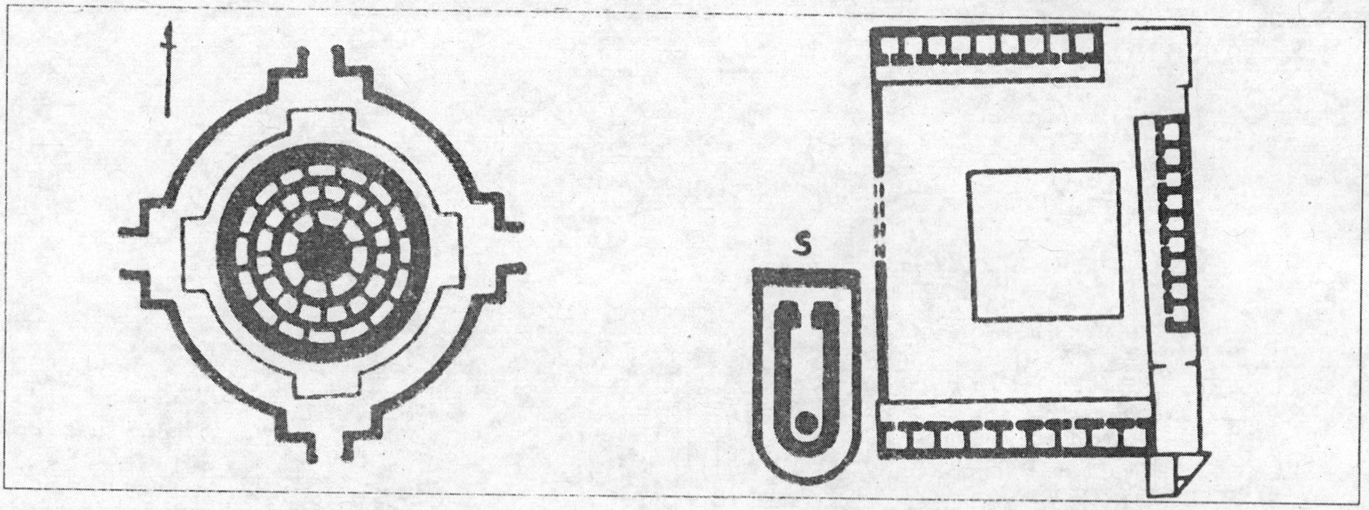

18. Plan of Site 1, Nāgārjunakoṇḍa (B. Forman after H. Sarkar, *Buddhist Architecture*, pl. XIII).

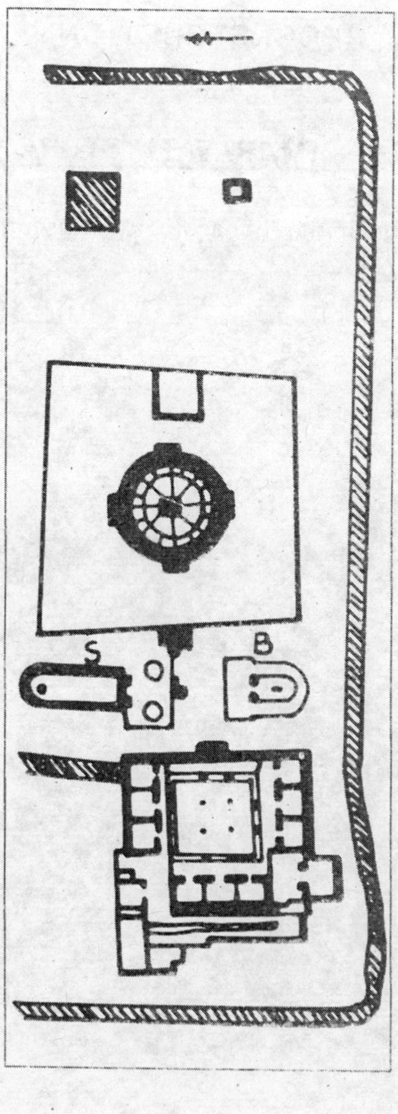

19. Plan of Site 9, Nāgārjunakoṇḍa (adapted by B. Forman from H. Sarkar, *Buddhist Architecture*, pl. XIII).

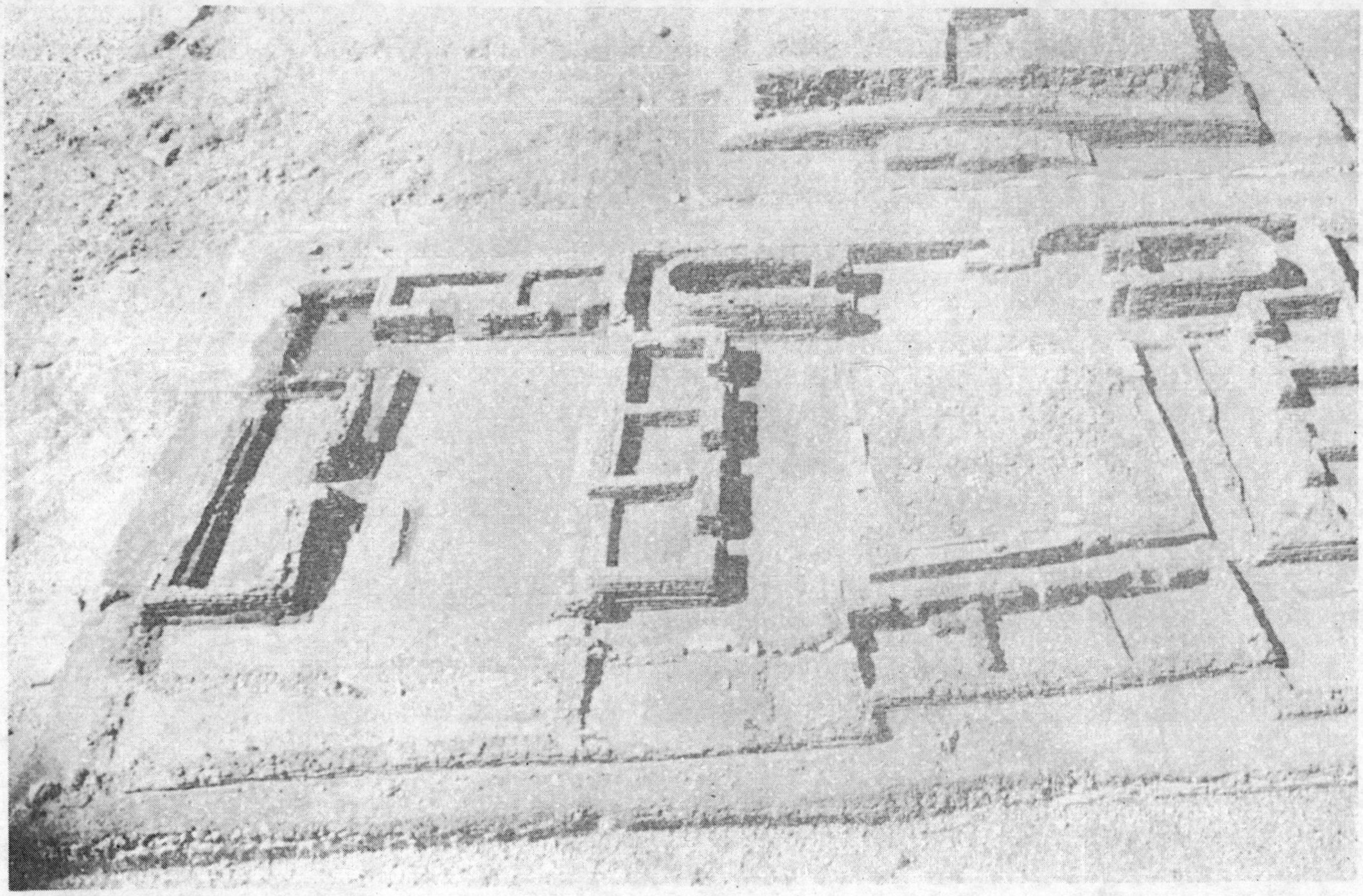

20. Model of Site 4.

21. Plan of Site 4 (adapted by B. Forman, from H. Sarkar, *Buddhist Architecture*, pl. XIII).

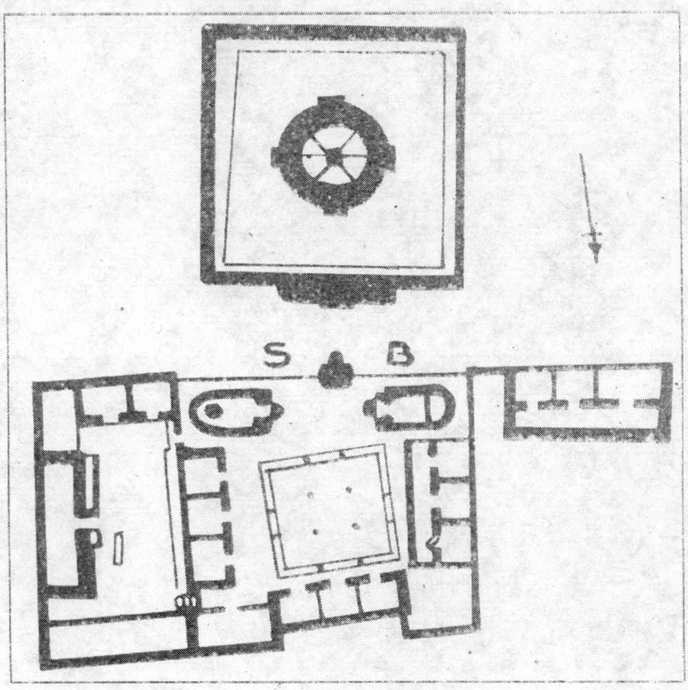

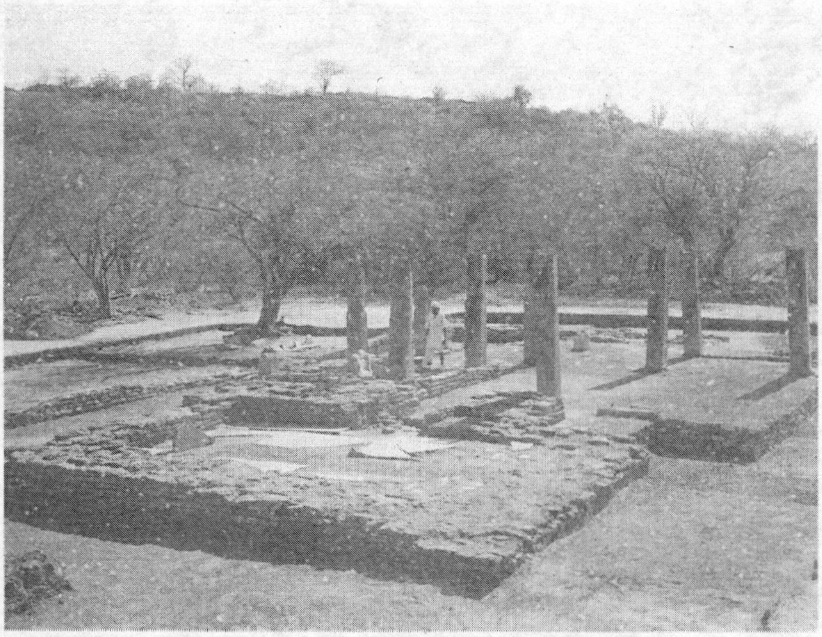

23. "Hāritī" temple, Nāgārjunakoṇḍa (Photo: Archaeological Survey of India).

24. Seated image, "Hāritī" temple, Nāgārjunakoṇḍa.

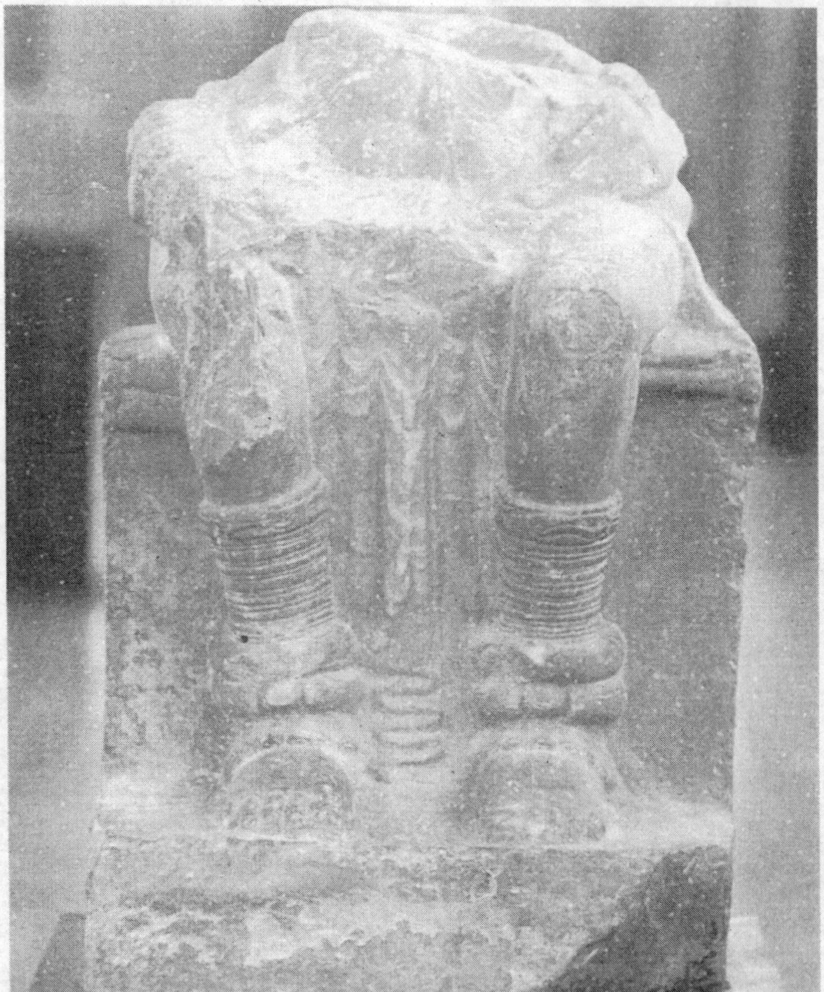

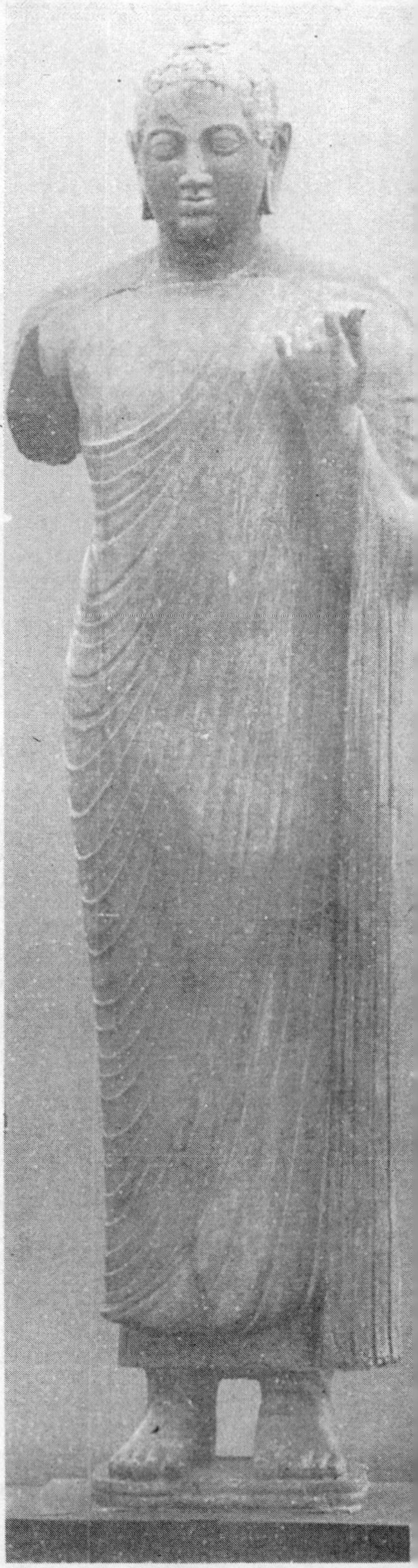

22. Buddha image, Site 4, face re-stored.

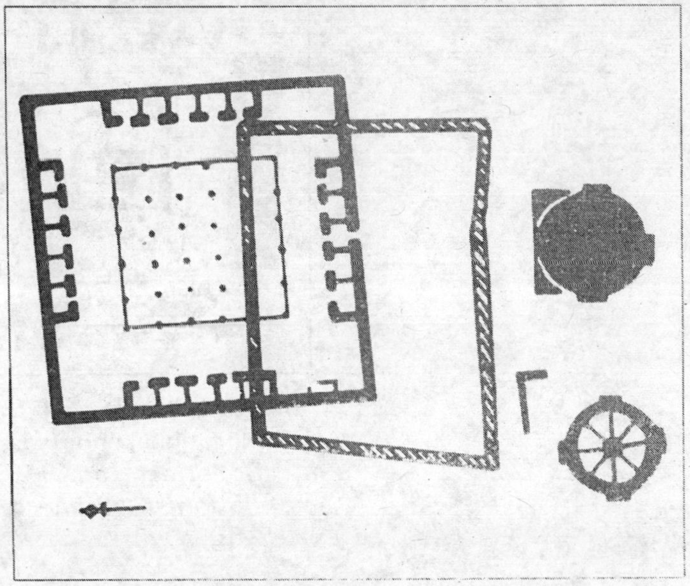

25. Ground plan of Site 7-8 (adapted by B. Forman after H. Sarkar, *Buddhist Architecture*, pl. XIII).

26. Ground plan of Site 5, Nāgārjunakoṇḍa (adapted by B. Forman after H. Sarkar, *Buddhist Architecture*, pl. XIII).

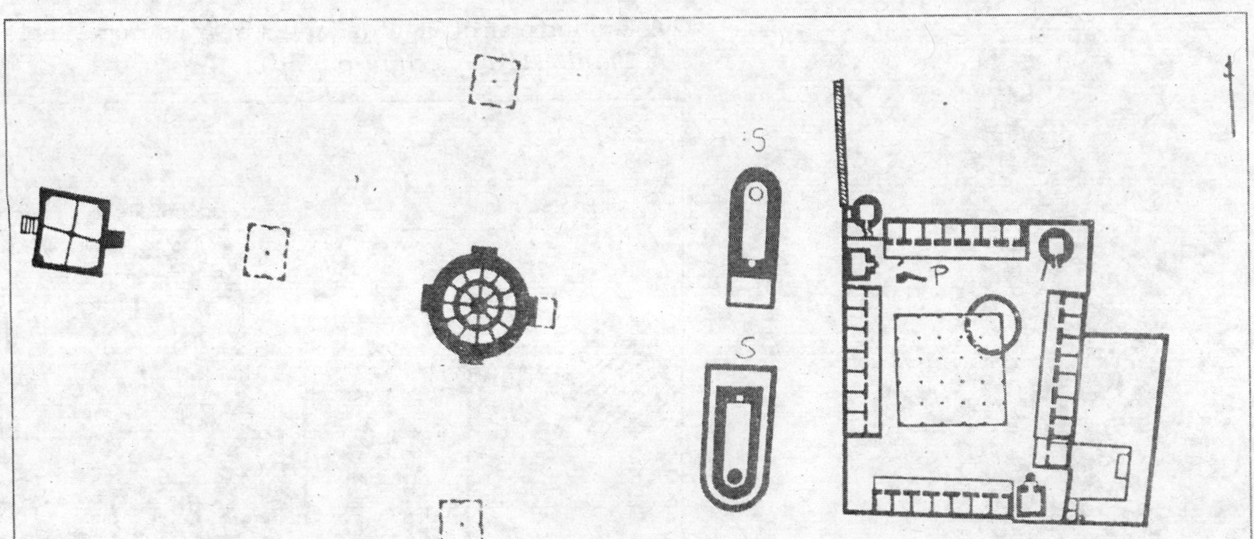

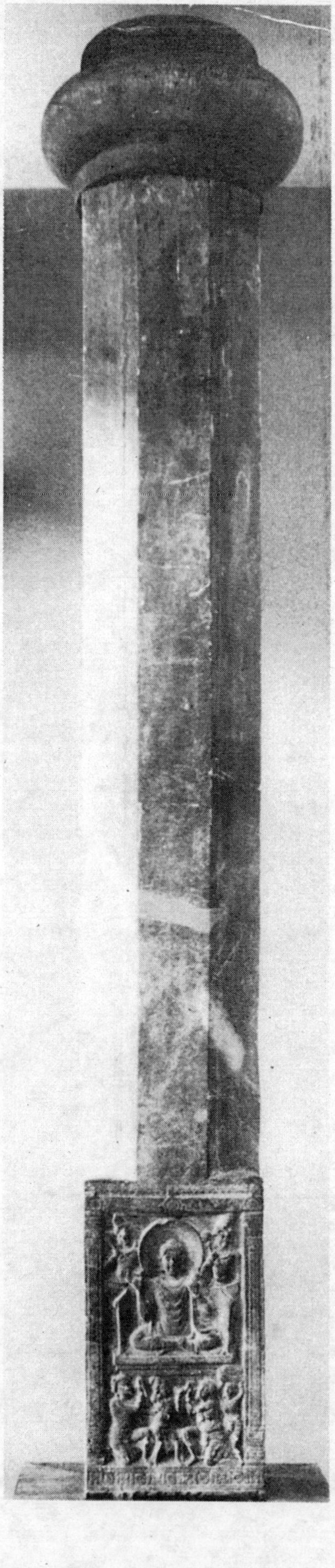

27. Pillar, Site 5 (Photo: Archaeological Survey of India).

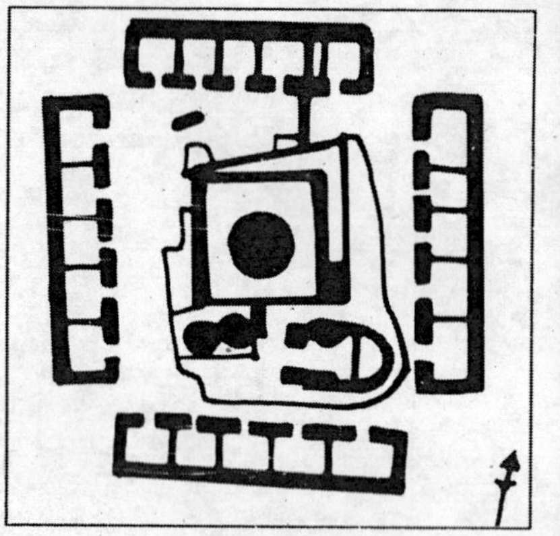

28. Ground plan of Site 38, Nāgārjunakoṇḍa (adapted by B. Forman from H. Sarkar, *Buddhist Architecture*, pl. XIII).

29. Ground plan of Site 43 (adapted by B. Forman after H. Sarkar, *Buddhist Architecture*, pl. XIII).

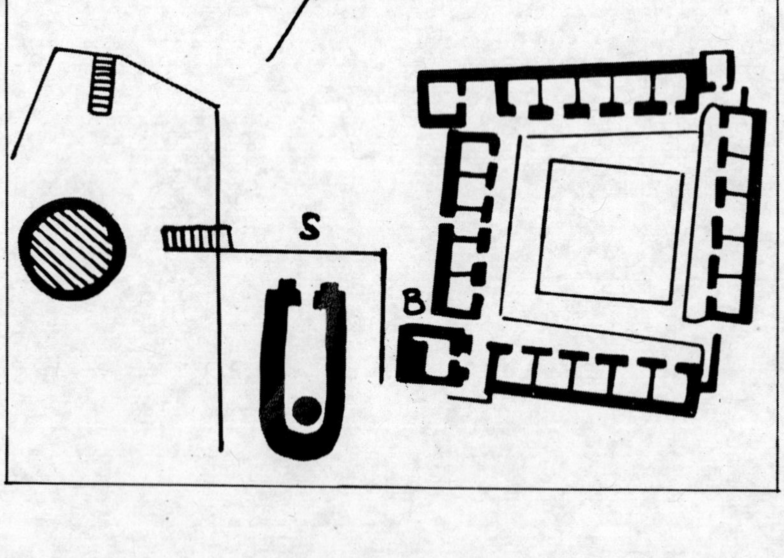

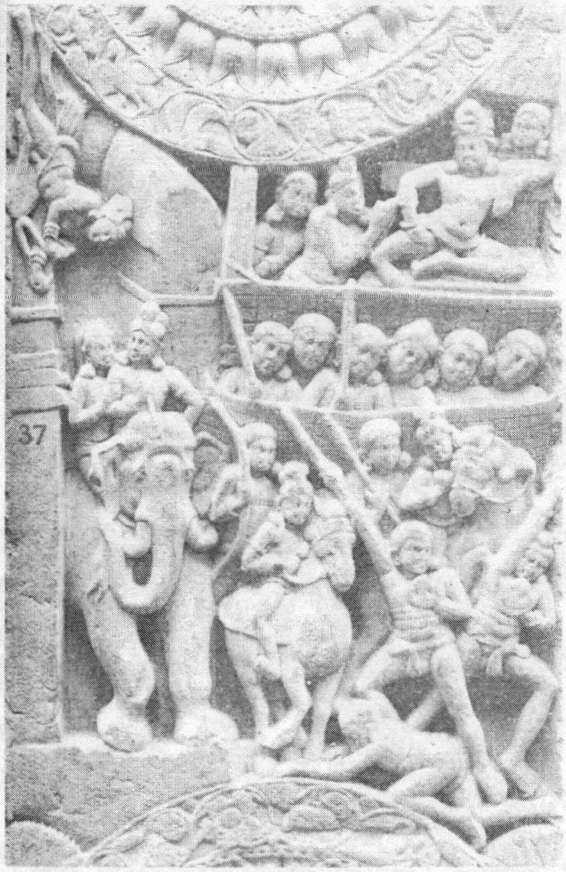

30. Scene of Valour (?), railing pillar from Amarāvatī, now British Museum (Photo: Trustees of the British Museum).

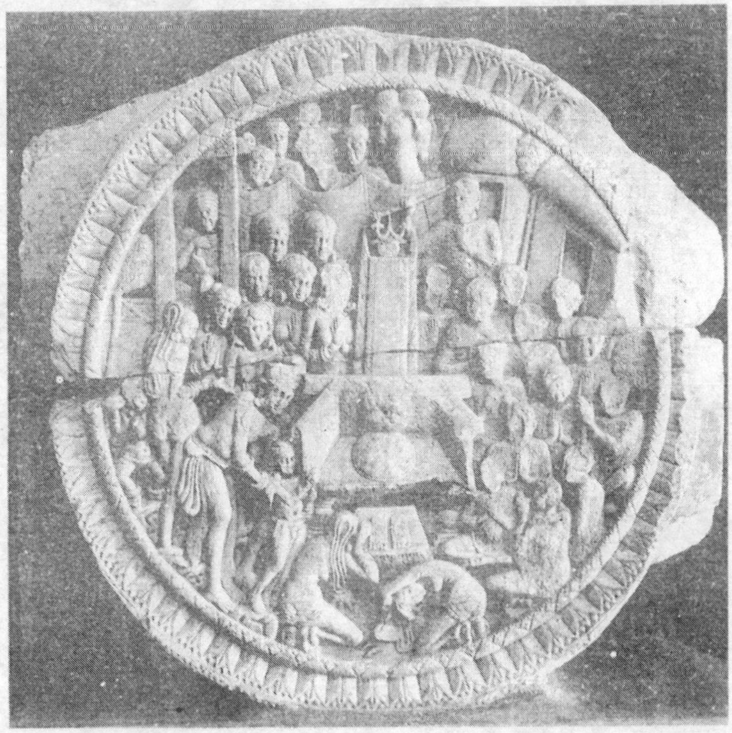

32. Presentation of Rāhula, crossbar from Amarāvatī railing Archaeological Museum, Amarāvatī (Photo: Archaeological Survey of India).

31. Return to Kapilavastu, coping stone from Amarāvatī, now British Museum (Photo: Trustees of the British Museum).

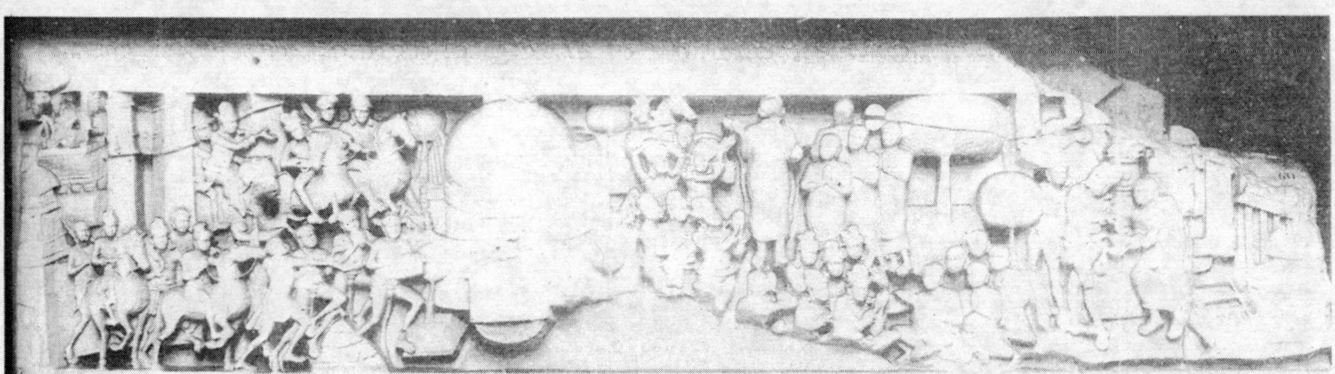

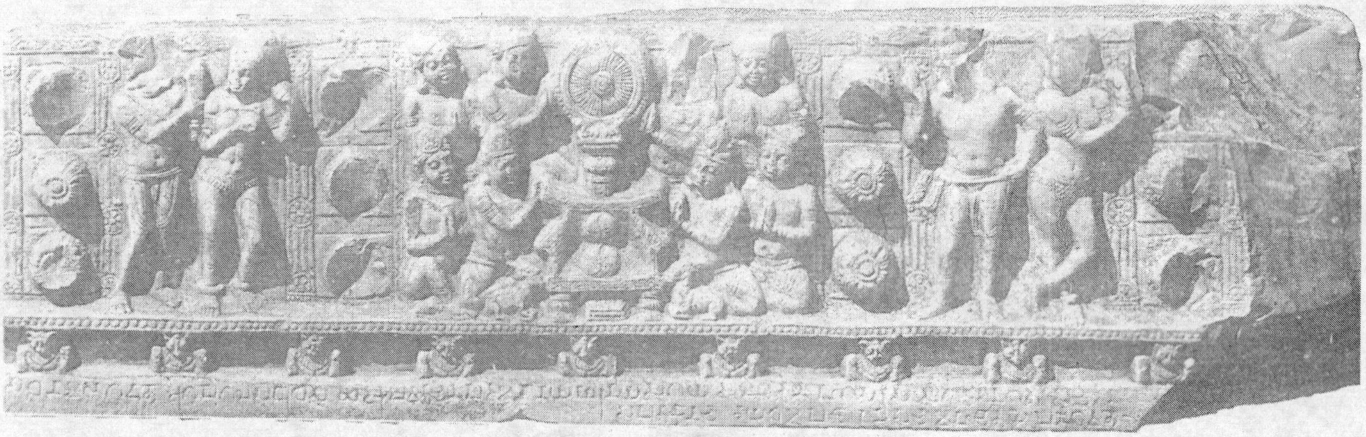

33. The First Sermon, part of an *āyaka* cornice from Nāgārjunakoṇḍa intended for the *Mahācetiya* (Photo: Archaeological Survey of India).

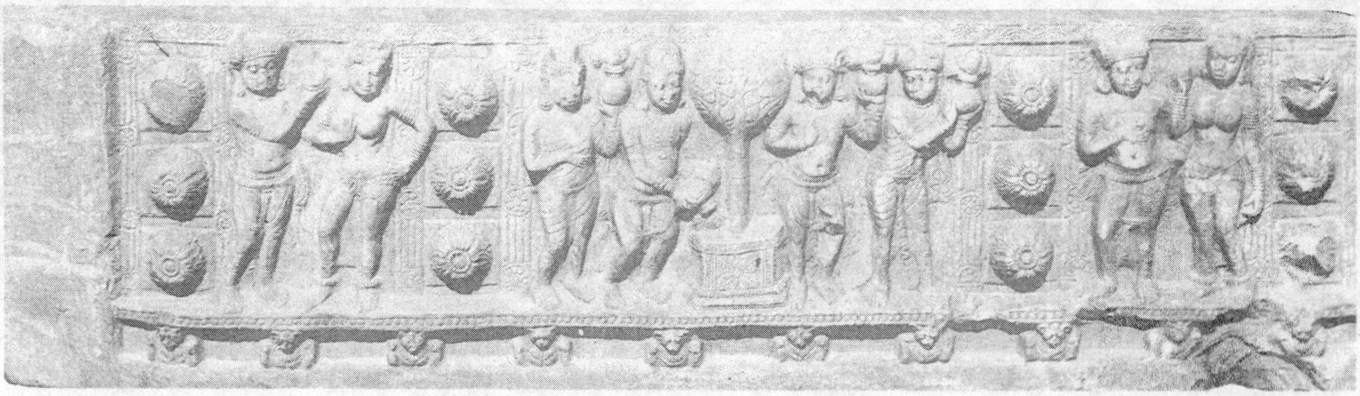

34. Worship of the Bodhi Tree, section of an *āyaka* cornice (Photo: Archaeological Survey of India).

35. Champaka Jātaka, fragment of an *āyaka* cornice (Photo: Archaeological Survey of India).

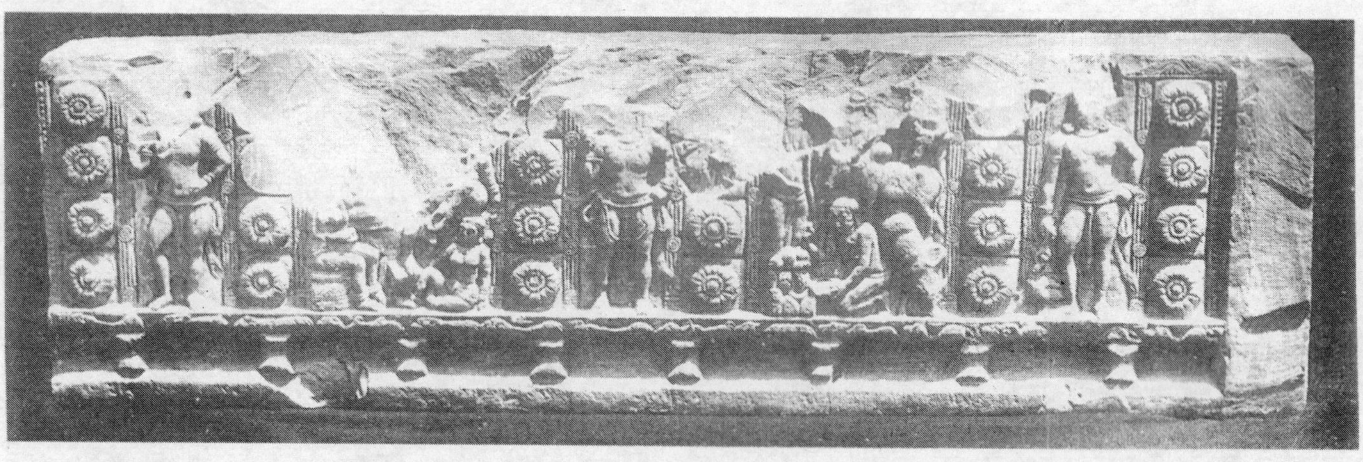

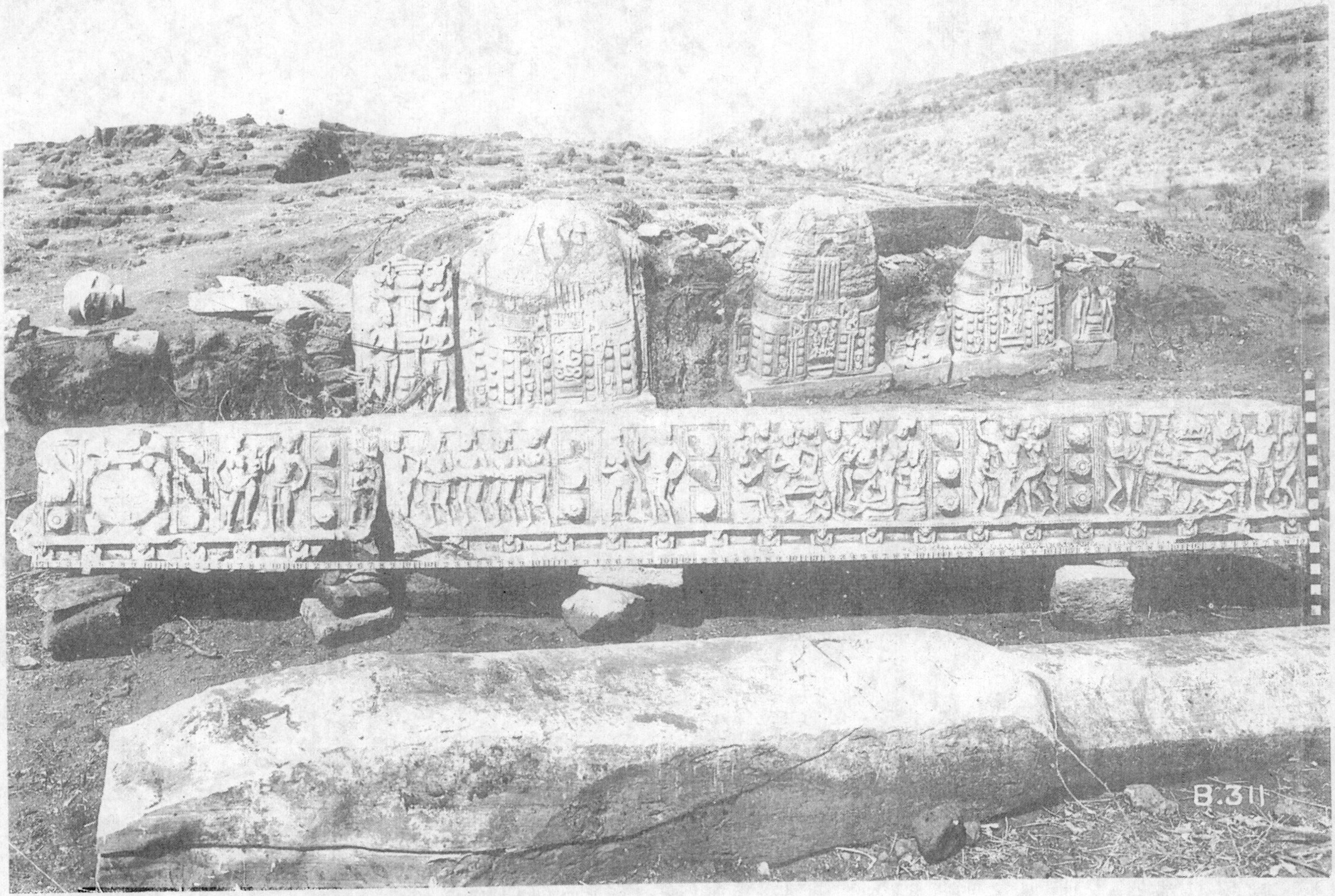

36. Site 6 (Photo: Archaeological Survey of India).

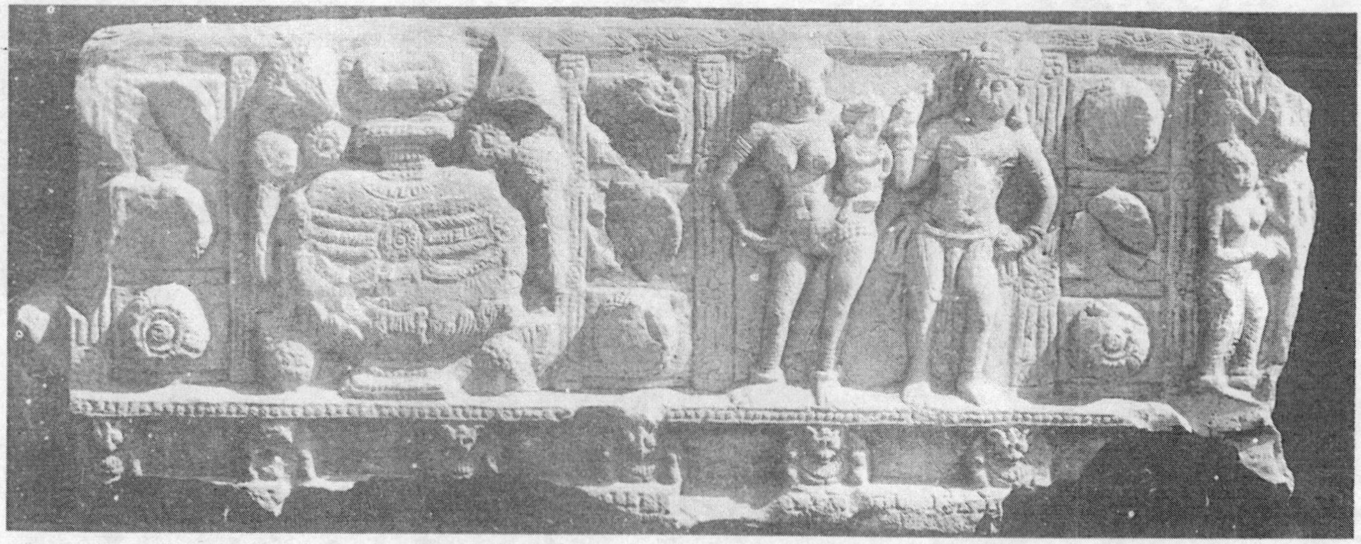

37. Fragment of an *āyaka* cornice, Site 6.

38. Fragment of an ivory throne from Begram, now *Musée* Guimet (Photo: RMN. Paris).

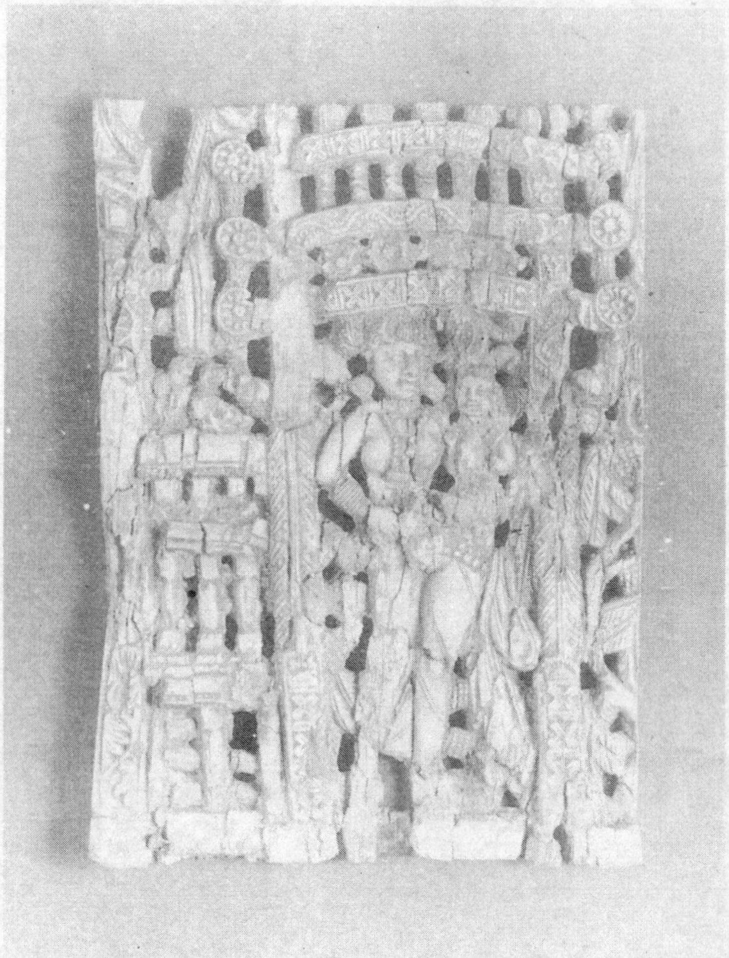

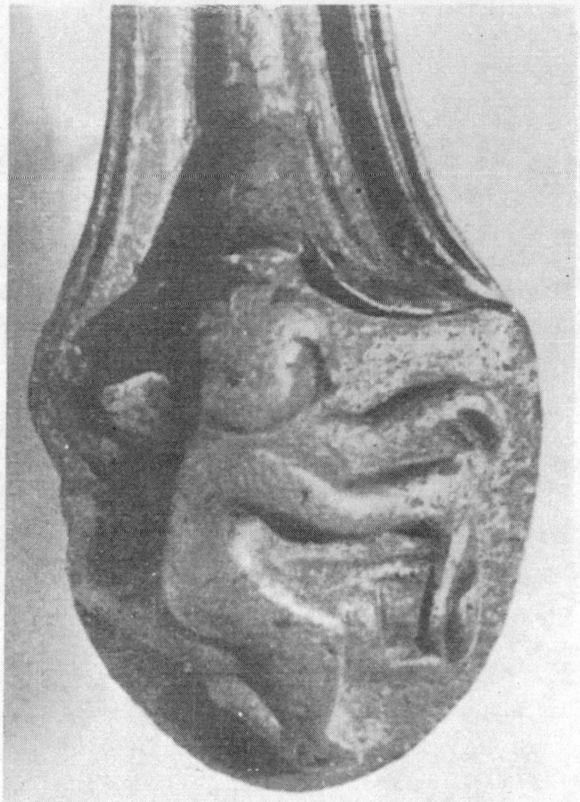

39. Bronze handle from Akota, now Baroda Museum and Picture Gallery.

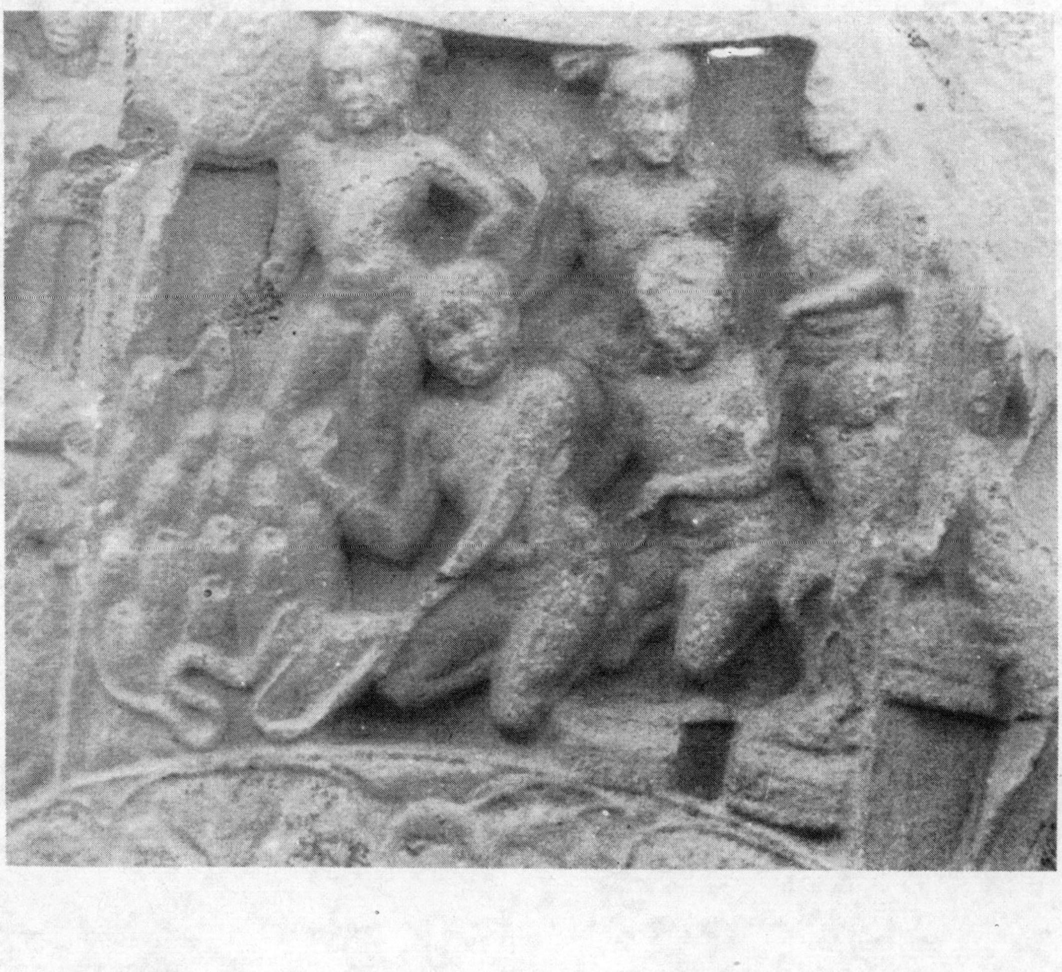

40. Champaka Jātaka, fragment of a railing from Amarāvatī, now Archaeological Museum, Amarāvatī.

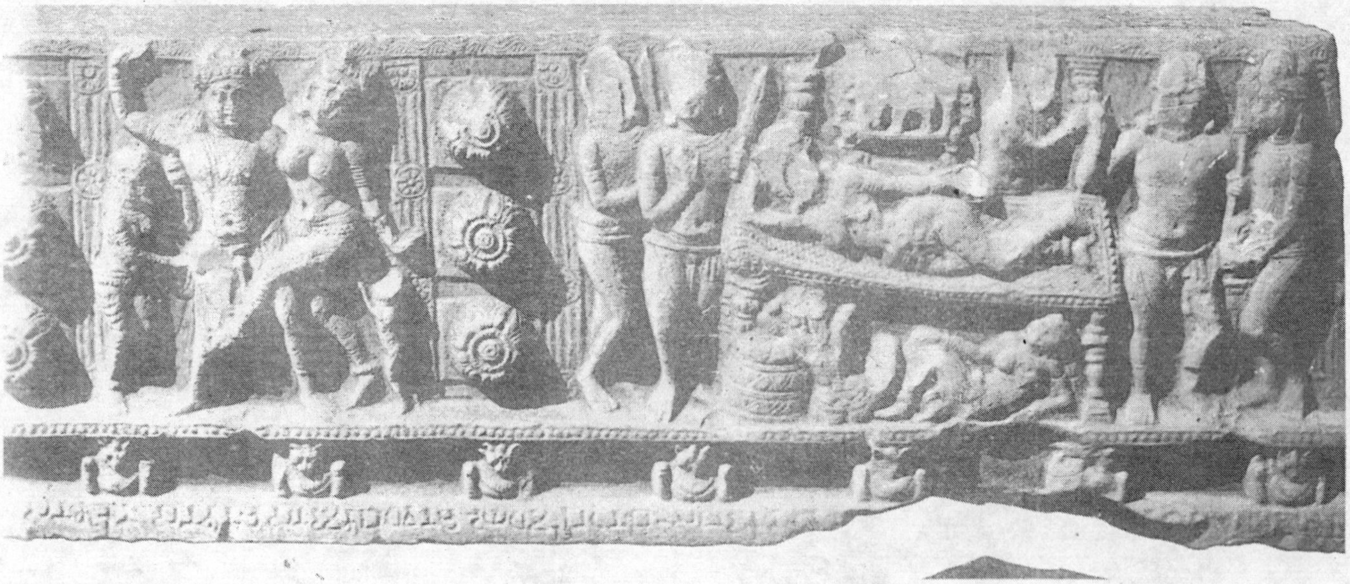

41. The Dream of Queen Māyā, detail of an *āyaka* panel from Site 6 (Photo: Archaeological Survey of India).

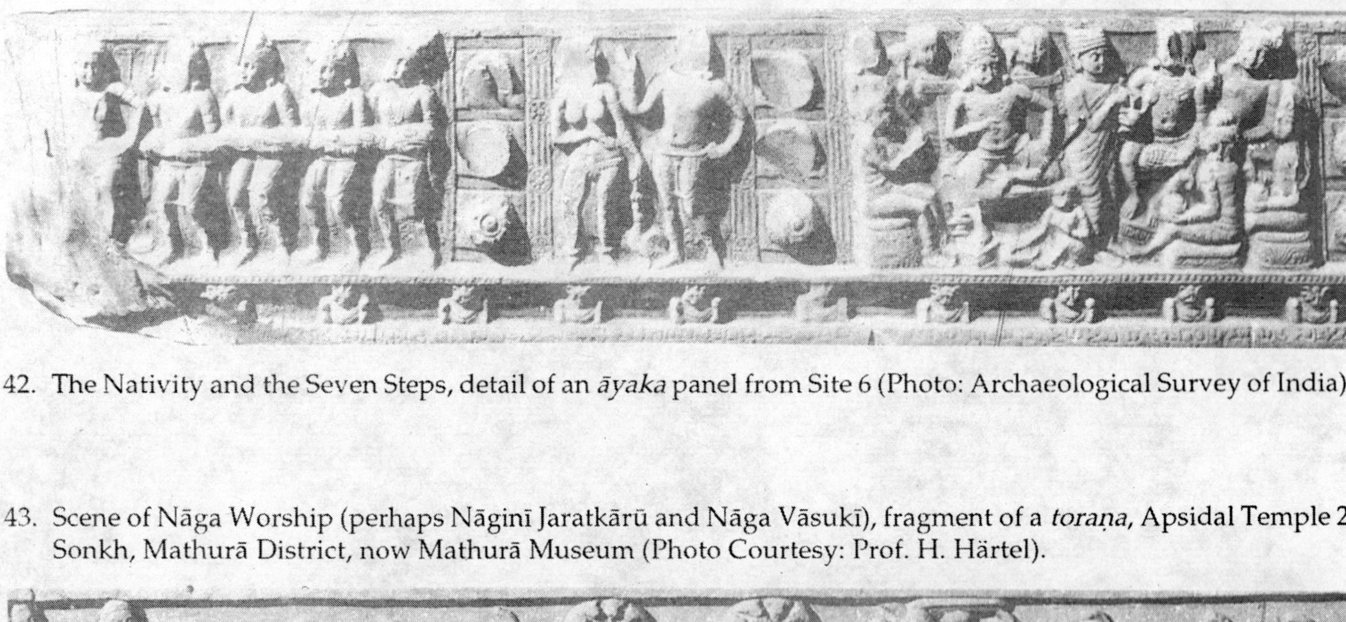

42. The Nativity and the Seven Steps, detail of an *āyaka* panel from Site 6 (Photo: Archaeological Survey of India).

43. Scene of Nāga Worship (perhaps Nāginī Jaratkārū and Nāga Vāsukī), fragment of a *toraṇa*, Apsidal Temple 2, Sonkh, Mathurā District, now Mathurā Museum (Photo Courtesy: Prof. H. Härtel).

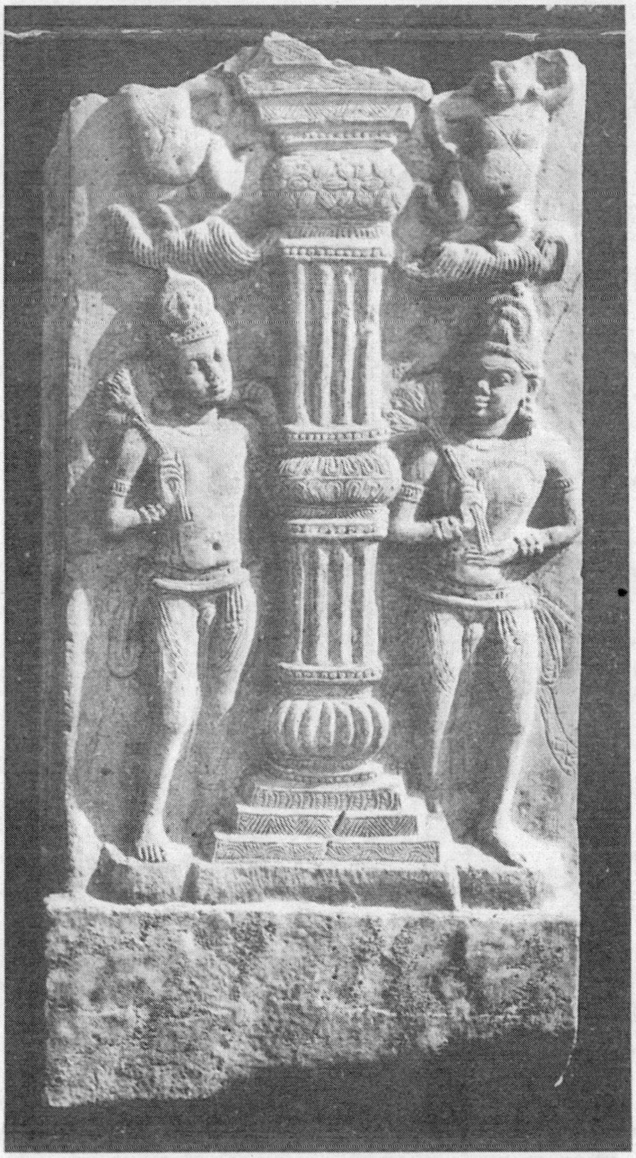

44. Adoration of a pillar, Site 6 (Photo: Archaeological Survey of India).

45. Imitation Roman gold coins found at Site 6 (Photo: Archaeological Survey of India).

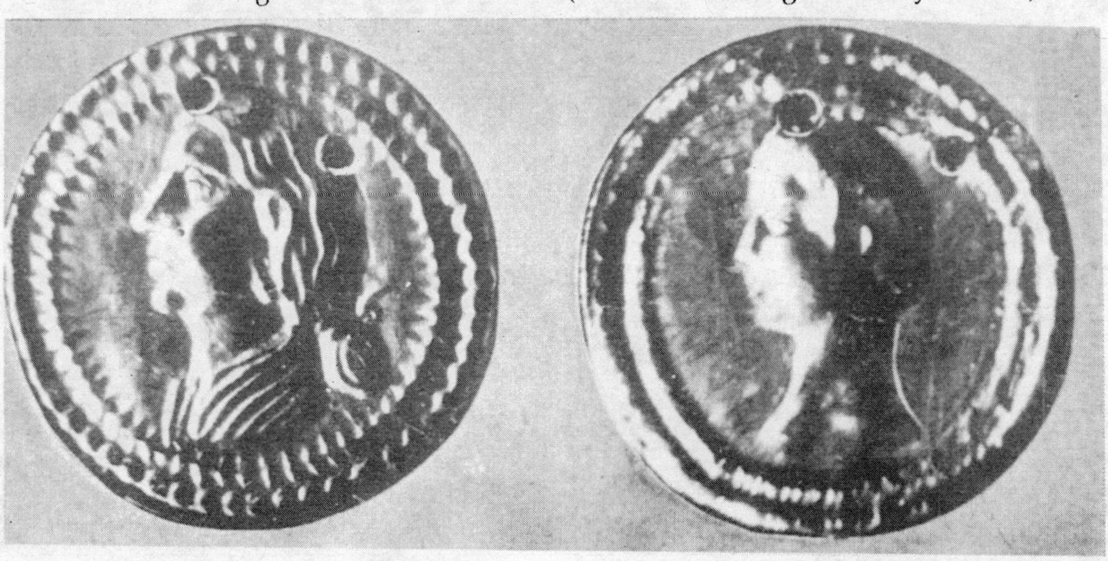

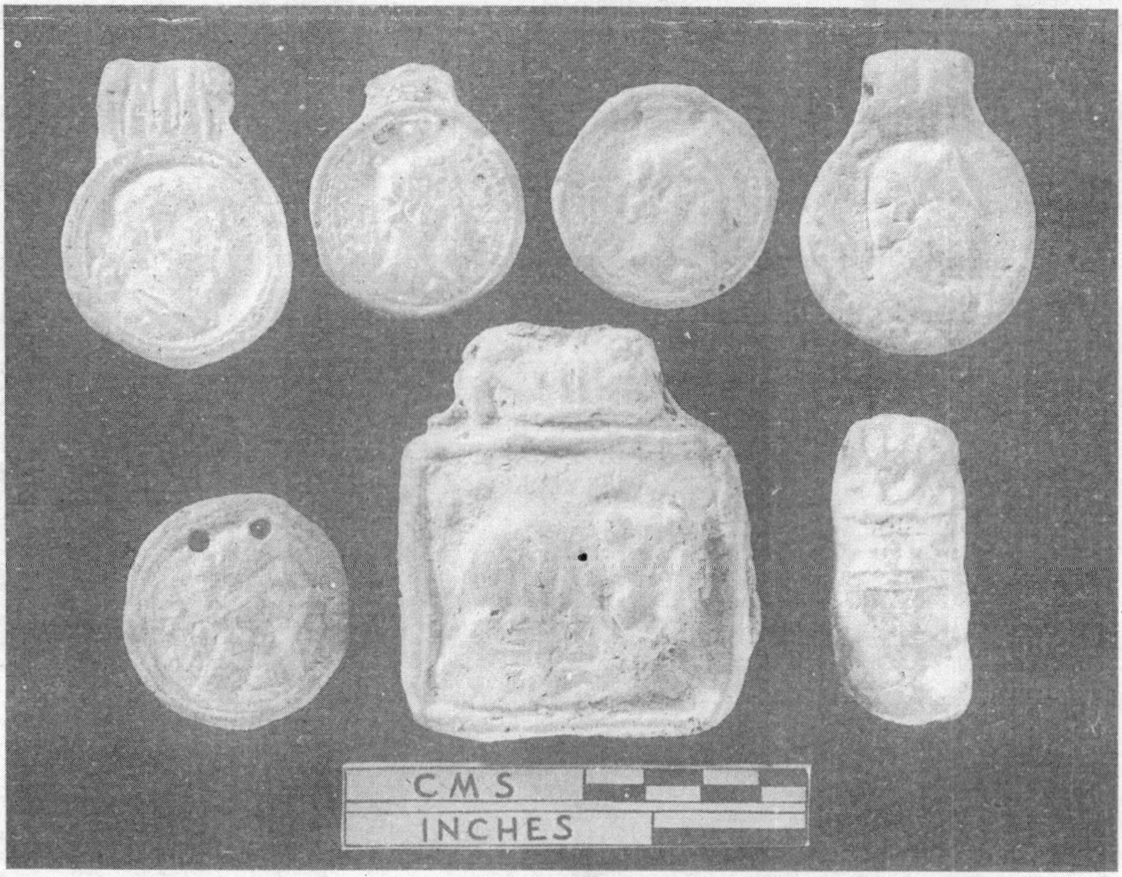

46. Clay *bullae* in imitation of Roman coins (Photo: Archaeological Survey of India).

47. Viśvaṁtara Jātaka, detail of a panel from Site 23.

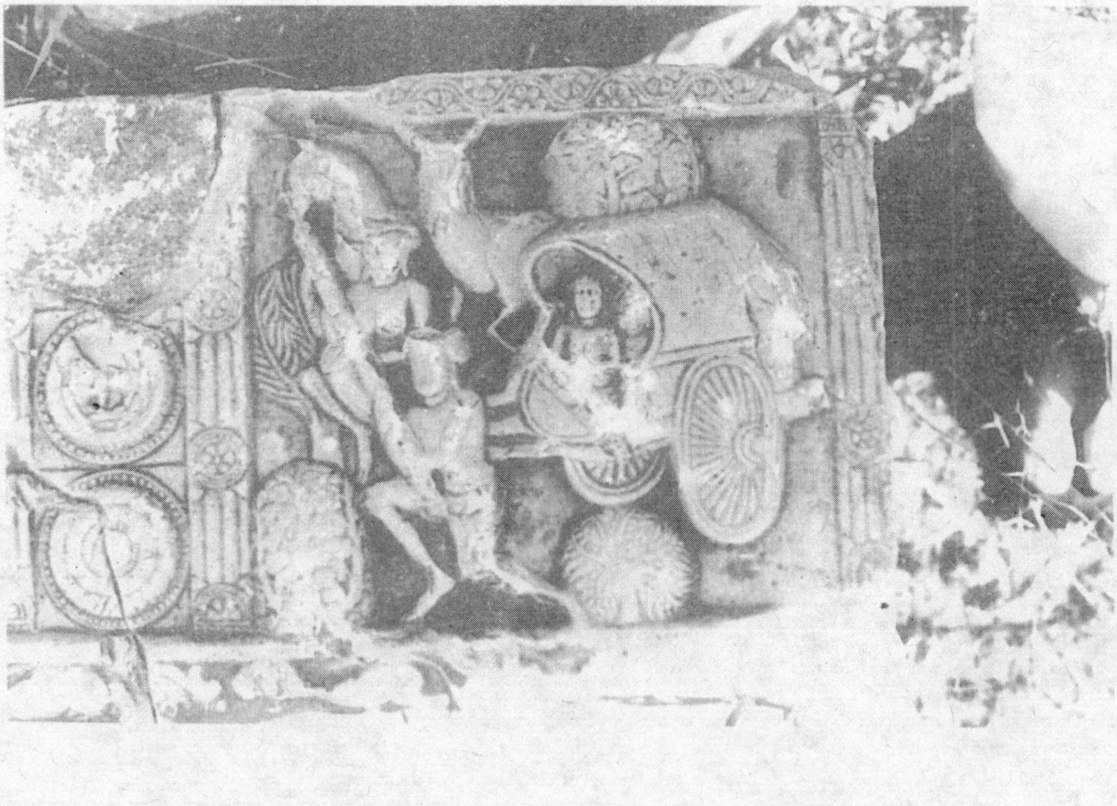

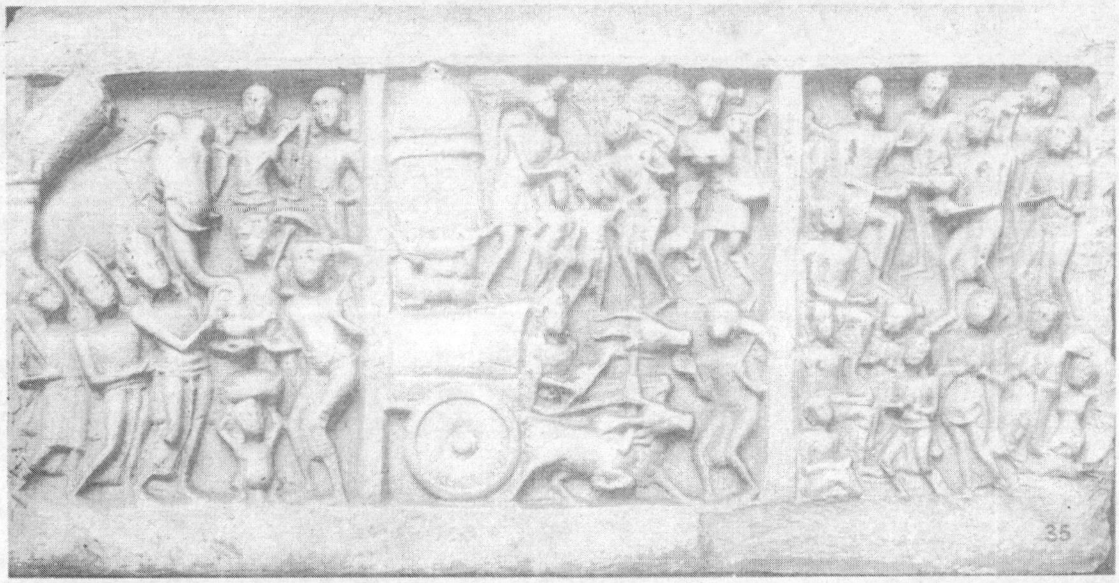

48. Viśvaṁtara Jātaka, detail of coping stone from Amarāvatī, now British Museum (Photo: Trustees of the British Museum).

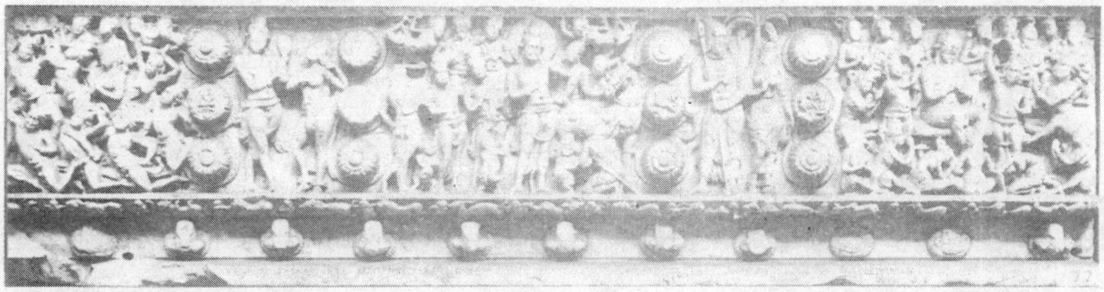

49. Frieze from Amarāvatī, now British Museum (Photo: Trustees of the British Museum).

50. The Elevation of the Headdress of the Buddha, detail of fig. 49.

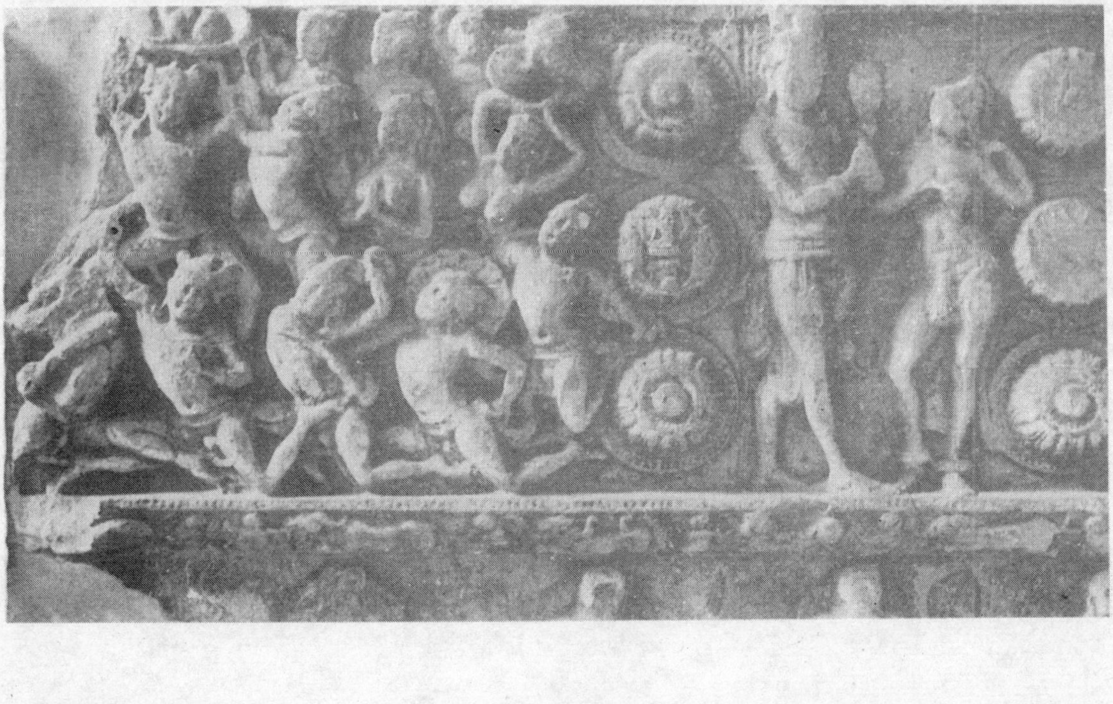

51. Memorial Pillar to Cāṁtamūla I found at Site 9, dated in the year *vijaya* of King Vīrapuruṣadatta (Photo: Archaeological Survey of India).

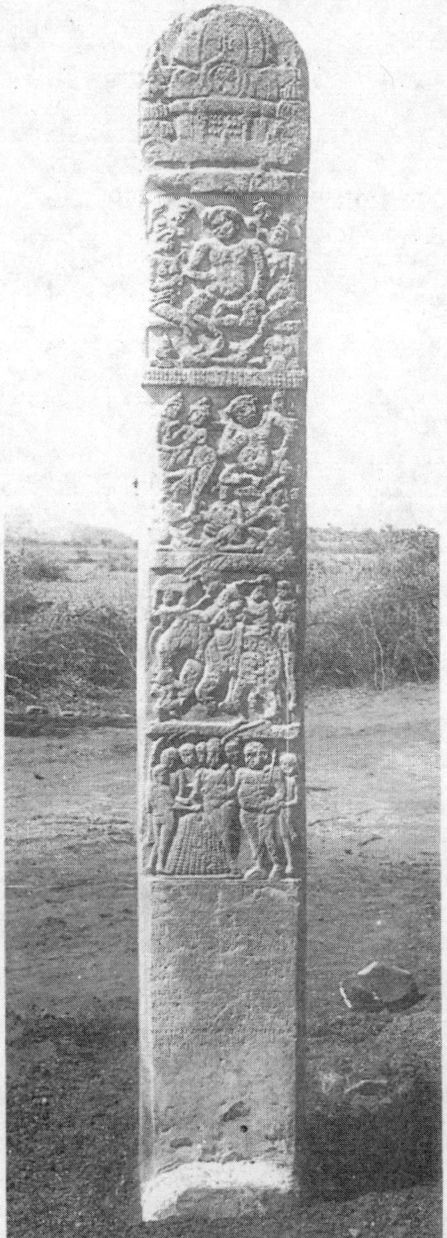

52. Detail of fig. 51.

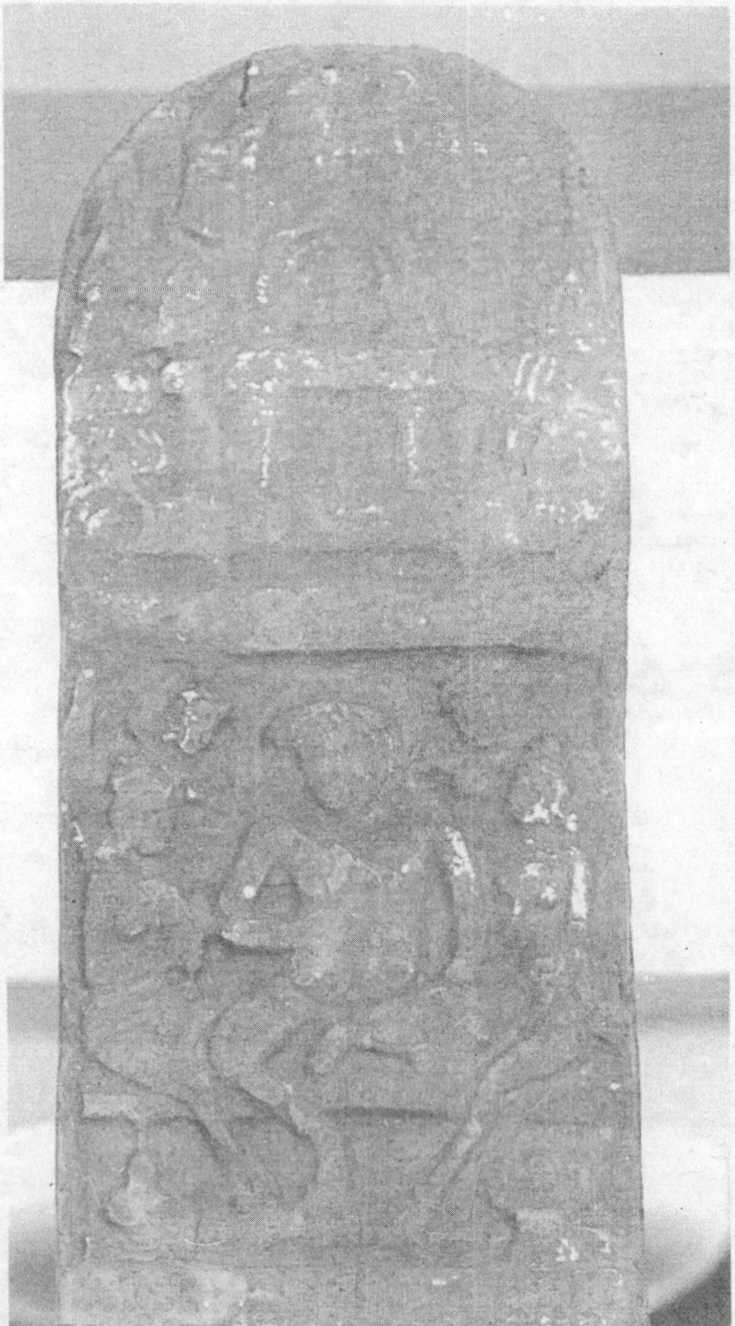

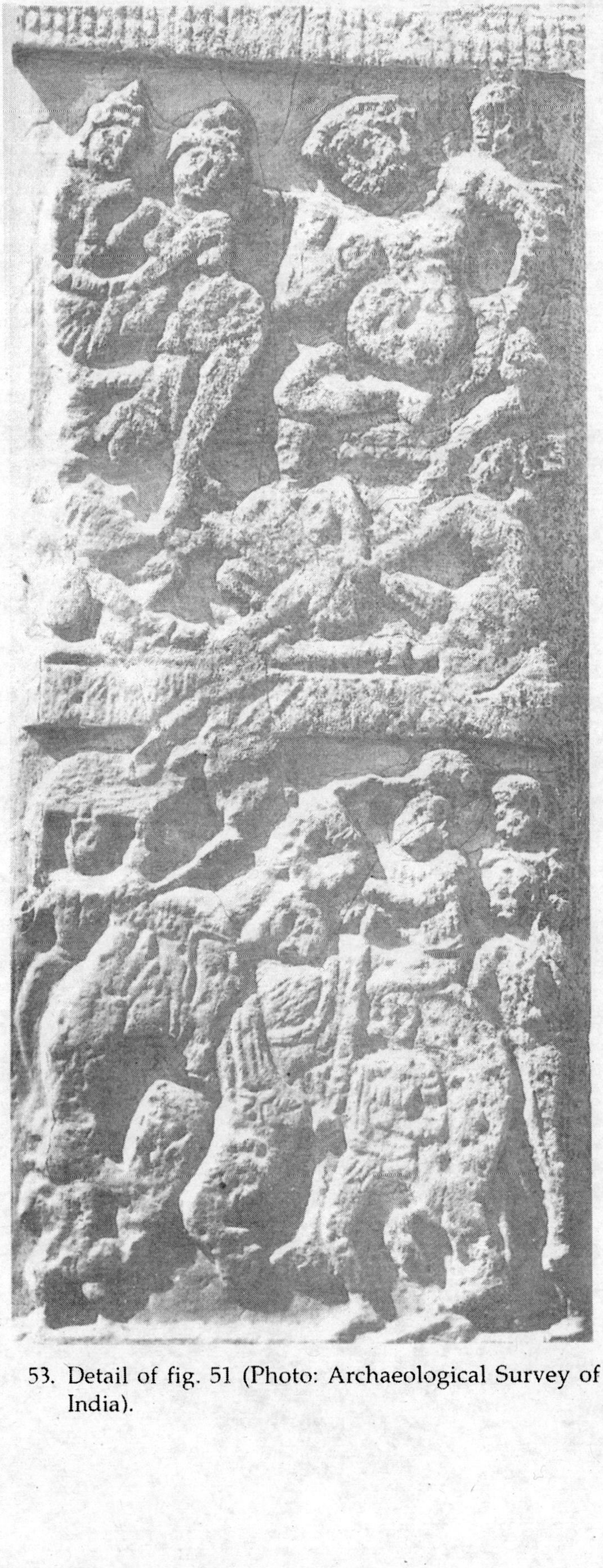

53. Detail of fig. 51 (Photo: Archaeological Survey of India).

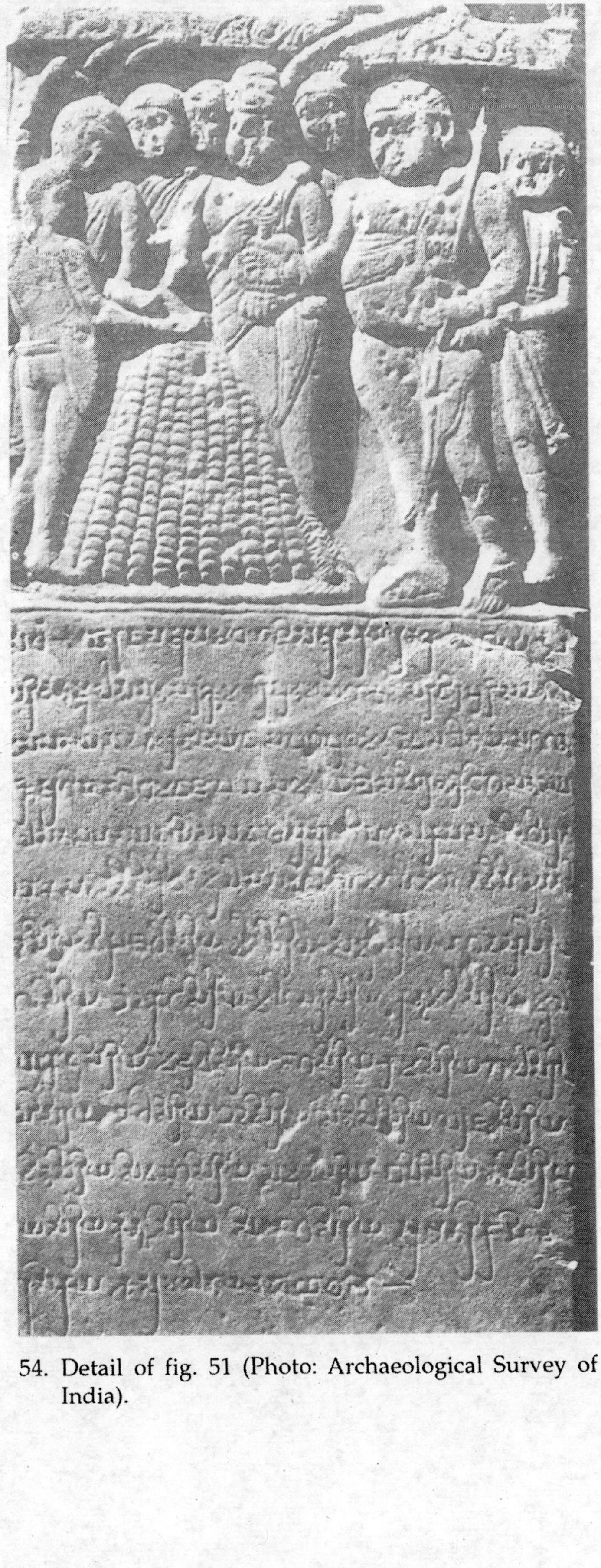

54. Detail of fig. 51 (Photo: Archaeological Survey of India).

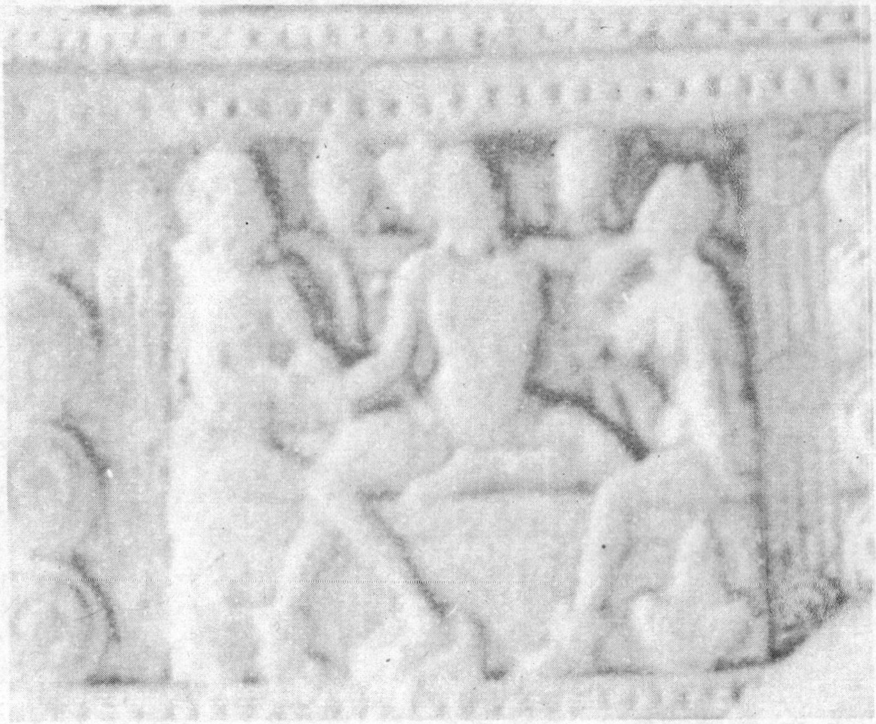

55. Detail of fig. 67.

56. Detail of fig. 67.

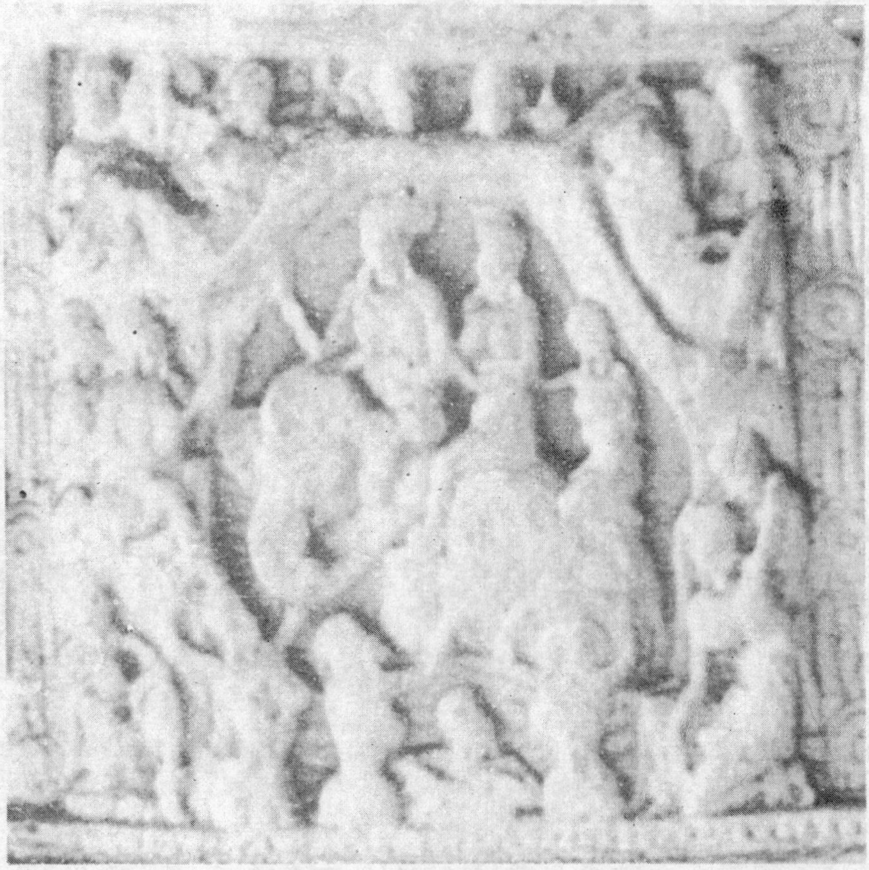

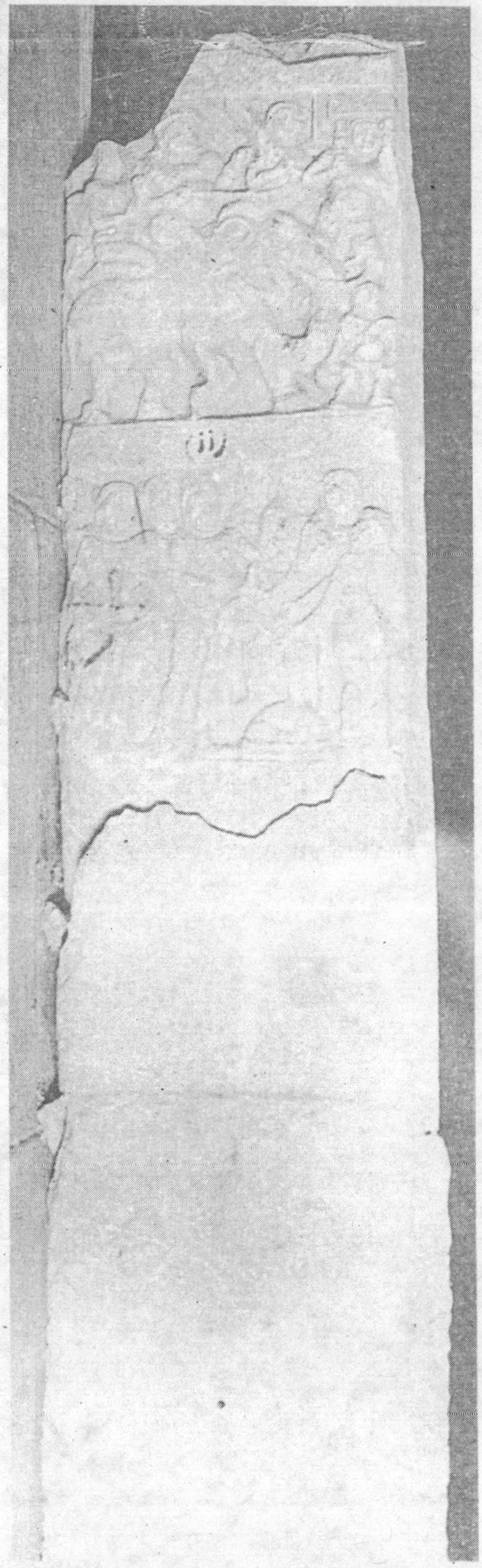

57. Memorial Pillar to Cāṁtamūla I (Photo: Archaeological Survey of India).

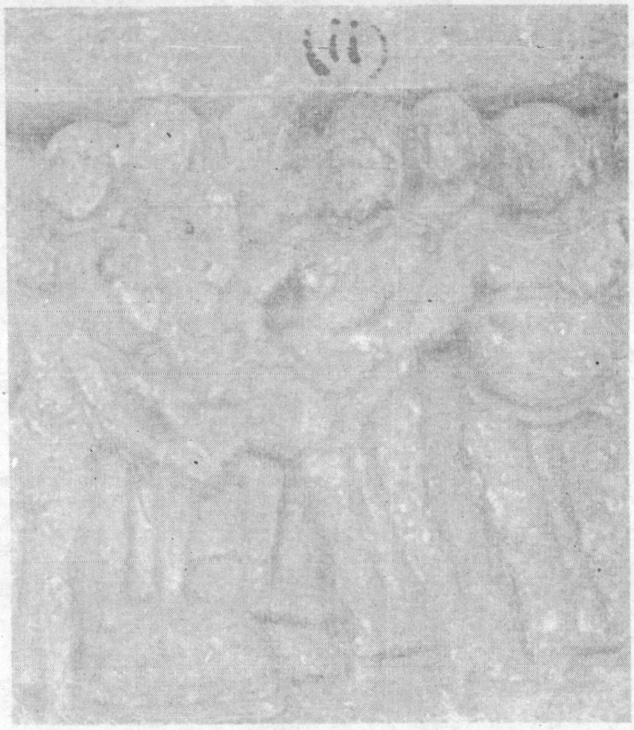

58. Detail of fig. 57.

59. Detail of fig. 57.

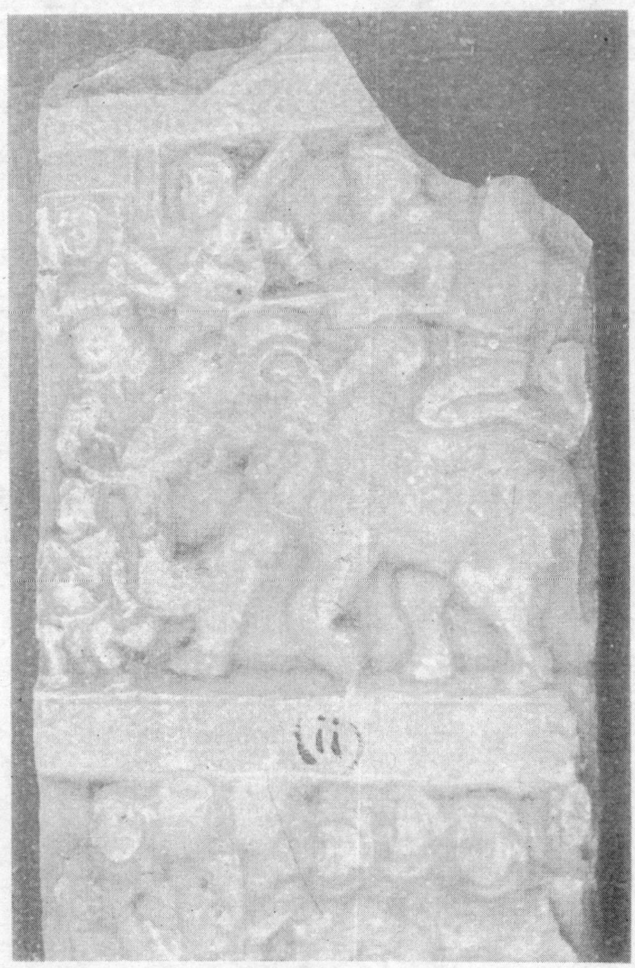

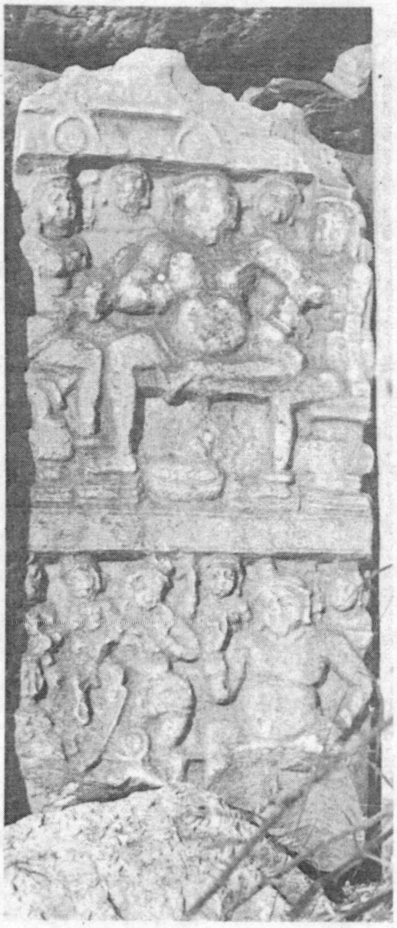

60. Fragment of a memorial pillar to Cāṁtamūla I.

62. Fragment of a memorial pillar.

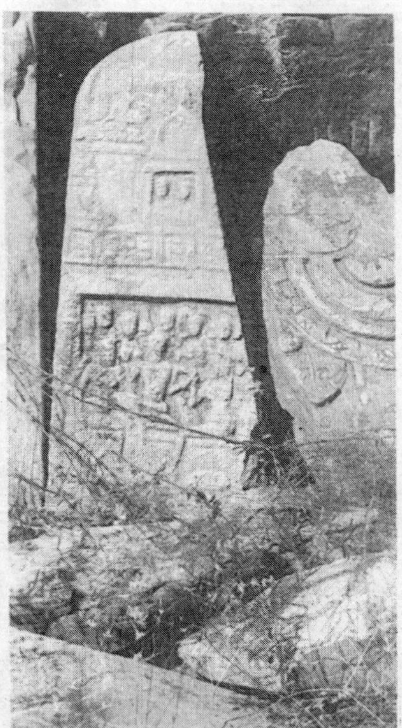

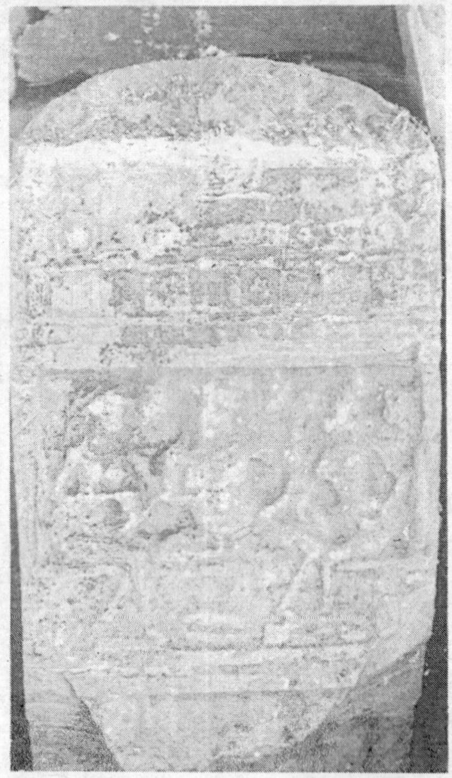

61. Fragment of a memorial pillar.

63. Fragment of a memorial pillar.

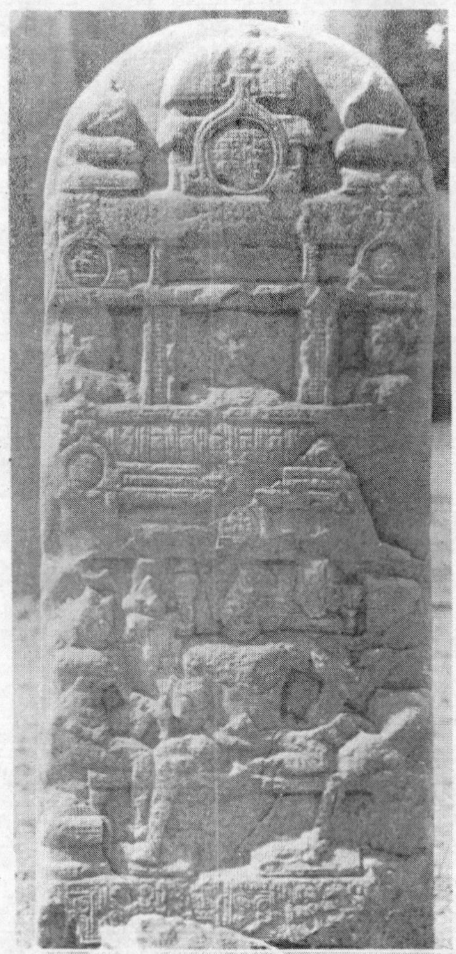

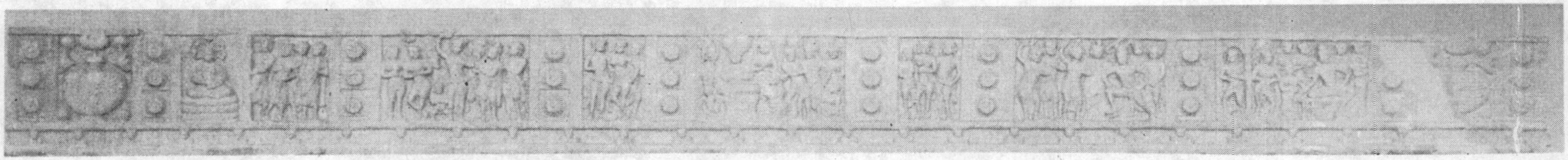

64. *Āyaka* panel 1, Site 9.

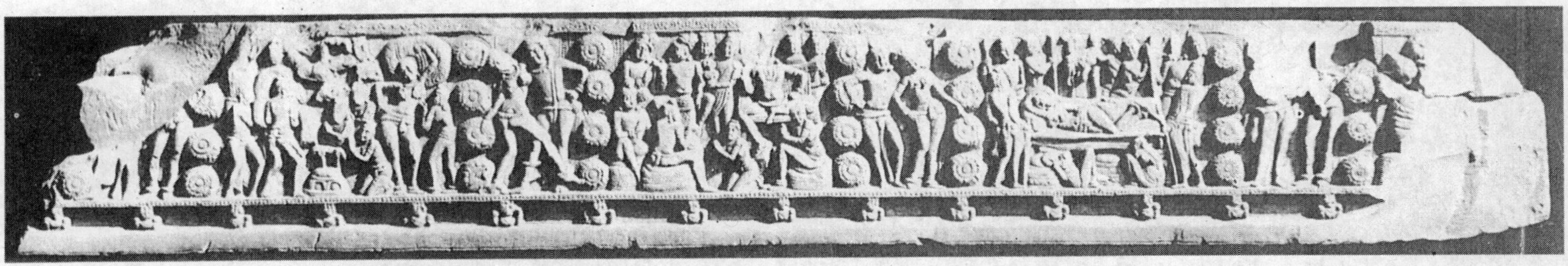

65. *Āyaka* panel 2, Site 9 (Photo: Archaeological Survey of India).

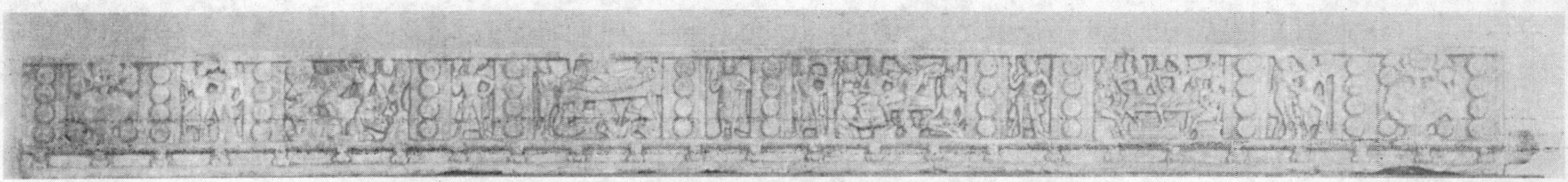

66. Champaka Jātaka, *āyaka* panel 3, Site 9 (Photo: Archaeological Survey of India).

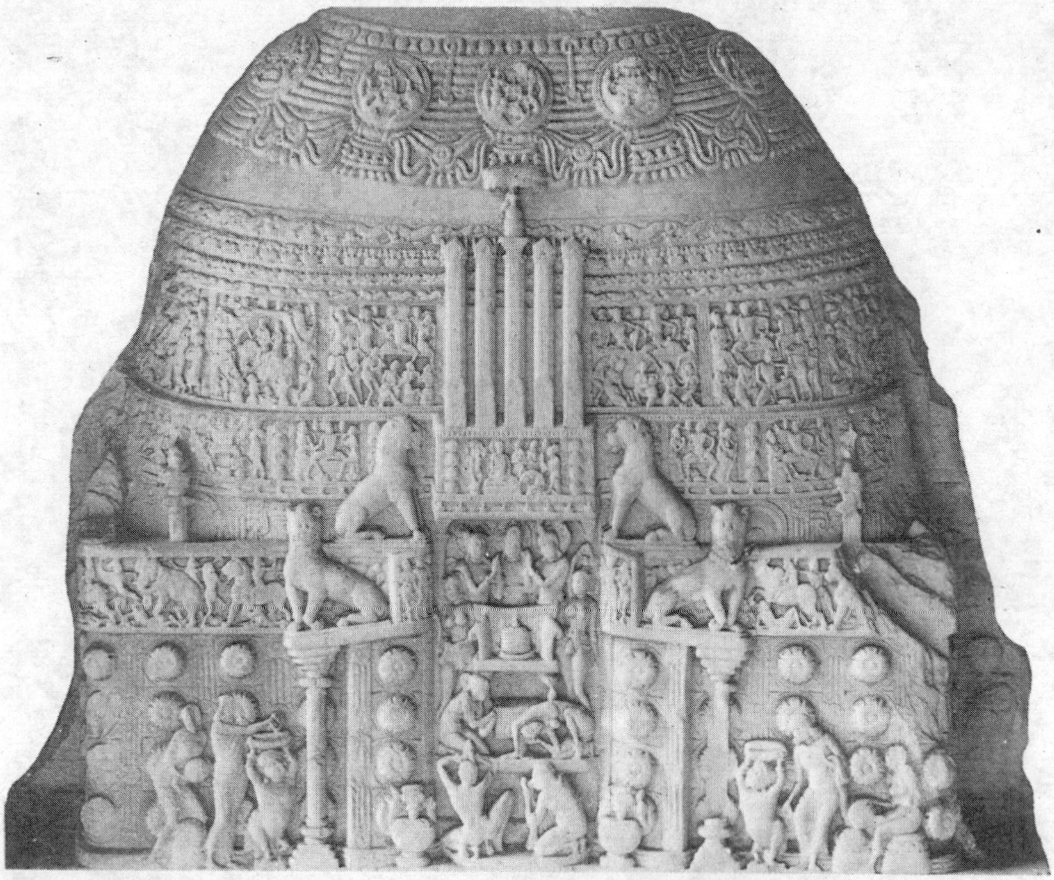

67. Drum slab from Amarāvatī, now British Museum (Photo: Trustees of the British Museum).

68. "The Man in the Well", detail of fig. 67.

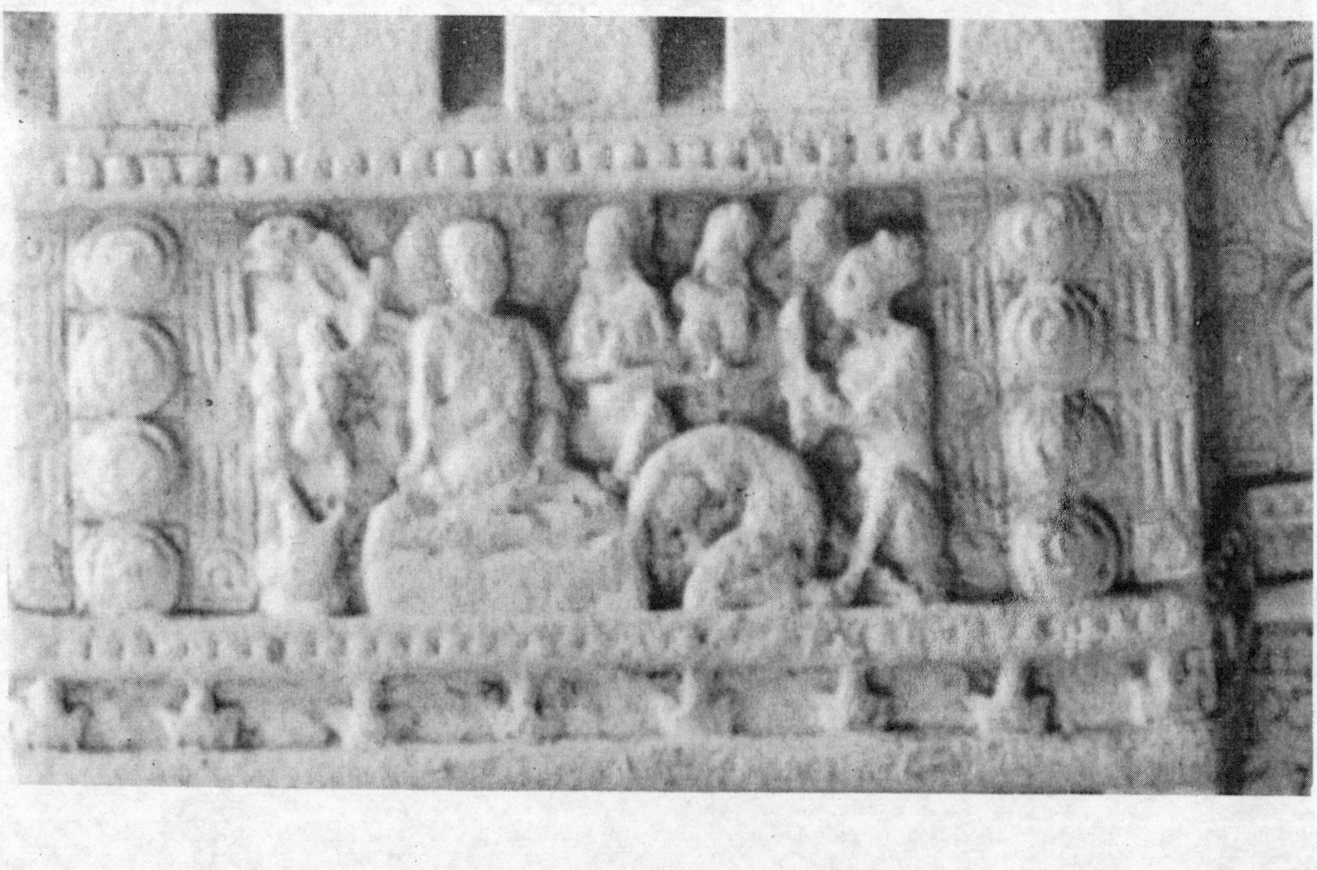

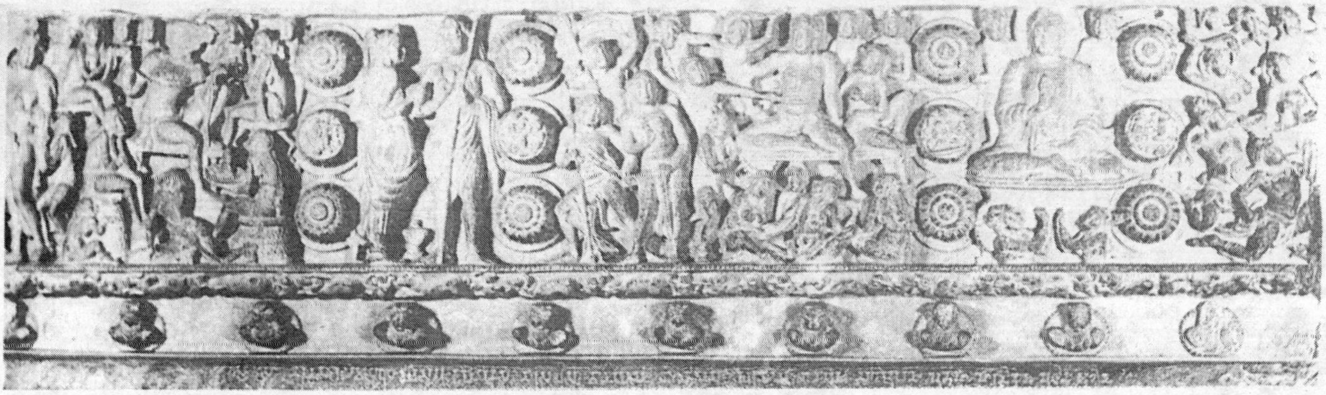

69. Frieze from Amarāvatī, now Madras Government Museum (Photo: Archaeological Survey of India).

70. Detail of fig. 69.

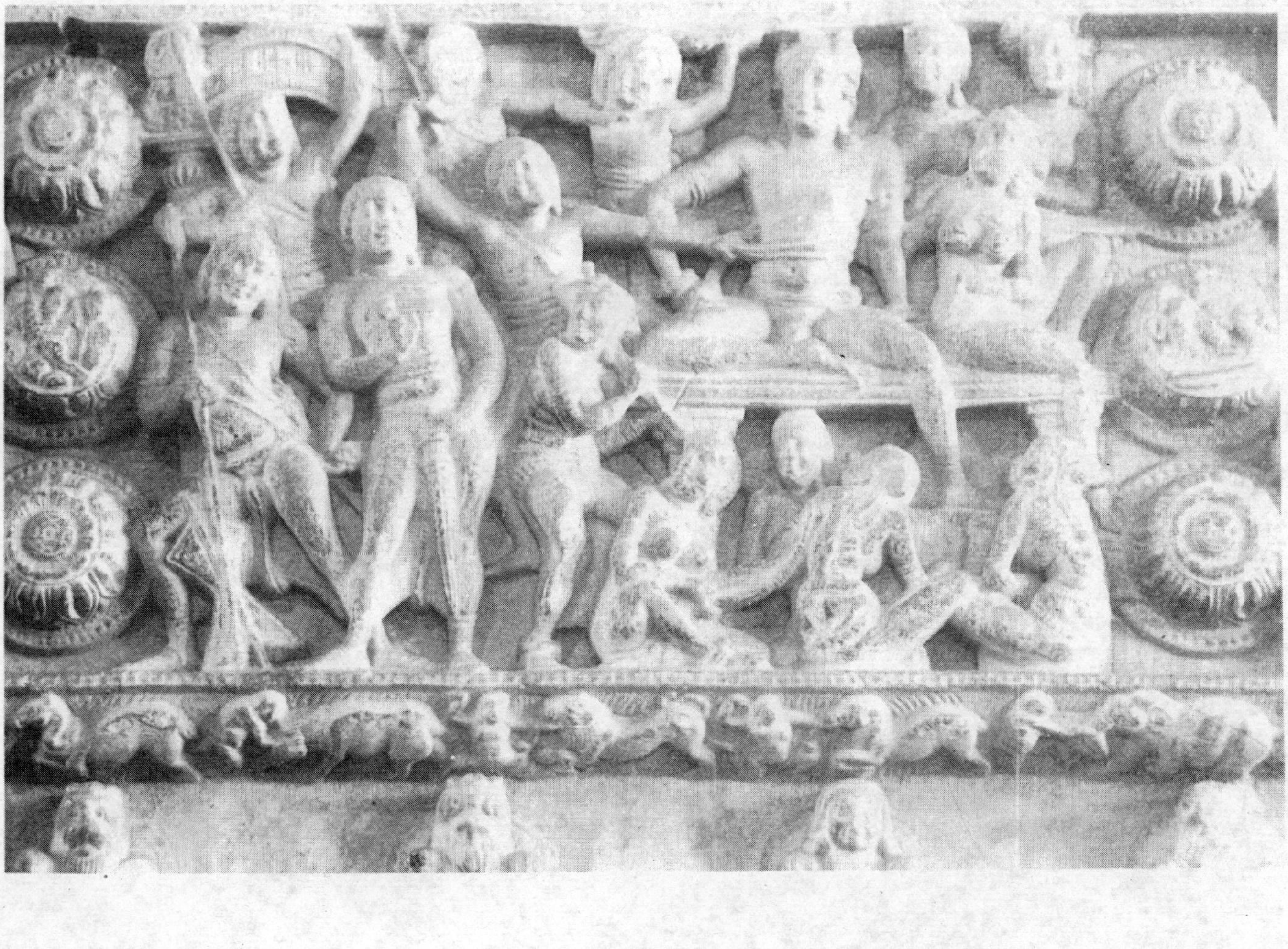

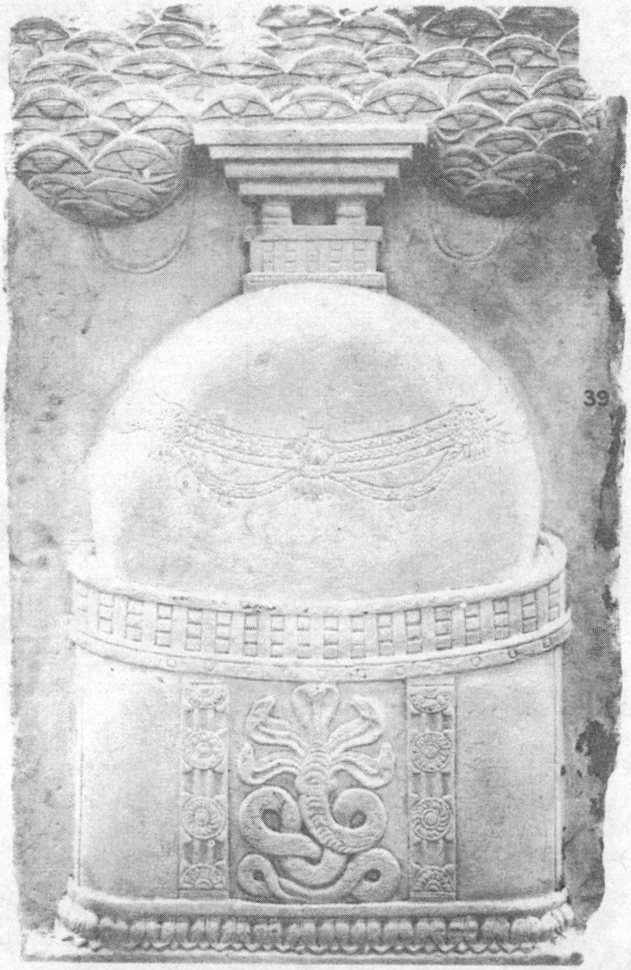

71. Drum slab from Amarāvatī, now British Museum (Photo: Trustees of the British Museum).

72. A votive *stūpa* from Amarāvatī (Photo: Archaeological Survey of India).

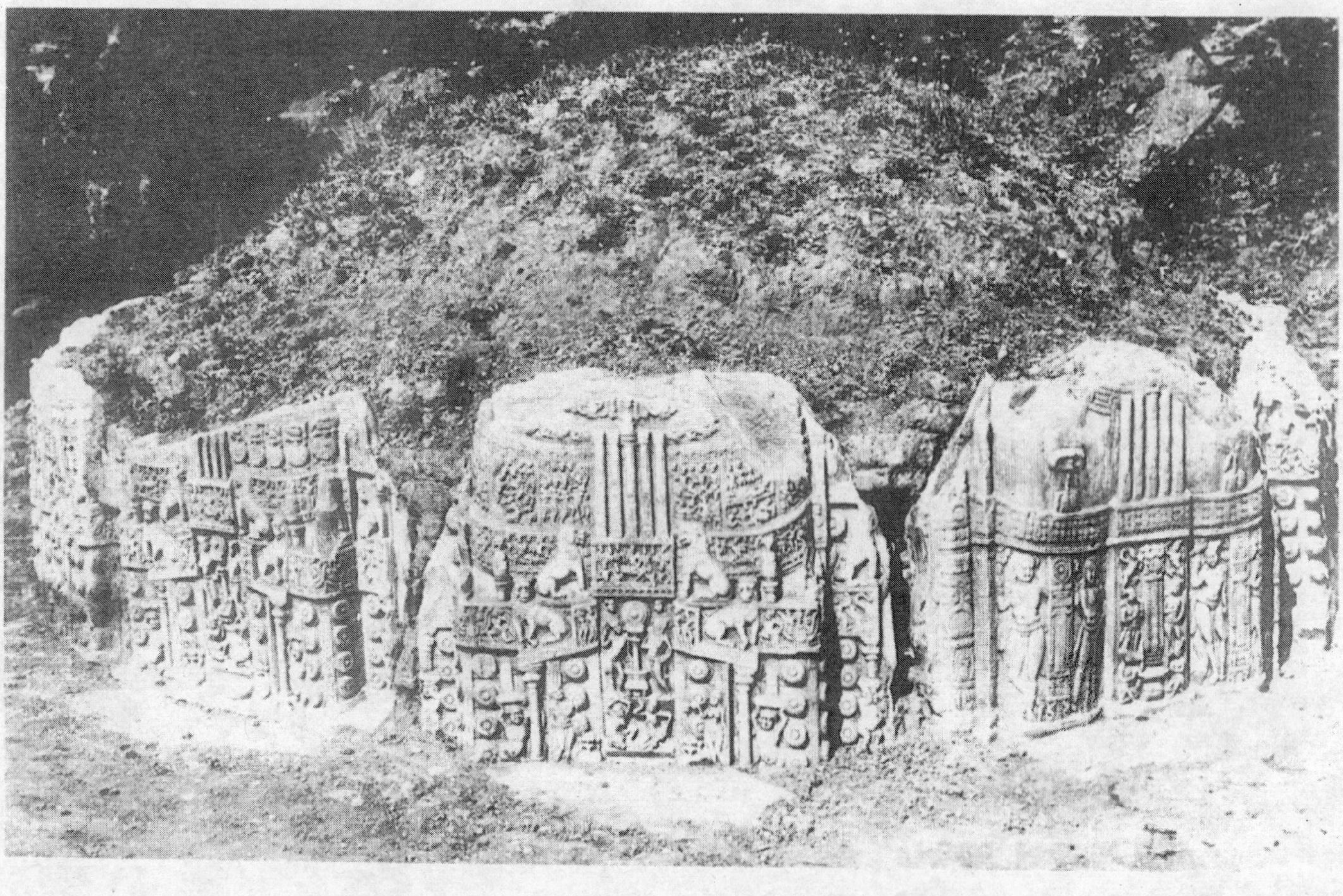

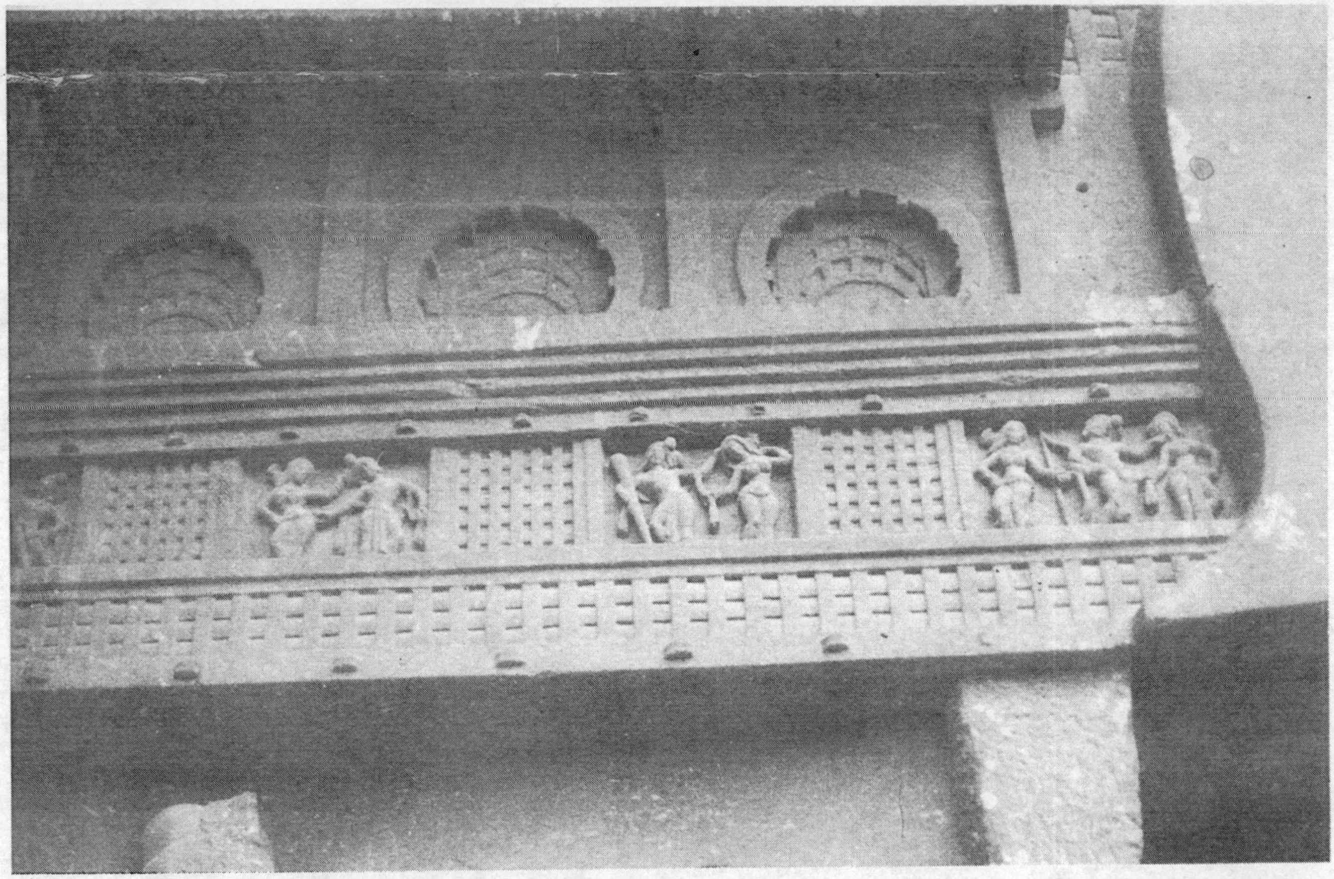

73. Detail of the façade of a Buddhist *caitya* hall at Kondāñe.

74. Detail of fig. 69.

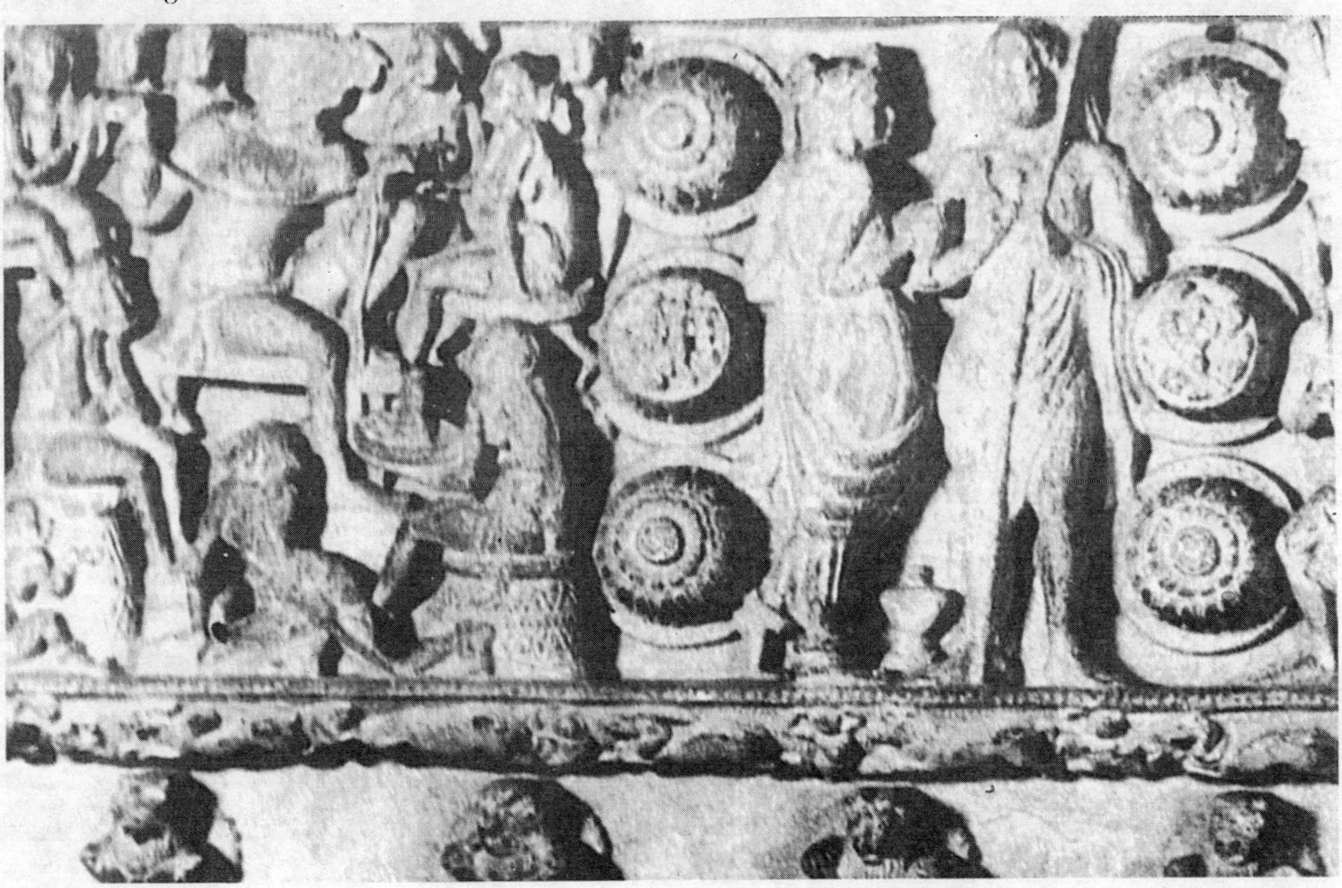

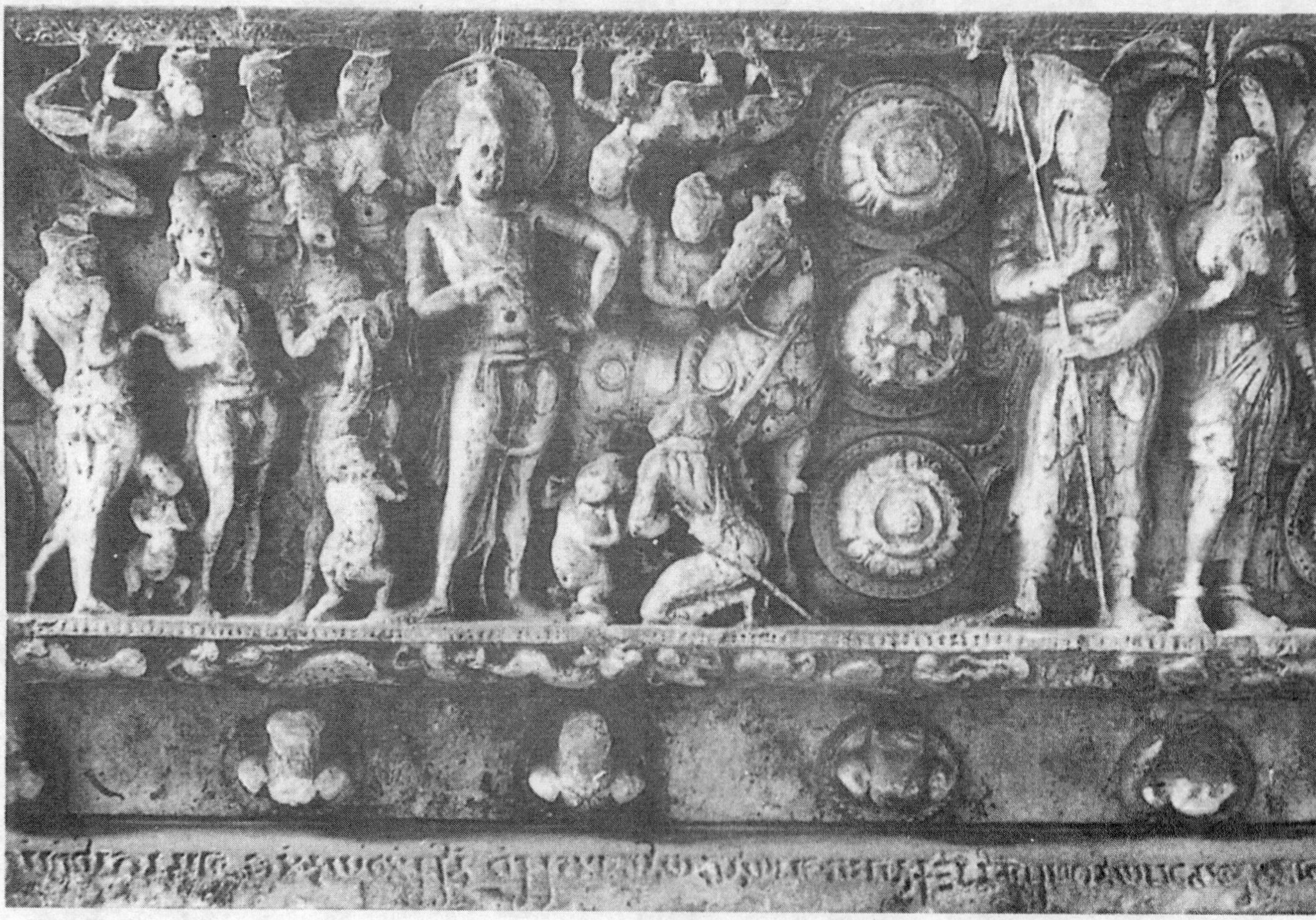

75. Detail of fig. 49.

76. Detail of Coffret IX, Begram, now Kabul Museum (Photo: RMN. Paris).

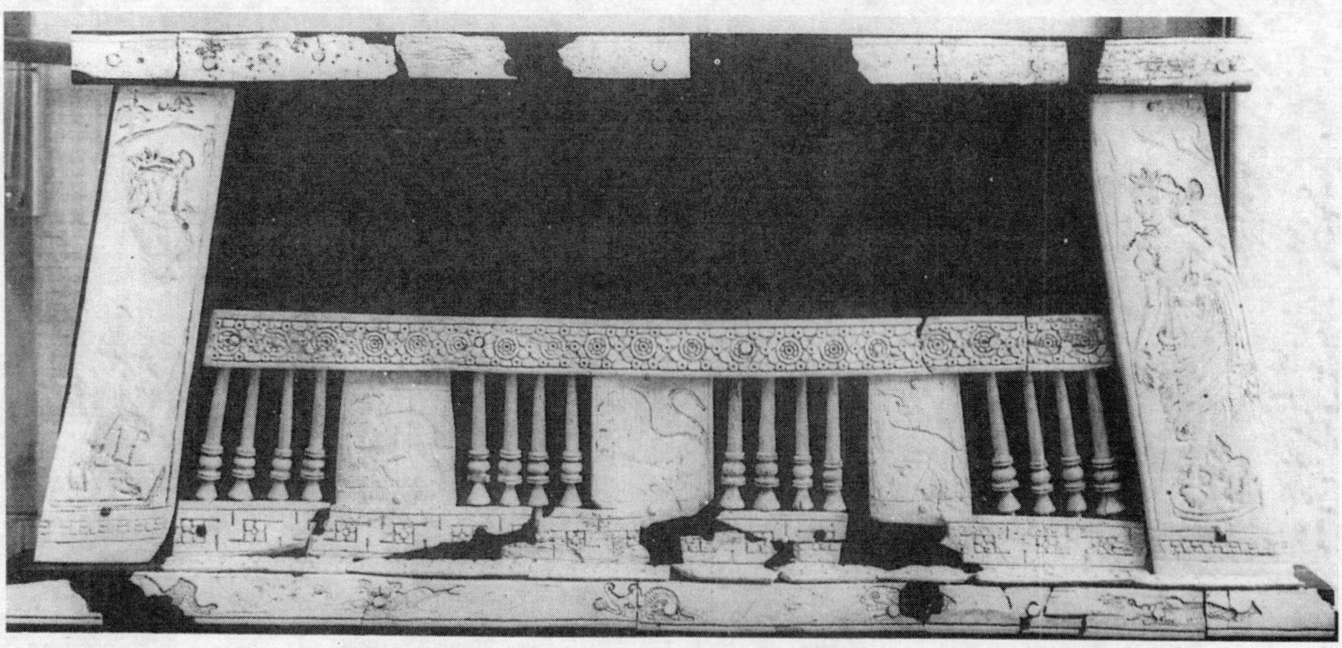

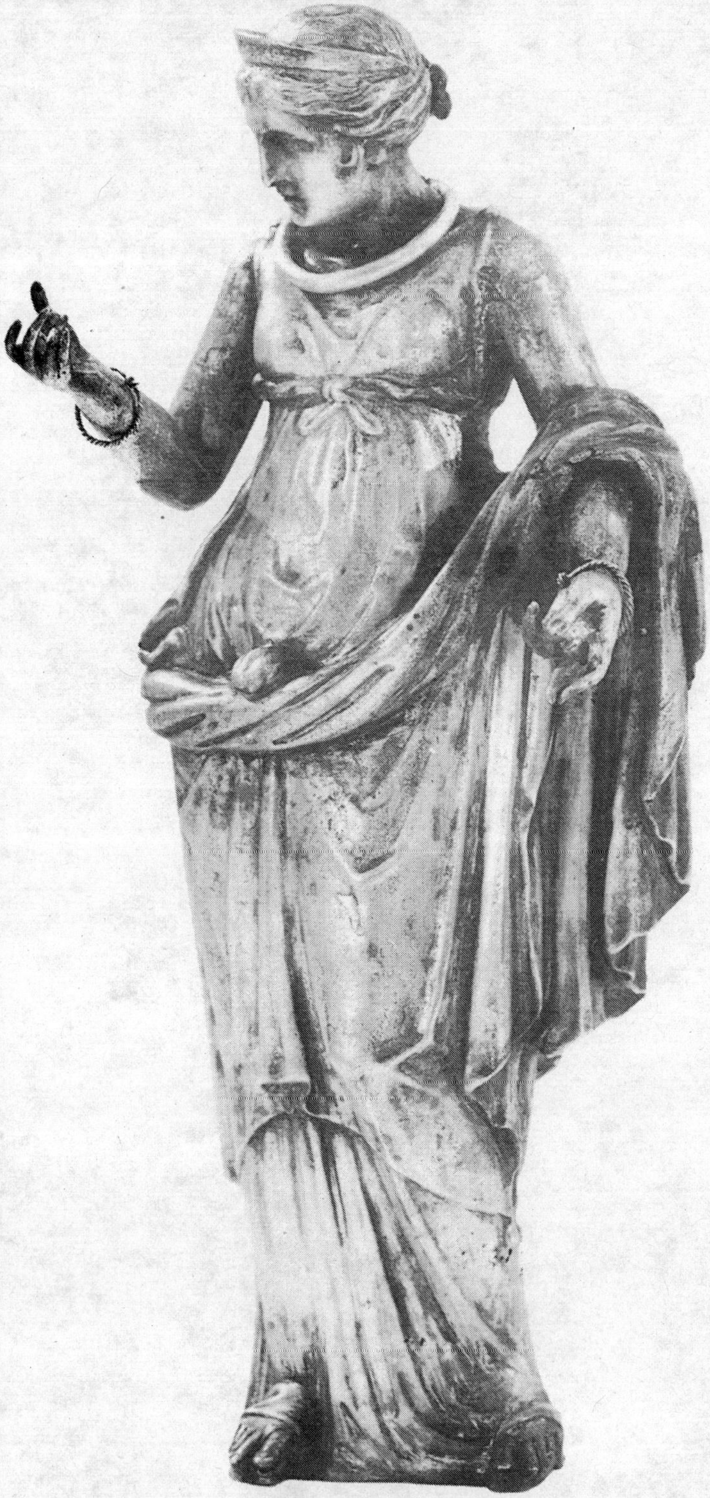

77. Silver statuette from Lebanon or Syria, now Toledo Muesum of Art, Gift of Edward Drummond Libbey, c. A.D. 150-230 (Photo: Toledo Museum of Art).

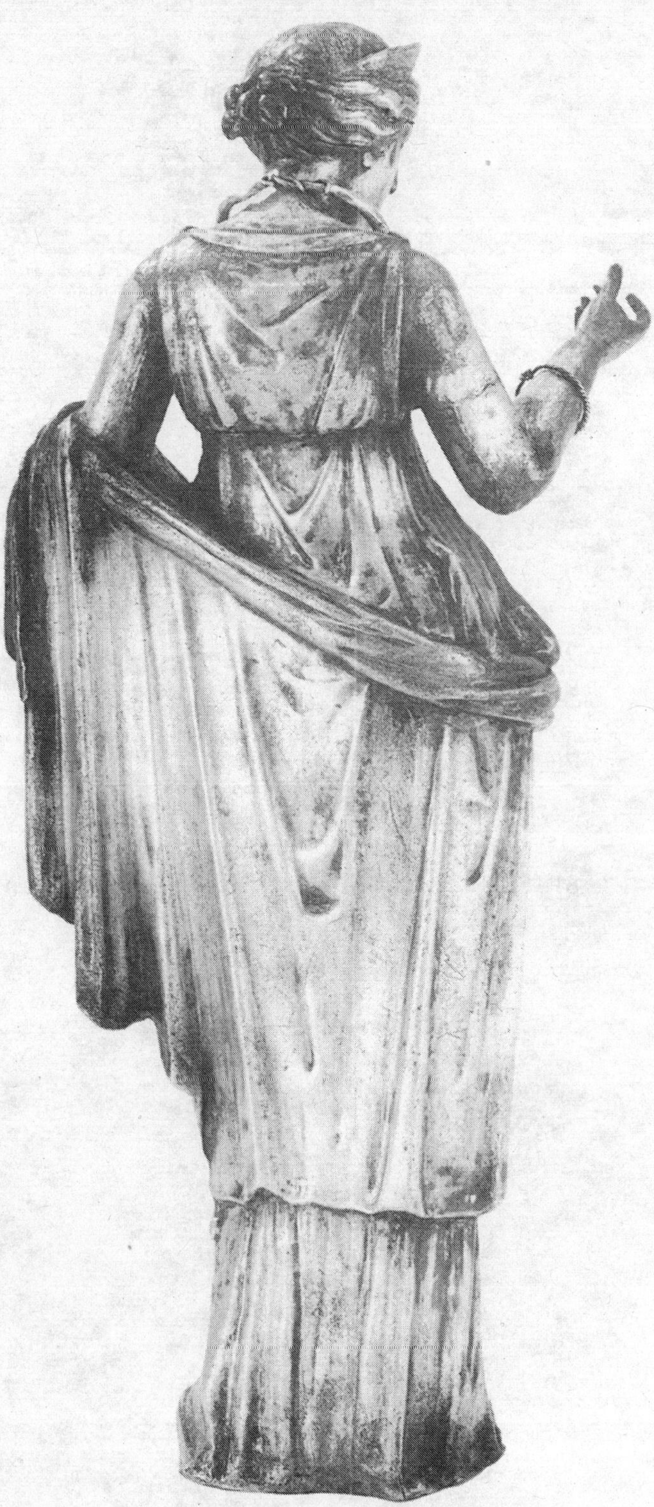

78. Rear view of fig. 77.

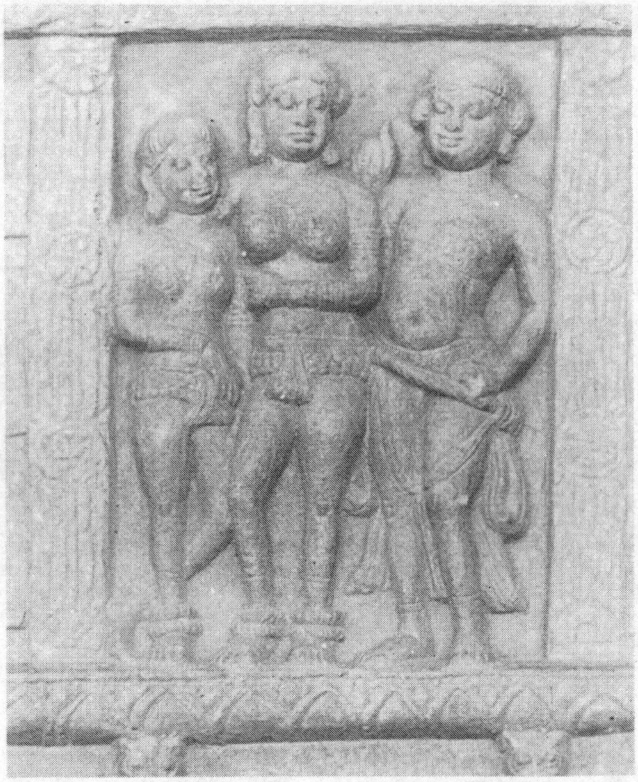

79. Detail of fig. 64.

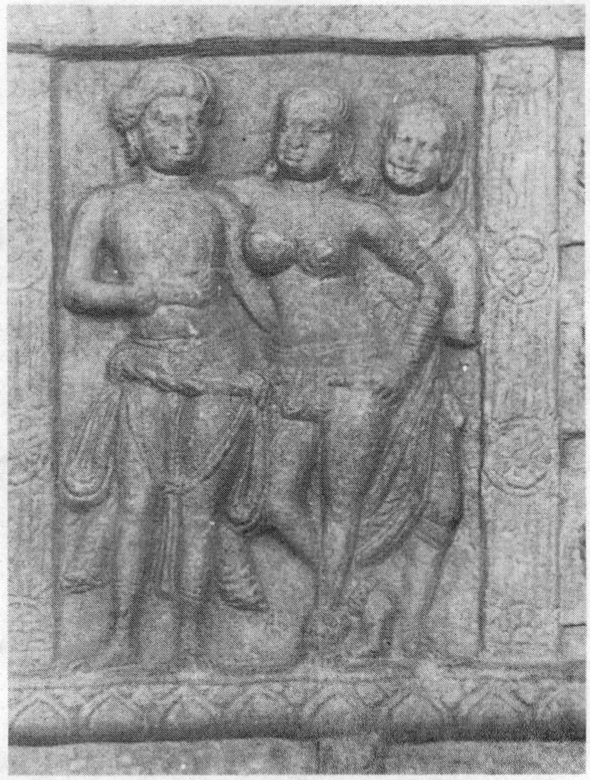

80. Detail of fig. 64.

81. Scene representing the episode of "The Man in the Well", detail of fig. 64.

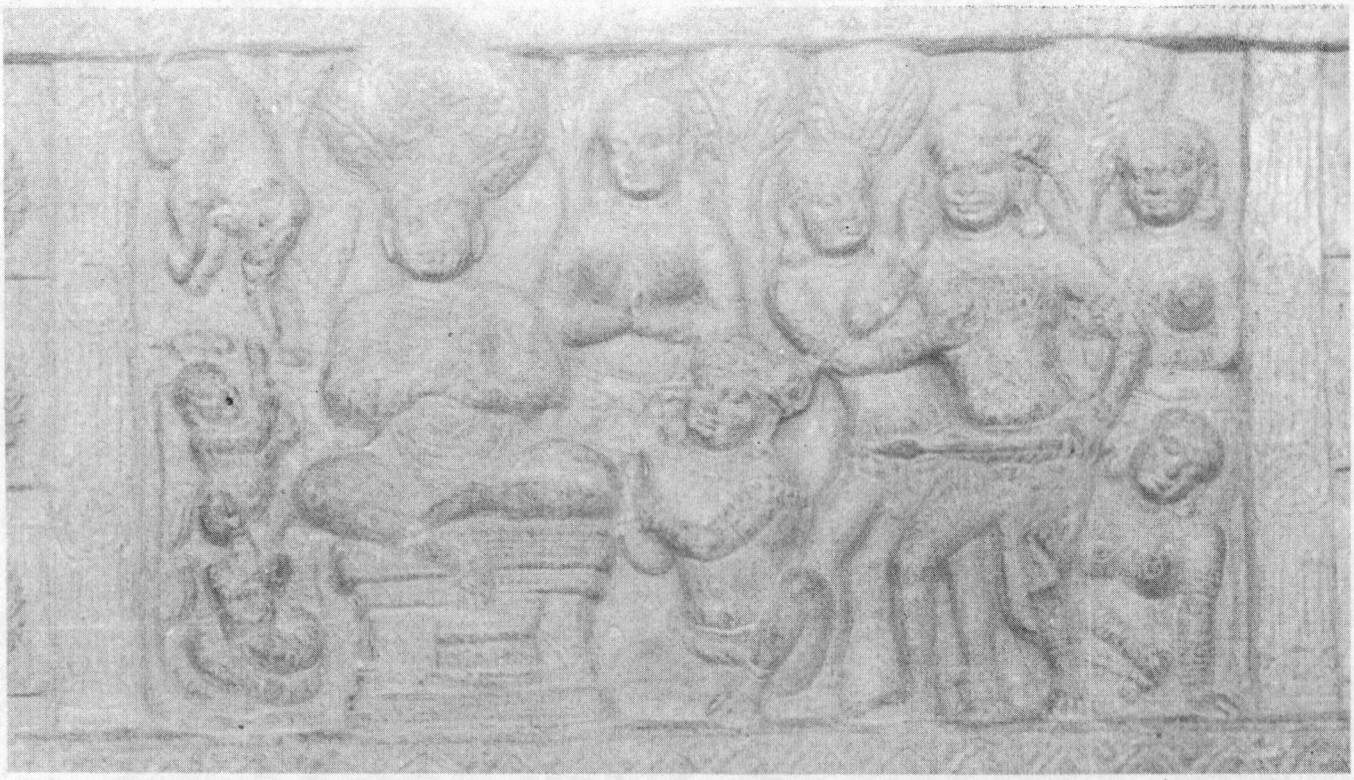

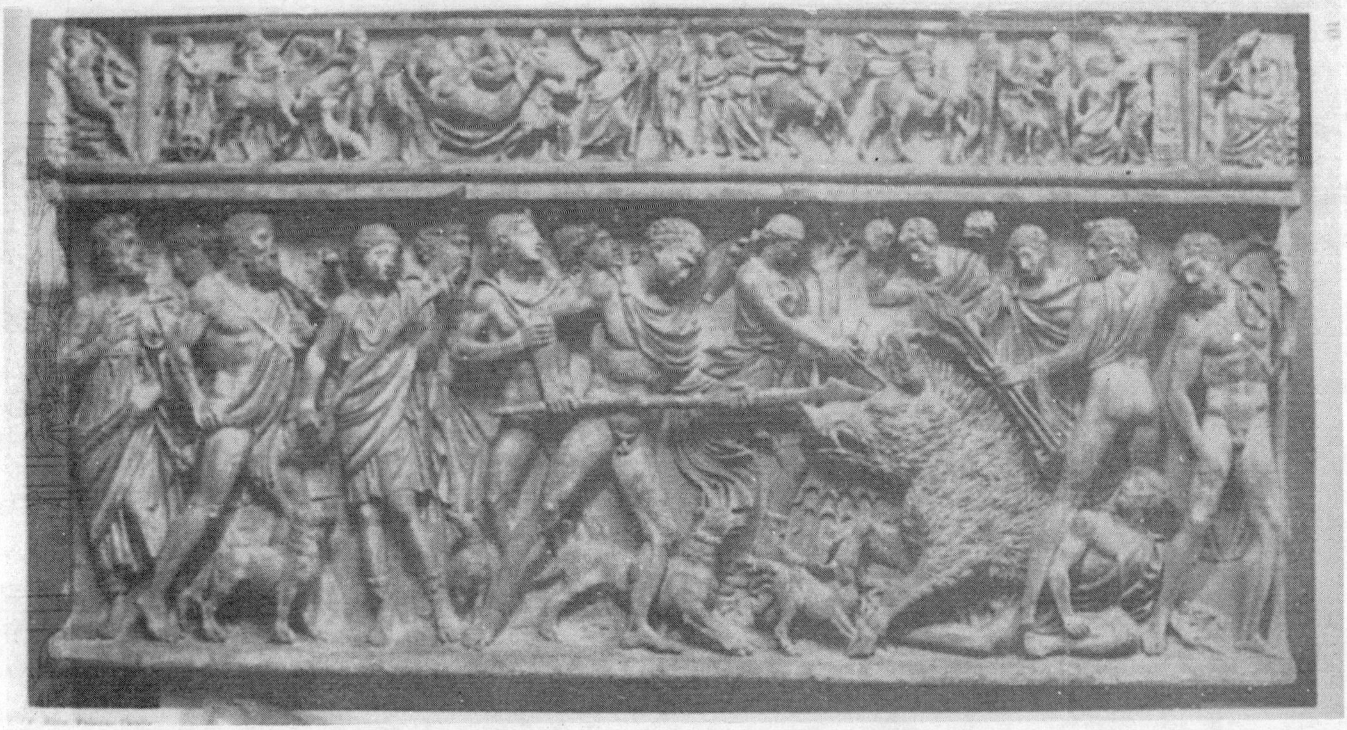

82. Meleager Killing the Boar, Roman Sarcophagus, second century A.D., Plazzo Doria, Rome (Photo: G. Koch, *Die Mythologischen Sarcophage*, Part 5, *Meleager*, Vol. 12, Berlin, 1957, pl. 10).

83. Dream of Queen Māyā, detail of fig. 65. (Photo: Archaeological Survey of India).

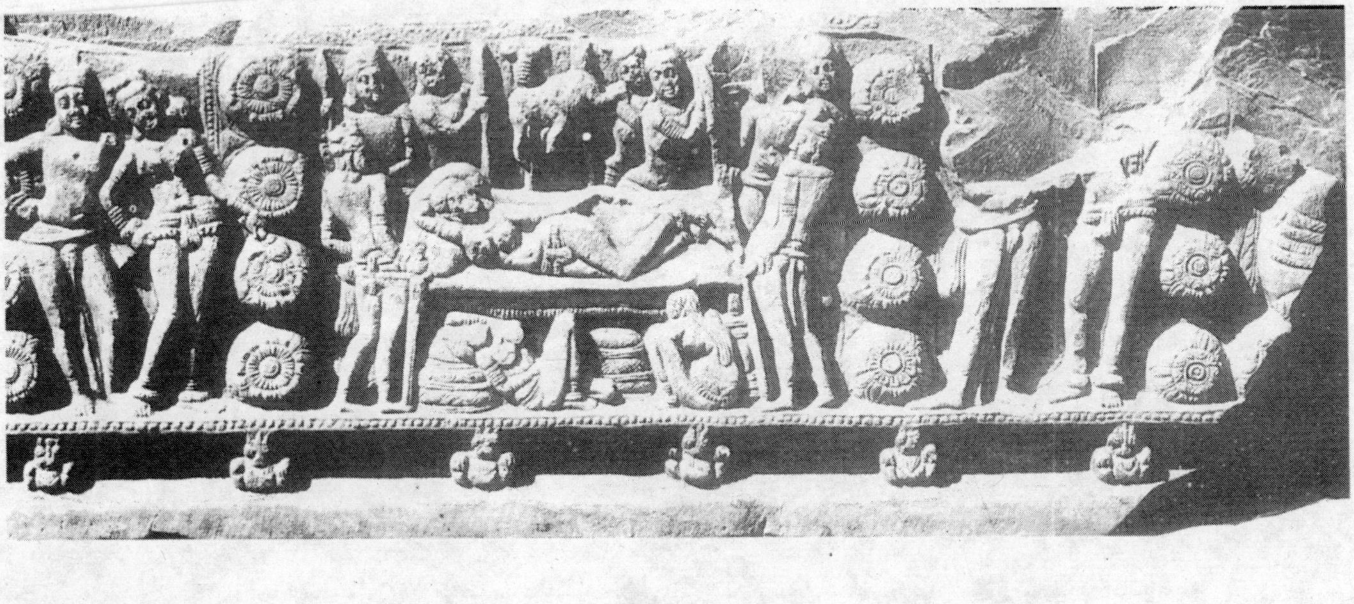

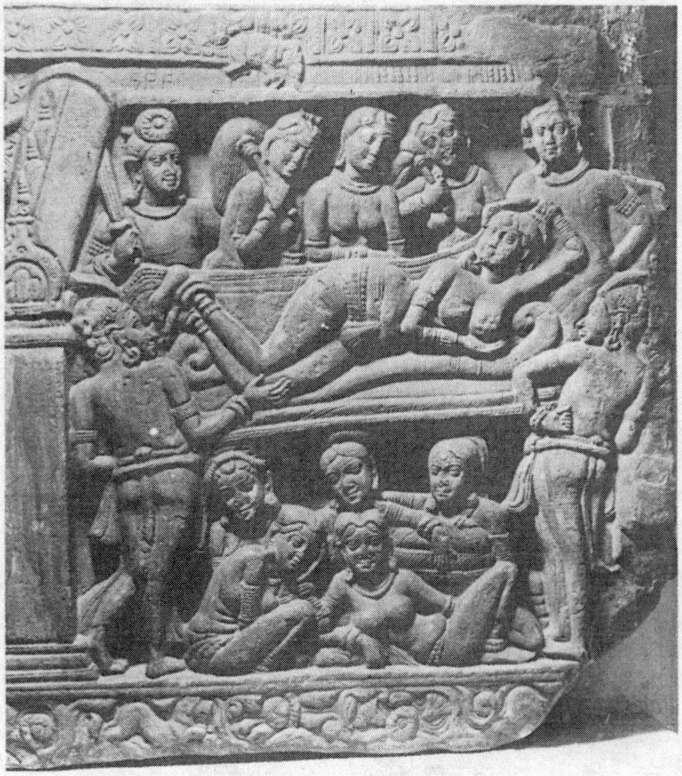

84. The Dream of Queen Māyā, detail of coping stone from Amarāvatī, now The Indian Museum, Calcutta (Photo: Archaeological Survey of India).

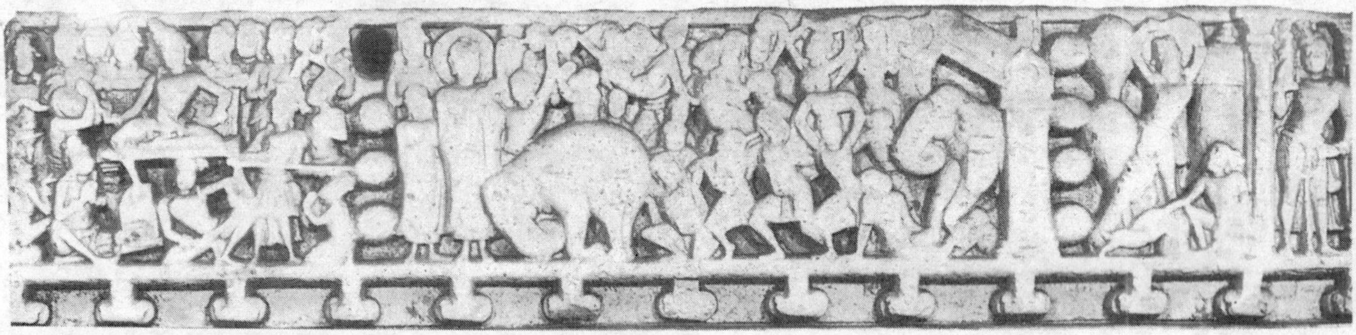

85. Śibi Jātaka, Subjugation of the Mad Elephant, and Sasa Jātaka, drum frieze from Amarāvatī, now British Museum. (Photo: Trustees of the British Museum).

86. King Ugrasena Visited by the Wife of the Nāga King, and a small panel of a standing Buddha in *abhaya mudrā*, detail of fig. 66.

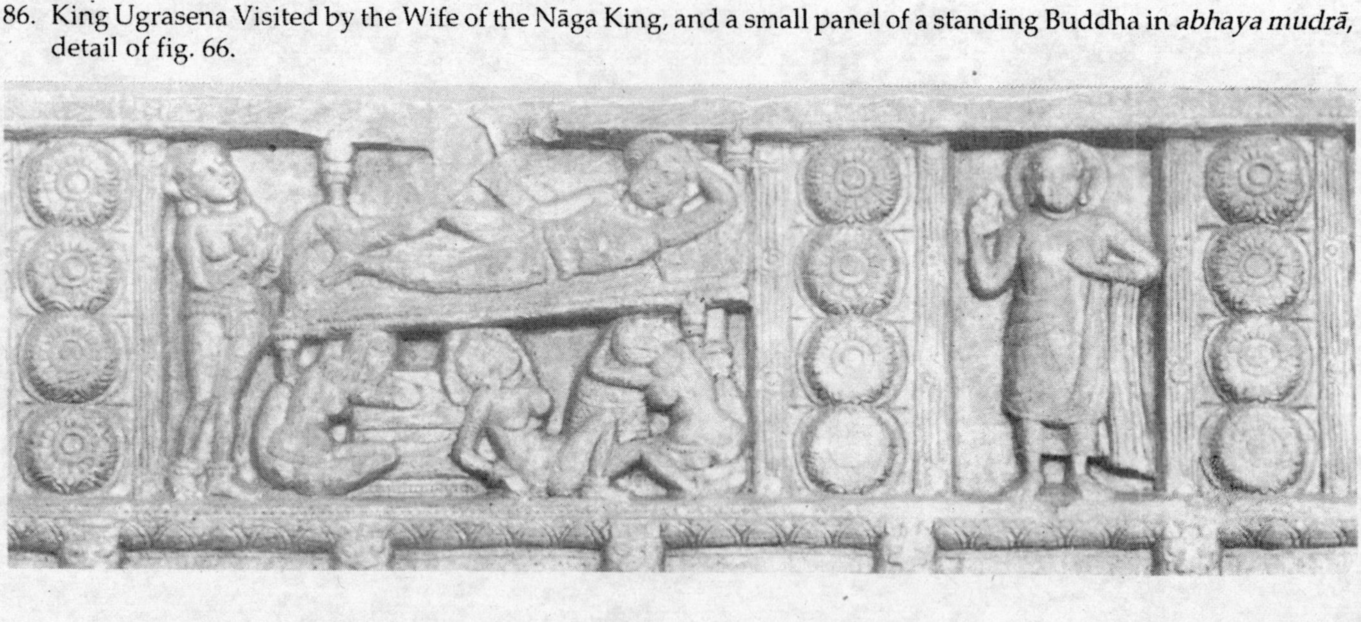

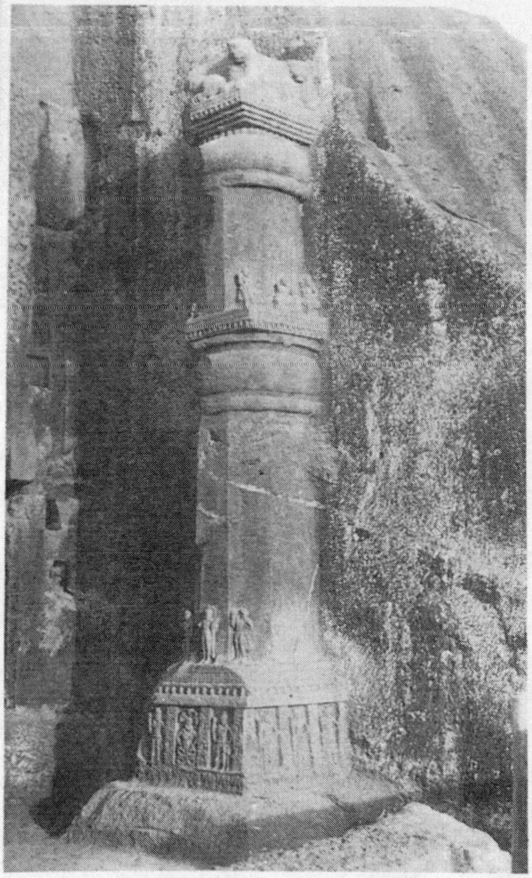

87. Rock cut pillar in front of the Buddhist *caitya* hall at Kanheri (Photo: Archaeological Survey of India).

88. Detail of fig. 66.

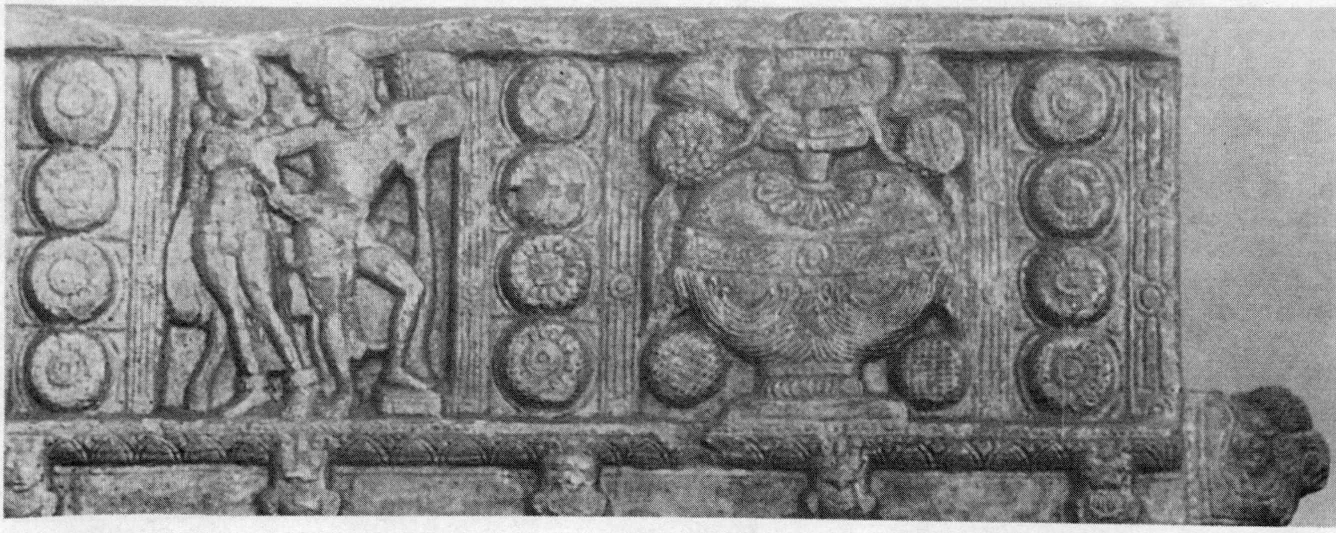

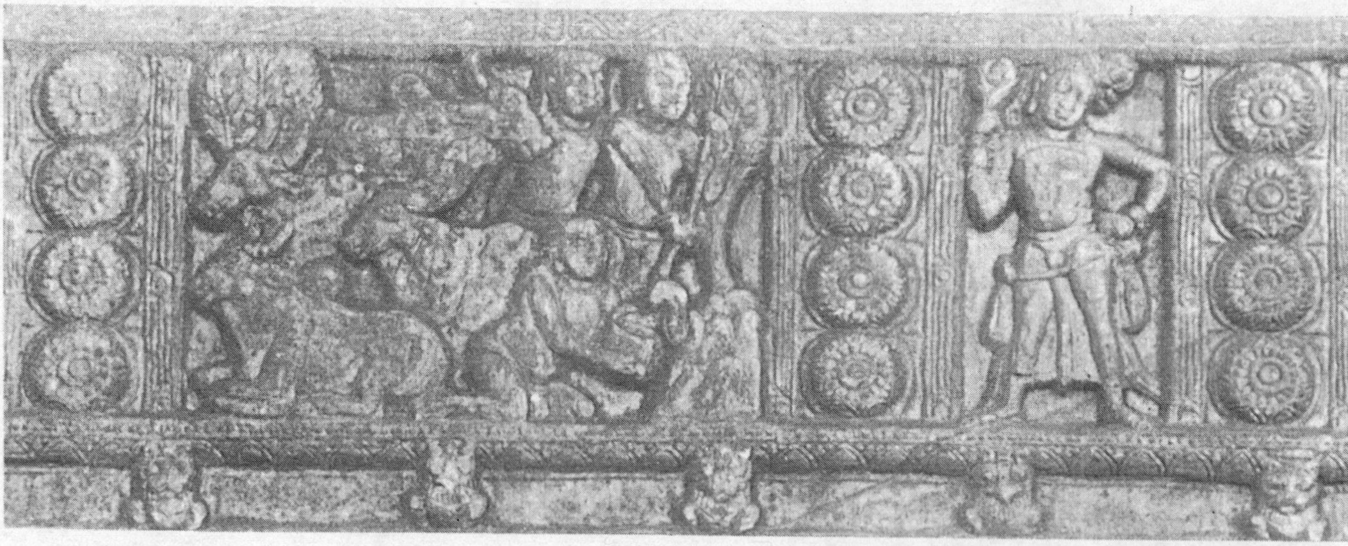

89. Snake Charmer Catching the Nāga King Champaka, detail of fig. 66.

90. Śibi Jātaka, *āyaka* panel from Site 9 (Photo: Archaeological Survey of India).

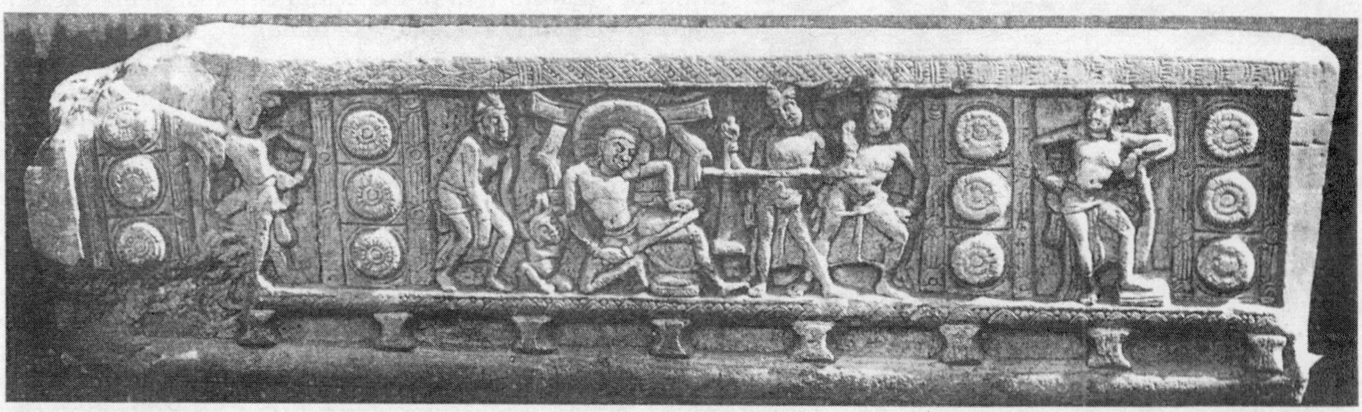

91. Subjugation of the Mad Elephant, *āyaka* panel, Site 9 (Photo: Archaeological Survey of India).

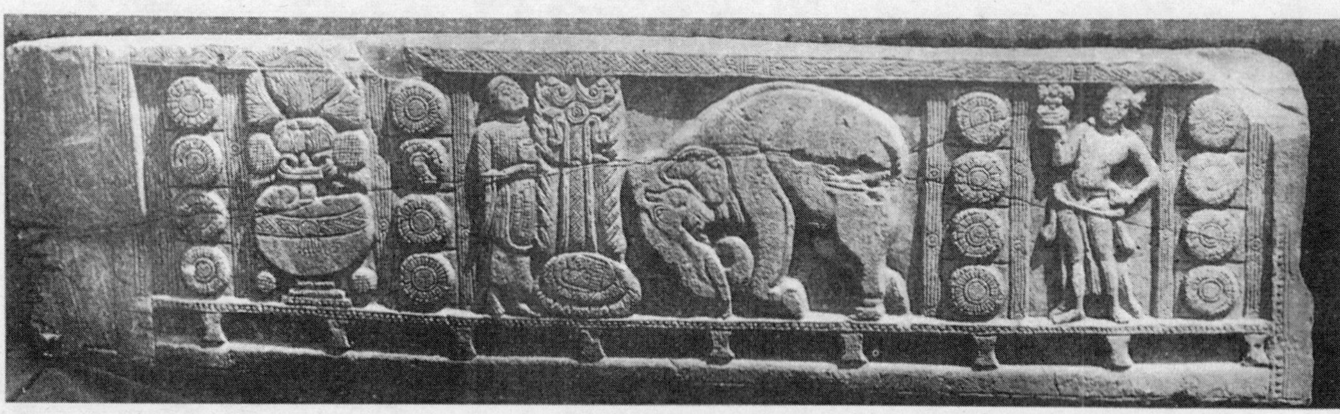

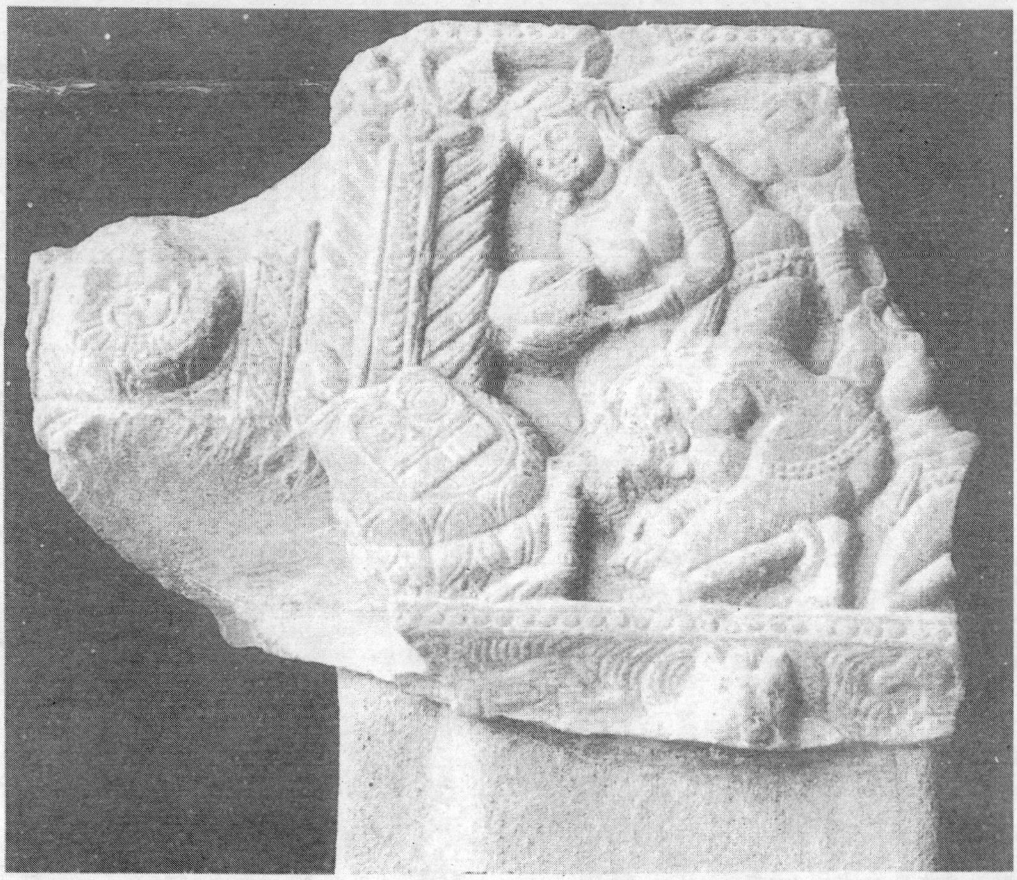

92. Worshippers Paying Homage to the Feet of the Buddha (Photo: Archaeological Survey of India).

93. Drum slab from Site 9 (Photo: Archaeological Survey of India).

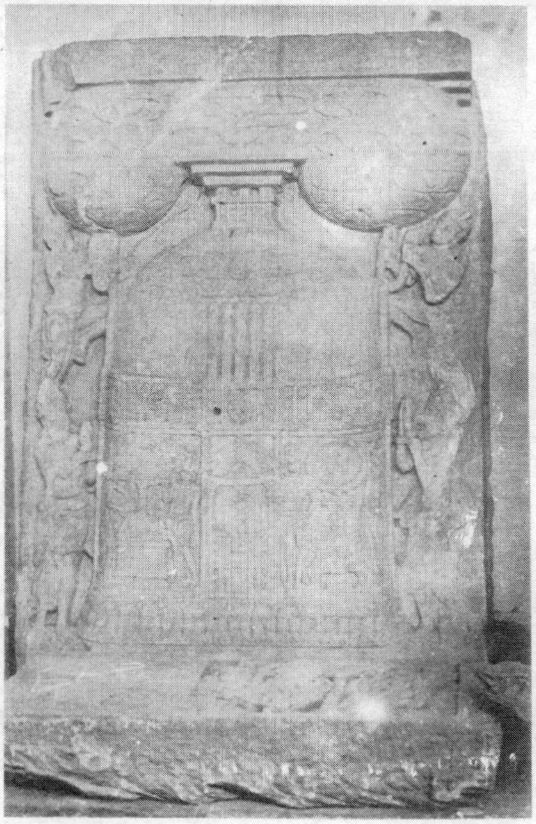

94. Drum slab from Site 9 (Photo: Prince of Wales Museum, Bombay).

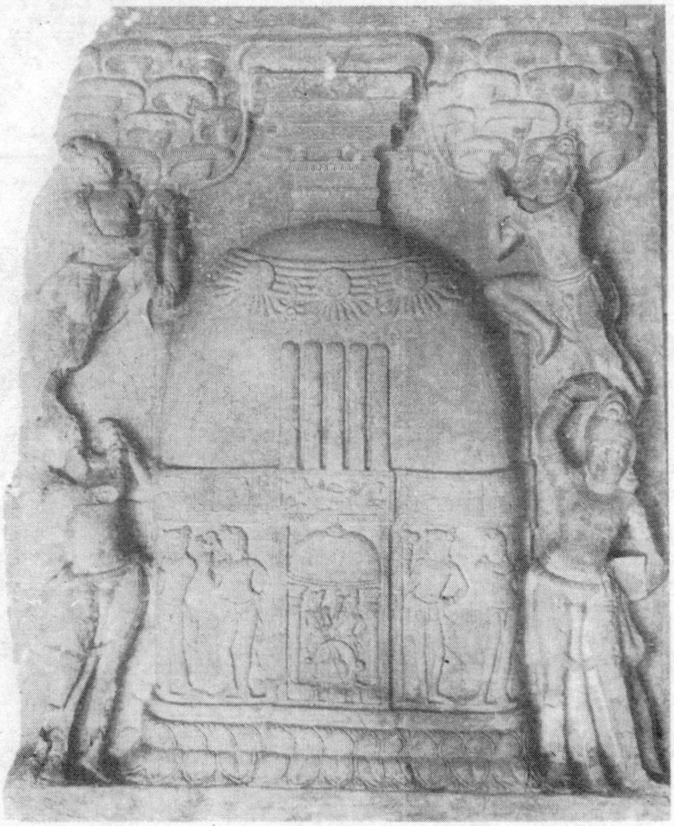

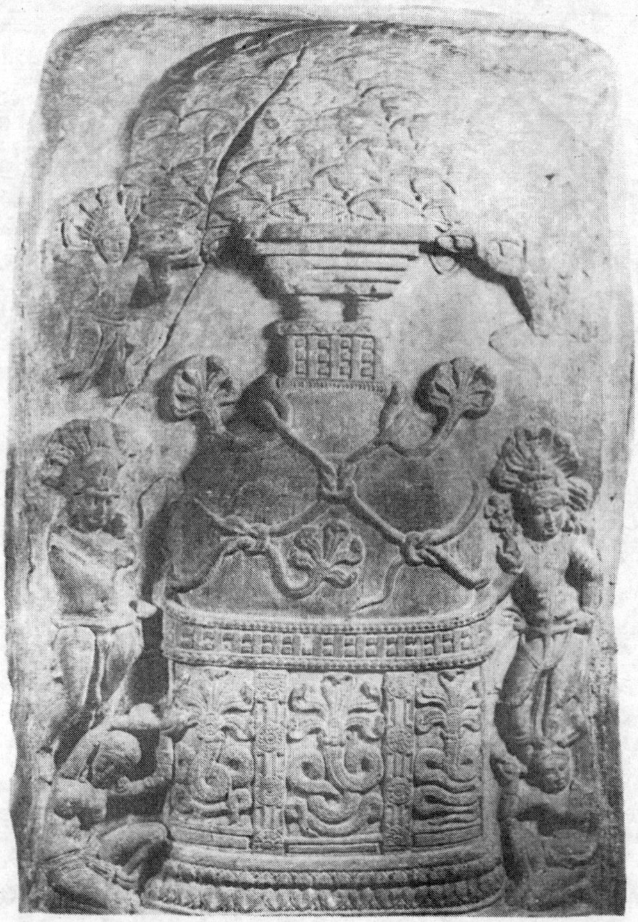

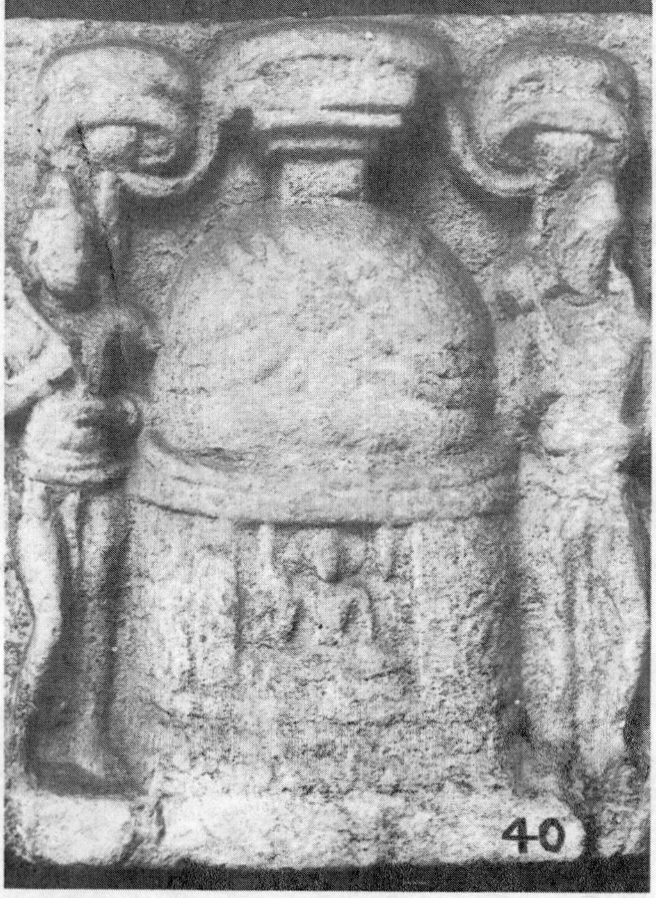

95. Drum slab from Amaravatī, possibly recut, now Madras Government Museum (Photo: Archaeological Survey of India).

96. Fragment of a dome slab from Amaravatī, now British Museum (Photo: Trustees of the British Museum).

97. Drum slab from a votive *stūpa* at Amarāvatī, now Archaeological Museum, Amarāvatī.

98. Drum slab from a *stupa* at Goli Village, now Los Angeles County Museum of Art, Gift of the Michael J. Connel Foundation (Photo: Los Angeles County Museum of Art).

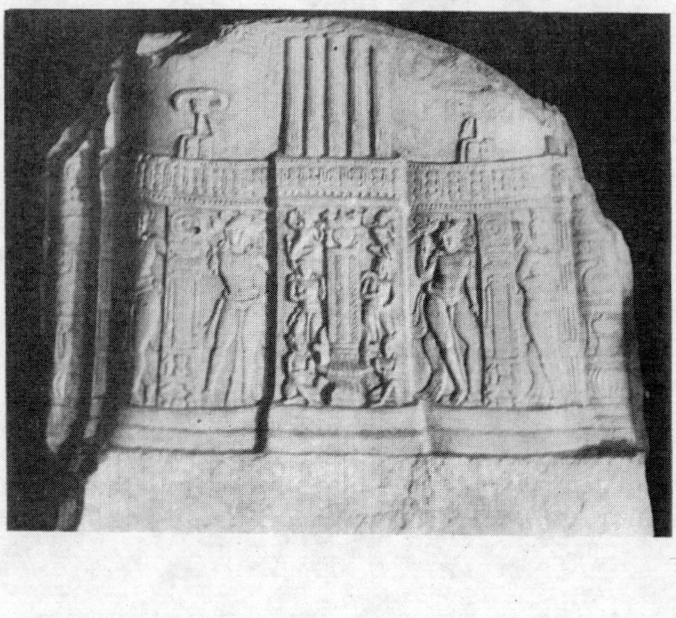

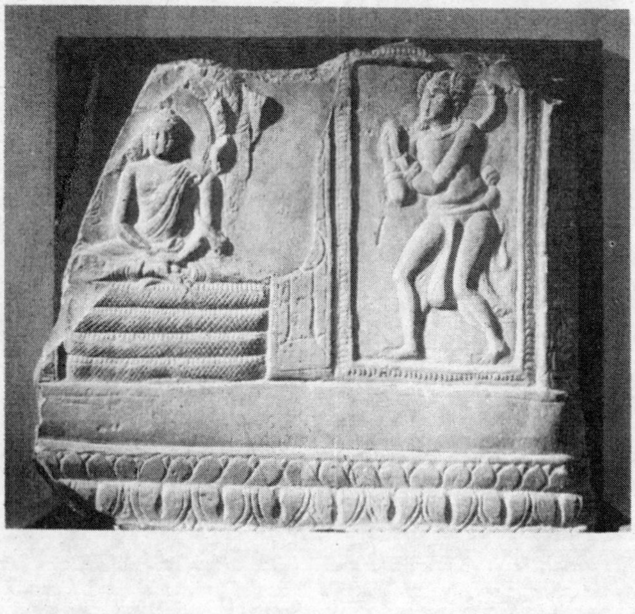

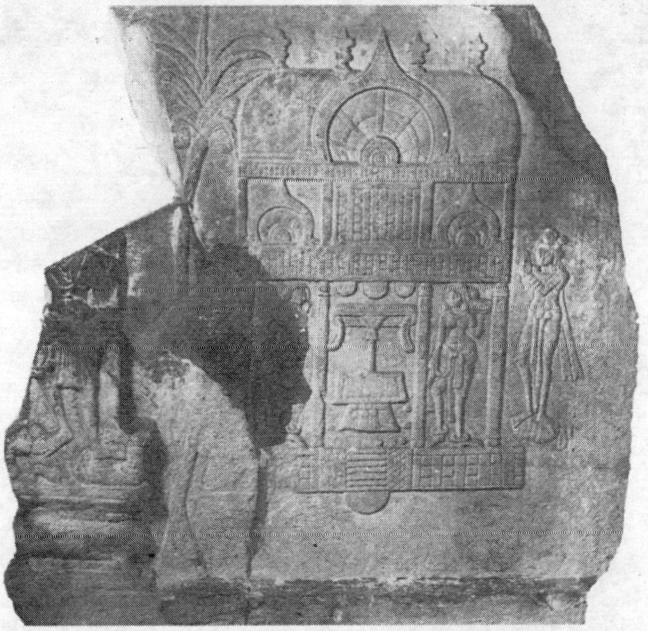

99. Fragment of a drum slab from Jaggayapeta, now Madras Government Museum (Photo: Archaeological Survey of India).

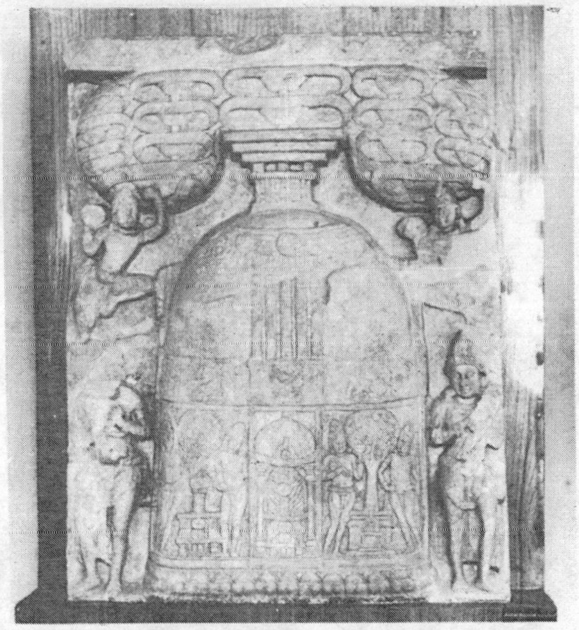

100. Drum slab of the Site 9 type (Photo: Archaeological Survey of India).

101. Drum slab of the Site 9 type.

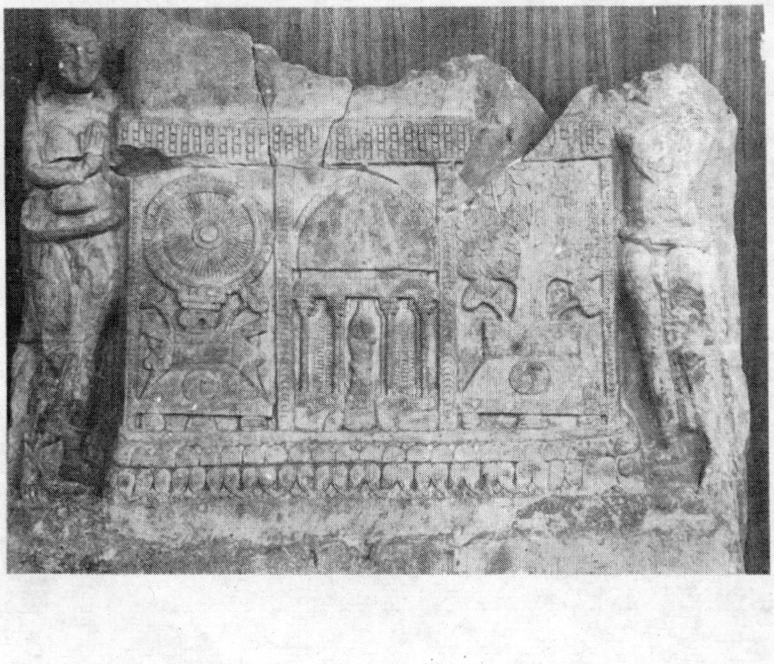

102. Drum slab from Amarāvatī, now British Museum (Photo: Trustees of the British Museum).

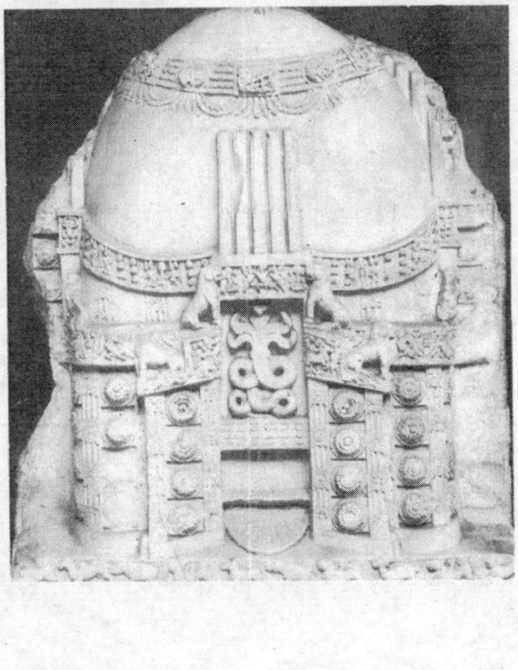

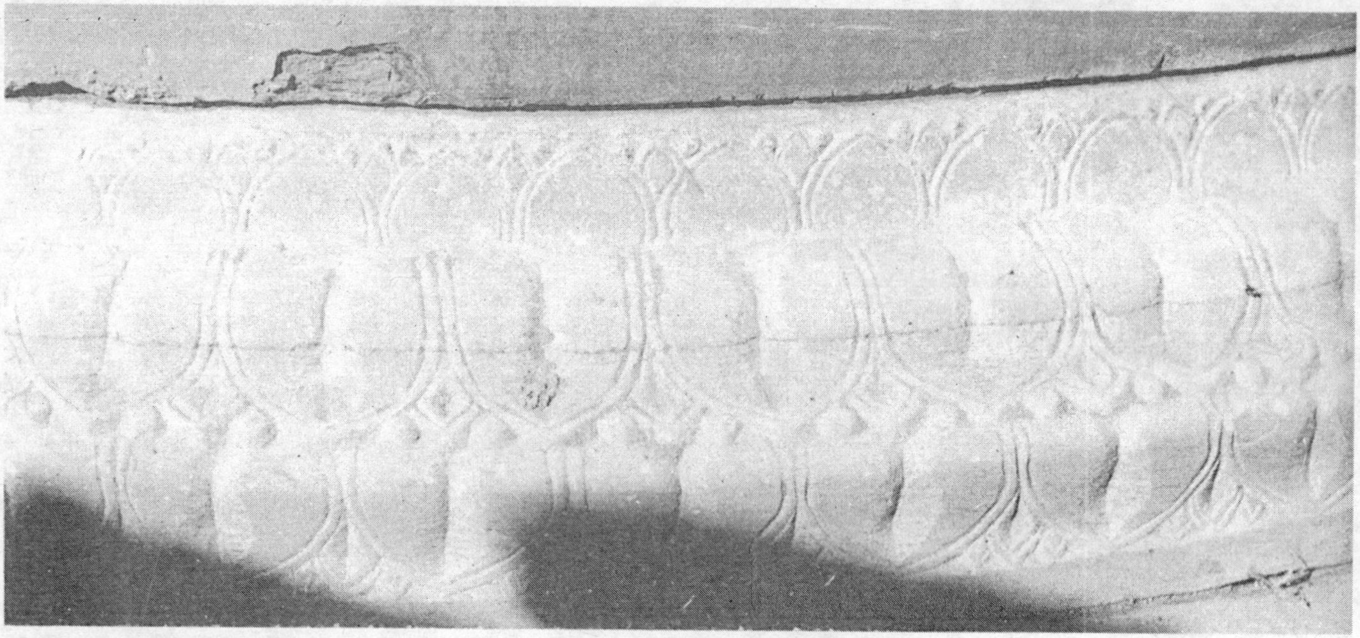

103. Molding at the base of a *stūpa* within a *caitya* hall at Nāgārjunakoṇḍa.

104. Drum slab of the Site 9 type (Photo: Archaeological Survey of India).

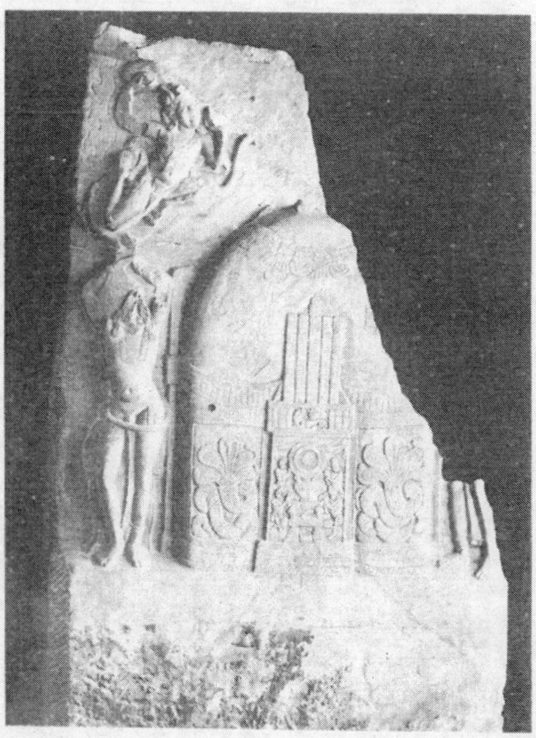

105. Drum slab of the Site 9 type.

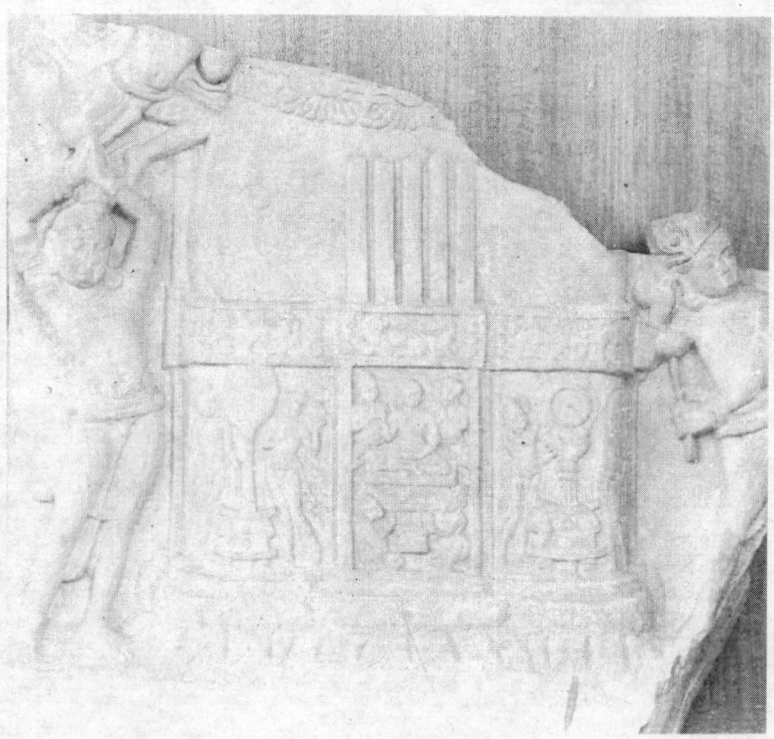

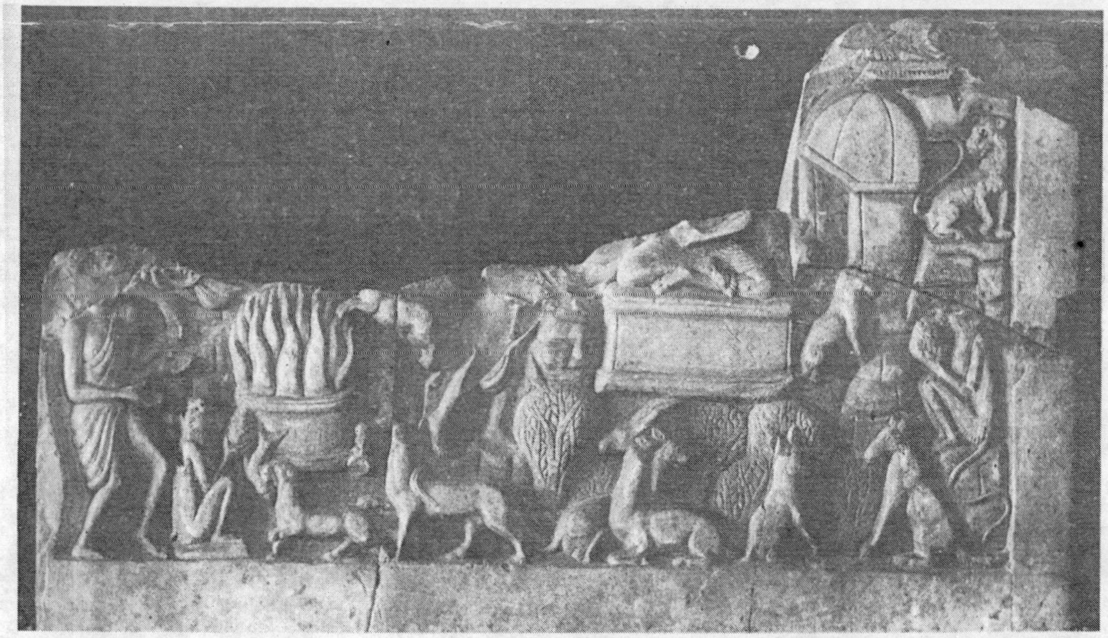

106. Sasa Jātaka, dome slab from Site 9 (Photo: Archaeological Survey of India).

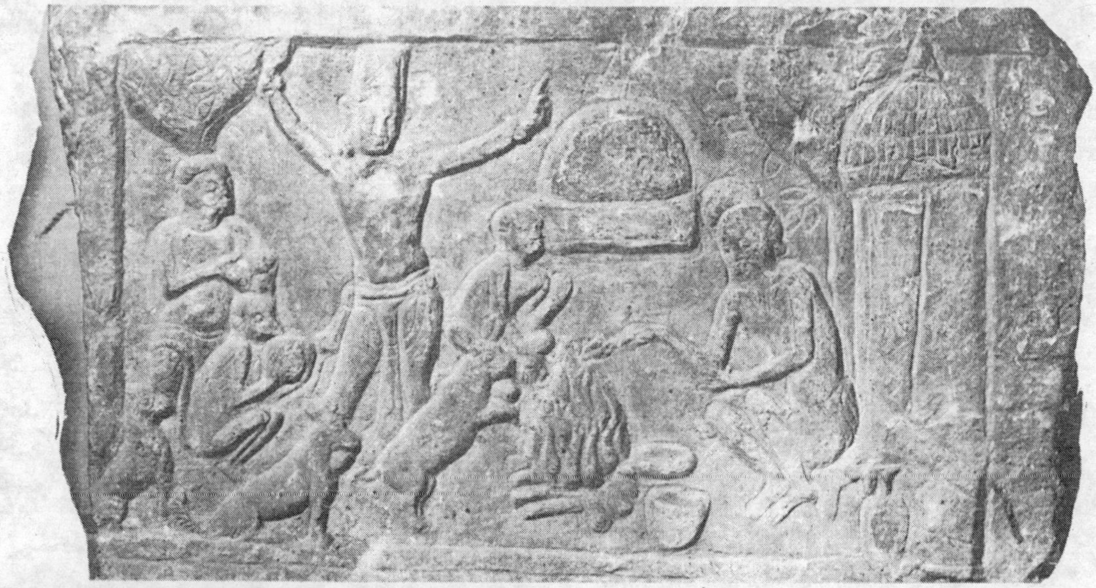

107. Sasa Jātaka from Goli Village, now Madras Government Museum (Photo: Archaeological Survey of India).

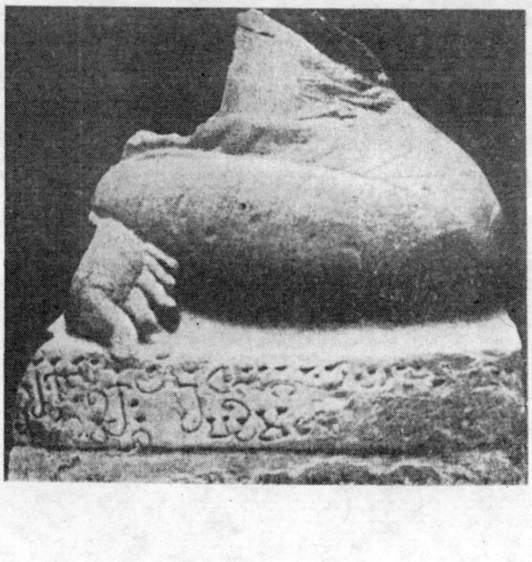

108. Fragment of an inscribed, seated Buddha image from Site 9 (Photo: Archaeological Survey of India).

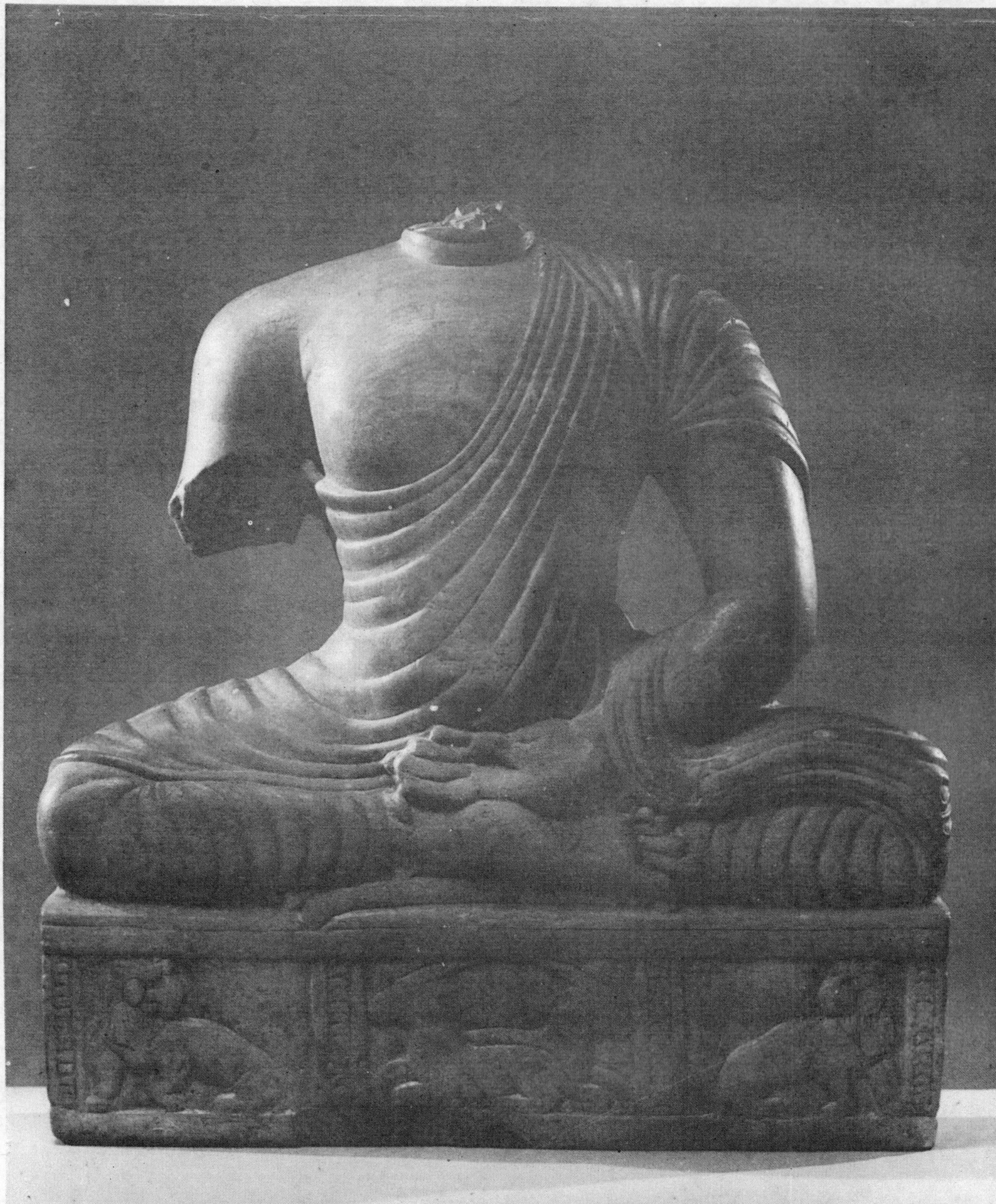

109. Seated Buddha image (after cleaning), now The Brooklyn Museum, gift of the Ernest Erickson Foundation, 86.227. (Photo: The Brooklyn Museum).

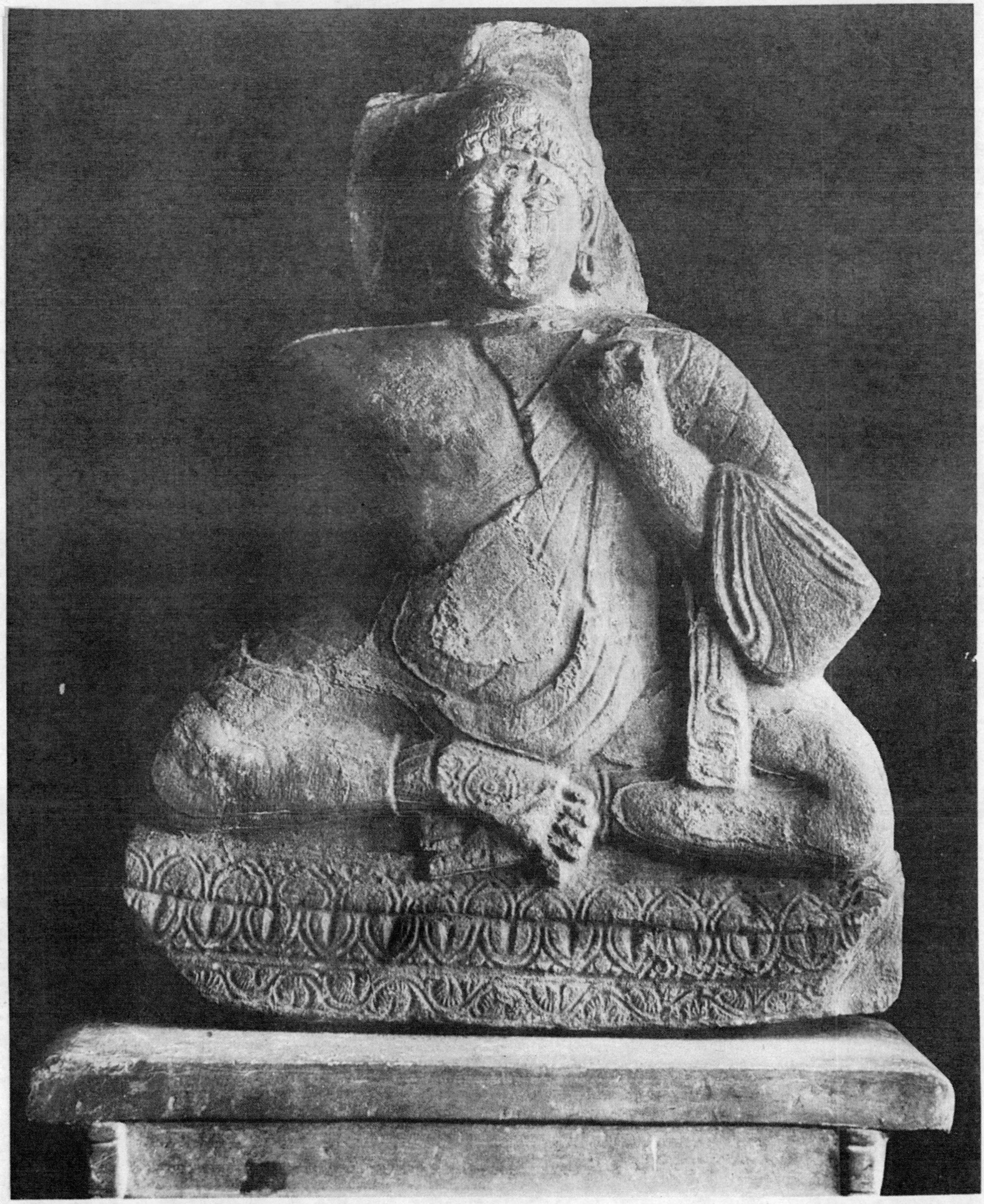

110. Seated Buddha (Photo: Archaeological Survey of India).

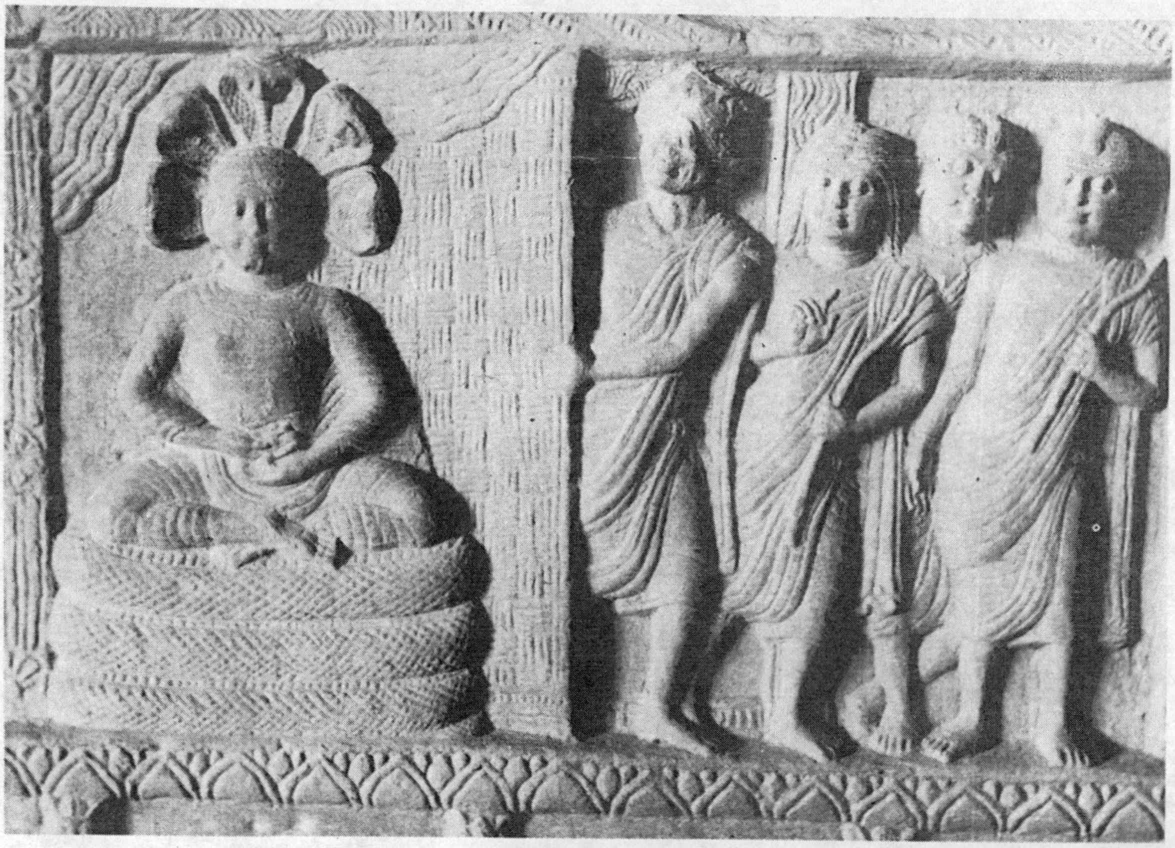

111. The Buddha Protected by Nāga Mucịlinda's Hood, detail of pl. 64 (Photo: Archaeological Survey of India).

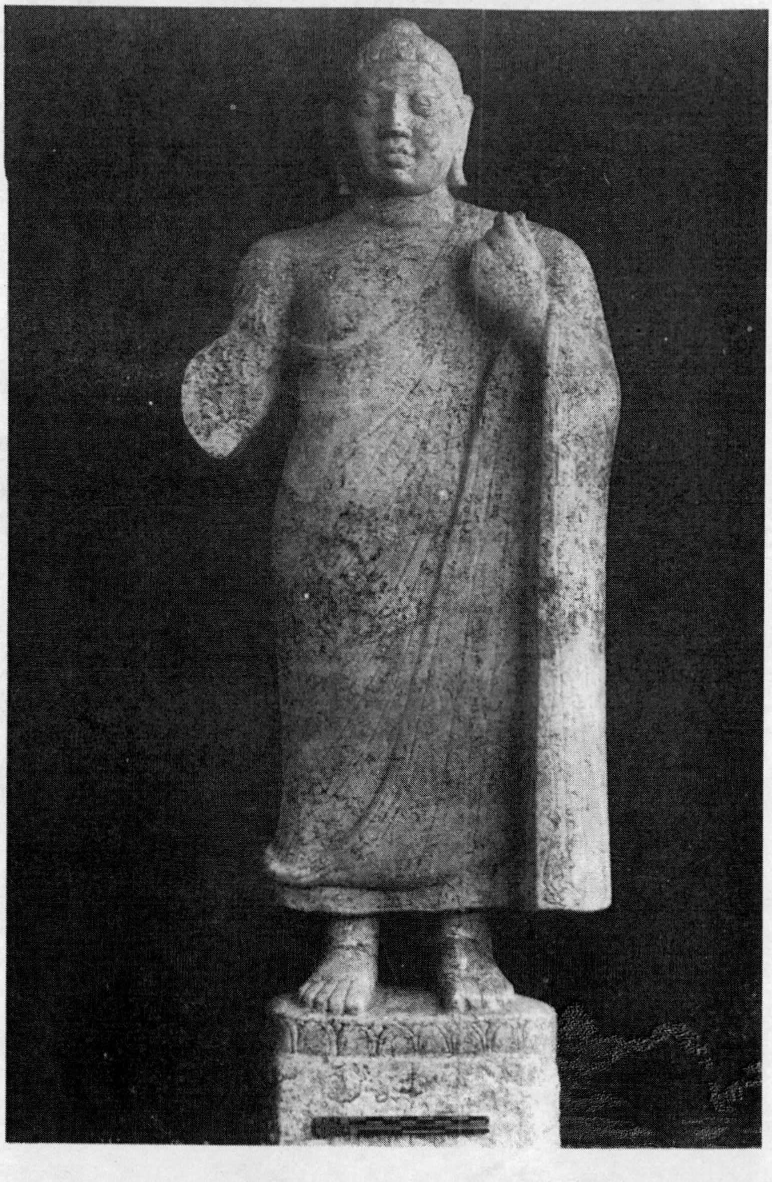

112. Standing Buddha from Guntapalli (Photo: Archaeological Survey of India).

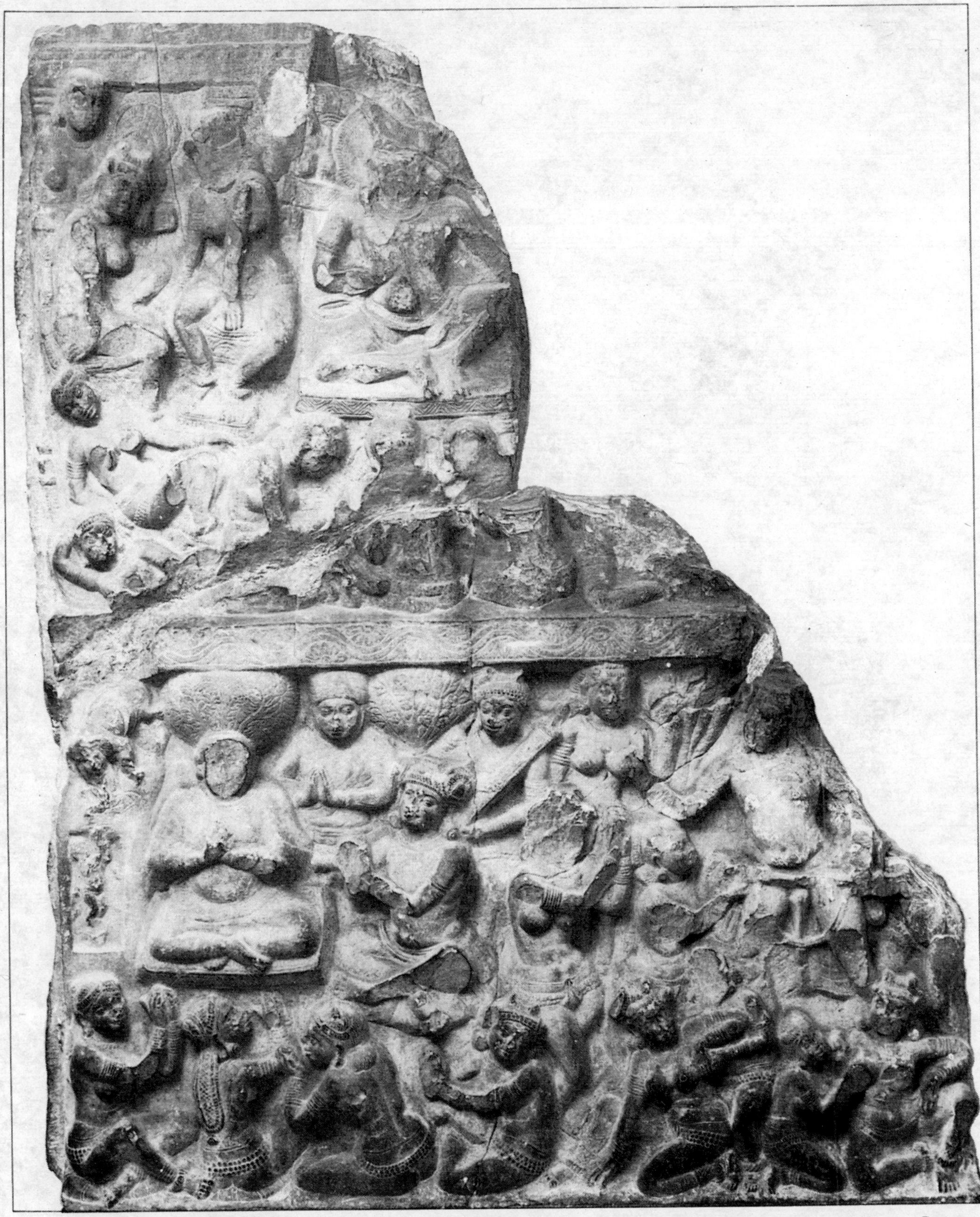

113. Siddhārtha in his palace and the story of "The Man in the Well", probably from Site 6, now Musée Guimet (Photo: RMN. Paris).

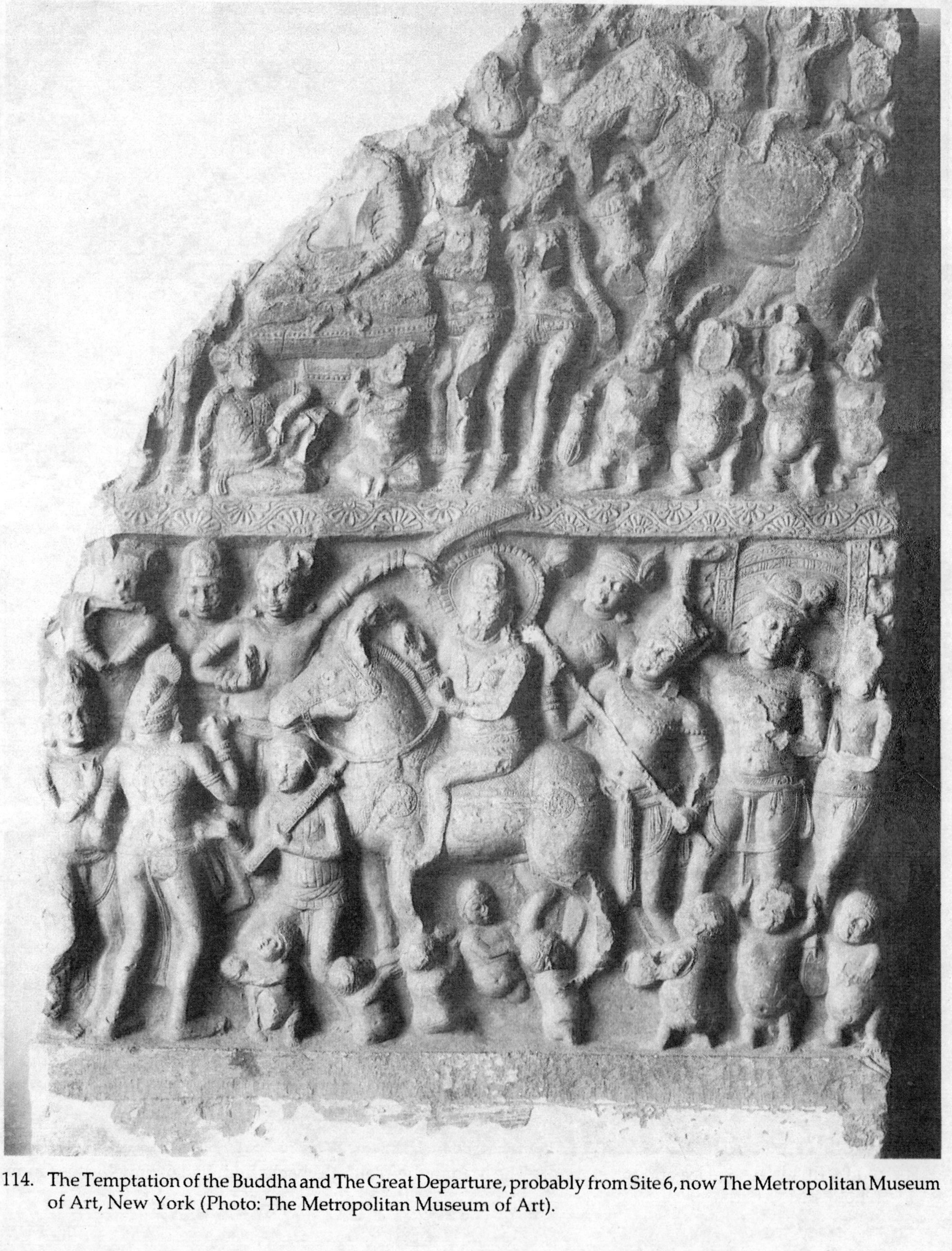

114. The Temptation of the Buddha and The Great Departure, probably from Site 6, now The Metropolitan Museum of Art, New York (Photo: The Metropolitan Museum of Art).

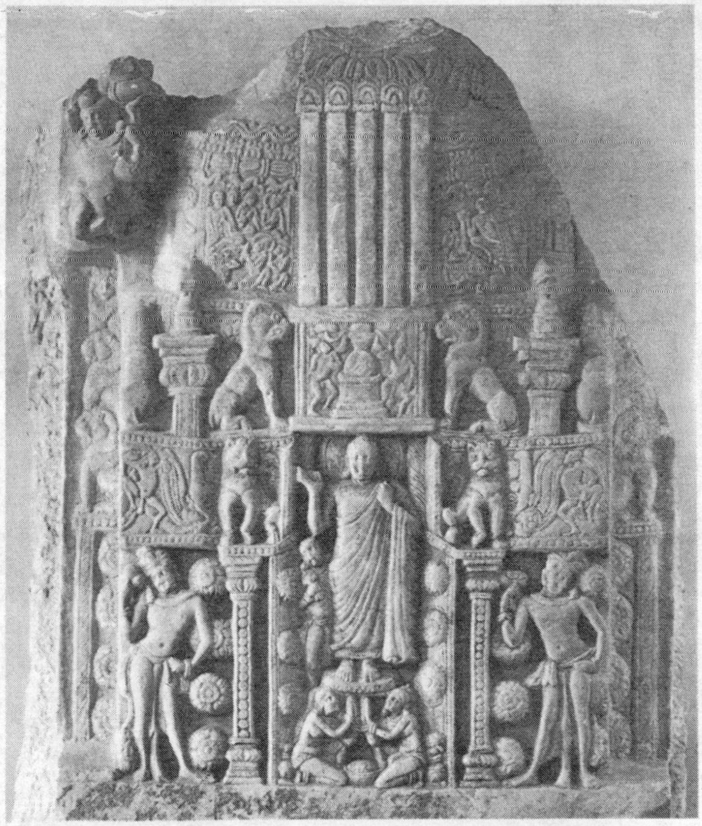

115. Drum slab, now The Metropolitan Museum of Art, New York (Photo: The Metropolitan Museum of Art).

116. Section of an *āyaka* pillar from Site 6. (Photo: Archaeological Survey of India). (Left below)

117. Fragment of an *āyaka* pillar from Site 6 (Photo: Archaeological Survey of India). (Right below)

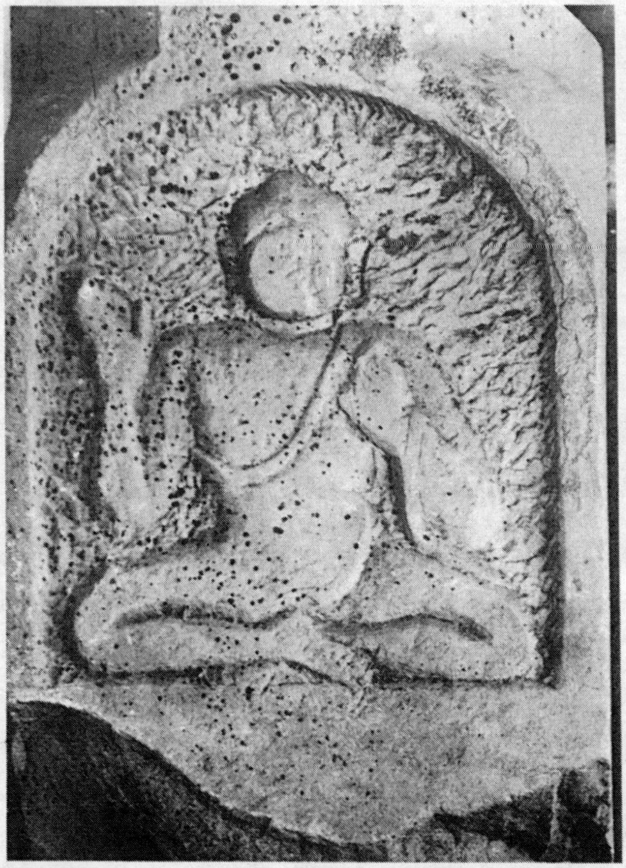

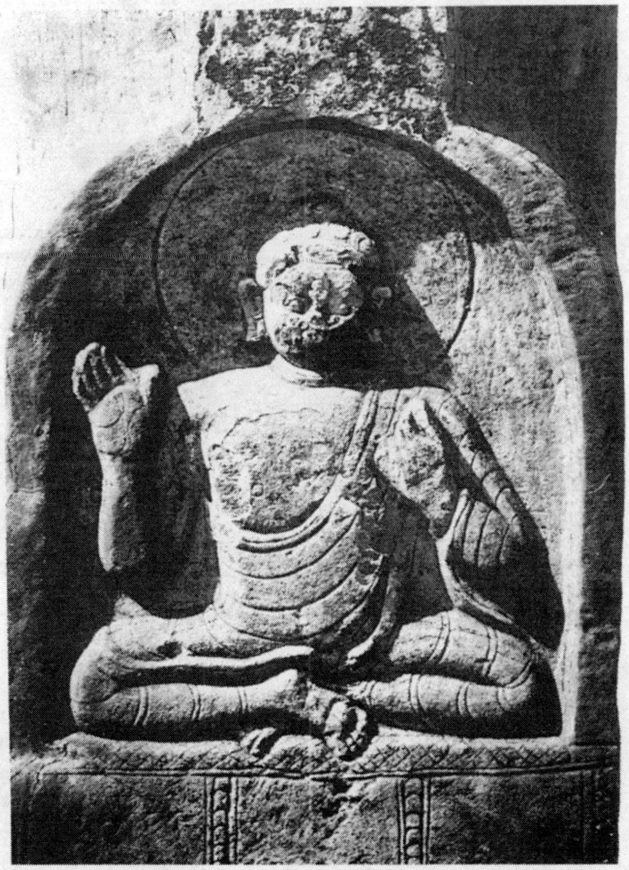

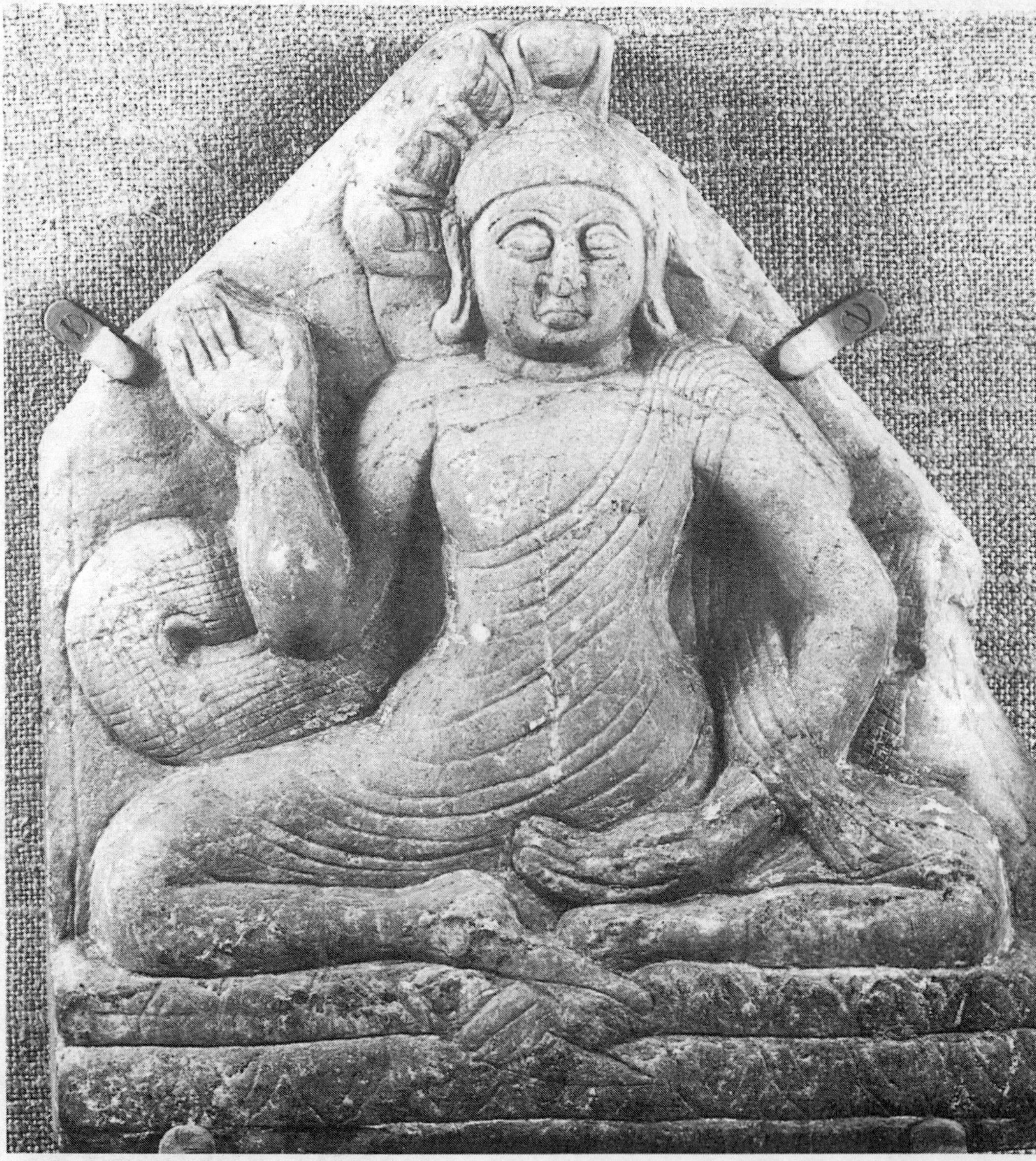

118. The Buddha Protected by Nāga Mucilinda's Hood, possibly from Site 6, now The Victoria and Albert Museum, London IM81-1936 (Photo: Reproduced by permission of the Trustees of The Victoria and Albert Museum).

119. Śrī Kinnarī Jātaka, base molding from Site 6 (Photo: Archaeological Survey of India).

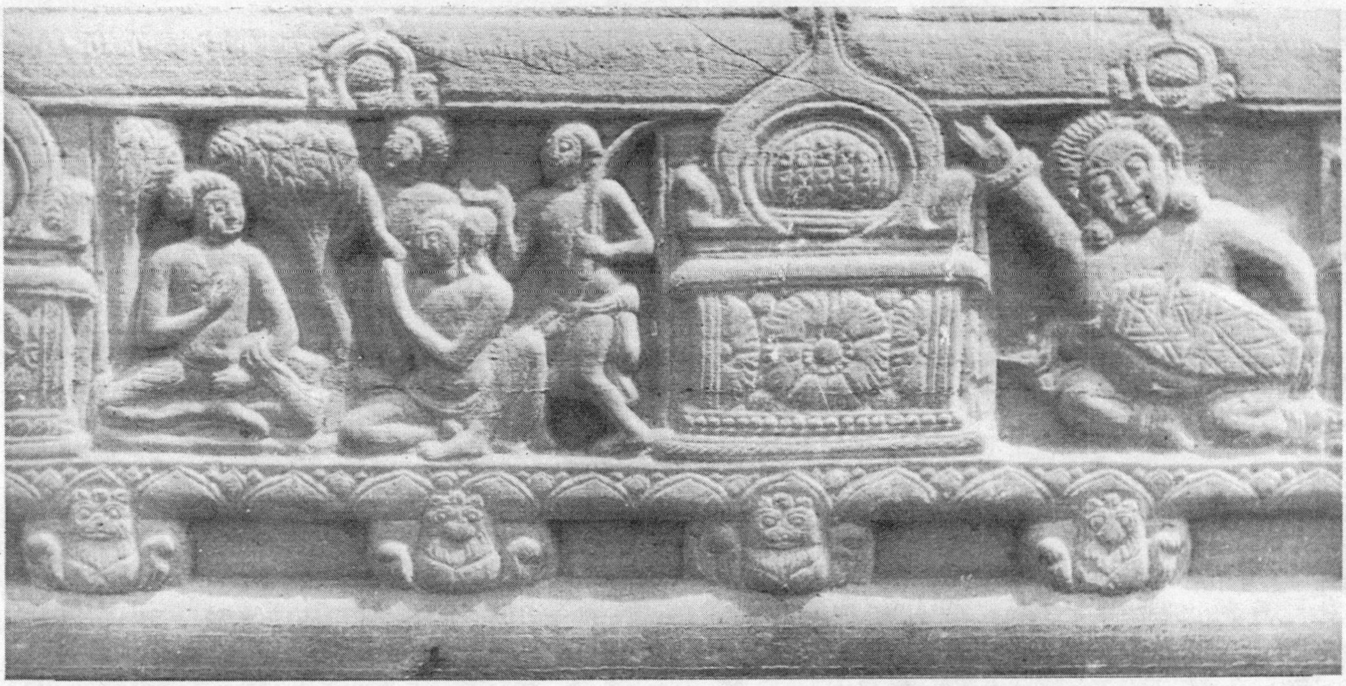

120. Prince Sudhanu seated before Kasyapa, detail of fig. 119 (Photo: Archaeological Survey of India).

121. Prince Sudhanu and His Companions Mounted on the Back of the Monkey King, detail of fig. 119 (Photo: Archaeological Survey of India).

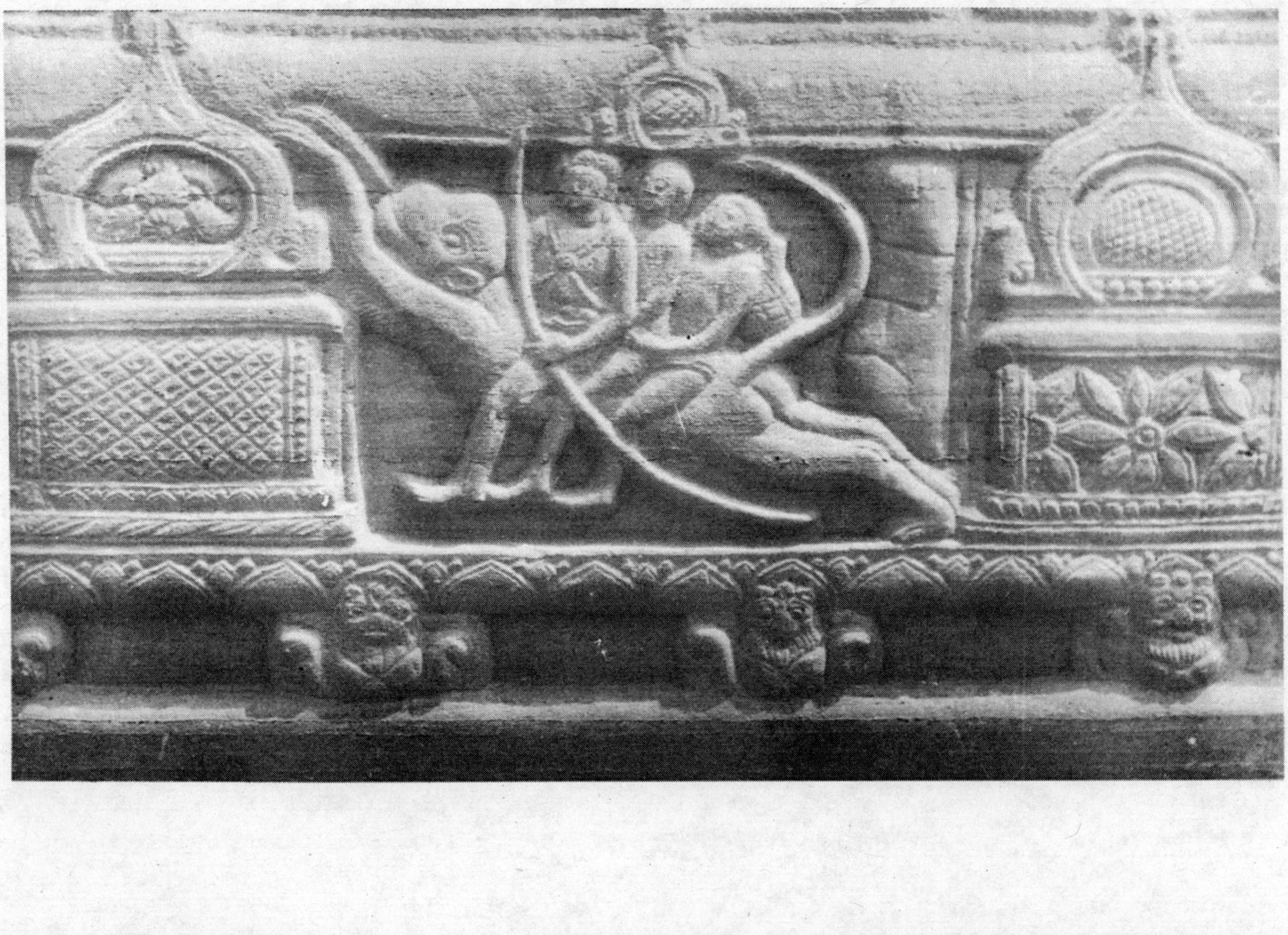

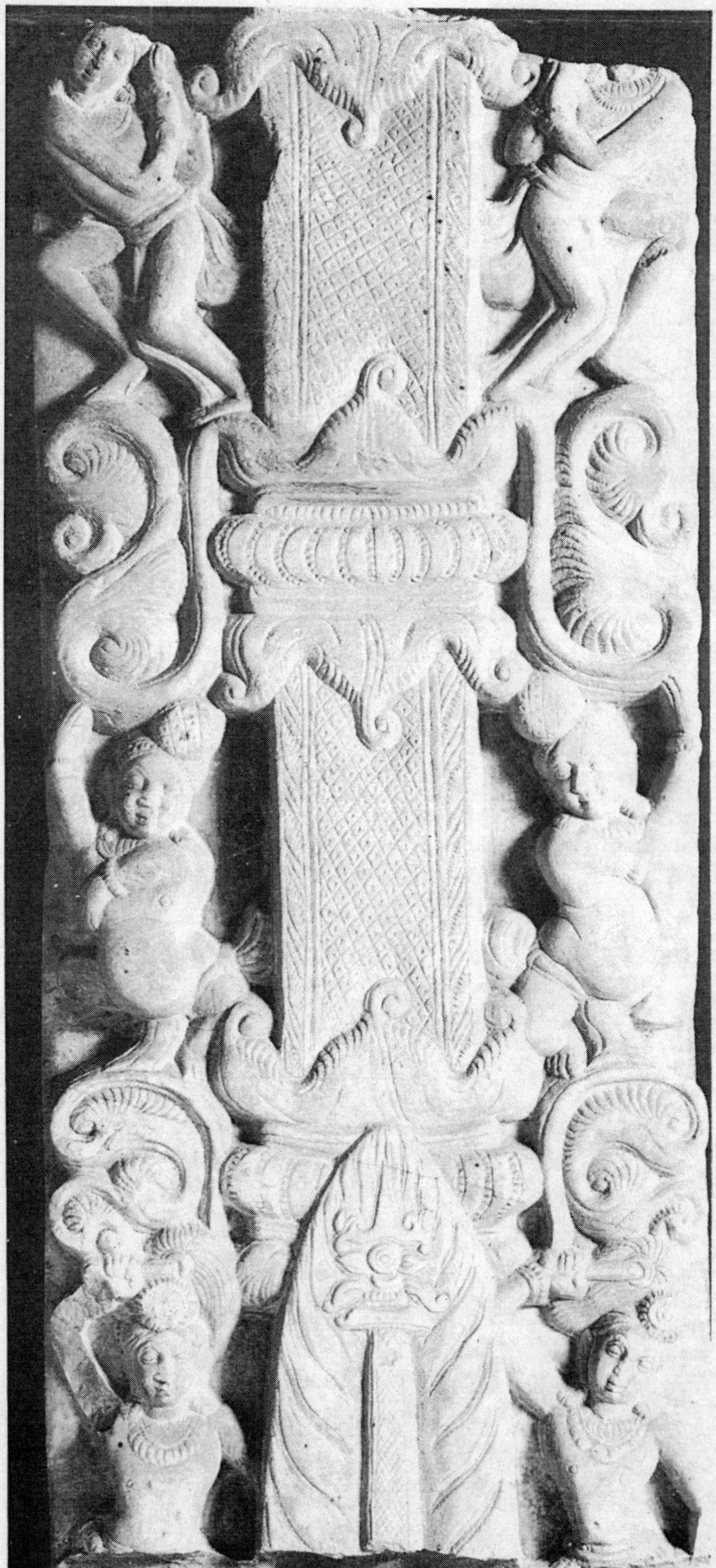

122. Drum slab, probably from Site 6, now The Cleveland Museum of Art, purchase, J.H. Wade Fund, 43.72 (Photo: The Cleveland Museum of Art).

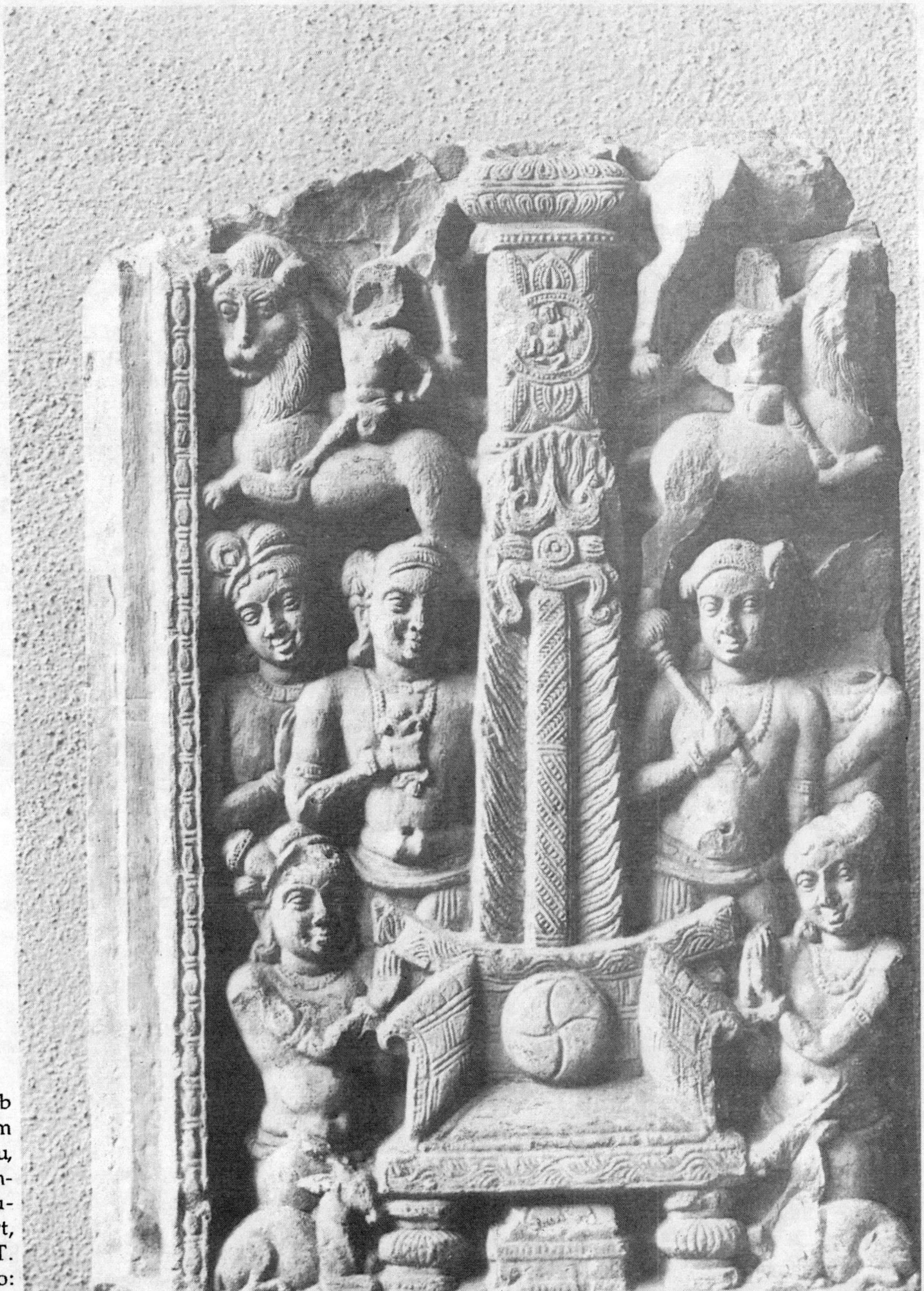

123. Drum slab from Gummididurru, now The Cincinnati Museum of Art, gift of C.T. Loo. (Photo: The Cincinnati Museum of Art).

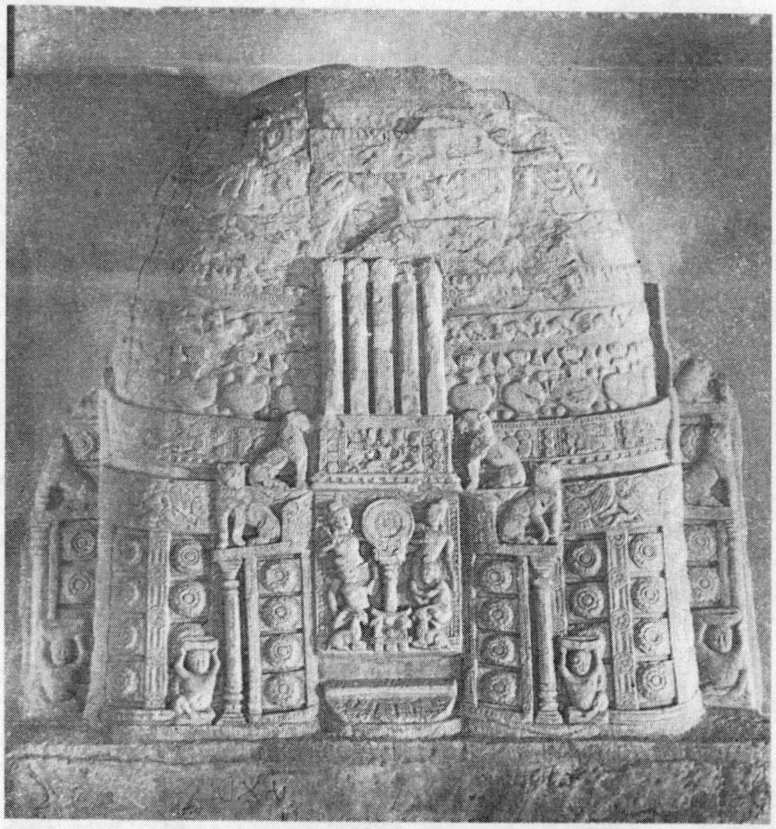

124. Inscribed Drum slab from Site 6 (Photo: Archaeological Survey of India).

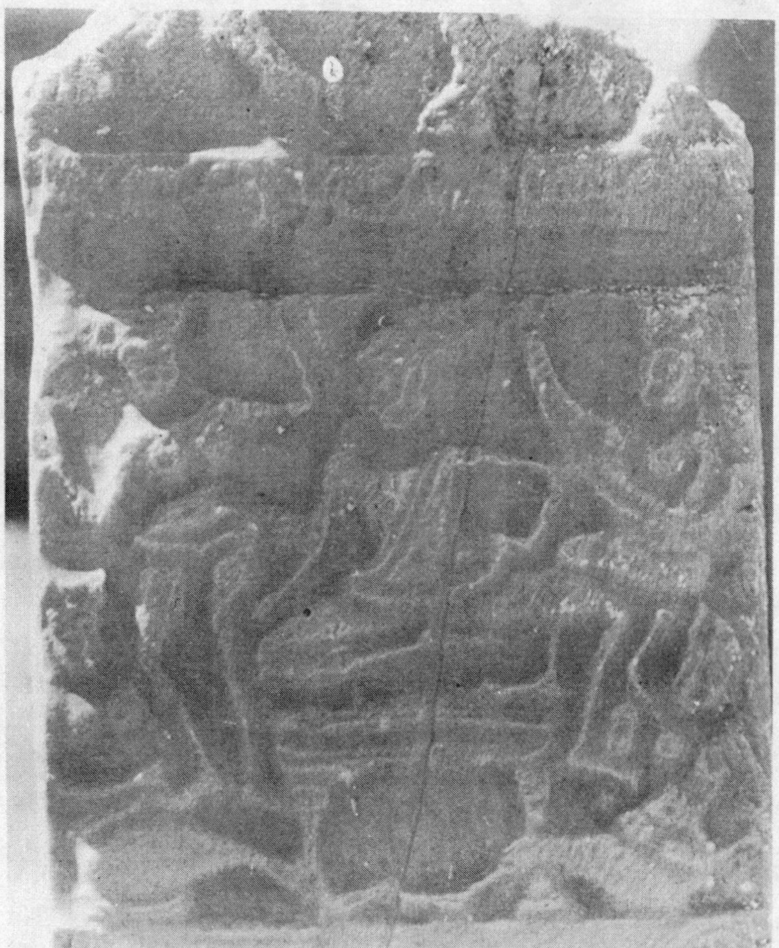

125. Memorial pillar of Mahāsenāpati Kumāra Elī Ehuvaladāsaṁnaka, dated in the thirteenth regnal year of Ehuvala Cāṁtamūla (c. A.D. 278-88), from Site 61.

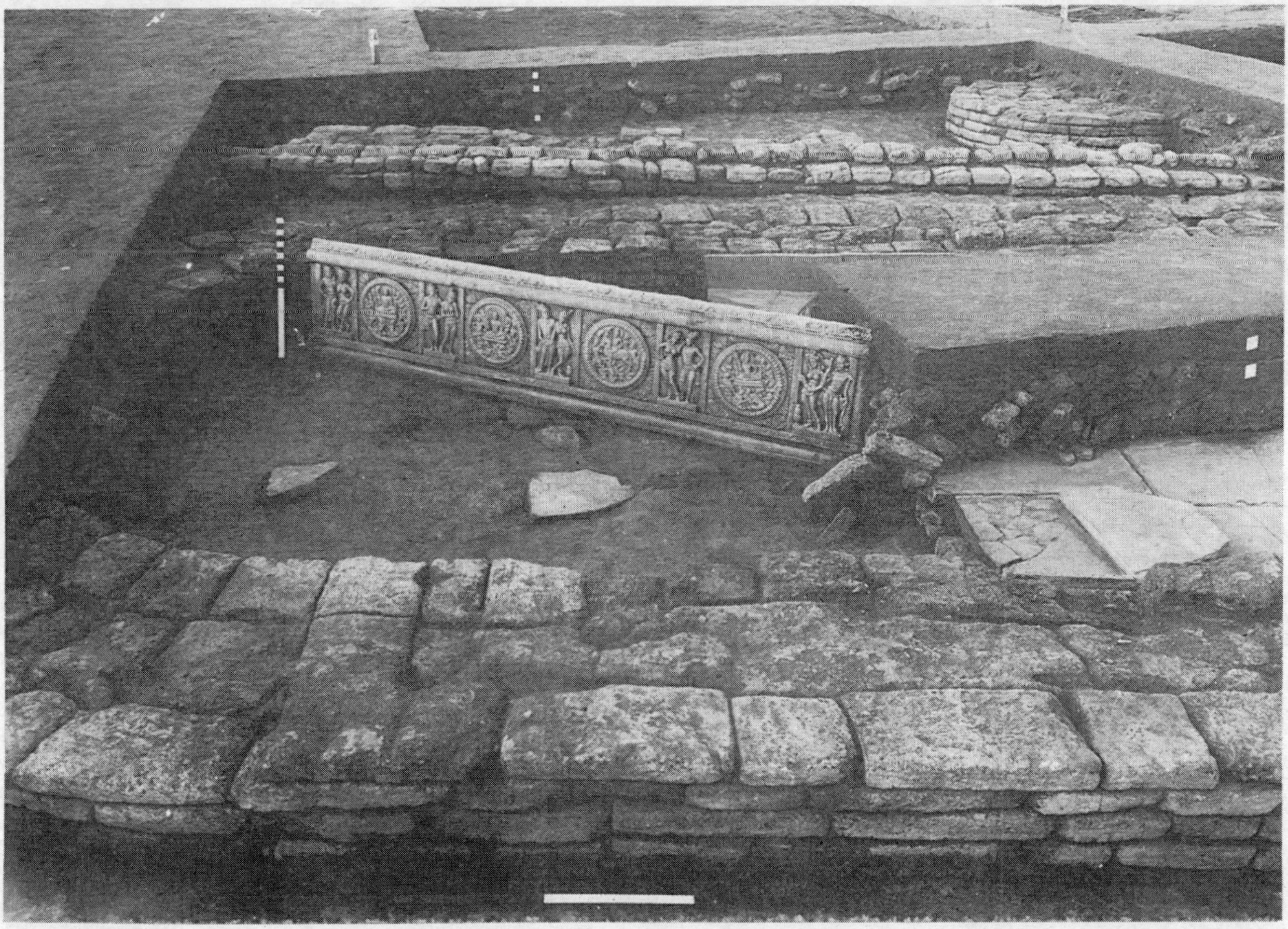

126. The Kumarānandin panel as found at Site 106 at Nāgārjunakoṇḍa (Photo: Archaeological Survey of India).

127. The Kumaranandin panel inscribed in the twenty-fourth regnal year of Ehuvala Cāṁtamūla c. A.D. 289-99.

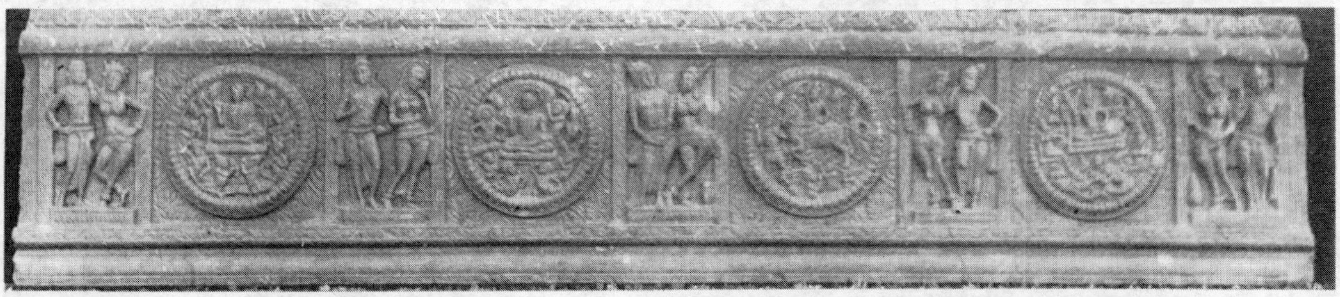

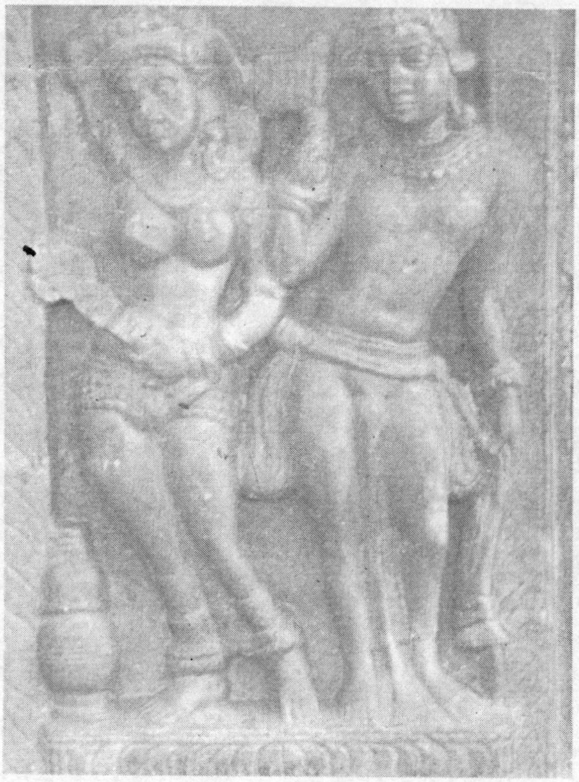

128. Detail of fig. 127.

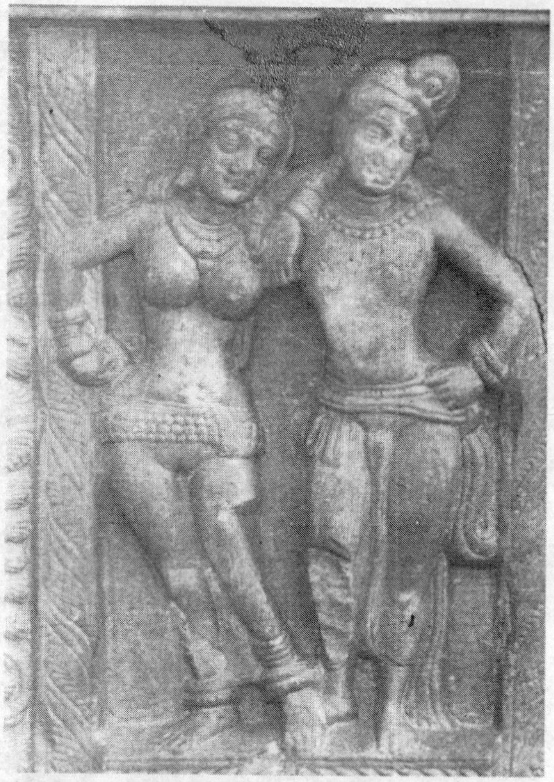

129. Detail of fig. 127.

130. Detail of fig. 127.

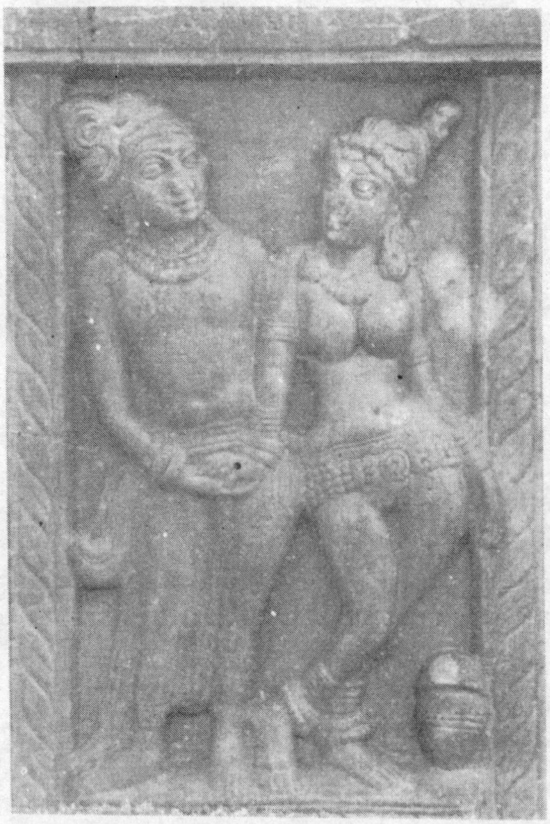

131. Detail of fig. 127.

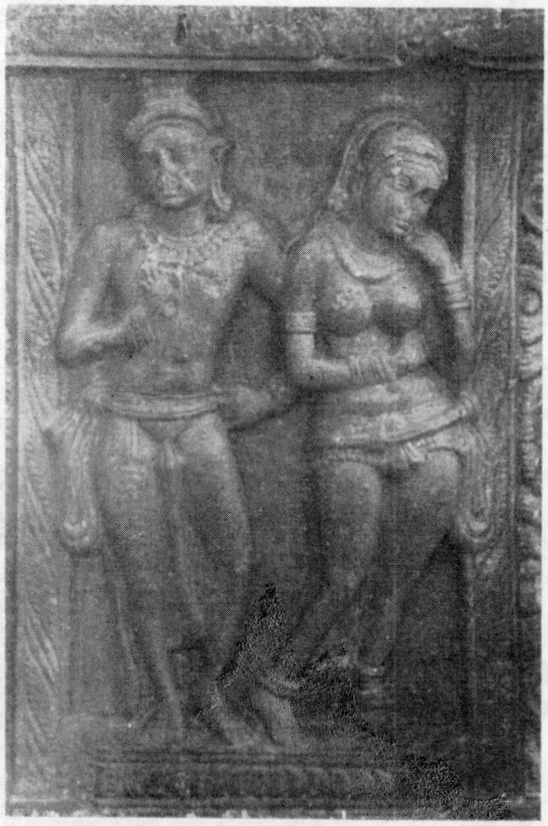

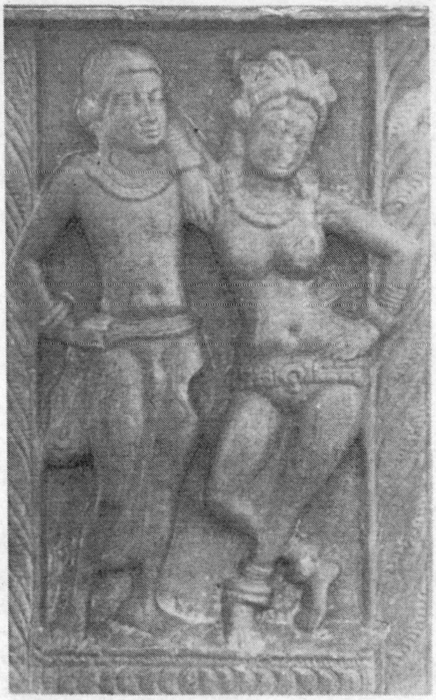

132. Detail of fig. 127.

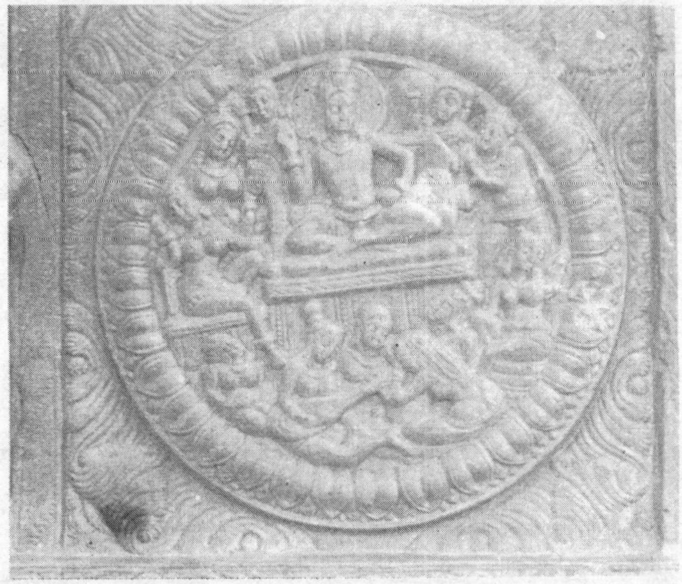

133. Siddhārtha in His Palace, detail of fig. 127.

134. The Great Departure, detail of fig. 127.

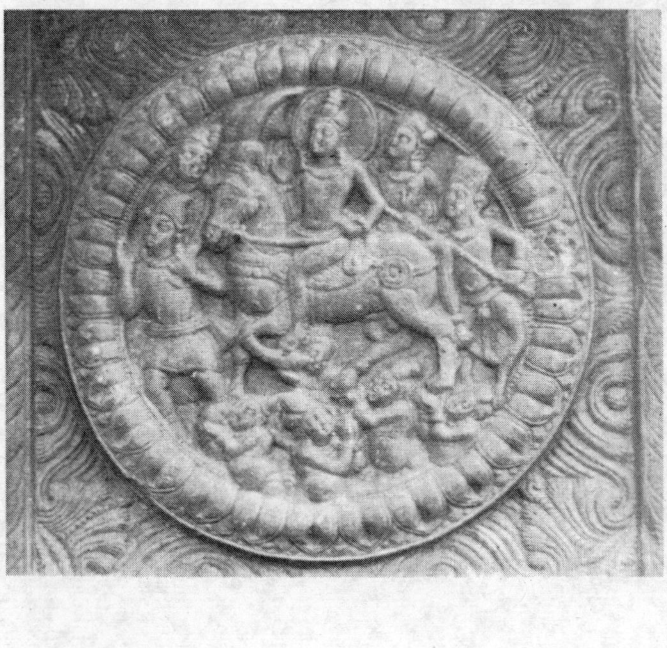

135. The Temptation, detail of fig. 127.

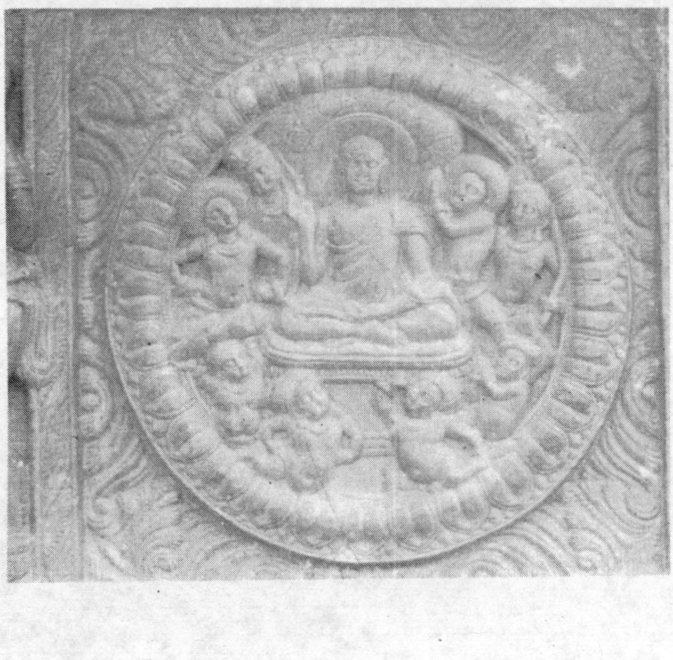

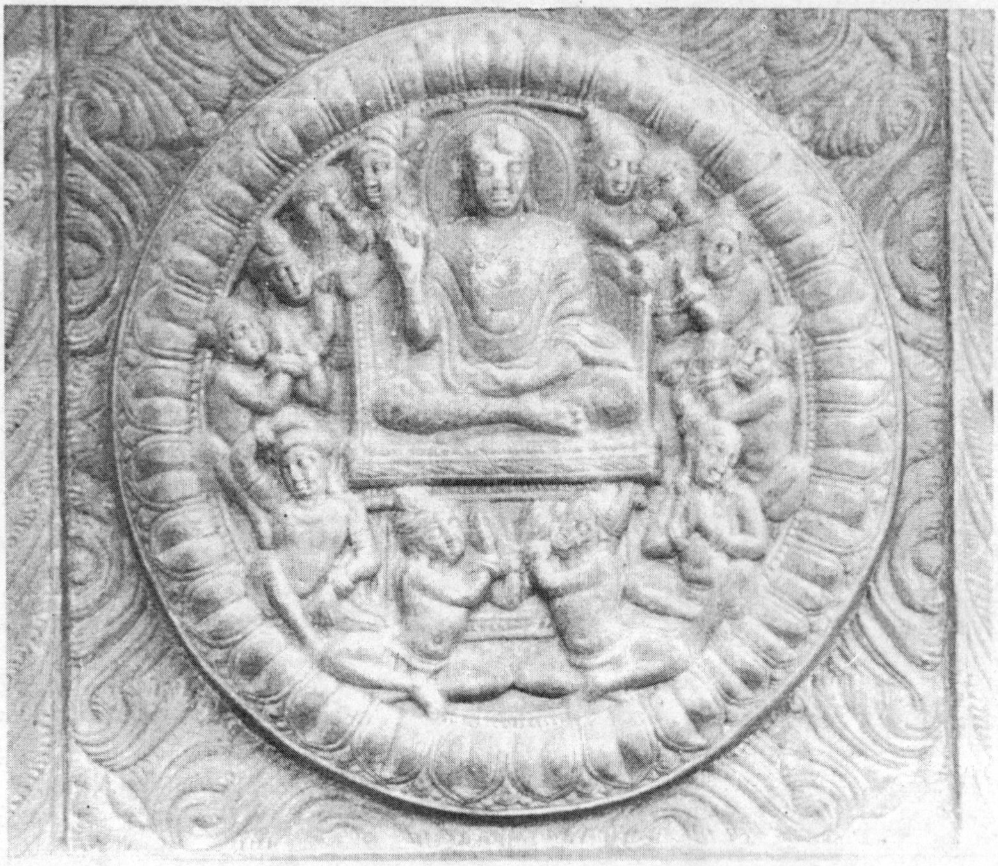

136. The Devas Congratulating the Buddha After His Enlightenment, detail of fig. 127.

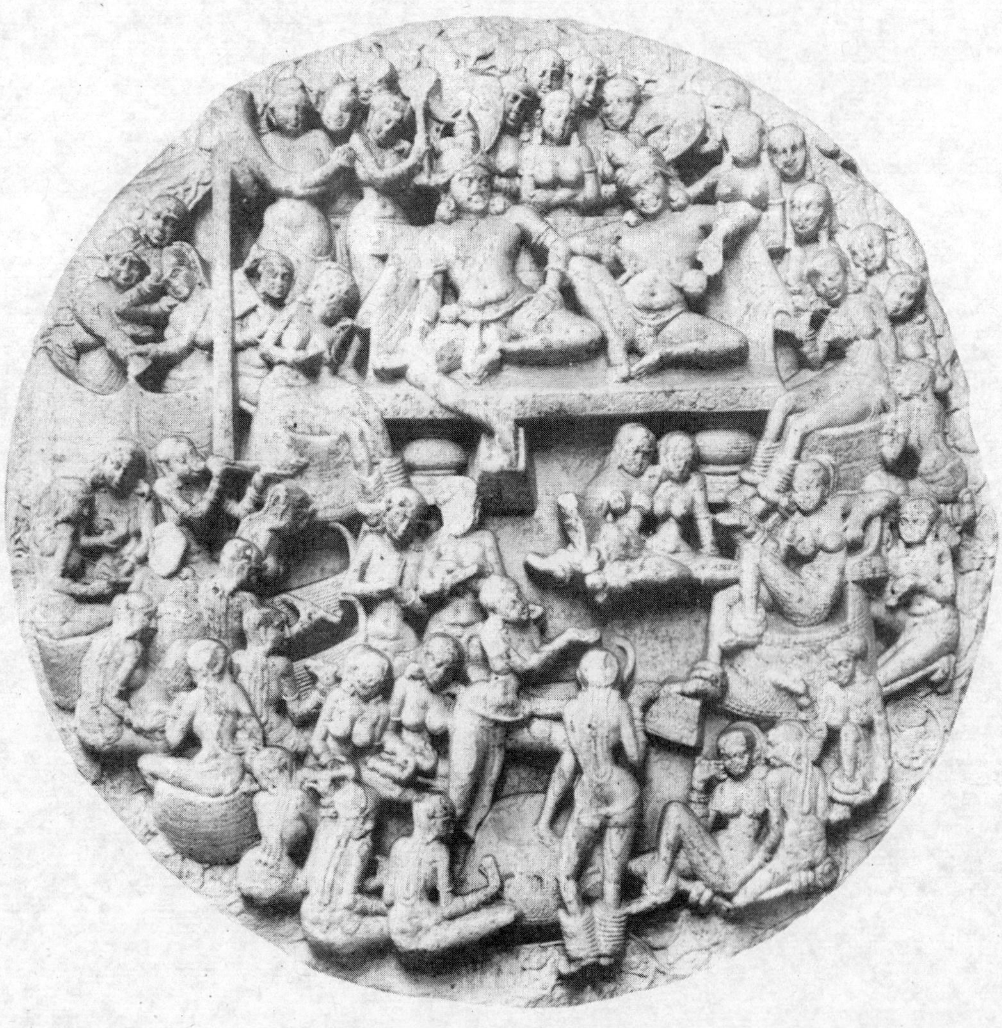

137. Muga Pakkha Jātaka, crossbar from the railing of the Amarāvatī *stūpa* now British Museum (Photo: Trustees of the British Museum).

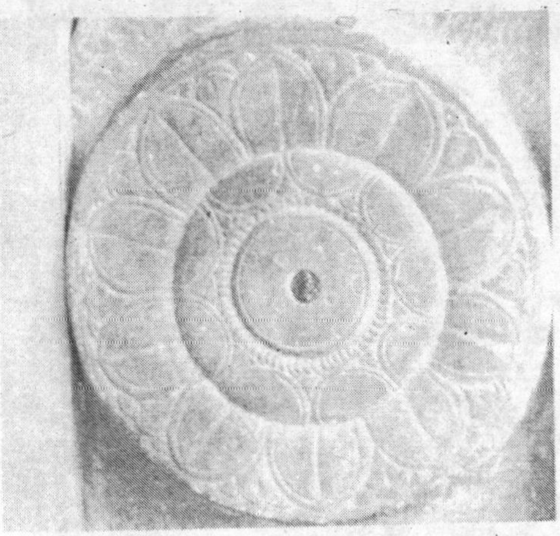

138. Crossbar with lotus decoration.

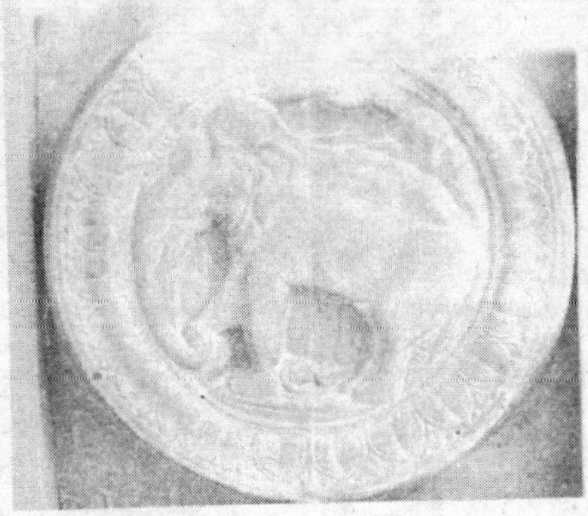

139. Elephants, crossbar, perhaps from Site 3.

140. Boxers within a decorated roundel (Photo: Archaeological Survey of India).

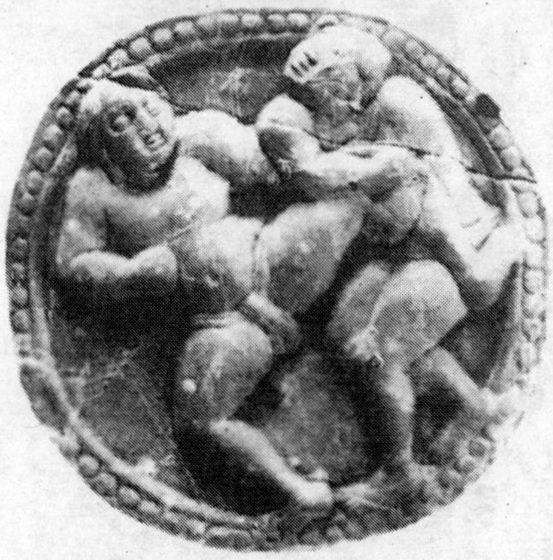

141. Dancing figure, reverse of fig. 140 (Photo: Archaeological Survey of India).

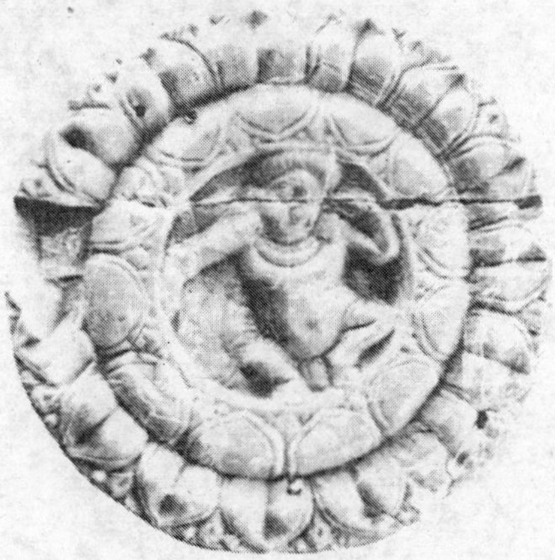

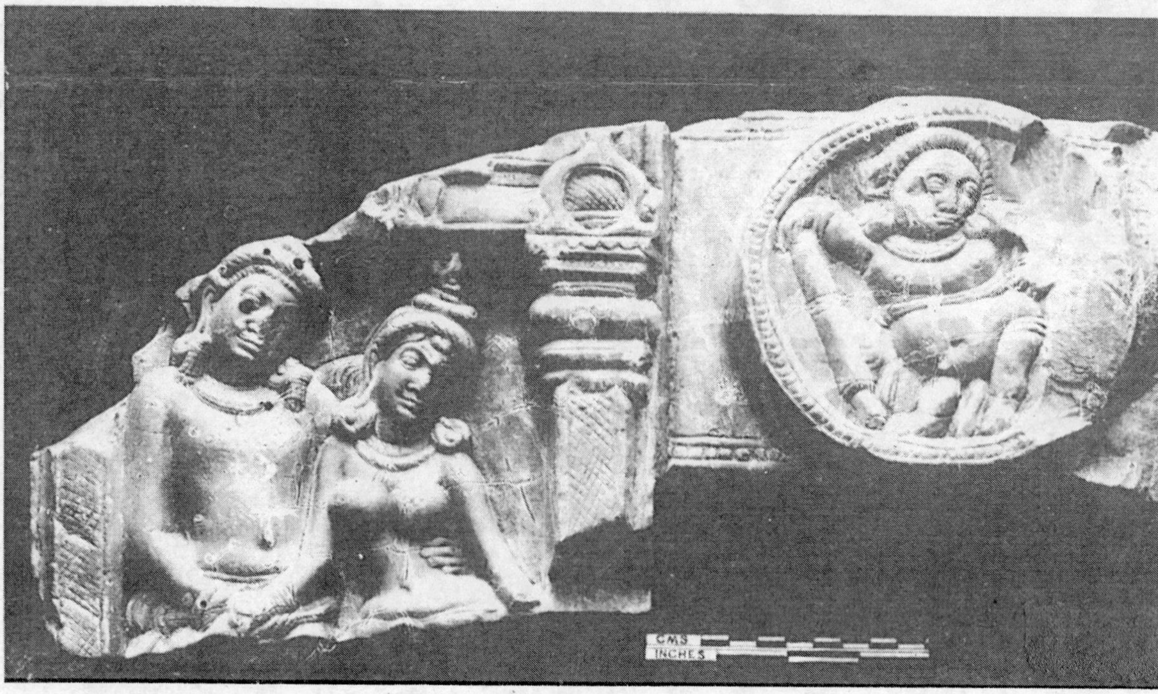

142. Fragment of a railing (Photo: Archaeological Survey of India).

143. Drum slab, probably from Nāgārjunakoṇḍa, now Madras Government Museum (Photo: Archaeological Survey of India).

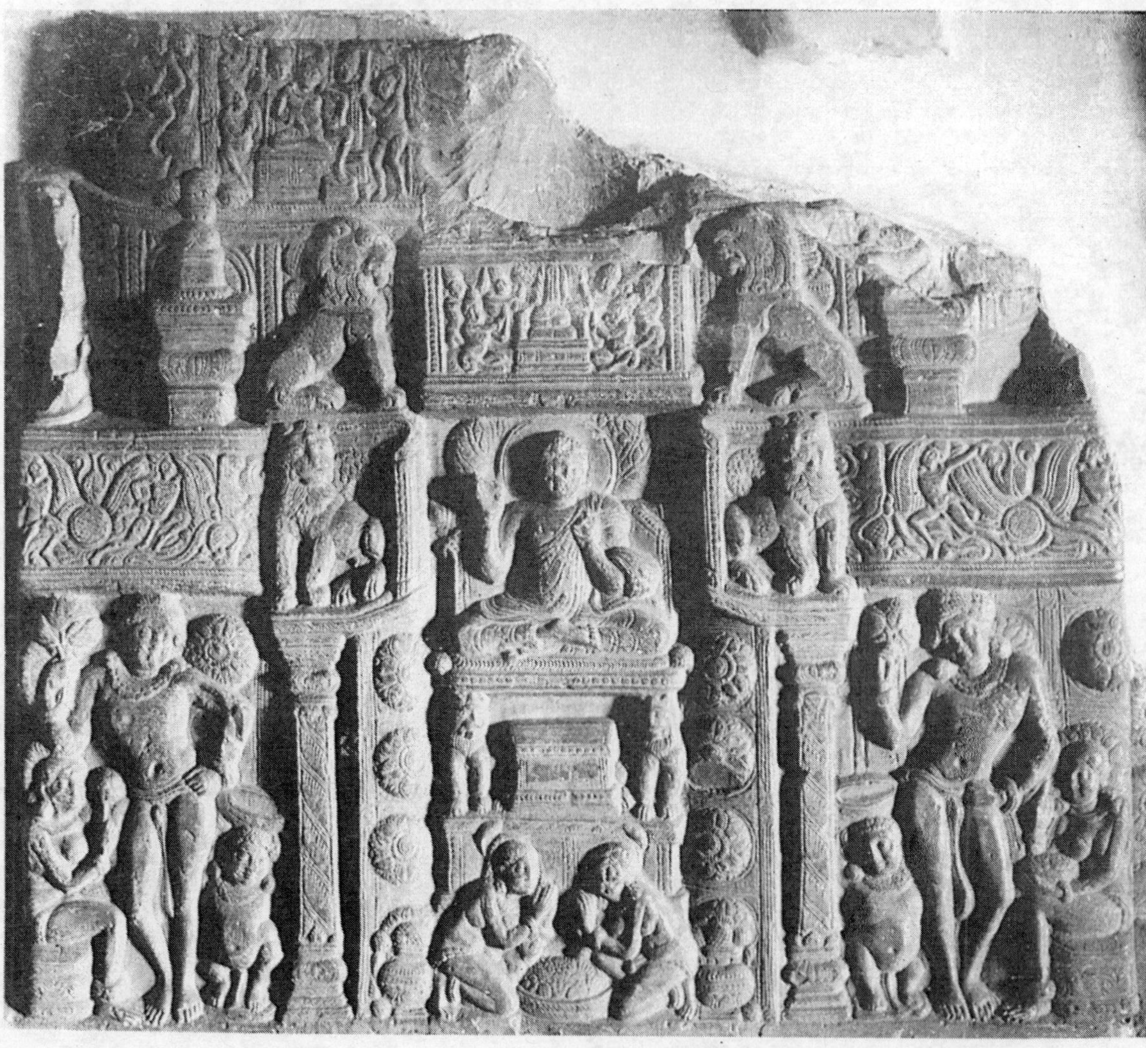

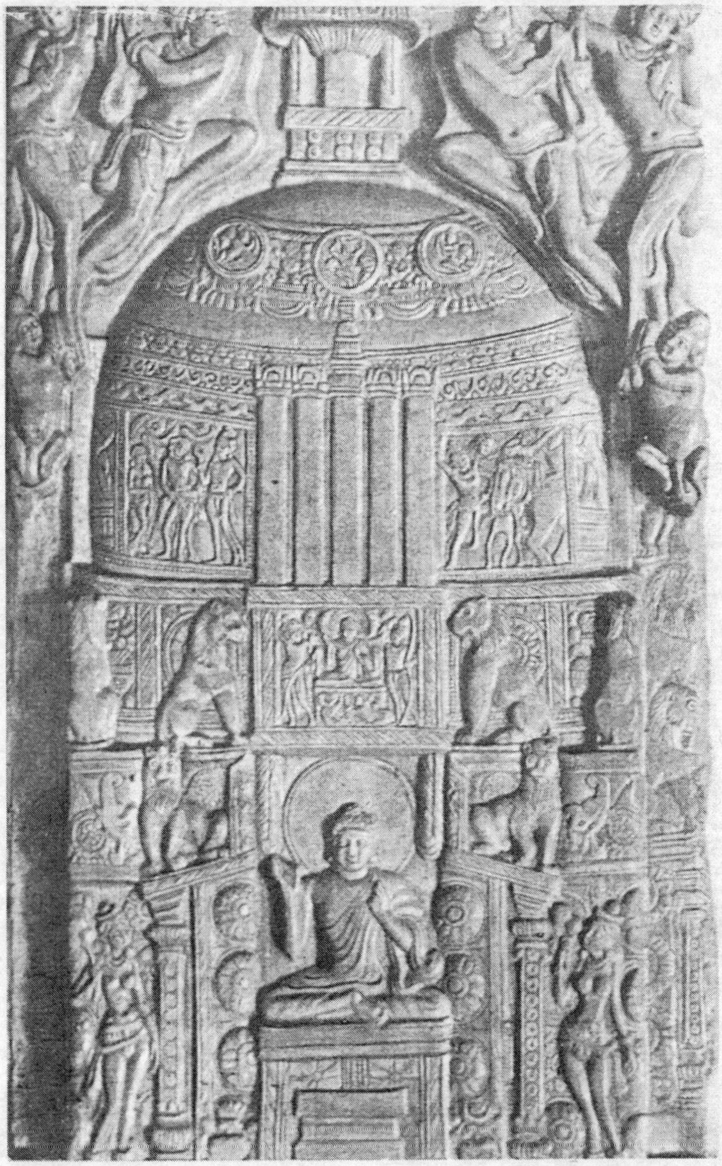

144. Drum slab (Photo: Archaeological Survey of India).

145. Drum slab (Photo: Archaeological Survey of India).

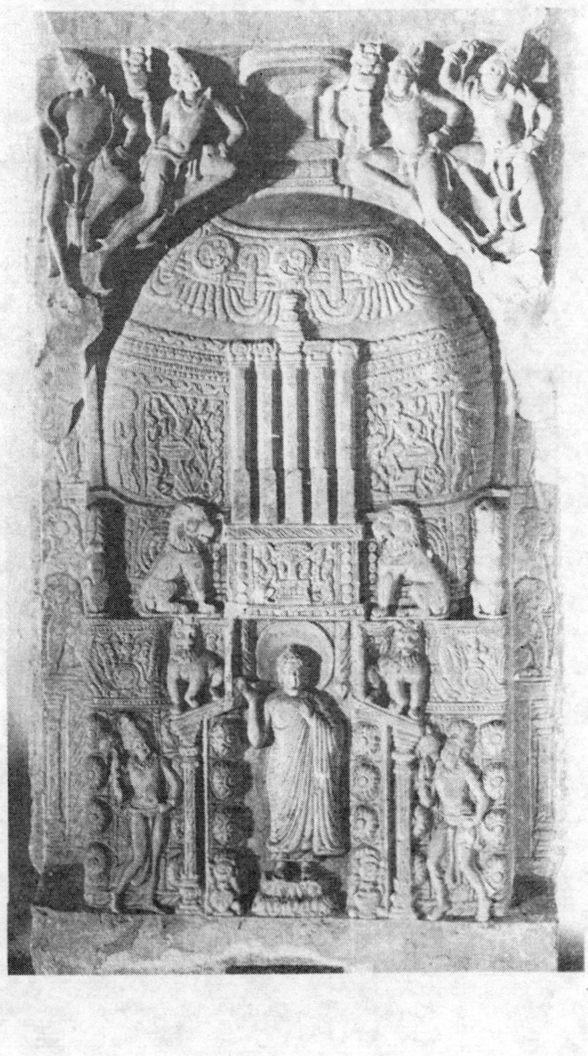

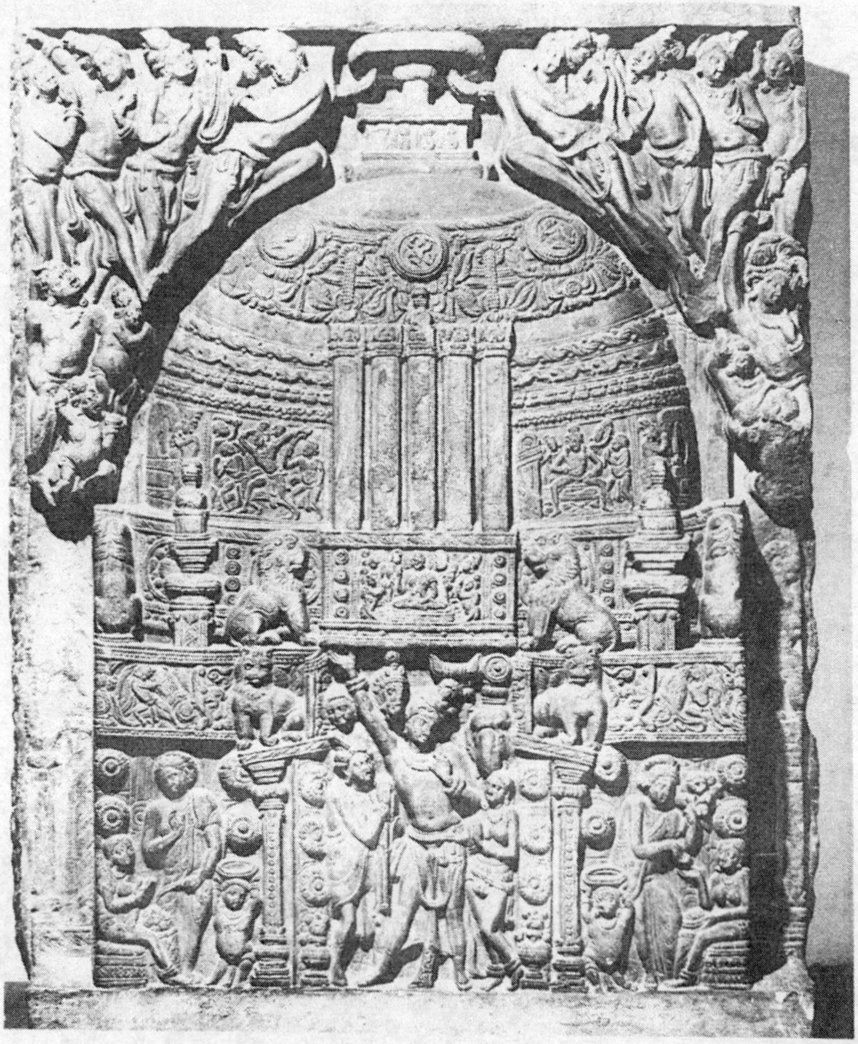

146. Drum slab, National Museum, New Delhi.

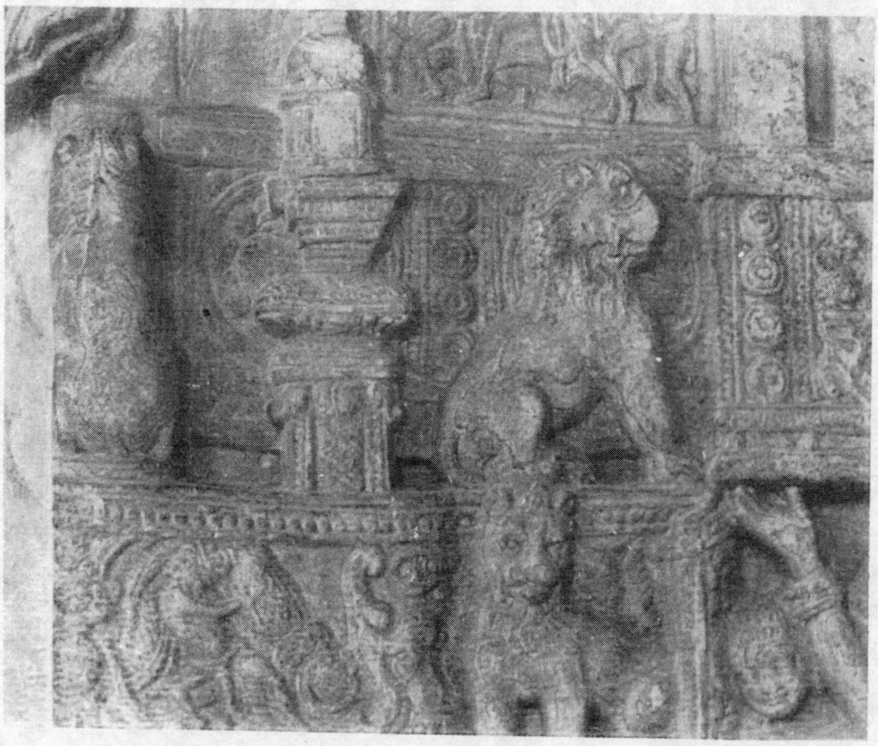

147. Detail of fig. 146.

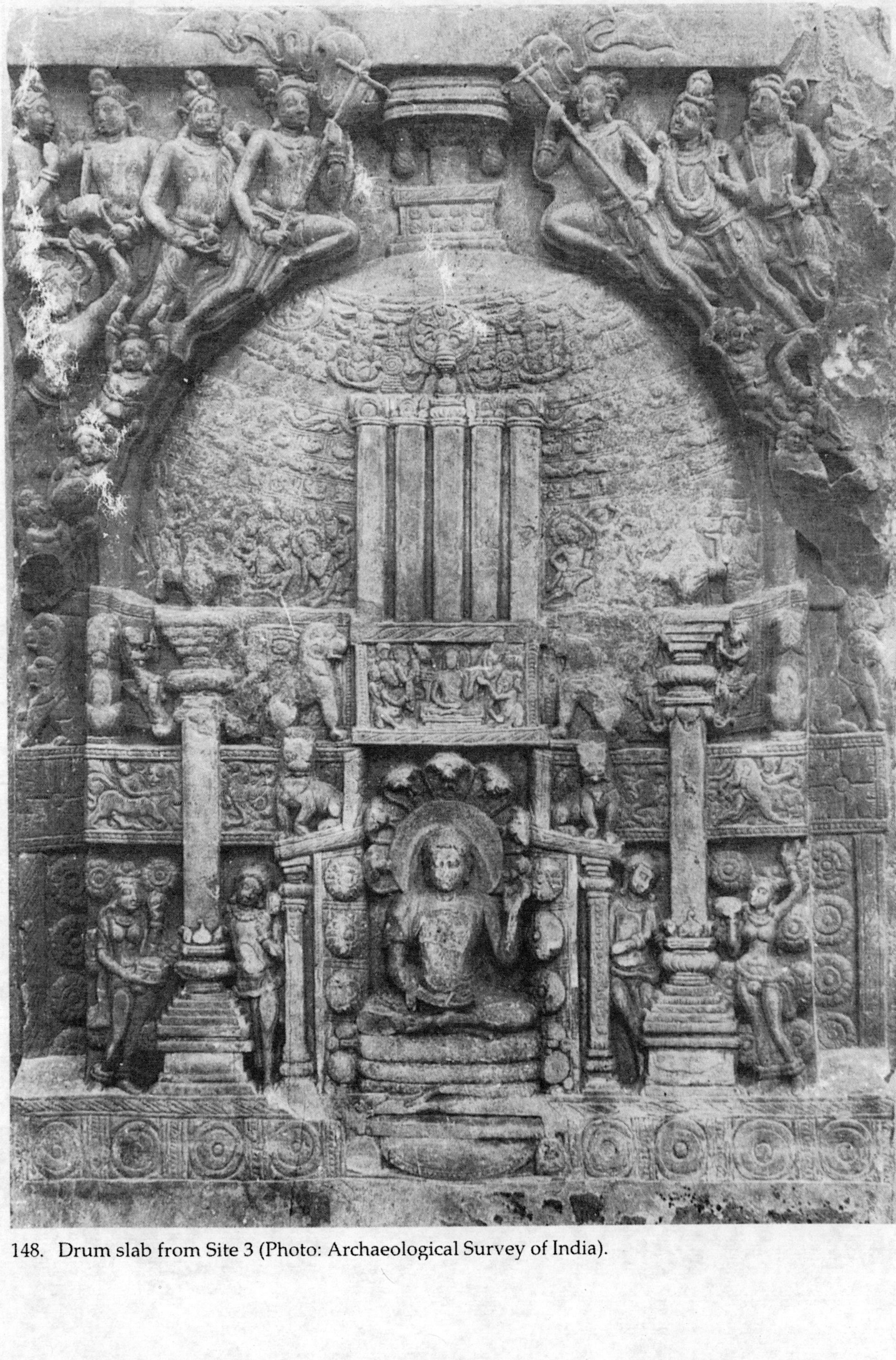

148. Drum slab from Site 3 (Photo: Archaeological Survey of India).

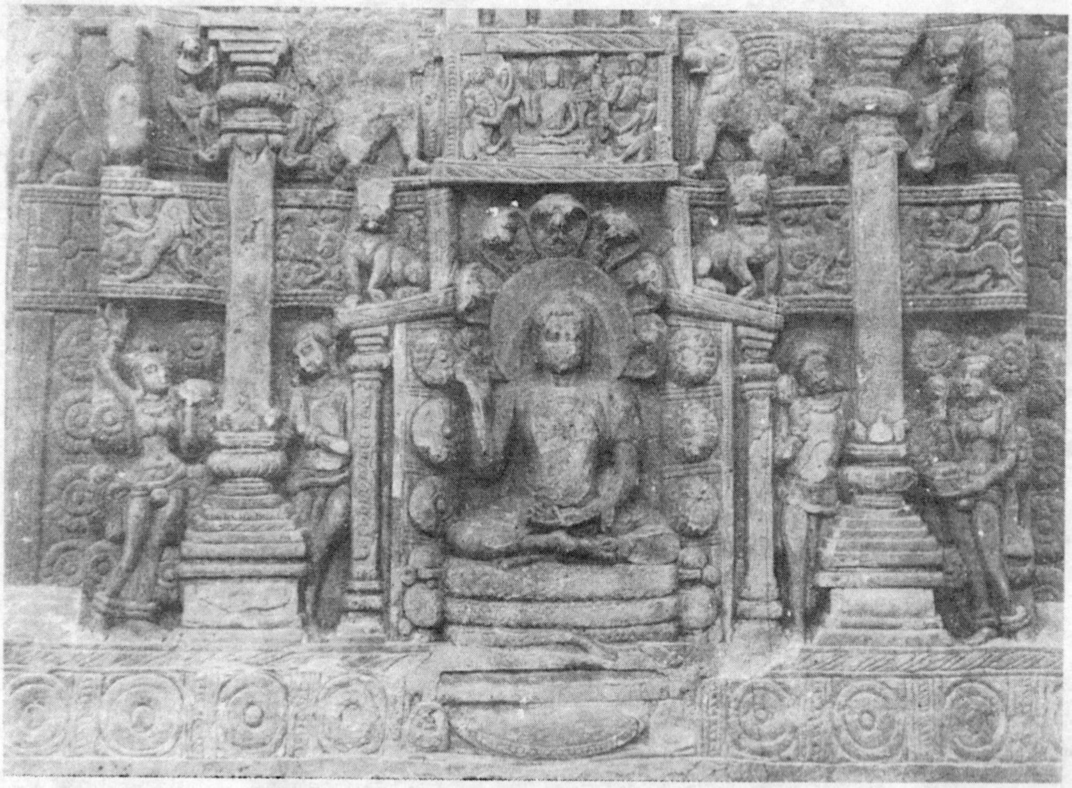

149. Detail of fig. 148 (Photo: Archaeological Survey of India).

150. Drum slab from Amarāvatī, now British Museum (Photo: Trustees of the British Museum).

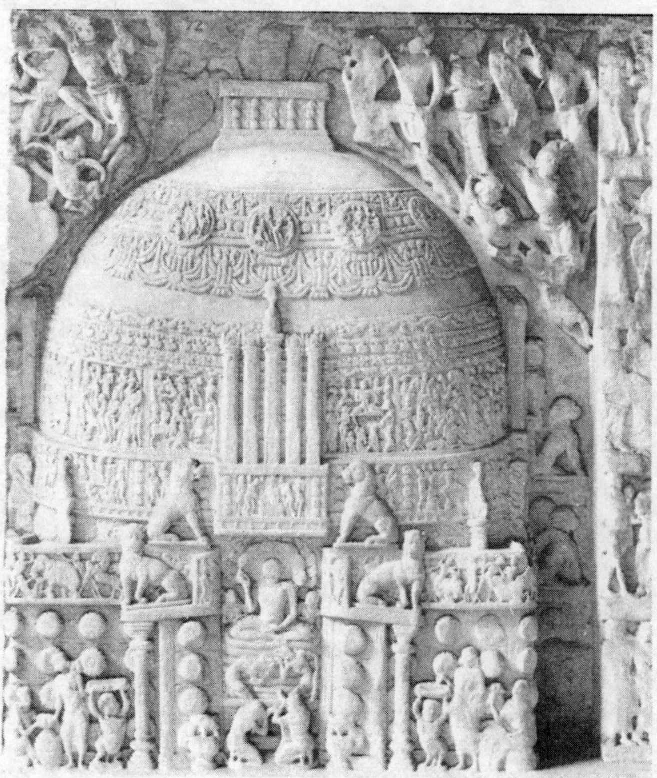

151. Drum slab from *Stūpa* 2.

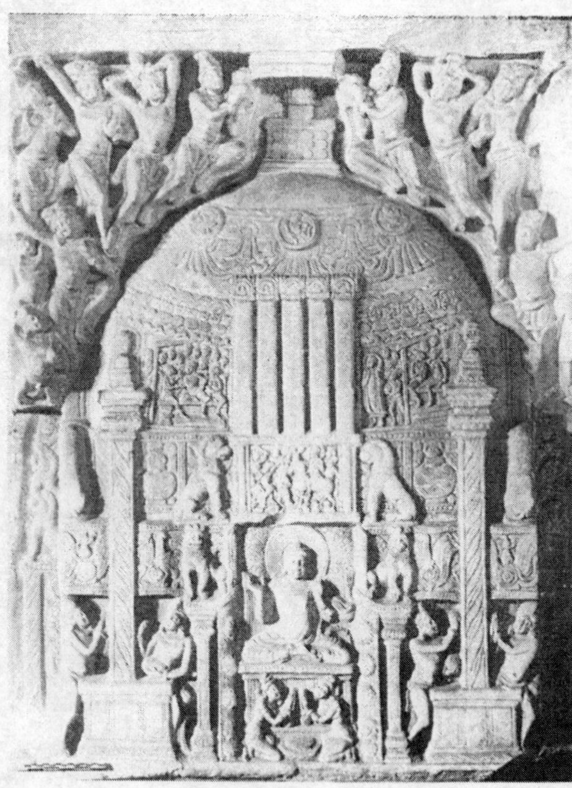

152. Drum slab (Photo: Archaeological Survey of India).

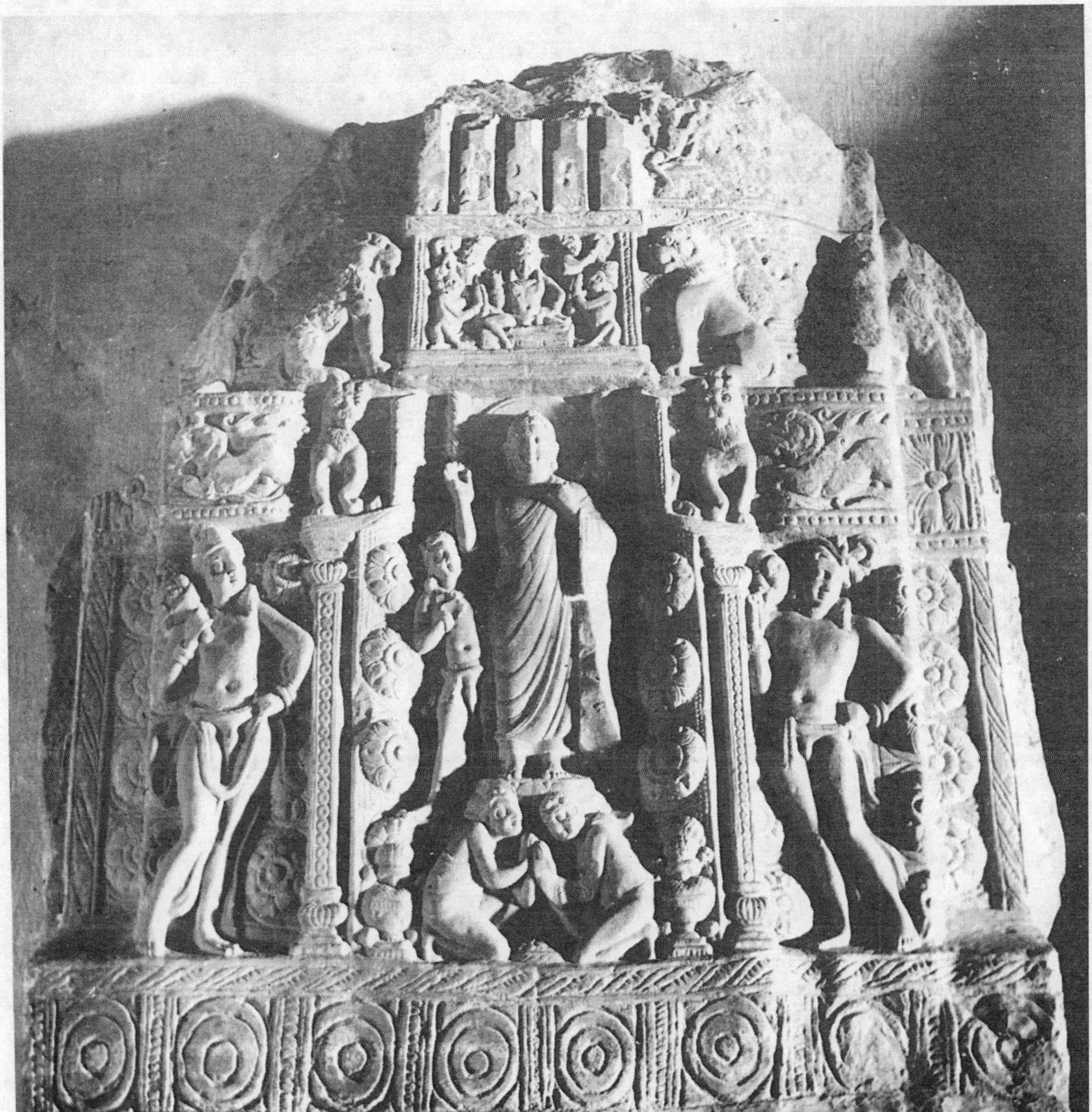

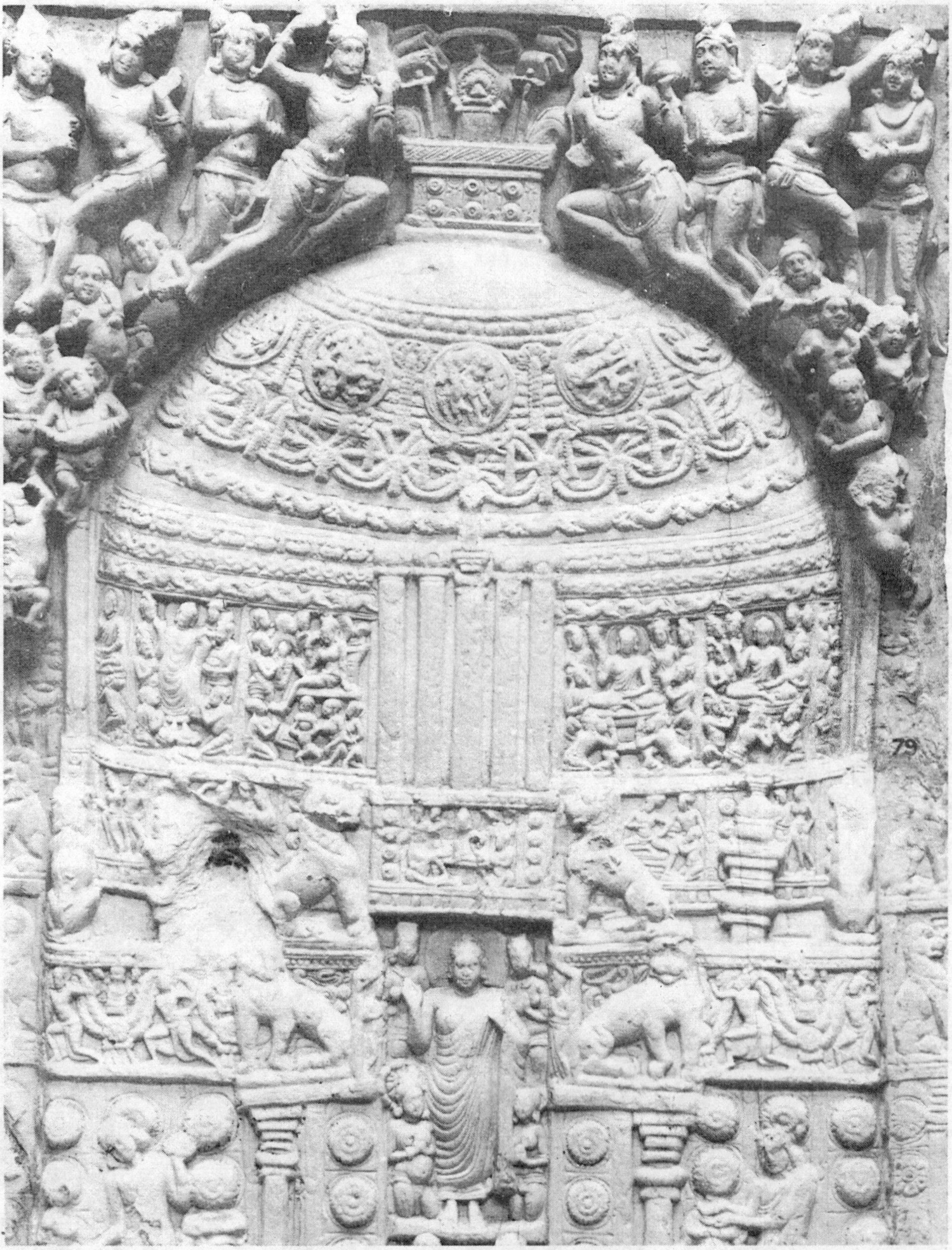

153. Drum slab from Amarāvatī, now British Museum (Photo: Trustees of the British Museum).

154. Drum slab from Amarāvatī, now British Museum (Photo: Trustees of the British Museum).

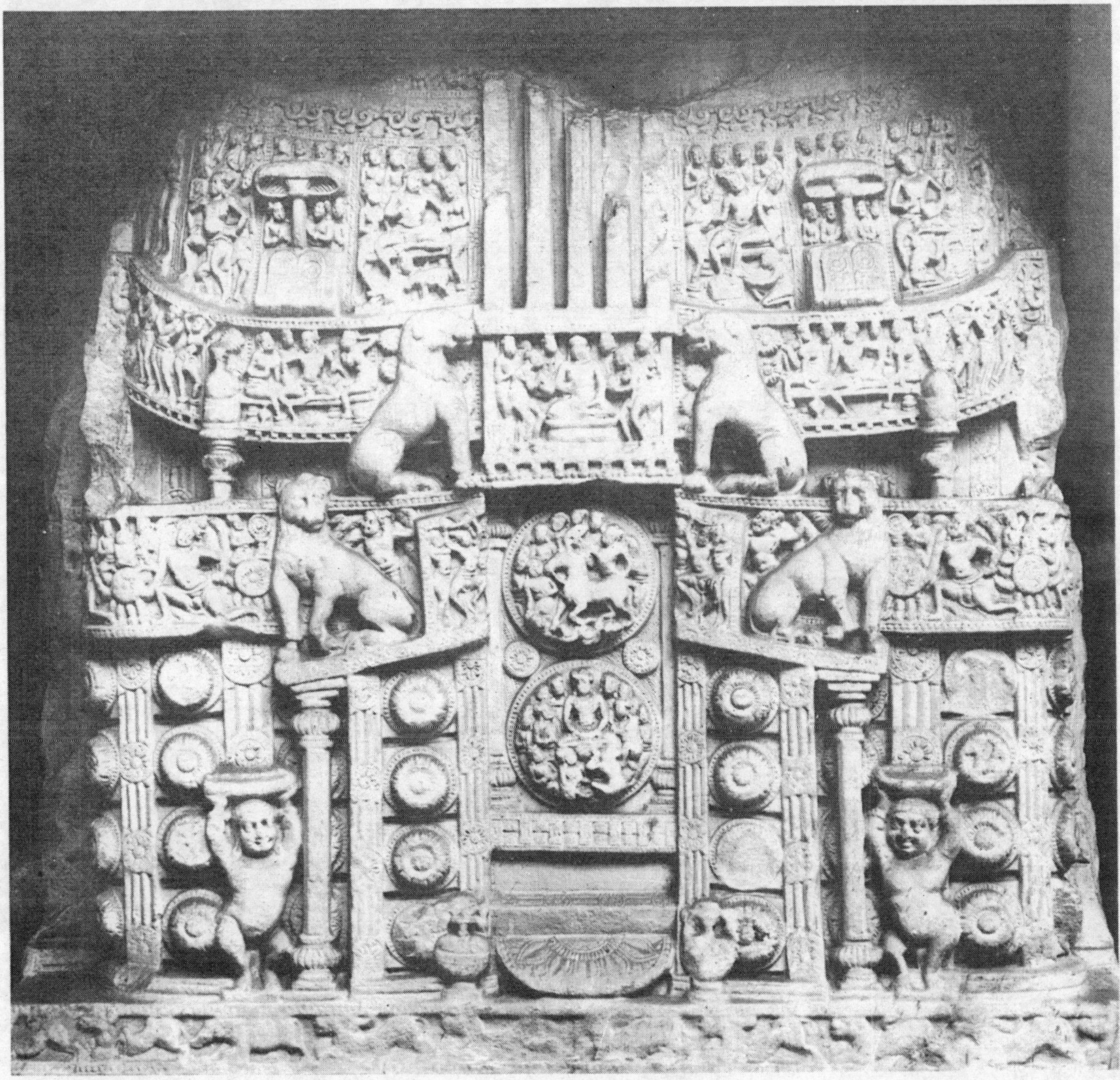

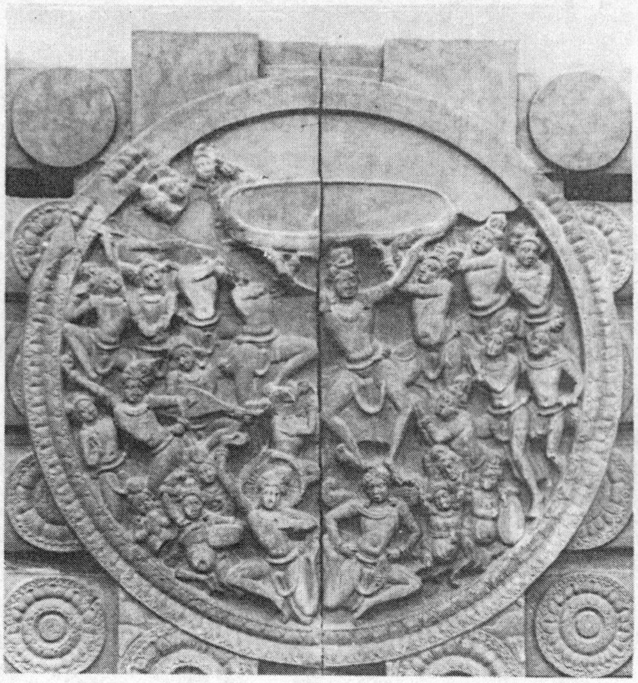

155. Transportation of the Buddha's Alms Bowl to Heaven, from an *āyaka* platform of *Stūpa* 3 (Photo: Archaeological Survey of India).

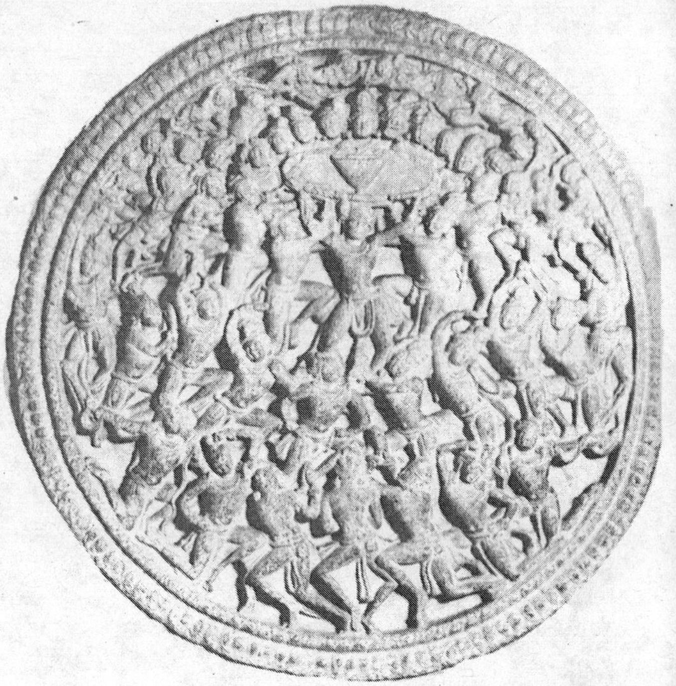

156. Transportation of the Buddha's Alms Bowl to Heaven, detail of railing from Amarāvatī, now Madras Government Museum (Photo: Archaeological Survey of India).

158. Scenes from the Life of the Buddha, *āyaka* panel from *Stūpa* 3.

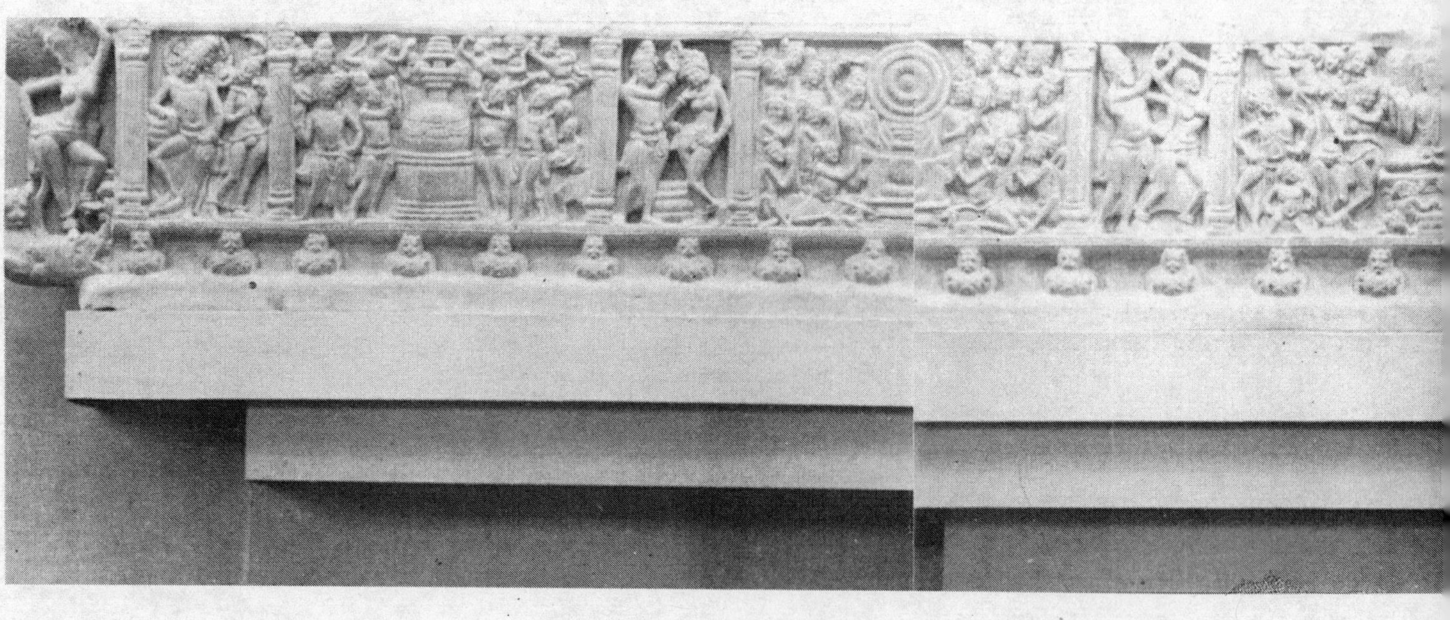

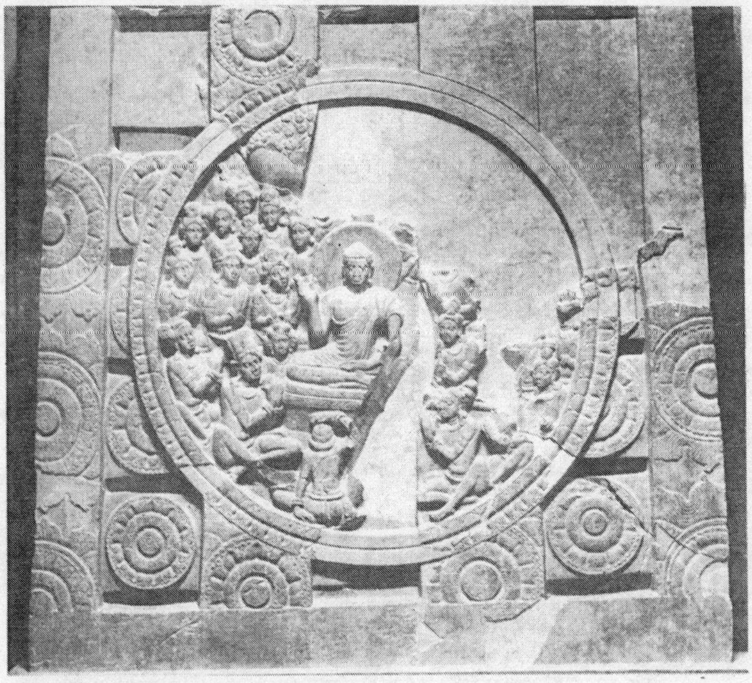

157. The Buddha and the Devas, from an *āyaka* platform of *Stūpa* 3 (Photo: Archaeological Survey of India).

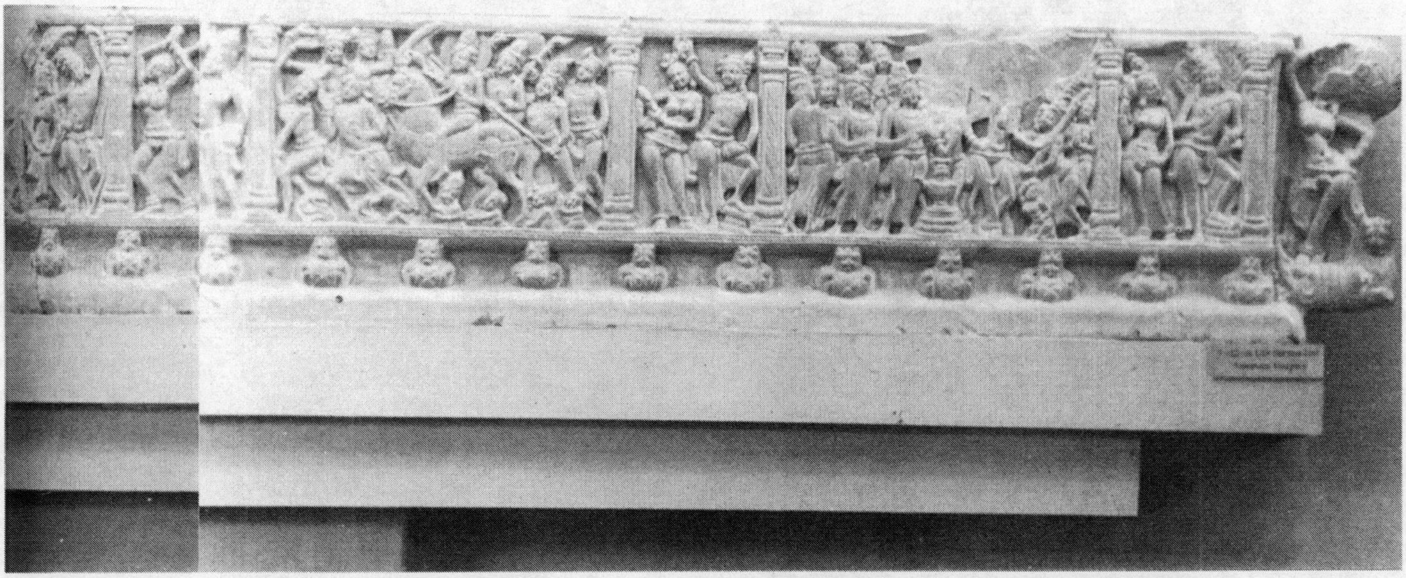

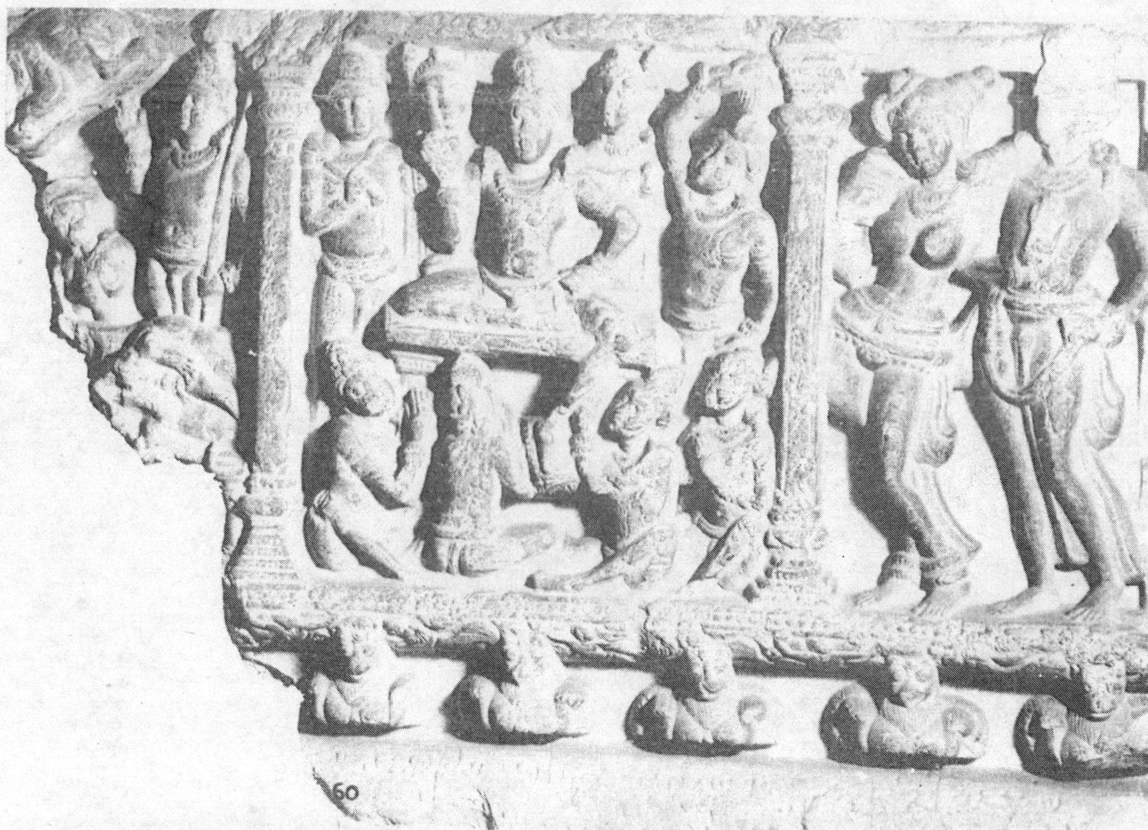

159. Interpretation of Queen Māyā's Dream, fragment of a frieze from Amarāvatī, now Madras Government Museum (Photo: Archaeological Survey of India).

160. Rāhula Asks for His Inheritance, fragment of a frieze from Amarāvatī, now Madras Government Museum (Photo: Archaeological Survey of India).

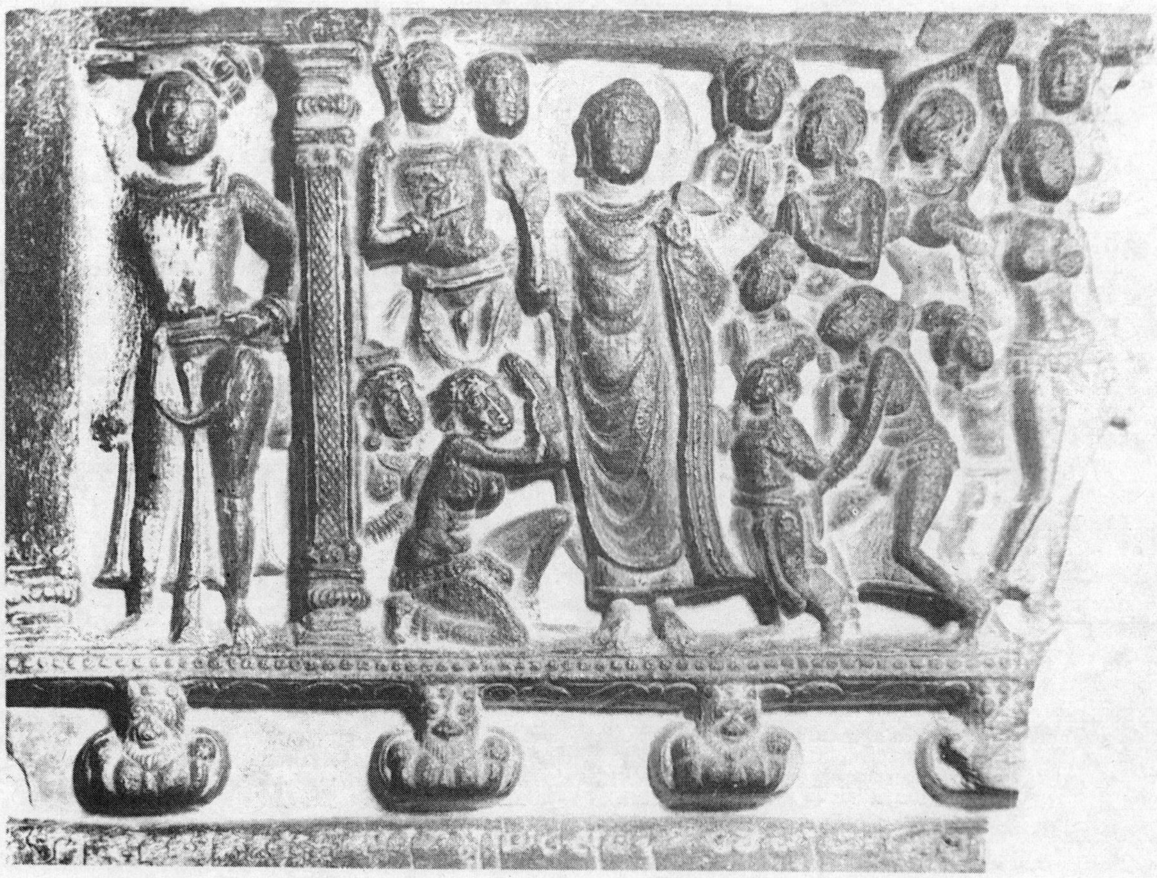

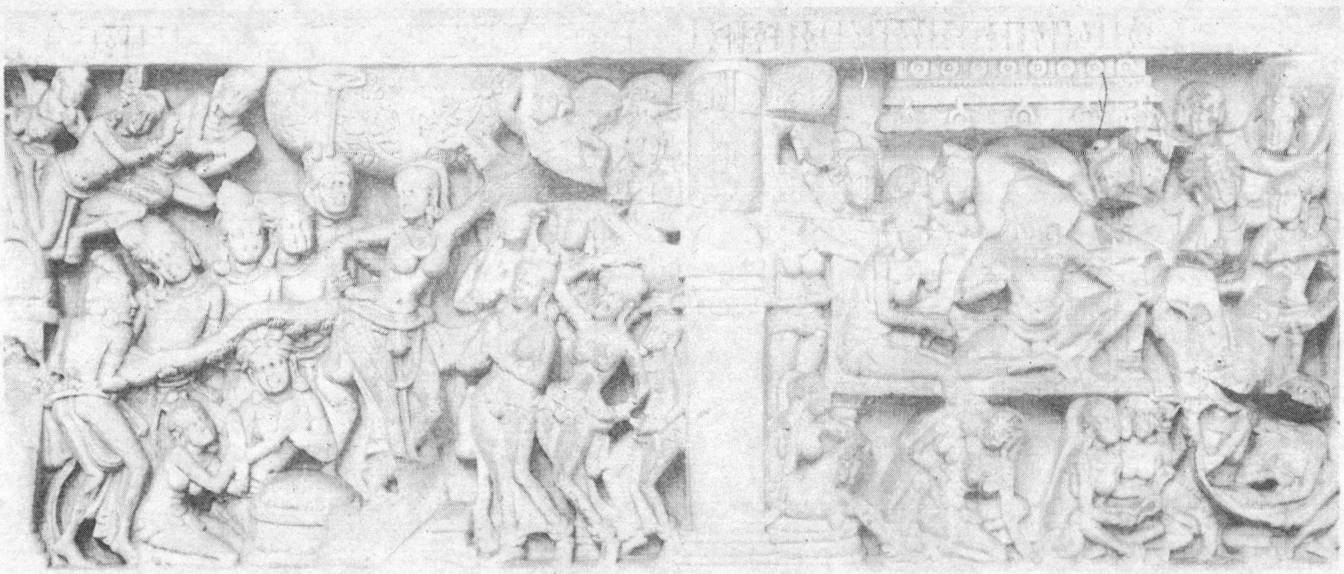

161. The Nativity and the Seven Steps and Prince Siddhārtha in His Harem, detail of a coping stone from Amarāvatī, now British Museum (Photo: Trustees of the British Museum).

162. The Nativity and The Seven Steps, detail of fig. 158.

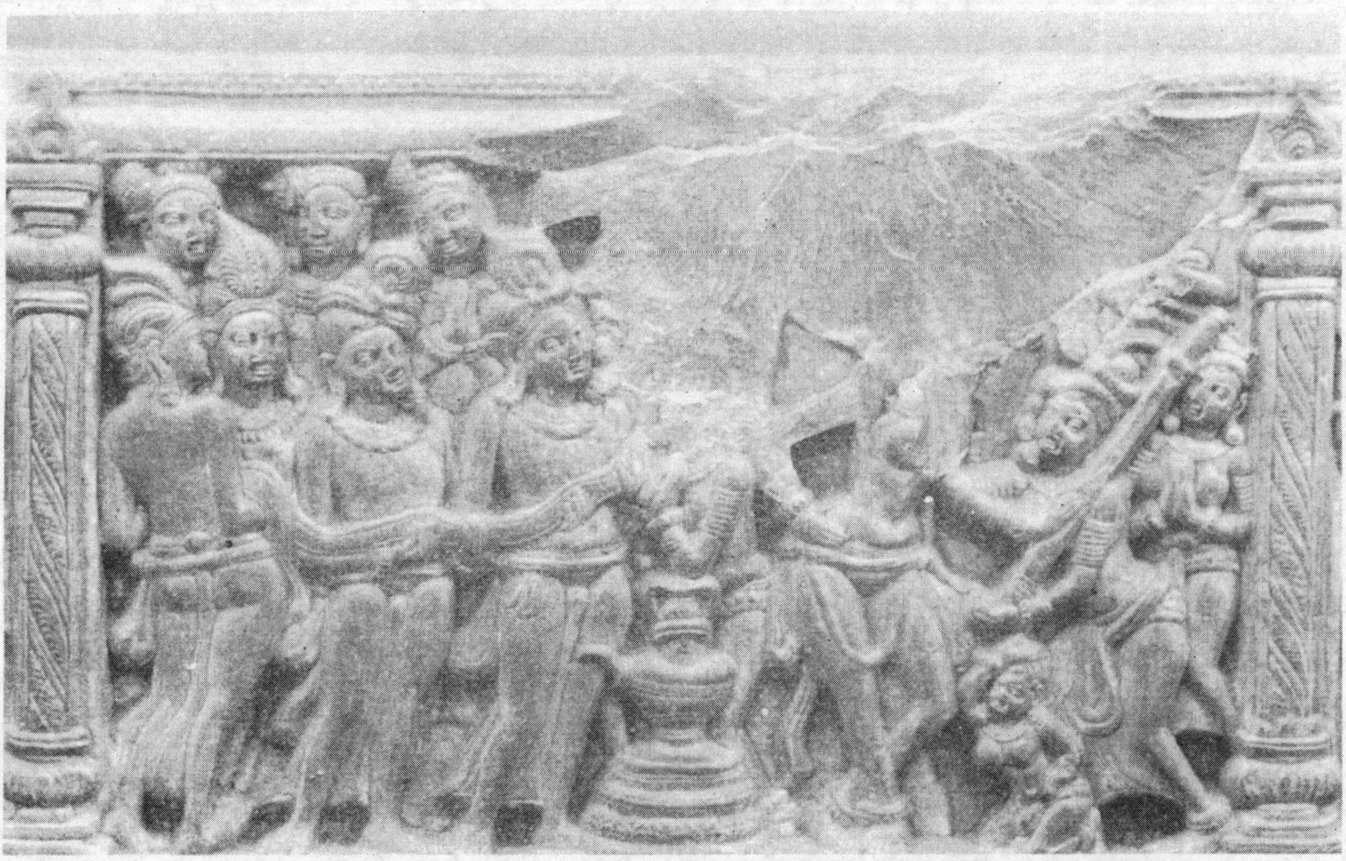

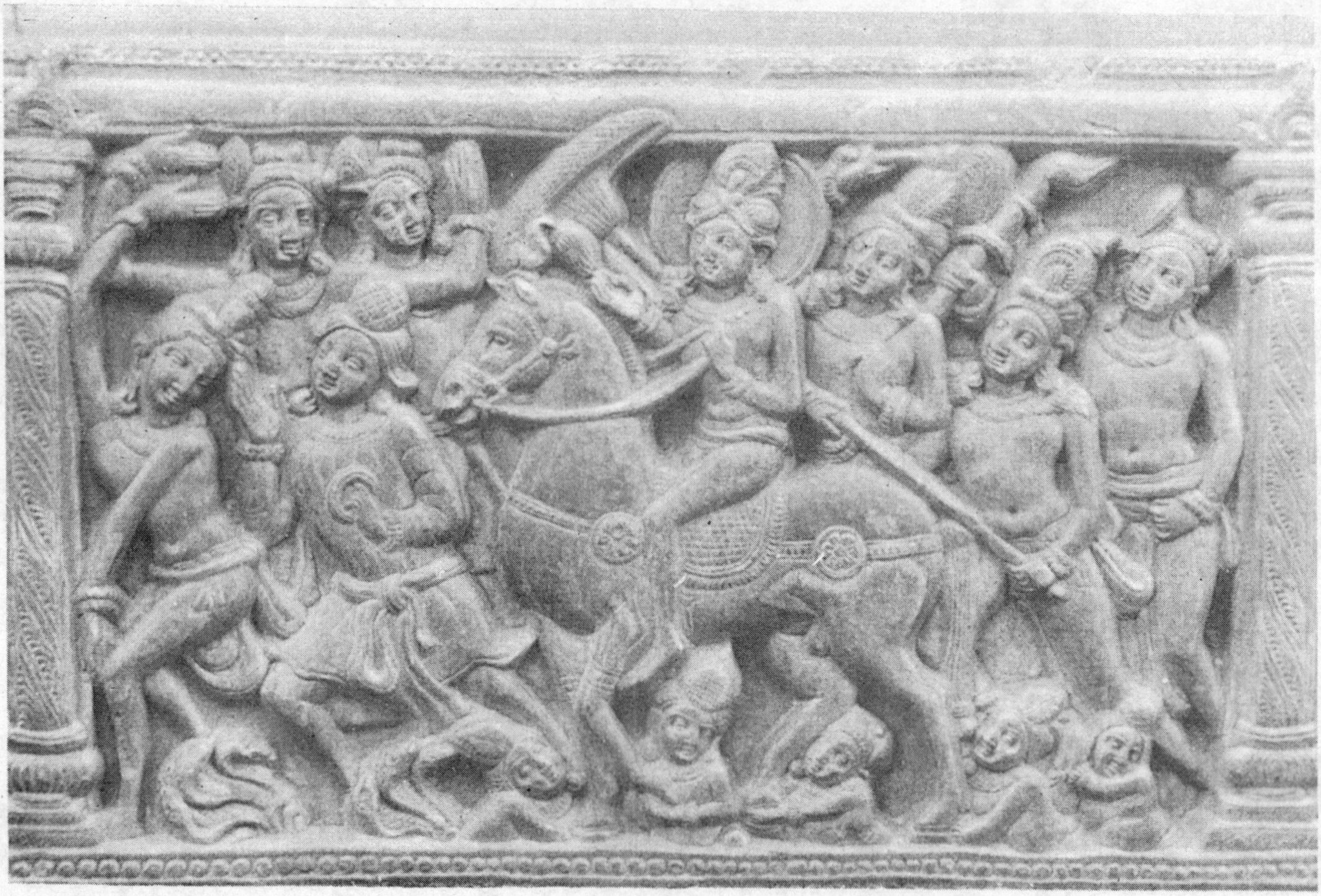

163. The Great Departure, detail of fig. 158.

164. Siddhārtha in His Harem, The Great Departure, Siddhārtha Taking Leave of His Groom Chandaka and His Horse Kanthaka, drum frieze from Amarāvatī, now British Museum (Photo: Trustees of the British Museum).

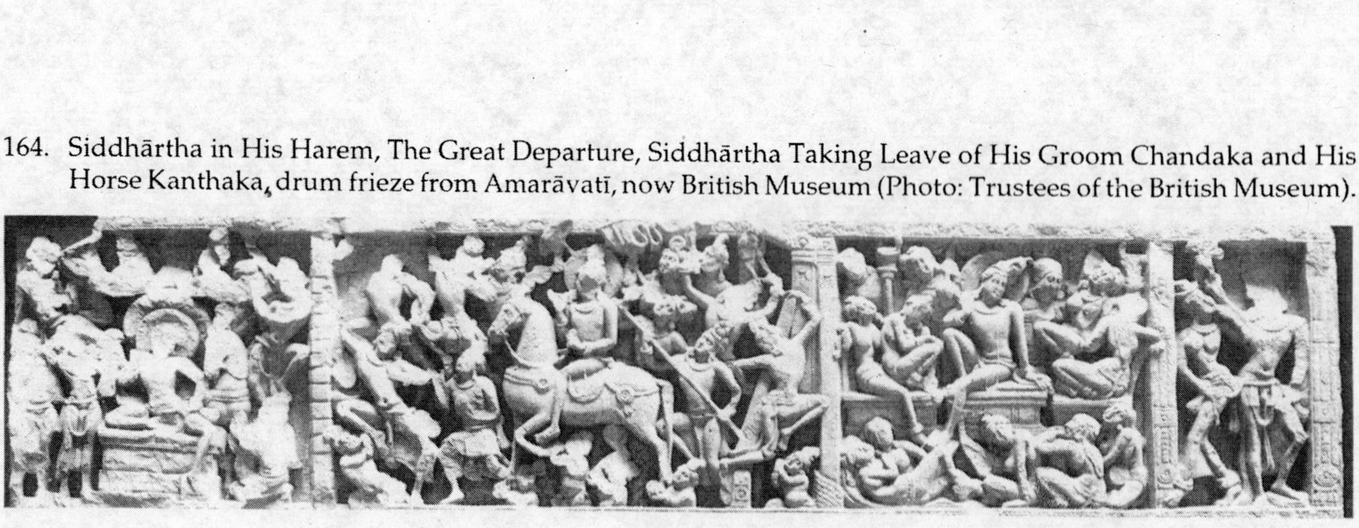

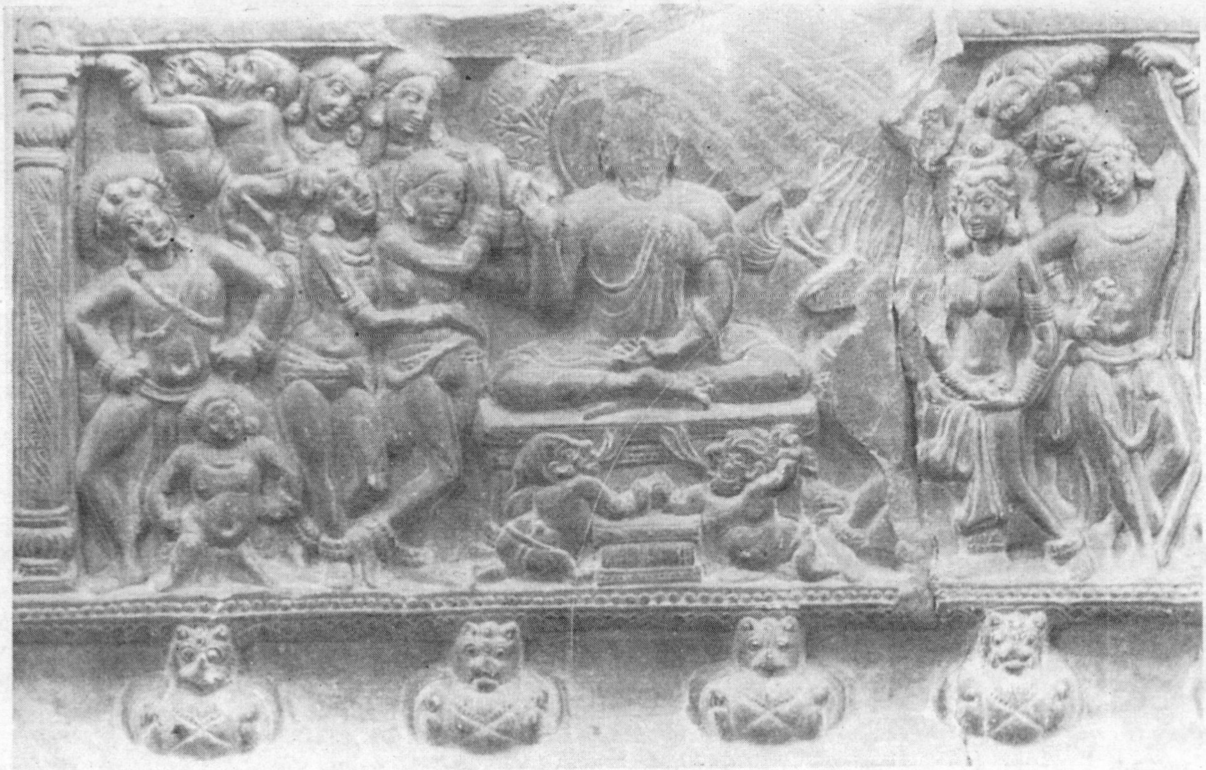

165. The Temptation of the Buddha, detail of fig. 158.

166. Māra and His Daughters, detail of fig. 165.

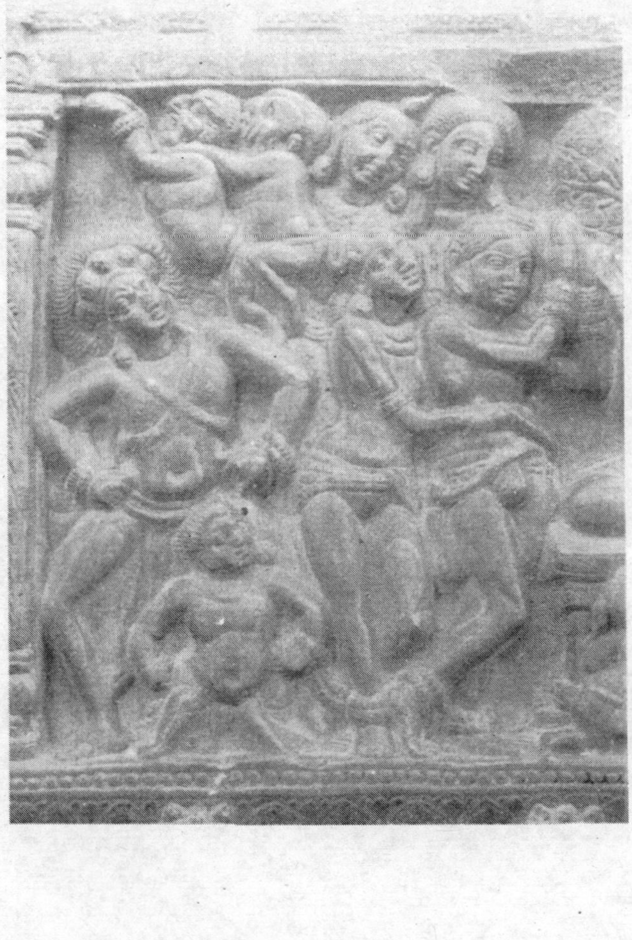

167. The *Parinirvāna* of the Buddha, fragment of a railing pillar from Amarāvatī, now Madras Government Museum (Photo: Archaeological Survey of India).

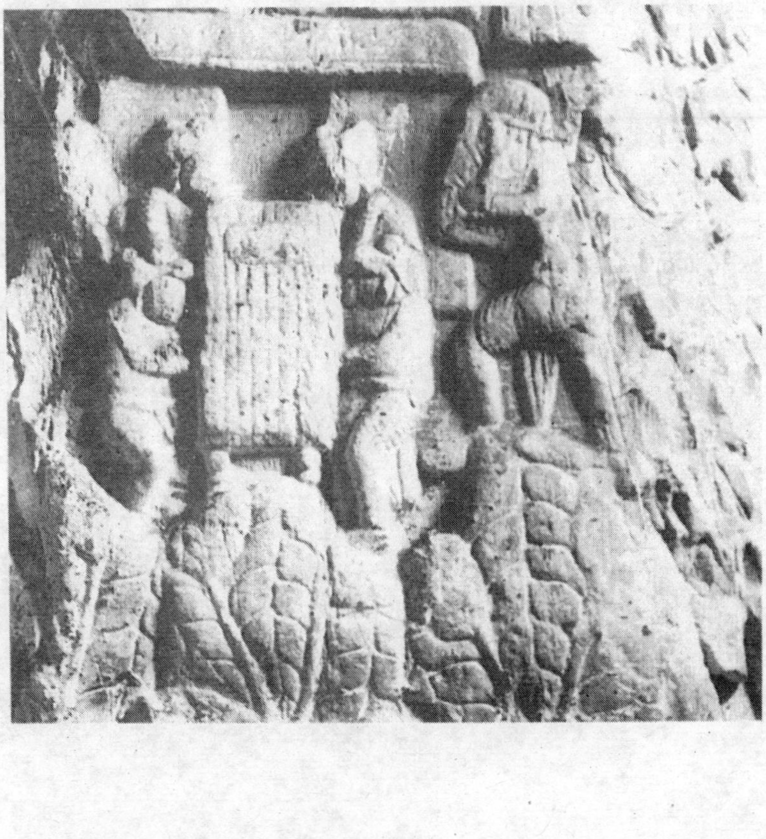

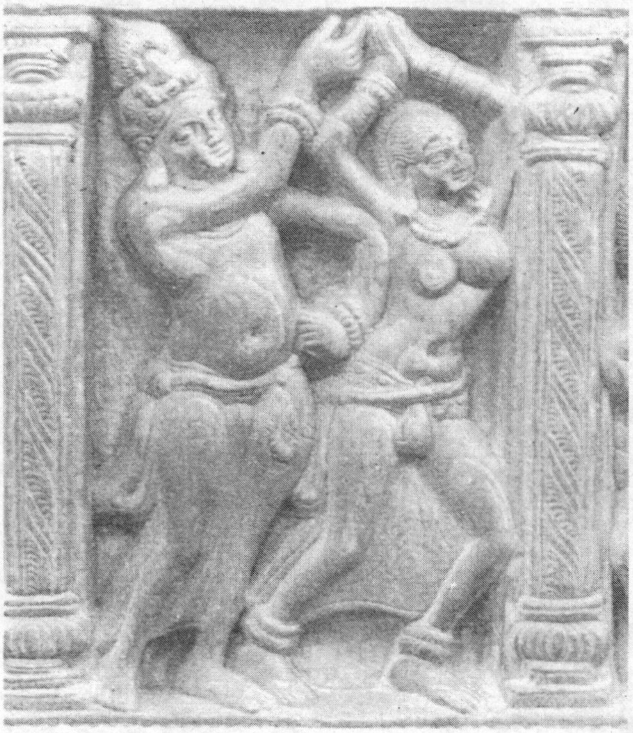

168. Detail of fig. 158.

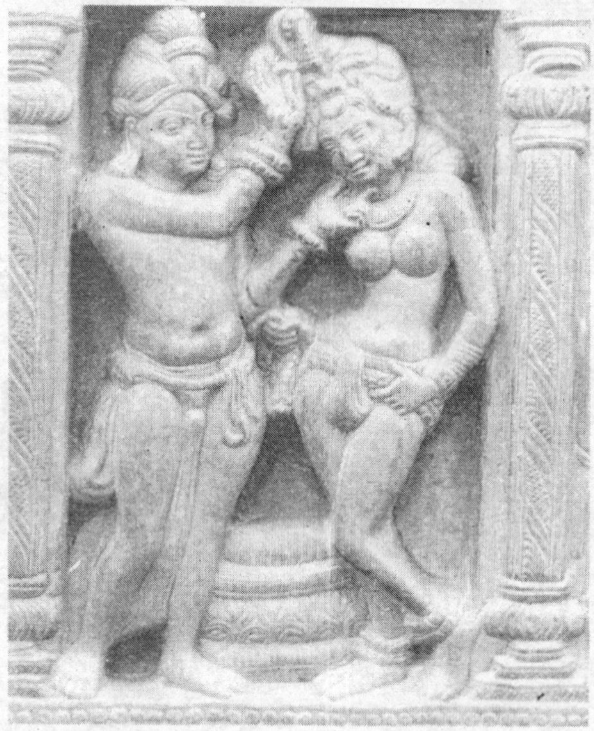

169. Detail of fig. 158.

170. Detail of fig. 158.

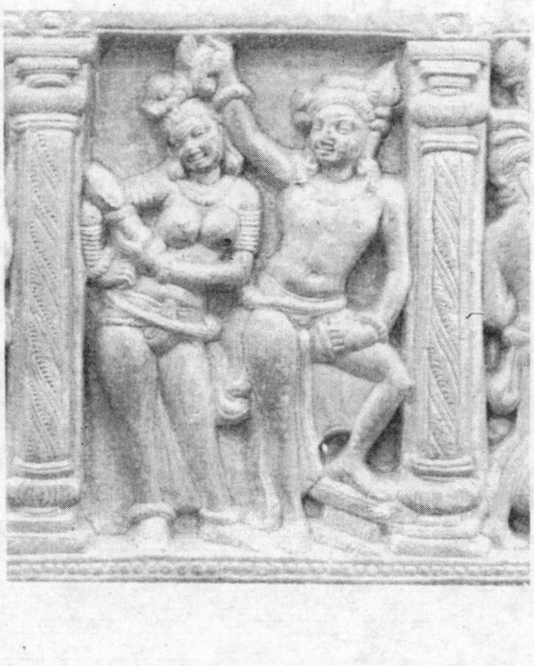

171. Detail of fig. 158.

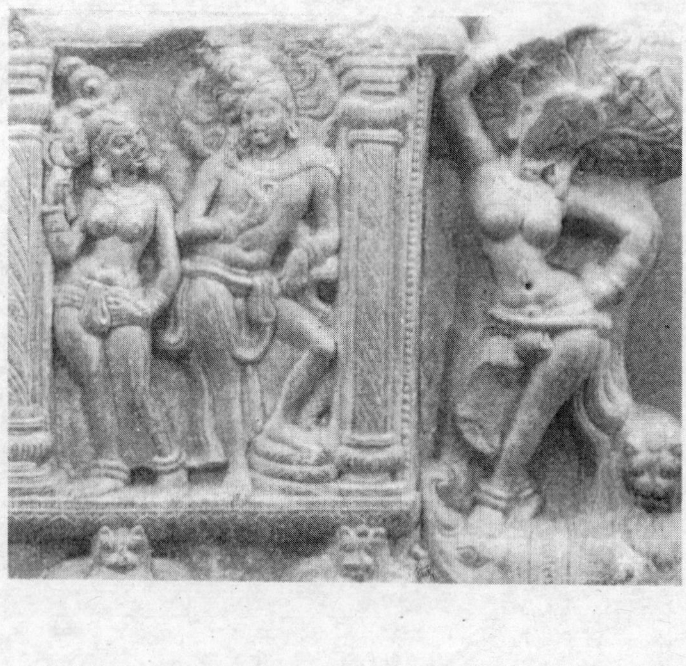

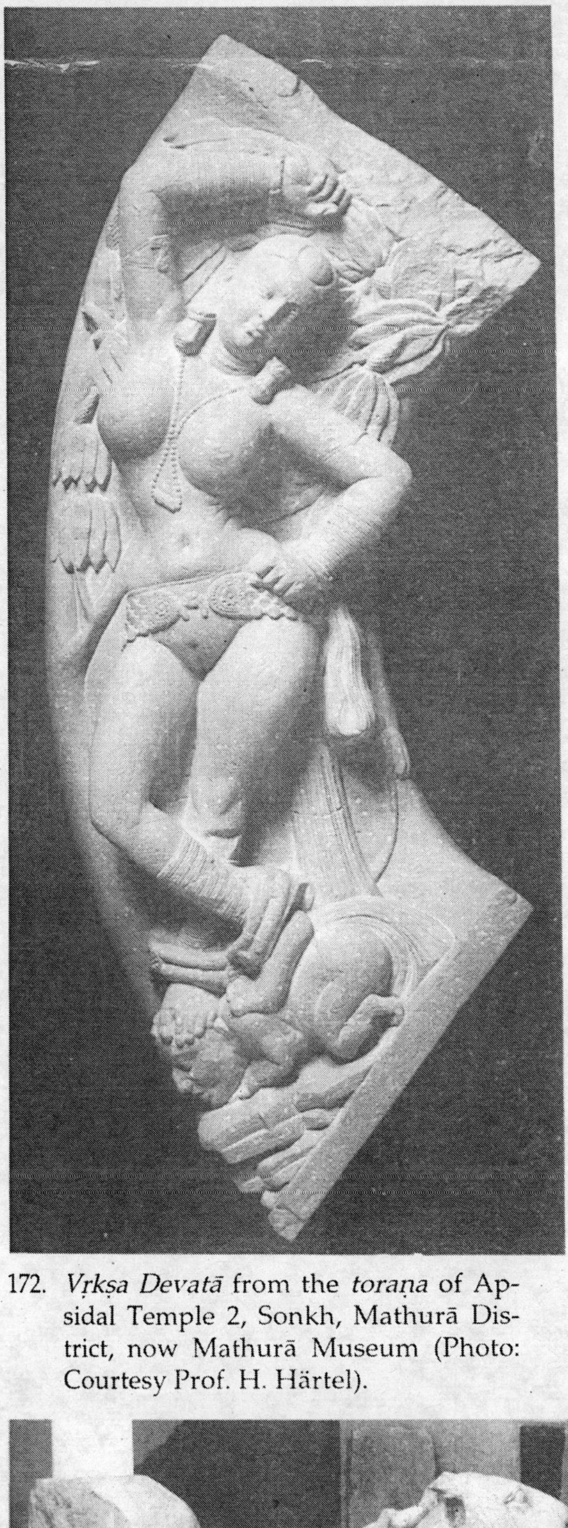

172. *Vṛkṣa Devatā* from the *toraṇa* of Apsidal Temple 2, Sonkh, Mathurā District, now Mathurā Museum (Photo: Courtesy Prof. H. Härtel).

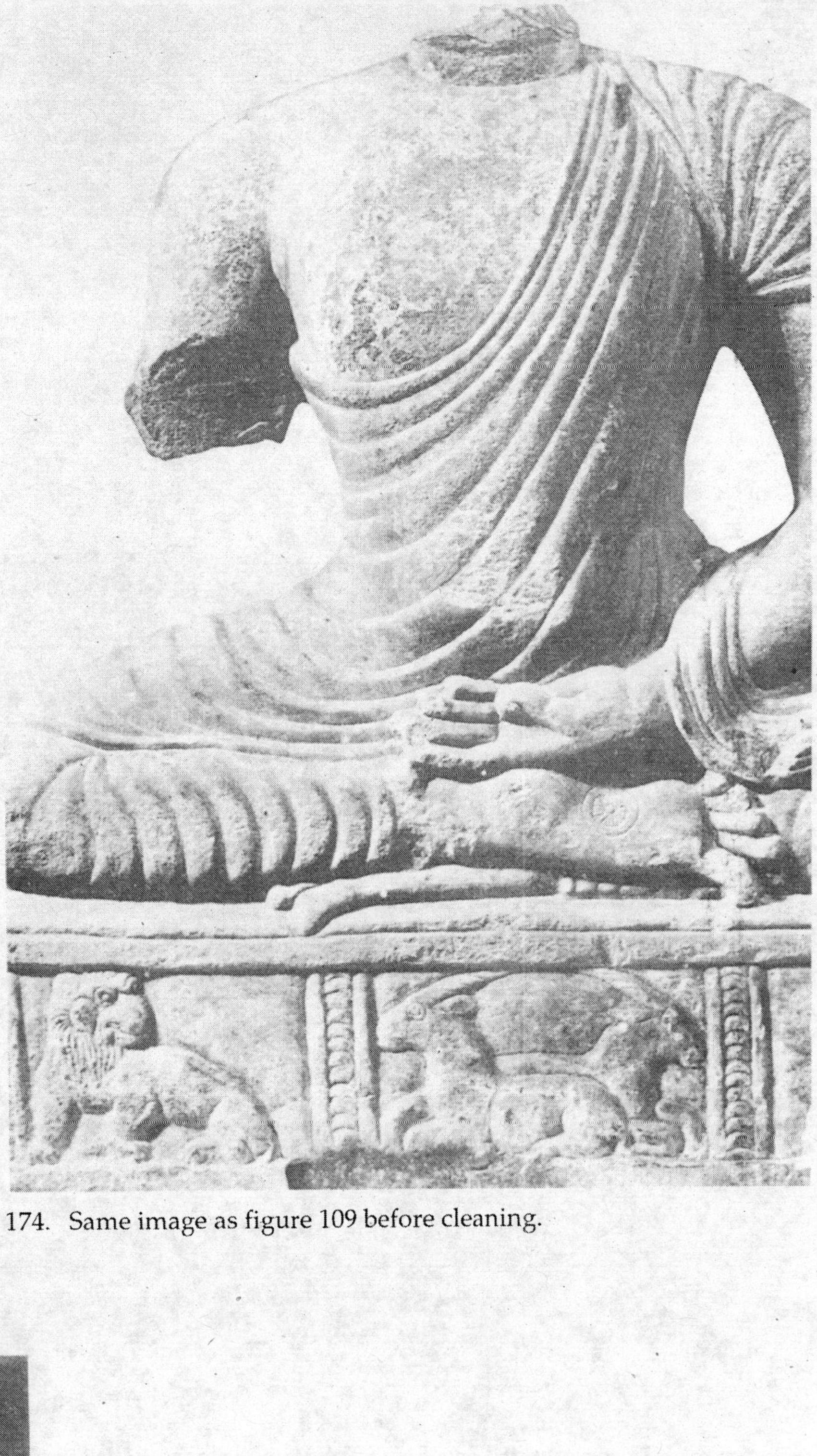

174. Same image as figure 109 before cleaning.

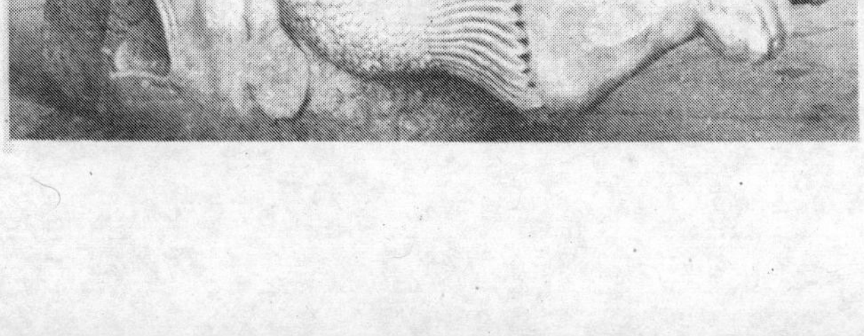

173. *Makara śārdūla* with rider, perhaps from Amarāvatī (Photo: American Institute of Indian Studies, Banaras).

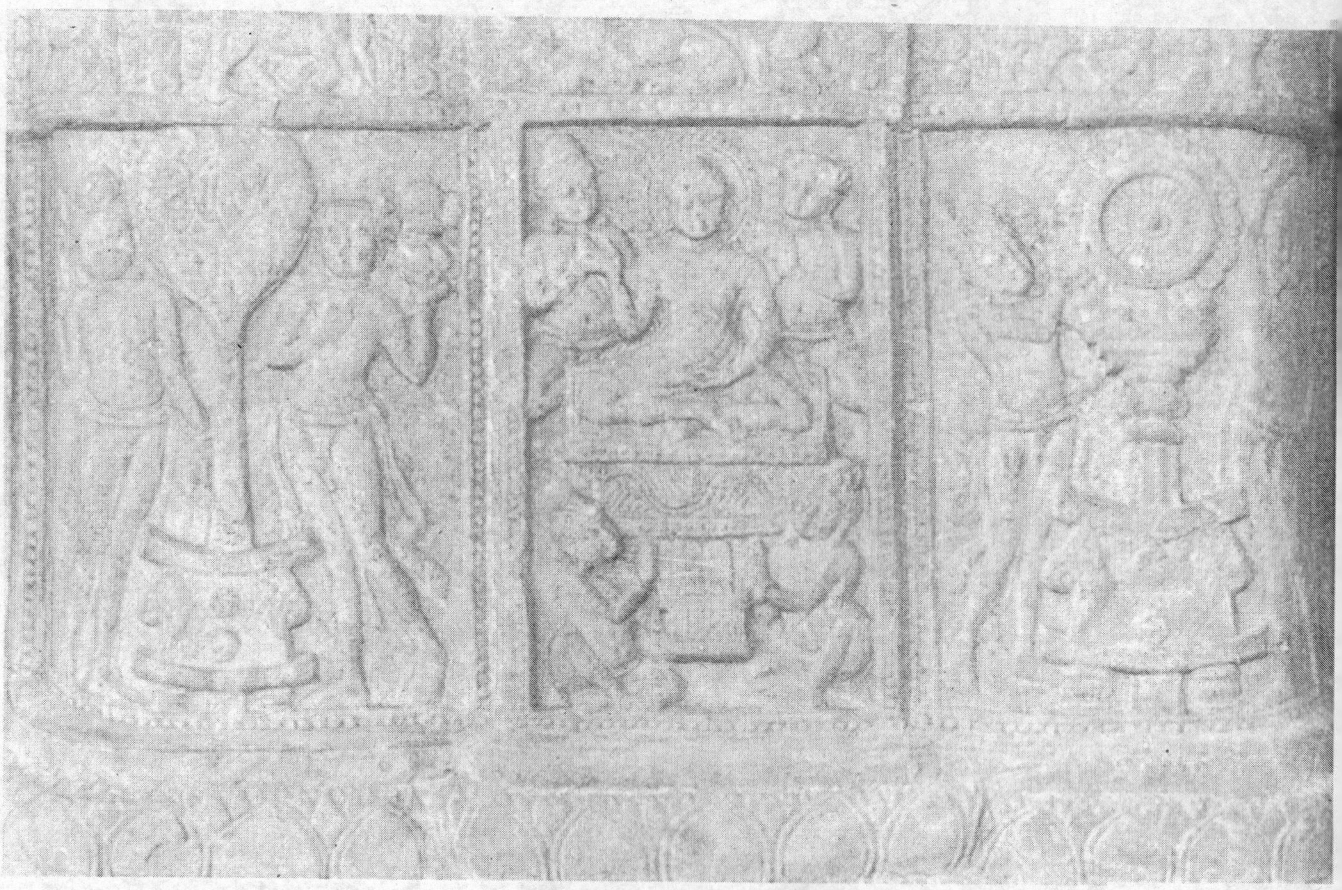

175. Detail of fig. 104.

176. The Conversion of Nanda, probably from Site 3.

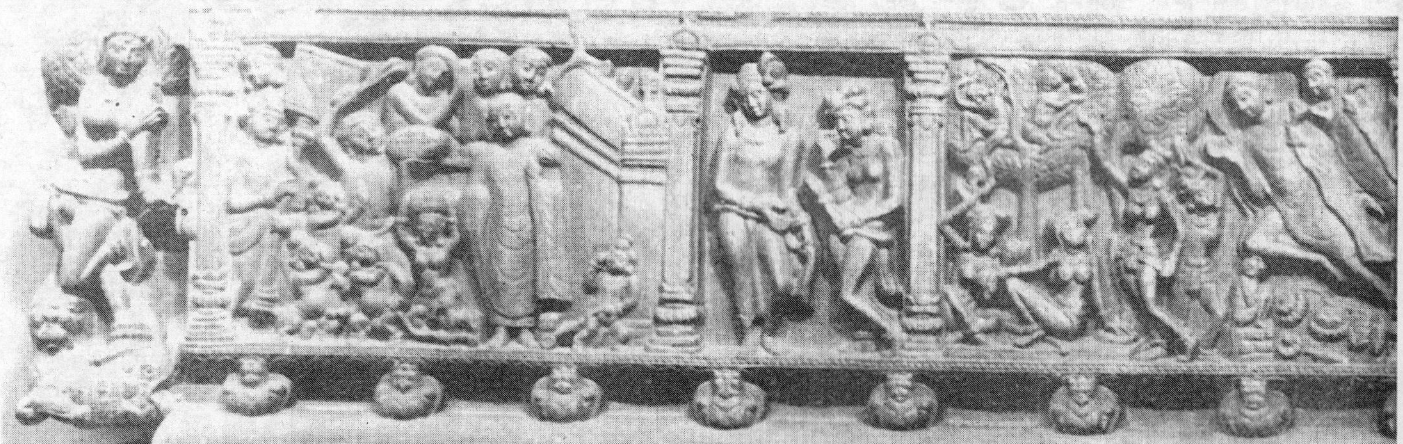

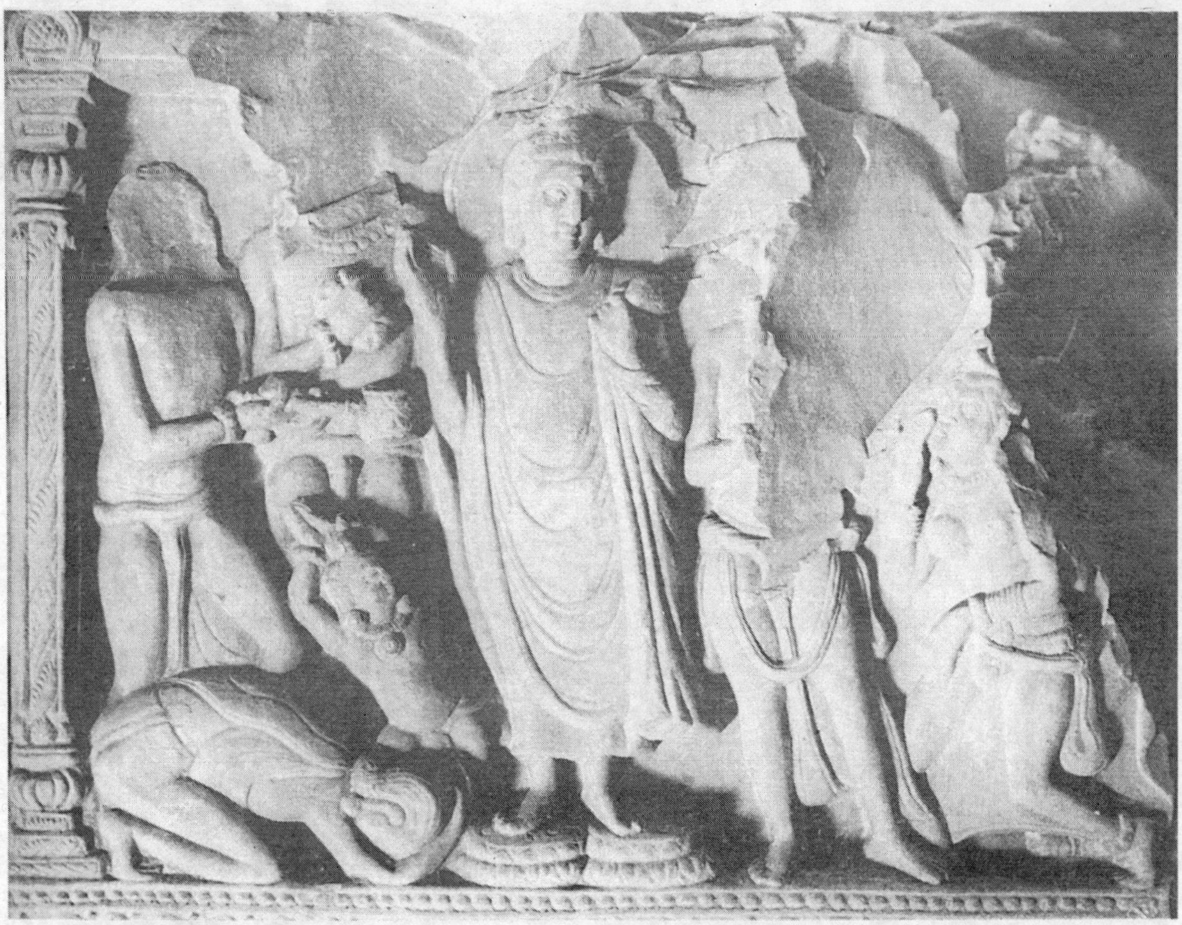

177. The Buddha and Nanda with Nanda's Wife Sundarī, detail of fig. 176.

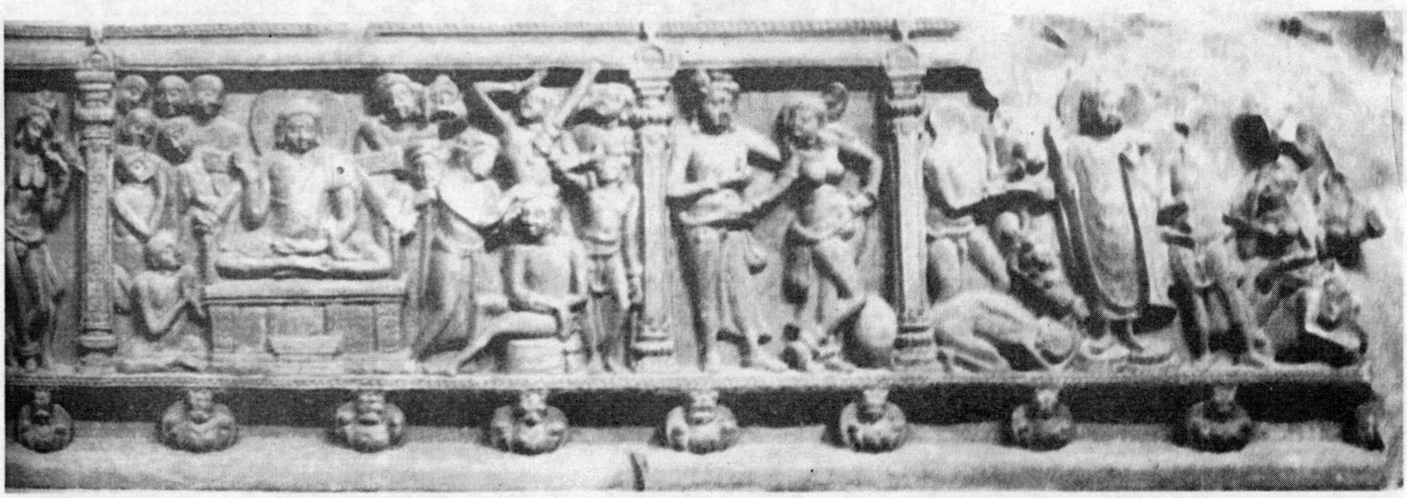

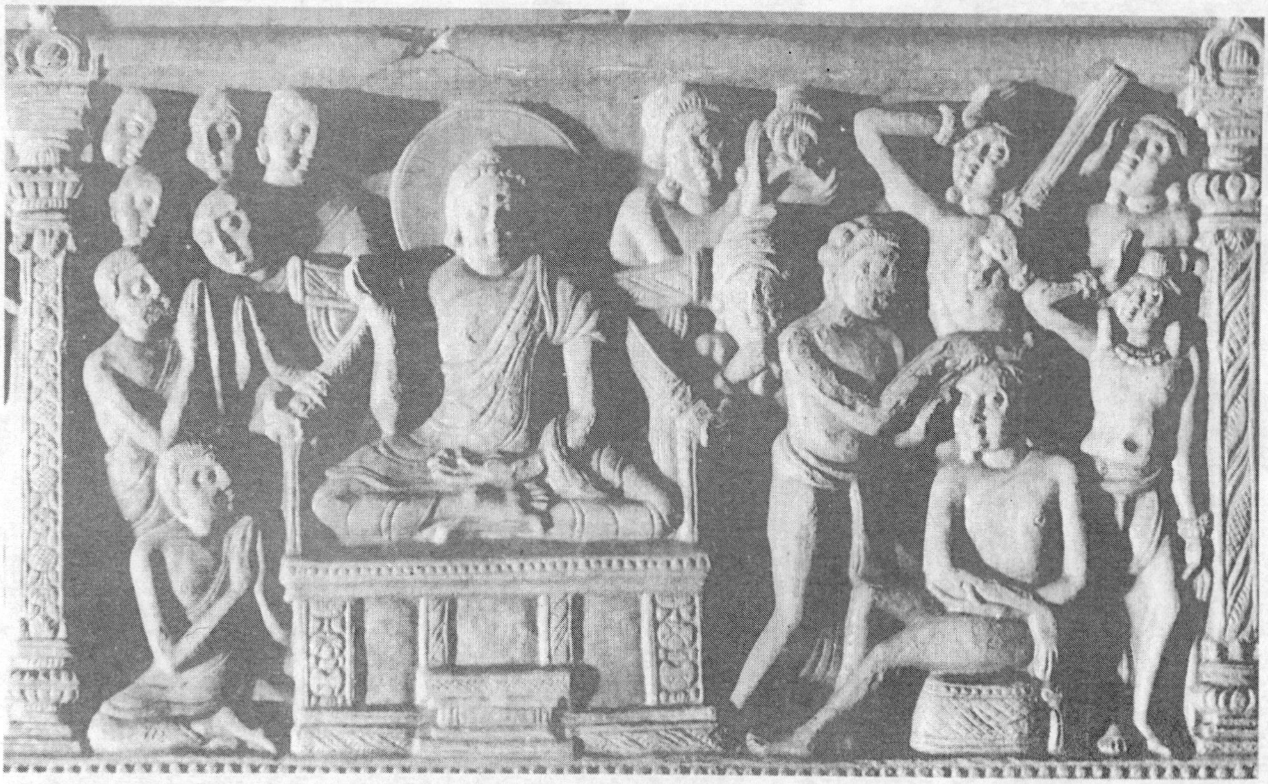

178. The Ordination of Nanda, detail of fig. 176.

179. The Buddha and Nanda Flying to the Celestial World, detail of fig. 176.

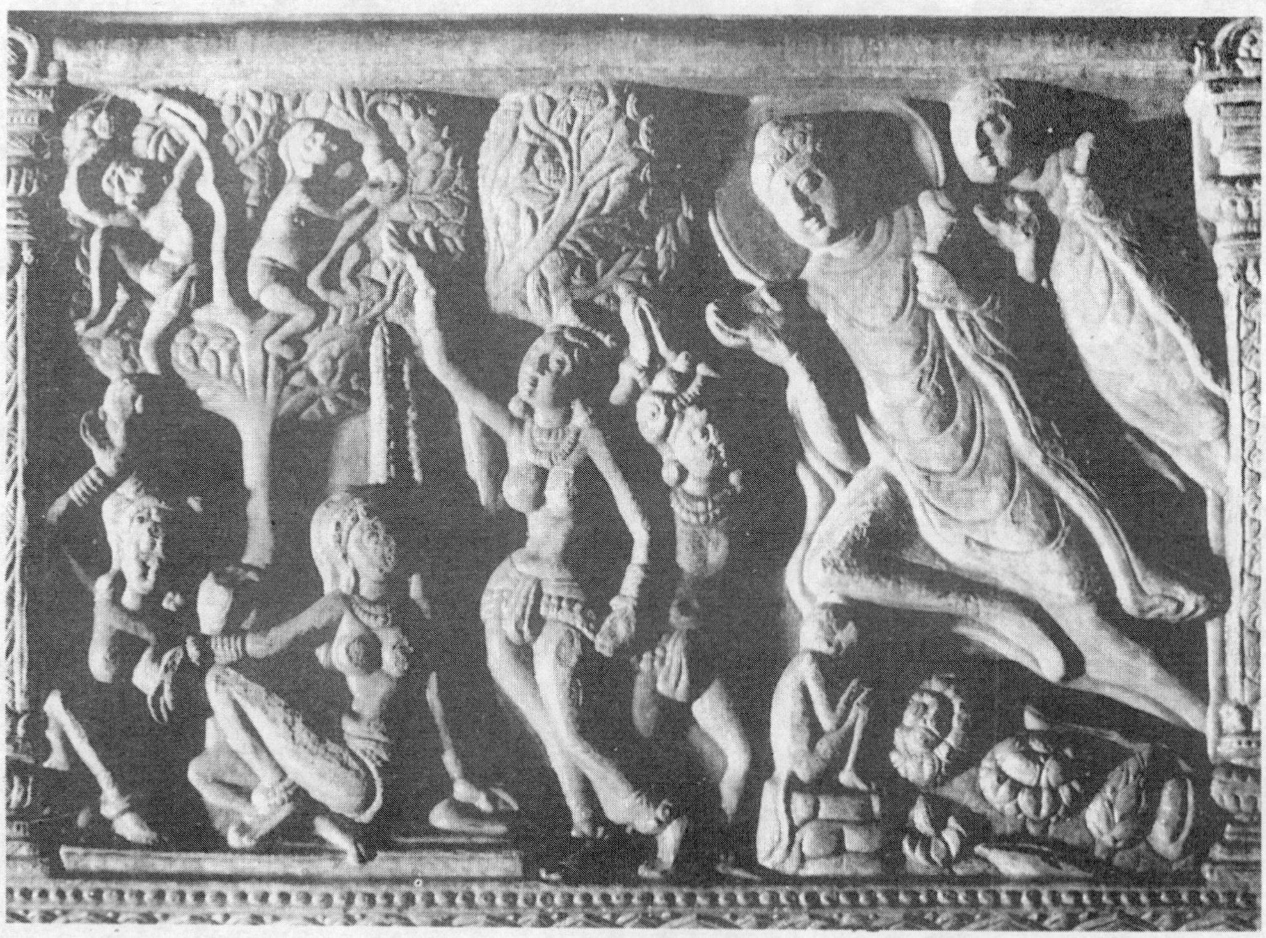

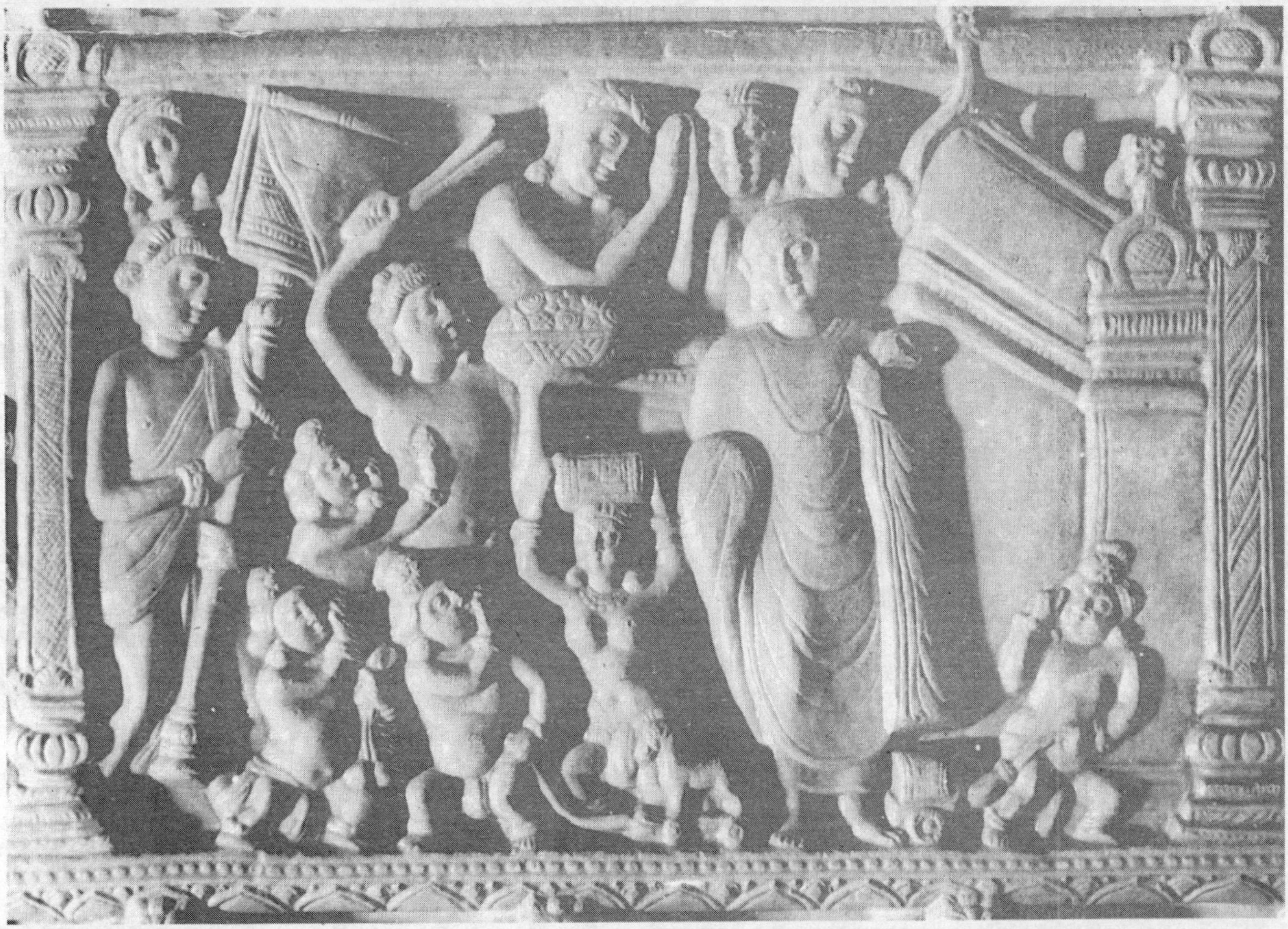

180. Perhaps Nanda Preaching to the People of Kapilavastu, detail of fig. 176.

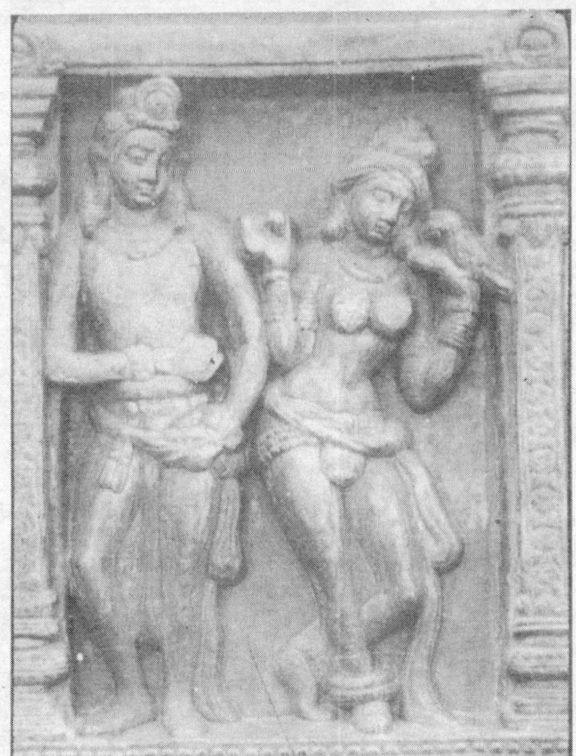

181. Detail of fig. 176.

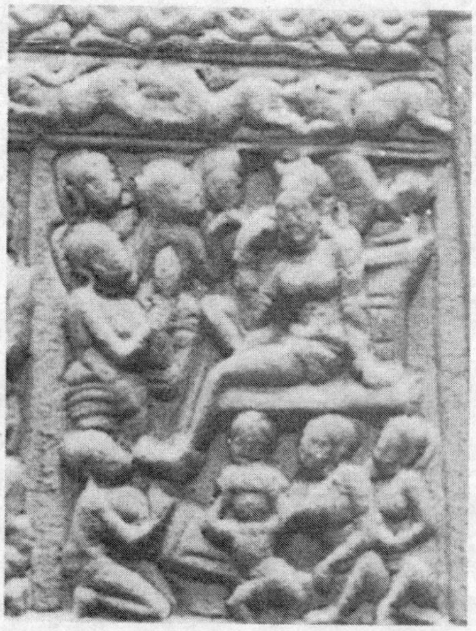

182. Sundarī at Her Toilet, detail of fig. 153.

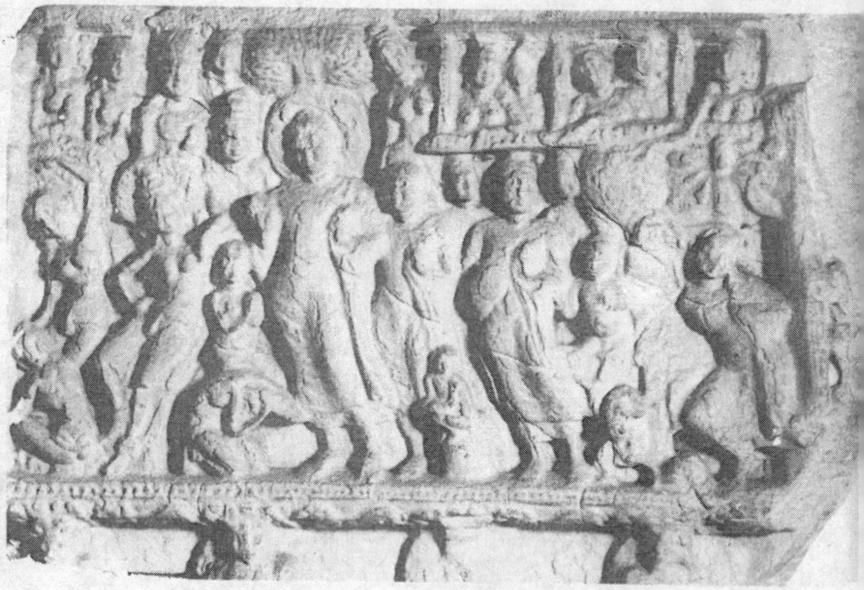

183. Scenes from the Conversion of Nanda: Nanda Leaving His Wife, Nanda Dreaming of His Wife, The Buddha and Nanda on the Way to Heaven, and the Celestial Grove; Drum slab from Amarāvatī, now Madras Government Museum (Photo: Archaeological Survey of India).

185. Scenes from the Conversion of Nanda, Goli Village, now The Metropolitan Museum of Art, New York (Photo: The Metropolitan Museum of Art).

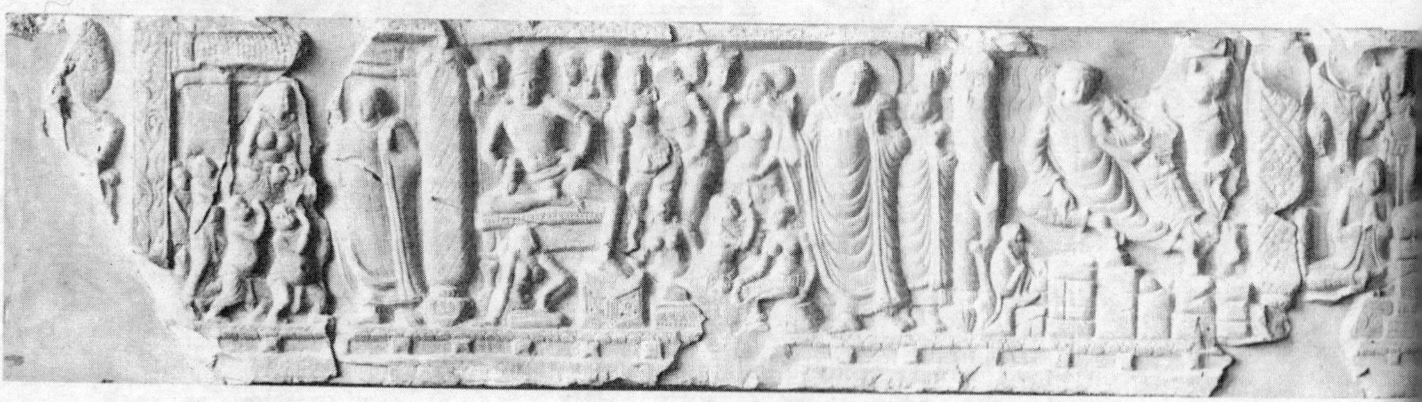

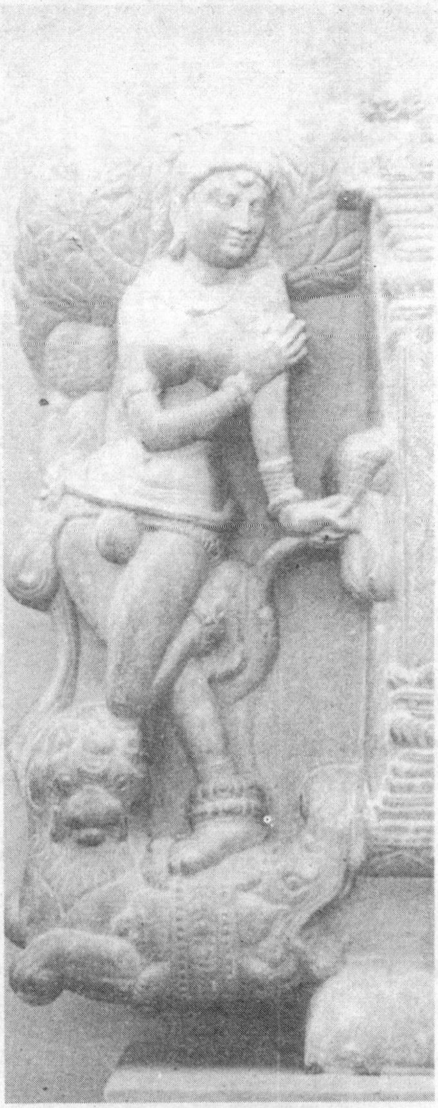

186. *Vṛkṣa Devatā,* detail of fig. 176.

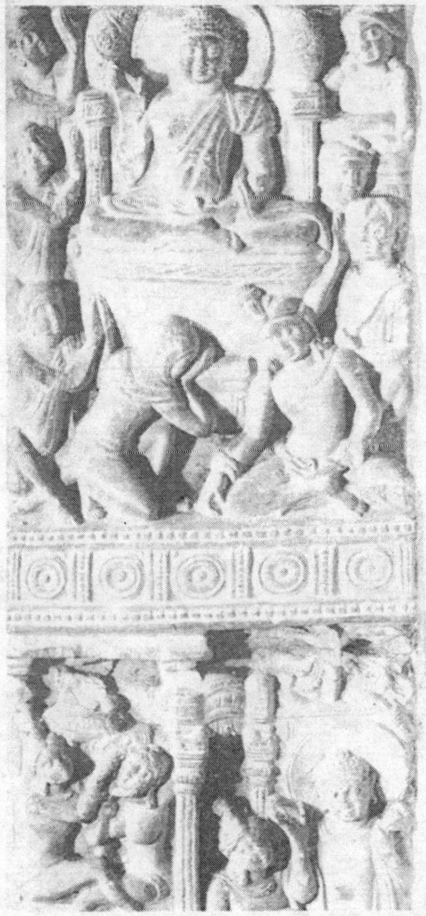

184. Scenes from the Conversion of Nanda, from bottom to top: Nanda and His Wife Sundarī and Nanda Following the Buddha, Nanda at His Ordination, and the Paradise of Indra; Drum slab from Amarāvatī, now Madras Government Museum (Photo: Archaeological Survey of India).

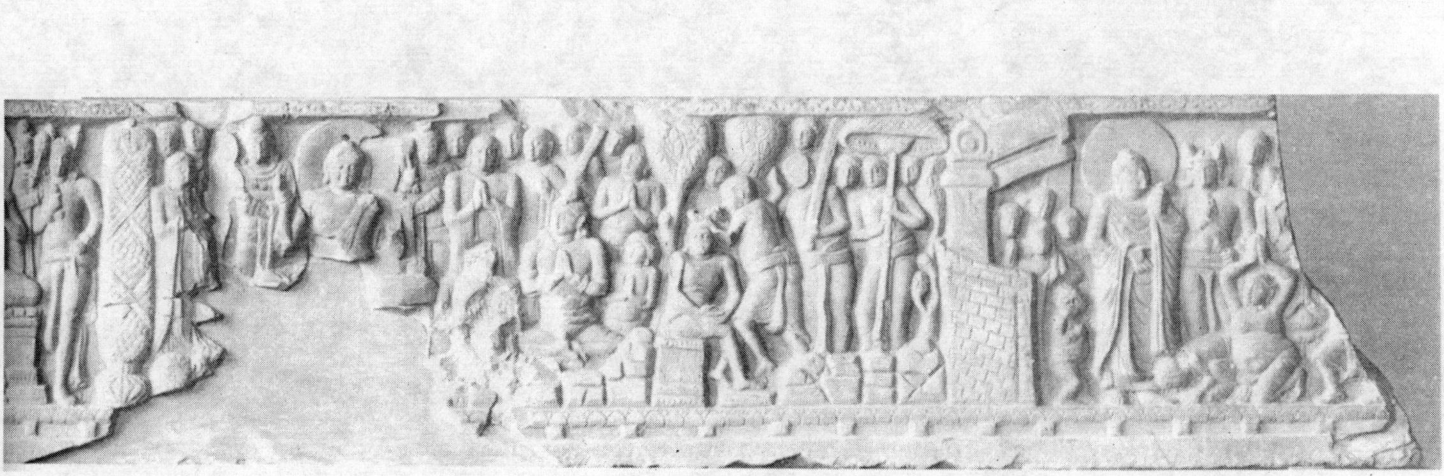

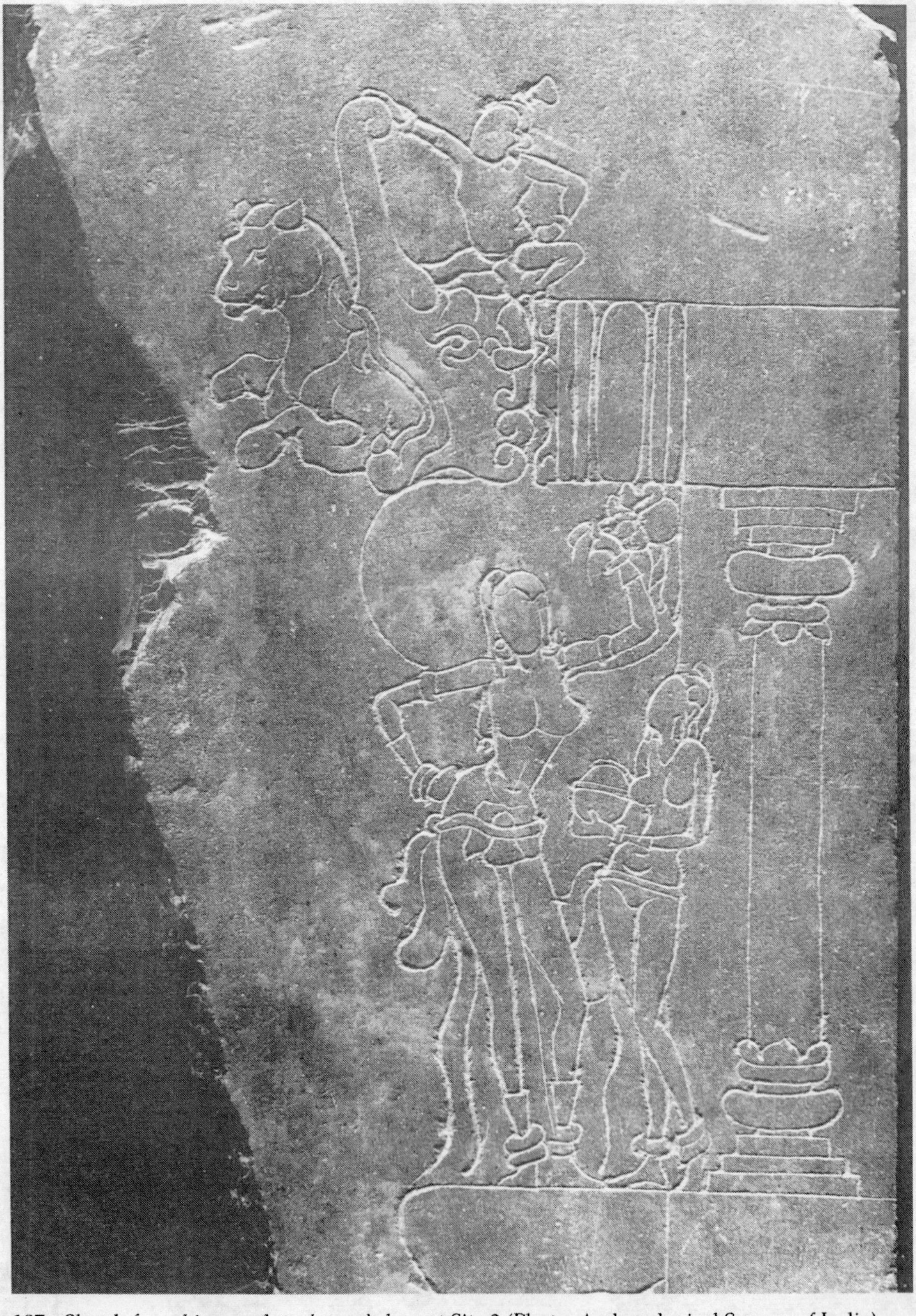

187. Sketch found in a sculptor's workshop at Site 3 (Photo: Archaeological Survey of India).

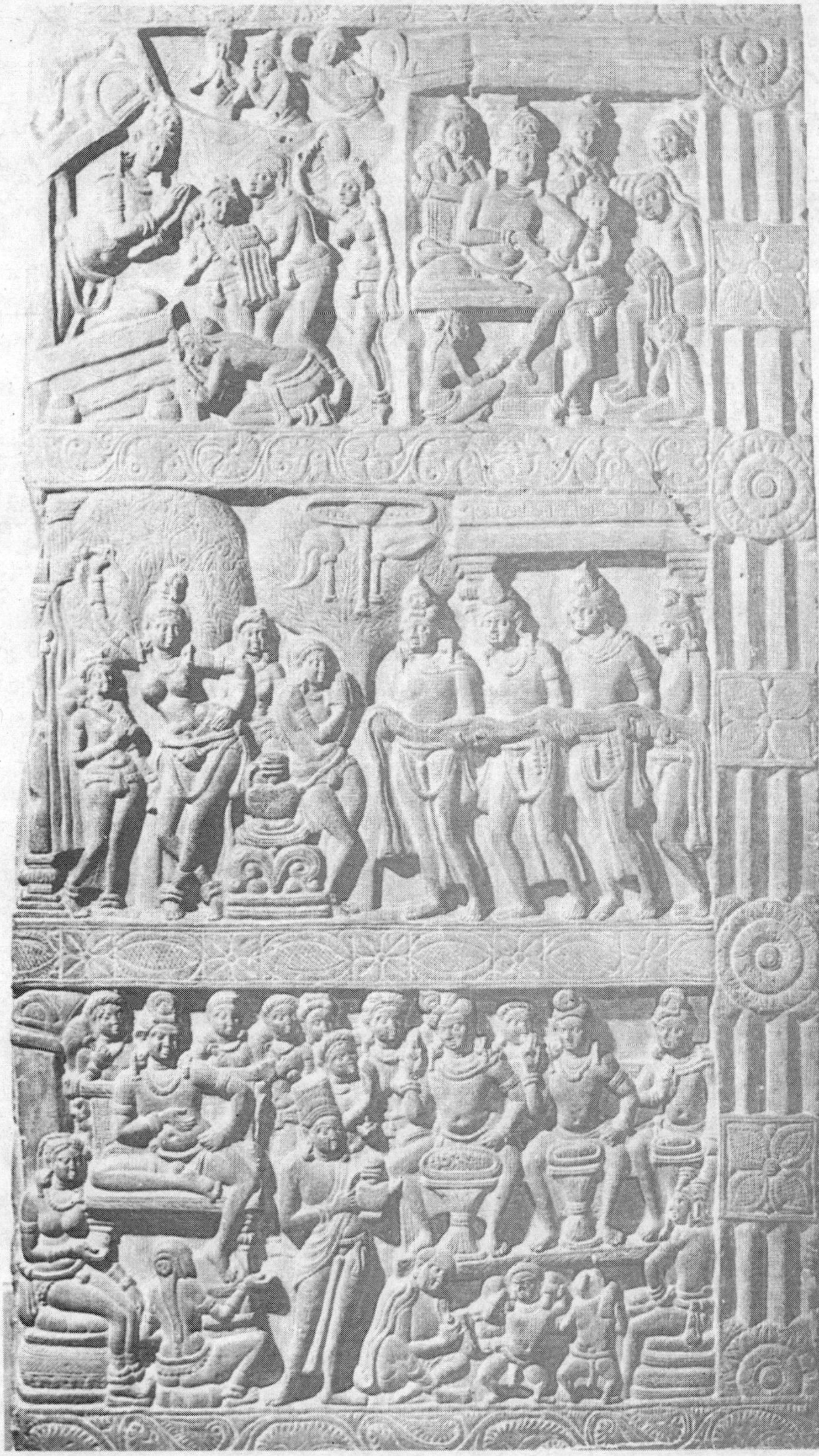

188. Top Panel: Asita's Visit to Śuddhodhana and the Presentation of the Child to the Śakya Temple; Middle: The Nativity and the Seven Steps; Bottom: Casting the Horoscope; Dome slab, probably from Site 3, now National Museum, New Delhi.

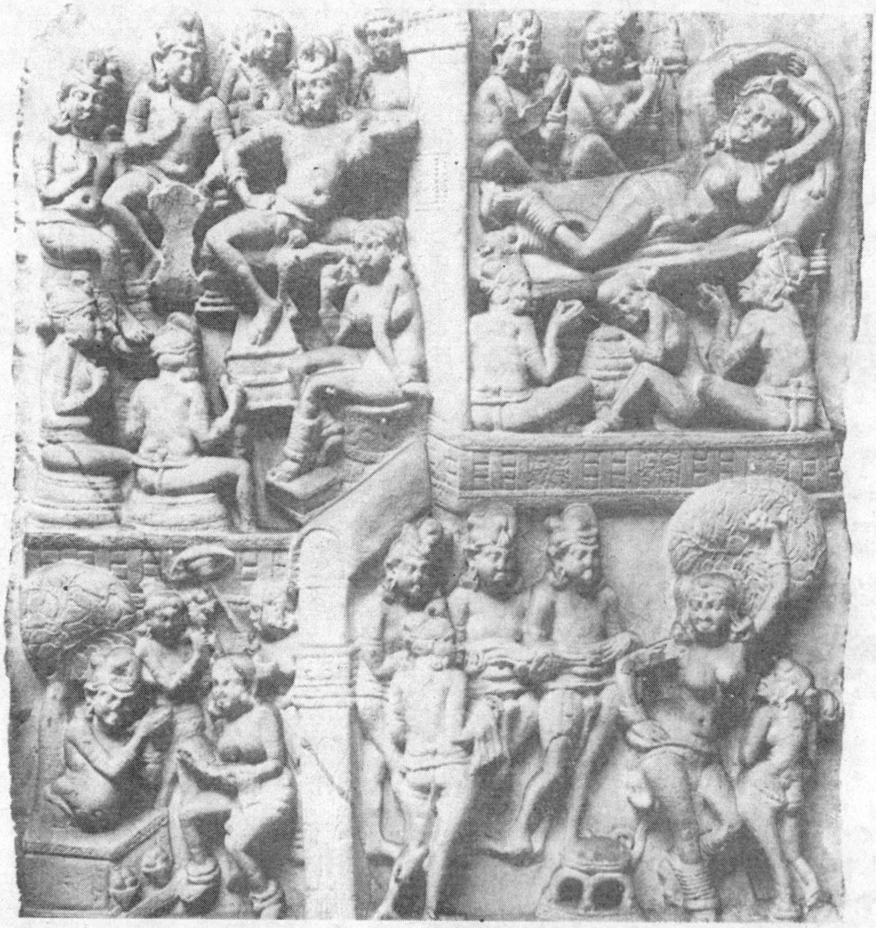

189. Top right: Queen Māyā's Dream; Top left: The Interpretation of the Dream; Bottom right: The Nativity and the Seven Steps; Bottom left: Presentation of the Child to the Śakya Temple; dome slab from Amarāvatī, now British Museum (Photo: Trustees of the British Museum).

190. Interpretation of Queen Māyā's Dream, continuation of fig. 161 (Photo: Trustees of the British Museum).

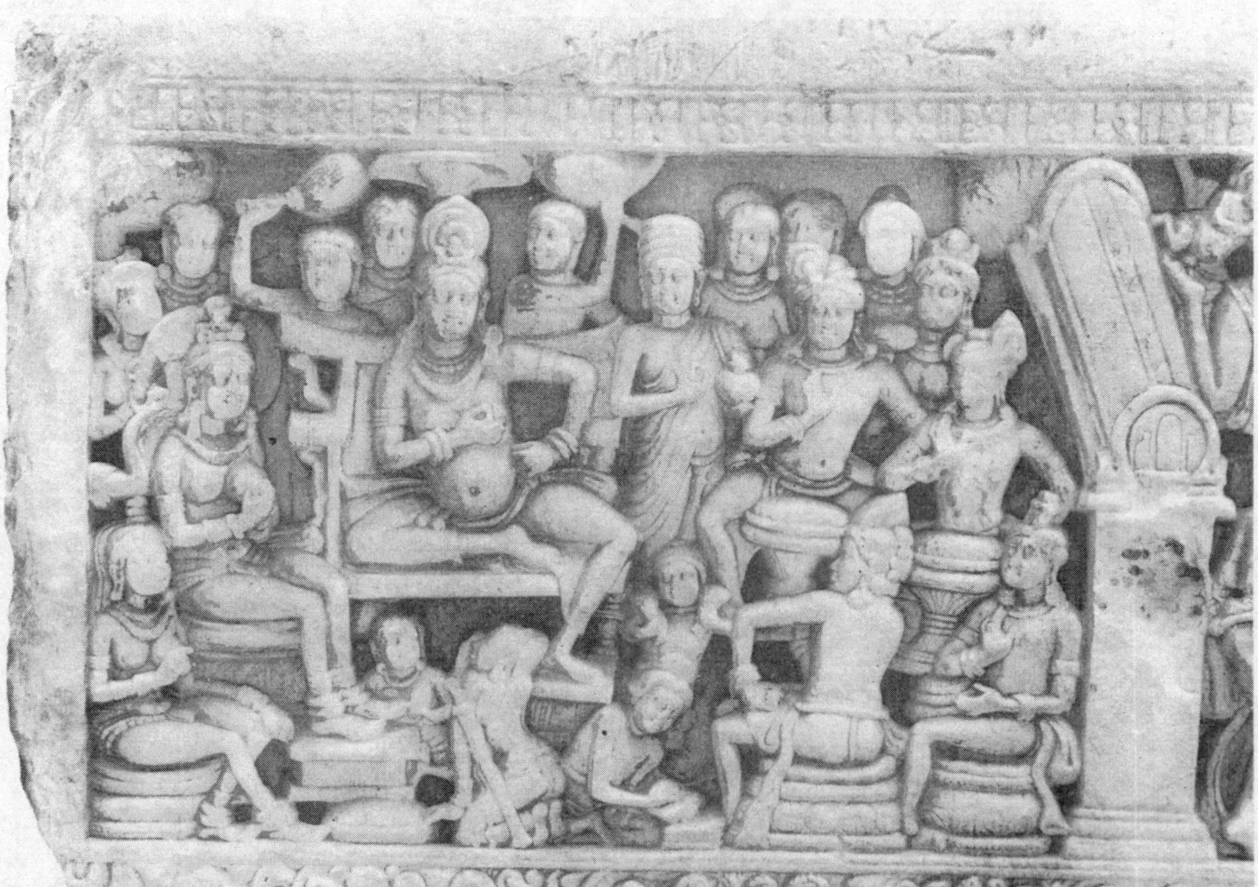

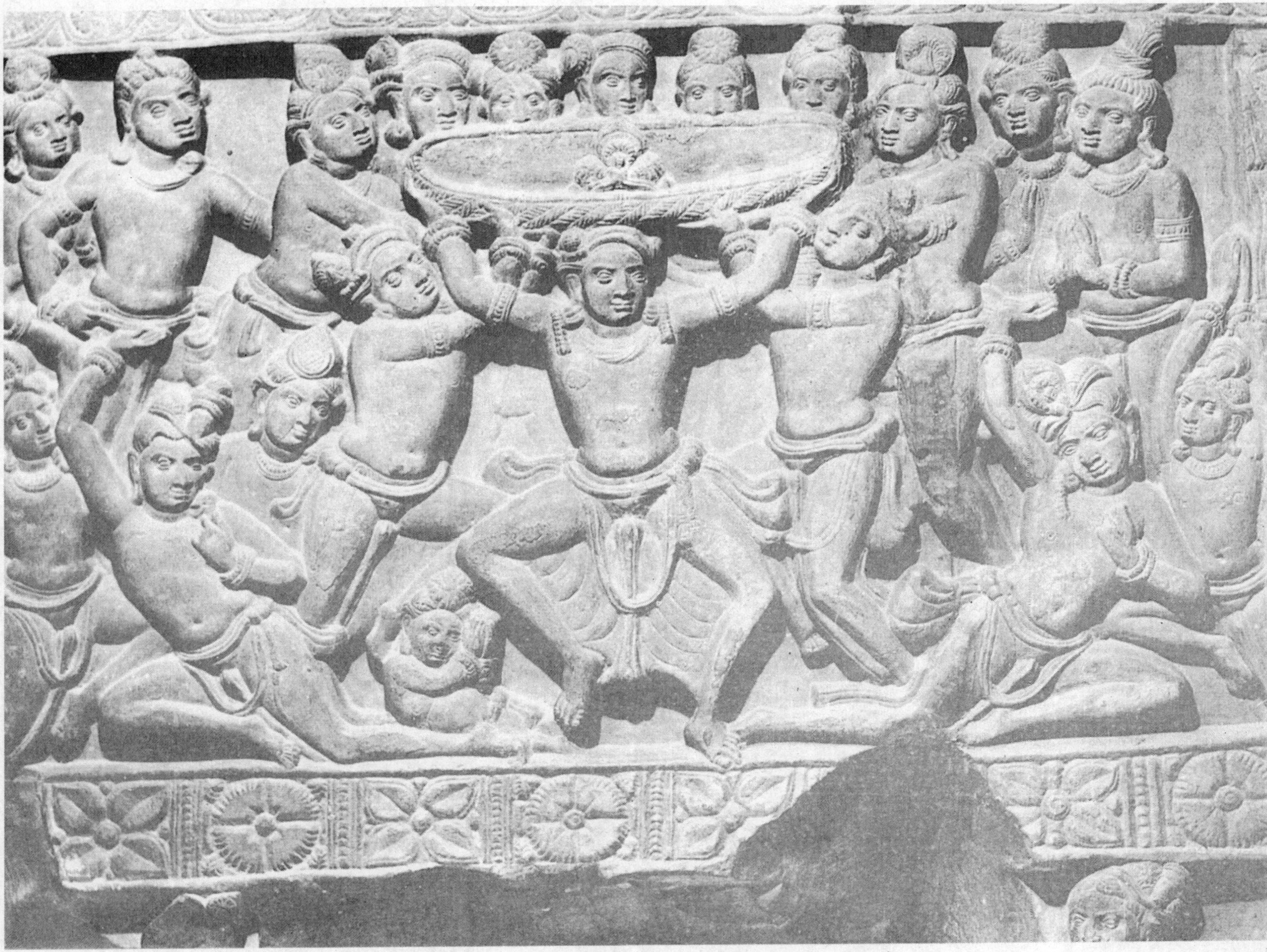

191. Transportation of the Buddha's Headdress to Heaven, possibly Site 3, Dome slab, now National Museum, New Delhi.

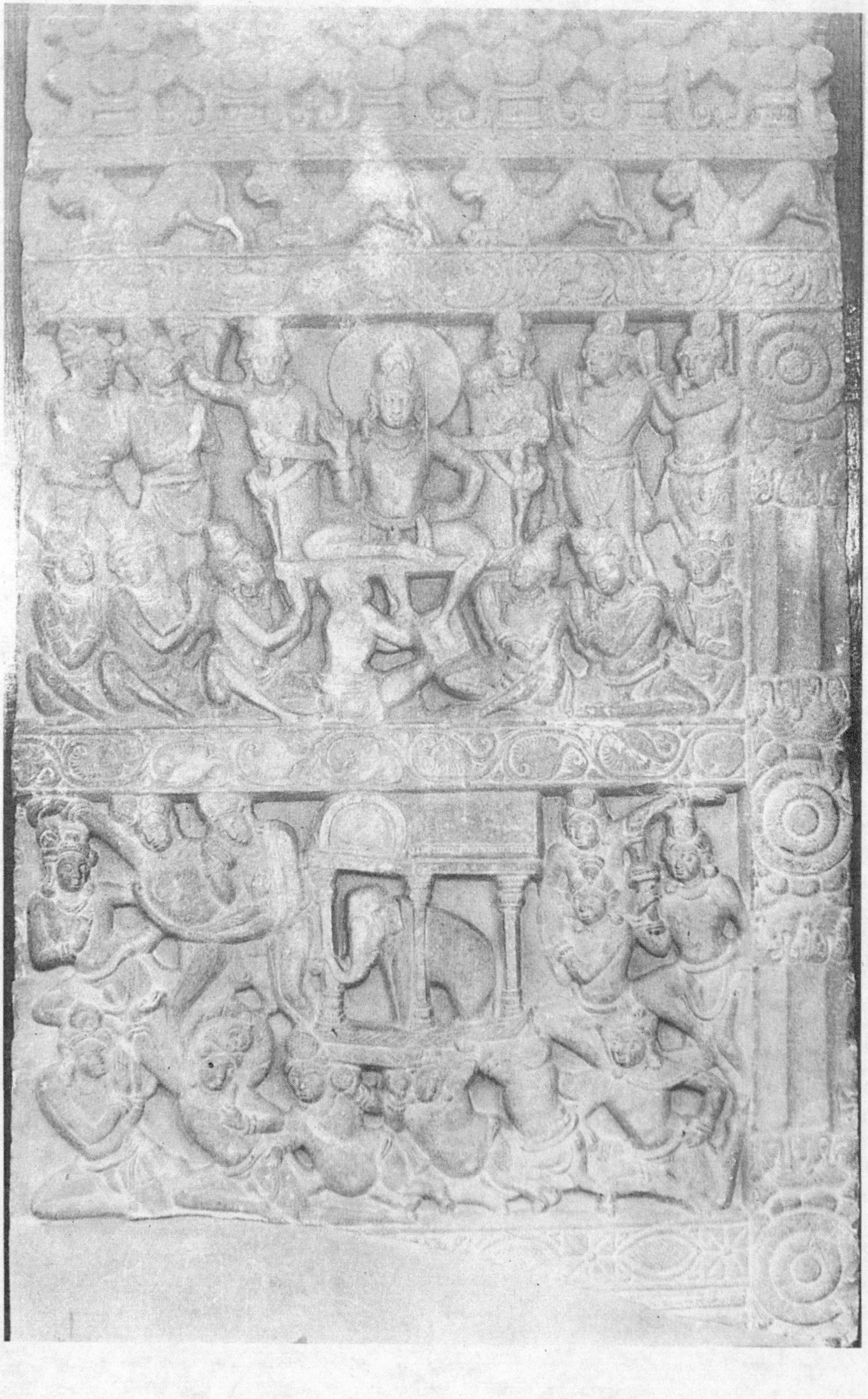

192. Exhortation of the Gods to the Bodhisattva, and the Descent of the Bodhisattva in the Form of a White Elephant, Dome slab, perhaps from Site 3 (Photo: Archaeological Survey of India).

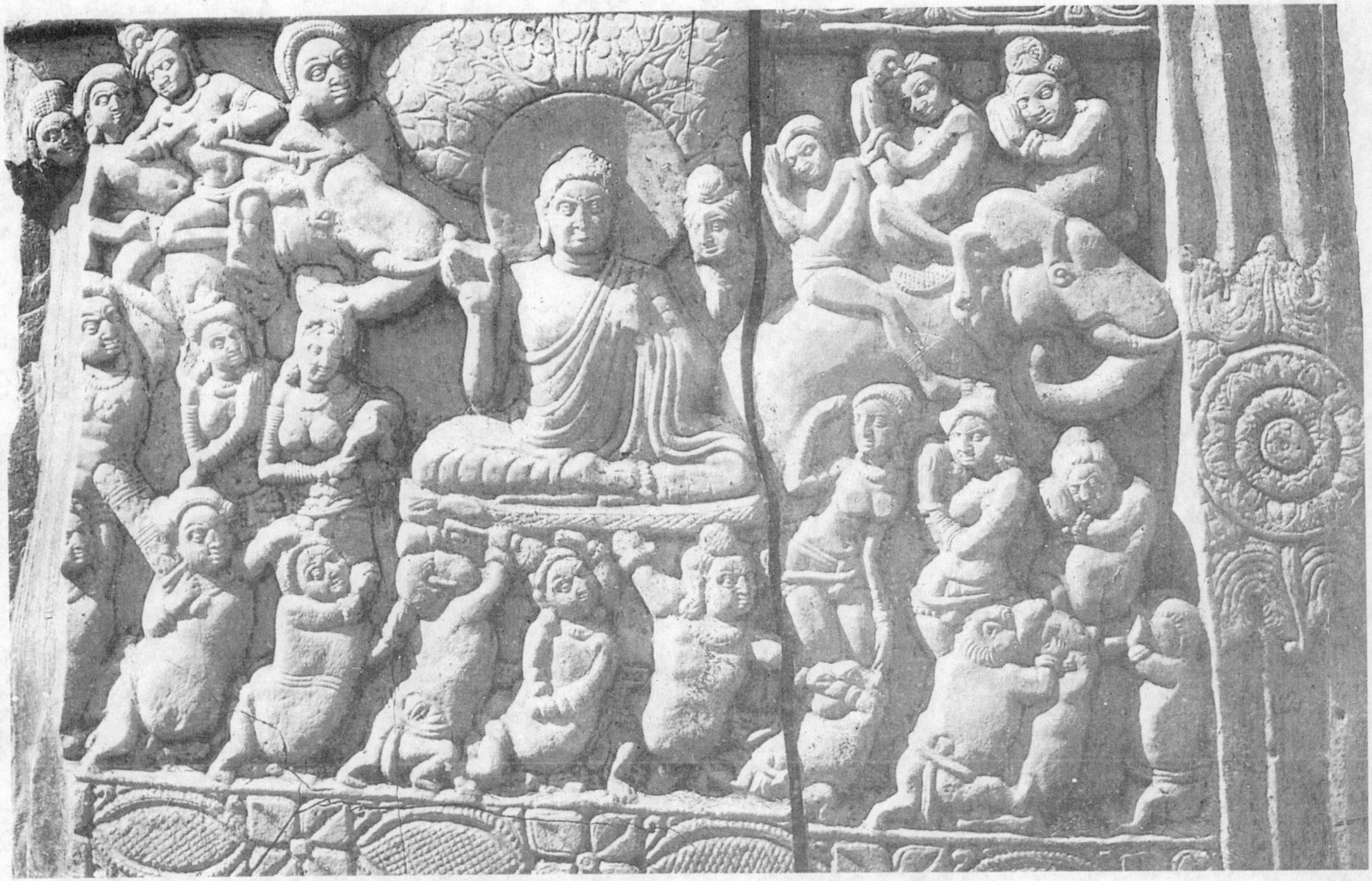

193. Māra's Assault, detail of a dome slab (Photo: Archaeological Survey of India)

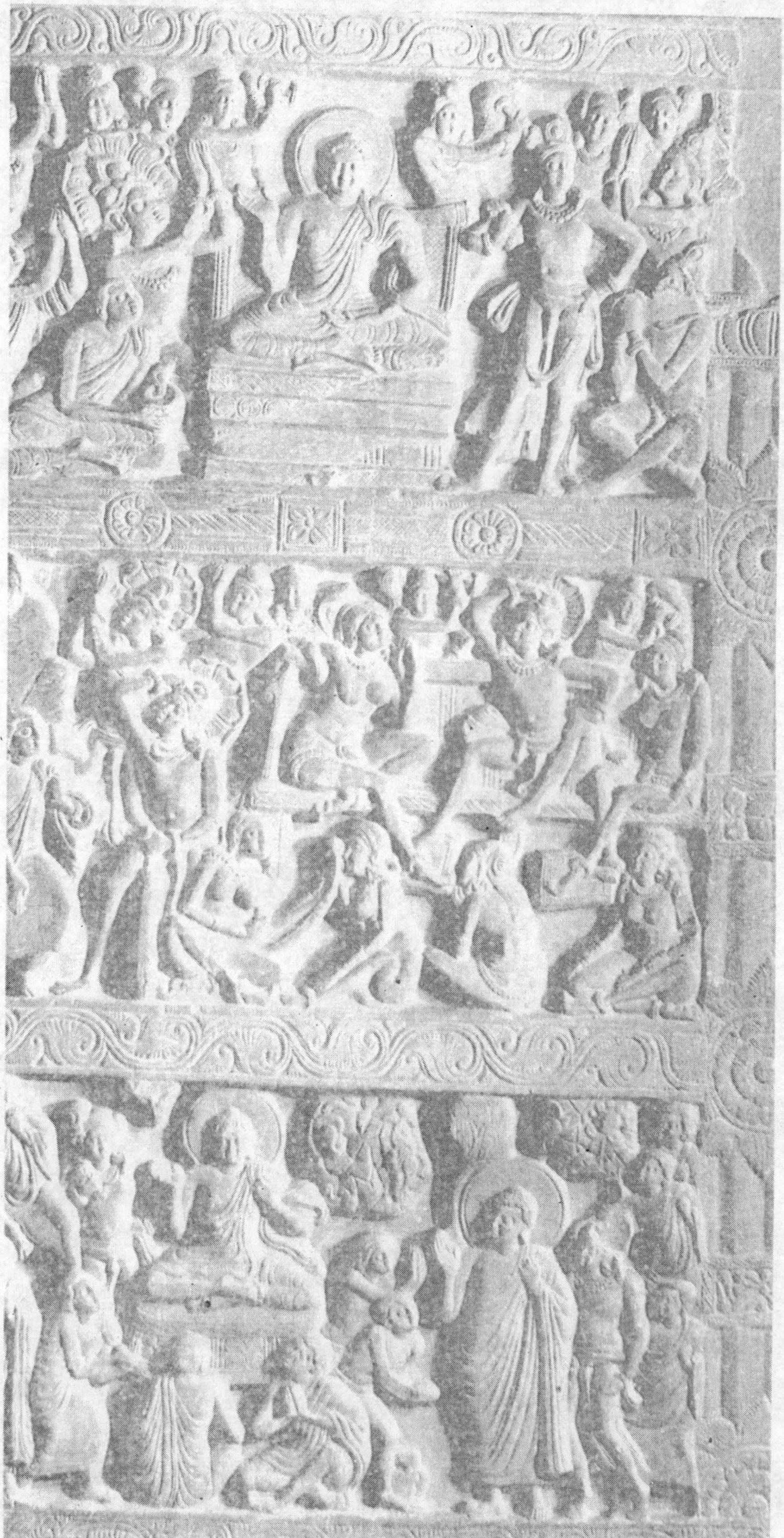

194. Top: The Conversion of the Kāśyapas; Middle and Bottom: Sāgata and the Nāga of Mango Ferry; dome slab probably from Site 3 (Photo: Archaeological Survey of India).

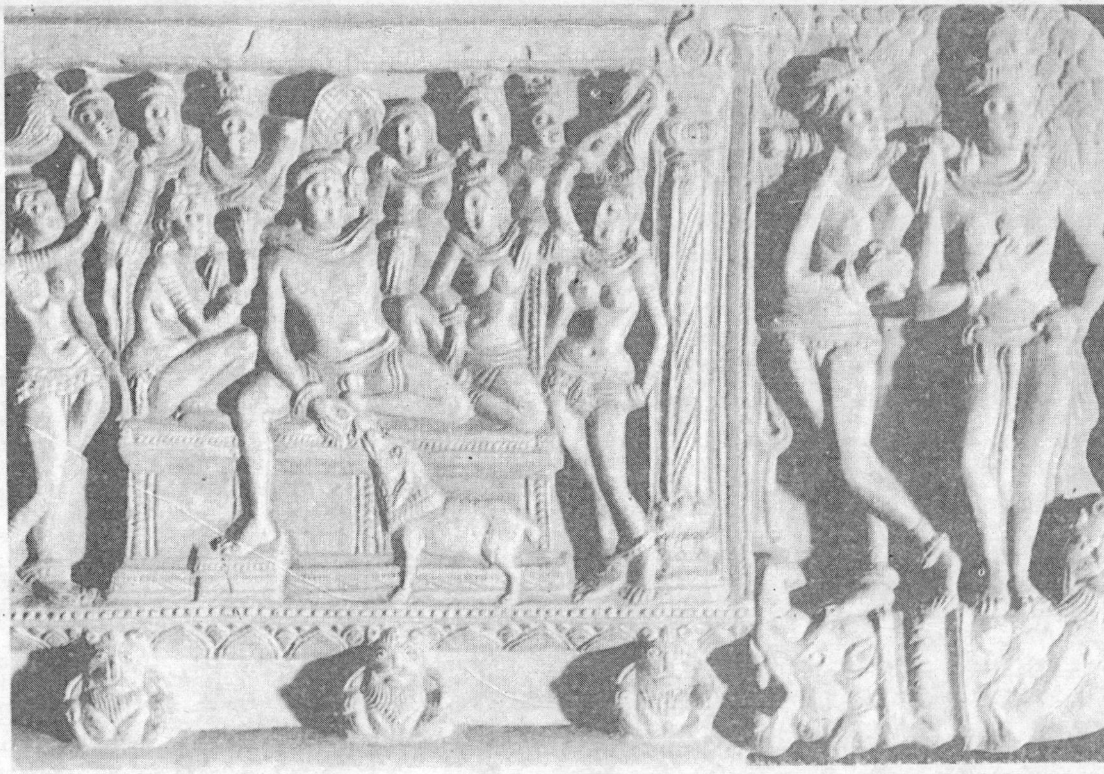

195. Detail of an unidentified section of an *āyaka* panel from Site 2 (Photo: Archaeological Survey of India).

196. Continuation of fig. 195 (Photo: Archaeological Survey of India).

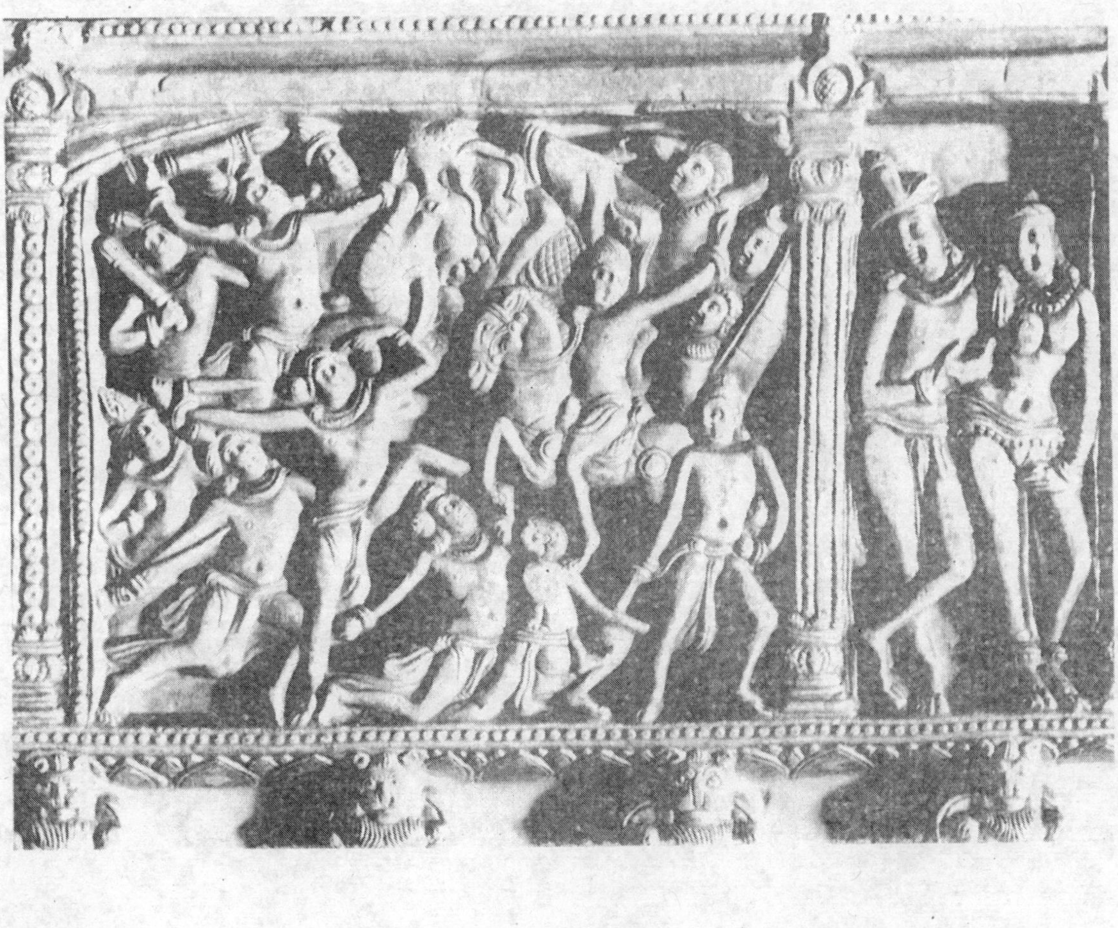

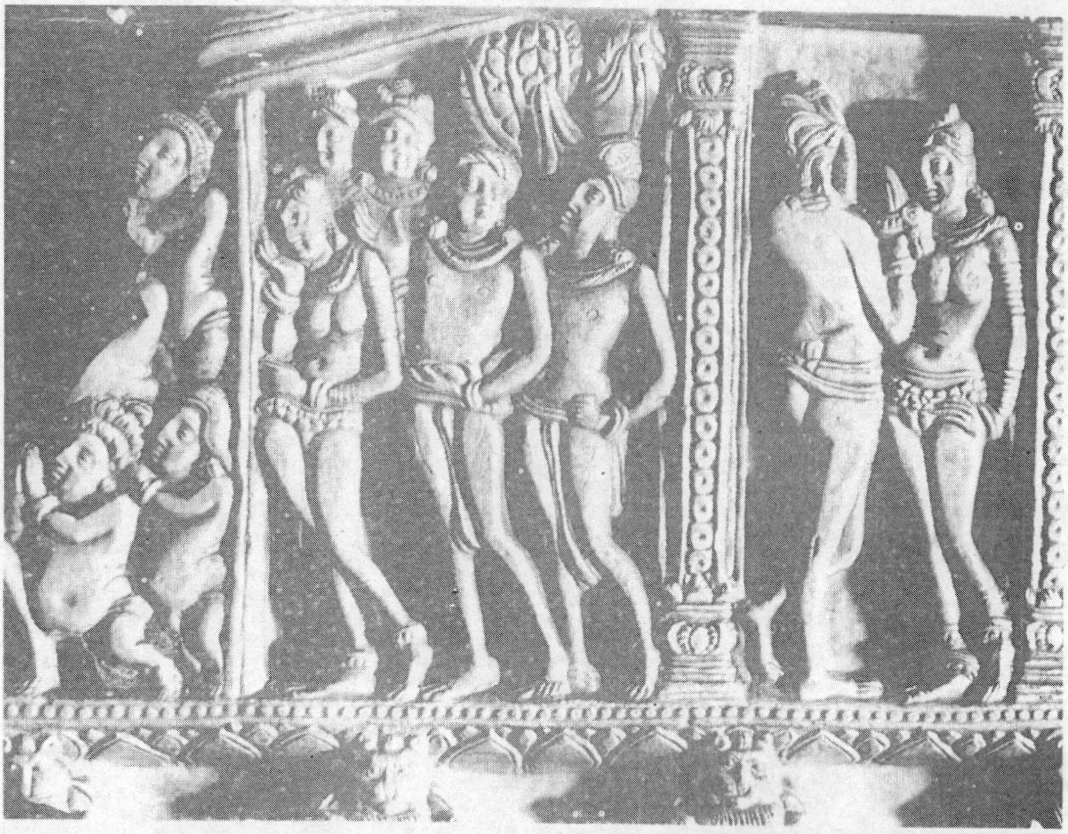

197. Continuation of fig. 196 (Photo: Archaeological Survey of India).

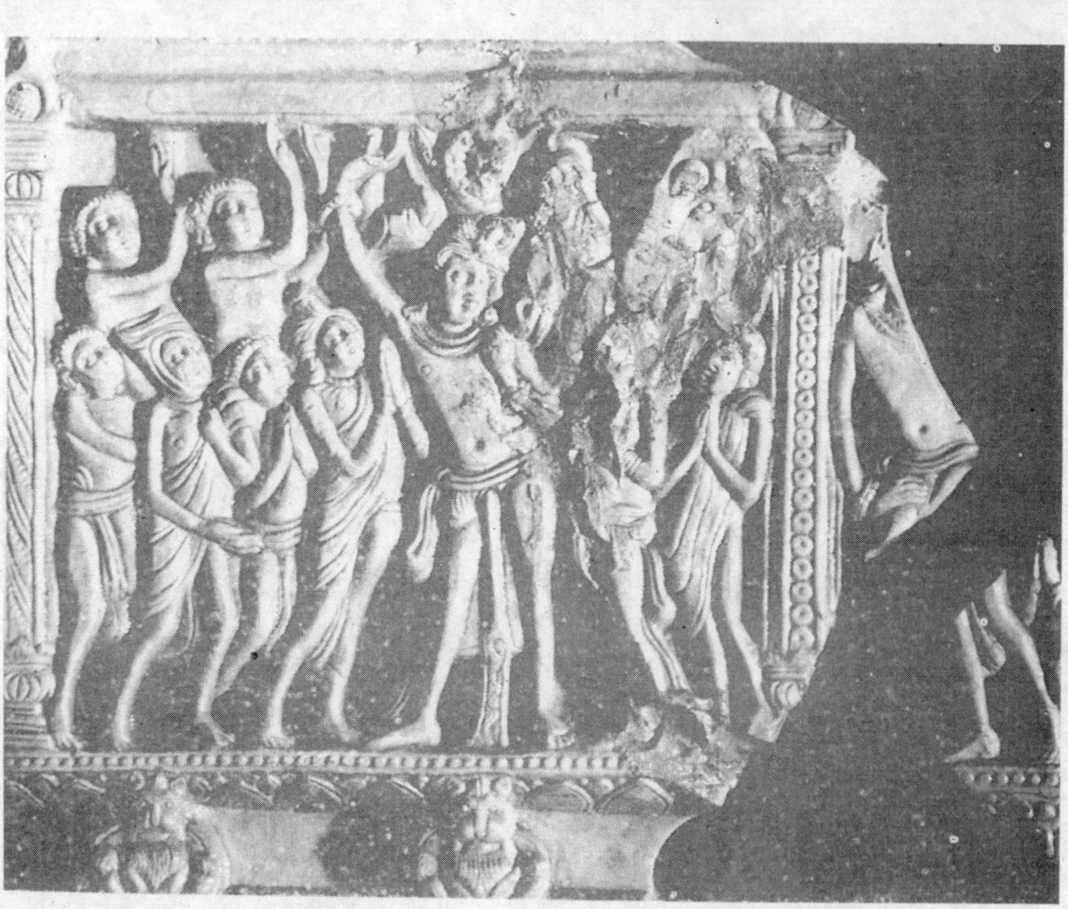

198. A Chakaravartin and His Seven Jewels, continuation of fig. 197 (Photo: Archaeological Survey of India).

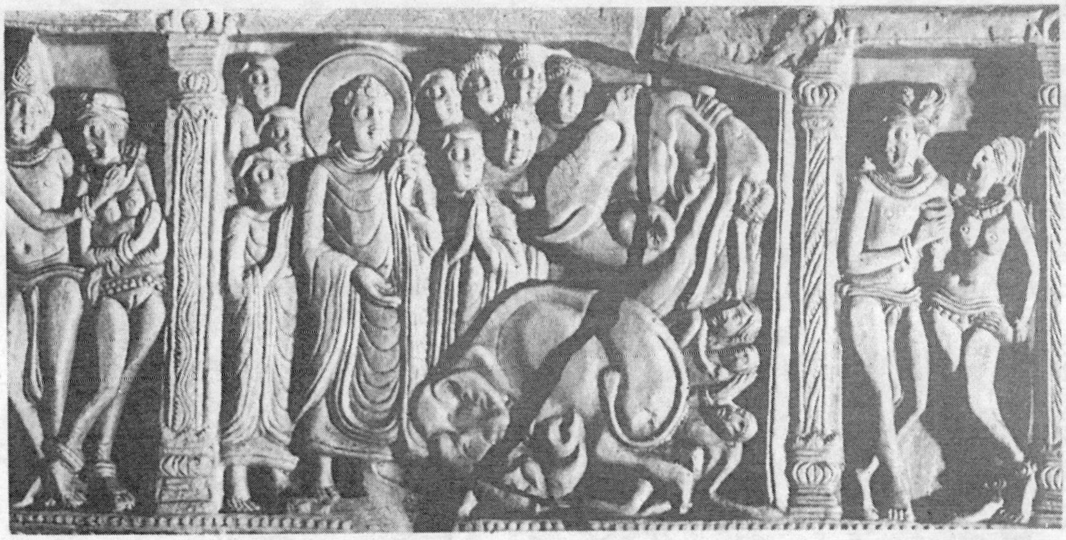

199. Subjugation of the Mad Elephant, continuation of fig. 198 (Photo: Archaeological Survey of India).

200. Siddhārtha and The Mighty Bow, continuation of fig. 199 (Photo: Archaeological Survey of India).

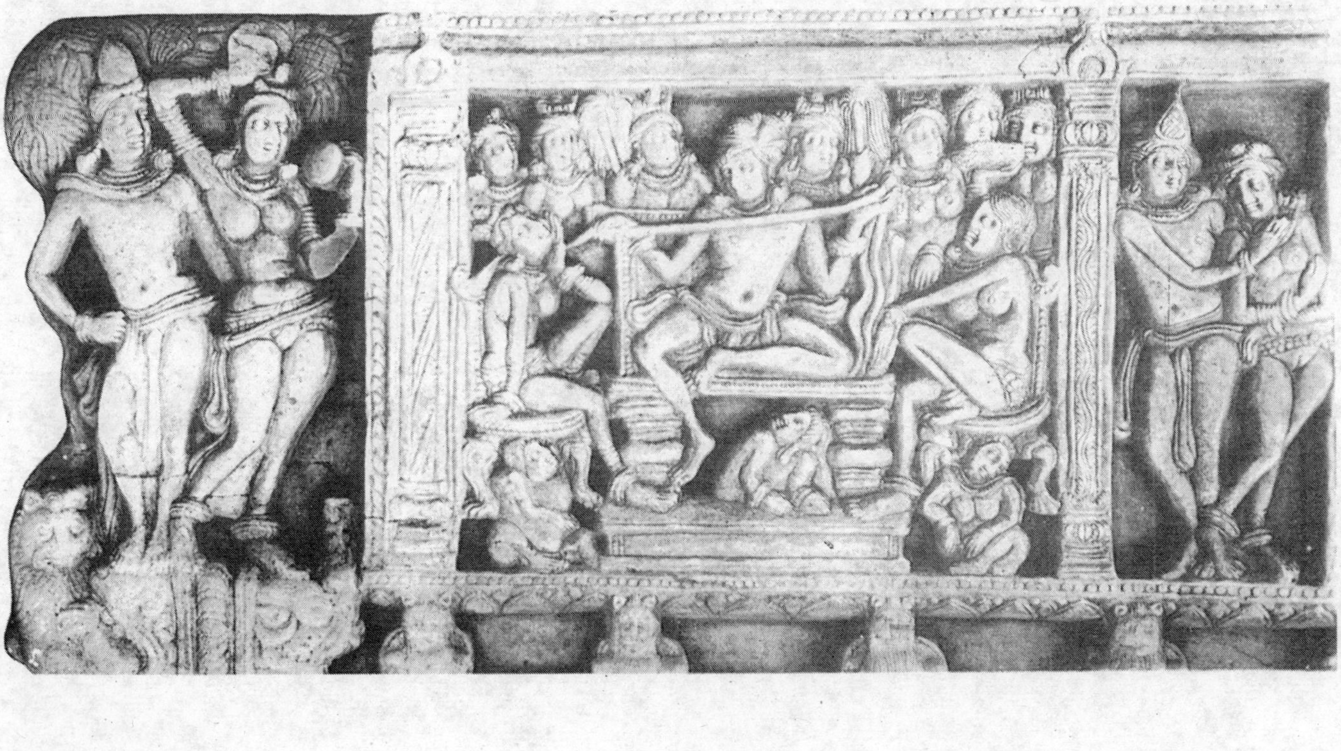

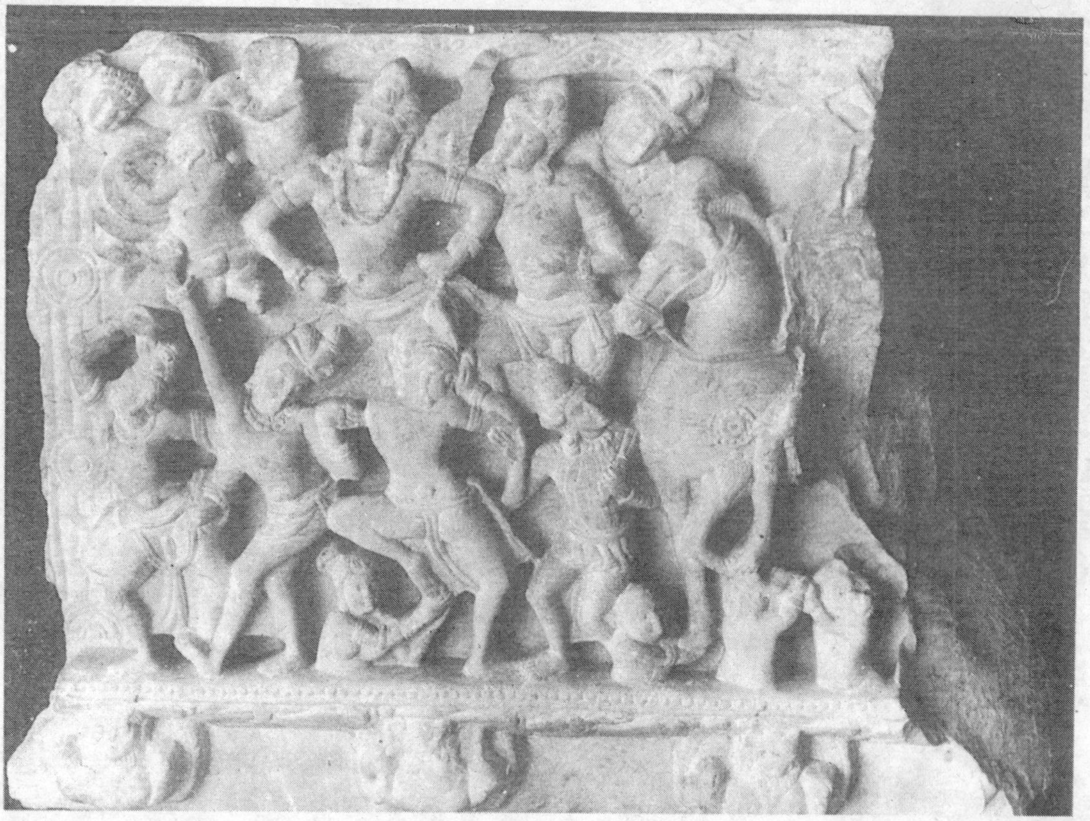

201. The Great Departure, from Amarāvatī, now Archaeological Museum, Amarāvatī (Photo: Archaeological Survey of India).

203. *Āyaka* panel, Site 2, now National Museum, New Delhi. (Photo Courtesy: National Museum, New Delhi)

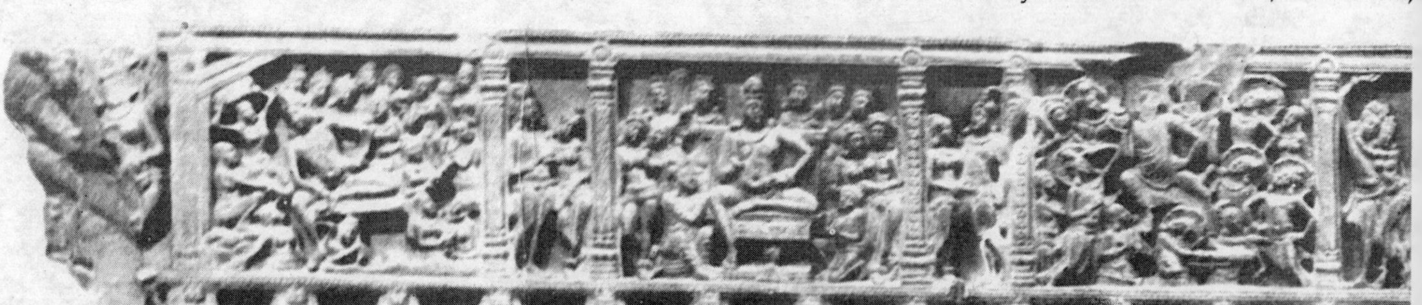

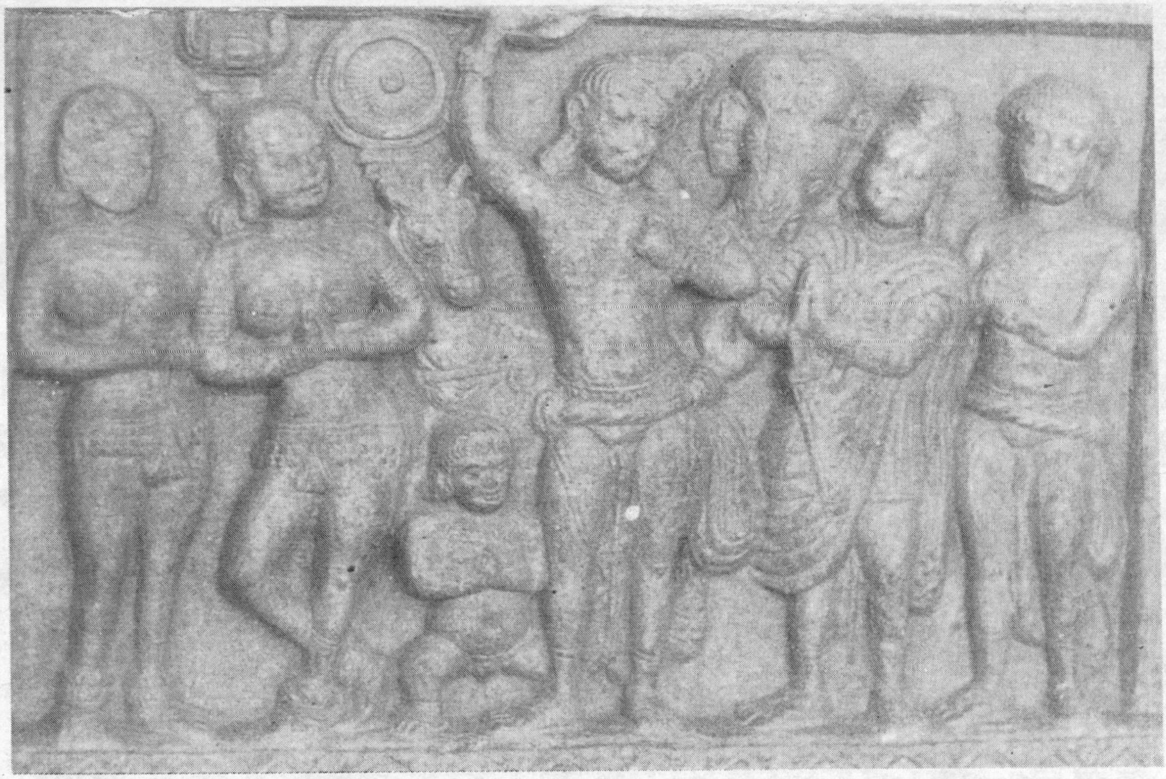

202. The Chakravartin and His Seven Jewels, detail of fig. 64.

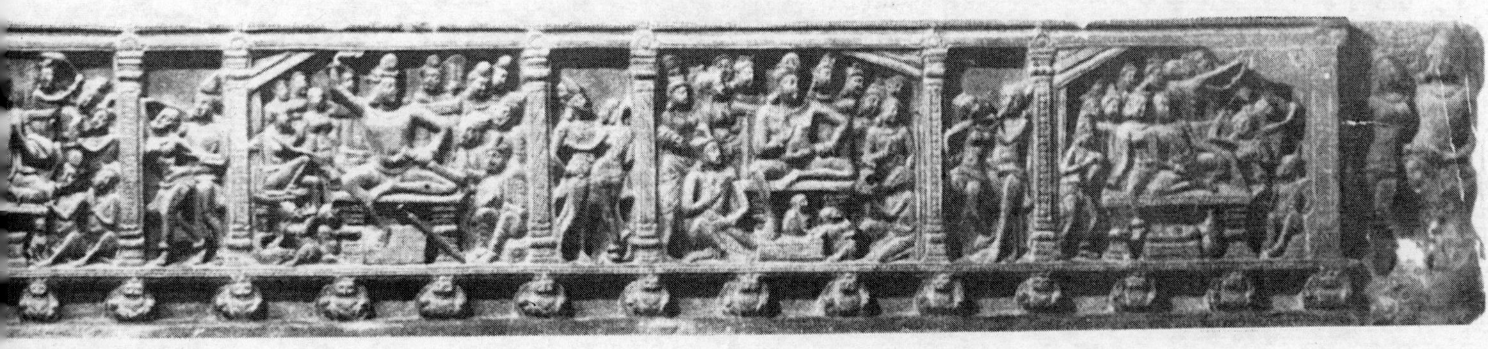

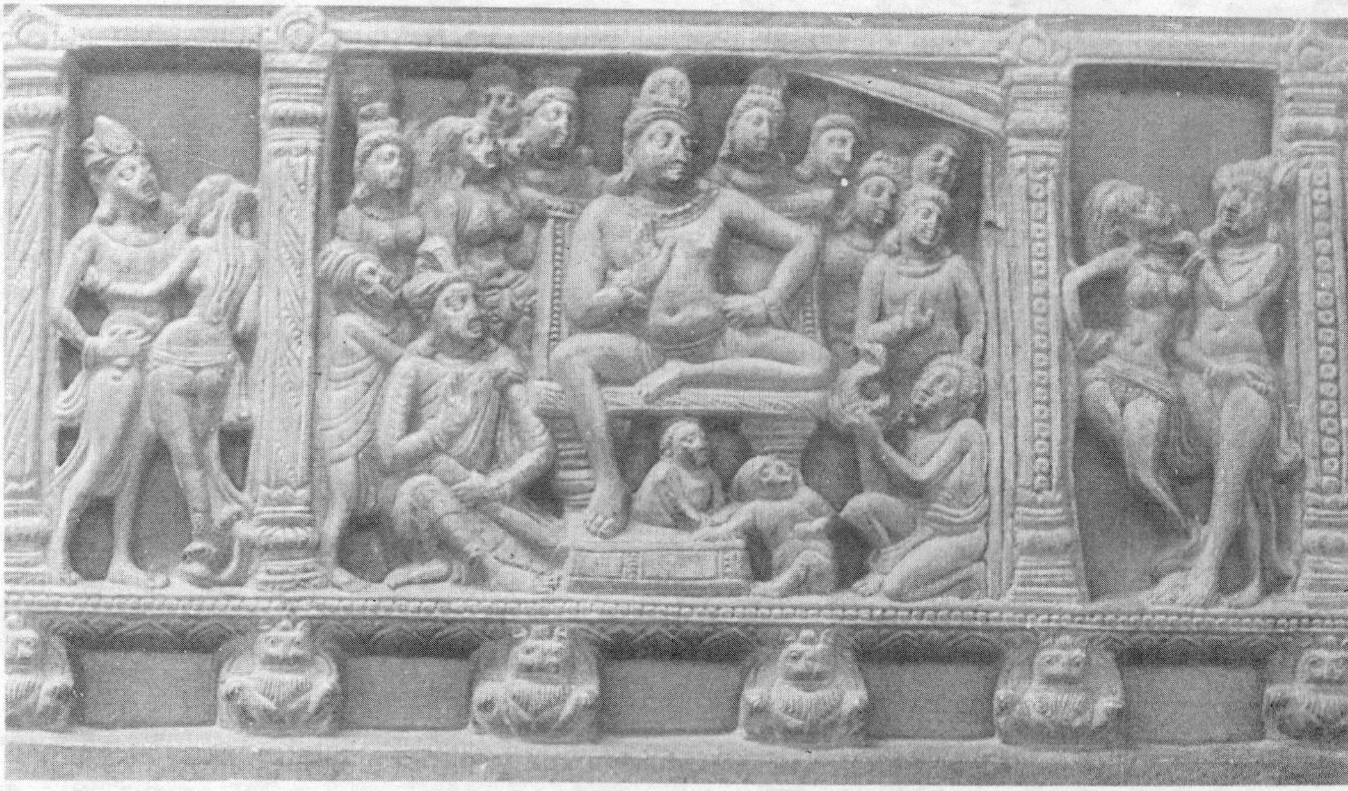

204. Champeyya Jātaka, detail of fig. 203.

205. Unidentified panel, detail of fig. 203.

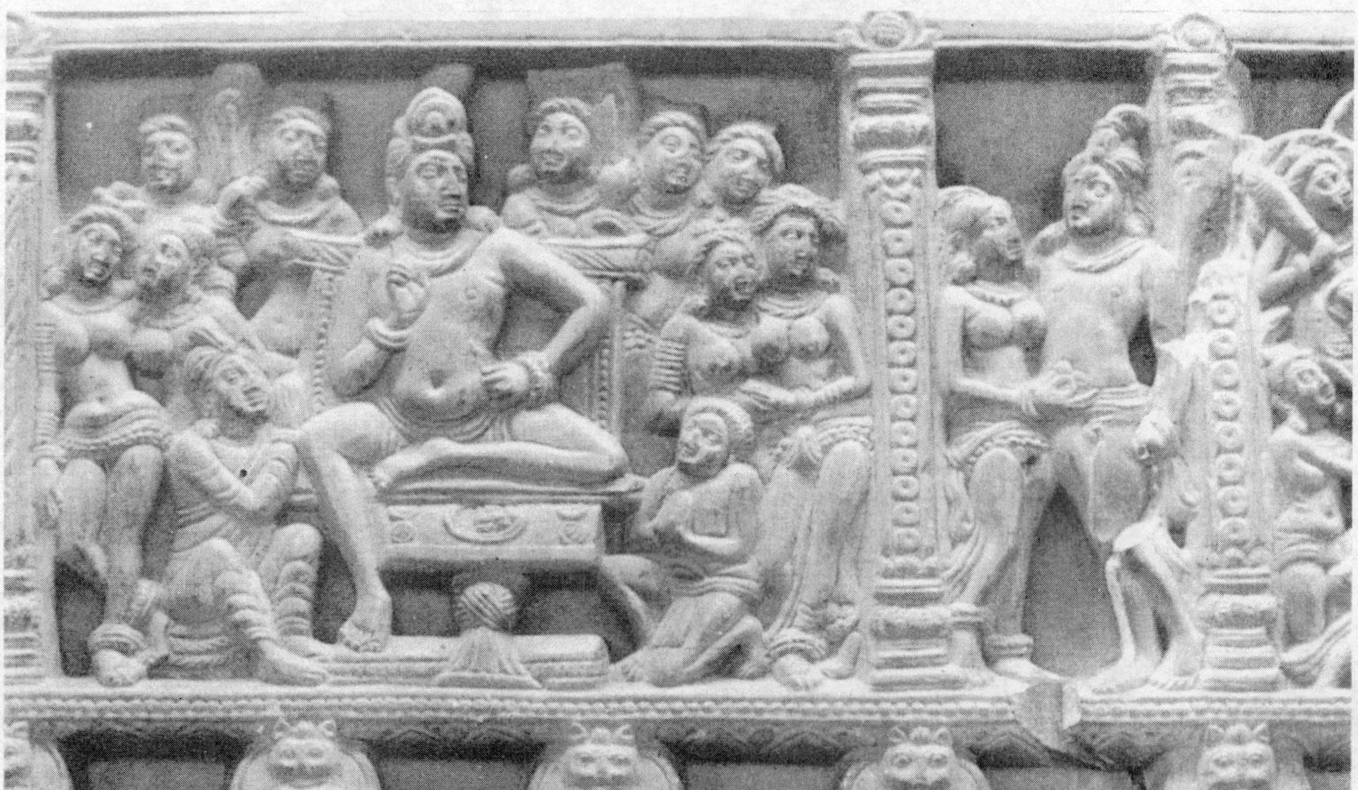

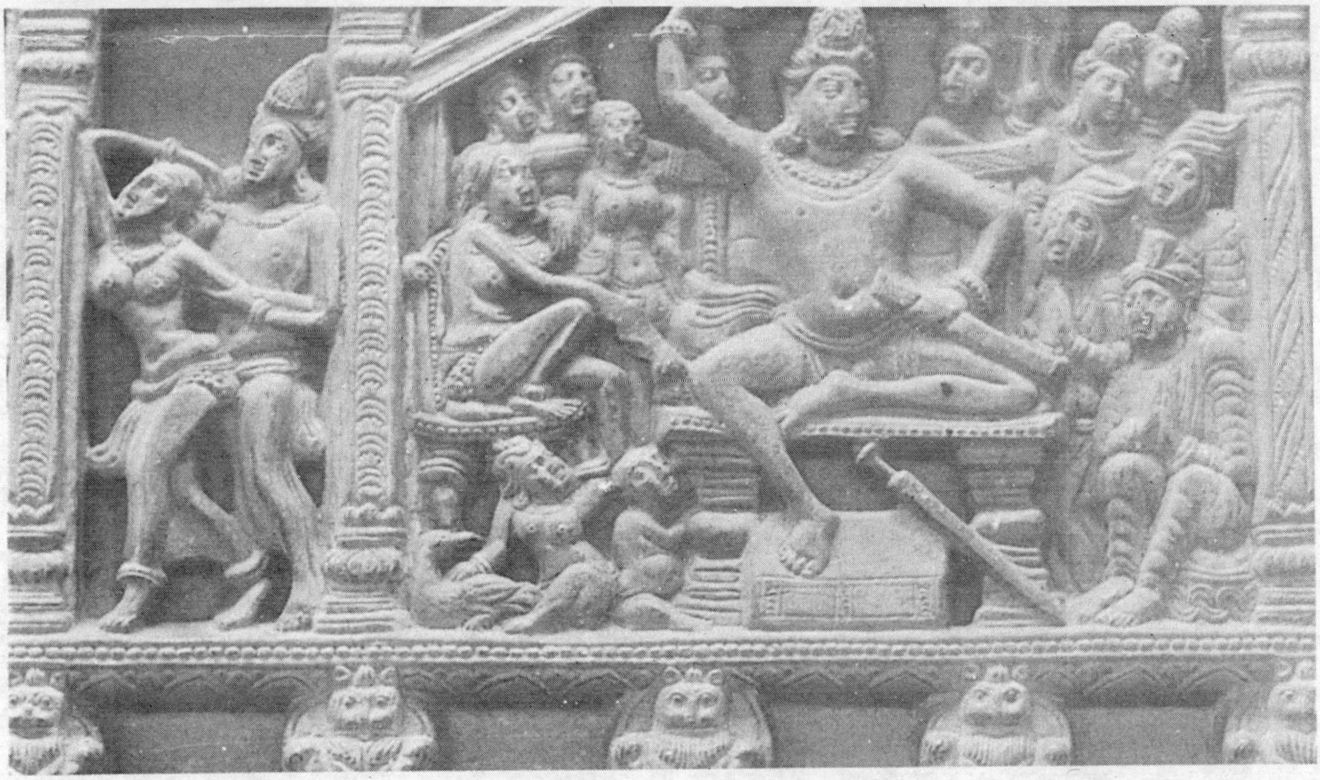

206. Lady Amarā and the Four Wise Men, detail of fig. 203.

207. Siddhārtha in His Pleasure Garden, detail of fig. 203.

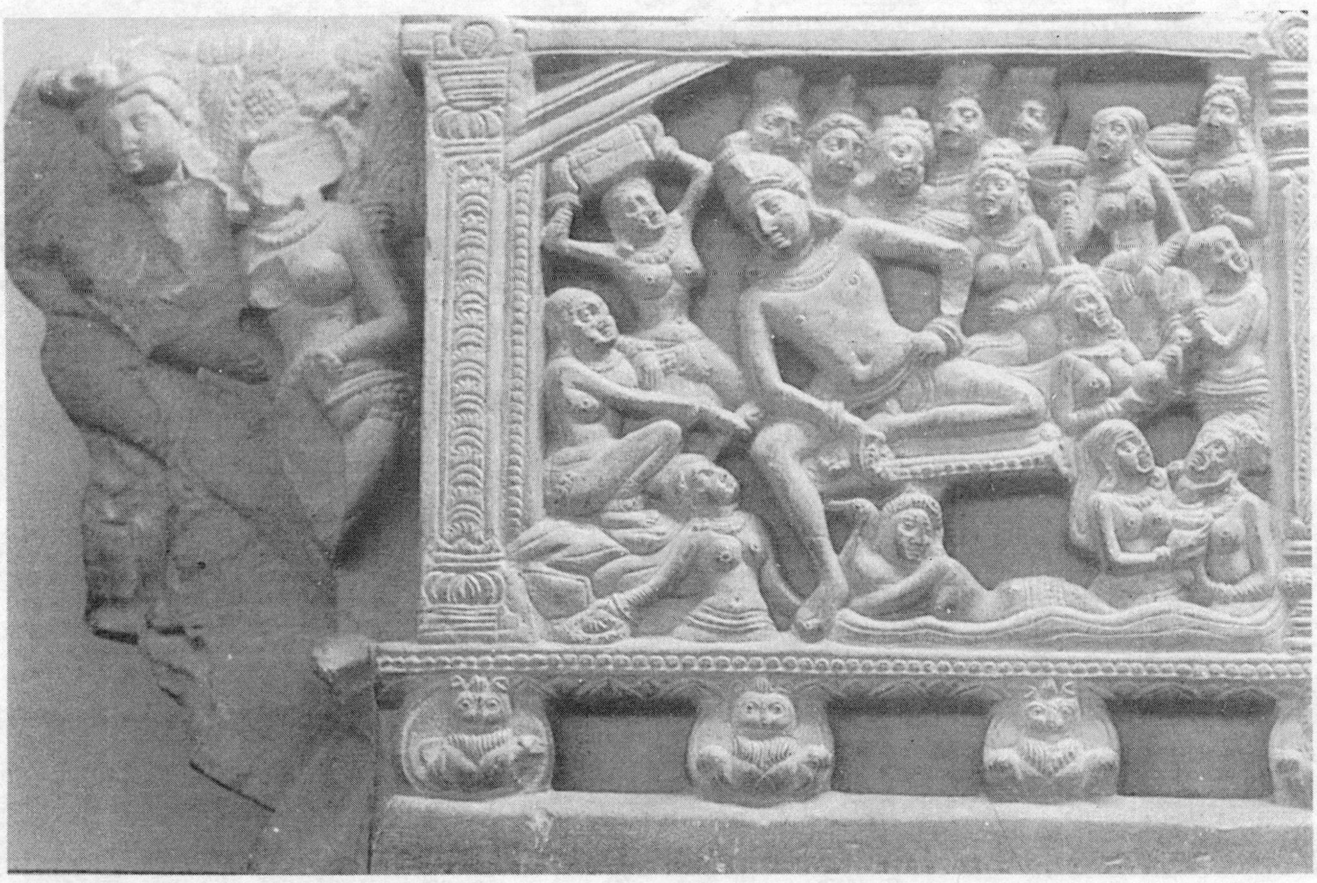

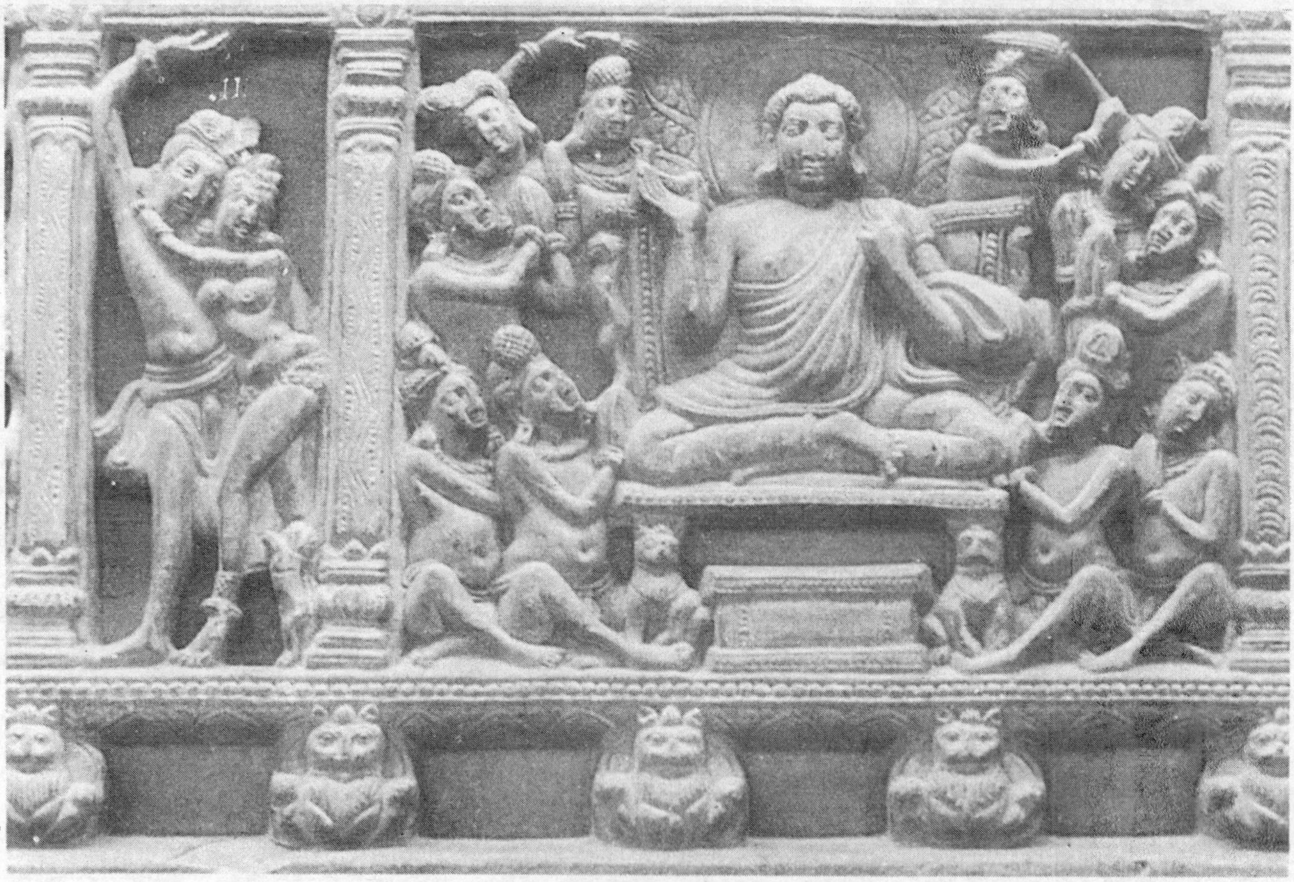

208. Devas Congratulating the Buddha After His Enlightenment, detail of fig. 203.

209. Scenes of the Life of the Buddha, *āyaka* panel (Photo; Archaeologial Survey of India).

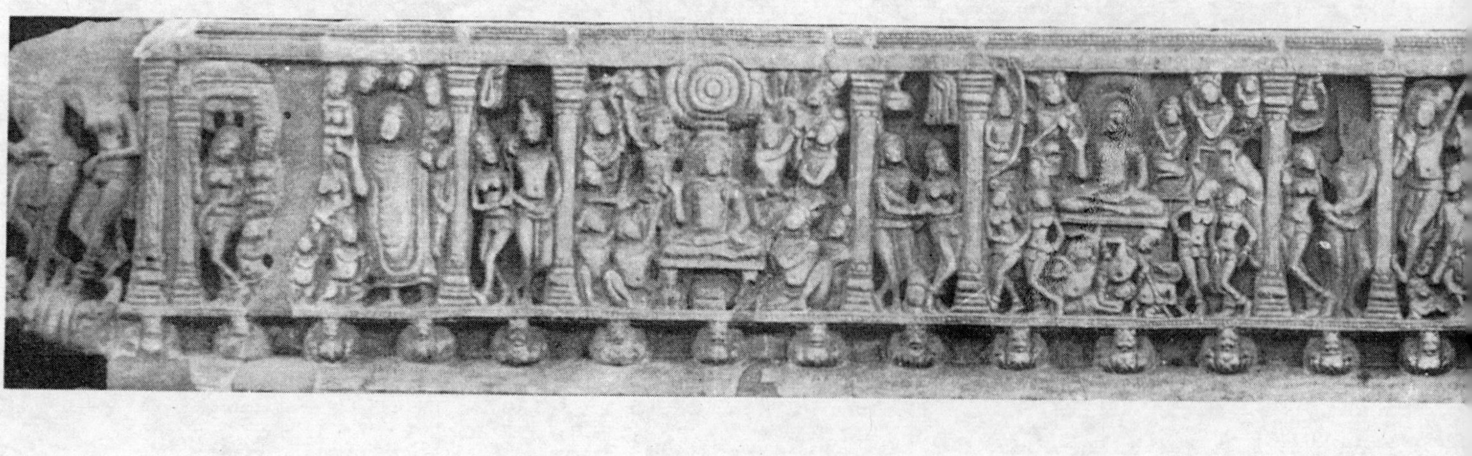

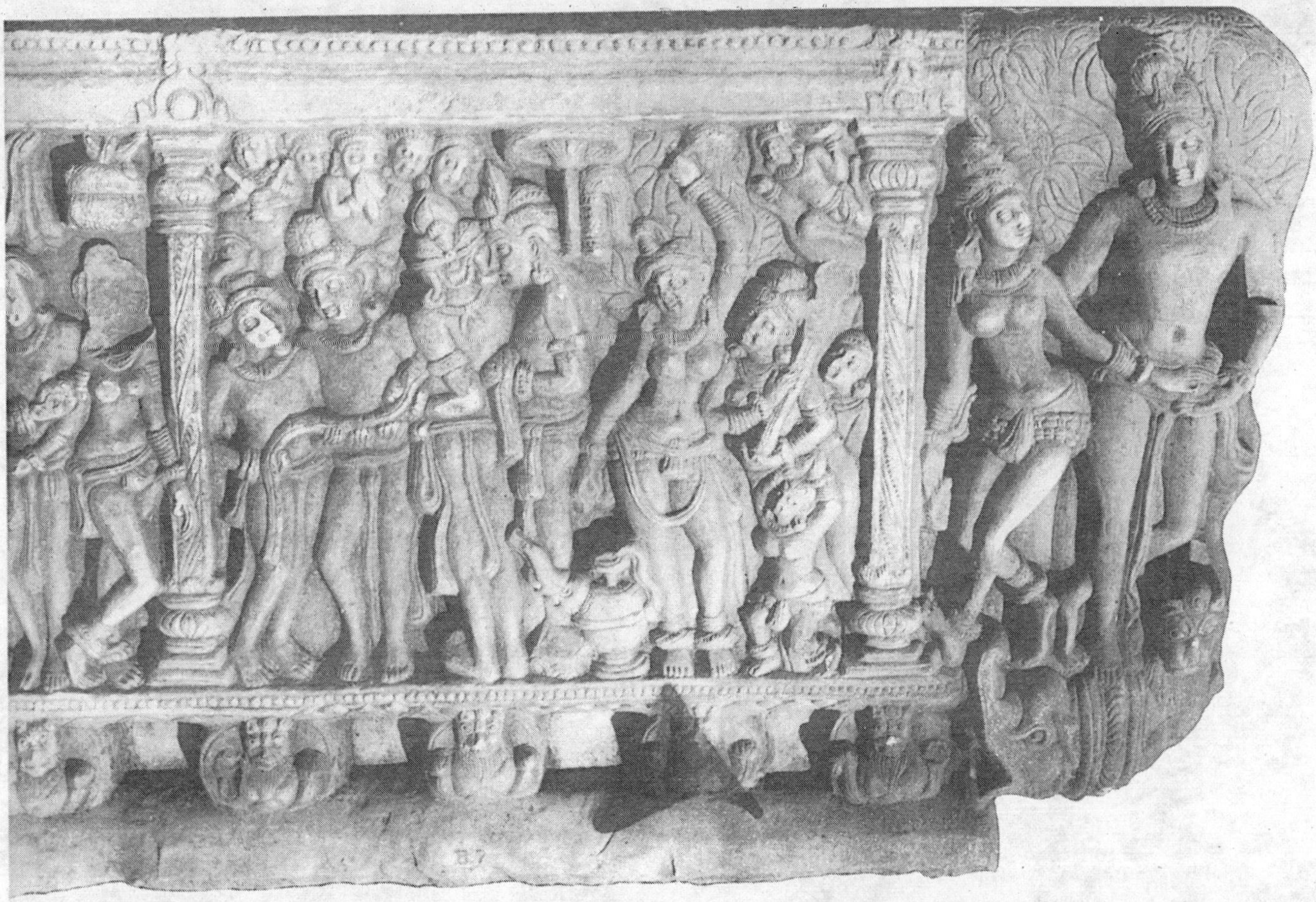

210. The Nativity and the Seven Steps, detail of fig. 209.

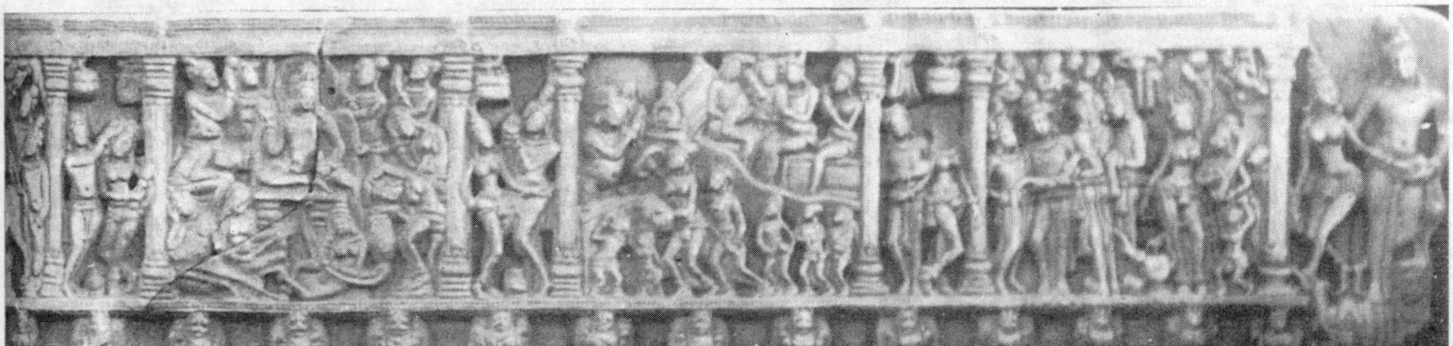

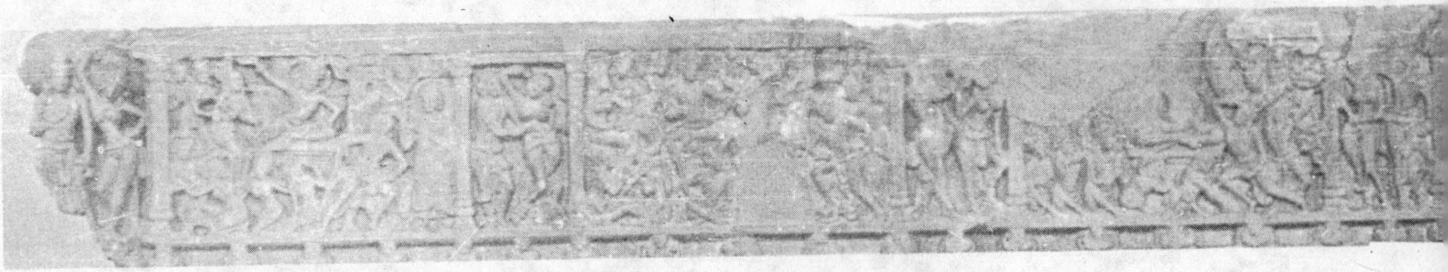

211. *Āyaka* panel (Photo: Archaeological Survey of India).

212. Bracket figure, detail of fig. 211.

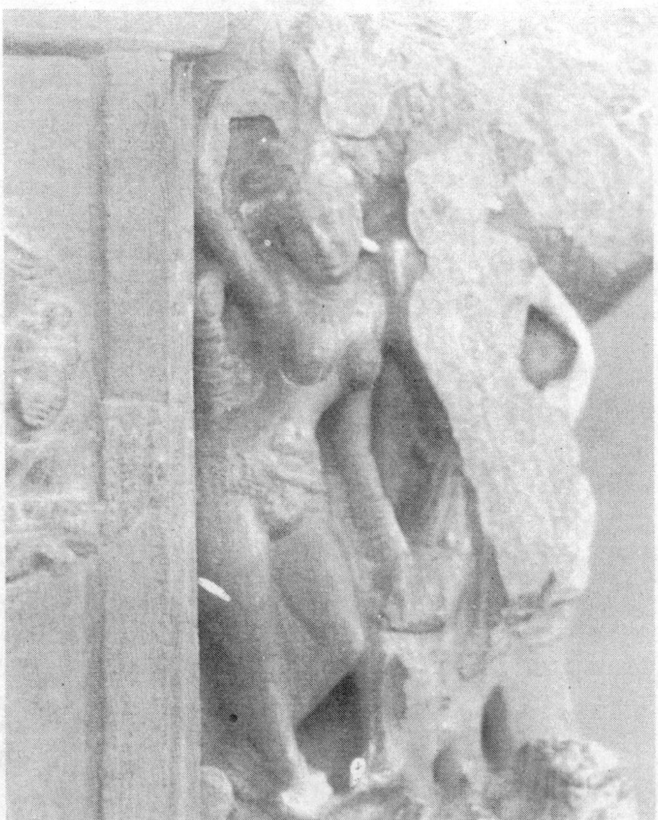

213. Bracket figure, detail of fig. 211.

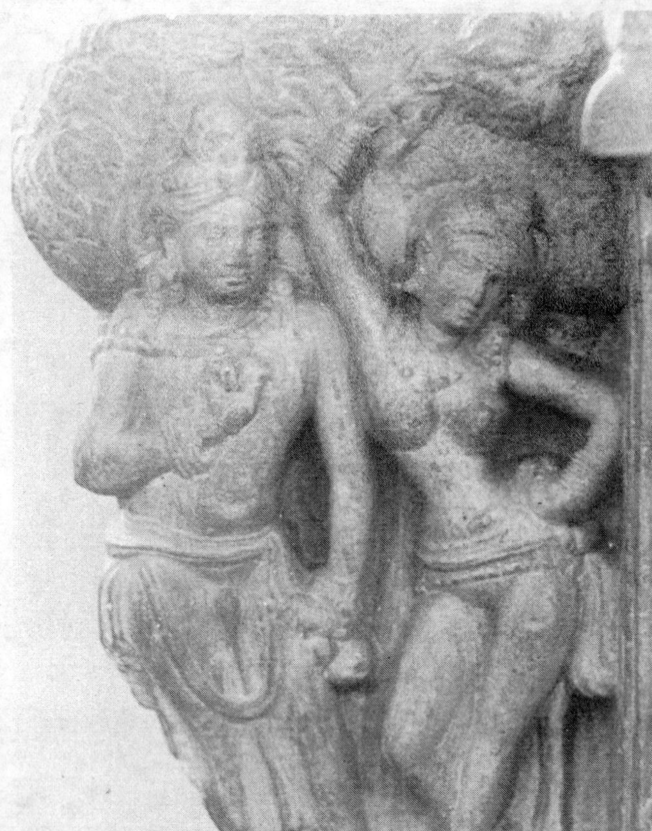

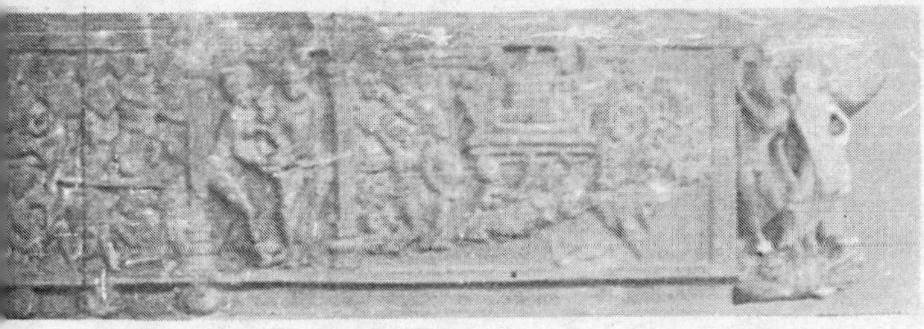

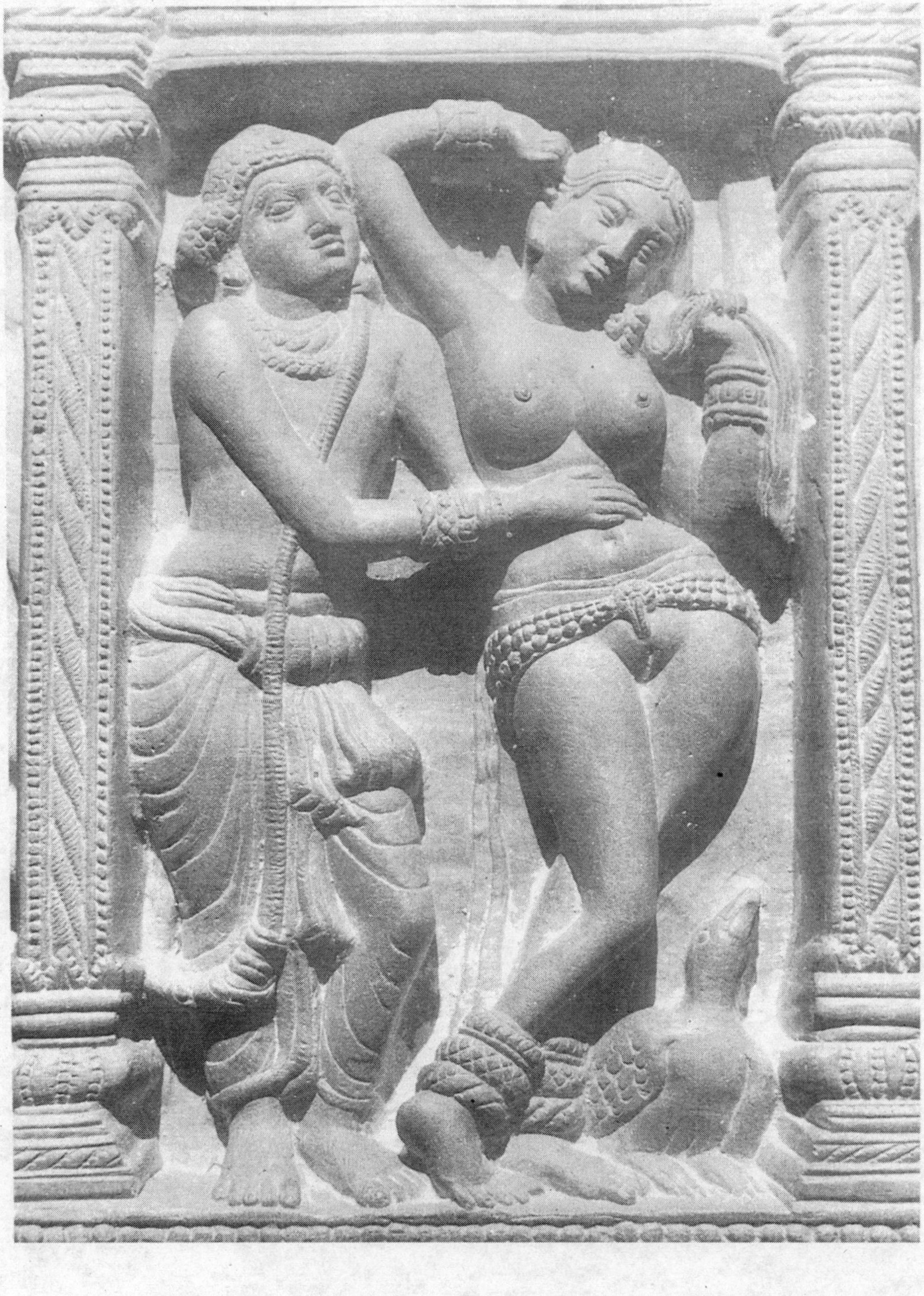

214. *Mithuna* couple, detail of fig. 211 (Photo: Archaeological Survey of India).

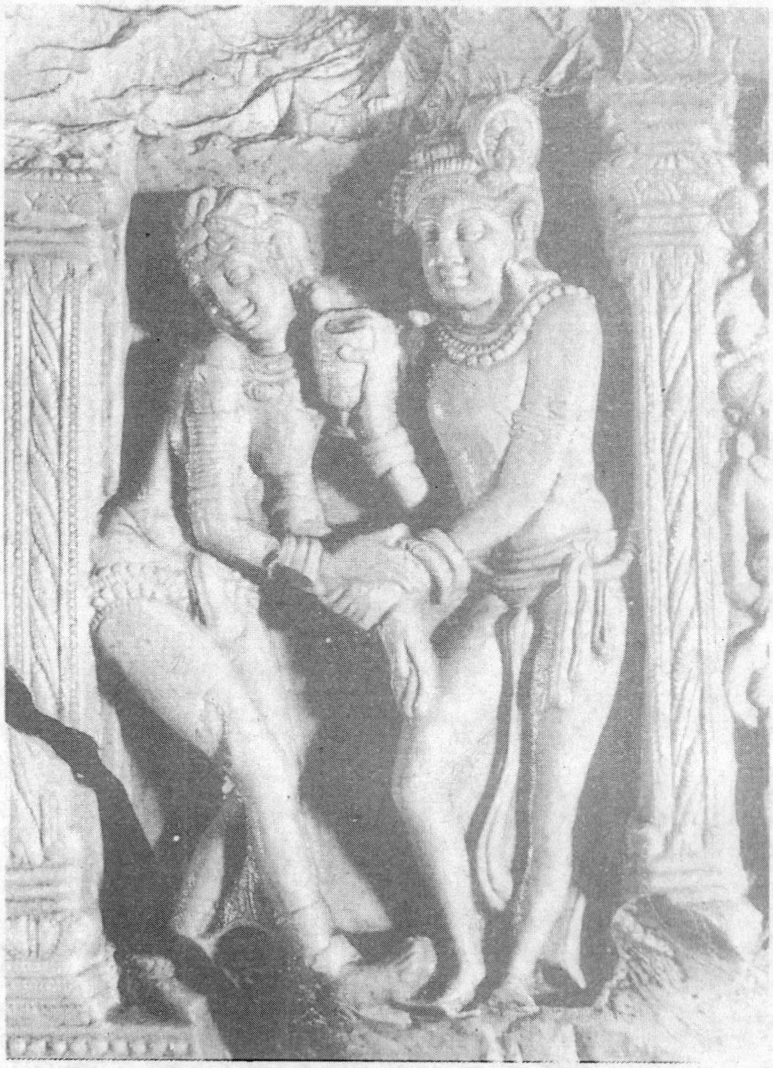

215. *Mithuna* couple, detail of fig. 211 (Photo: Archaeological Survey of India).

216. The Śibi Jātaka, detail of fig. 211 (Photo: Archaeological Survey of India).

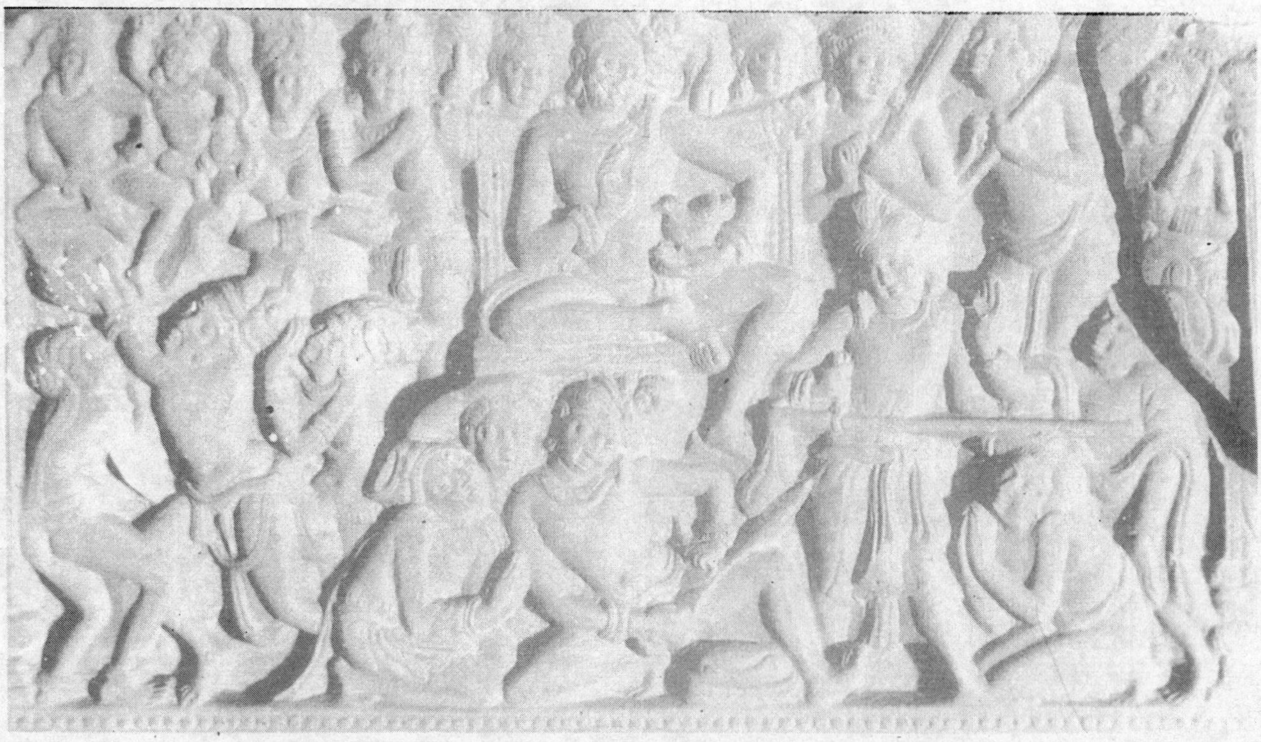

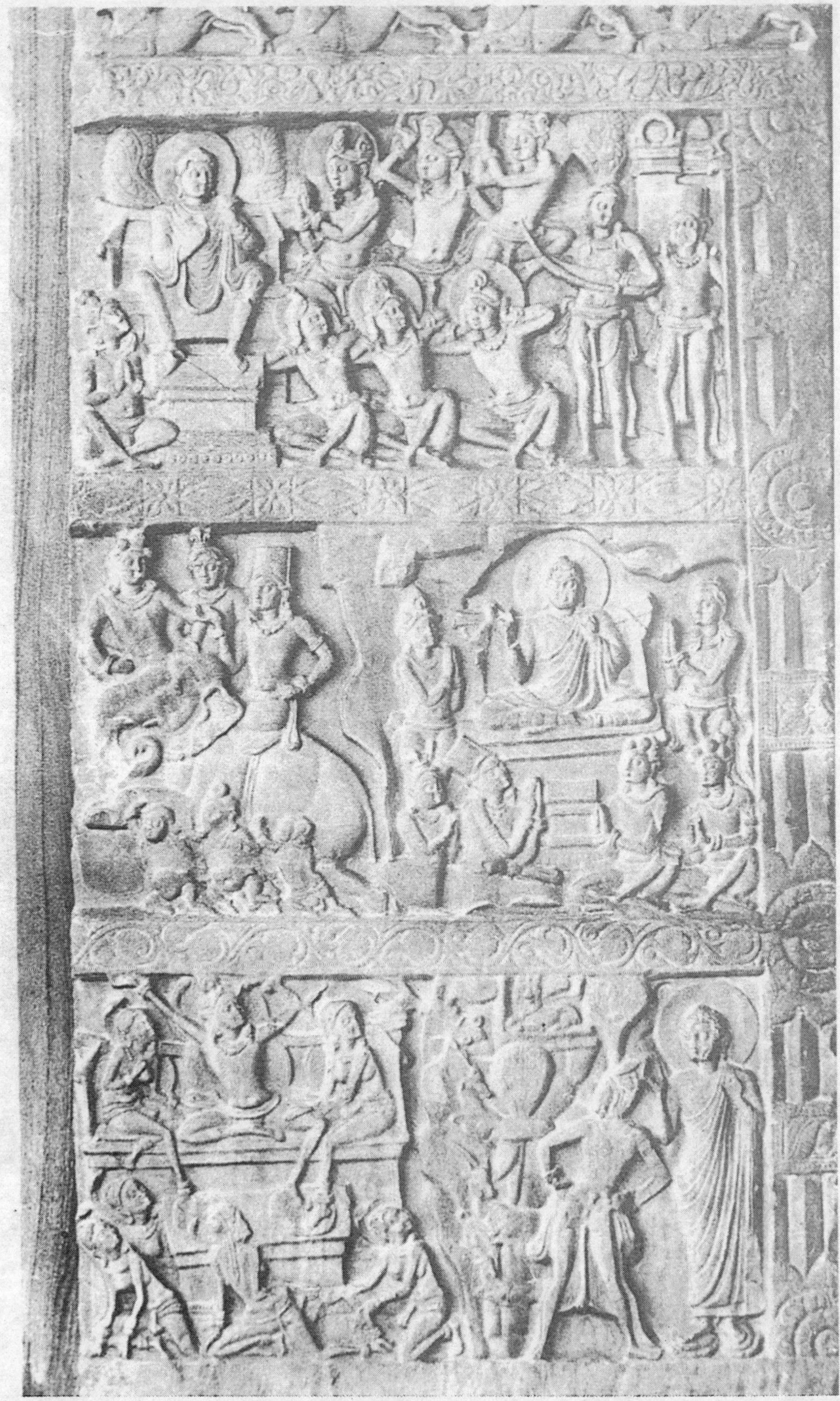

218. Top: The Buddha Visited by Indra and the Minstrel Pañcasikha; Middle: The Buddha Visited by Indra in the Cave of Indraśaila; Bottom: The Nāga Apalāla Subdued by the Buddha, dome slab. (Photo: Archaeological Survey of India).

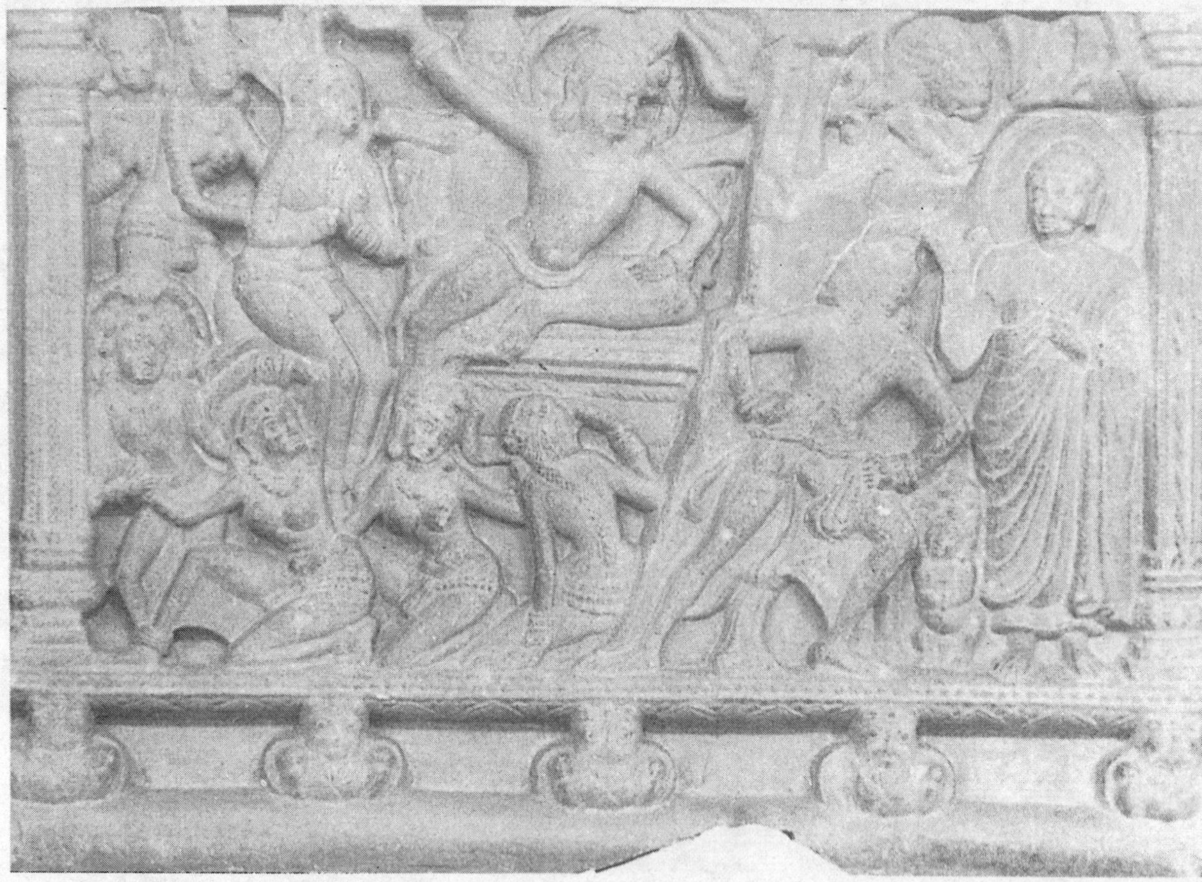

217. The Nāga Apalāla Subdued by the Buddha, detail of fig. 211.

219. The Nāga Apalāla Subdued by the Buddha, detail of a dome slab (Photo: Archaeological Survey of India).

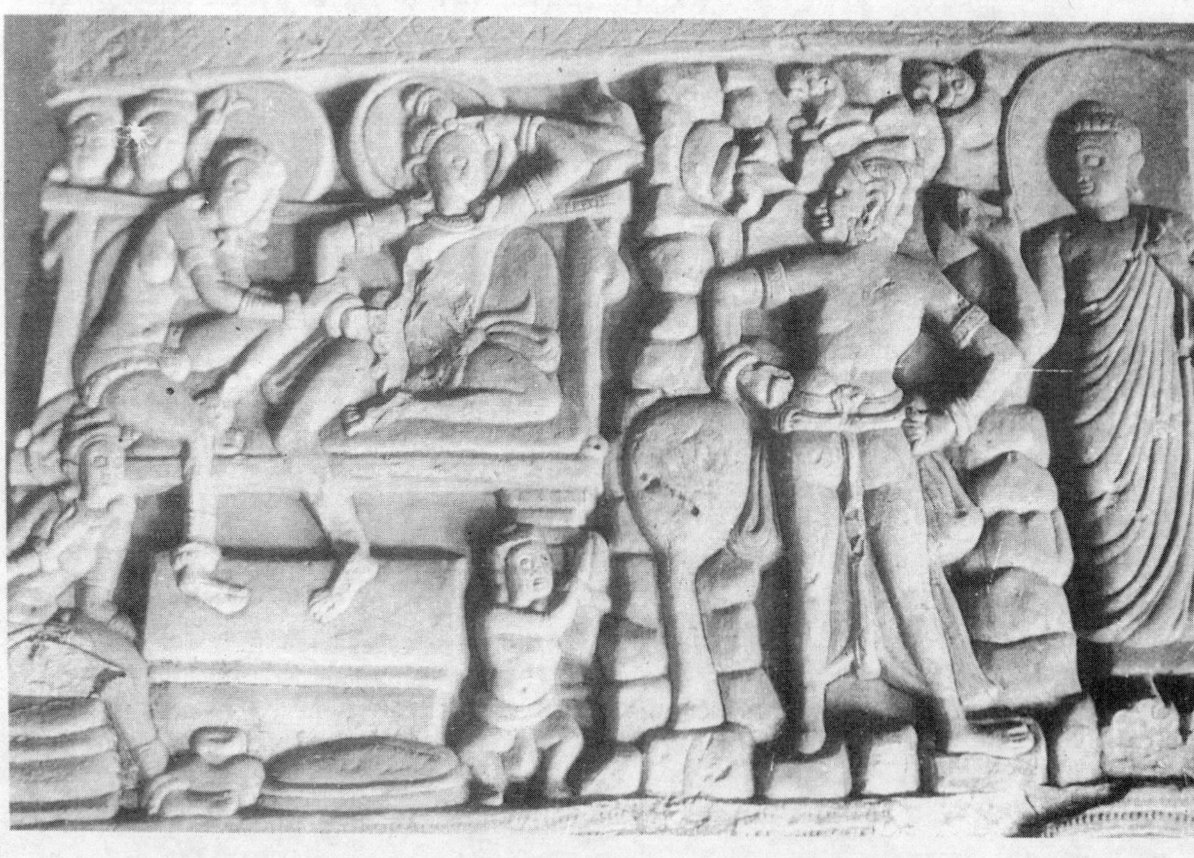

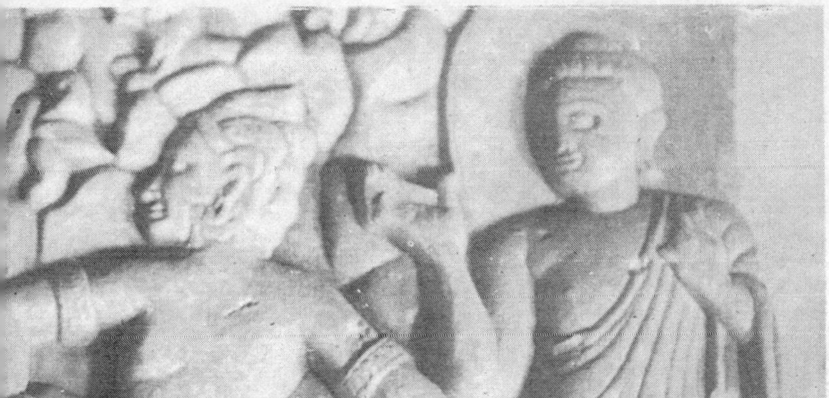

220. Detail of fig. 219. (Photo: Archaeological Survey of India).

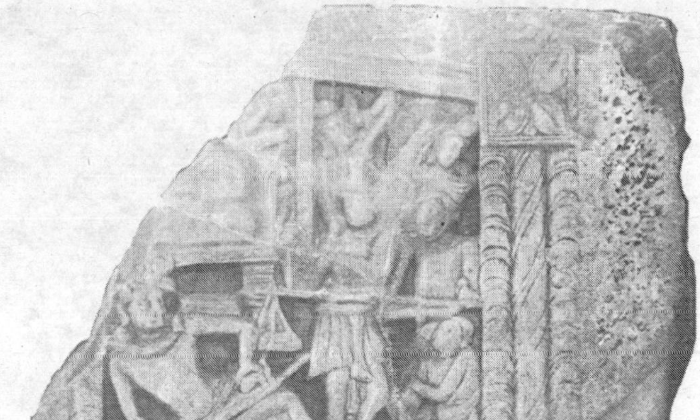

222. Top: Śibi Jātaka; Bottom: The Story of "The Man in the Well", dome slab, Site 2 (Photo: Archaeological Survey of India).

221. The Buddha's Victory Over Māra, *āyaka* panel, Site 2 (Photo: Archaeological Survey of India).

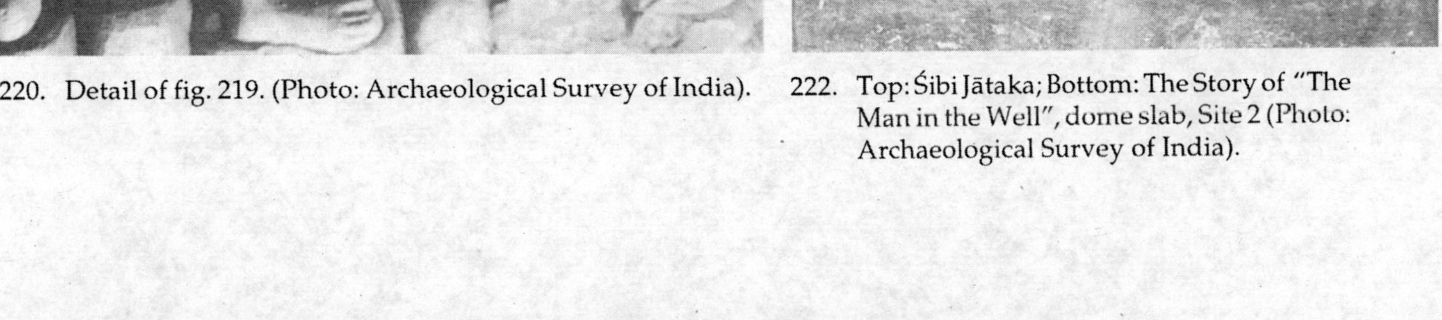

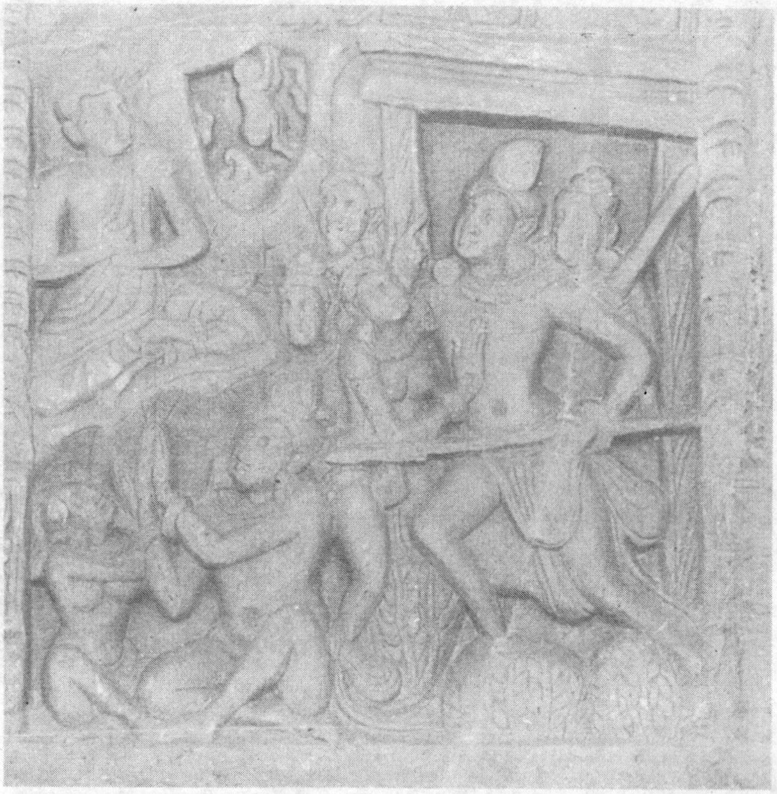

223. "The Man in the Well", detail of fig. 222.

224. One of the "Four Sights" (Siddhārtha Sees a Corpse), detail of a dome slab (Photo: Archaeological Survey of India).

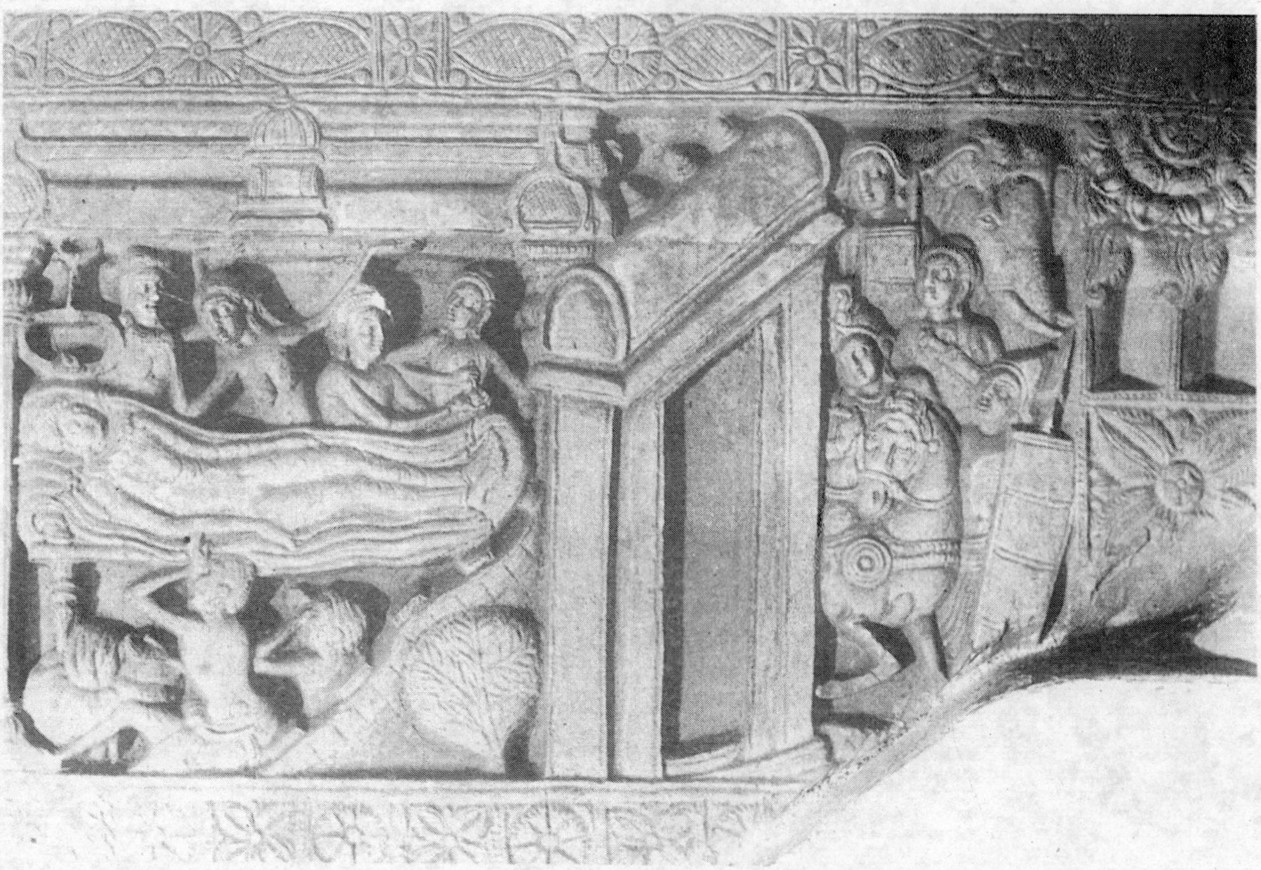

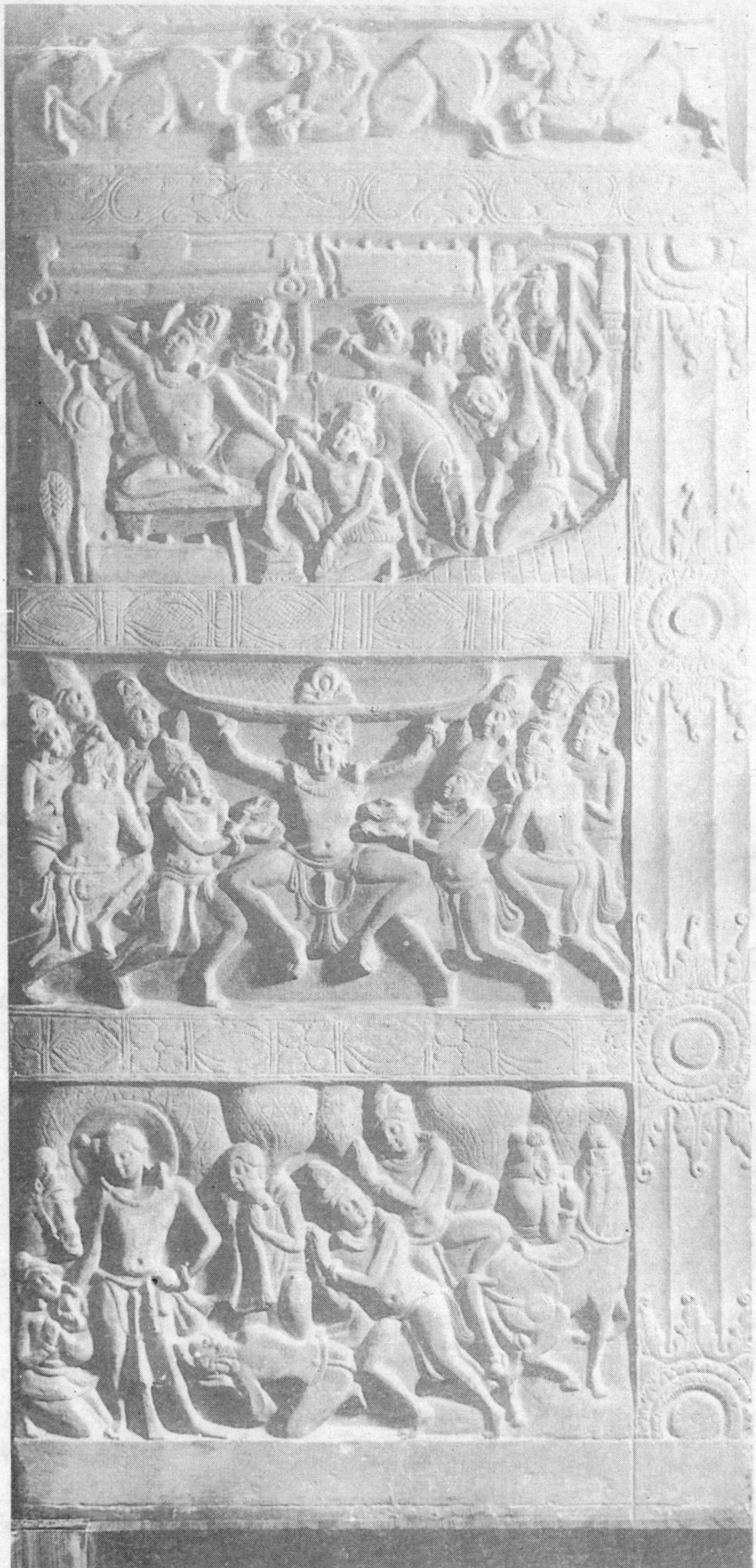

225. Top: Śuddhodana's Grief Upon the News of His Son's Renunciation; Middle: Transportation of the Buddha's Turban to Heaven; Bottom: Śākyamuni Changing Clothes with the Hunter; dome slab from Site 2 (Photo: Archaeological Survey of India).

226. Unidentified scene, detail of a dome slab from Site 2 (Photo: Archaeological Survey of India).

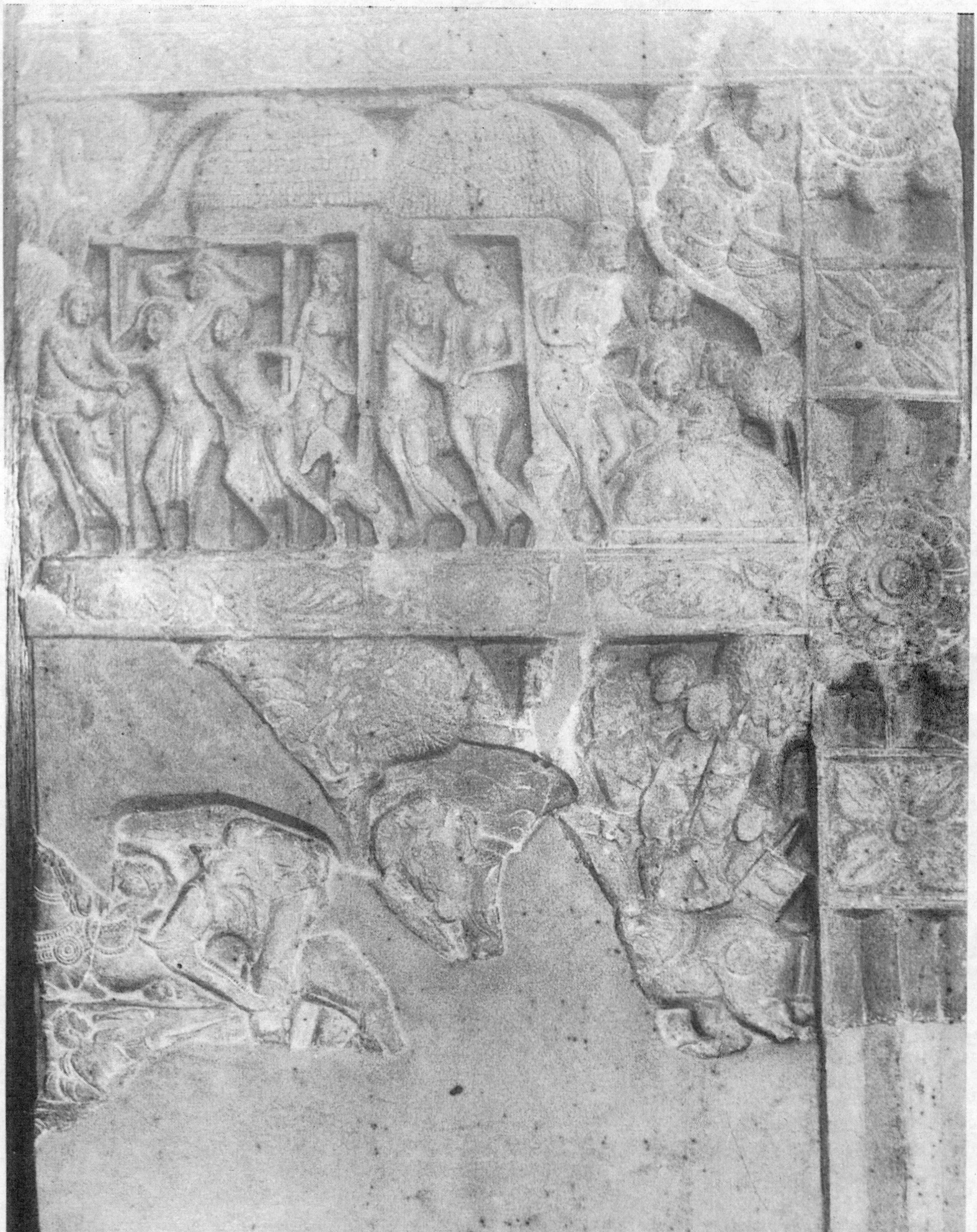

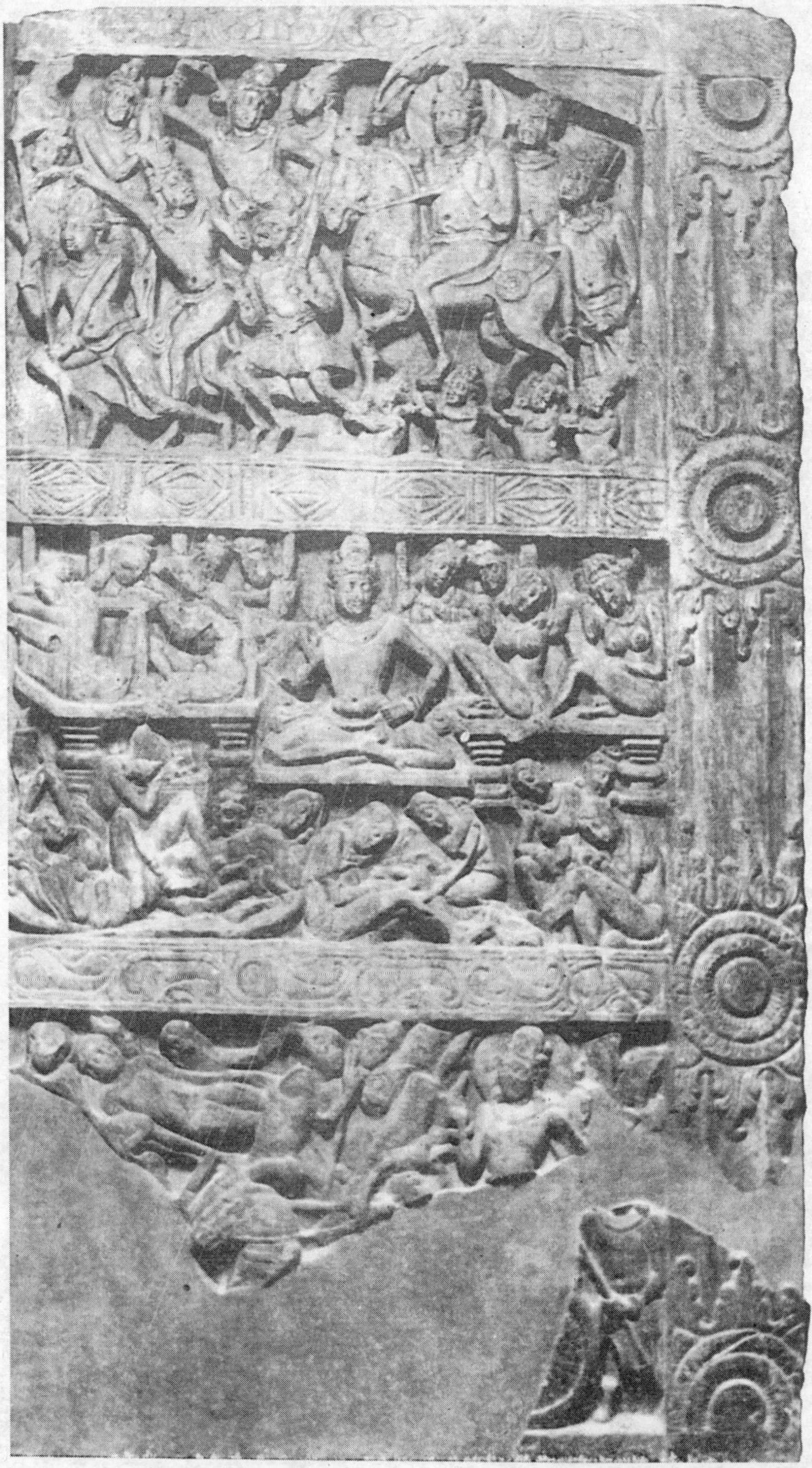

227. Top: The Great Departure; Middle: Siddhārtha in His Palace; Bottom: One of the "Four Sights" (Siddhārtha Sees a Corpse) (Photo: Archaeological Survey of India).

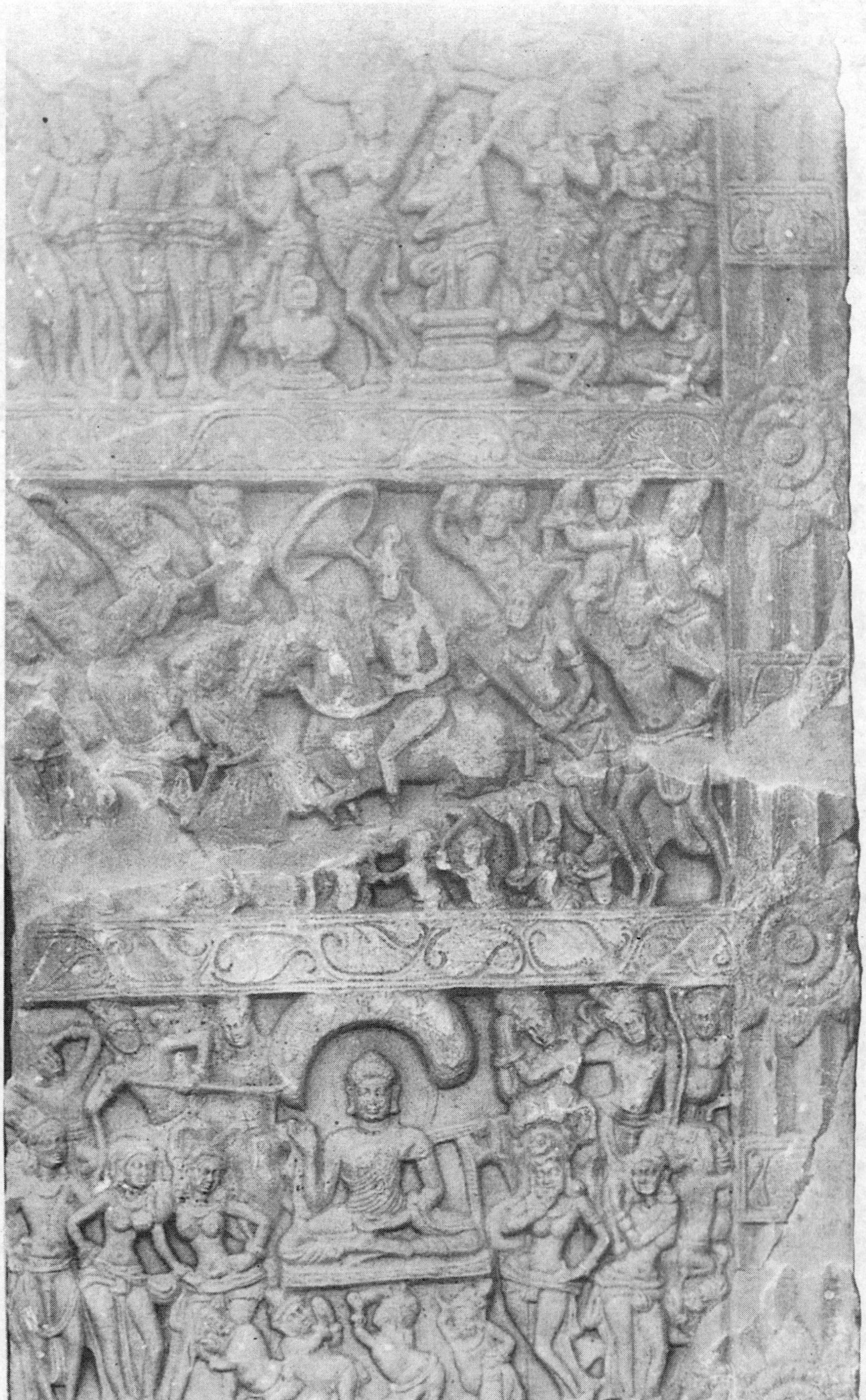

228. Top: The Nativity and the Seven Steps; Middle: The Great Departure; Bottom: The Temptation of the Buddha, dome slab (Photo: Archaeological Survey of India).

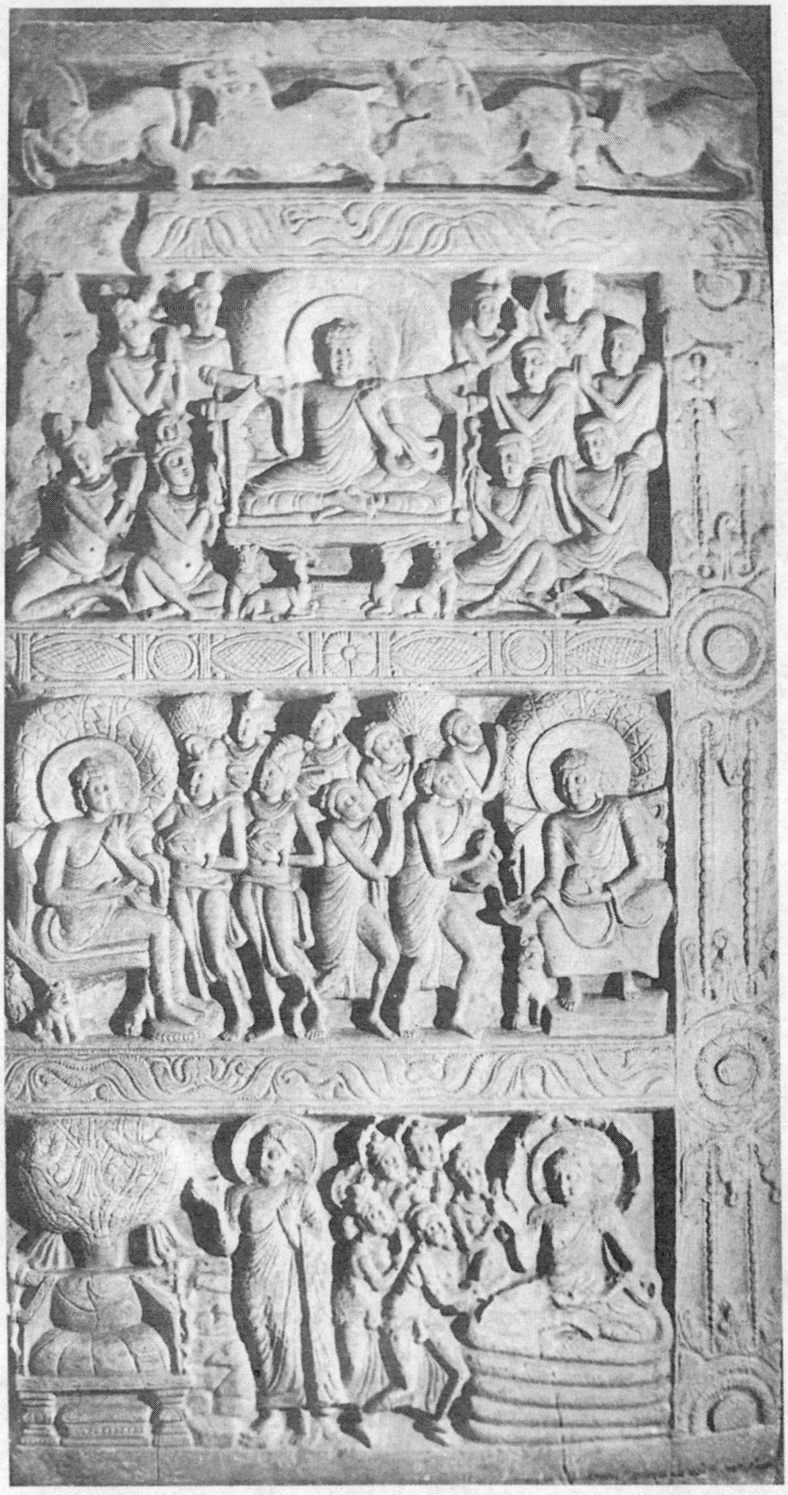

229. Top: The First Sermon in the Deer Park at Banaras; Middle: Two Episodes in which Merchants Feed the Buddha After His Enlightenment and the Buddha Protected by Nāga Mucilinda, dome slab reported to be from Site 2.

230. Memorial Pillar to Queen Varmabhattā, dated in the 11th regnal year of King Rudrapuruṣadatta, c. A.D. 301-11.

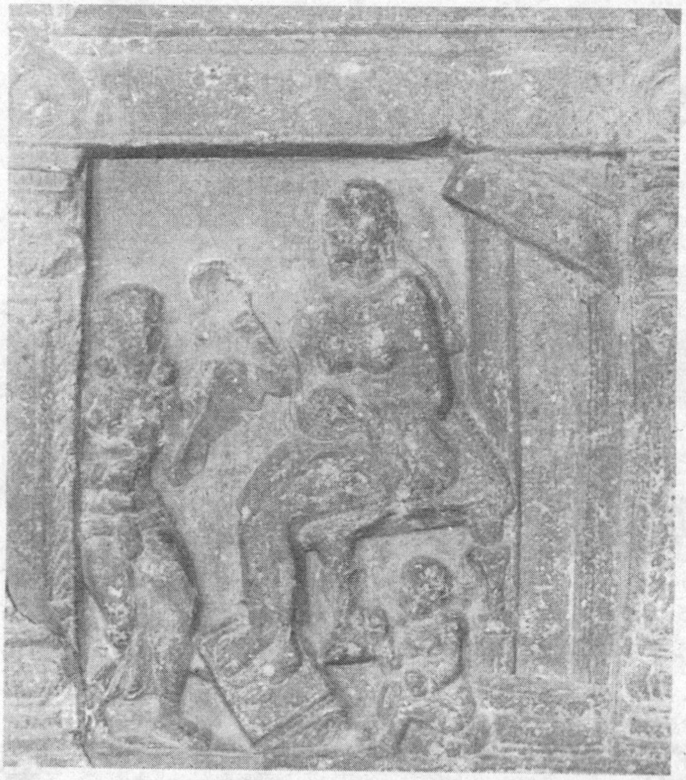

231. Detail of fig. 230.

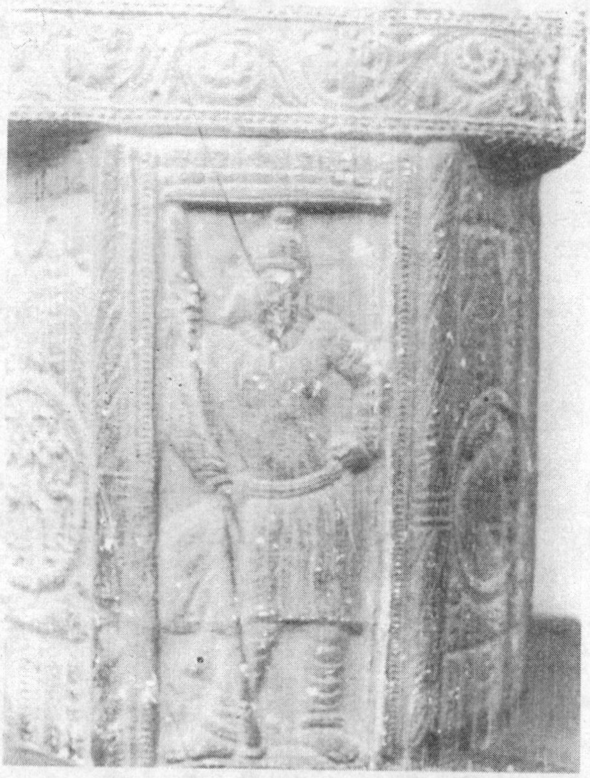

232. Scythian type guardian figure on a pillar from Site 37, now National Museum, New Delhi.

233. Adonis Sarcophagus (fragment), Rome, Villa Borghese, (line drawing: C. Robert, *Die Antiken Sarkophag-Reliefs III,* Vol. 1961, pl. II, No. 10).

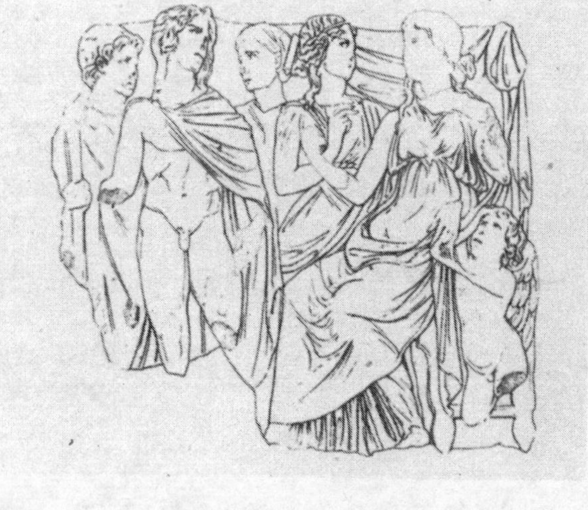

234. Adonis Sarcophagus (fragment), Rome, Villa Medici (line drawing: C. Robert, *Die Antiken Sarkophag-Reliefs III,* Vol. 2, Rome, 1969, pl. II, No. 9).

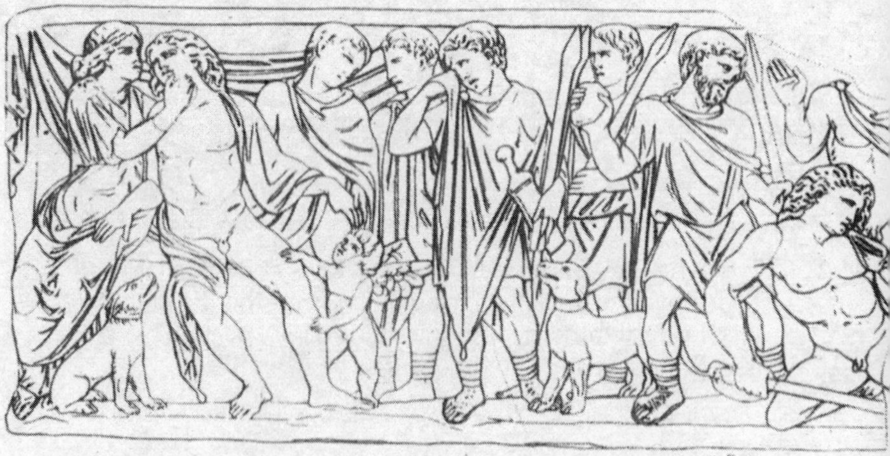

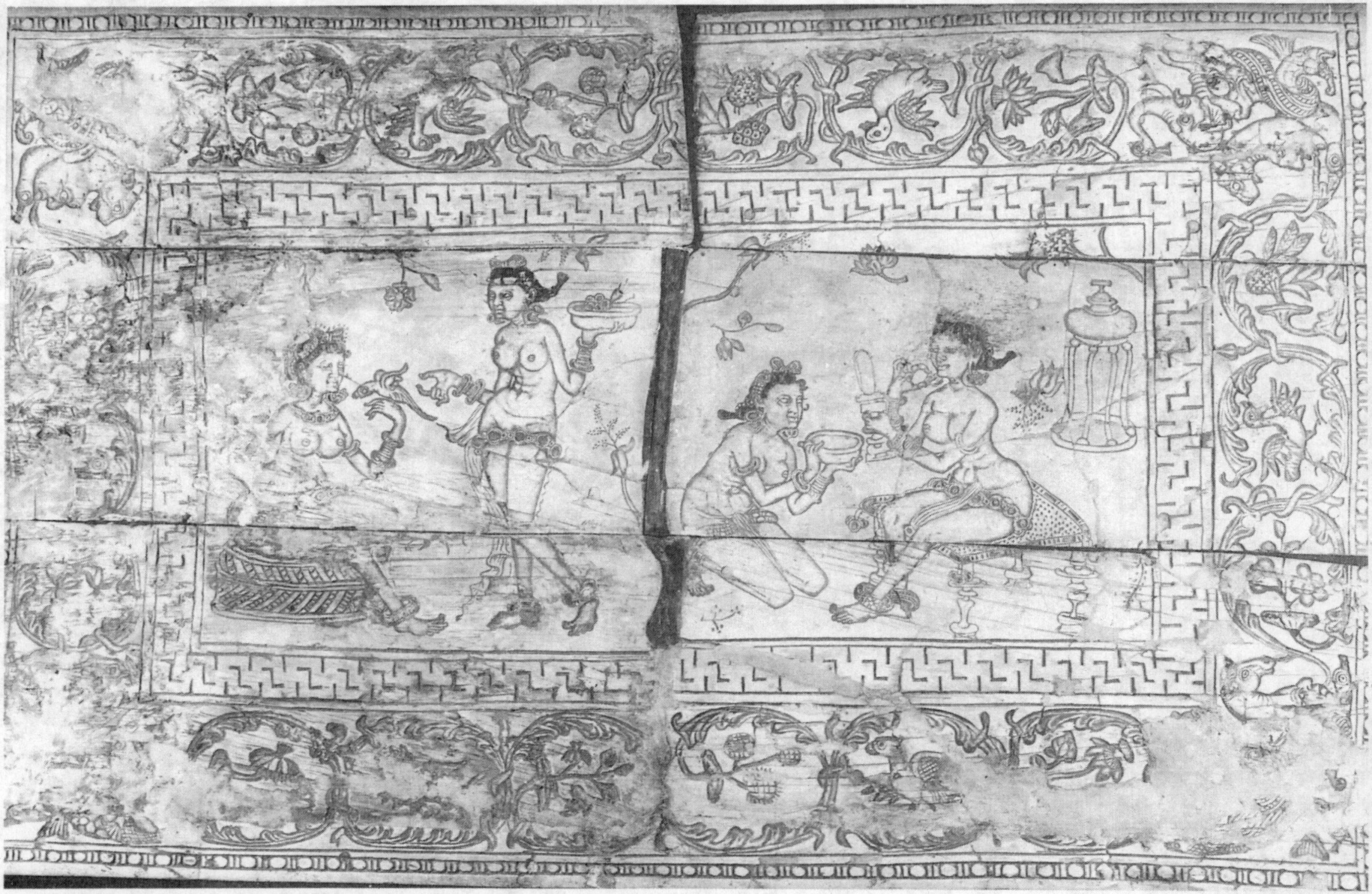

235. Detail of Coffret IX, Begram, now Kabul Museum (Photo: Dominique Darbois).

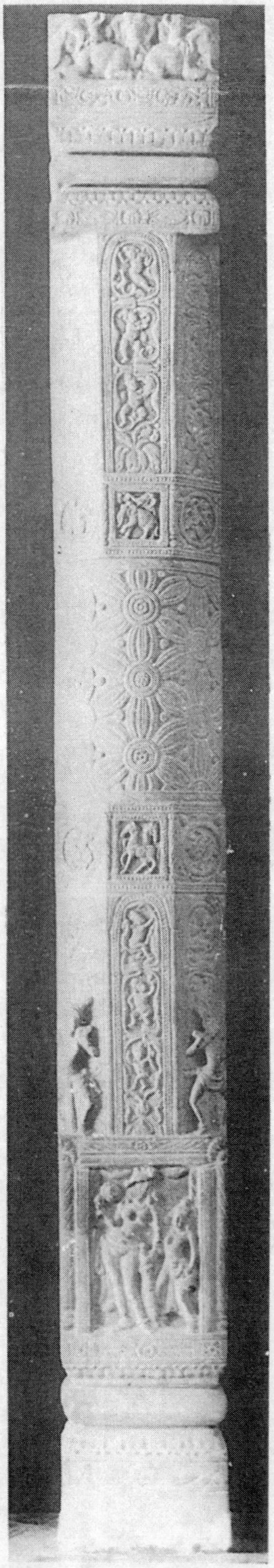

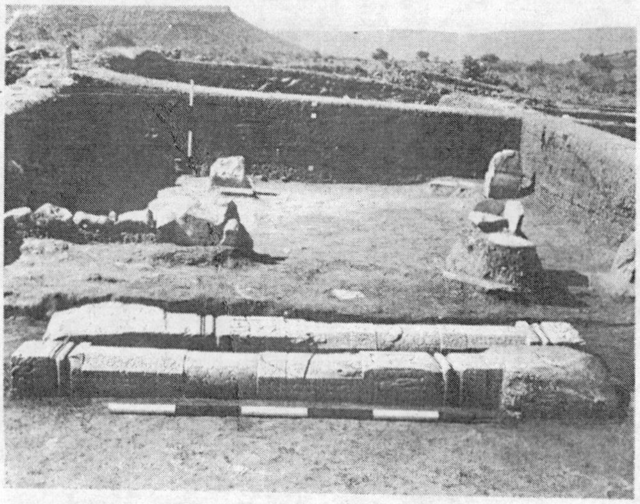

236. Pillars from the Aṣṭabhujsvāmin Temple *in situ* (Photo: Archaeological Survey of India).

237. Pillar from the Aṣṭabhujsvāmin Temple (Photo: Archaeological Survey of India).

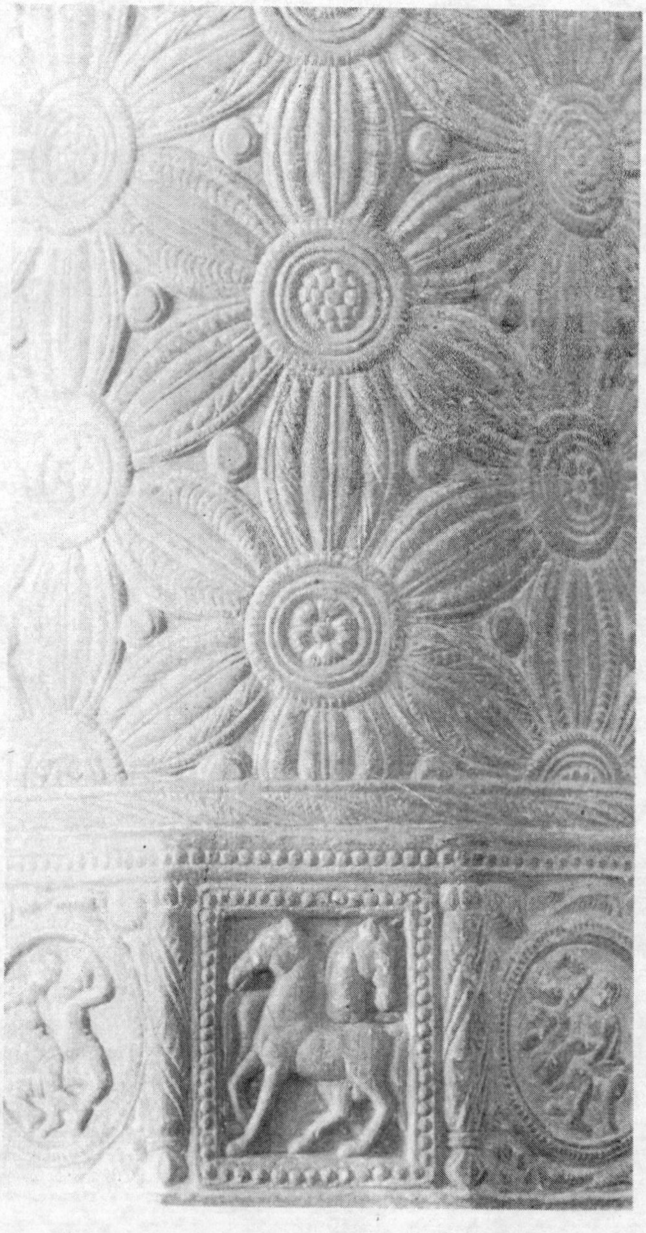

238. Detail of fig. 237.

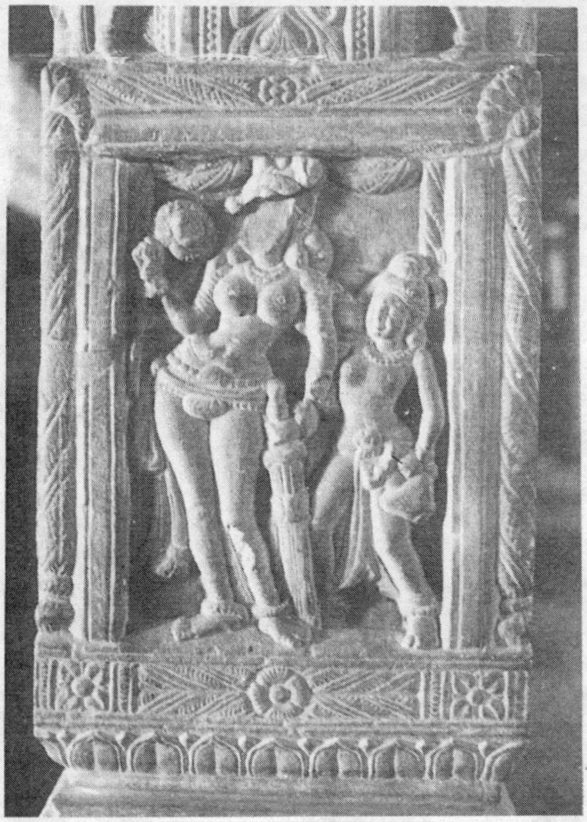

239. Detail of fig. 237.

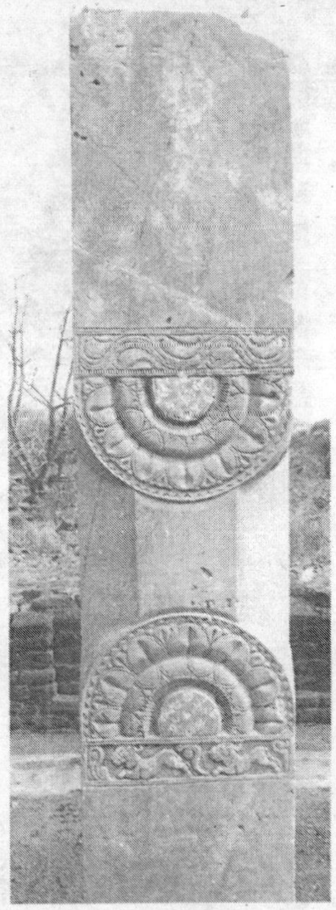

240. Pillar, Site 4.

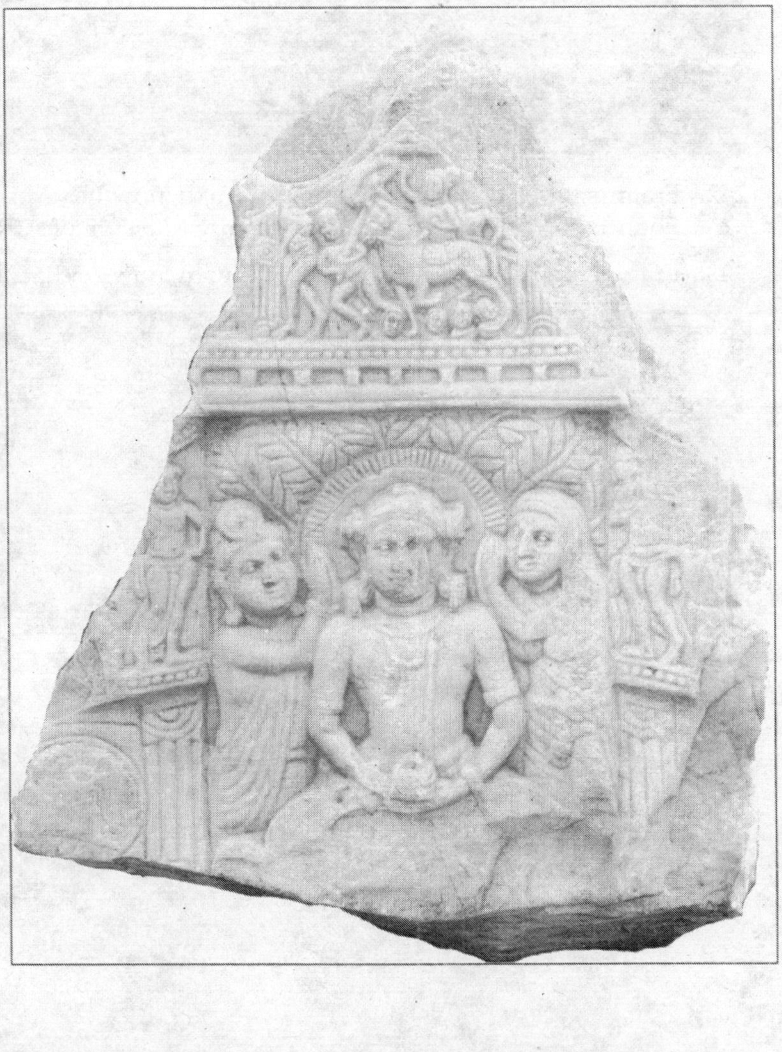

241. Siddhārtha Meditating Under the Jambu Tree and the Great Departure, fragment of a *caitya* slab, Gummididurru, now Los Angeles County Museum of Art, Gift of the Ahmonson Foundation (Photo: Los Angeles County Museum of Art).

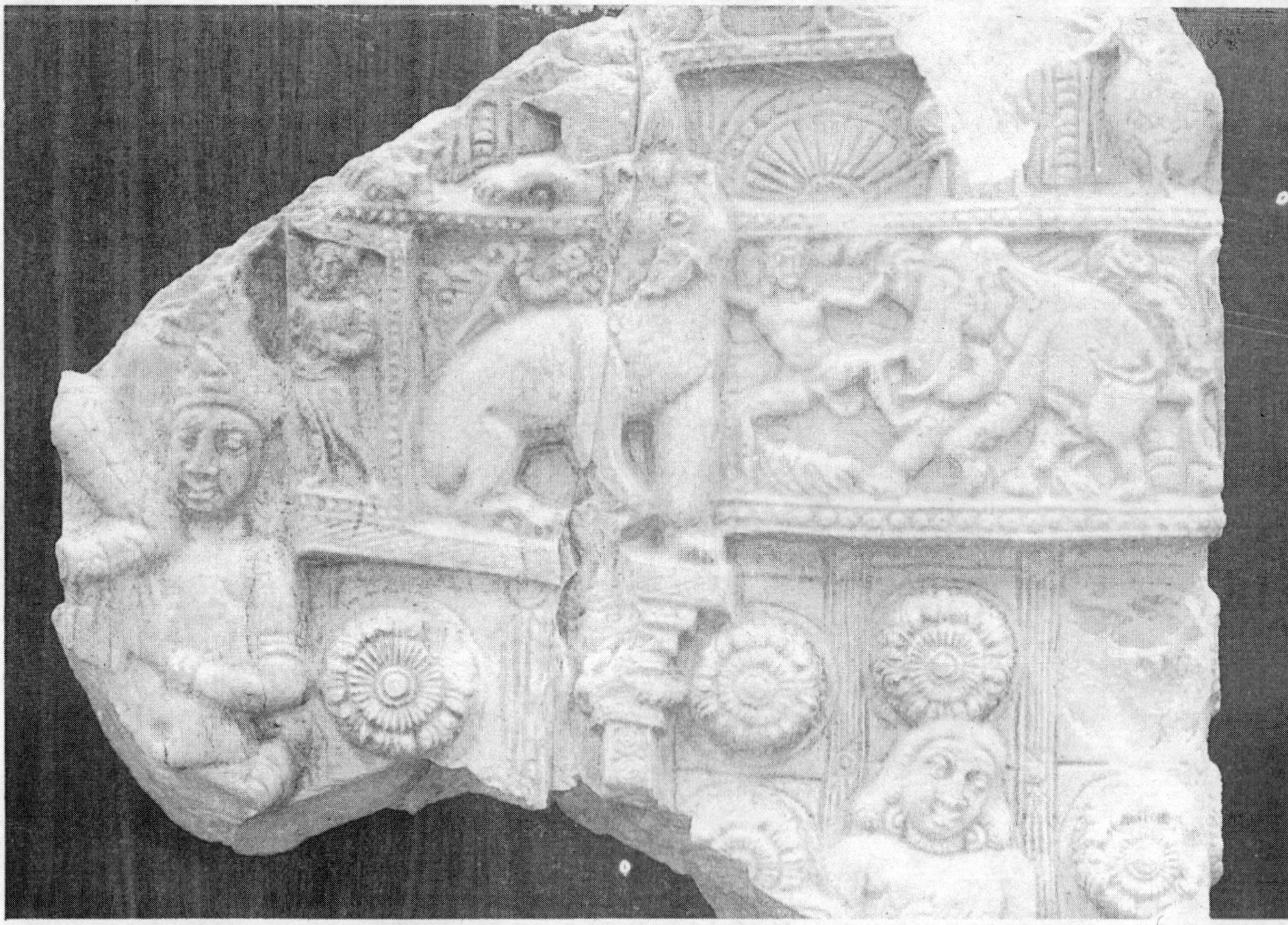

242. Fragment of a *caitya* slab, Gummididurru, now Los Angeles County Museum of Art, Gift of the Ahmonson Foundation (Photo: Los Angeles County Museum of Art).

243. Fragment of a *caitya* slab, Gummididurru, now Archaeological Museum, Amarāvatī.

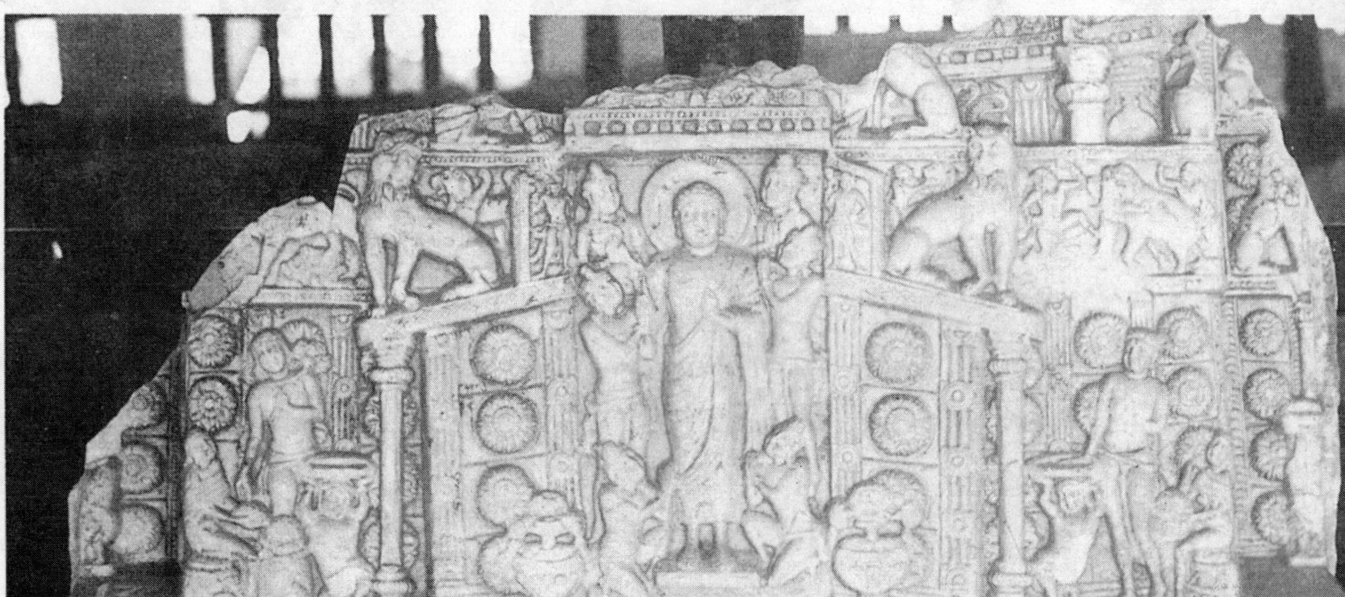

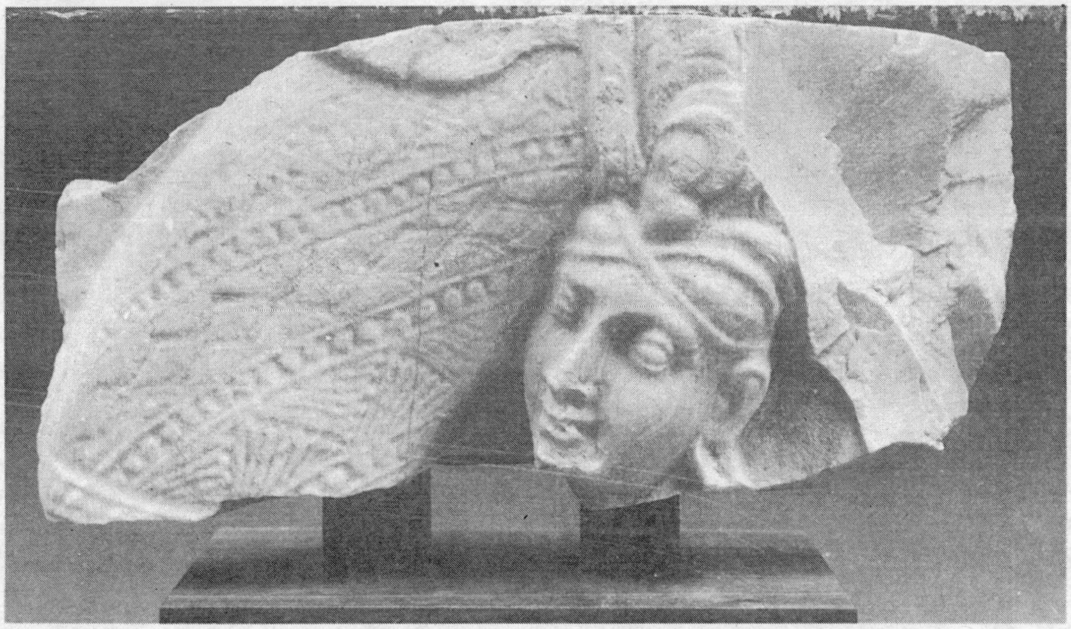

244. Fragment of a coping stone, Gummididurru, now Los Angeles County Museum of Art, Gift to the Ahmonson Foundation (Photo: Los Angeles County Museum of Art).

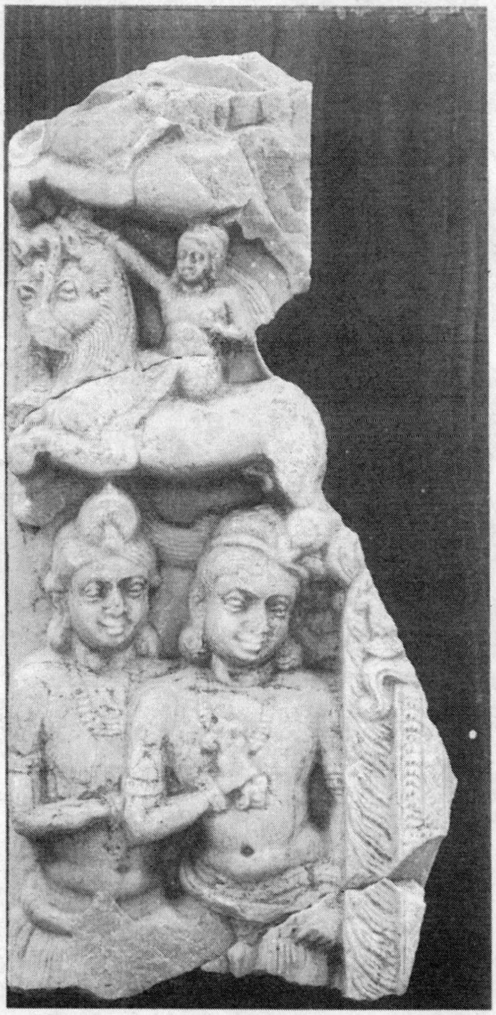

245. Fragment of a drum slab, Gummididurru, now Los Angeles County Funds (Photo: Los Angeles County Museum of Art).

246. Detail of fig. 114.

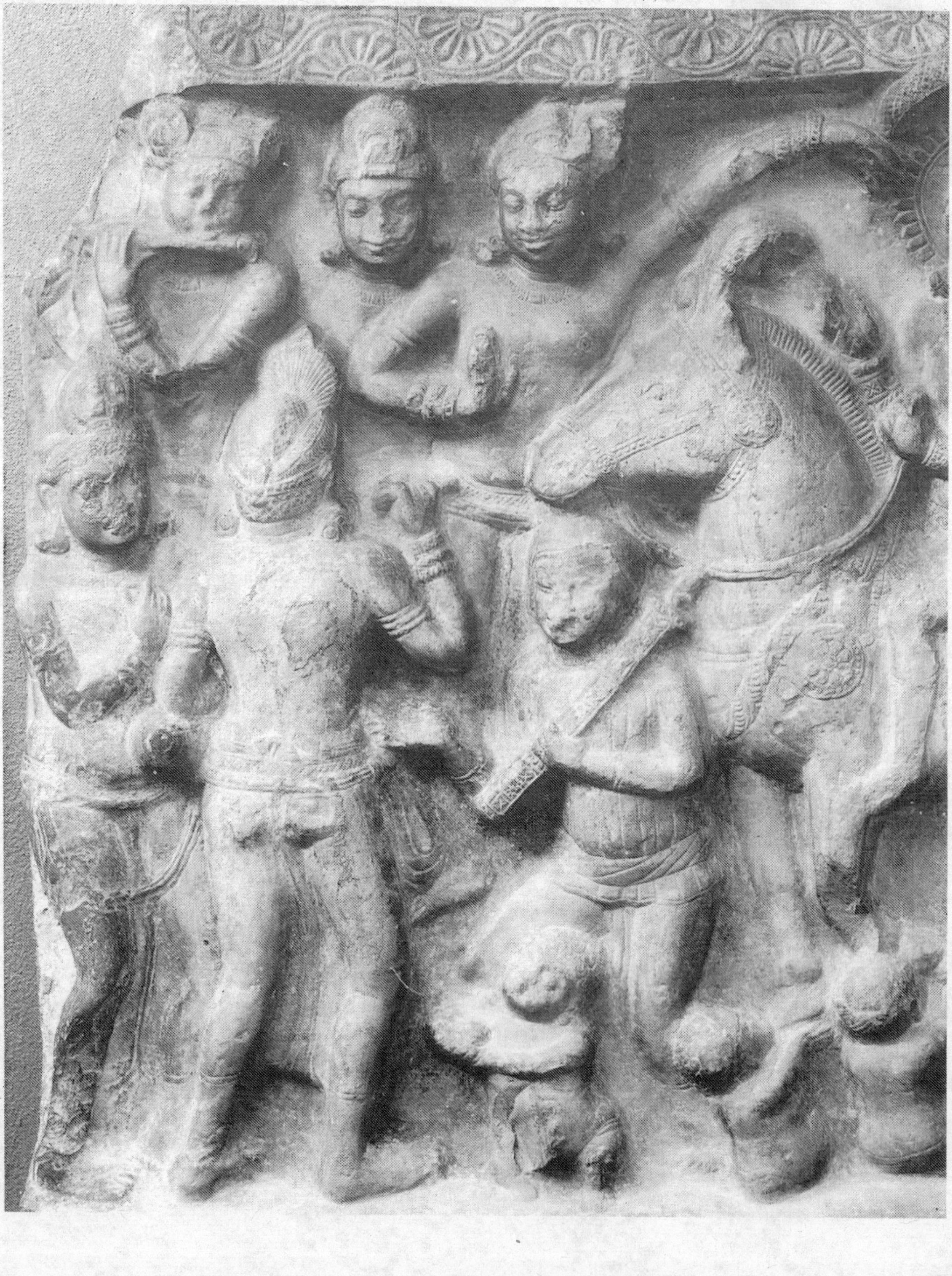

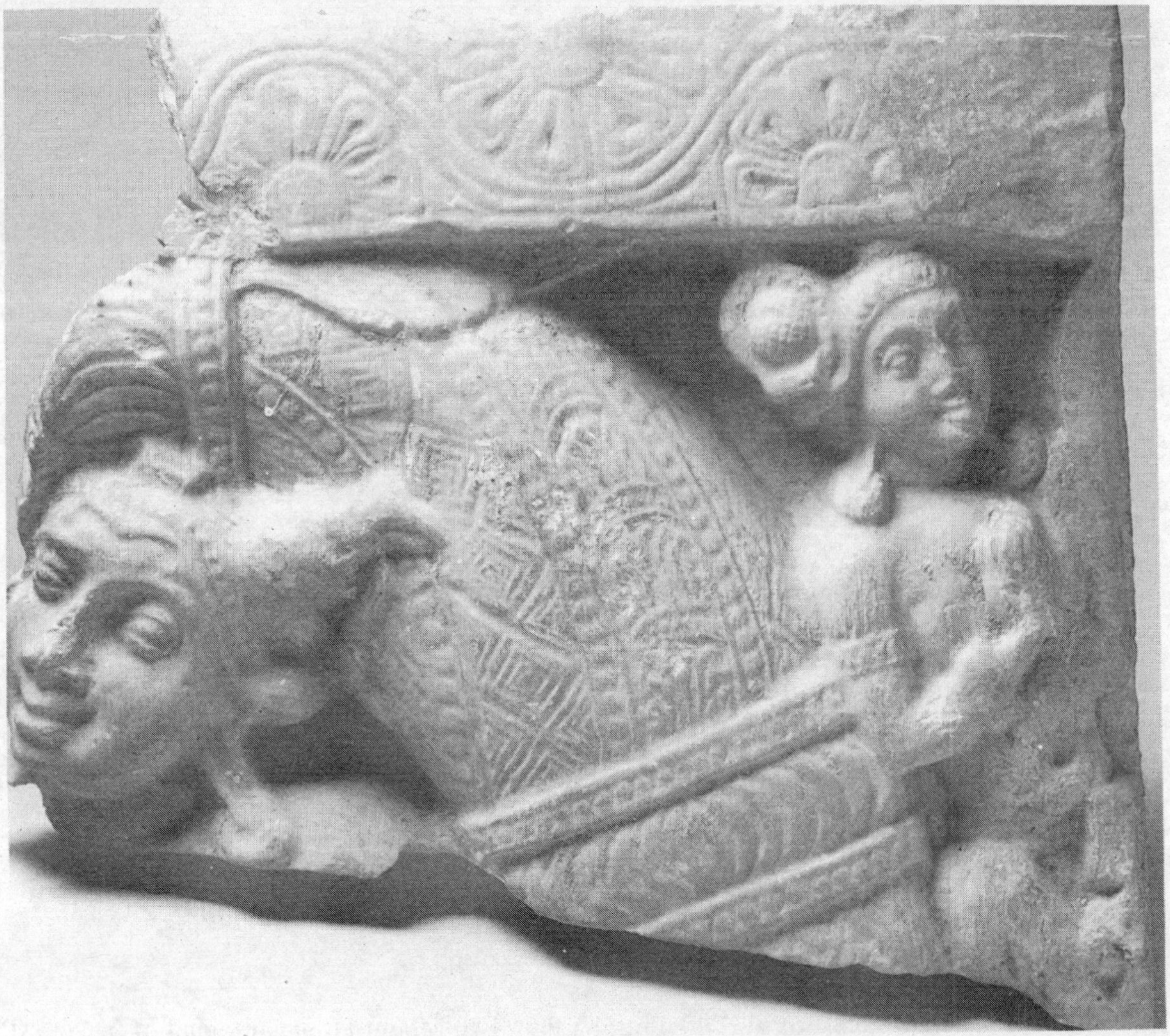

247. Fragment of a coping stone, Gummididurru, now Asian Art Museum of San Francisco: The Avery Brundage Collection (Photo: Asian Art Museum of San Francisco).

248. The Mandhātu Jātaka, detail of fig. 64.

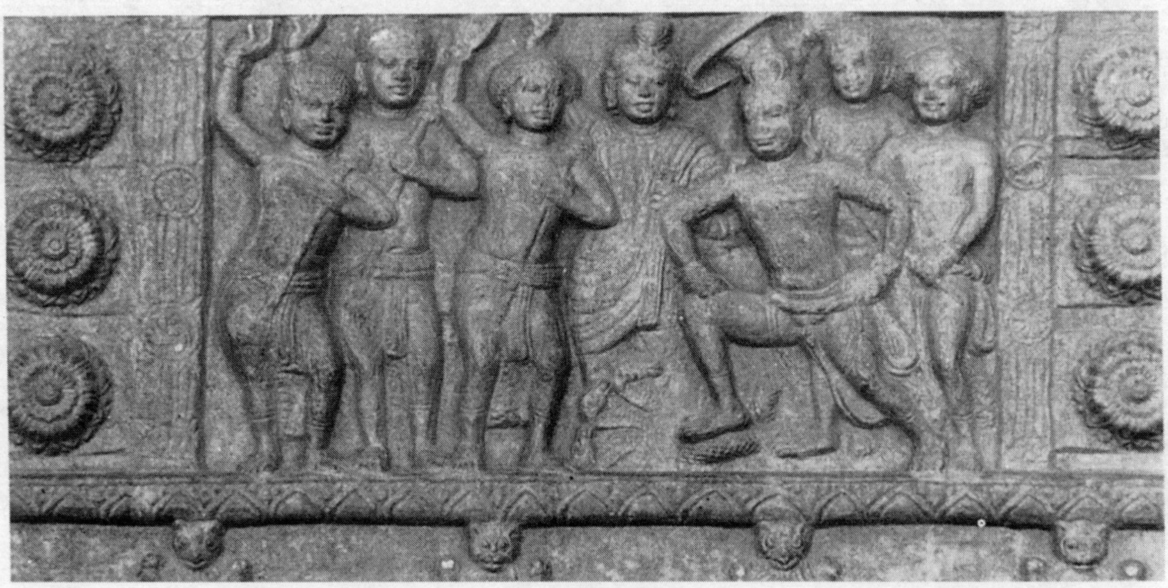

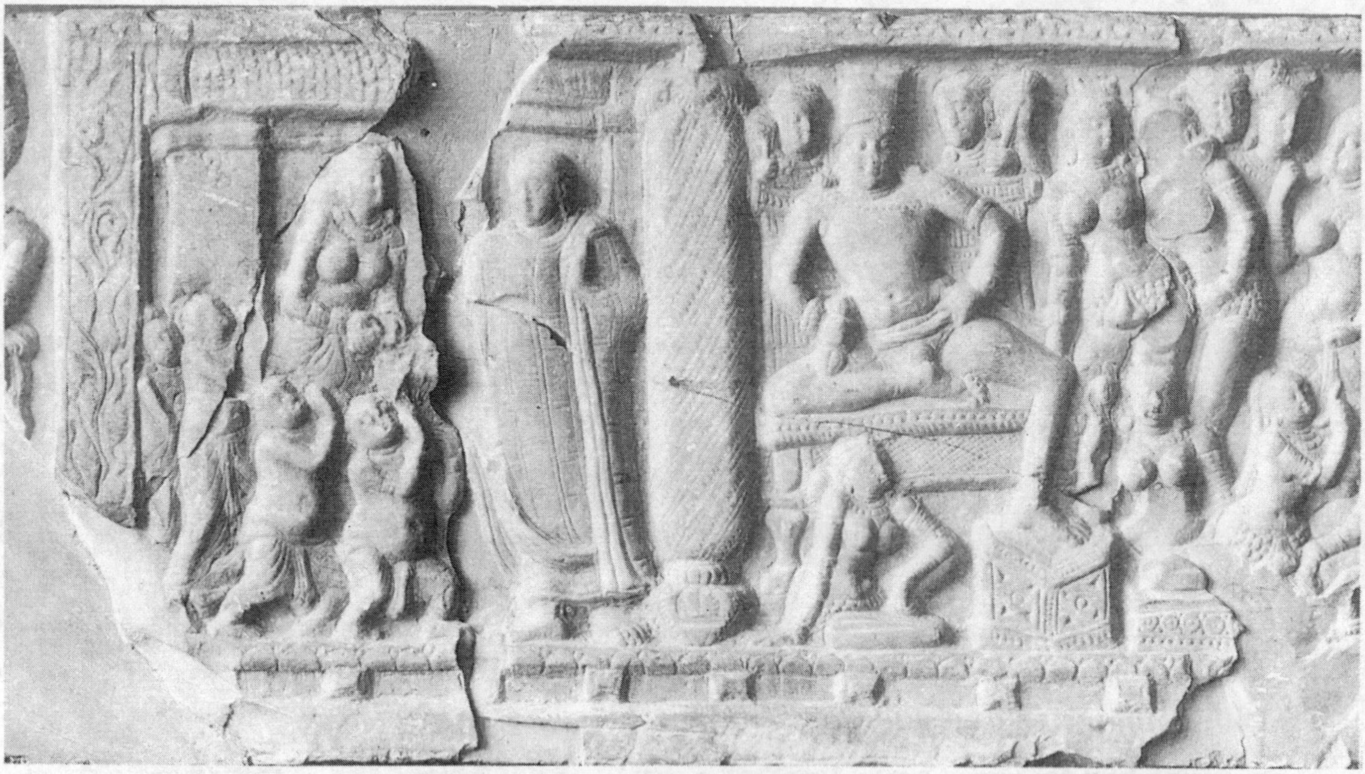

249. The Paradise of Indra and Nanda Preaching, detail of fig. 185 (Photo: The Metropolitan Museum of Art).

250. The Buddha Preaching to Nanda and the Buddha Flying to Mount Himavat, detail of fig. 185 (Photo: The Metropolitan Museum of Art).

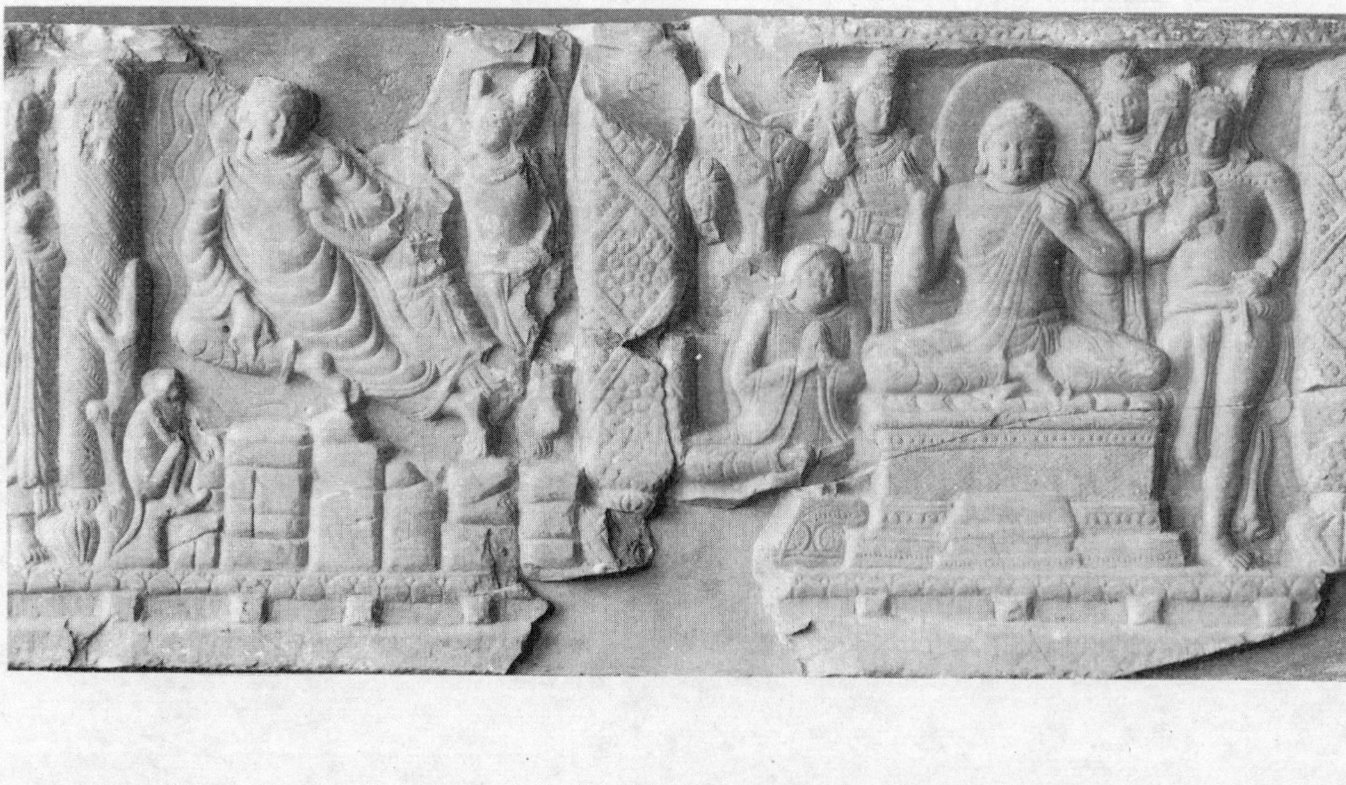

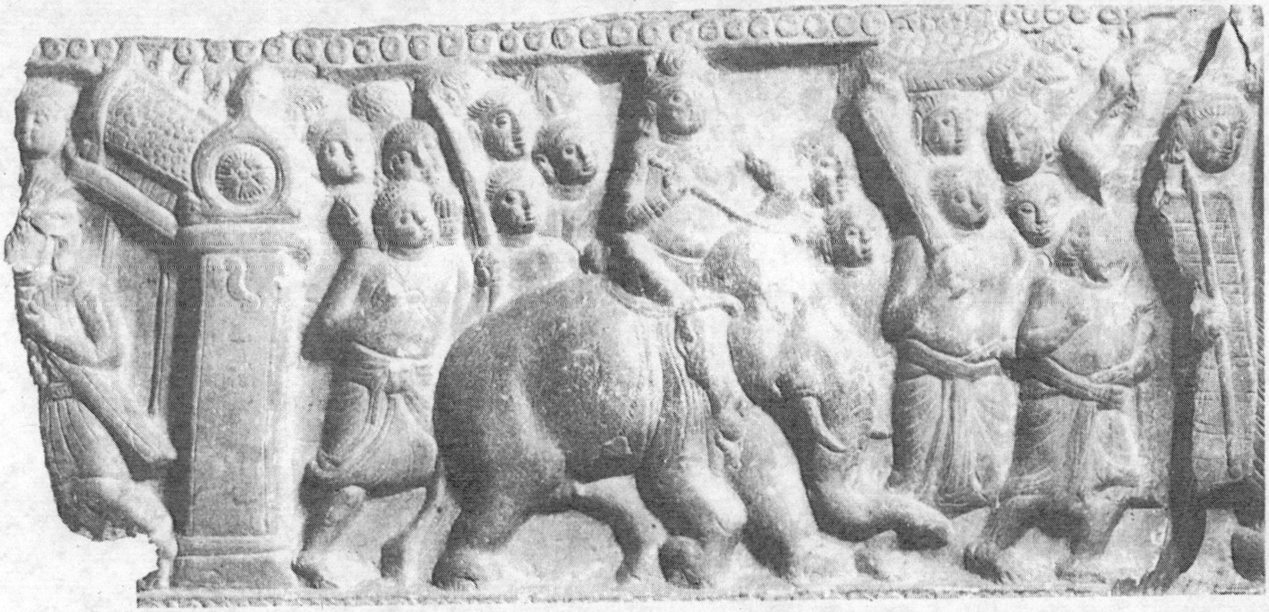

251. The Prince Goes to His Alms House, Viśvaṁtara Jātaka, frieze 2, Goli, now Madras Government Museum) (Photo: Archaeological Survey of India).

252. The Presentation of the Elephant, continuation of fig. 251 (Photo: Archaeologieal Survey of India).

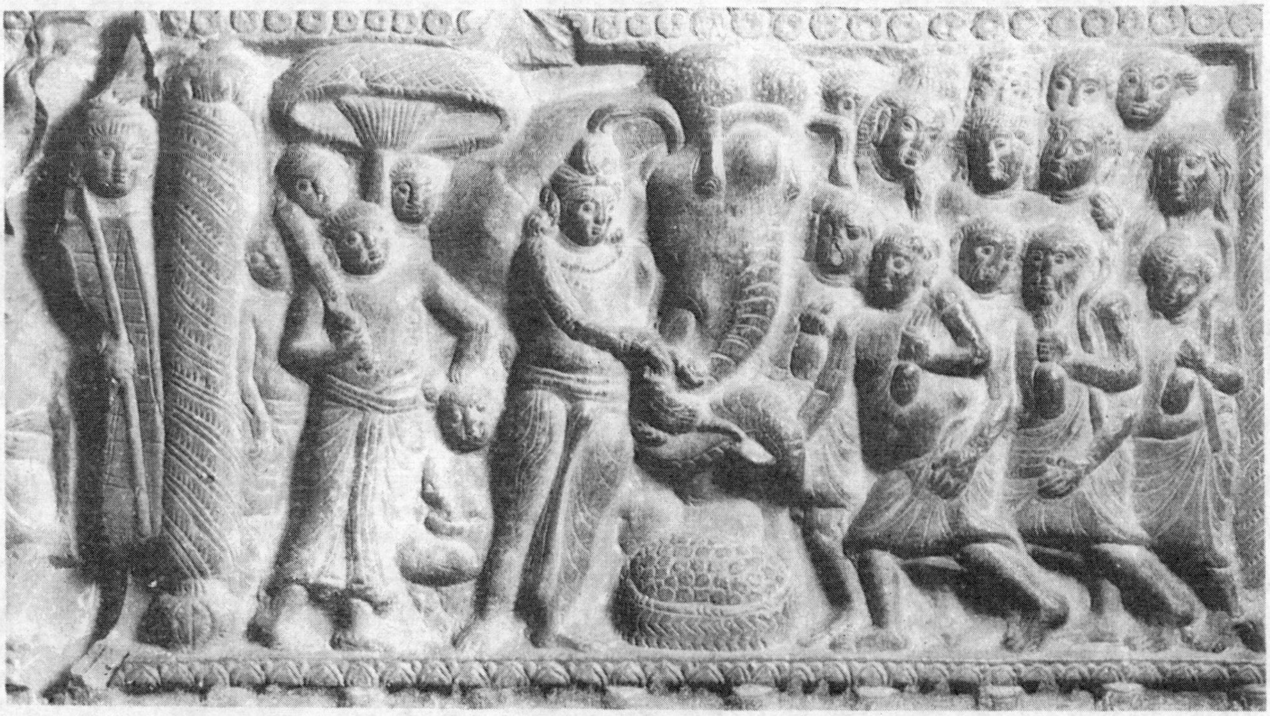

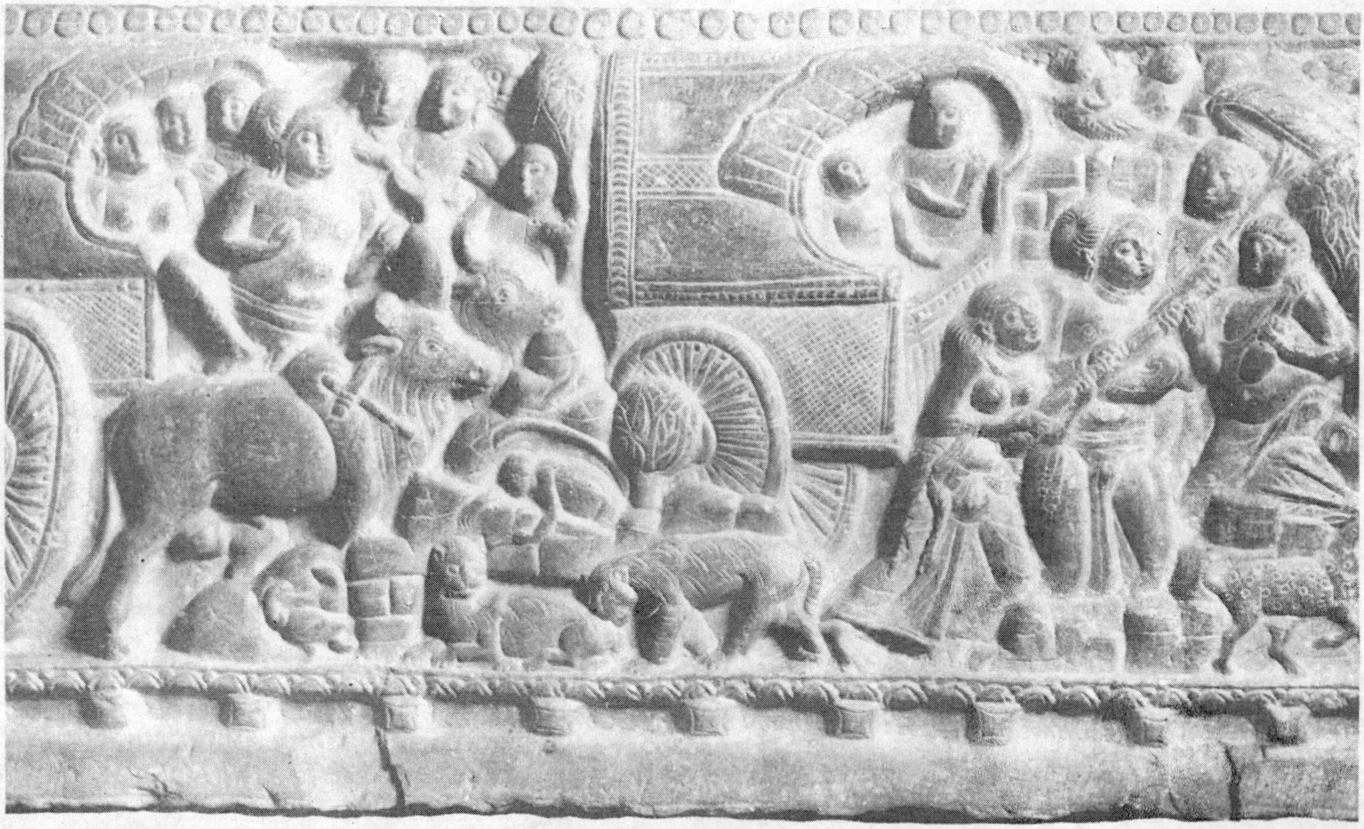

253. Presentation of the Two Bullocks and Presentation of the Cart, continuation of fig. 252 (Photo: Archaeological Survey of India).

254. The Prince and Princess Carrying Their Children and the Presentation of the Children, continuation of fig. 253 (Photo: Archaeological Survey of India).

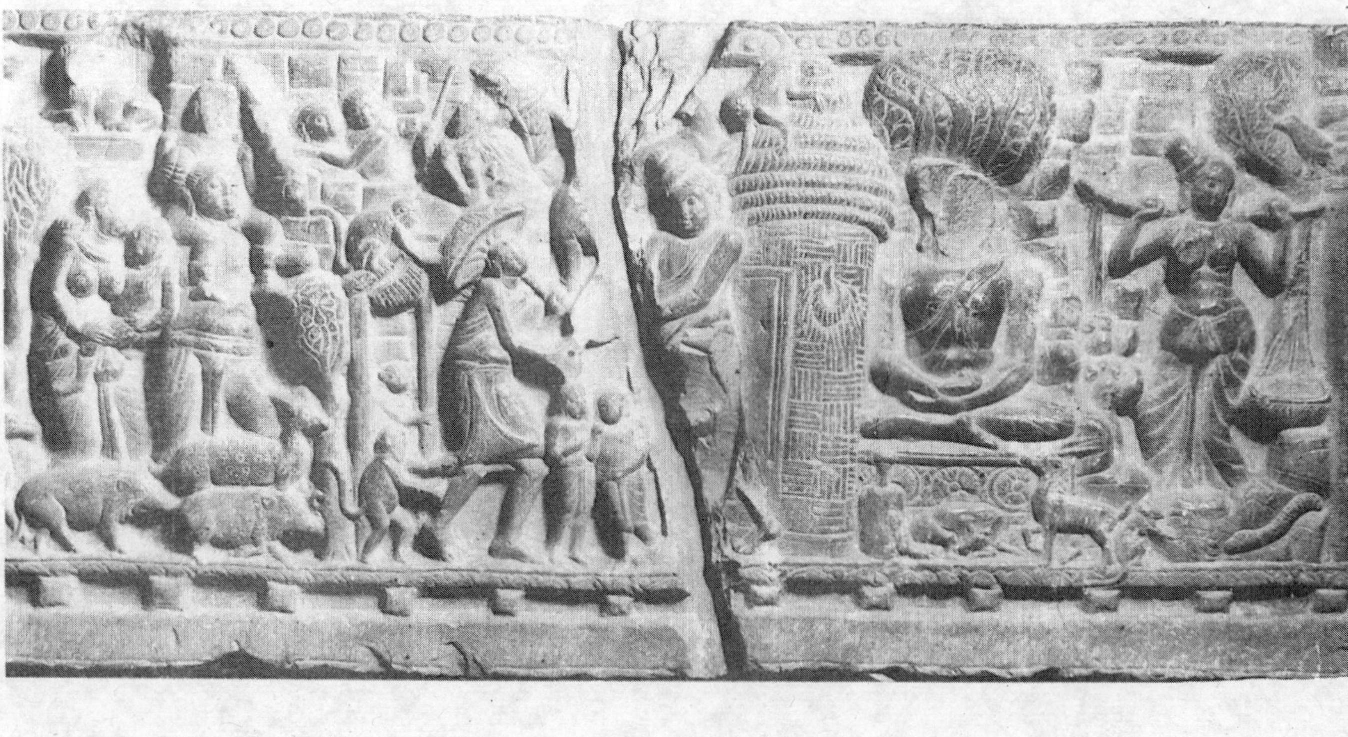

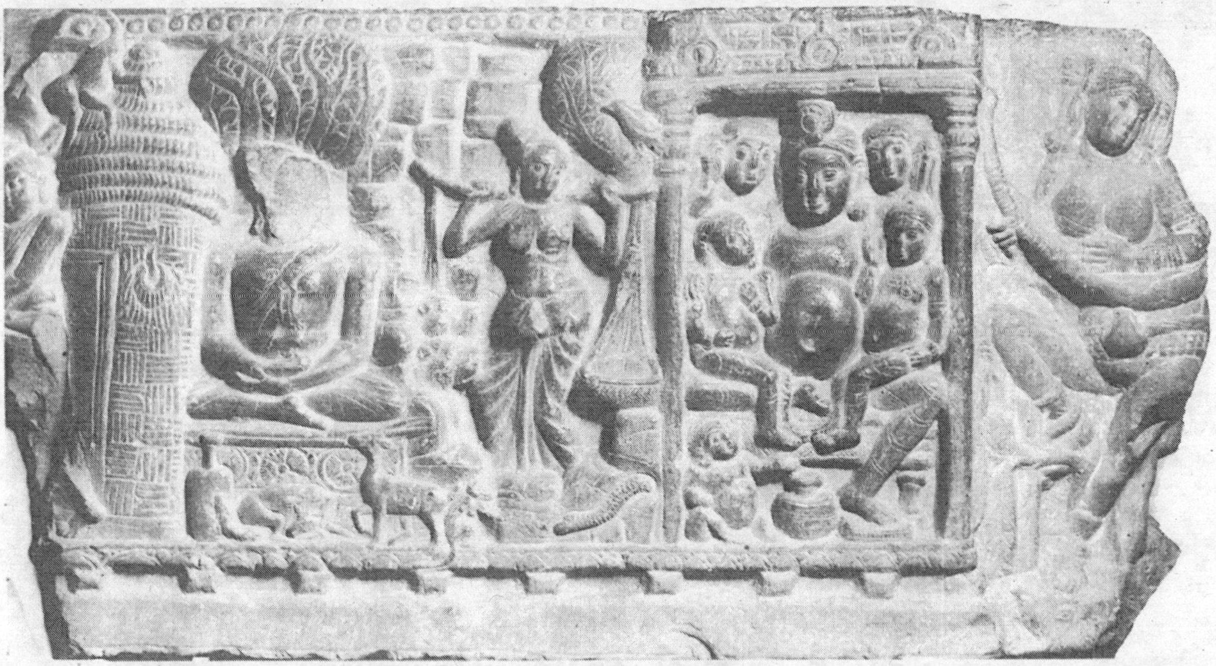

255. The Return of the Princess to the Hermitage, and the Children Liberated by Their Grandfather, continuation of fig. 254 (Photo: Archaeological Survey of India).

256. Javasakuṇa Jātaka, Goli, now The Cleveland Museum of Art, Gift of George P. Bickford, 70-350 (Photo: The Cleveland Museum of Art).

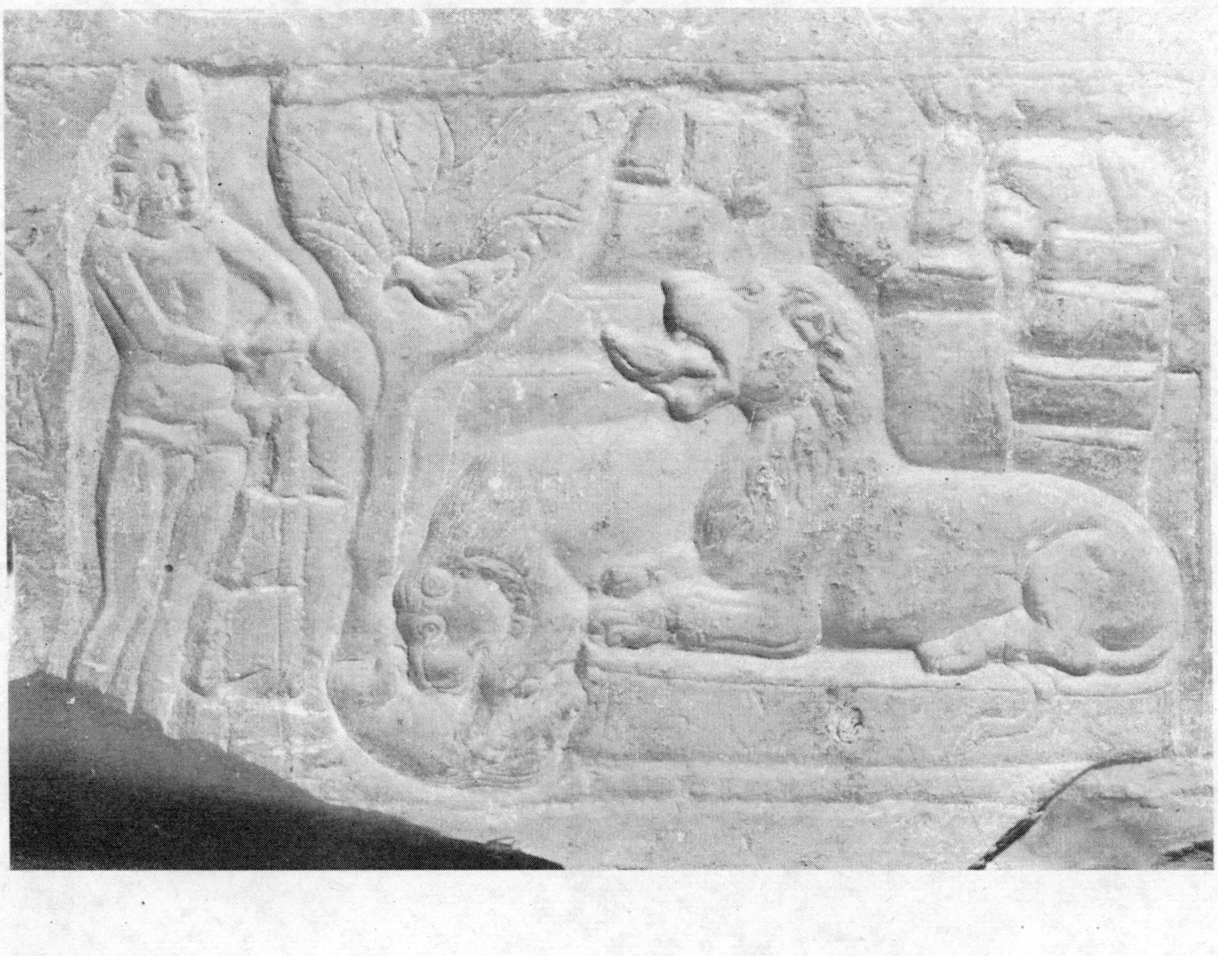

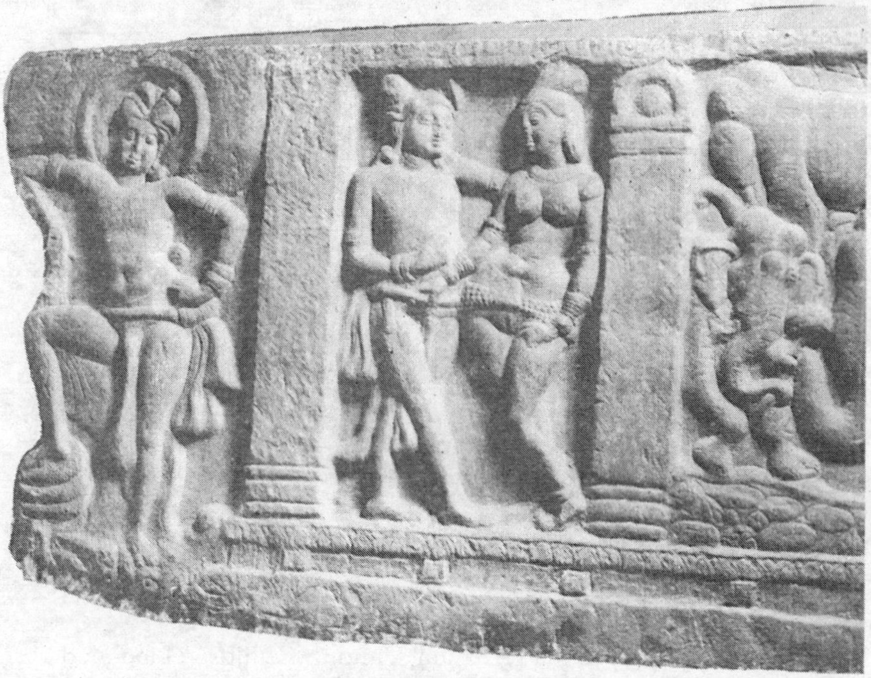

257. Section of Frieze 1, Goli, now Madras Government Museum (Photo: Archaeological Survey of India).

258. Chaddanta Jātaka, continuation of fig. 257 (Photo: Archaeological Survey of India).

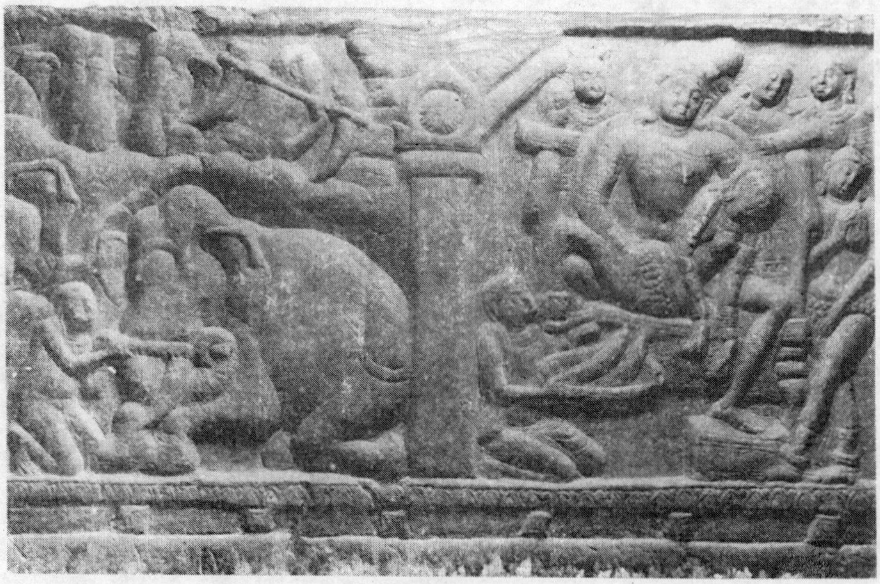

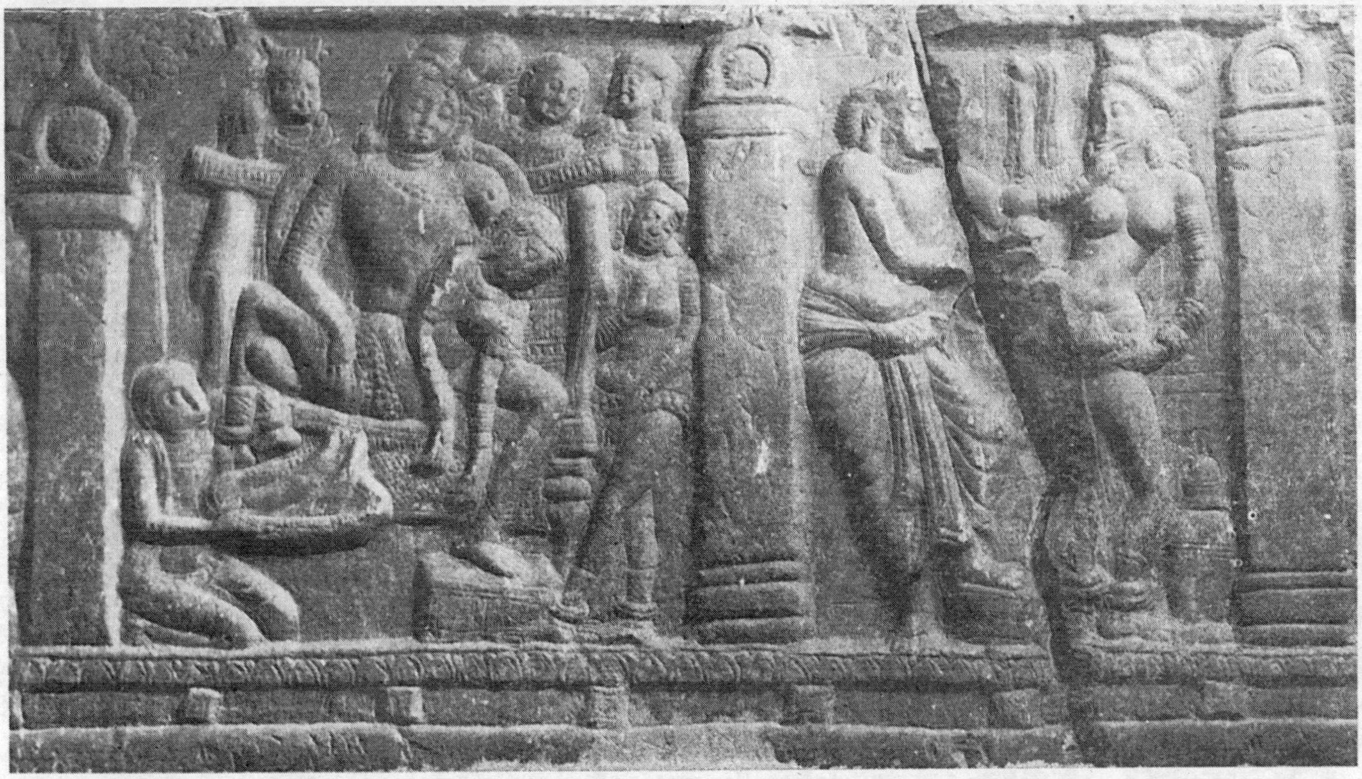

259. Continuation of fig. 258 (Photo: Archaeological Survey of India).

260. The Buddha's Visit to Yaśodhara (Photo: Archaeological Survey of India).

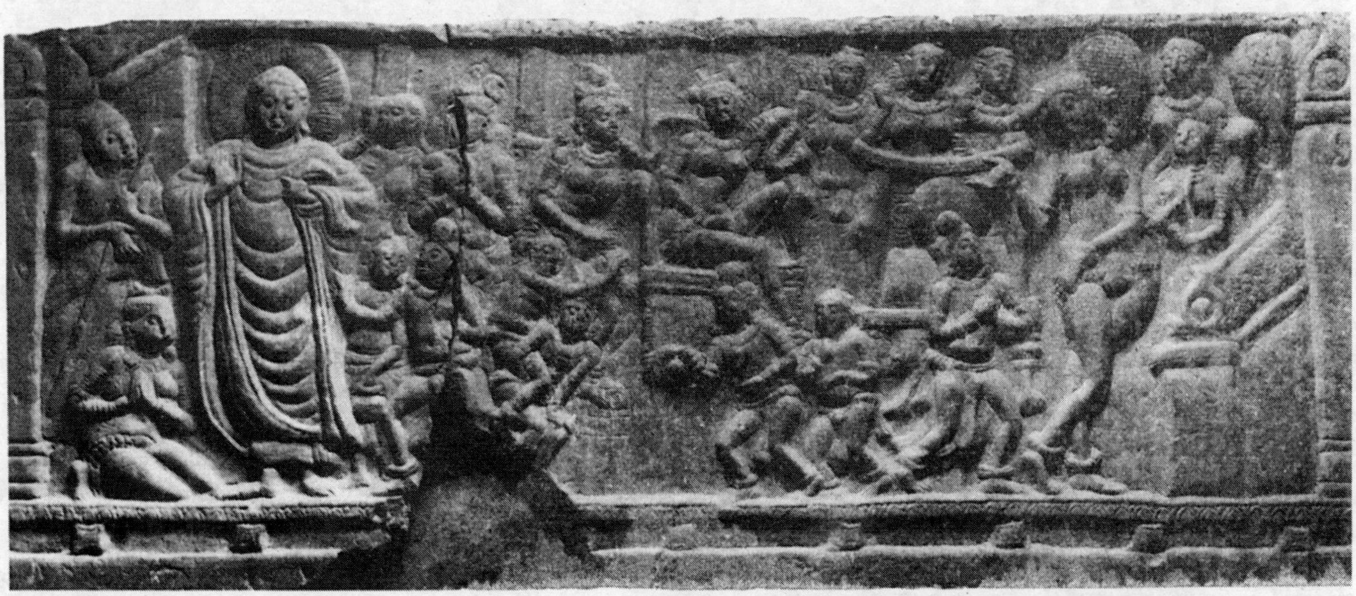

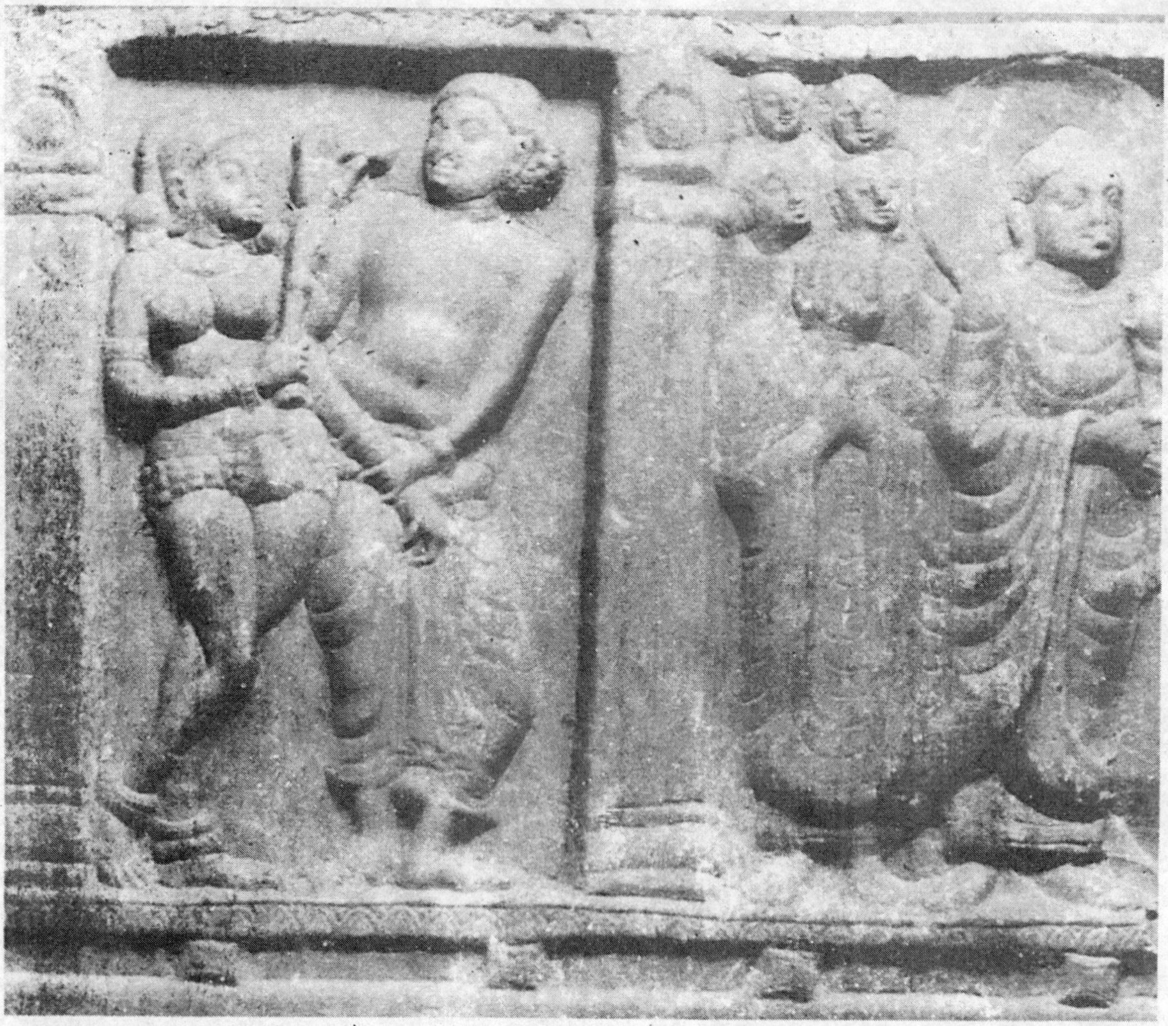

261. Continuation of fig. 260 (Photo: Archaeological Survey of India).

262. Subjugation of the Elephant Nālāgiri, continuation of fig. 261 (Photo: Archaeological Survey of India).

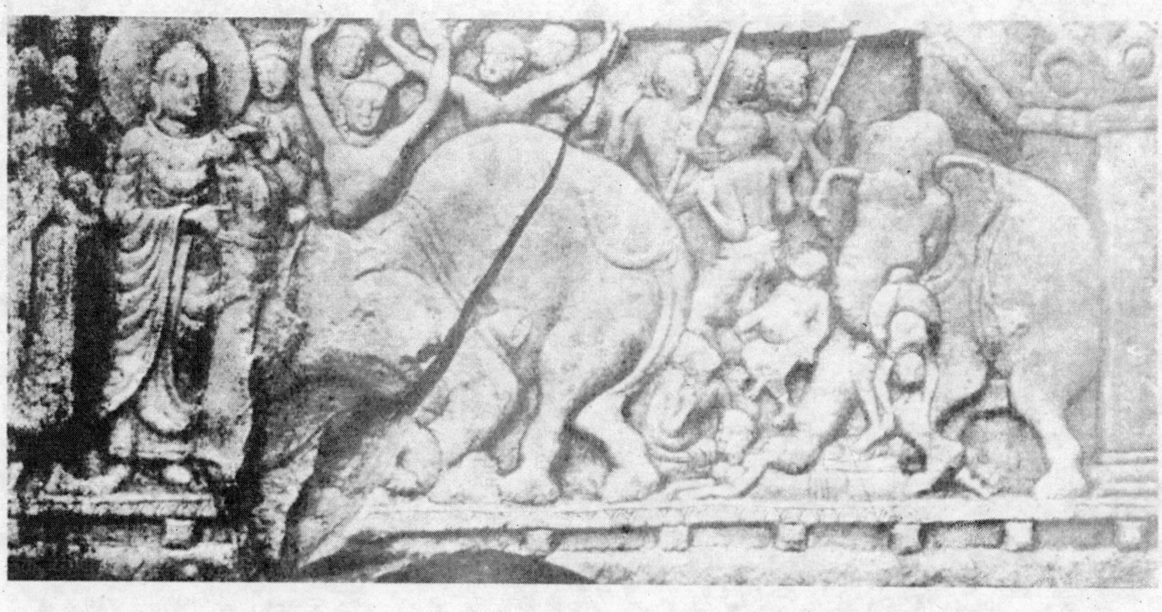

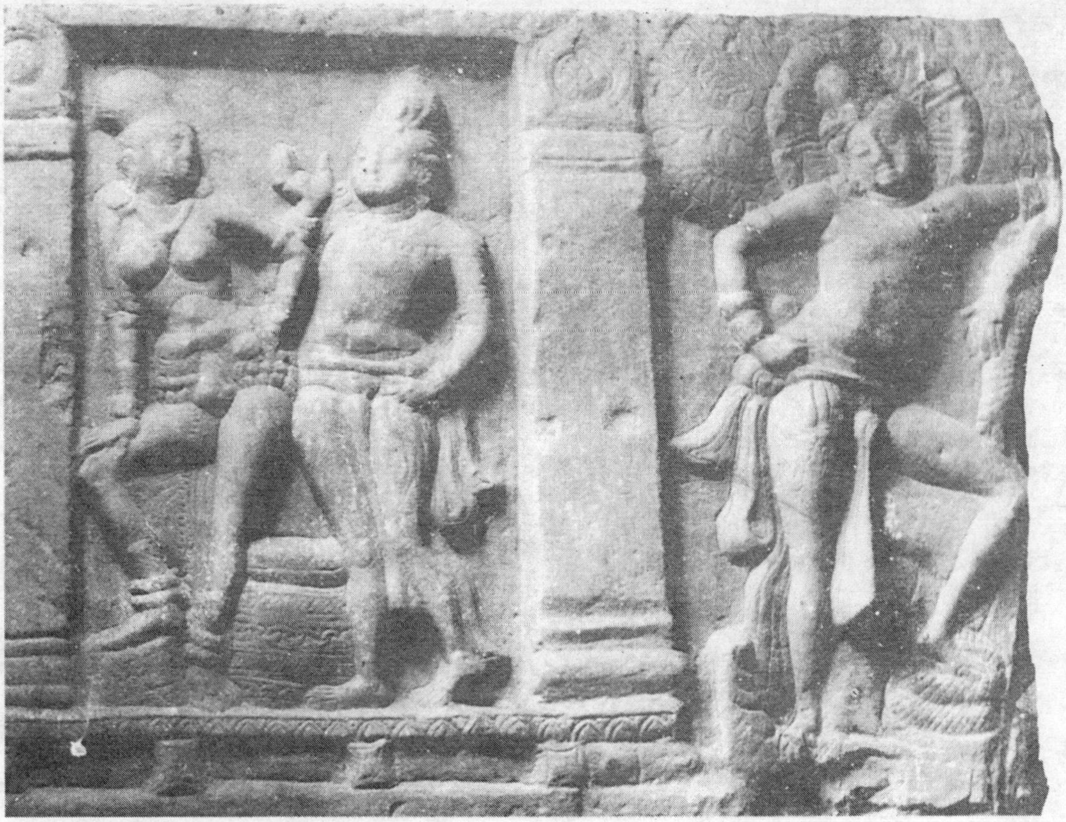

263. Continuation of fig. 262 (Photo: Archaeological Survey of India).

264. Temptation of the Buddha, frieze 3, Goli, now Madras Government Museum (Photo: Archaeological Survey of India).

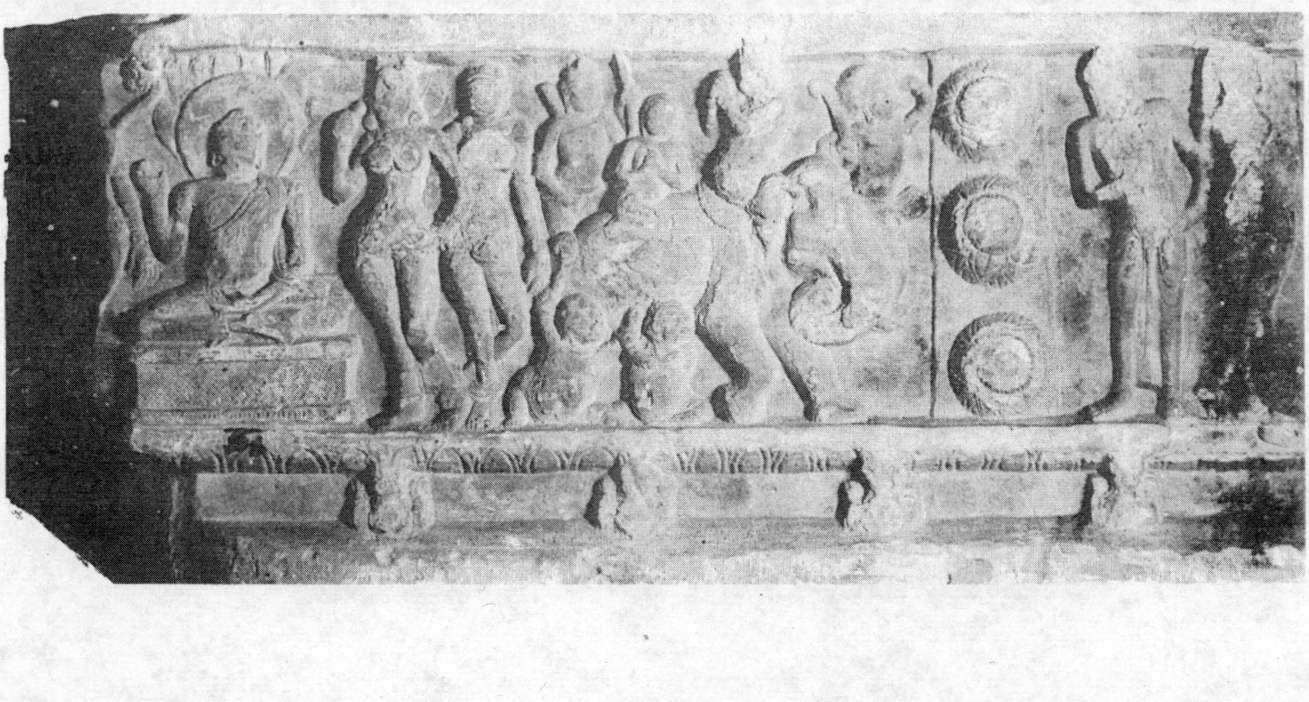

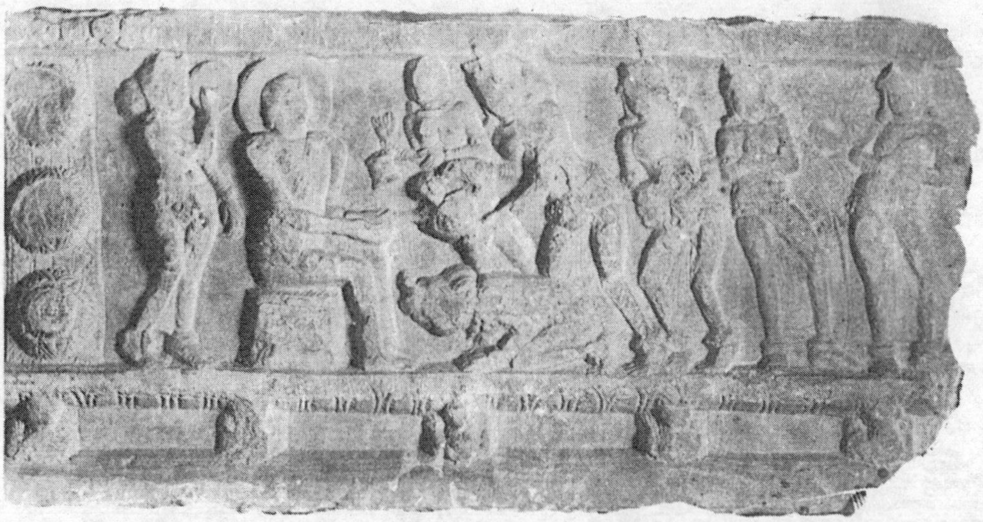

265. Sujātā Offering Food to the Buddha, continuation of fig. 264 (Photo: Archaeological Survey of India).

266. Representation of a throne, drum slab.

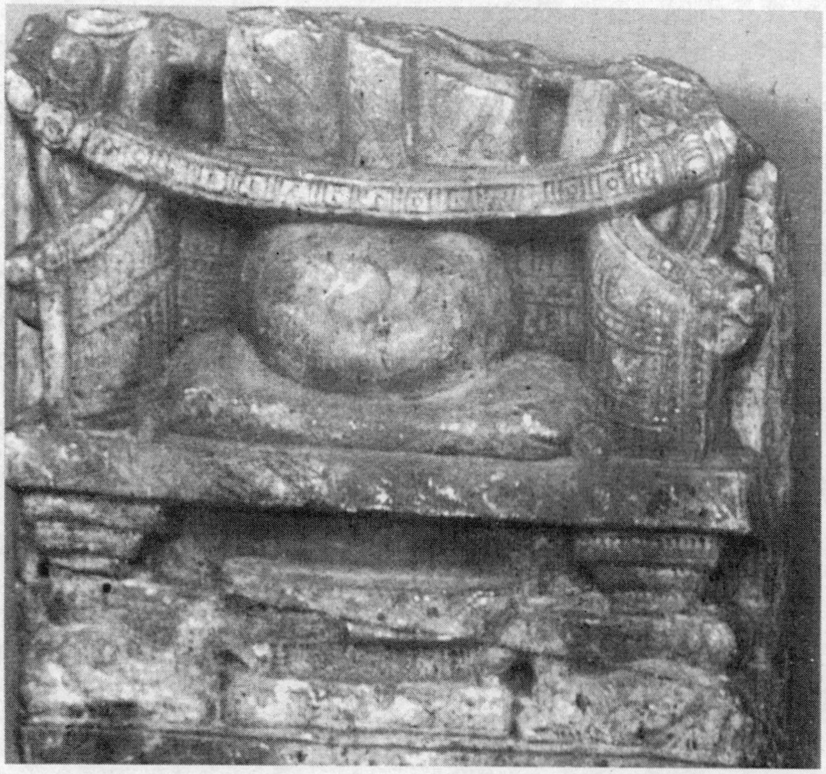

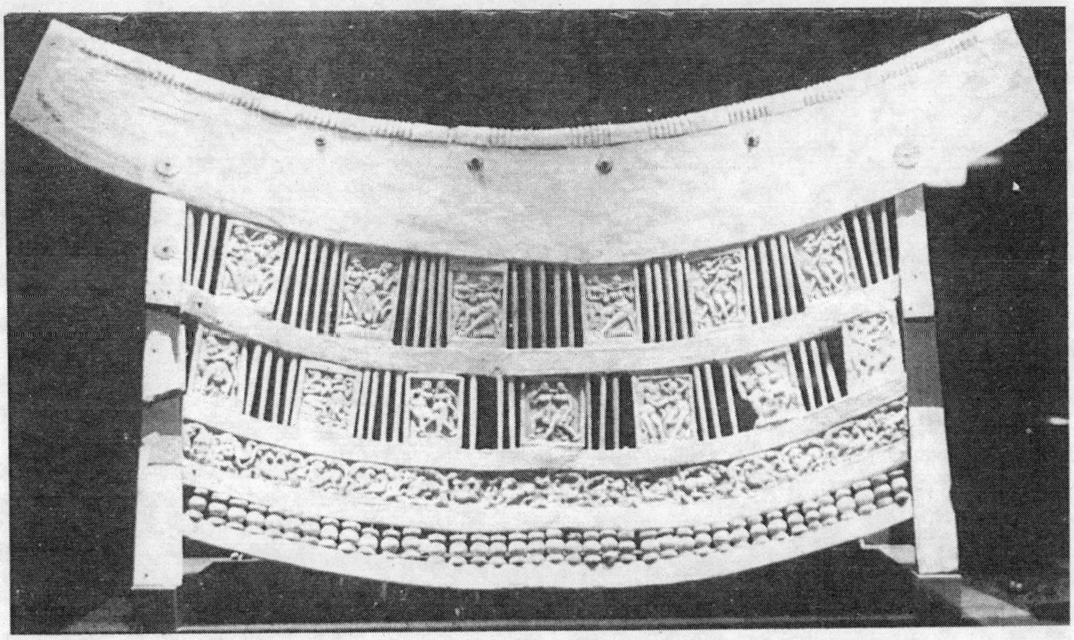

267. Ivory throne back, Begram, now Kabul Museum.

268. Detail of fig. 267.

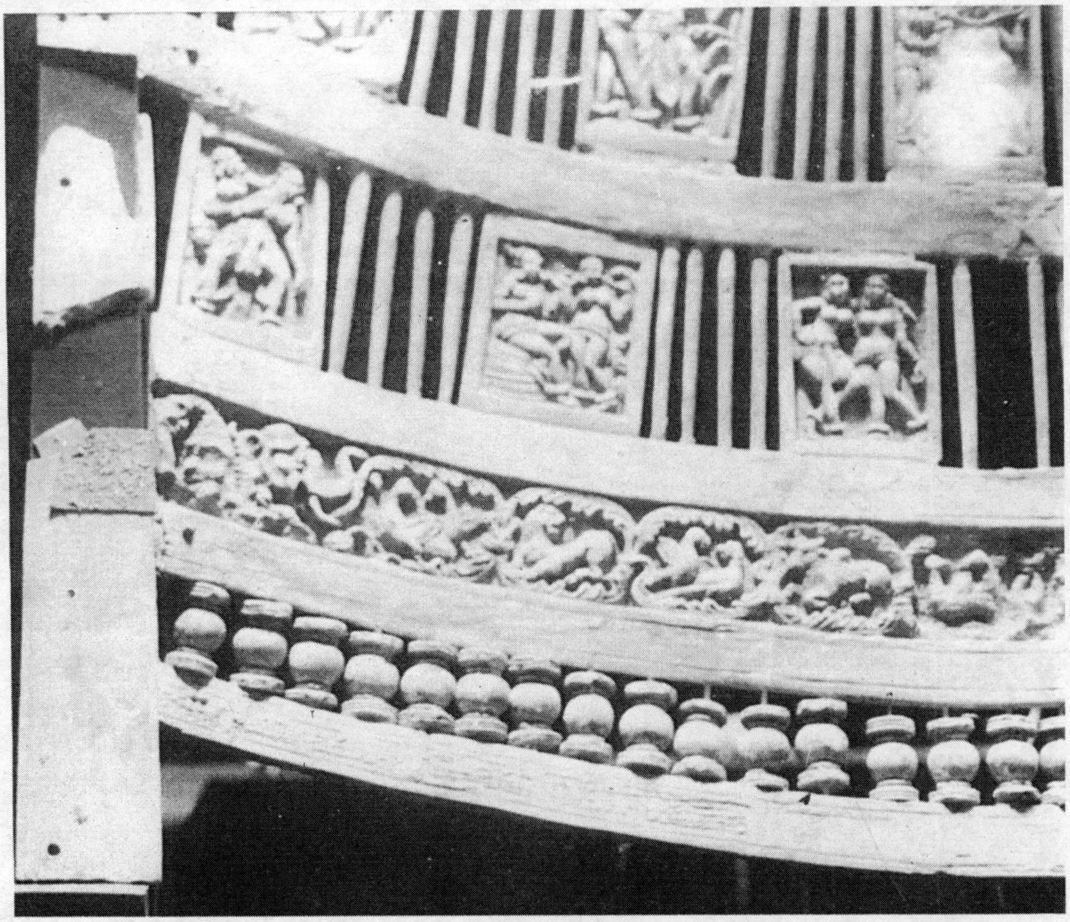

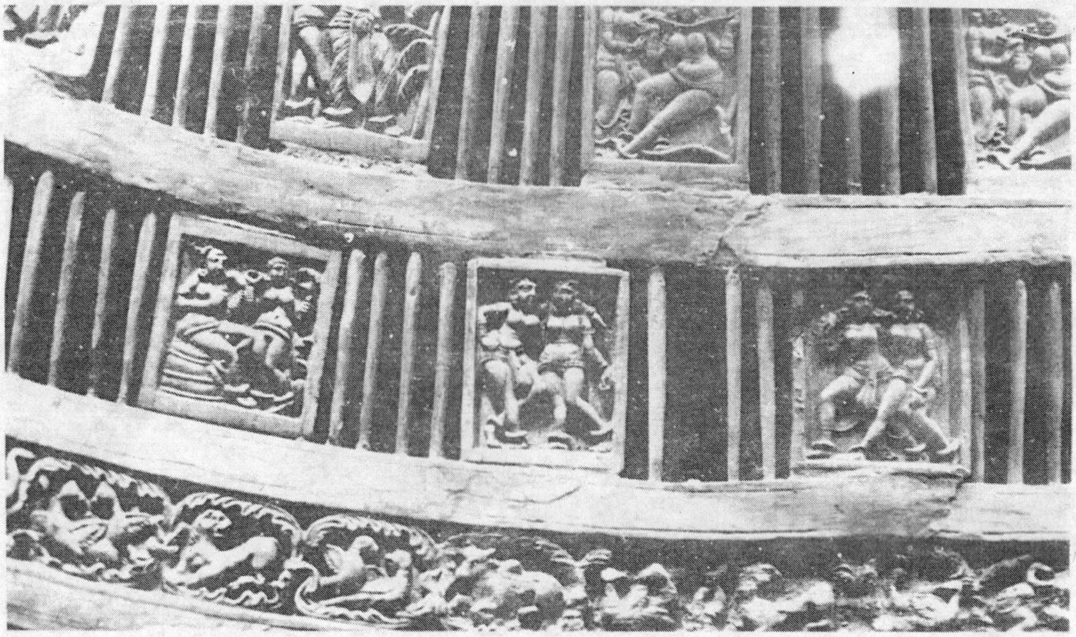

269. Detail of fig. 267.

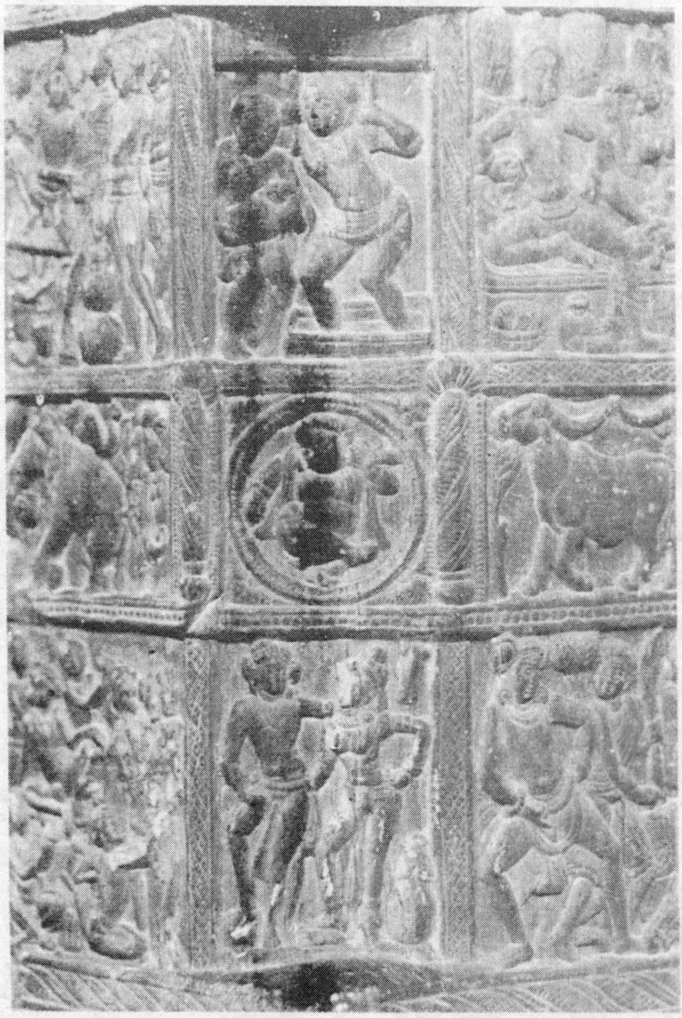

270. Detail of a pillar from Site 37.

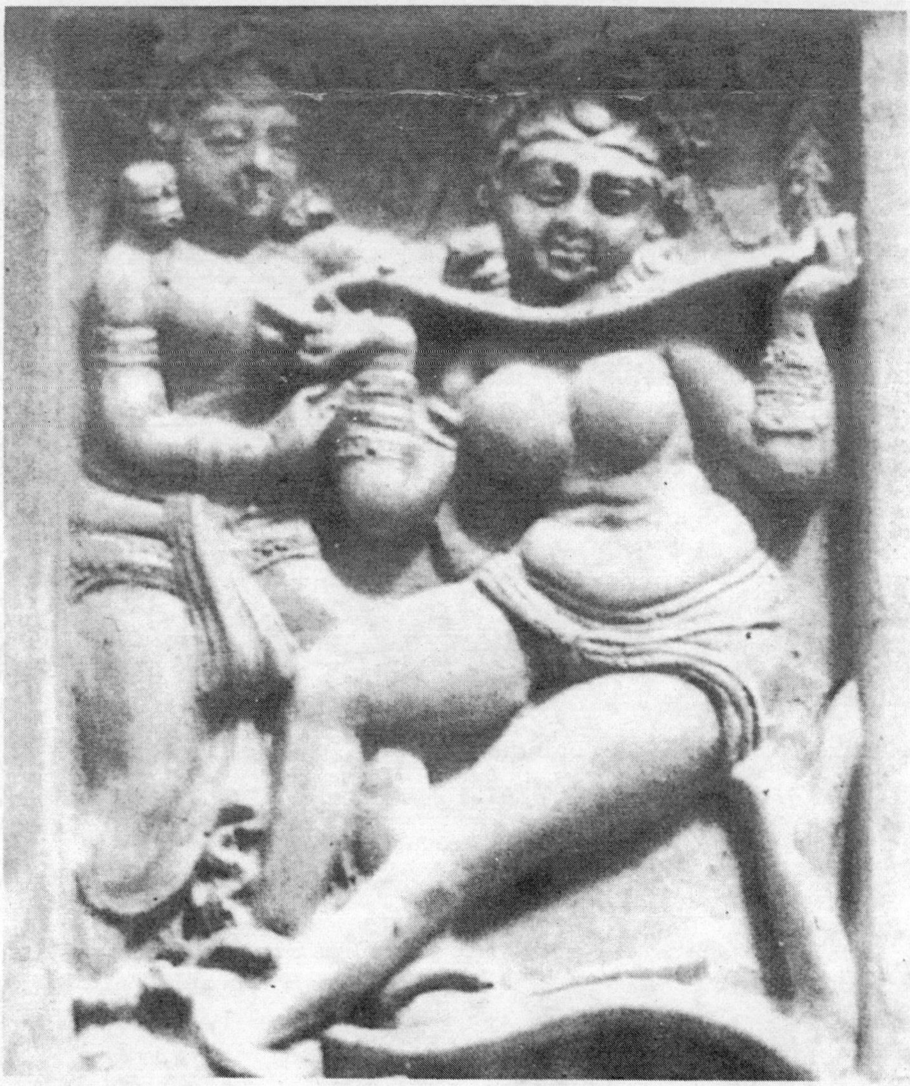

271. Detail of fig. 267.

272. Stone "throne back" Site 3.

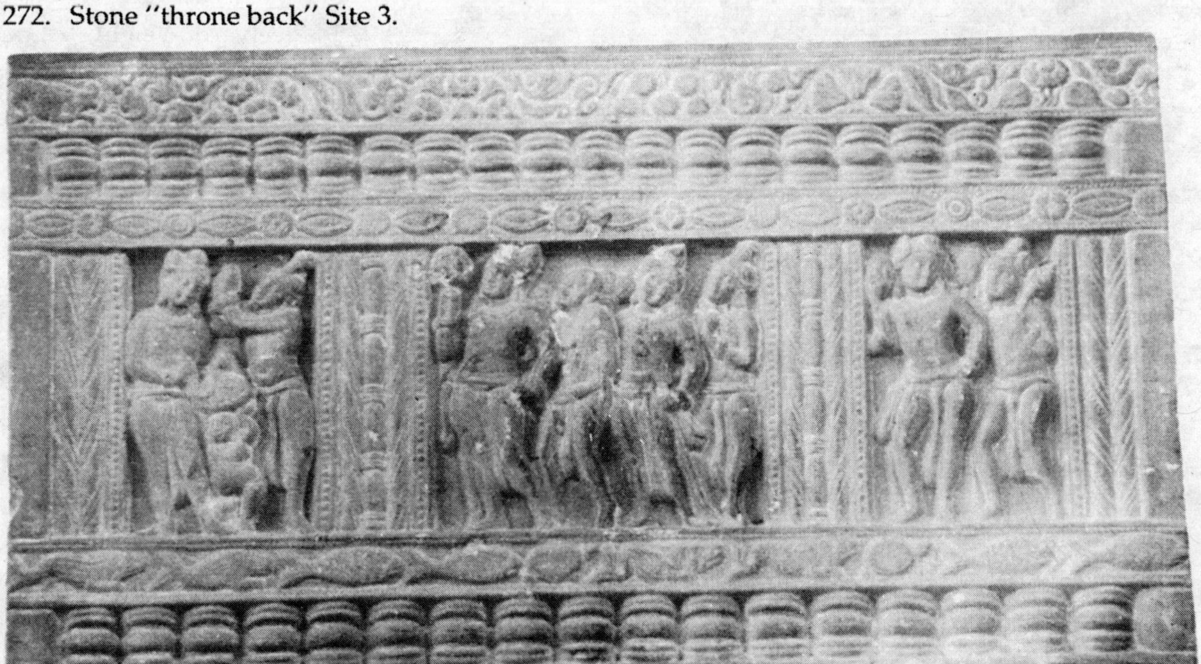

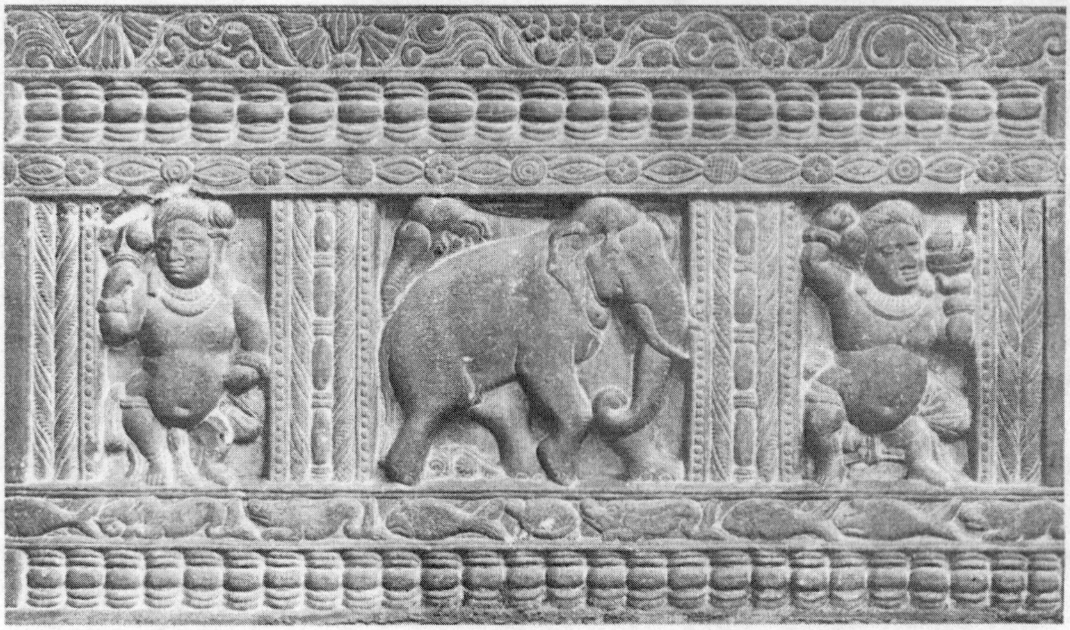

273. Reverse of fig. 272 (Photo: Archaeological Survey of India).

274. Ivory plaque, Begram, now Kabul Museum (Photo: RMN. Paris).

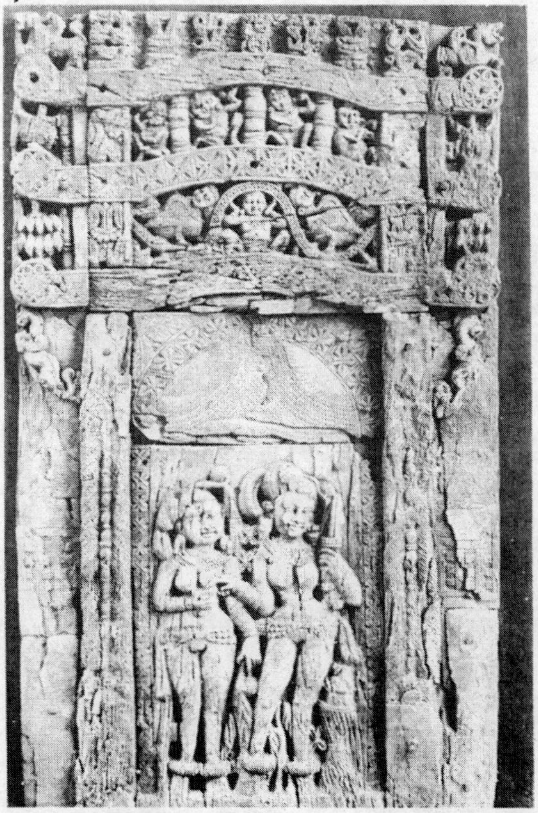

275. Steelyard Weight, Begram (Photo: B. Rowland and C.M. Rice, *Art in Afghanistan*, London, 1971, fig. 3).

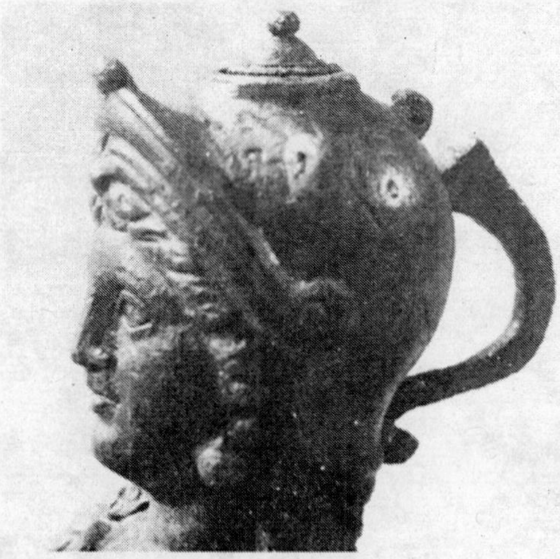

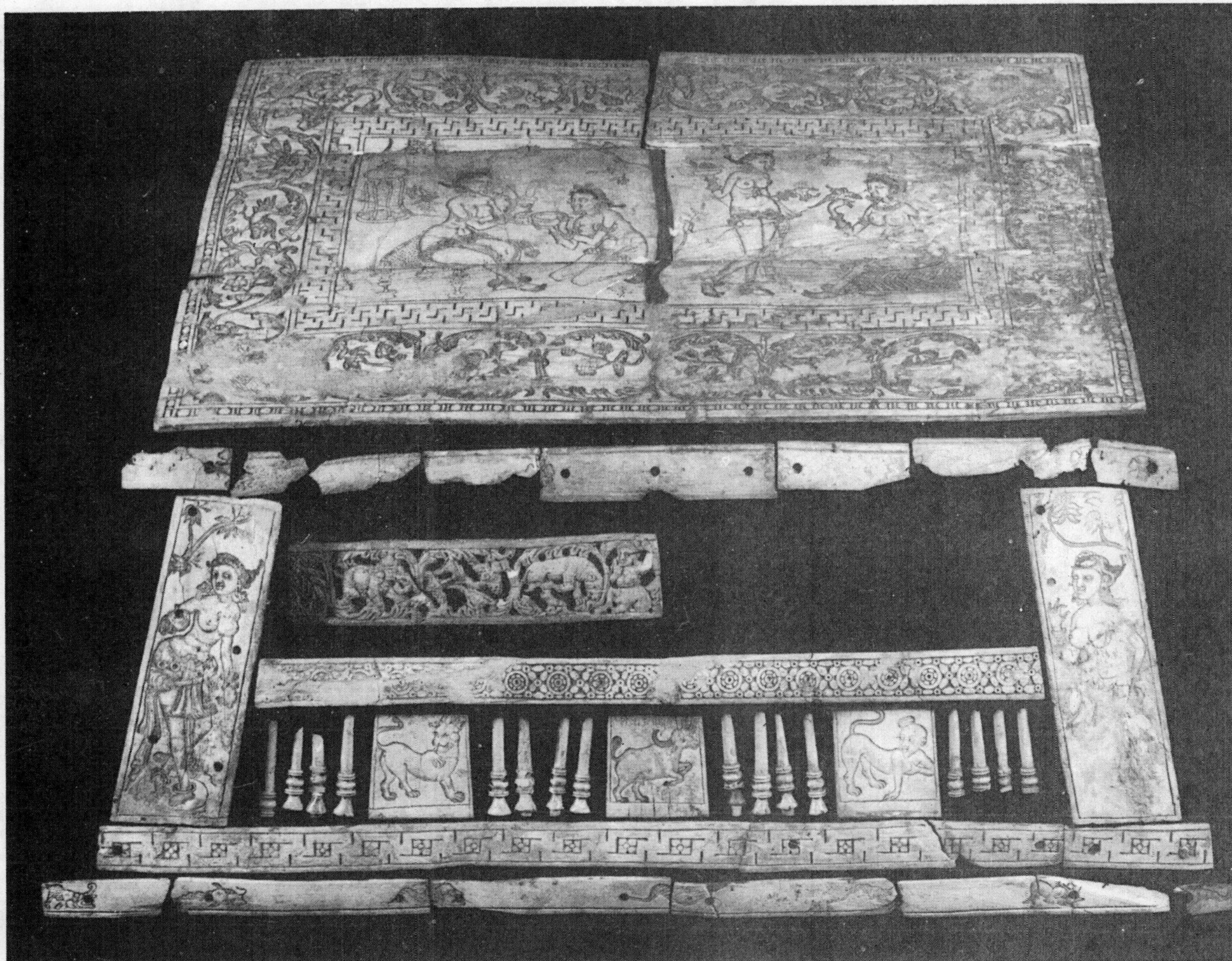

276. Coffert IX, Begram, now, Kabul Museum (Photo: Dominique Darbois P. Kneebone, Prague, 1968, fig. 32).

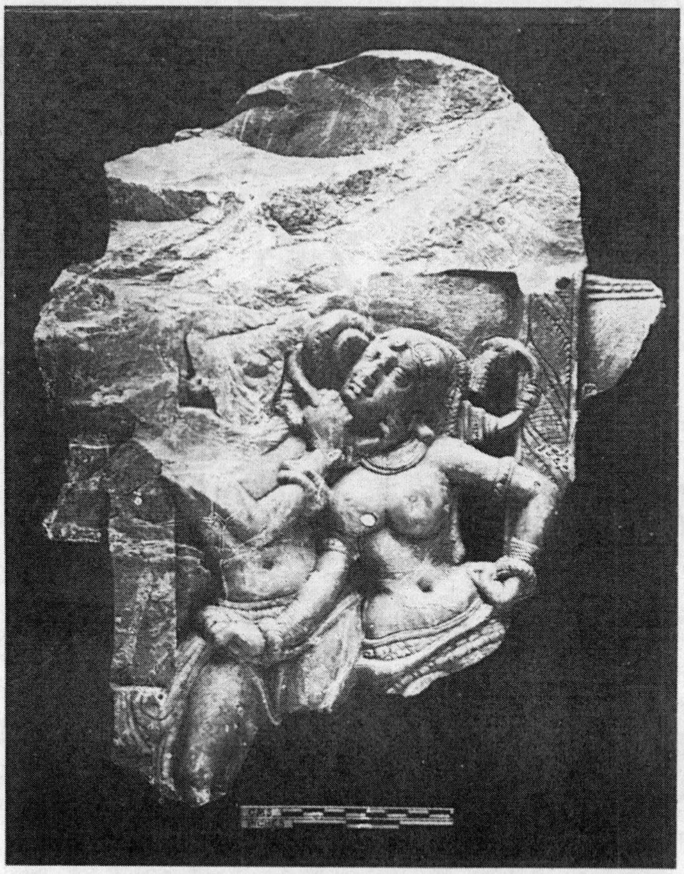

277. *Mithuna* couple.

278. Lid of a Sarcophagus, Tripoli Castle (Photo: J.M.C. Toynbee and J.B. Ward-Perkins, "People Scrolls: A Hellenistic Motif in Imperial Art", *Papers of the British School at Rome,* Vol. XVIII, N.S. Vol. V, 1950, pl. XXI, No. 3).

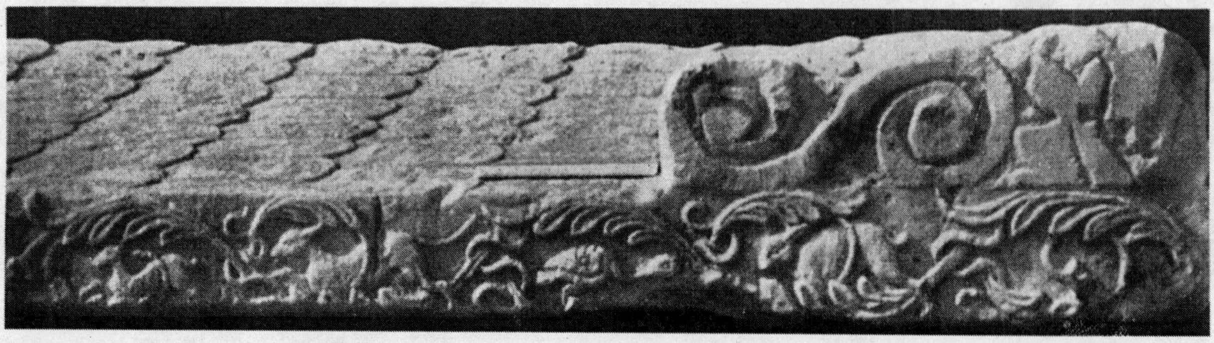

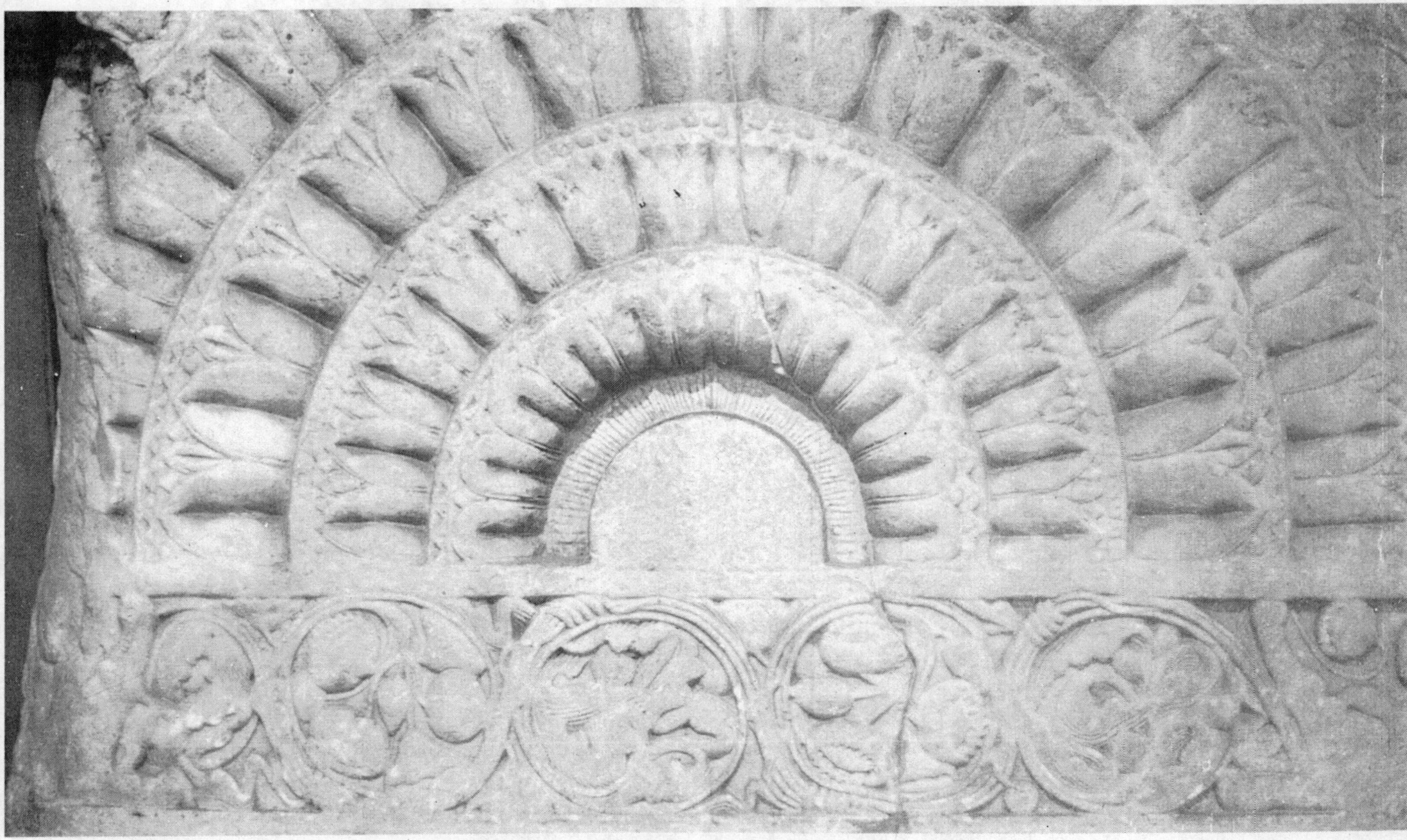

279.Detail of a pillar from Amarāvatī, now National Museum, New Delhi.

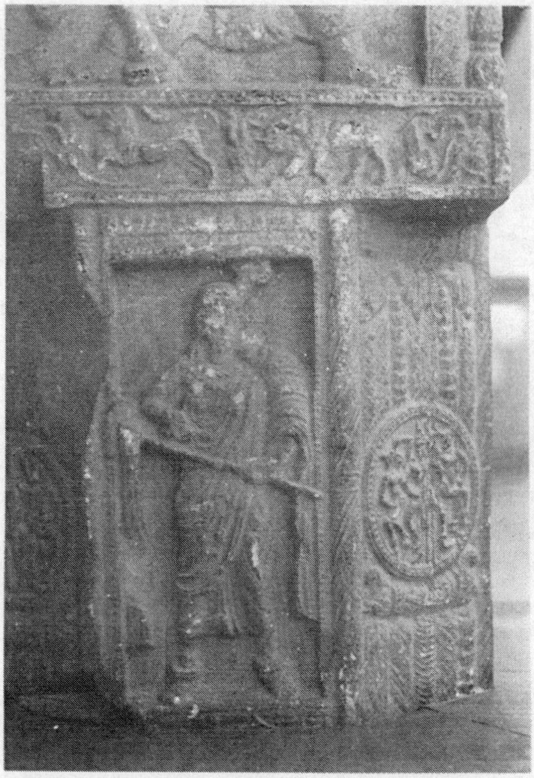

280. Detail of a pillar, same as fig. 232.

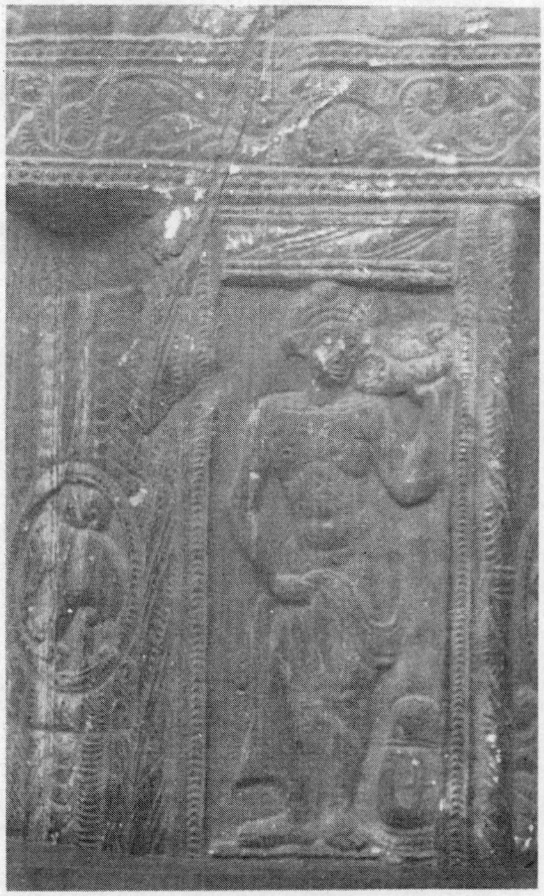

281. Detail of a pillar, same as fig. 232.

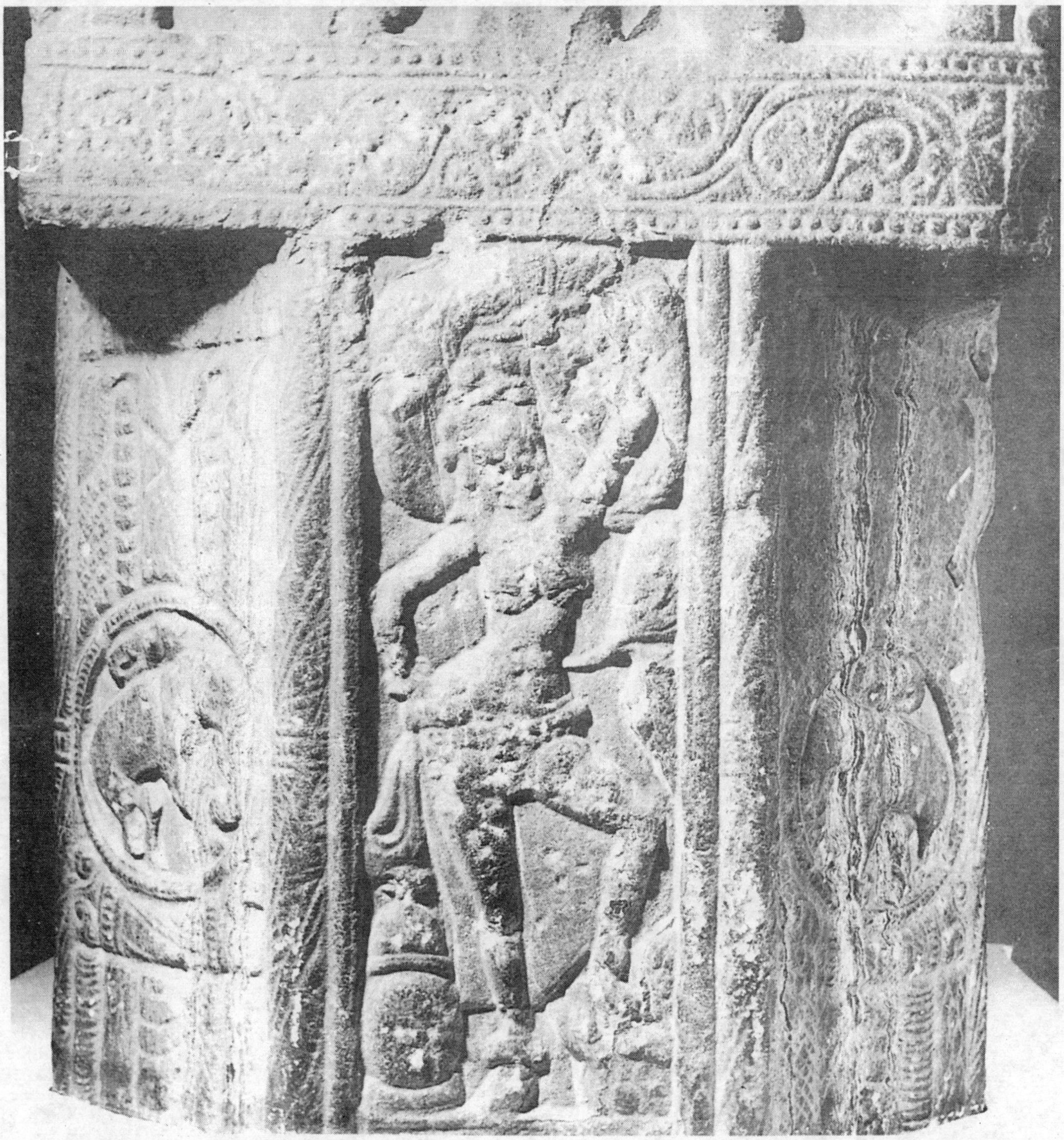

282. Detail of a pillar, same as fig. 232.